The Banks and the Monetary System in the UK 1959-1971

The Banks and the Monetary System in the UK 1959-1971

A banking view of developments from the Radcliffe Report to the monetary reforms of 1971, comprising articles selected from the Midland Bank Review

Edited and with an introduction by
J. E. WADSWORTH

Methuen & Co Ltd
11 New Fetter Lane London EC4

First published 1973 by Methuen & Co Ltd
11 New Fetter Lane, London EC4
Reprinted 1973

Printed in Great Britain by
Butler & Tanner Ltd, Frome and London

SBN *hardbound 416 18730 7*
SBN *paperback 416 20420 1*

Distributed in the USA by
HARPER & ROW PUBLISHERS INC.
BARNES & NOBLE IMPORT DIVISION

Contents

SECTION B LONDON'S MARKETS FOR MONEY

SECTION C THE ANNUAL MONETARY SURVEYS 1959–1971

SECTION D APPENDICES

Acknowledgements

Throughout the years articles and statistics in the *Midland Bank Review* have relied upon contemporary business, banking and official publications, as well as on experience and statistical work within the Bank. Where thought to be required, sources and references are given in the text, tables and charts, but here we acknowledge our continuing indebtedness to: *Economic Trends*; the UK Balance of Payments 'Pink Book'; the *Annual Abstract* and *Monthly Digest of Statistics*; *Financial Statistics*; *International Financial Statistics*; press releases of government departments; the quarterly bulletins and annual reports of the Bank of England; statistics of the British Bankers Association, the Committee of London Clearing Bankers and other banking figures; the *National Institute Economic Review*; the *London and Cambridge Economic Bulletin* and the industrial trends surveys of the Confederation of British Industry. We are grateful to the Bank of England for permission to reproduce in Appendix 4 the memoranda introducing the new methods of credit control. Then, too, we have benefited from the experience of other city institutions in day-to-day meetings, and from discussions with many economist friends engaged in business, teaching and research. Indeed, for many years past our efforts have sought to help in bridging gaps between the City and the business and academic worlds.

The surveys and other articles are written and statistics compiled by the team of economists and statisticians in the Economics Department of the Midland Bank and since 1966 the names of the editorial panel for the issue have appeared in each *Review*. To these full acknowledgement is now made. Editorial work and responsibility has rested with the principal economist of the Bank and drafting has been under the leadership of the managers of the Department. When the surveys began, the encouragement and surveillance of them was undertaken by W. F. Crick, General Manager for Research and

Statistics who retired in 1961, and I introduced them and produced the drafts. Later, editorial responsibility passed to me and thereafter to J. E. Maycock. Work on the production of drafts has been in the hands of the manager of the Department, who since 1967 has been P. K. Marks, and he has been closely supported by his colleagues, particularly S. R. Maycraft, B. D. Wesson and K. F. G. Clarke. The team has been of great assistance to me when, as Economic Consultant, I prepared this volume, but my especial thanks are due to F. D. Caunt, the assistant manager who has been directly concerned with the preparatory work for this book.

The writing and publication of the *Review* could not be undertaken without the support of the Chairman and Board of Directors of the Bank, and help and guidance from the management and colleagues throughout its service. With their assistance always at hand, the *Midland Bank Review* aims to continue to interest its readers, now numbering about 50,000 in most countries of the world, by objective commentaries that may be described as providing a running text book covering the ever-changing field of money and banking in Britain.

Introduction

This volume consists of reprints of major articles published in the *Midland Bank Review* during the twelve years since the Radcliffe Report* appeared. By that time the long period of post-war financial and monetary readjustment was over, and Britain was entering upon the 1960s, years that seen in retrospect constitute a heroic decade in her economic development, notably in its monetary aspects. The low rate of growth long characteristic in Britain's industrial activity was less evident in the early 1960s and inflationary tendencies appeared to have been checked, only to re-emerge with gathering virulence as the improvement in production made little headway, and pressures on sterling at first eased, but later repeatedly threatened stability in external conditions. Thus in the nation's affairs the situation was swinging from achievement to near calamity, and in the monetary field policy responded, moving from convertibility for current transactions and comparative freedom from credit restraints to ever more severe restrictions, and eventually to devaluation. Thereafter the balance of payments situation improved markedly but domestic conditions continued to suffer from accelerating inflation and rising unemployment.

During these years, when general economic policy tended to be overwhelmed by events, the authorities were driven time and again to resort to 'packages' of credit restrictions, with controls over bank lending central to them, as had been prescribed in the Radcliffe Report. These provided no lasting remedy and brought serious disadvantages that were plain to all. Meanwhile, the commercial banks were under fire for alleged lack of enterprise, monopolistic attitudes and obscurantism. After Radcliffe they were

* *Report of the Committee on the Working of the Monetary System* (Cmnd. 827), published August 1959. The volumes of evidence followed in 1960.

confronted with two further wide-ranging public inquiries* and innumerable articles, generally critical in tone. The Bank of England likewise was the subject of yet another searching official investigation.† Nevertheless, it was in this period that new markets for money made remarkable progress in London and sweeping institutional changes took place in banking structures at home and abroad, partly for reasons discussed below (see p. 12).

After such frustrating experiences in monetary arrangements the authorities made radical changes in the techniques of debt management, interest rates and methods of influencing banking activities. Thus the period ends with the introduction in September 1971 of quite different forms of monetary regulation in Britain, to bring about the most profound change in credit control of our times. About then, also, currency markets in financial centres were confronted with the explicit break with gold of the United States dollar, a situation likewise foreshadowing fundamental changes in international monetary arrangements. The boundaries of our period thus are neatly delineated: in domestic matters it runs from the Radcliffe Report to the introduction of reserve assets ratios, and in external affairs from the adoption in 1959 by Britain and several other countries of convertibility for current transactions, with fixed exchange rates under the International Monetary Fund system, to the floating rates of 1971.

Over the same turbulent years while Britain's financial policies were so hard pressed, developments of weight and significance occurred in her money markets and financial institutions. From time to time these pressures and developments were examined and analysed in articles in the *Midland Bank Review*, on occasion more than once, and some of the commentaries broke new ground that was subsequently to be well ploughed. The *Review* articles discussed money supply and bank deposits in 1957, 1969 and again in 1970; the techniques of managing government debt and inescapable conflicts in policy were noted, and important changes were examined in 1958, 1969 and 1971; methods of regulating the banking system were discussed in 1967, 1970 and 1971. Reminders and records provided were, for example, by an outline of the views on banks and banking in the Radcliffe Report, by a comparison of credit squeezes up to 1965 – these and subsequent 'squeezes' are mentioned in the Monetary Surveys for the relevant years – and by notes covering the devaluation of sterling.

All have proved popular with readers having more than a passing interest in monetary affairs, and public demand has been sustained likewise for articles in 1961, 1966 and 1969 dealing with activities of the London money market, and the emergence of new markets for money, handling funds far

* National Board for Prices and Incomes, *Bank Charges* (Cmnd. 3292), May 1967. The Monopolies Commission, *Report on Proposed Merger – Barclays, Lloyds and Martins Banks*, July 1968, No. 319.

† Select Committee on the Nationalized Industries, 1969–70, *The Bank of England*, No. 258.

exceeding those moving through traditional channels. Despite the persistent weakness of sterling throughout much of this period, London became a leading international centre for dealing in Eurodollars, attracting large numbers of banks from abroad and especially from the United States. Barriers to the establishment of banks and branches in Britain were by no means prohibitive and the number of overseas banks operating offices in London rose from 77 in 1960 to 172 in 1971, or well over 200 if participations in London registered banks are included.

A strong thread binding the articles together comprises the annual Monetary Surveys. For the past twenty-one years the *Midland Bank Review* has published a Monetary Survey in each May issue covering developments in money and banking during the preceding twelve months: in May because this number in the *Review's* quarterly issues follows closely upon the publication of official statistics and economic assessments appearing regularly each spring and associated with the end of the government's financial year. The Surveys tell an absorbing story year by year of the battle seen against the devaluation of sterling, of how it was lost in November 1967, and of the consequences for Britain's monetary and banking arrangements and her domestic economy. They deal with the failure of domestic economic policy to maintain progress with stability in Britain's affairs, even by resort to increasingly severe 'packages' of credit restrictions, and of the extent to which this was attributable to international monetary arrangements that could not prevent the crippling blows delivered from time to time against sterling and other currencies.

The first Survey, appearing in May 1950, was prompted by the considerable improvements in statistics and other information upon monetary and economic affairs in Britain, as well as by the devaluation of sterling in the previous autumn. Thus the enterprise was justified by noting that, although this first post-war devaluation brought to a head monetary tendencies that had been in operation for some years previously, yet, notwithstanding the better documentation and statistics, 'in no official document – not even in the annual report which the Bank of England began to issue following nationalization – do we find a considered, comprehensive yet specialized review of monetary conditions as they have developed over the year'. Indeed at that time 'the most authoritative and firmly established record of monetary developments in Great Britain' was produced abroad as part of the annual report of the Bank for International Settlements. (Economic historians will recall that until the history of the Bank of England by W. M. Acres appeared in 1931 and Sir John Clapham's two volumes in 1944, a familiar history of the Bank* was written in French by a Greek scholar and translated into English.)

* A. Andreades, *Essai sur la fondation et l'histoire de la Banque d'Angleterre 1694–1844*. In 1906 it was expanded into *Histoire de la Banque d'Angleterre 1694–1903*. The edition in English appeared in 1909.

In this original Monetary Survey we expressed the hope that it would provide a useful supplement to the regular quarterly summaries and charts constituting long-established features of the *Review*, and that if so it would become an annual contribution, embodying such improvements as might be practicable. These modest expectations were fulfilled, if we are to rely upon comments from readers, the frequent quotations and requests for reprints and the restrained expansion of our Survey over the years. The first Survey occupied barely five pages, including four short tables. Ten years later the issue for May 1959 was more than twice as long and supported by far more statistical material. Within a few months the Radcliffe Report appeared (our Survey in May 1959 described it as 'eagerly awaited') and later the four volumes of evidence, providing detailed analyses and a wealth of new information and statistics, with many tables that thereafter were to be published regularly. Thus the Radcliffe Report represents a turning point in the documentation of banking and monetary affairs in Britain, and hence the year of its appearance is an appropriate one with which to begin this volume. The Report and evidence furnish enough and to spare of the monetary background as it developed over the preceding post-war years. The annual Monetary Surveys and other articles of the *Review*, having likewise covered that period, have continued the story thereafter, and are now presented in a convenient form to bring the record up to date.

For some years it was uphill work, and in the concluding paragraph of the 1959 Survey, with which we begin Section C of these reprints, we commented: 'In the ten years over which this Monetary Survey has appeared we have been conscious of how much more information is needed, particularly about official operations, if widespread appreciation and truly objective criticism are to be fostered in the interest of healthy management of the nation's monetary system. Private surveys can at the best be only inadequate contributions to public education in these matters by comparison with the fully documented reports having all the authority of complete knowledge of the facts and of the considerations entering into the determination of policy.' Private efforts do, however, have a part to play and our annual Monetary Survey, with ten years' experience of record and analysis, continued into its second decade. The reasons were expressed a year or so later, after information about Britain's monetary affairs had been greatly expanded by the Bank of England giving much more material in a considerably extended annual report and by the issue of its *Quarterly Bulletin*. Our Monetary Survey for 1961 warmly welcomed the help from these sources and added that the Surveys would continue, because of the large readership of the *Review* and of the particular interest in this annual compilation. The comment went on to say: 'It (the Survey) presents an independent, unofficial account of monetary conditions which is intended to be entirely objective and should be all the better for the added material that can now be drawn upon.'

In several ways this collection of articles reflects and continues a well-established tradition of the *Midland Bank Review*. The selection has been directed to those articles dealing with the interrelations of monetary policy and banking activity, always examining the ways in which policy was implemented. But long before the Surveys began to appear the *Review* gave prominence to discussions of the techniques used for influencing monetary conditions. Early in 1939 a leading article stressed the importance, as regulators of the credit situation, of assets ratios in Britain's banking arrangements, identifying these as the cash ratio ('a little over 10 per cent' – in later years it became 8 per cent), and the liquid assets, or as it came to be described, the liquidity ratio ('at least 30 per cent' – later to become 28 per cent). After the First World War the cash ratio was the leading indicator, but after the Second the liquidity ratio moved to pride of place, to become officially adopted in the early 1950s as the principal gauge for credit control. In this sense it constituted a forerunner of the reserve assets ratios introduced in 1971. Meanwhile, the liquidity ratio had been strengthened by Special Deposits, bringing into operation a further ratio of control, for which an incongruous use was found when in 1969 the rate of interest allowed was reduced by one half to mark the displeasure of the authorities at the failure of the banks to curtail further the growth in their advances (see p. 402). The part played by liquidity ratios, as buttressed by Special Deposits, is illustrated by the chart showing the assets distribution of the London clearing banks in Appendix 3(g).

Throughout this volume the significant and lively contribution of the Radcliffe Report to monetary thought and policy is made clear by frequent quotations and references to its findings and recommendations. However, the Report was concerned with the working of the entire monetary and credit system: it stressed the importance of looking at the whole picture, insisting that the market for credit is a single market. This opened a wider view than the concentration upon banking affairs in these pages, though in the Radcliffe analysis the banking system was often deeply involved. For example, in the Report doubts were cast upon long-accepted views on the quantity theory and of methods of regulation based largely upon influencing the money supply. Instead, as a loosely applied replacement, Radcliffe insisted that in the main attention ought to be directed to the general liquidity of the whole economy. For the commercial banks this meant that their deposits were no longer to be seen as the main field for monetary action; this should be directed more particularly to their lending activities.

As may be seen from our commentary on the new monetary arrangements of 1971 in Chapter 5, the authorities turned away from the direct regulation of bank advances to give closer attention to monetary aggregates. An important aspect of the Radcliffe Report was the consideration given to other financial intermediaries and the growth of their activities at a time when those of commercial banks were restricted. The part played by 'money substitutes' provided largely through those institutions was noted. But above all the Report saw monetary regulation for credit conditions as a whole as relying mainly upon the influence to be exerted by the authorities through their management of the national debt and so changing the structure of rates of interest. Here, too, banking activities are closely implicated, but so are those of other institutions and individuals.

In our articles the views of the Radcliffe Report are discussed and analysed whenever they bear directly upon banking conditions, beginning with Chapter 1, which simply brings together extracts of this nature from the Report itself. For its more general and more weighty pronouncements the Report has been examined extensively elsewhere, and after more than a decade it is still the subject of discussion and controversy.* But there can be no argument about one aspect: the great contribution to the understanding of monetary affairs that followed upon the publication of the Report itself and supporting evidence, and that has been continued in large measure by the implementation of its recommendations for improvements in the issue of financial information and statistics. From this flow of fresh material, still being improved and refined, our articles themselves have greatly benefited.

To return to the background of our period, during 1960 sterling required no assistance whatever from abroad and our Survey in May of that year referred to the preceding twelve months as 'the best of the post-war period', with convertibility virtually restored for current sterling, taxes reduced, and credit controls lifted. Over a wider field the managing director of the International Monetary Fund at the annual meetings of the previous September had asserted that internationally post-war inflation was at an end, and in February 1961, article 8 of the Fund rules, providing convertibility for current transactions, was accepted by Britain and nine other countries, thus formally confirming the *de facto* convertibility of fourteen months previously. The governor of the Bank of England speaking in November 1959 saw Britain 'as entering into a new sphere. After the distortions and controls of the war and post-war periods, we seem now to have come, both domestically and internationally, to a position of more stability with the freedom of markets largely restored.'

But for Britain the good times did not last. True, despite relatively small borrowings in 1961, sterling was not again in need of external support for the ensuing two years. But thereafter a period of economic uncertainties and disappointments, with overstimulated activity in 1964, led to a relapse, bringing massive deficits on Britain's external payments. Formidable 'packages' of restrictive measures were applied, but nevertheless the govern-

* See, for example, *Money in Britain 1959–1969*, edited by D.R. Croome and H.G. Johnson (Oxford University Press, 1970). This prints the papers and proceedings of a conference held in October 1969 under the title 'The Radcliffe Report – Ten Years After'. See also *Monetary Theory and Monetary Practice in the 1970's*, edited by G. Clayton, J.C. Gilbert and R. Sedgewick (Oxford University Press, 1971).

ment was obliged to 'liquefy' Britain's holdings of dollar securities, and loans and credits in support of sterling were raised from financial centres throughout the western world. Even so, sterling could not escape devaluation in November 1967. For several months thereafter further support continued to be required, and was generously forthcoming, and by the end of 1968 the stupendous total of over £3300 million was reached, with other help also needed.

The Survey in May 1968 described the preceding twelve months as 'the most eventful in monetary affairs of the whole of the post-war period. It included the devaluation of sterling, the subsequent measures – among them an 8 per cent bank rate . . . the most severe budget since the war . . . and a crisis in the international payments system.' In Chapter 11 the subtitle refers to it grimly as the 'worst post-war year'. The gold market in London was closed in March 1968 at the request of the United States government, to reopen some time later on a two-tier price system. Mortifying witness to the depths plumbed are the Letters of Intent (the texts are given in Appendix 4(a) and (b)) sent to the International Monetary Fund in November 1967 and May 1969 requesting support for sterling and giving undertakings about Britain's financial intentions and objectives. The Basle agreement for assisting sterling and the UK dollar guarantees for the sterling balances had soon followed upon devaluation.

Throughout the succeeding stringent years business and banking were hamstrung by the reapplication of ferocious credit restrictions, including 'ceilings' pressed downwards and more narrowly selective priorities on bank advances to the private sector, the maintenance of Special Deposits, and bank rate running at a high level. Not until 1971, in the last of our Surveys now reprinted in full, could it be said with almost palpable relief, that, in marked contrast with the situation in preceding years, Britain's 'external situation ceased to be the dominant consideration in the application of domestic policies'. By that time, however, further inflationary developments, stagnation and rising unemployment, called for different remedies while the changes in the system of credit control brought a new approach in financial matters.

Over such a period the annual Surveys of monetary conditions are more than chronological reminders, even if seen as recent history. For many they will have a special interest as reflecting the nature of pressures on a currency widely used in international trade and as describing some of the consequences for Britain's domestic conditions. A clear path is not easy to find in Britain's monetary affairs, if only because they are complex and often associated with external developments. Thus the application and adaptations of techniques in sophisticated monetary arrangements present a remarkable story, including the emergence of anomalous effects, such as when a drain on central reserves strengthens the government's short-term borrowing position, or when the gilt-edged market responds perversely to official actions. Again, all too often background analysis has been uncertain and conflicts in objectives have led to ineffectual procedures.

Some years before our period begins the regulation of the note issue had been replaced, in effect, by no more than a biennial opportunity for parliamentary review under the Currency and Bank Notes Act, 1954, and long before then attention had ceased to be given to 'the proportion' of cash to total deposits in the Banking Department of the Bank of England. The term 'fiduciary issue' altogether lost its pejorative implications and was rarely to be heard in discussions of monetary affairs. The Radcliffe Report dismissed legislative control of the note issue as 'otiose', and could suggest no way of 'restricting by statute the supply of money' (para. 523). This followed hard upon a comment by the Chancellor of the Exchequer in 1957, when he declared that 'there can be no remedy for inflation . . . which does not include, and indeed is not founded upon, the control of the money supply.' Around the same time the governor of the Bank of England remarked that 'the level of bank advances is by no means the whole story. The total level of bank deposits . . . is no less important' (see Chapter 4, p. 79). Whether regulated by statute or otherwise, thereafter a seemingly conspiratorial silence about money supply was to prevail for a full ten years in statements from Whitehall and Threadneedle Street. It was brought back, at least into discussion, with the Letters of Intent, embracing the more abstruse concept of 'domestic credit expansion'.

Likewise, in managing government debt, official analysis has wavered and the emphasis in policy has changed as the objectives of marketability, confidence of investors and fairness have not always harmonized with other and more insistent requirements. Over ten years ago a government spokesman exclaimed, when the banks were sellers of gilts: 'We do not think it is right that the government should be a kind of sink for unwanted government stock at an artificially high price' (p. 230). Shortly before then the Radcliffe Report had been published expressing the view that the main instrument of monetary operations should be by influencing rates of interest through the management of the government debt. Possibly the government's *cri de coeur* marked recognition of the inescapable limitation on action, as expressed in the Radcliffe Report, that the authorities could not 'simultaneously choose both the structure of interest rates and the structure of the debt' (para. 375); clearly as was soon evident, it did not signal a return to dependence on regulating the money supply. Not until September 1968 did the curve for bank deposits turn downwards, then to follow a more or less level course for the ensuing two years.

This brought to the forefront conflicts in objectives. By mid-1969 the complexities and difficulties of reconciling satisfactory management of the national debt with restraining the growth of the money supply had led to a 'memorandum of objectives to be followed', agreed upon between the Bank of

England and the Treasury. The Bank of England have stated that in open market operations they 'work to it', but the terms of that, or any subsequent version of the memorandum, have not been disclosed, not even to members of the Parliamentary Select Committee on Nationalized Industries, who commented with some acerbity upon such close secrecy on a matter of public importance. However, radical changes in methods of control by the authorities were on the way and were introduced in 1971.

A year or two earlier, a significant indication of readiness for reform in banking practice had been evident in the announcement that the clearing and Scottish banks were to give up exemptions they had long enjoyed under company legislation, and to disclose in their published annual accounts for 1969 'true' profits and 'inner' reserves. Considerable changes in accounting procedures were made in order to establish, as closely as possible, uniform treatment in banking figures. The rearrangement of balance sheets resulted in a steep reduction in the published figures of aggregate deposits and, more to the point, brought to light differences between the leading banks in accumulated reserves and in business results. It thus sharpened the edge of bank competition, which was to be whetted yet again with the new arrangements for monetary regulation, including the abandonment of the long standing collective agreements on rates of interest charged and allowed.

A further step consisted of the modification of policy in the gilt-edged market, and this is discussed in Chapter 3. Broadly the new policy seeks to reduce official intervention in the market and so to promote greater freedom and competition. Thus the fresh approach involves increased reliance on changes in interest rates for the implementation of monetary policy, associated with the possibility of wider swings in market prices of gilts. The change in emphasis is not simply a return to earlier conditions, and can hardly be compared with the old-style bank rate operation, when modest shifts in the rate, supported by open market transactions, could result in major changes in the domestic and international situation. Nowadays, bank rate is no longer so dominant in the structure of interest rates: the finance houses established their own 'base rate' in 1970, and in the following year the clearing banks were at last enabled to move away from the old guide-line. On several occasions before then bank rate had run at 7 and 8 per cent, and rates in the complementary money markets had been much higher, so that it was indeed a far cry from conditions at the time of the Macmillan Report,* where bank rate was described as 'a most delicate and beautiful instrument for the purpose' of managing the monetary system. The new arrangements covering operations in the gilt-edged market were carried further in 1971, though the stern reference to bank selling (see p. 69) was not then tested. Moreover, in the closing words of Chapter 3, the new system has still to

* Committee on Finance and Industry (Cmd. 3897), 1931, para. 218.

show any way of escape from the underlying dilemna in this field – that monetary and debt management objectives do not run in harmony'.

In September 1971 came the radical change in methods of regulating Britain's monetary and banking system, and the new arrangements are examined in Chapter 5. These are of such interest that an indication of their first effects has been given by adding a few paragraphs from the following Monetary Survey, for May 1972, under the heading 'Banking enters a new era'. This bold transformation in regulatory technique sweeps away a number of venerable observances: a single 'reserve assets ratio' of $12\frac{1}{2}$ per cent replaces both the former cash and liquidity ratios, with assets and liabilities each newly defined; the new ratio is to be applied to other financial institutions besides the clearing banks and it may be reinforced by Special Deposits called from all of them, instead of from the clearing and Scottish banks alone. Meanwhile, outstanding Special Deposits have been released, though the clearing banks, with reserve assets far in excess of the new ratio level, agreed to subscribe to special issues of government stock. Above all, the 'ceilings' and restraints on advances were lifted and the clearing banks gave up their agreements on interest rates. In these and other directions the way is prepared for banking conditions in the future to operate with less discrimination and more competition.

The new arrangements were preceded by the distribution of explanatory memoranda from the Bank of England, an action of itself without precedent and contrasting with the manner in which Special Deposits were introduced.* The memoranda are reproduced in Appendix 4. Nevertheless, the regulatory changes, made without benefit of Parliament, did not attract widespread public interest. The clearing banks have expressed support for them, though with some reservations. As is noted in Chapter 5, they will still be required to hold a larger proportion of unremunerative assets than will rival financial institutions, particularly by reason of the curious exclusion of cash in tills from among their 'reserve assets'; they suffer other competitive disadvantages, and they continue to remain vulnerable in emergency conditions. For example, although the Radcliffe Report regarded discriminatory action against the banks as unjustified, it went on to say: 'A monetary authority in a tight corner may well decide to strike directly at the banks. It is . . . at bank advances that they should strike.' (para. 397). Thus, for all the freshness and rationality now brought to bear in methods of regulation, it is to be expected that well-tried practices will live on.

Again, it was, after all, for banking purposes that the old working ratios of cash and liquidity were devised by the clearing banks, becoming adopted much later by the authorities as levers for monetary regulation. In such essentials banking needs do not change, so that in the nature and distribution of their

* See A. W. Tuke's evidence to the Radcliffe Committee (Q. 13054, see footnote, p. 1).

assets the banks will doubtless continue to look to the primacy of liquidity. 'Cushions' of maturing securities may be held to protect the new reserve asset ratio, just as they defended the old liquidity ratio, and the abandonment of the cash ratio as an official requirement does not lessen branch needs nor alter the fact that cash is shown monthly in the published statements of the banks. As the governor of the Bank of England told the Select Committee on Nationalized Industries (Q. 375, see footnote, p. 2): 'The whole purpose of the 8 per cent cash ratio is that cash has got to be seen there constantly. This is part of the confidence in banks.'

Inevitably, for the banks as institutions our period was one of stress, change and interrupted development in responding to the pressures of business needs as well as to the demands of abrupt variations in government policy. In the immediate post-war years the Bank of England had passed into public ownership and banking activities remained closely regulated to meet the needs of war and post-war finance. The banks have been required to accommodate their assets structures and lending policies, first to the consequences of the reintroduction of the use of interest rates in monetary policy from 1951 onwards, then to the adoption by the authorities of the official liquidity ratio and thirdly to the suspension of restrictions on advances in 1958 and again four years later. In the mid-1950s government policy resulted in heavy falls in market prices of the banks' portfolios of gilt-edged securities at a time when holdings were inescapably large, and thus brought changes in bank practices, with the need to regard their investments as among risk assets and hence to favour short-term maturities. Then, too, as the new-found weapon of the authorities consisted of requiring the liquidity ratio to be held at 30 per cent – the official ratio was lowered to 28 per cent in 1963 – it was convenient for individual banks to arrange their investment portfolios with maturities spread as evenly as practicable in the years immediately ahead, in 'echelon' as the practice is described.

Nor was this all. The composition of liquid assets held by the banks was greatly changed as less use was made of Treasury bills in government finance and, as may be seen in Appendix 2, Table 4, as the out-turn changed from heavy deficits in the financial years preceding 1968 to substantial repayments thereafter. As Chart (h) in Appendix 3 shows, Treasury bill holdings of the clearing banks declined and were replaced by other liquid assets, until early in 1970 the total for the clearing banks' holdings of Treasury bills was under £100 million, as compared with ten times as much a decade before. The Radcliffe Report had spoken of the importance of the Treasury bill as a component of liquidity and had indicated that the 'funding of Treasury bills beyond a certain (not very remote) point would cause a major upheaval in our financial institutions' (para. 543). In the event, the banks, aided by a considerable revival in the use of commercial bills and the flexibility of the money market, displayed a noteworthy adaptability in substituting other liquid assets.

Above all, when official restrictions on lending were lifted late in 1958 an uninhibited upsurge during the next five years carried the proportion of advances to gross deposits of the clearing banks from less than one third to well over one half, with a consequential fall in the proportion of investments. But by the spring of 1961 inflationary developments at home, and speculation following currency revaluations abroad, brought heavy pressure to bear on sterling. With the summer came the 'little budget', the 'pay pause', and the return of restrictions on bank lending, even stricter than on previous occasions. Thereafter the situation became steadier until by the autumn of 1962 all the credit restraints had been lifted once more and bank lending was again free. Two years later, with home conditions 'overheating' and a growing external deficit, restrictions on credit and on bank advances returned. When restrictions had been suspended innovation and expansion had followed in banking activities, to be discouraged with the reimposition of restraints. The third release from controls on lending took place in 1971, this time accompanied by the wide-ranging changes in monetary regulation of September of that year.

Structural development in the banking system was likewise conditioned by official attitudes and policies. As we have seen, controls on lending returned after being suspended. They were reinforced by calls for Special Deposits, and both restraints were to remain to hamper banking development until 1971. Meanwhile the clearing banks, as encouraged by the authorities until then, had continued to follow the regular pattern of interest rates in accordance with their agreements, and so left the field open for other financial intermediaries to develop by attracting funds at relatively high rates of interest to lend on correspondingly costly terms. These institutions were not only outside the agreements on interest rates of the clearing banks, but also they were not similarly hobbled by cash and liquidity ratios or Special Deposits. An embryonic cash deposits scheme, announced in 1968 as a means of controlling their activities, proved abortive, though restrictions on lending to the private sector were extended beyond the clearing banks to them. The swift growth of such non-bank financial intermediaries, and of the complementary money markets in which they operated, is explored in several of the *Review* articles we reprint (see Section B). Since then growth has continued, and the sterling deposits of the accepting houses, overseas and other banks have risen from about £1000 million in 1959 to nearly £6500 million by December 1971, with a further £2000 million of sterling certificates of deposits. Meanwhile, the explosive thrust of the Eurodollar market is reflected in the increase in foreign currency deposits from the equivalent of no more than a few hundred million pounds in 1959 to £23,000 million in December 1971, with the addition of a further £1900 million of dollar certificates of deposit. However, here the point is made that one consequence was the development of subsidiaries of the clearing banks. These were not subject to the ratio clogs hampering the parent banks and so competed with other financial intermediaries for funds at going market rates, and for lending business of a kind not traditionally undertaken in this country by ordinary deposit banks.

Here was an aspect of competition sometimes overlooked in contemporary discussions of banking activities. As the governor of the Bank of England remarked at his Jane Hodge Memorial Lecture in December 1970: 'I sometimes feel that the clearing banks attract more than their fair share of criticism for being – it is alleged – unadventurous and slow to react to a changing world. Yet from small beginnings the clearing banks' subsidiaries have grown rapidly to account for well over 10 per cent of deposits with these "other" banks as a whole. If we consider sterling business only, their performance has been even more striking. In the past five years the clearing banks' subsidiaries have increased their sterling resources fivefold, and in the course of doing so they have gained over one third of all the growth in the sterling resources of these "other" banks as a group. I wonder whether those who like to characterize the clearing banks as sleeping giants are really aware of all these developments.'

Another major structural change was a strange by-product of the report on bank charges of the National Board for Prices and Incomes to which reference has been made earlier. Since the end of the First World War the large banks had observed loyally an undertaking not to arrange further amalgamations except with the consent of the authorities. An almost incidental comment in the report indicated that the authorities 'would not obstruct some further amalgamations, if the banks were willing . . .' (para. 154). Even so, the official attitude was far from plain,* and the long-standing weakness in communications continued, but when an amalgamation between the National Provincial and Westminster banks was put forward in 1968, and agreed, it was clear that mergers between large undertakings were not ruled out. Nevertheless, the proposal for an amalgamation between three banks – Barclays, Lloyds and Martins – was referred to the Monopolies Commission and then disallowed, though subsequently Barclays arranged to take over Martins Bank. Recent mergers between major deposit banks in Britain are listed in Appendix 5 (see also p. 370).

In their everyday affairs the banks have been heavily engaged, quite apart from observing official guidance on lending. In general, administrative pressures have increased considerably. The volume of transactions has grown in all directions; adequate staff has been hard to find; days and times of opening have had to be adjusted and policies towards branch development reconsidered. In the mid-1960s new bank branches were being established at a rate of four or five in each week, largely to build up again after the wartime standstill, but in recent years branch expansion has been slower and a number have been closed as a consequence of mergers and the changing environment.

* See Monopolies Commission (see footnote, p. 2), para. 48.

Some lightening of the burden of book-keeping has been achieved by substantial investments in computers. Then, too, with repeated robberies at branch counters and during cash movements, further protective measures have had to be taken at offices and in the transport of notes and coin. Such innovations as personal loan accounts, term loans, credit cards and cheque cards have been introduced and continue to contribute to Britain's financial facilities. Improvements in money transmission services have been considerable with the introduction of, in the early 1960s, a credit clearing – later designated bank giro – and subsequent refinements such as direct debiting. The links made in the late 1950s with hire purchase companies have been retained and on occasion have provided a channel for the clearing banks to enter into new extensions of the instalment credit field such as leasing and factoring. It is noteworthy that the transfer to decimal currency was made smoothly and satisfactorily with the banks playing a central role, notwithstanding a postal strike.

In international developments the banks have been forging fresh ties with banks abroad, often by setting up new organizations to meet the ever-increasing needs of the large multinational companies for longer-term credits. Meanwhile the clearing banks were required to provide, in the national interest, large credits, at relatively low rates of interest and long terms, for the finance of exports. Throughout post-war years the usual flow of revisions in regulations affecting foreign exchange transactions has continued with the banks as the main operating agents. To these and other changes frequent references are made in the annual Surveys.

The special articles chosen for reprint have been selected rigorously from the wealth of material available, as may be seen from Appendix 6, and have been kept closely to our period. Out of seventeen, only two appeared just before the Radcliffe Report and these are included because they began discussions on money supply and debt policy that were to be continued in later years. By contrast we have not included bold attempts to establish the resources behind the pound, giving as it were a balance sheet of external assets and liabilities for sterling, in the issues for February 1956 and August 1960. Again, two articles on changes in investment conditions and practices are not reproduced: 'Corporate Investment in Equities' published in February 1959, and 'Analysis of the Reverse Gap' published in May 1960. As is shown by the chart on interest rates and yields (Appendix 3(c)), the curve for equities moved below that for Consols in the second half of 1959, so establishing the 'reverse gap' that has lasted throughout our period. Indeed the gap has widened considerably and by 1971 equities were lording it over gilts with the average yield standing more than 5 per cent below that on Consols. As a last example of other commentaries of monetary interest, we have not reprinted an article, 'The Nuisance of Stamp Duties', which in May 1959 opened a campaign, to be supported over a wide front, against these uneconomic imposts. In 1961 the *ad valorem* stamp duty on bills of exchange was replaced by a flat twopenny (2*d.*) stamp, as for cheques, and ten years later the duty was withdrawn altogether.

The book is set out in four sections: Section A – Banking and Credit Policy since the Radcliffe Report – includes twelve special articles, comprising Chapters 1 to 5, dealing in the main with official activities in the management of the government debt, the regulation of the money supply, and banking activities. Section B – London's Markets for Money – covers five articles describing and analysing recent developments, especially operations in the new markets, and contained in Chapters 6 and 7. These special articles are followed by Section C, consisting of the thirteen annual Monetary Surveys from 1959 onwards, occupying Chapters 8 to 12, arranged in groups in accordance with the pattern of events over the period. The year at the head of each survey is for the twelve months to April. Most of the annual surveys fall into three parts: first, the background of economic conditions in Britain; next, the external situation and position of sterling; thirdly, developments in monetary and banking conditions. The space devoted to each section varies with the circumstances of the year under review. For the most part the articles have been reprinted as they stand, with only essential editorial compression and rearrangement, and this has been largely confined to the introductory paragraphs of the Annual Surveys. The views and attitudes that were held at the time of writing have an interest of their own, and indeed, no doubt, illuminate the subsequent course of events. Hence the dates of articles and surveys are given in the titles.

A fourth Section D consists of appendices including: statistics; charts, generally with 1958 as the base year; illustrative documentary material and schedules relating to the banking structure. With such considerable changes in monetary affairs it is helpful to have at hand the precise dates of the more important among them. The chronology in Appendix 1 pinpoints the major monetary events, and constitutes a selective and severely abridged abstract from the detailed chronology we have maintained for many years past. Each year's survey was supported by statistics and charts, but some of the official figures were revised subsequently, while on occasion the basis was changed for a regular series. To avoid confusion and repetition most of the statistical material has been brought together for the whole of the period in Appendices 2 and 3, with consistent figures in the latest form down to 1971, for use in conjunction with the articles. Then, too, we have thought it of interest to provide a few examples of the texts of leading monetary documents, such as guidance from the Chancellor of the Exchequer and the Bank of England on bank lending and the Letters of Intent to which reference has been made earlier. Appendix 5 provides lists of banks and recent mergers and Appendix 6 gives the titles of other articles of monetary interest in the *Midland Bank Review*.

A point worth making is that all with editorial responsibility for the *Review* have been involved also in the everyday work of the bank, as well as concerned with monetary developments, and the analyses and interpretations thus are rooted in practice. This is evident in frequent references to the Midland Bank's experience in the articles.

December 1971 J. E. WADSWORTH

SECTION A

Banking and Credit Policy Since the Radcliffe Report

1

The Radcliffe Report and the Banks November 1959

In this first chapter we call attention to observations and recommendations in the *Report of the Committee on the Working of the Monetary System** (Cmnd. 827), generally known as the Radcliffe Report, bearing directly on the joint stock banks and the banking system, because of the influence it exerted upon views and practices in Britain's monetary affairs, and also because it provides a convenient benchmark upon which to begin these reprints of articles from the *Midland Bank Review*. We do so simply by drawing together extracts – giving the paragraph numbers – from the Report. The Committee itself, in its unanimous report on the way in which the monetary system of Britain operates today insists on the need to see monetary operations as part of general economic developments. 'Monetary policy is necessarily moulded by the world in which it takes shape . . . [and] . . . conditioned by the facts of the economic situation and ideas of the time.' (17) In Britain economic conditions and opinion have changed greatly since the Macmillan Committee reported in 1931, and 'it is . . . no longer appropriate to charge the monetary authorities with unambiguous tasks that can be sharply differentiated from other governmental action'. (52) Nowadays, monetary measures may be employed in furthering five aims of government policy: 'a high and stable level of employment; reasonable stability of the internal purchasing power of money; steady economic growth and improvement of the standard of living; some contribution, implying a margin in the balance of payments, to the economic development of the outside world; and a strengthening of London's international reserves, implying further margin in the balance of payments.' (69) 'There are serious possibilities of conflict between them . . . and the freedom of governments in making these choices is not absolute', (70) but 'they must in the last resort be settled by government'. (64)

* Reference to the significance of this Report in monetary thought and policy is included in the Introduction.

When discussing financial institutions, the importance of looking at the whole is likewise stressed; despite the great differences that exist in their activities and the facilities they offer, 'we have been impressed . . . not by these differences but by the fact that the market for credit is a single market . . . It does not seem that any hard and fast lines are drawn, for instance between the supply of short finance and the supply of long finance.' (125) Hence the authorities must act 'not upon the "supply of money" (however that is defined) but on the liquidity position of the system as a whole'. (125) 'The authorities thus have to regard the structure of interest rates rather than the supply of money as the centrepiece of the monetary mechanism. This does not mean that the supply of money is unimportant . . . nor . . . that the authorities have no special interest in the behaviour of the banks. As the most accessible lenders, they are peculiarly important in the total liquidity position. . . .' (397)

By separating, as we now do, the comments on banking, notwithstanding the emphasis of the Committee on the fact that the market for credit is one, we seek to bring to the forefront the fresh view thus presented of banking in a modern economy. It is with the banks as part of monetary arrangements that the Committee is concerned, and not with their duties as business undertakings in competition with one another. Thus the tasks of administering a large clearing bank, with its widespread branch system and highly developed overseas business, are not examined by the Committee. It does not discuss concentration in banking, the capital structure of the banks, relations between ownership and control, or the return to shareholders – 'the total profit position of the clearing banks [is] a subject into which we have made no inquiry'. (168) It is, however, remarked that the banks are 'essentially commercial undertakings, in the sense that in form their first duty is to conduct their business in the interests of their owners', but 'this commercial interest has often been tempered by regard for a wider public interest'. (127)

The Committee comments that bank deposits on current account (demand deposits) are 'peculiarly significant both from the point of view of economic policy and from that of banking policy (in the commercial sense)', in that they 'are "money" to a degree shared by no other asset except, for the smaller transactions, notes and coin'. (129) 'All the larger transactions in the ordinary business of the country, and many of the smaller transactions, are settled by transfer of these deposits.' Hence the banks 'can always rely on the maintenance of a very large total of balances . . . Individual balances go up and down, depositors come and depositors go, but the total on current account goes on for ever.' (128) The 'theoretical mobility of the current account' balance has 'great force when banks are small and insecure, but firmly established banks as large as the present English banks can . . . safely regard their demand liabilities in total as containing a hard core of permanent resources.' (130)

In recognizing the convenience and efficiency of the cheque service, the Committee observes that one bank (the Midland) recently introduced a personal cheque service for people requiring simply a cheque service at a low, established cost, though the other banks 'have doubts as to whether the public really wants a "utility" banking service'. (958–9) Even so, it thinks that there may be 'room for extending the means of transferring payments in the whole range of transactions to and by persons which are rather larger, or more occasional, than the small everyday transactions for which notes and coin are the obvious means of settlement'. (955) It refers to the successful development of 'giro' systems on the Continent, adding that 'in the absence of an early move on the part of existing institutions to provide the services . . . there would be a case for investigating the possibility of instituting a 'giro' system to be operated by the Post Office', with 'the possibility of co-operation with the joint stock banks and savings banks'. (964) No doubt the Report was completed before the announcement in July 1959 that 'the Clearing Banks are actively engaged in a re-examination of the whole problem of the transmission of payments, with a view to considering whether new procedures, or an extension of the existing arrangements for the settlement of debts by credits to an account, might widen the services now available to customers without sacrificing the highly developed cheque system operated through a country-wide branch organization.'

The Committee notes that 'historically the great English banks depended little on the attraction of "small savings" . . . and in recent times the clearing banks have broadly, as a matter of deliberate and concerted policy, stood aside' from this type of business; 'in evidence to us the banks confirmed their adherence to this policy . . . The banks' restrictive attitude . . . has been supposed to set corresponding limits on the kind of lending they could safely engage in; the truth is rather that it has limited their quantitative share of the total lending in the economy.' (132) For monetary regulation, little significance is attributed to distinguishing balances held on deposit accounts (time deposits), which have 'advantages in liquidity and convenience not fully shared by any other interest-bearing asset . . . Bankers . . . in practice appear to lump all their deposit liabilities together, and to treat them as in effect repayable on demand.' 'From the point of view of economic policy, therefore, the total of balances on deposit account has to be reckoned almost, but not quite, as relevant as are current account balances to the pressure of demand.' (131)

In monetary policy bank deposits are seen as important but not as the main aspect of bank activity to be brought under investigation. Thus 'the amount of money, in the sense of the amount of notes and bank deposits, is of considerable significance' (392) but it is 'only part of the wider structure of liquidity in the economy'. (389) 'The spending is not limited by the amount of money in existence; but it is related to the amount of money people think they can get hold of, whether by receipts of income . . . by disposal of capital assets or by borrowing.' (390) Hence 'it is the level of bank advances rather than the level of bank deposits that is the object of . . . special interest; the behaviour of bank deposits is of interest only because it has some bearing, along with other influences, on the behaviour of other leaders.' (395)

The Committee not only attributes less significance to the quantity of money in interpreting monetary developments, but also it finds little use for the associated concept of the velocity of circulation of money. After noting that velocity has increased in recent years, the Committee observes that it 'cannot find any reason for supposing, or any experience in monetary history indicating, that there is any limit to the velocity of circulation; it is a statistical concept that tells us nothing directly of the motivation that influences the level of total demand.' (391) In modern conditions, the Committee dismisses the existing statutory control of the note-issue as 'otiose', (523), and quotes the view of the authorities, who 'do not regard the supply of bank notes as being the only, nor nowadays the only important, supply of money . . . The government's function in issuing notes is simply the passive one of ensuring that sufficient notes are available for the practical convenience of the public . . . Bank notes are in effect the small change of the monetary system.' (348) Nor can the Committee find 'some up-to-date close parallel with the restriction of the note issue: some way of restricting by statute the supply of money . . . Regretfully, we cannot identify any quantity, the statutory restriction of which would solve the problem.' (523)

Though the Committee looks at the level of bank advances primarily as of importance in monetary regulation, it also has something to say of bank activities as lenders, and these comments will be noted first. The Committee reports the emphasis placed by the banks on the short-term and self-liquidating character of advances, but goes on to point out that exceptions could always be found to the general rule, and that the attitude of the banks is changing, so that the range of acceptable proposals is increasing. With the observations on the 'hard core' of deposits in mind, the adherence to short-term lending need no longer be required as providing assets that may be turned readily into cash (130), but it is a preference that 'still has some sound basis in that it limits the range of judgement required in the lending banker. The great majority of overdraft agreements made by the banks must be based, at least in large part, on the judgement of branch managers, and these managers may reasonably be expected to assess the capacity of a borrower to repay in a short time, though they could have no assurance in estimating long-term profitability.' (136) However, 'as long as the banks remain in [the] position of feeling that they could comfortably lend more on overdraft if only they could find more credit-worthy customers, they are likely gradually to modify their theoretical confinement to short-term lending. . . . The tendency to broaden the basis of lending is bound to continue.' (142) The Committee remarks upon the ways in which the field of lending has been extending, through medium-term credit for exports, participation in tanker finance and 'personal loans', and itself suggests further expansion in two directions: term loans to farmers and to small businesses.

'Whether for short-term credit ("seed-time to harvest"), medium-term credit for the purchase of livestock and machinery, or long-term credit for the purchase or improvement of lands and buildings, it is clear that the principal institutional source of credit [for agriculture] has in the past been, and still is, the joint stock banks.' (915) 'The joint stock banks regard the financing of farmers as one of their special concerns. . . . The banks are in practice able and willing to meet all creditworthy applicants for short-term credit and medium-term credit, and often for long-term credit also.' (918) The Committee therefore sees no need for the establishment of a special institution to guarantee bank loans to farmers or of a new government institution to provide medium-term credit for agriculture, two of the proposals made by the farmers' unions, but recommends 'that the banks should be ready to offer term loan facilities within reasonable limits, having due regard to their liquidity requirements, as an alternative to a running overdraft for credit-worthy farming customers.' (922) The banks' lending facilities should also be made better known to farmers. Almost immediately after the publication of the Report one bank (the Midland) announced term loans to farmers on lines similar to those suggested by the Committee.

Looking at borrowing by small businesses, especially those developing industrial innovations, the Committee draws attention to the sources of finance now available, including special institutions, hire purchase undertakings and the banks. It finds that 'the banks recognize that small concerns stand in special need of their support and help them to the best of their ability', (941) but that the usual terms of advances are not always suited to their needs. It therefore recommends that 'the banks should be ready to offer term loan facilities within reasonable limits, having due regard to their liquidity requirements, as an alternative to a running overdraft for credit-worthy industrial and commercial customers.' (942) It stresses the importance of ensuring that 'bank managers, solicitors and accountants who are the professional advisers of small businesses should be well informed about the existing institutions and what they have to offer'. (940) It also suggests that the upper limit for loans provided by the Industrial and Commercial Finance Corporation, of £200,000, should be increased and that consideration should be given to establishing an Industrial Guarantee Corporation, with government support, to facilitate the commercial exploitation of technical innovation (946 and 949).

The rate of interest payable by farmers on bank overdrafts varies with bank rate, and the Committee does not accept the contention of the farmers' unions that the price of credit, from whatever source, was too high and should be stabilized in some way at the lowest possible level, irrespective of market rates. This would, in effect, represent a further government subsidy, in a form less satisfactory than the direct subventions now provided for agriculture.

For bank advances generally, the effect of movements in short-term interest rates on borrowing is not large, and 'the banks do not ordinarily take any action independently of bank rate to deter or encourage overdrafts by altering the general level of overdraft charges.' (137) The Committee thought that borrowers seemed to view interest rates as shifting through 'three gears', and movements within the high, middle or low range had little effect. A change of gear, as for instance the movement into high in September 1957, does have an impact, depending for its force and effect on long-term rates, on how long the new level is expected to persist. (442–7) Broadly speaking, large undertakings, including the nationalized industries and local authorities, showed 'independence of interest rate changes', (451) but small firms in various trades were likely to be influenced by a 'change of gear'. (452) The evidence of the consequences of the direct restriction of lending by banks 'was generally firmer than the evidence on the effects of changes in the cost of credit', (455) but 'the main effect . . . was to drive frustrated borrowers to other sources of credit, where borrowing was more expensive and sometimes more onerous in other ways'. (460)

Among comments on borrowing by local authorities, for other than temporary purposes, it is suggested that the Treasury should assist by 'not restricting their access to the Public Works Loan Board at prevailing gilt-edged rates'. (597) When borrowing from the banks for temporary purposes, the local authorities – like the nationalized industries – should, the Committee suggests, receive preferential treatment for rates of interest charged, being required to pay a rate below that usual for industrial borrowers but above the Treasury bill discount rate, because 'there is in practice no risk of default, and . . . irregularity of borrowing is a convenience at the expense of the banks for which local authorities should pay'. (599) The Treasury does not wish to see an extension of borrowing on bills by local authorities 'on the principle that bill finance is proper only for self-liquidating transactions'. The Committee observes that 'the Treasury ignores this principle in its own borrowing operations'. (600)

In comments upon the fact that the proportion of bank advances to deposits is still below the pre-war figure, the Committee notes that 'in evidence to us the bankers appeared to be uncertain whether they would ever wish to get all the way back to the pre-war proportions, but there was no doubt whatever that they would like to see, and indeed expect to see, a decided increase over present levels.' (140) Hence measures aimed at restricting advances 'must be powerful enough to overcome this strong expansionary push'. (141) 'Under present circumstances the total of bank advances is thus a function of the demand by customers who satisfy the slowly broadening standards of the banks', while 'the investments are the final residual item'; 'given the availability of liquid assets, the amount of investments follows from the amount of advances, a rise in advances being compensated by a fall in investments and vice versa.' (143)

In this orthodox view of the relationship between investments and advances, it is usually assumed that a rise in interest rates will impose a penalty on further growth in advances because the banks, obliged to sell investments to provide for the growth, will do so at a loss, since market prices will have fallen. The Committee finds that nowadays the force of this restriction on the activities of the banks is greatly reduced. It is made clear that, in regulating monetary conditions generally, interest rates and bond prices are of leading importance: the Committee looks upon 'the structure of interest rates . . . as the centre-piece of monetary action', (395) and 'the management of the national debt' as 'an instrument of singular potency' for influencing the structure of interest rates. (982) With the great increase in the national debt over the past twenty years, accompanied by a rise in the proportion of bank resources lent to the government, the sensitiveness of the banks 'to changes in the terms and forms of borrowing by the public sector, and therefore . . . to the monetary policy of the authorities as exercised through debt management, have also greatly increased.' (148) But the banks have so arranged their portfolios as to be insulated for long periods from influence in this form; 'much the greater part [of their investments] is in bonds with less than ten years to run to maturity' and since 1951 'their total holdings . . . have been more or less evenly divided between bonds with less than five years and bonds with more than five years to run to final maturity date.' (144)

In these circumstances, the banks have 'beyond their "liquid assets" (in the technical 30 per cent sense), a substantial cushion of short government bonds; by selling these bonds they can expand activities despite the restraint on their liquid assets.' (506) Moreover, by arranging their holdings with maturities in echelon, 'as long as they have a steady and substantial stream of maturities year by year in their bond portfolio, no manipulation of interest rates by the authorities can impose a penalty on banks that wish to expand advances by running down investments. . . . In recent years bond portfolios . . . have been such that even sharp rises in interest rates have not imposed on the banks a penalty sufficient to check them in their efforts to satisfy the needs of their borrowing customers.' (145) And thus the Committee concludes that 'unless the shape of the national debt is to be completely transformed by radical measures, the banks will always be able to hold a close succession of maturities to give themselves this facility in increasing advances.' (507)

Yet this protection from the effects of rising interest rates has limits because 'no bank will denude itself entirely of the nearest maturities', and so a 'rapid and sustained expansion of advances' would eventually involve sales of longer dated stocks, which 'are more vulnerable to rising interest rates. This interest rate brake on the expansion of advances . . . can be enough to make the banks think twice about a rapid and sustained expansion.' (507) Then, too, the Committee finds that 'the total demand for short bonds . . . is substantial . . . [and] . . . no great progress in funding might bring supplies of short bonds down to uncomfortably low levels.' (546) Similarly, the 'funding of Treasury bills beyond a certain (not very remote) point would cause a major upheaval in our financial institutions.' (543) It seems possible that 'if . . . the banks (whose figures are the really big ones) find in the future that they can maintain an advances ratio near to pre-war standards, they may well prefer to fill their correspondingly reduced investment portfolios mainly with short bonds.' (548) As the banking practices are changing, 'the composition of the banks' investment portfolios should be closely watched' by the authorities. (508)

With the orthodox methods of influencing bank lending weakened in these ways, and deposits seen as an aspect of general liquidity, the Committee discusses how banking activity should be regulated as part of monetary control. It points out that 'the Bank of England does not formally inspect or supervise the policies or operations of the clearing banks', and that no use has ever been made of the qualified powers given in the Bank of England Act, 1946, whereby the Bank, on the authority of the Treasury, may give directions to bankers. (350) It describes (354) the arrangements whereby 'the Bank of England is in continual touch with the clearing banks both on operational matters and on questions of policy', and quotes 'one of the representatives of the Committee of London Clearing Bankers' as saying in evidence: 'We listen with great care to what the governor says to us at any time. He might give us a hint and we should not be likely to ignore it. We might even be asked to be especially liquid.' (350) The Bank 'will remonstrate with a bank whose liquidity ratio falls below 30 per cent.' (352)

The Committee regards as 'overwhelming' the argument for maintaining the two conventional ratios of assets to deposits of the banking system comprising 8 per cent cash and 30 per cent liquid assets, (505) and confirms that 'the effective base of bank credit has become the liquid assets (based on the availability of Treasury bills) instead of the supply of cash.' (376) Moreover, 'the Bank has used its influence to give a binding power rather stronger than that of mere custom to the conventions of bankers as to their cash and liquid assets ratios.' (351) This represents a further recently introduced form of regulation; 'the Bank of England in 1955 insisted on the 30 per cent liquid assets ratio in the London clearing banks – a device of control whose existence had never been officially admitted before that date.' (429) The Committee finds it 'difficult to believe that ordinary banking prudence' would require such high ratios to be maintained today, although the bankers had 'made it clear that they would feel discomfort if the liquidity ratios of their own banks went much below 30 per cent'. (352) However, the Committee also found that while 'the 8 per cent cash rule appears to be accepted with almost rigid strictness . . . the 30 per cent rule is not accepted quite as unreservedly by the banks; nor has it even been propounded in altogether unequivocal terms by the authorities. . . . We therefore recommend that the 30 per cent rule . . . should be made absolutely explicit, though this need not be by statutory enactment or direction.' (505)

Since the Committee regards the supply of money as part of the liquidity of the whole economy, monetary measures aimed at the banking system should be 'as key lenders in the system and not at the banks "as creators of money."' (395) Yet, 'advances are of very high importance, because this is for most companies and individuals the easiest and most convenient form of borrowing; an interference with bank advances . . . is a major alteration in the credit situation in the economy.' (135) 'The authorities therefore need to have a special care, in framing a particular course of action, for its effects on the banks.' (395) Although 'regulation of the banks is required . . . because they are the biggest lenders at the shortest (most liquid) end of the range of credit markets . . . any severely restrictive control of their operations is certain, over a period of time, to be defeated by the development of rival institutions' and 'we therefore begin with some presumption against discriminatory control of banks, at any rate in ordinary times.' (504)

Even so, 'there must be some restraints on the activites of the banks', since 'bank deposits are so favoured as highly liquid assets in the hands of the public, and the amounts involved are relatively so large, that the banks are in a uniquely strong position to defeat, or at least to embarrass, any policy of the authorities in influencing rates of interest.' (505) After recommending that the 30 per cent liquidity ratio should be made explicit, the Committee considers various 'proposals for raising "reserve requirements" or similar devices'. They 'incline towards a straightforward power to raise the 30 per cent liquidity requirement to some higher percentage'. But 'any requirement of this kind . . . would have to be drastic if it was to influence the banks in their lending operations . . . In any ordinary situation we cannot find that there would be sufficient advantage to justify discriminatory action against the banks' – that is, 'unaccompanied by general restrictions on all classes of lenders.' (508)

'In times of emergency', however, the Committee considers that the authorities 'may choose to exercise a direct control on the lending operations of the banks'. (395) 'A monetary authority in a tight corner may well decide to strike directly at the banks. It is . . . at bank advances that they should strike.' (397) Emergencies of two sorts have to be treated differently. 'In the event of catastrophic slump . . . a government must place its reliance on other measures. Monetary conditions can be made propitious, but that is all.' (521) For the opposite danger, of headlong inflation or threat of it, the Committee considers that 'there should be standing provision for such monetary measures as could substantially help to check such a development . . . . We regard a combination of controls of capital issues, bank advances and consumer credit as being most likely to serve this purpose', (524) these being 'the most important and efficient sources of credit for those wishing to raise additional credit'. (525) Quantitative control of bank advances is recommended, preferably by way of 'a restriction of the proportion of advances to deposits, defining "advances" in such a way as to include all lending to the private sector'. The proportion would be 'uniform for all banks within a group (e.g. the London clearing banks)'. (527)

After surveying the available information about financial and monetary affairs, the Committee makes many suggestions as to how it might be improved and published more widely, either 'for monetary management or for greater understanding by informed opinion of monetary affairs'. (794) It believes that there is 'scope for more regular comment by the authorities on monetary and financial affairs', (859) particularly in the Annual Report of the Bank of England, possibly with, in addition, regular bulletins and occasional monographs. (861) In the amplification of banking statistics, the Committee explains that it is interested in 'statistics of banking as a whole and . . . the aggregates for the various transactions in which banks engage', and thus 'treat as banking institutions for statistical purposes not only the commercial banks but the discount houses'. (811) Indeed, since 'changes in bank liabilities and bank lending may be offset or reinforced by simultaneous changes in . . . other financial institutions . . . it would be desirable to draw up a single account for financial institutions as a group.' (808) But 'since it is more particularly the flow of short-term funds that reveals changes in liquidity, we have given particular attention to banking statistics.' (810)

The 'two principal requirements of banking statistics that up till now have not been adequately met' are 'that the figures should cover all banks' and that 'the figures of deposits and advances . . . should . . . exclude extraneous elements'. (812) On the second point, the clearing banks have already made considerable improvements, so that remaining imperfections 'are so small that they may be disregarded'. (816) To make the figures comprehensive, 'we see no reason why other banks should not provide and publish regular statements of assets and liabilities on a comparable basis with those of the clearing banks', so as to give 'aggregate monthly figures for each of the main groups'. (814) These would include the discount houses, Scottish banks, Northern Irish banks, other joint stock banks, accepting houses and merchant banks, and overseas and foreign banks. (813) The Committee would like to see published, at intervals, various statistics that the clearing banks now submit confidentially to the authorities (817), and also suggest 'a quarterly analysis of deposits with the clearing banks in parallel with the analysis now undertaken for advances', (818) probably by way of an analysis of large deposits only. For 'the joint stock banks, the accepting houses and the discount houses as a single group', the Committee suggests that the Bank of England should collect and publish 'quarterly figures of the holdings of gilt-edged securities . . . distinguishing between those with five years or less to run to maturity (short bonds) and those with more than five years to run', (819) and also 'quarterly figures of net cash transactions in gilt-edged securities'. (820)

Several other suggestions are made for statistics from financial institutions relating to home and overseas transactions. This is because the Committee believes that 'the successful use of monetary policy depends in the end upon a clear perception of a few underlying concepts which are basic to financial conditions in the modern economy', (979) and that 'what is needed is . . . a constant and profound diagnosis of the state of the economy . . . and a clear perception of the likely effects . . . of any particular measures'. (983)

2

The Failure of 'Packages' of Restrictions

Three Credit Squeezes
November 1965

In the ten years to 1965 the desirability of maintaining a steady rate of economic growth has been recognized widely, and the avoidance of 'stop-go' has come to the forefront in official programmes. But for the third time within that decade restrictive policies are once more being applied in Britain. The failure of achievement to match hopes is by no means novel, and especially is this so when the complex influences and forces of human society are involved. Accordingly we propose to examine briefly the circumstances that have made restrictive policies necessary on these three occasions, and to analyse the similarities and differences between the measures taken, giving particular attention to monetary developments.

The periods dealt with are around 1957 and 1961, and then from the autumn of 1964 to late 1965, and all have as their starting point crises of confidence in sterling. In 1957 the pressure reached a climax in September. Previously, the external situation had been giving rise to little concern as the measures taken to deal with the Suez crisis of 1956 took effect; indeed, over the first half of 1957, a substantial surplus was being earned on the balance of payments on current account, and despite a high net outflow of long-term capital the central gold and dollar reserves were increasing. Industrial production was expanding, after falling over the previous year. But some large wage settlements in the spring, a tightening of the labour market, and above all a sharp rise in the level of retail prices indicated an intensification of inflationary pressures. In overseas opinion, an uneasiness about sterling on account of these developments was heightened in the summer by rumours of an impending revaluation of the Deutschmark and also by the effective devaluation of the French franc in August.

From July 1957 the reserves began to fall at an accelerating pace, and the sterling-dollar spot rate, which incidentally had not been above parity since the middle of 1956, began to bump upon the floor of US $2·78 to the pound. So in September, bank rate was raised two full points to 7 per cent, this then representing an unusually big leap to an exceptionally high level. At the same time other restraints were applied, to which we refer later, with the object, in the words of the Chancellor of the Exchequer, of striking at 'the root of any inflation – namely the supply of money'.

In 1961 decisive action was taken in July, but on this occasion inflationary pressures had been causing concern, and had already resulted in preliminary safeguarding measures. In the April budget the Chancellor of the Exchequer had increased taxation and had then proposed the introduction of two new economic regulators – powers first to vary indirect taxes quickly and secondly to impose a surcharge on employers, 'analogous to a payroll tax'. Labour resources had been fairly fully stretched since the spring of 1960, and soon afterwards retail prices had begun to rise rapidly.

In addition, the balance of payments position was much less satisfactory than it had been four years earlier. A current account deficit of £273 million had been recorded in 1960, the greater part of it in the second half of the year. This had been offset by a large inflow of overseas funds, but it was appreciated that such a situation could not be expected to continue. As it happened, by the first half of 1961 the current balance of payments was improving, though not yet in surplus, but meanwhile the movement of short-term funds had been reversed. This was due partly to the unfavourable developments in the internal situation, but even more perhaps to uncertainties regarding exchange parities.

In the early months of the year, expectations of a revaluation of the Deutschmark led to large movements of funds into West Germany, and in fact the Deutschmark and the Dutch guilder were upvalued slightly in March. Even so, uncertainties persisted, particularly about the possibilities of changes in other currencies, including sterling. By June 1961 the spot rate had fallen below US $2·79, and once more the outflow from Britain's reserves was accelerating. Before the end of the month bank rate had again been raised from 5 to 7 per cent, and a range of other measures introduced.

The course of events leading to the crisis in the autumn of 1965 differed in some respects from that of either of the previous two. On this occasion the balance of payments was not only in deficit, but also it was deteriorating. Although retail prices were rising, it seems to have been the unsatisfactory external situation rather than indications of inflationary pressure that aroused particular disquiet abroad, even though for a time the drain was partly offset by an inflow of short-term funds.

Early in the year, bank rate had been raised from 4 to 5 per cent, and the budget was designed to slow down the relatively fast rate of growth at which the economy was then expanding, without bringing it to a halt. But it was now much more explicitly accepted than previously that in the initial stages of expansion, as the Chancellor of the Exchequer said in presenting his budget for 1964, this situation was 'a proper subject for financing through the use of our external credit, so long . . . as our domestic economy remains sound'.

No doubt this was the main reason why, despite the big swing into deficit in the current balance of payments in the first quarter of 1964, and further deterioration in the second, the external pressures led to no additional corrective measures. However, the rate for sterling began to weaken in May and in the second half of the year the size of the deficit became more evident, while the hoped-for expansion in exports did not materialize. Thus doubts about the position of sterling began to increase, and these were further exacerbated by the approach of the general election, which resulted in a change of government in October. Subsequently the pressures on sterling quickly gathered strength, necessitating the introduction of both old and new remedies. In 1965, too, the leads and lags in payments, on the part of traders at home as well as abroad, were particularly heavy in their cumulative effect.

The principal measures taken to deal with each of the three crises are described below. These were accompanied – and in 1961 and 1964 immediately preceded also – by generous assistance in the form of special arrangements of various kinds with monetary institutions in other countries, which were designed to reduce the pressure on, or to reinforce, Britain's central reserves of gold and convertible currencies. In the second half of 1956, a drawing of $561·5 million was made from International Monetary Fund. A standby credit of $738·5 million had also been arranged with the Fund, and in addition a line of credit of $500 million with the United States Export-Import Bank. Neither facility was drawn upon before the rise in bank rate in September 1957, and only when returning confidence in sterling was already evident in October was $250 million of the Export-Import Bank credit taken. The IMF standby arrangement was not utilized, but as a precautionary measure it was renewed at the end of the year for a further twelve months.

Before the next crisis came to a head, a major step forward had been taken in the development of international monetary cooperation. Following the revaluation of the Deutschmark and Netherlands guilder in March 1961, other currencies, and particularly sterling, came under pressure. The governors of eight European central banks then issued a statement that rumours of further currency adjustment were without foundation, and that 'they were co-operating closely in the exchange markets'. Nevertheless, the outflow of funds from the United Kingdom continued, and the 'Basle arrangements', as they came to be described, were called into play; assistance given thereunder by overseas central banks amounted to $900 million. This 'holding' action, however, was not by itself enough to avoid further and more positive measures to deal with the situation, to which we refer below. After July the credits were repaid from $1500 million drawn from the IMF, which also permitted a reinforcement of the reserves.

Before the 1965 sterling crisis was upon us, international monetary cooperation had made further substantial advances, and the various arrangements were fully utilized in 1964. One of these was the reciprocal 'swap' facility between the Bank of England and the Federal Reserve Bank of New York, then standing at $500 million; this was increased in November 1964 to $750 million. Additional short-term support was provided, as in 1961, from overseas central banks on a cooperative basis, to the extent of $500 million as pressure against the pound grew heavier. In November, when bank rate was again raised to 7 per cent, the reaction seemed to be perverse, and the step increased rather than diminished anxieties abroad. In these grave conditions many central banks abroad, in association with the Bank for International Settlements and the US Export-Import Bank, pledged support for sterling to a total of $3000 million.

Subsequently the amounts actually used were repaid from drawings on a longer-term basis from the Fund. For this purpose, the Fund itself, for the first time, found it necessary to obtain additional resources from the countries participating in the 'General Arrangements to Borrow' which had been agreed at the end of 1961. Finally, in September 1965, new arrangements were announced for the support of sterling, should the need arise, by a number of central banks, though the amount and forms of assistance were not disclosed.

These various 'holding' actions need to be distinguished from the other measures that have been taken on each occasion to moderate the pressure of internal demand, and in other directions, so as to bring about an improvement in the external balance. Official action outside the monetary field can be indicated fairly briefly. In 1957 the economy was already being restricted by measures introduced in 1955 and 1956, including, for example, a high rate of purchase tax – 60 per cent – on motor cars and domestic electrical appliances. Hire purchase controls had been adjusted several times, and in mid-1957 a minimum deposit of one third was required for motor cars and plant and machinery, and of one half for domestic appliances, with a maximum repayment period of two years.

Tax concessions amounting to about £100 million had been announced in April, but the overall deficit was expected to be smaller than in the previous year, and the budget was judged to be slightly deflationary. Thus the further measures were relatively modest. Apart from the raising of bank rate to 7 per cent and the imposition of restrictions on bank lending, reliance was placed upon a curtailment of public sector spending; current expenditure was to be limited while the total for investment outlays was to be held at the current year's level instead of rising substantially – as had been planned – during the ensuing two years.

The measures of July 1961 represented a more formidable 'package' than those of September 1957, but again they followed earlier action to deal with growing signs of inflationary pressure. In the first half of 1960 hire purchase restrictions had been reimposed, the first call was made for 'Special Deposits' from the banks (the introduction of this form of regulation is mentioned later), and it was announced that the level of capital spending in the public sector in 1961–2 was to be held at the level of the programme for 1960–1, but hire purchase controls were eased slightly in January 1961. When bank rate was raised to 7 per cent in July 1961, use was immediately made of one of the new economic regulators: a special surcharge was imposed on the main customs and excise duties and on purchase tax, expected to yield £210 million in a full year. Otherwise, apart from efforts to impose a 'pay pause', the measures were on familiar lines, being directed at bank lending and public expenditure. The surcharge on employers was not used, and the power to impose it has been allowed to lapse.

As the 1965 crisis developed, the only restrictions that were already operating were minimum deposits and maximum repayment periods for hire purchase transactions, but no 'package' of measures was introduced. Yet, because the external situation was far more critical than previously, the measures taken eventually ranged more widely, and were introduced over a prolonged period, as each individual remedy was found to be inadequate. Initially, on 26 October, a surcharge of 15 per cent was placed on imports of all manufactured and semi-manufactured goods, and a scheme for granting rebates to exporters was announced. Fresh attempts to restrain rises in prices and incomes were initiated, and a ban was placed on new office building in London and a wide area around it. An autumn budget followed, which among other changes brought an increase of 6*d.* a gallon in the duty on petrol and announced that the standard rate of income tax would be raised the following April. It also proposed improvements in welfare payments and an increase in contributions.

A fortnight later – on 23 November – bank rate was raised from 5 to 7 per cent, while within a few days it was announced that an international credit of $3000 million had been arranged. In December 1965 the first of three requests regarding their lending activities, to which we refer later, was made to the banks and other financial institutions. The April 1965 budget had brought further increases in taxation and the announcement of new taxes to come; subsequently hire purchase controls were tightened while fresh restrictions were placed on industrial and office building. It was not until eight months after the raising of bank rate to 7 per cent that cuts were announced in public sector investment and expenditure.

Exchange control regulations were applied more strictly in the recent crisis. In 1957, only usance draft and re-finance facilities were restricted, and in 1961 action was taken to ensure that direct overseas investment was limited to projects offering a quick return and to securing repatriation by companies operating outside the sterling area of a higher proportion of overseas earnings. In 1964–5 action had been taken on a broader front, with the main objects of bringing a higher proportion of foreign currency receipts of residents into the official reserves, of restricting overseas investment by United Kingdom companies, and of encouraging larger remittances of earnings from all overseas subsidiaries or branches. Restraints were placed on foreign travel facilities, and control over borrowing by United Kingdom companies controlled from outside the sterling area was tightened appreciably. Like the other measures, action in the field of exchange control was extended over several months.

Turning now to action taken in the monetary field, marked similarities are apparent in methods used in the three crises, but also some significant differences. On each occasion bank rate was raised sharply, from 5 to 7 per cent, but whereas in 1957 and 1961 the announcement of the increase and of other measures marked the peak of the crisis, in 1964 the rise came only after it was clear that the immediate effect of other measures taken in previous weeks was less decisive than had been hoped. And it had to be supported by further action.

On each occasion, too, the banks were asked to restrict the rate of growth of advances. In 1957, the request was that the average level of advances during the following twelve months should not exceed the average for the previous twelve. In 1961, the request was less specific – only to cut the rate of increase in lending considerably by the end of the year. On the third occasion, the initial request – in December 1964 – was similar to that of 1961, namely that the rate of growth should be reduced, but in May 1965 the banks were told that the increase in lending to the private sector during the twelve months to March 1966 should not exceed an annual rate of about 5 per cent.

In the third crisis, as in 1961 but not in 1957, the categories of borrower to be given priority and to which special restraint was to be applied were indicated. The absence of selective criteria in the original 'directive' of 1957 – other than the specific exclusion from restraint of medium-term advances guaranteed by the ECGD – was unusual, both as compared with most previous credit squeezes as well as the subsequent ones.

The guidance given to the banks in 1961 and 1964–5 followed a common pattern, with advances related to consumption at home, notably personal and professional borrowing, hire purchase finance companies, speculative building and property development, and other speculative transactions of all kinds marked out for special restraint; and finance to assist exports given priority. Within this general pattern, some changes of emphasis should be noted. After the first quantitative request of 1957, it was subsequently stated that finance for projects for 'sound' development within areas in which unemployment was substantially above the national average should be given specially favourable consideration, and again in December 1964 the banks were asked to have full regard to the aims of the government on regional development.

In the third period three letters of guidance were sent to the banks. In the second letter, in May, the criteria indicated in the previous December were reaffirmed, although the references to the importance of facilities for strengthening productive investment by manufacturing industry and to regional development were not repeated and first priority was specifically given to exports. In the third letter, of July 1965, the importance of encouraging exports was again emphasized; for the first time, too, the banks were categorically asked to restrain the growth of finance for imports and to examine requests for credit for this purpose even more carefully than before, particular reference being made to imports of manufactured goods for home consumption and imports for stockbuilding.

As time went on, new ways of reinforcing the 'directive' method of restricting credit were developed. One was by calling for 'Special Deposits' from the banks, under the arrangements drawn up in 1958. These act, in effect, as variations in the liquidity ratio, and when introduced it was hoped that use of them would make directives unnecessary. In fact, in 1961 and since, both directives and Special Deposits were used, although for the last the pattern of calls differed considerably. By July 1961, 2 per cent of gross deposits of the clearing banks, and 1 per cent of those of Scottish banks, were already on Special Deposits, but when bank rate was raised to 7 per cent further calls, of 1 and of ½ per cent respectively, were made. In 1965, it was only in April, five months after the bank rate increase, that the call for Special Deposits was made, of 1 per cent for the clearing banks and of ½ per cent for the Scottish. Both in July 1961 and in May 1965 it was clearly indicated that the impact of the call was to fall on bank advances, and in 1965 that 'It should . . . be mitigated as little as possible by the sale of investments'. Here, then, was a further refinement in the weapons used by the monetary authorities.

In 1957, the combined liquidity ratio of the clearing banks remained relatively high, notwithstanding funding operations by the authorities. In 1961, a vigorous funding policy had been followed, thus reinforcing the calls for Special Deposits, but in the middle of that year, before the further call was made, the ratio was comfortably above the minimum, then of 30 per cent. In 1964, however, liquidity remained under continued pressure, and at the end of the year, with the seasonal outflow of funds about to begin, the ratio was only 2½ points above the new minimum of 28 per cent. This may explain why a call for Special Deposits was not made until some months later, despite the strong upward trend in advances.

The effectiveness of the restrictions on credit was strengthened in two other ways. By July 1961, it was apparent that earlier measures to restrict bank advances were being offset, to some extent, by increasing use of commercial bills, and the banks were then asked to do nothing to encourage any further development of this tendency. In 1965, when the banks were asked to limit the rise in their advances, they were also requested to curtail similarly their acceptances and purchases of commercial bills.

The other way in which the effectiveness of official policy was strengthened was by widening the range of institutions to which requests were addressed. In 1957, they were sent only to the clearing banks, although the rest of the banking system was asked to give support to the measures; the situation was somewhat different at that time in that all applications to raise new capital then required the approval of the Capital Issues Committee. The Committee was asked to take 'a more restrictive and critical attitude towards applications to borrow, and in particular towards applications for large amounts'.

In 1961, however, the net was cast wider. The associations of overseas and foreign banks were also asked to seek to achieve a considerable reduction in the rate of growth of their advances in the United Kingdom and to apply the same general criteria as applied elsewhere when considering advances; the British Insurance Association was asked that its members should observe, in respect of their own lending, a policy similar to that requested of the banks; and the attention of the Finance Houses Association was drawn to the wish of the authorities that restrictions of credit should fall primarily on consumers' expenditure, and that hire purchase finance houses should not have recourse to the public in order to finance expansion of business other than that to which they were already committed.

Action was on similar lines in December 1964, with a further addition to the Bank of England's mailing list, namely the Building Societies Association, though it was made clear that the request was not intended to affect lending by societies in the field of housing for the owner-occupier. When the further request was made to the banks in the following May, indicating a quantitative limit on the growth of their lending, the same organizations were asked to exercise a comparable degree of restraint in their own activities, and again the list was widened, to include the National Association of Pension Funds. Later it was confirmed that a similar request had also been sent to leading hire purchase finance houses that did not belong to the main associations.

Like the measures themselves, the accompanying movements in financial indicators have shown similarities and differences in the three periods under review. For comparative purposes it is perhaps most convenient to take the raising of bank rate to 7 per cent as the common point of reference, as the eye of the storm, so to speak, even though this is not altogether satisfactory: first, because on each occasion the raising of bank rate occurred in a different month of the year and hence at varying points in the seasonal pattern; secondly because of differences in the time of application of other measures;

and thirdly because remedies were, in fact, applied at varying stages in the cycle. Thus the raising of bank rate and related measures taken in September 1957 and July 1961 in effect represented the final tightening of the screw, whereas in 1964–5 it was to be followed by further action extending over the next eight months.

In 1957 bank deposits had been rising quite sharply in the spring but had been tending to level out for several months before September. In 1961, too, net deposits of the clearing banks, seasonally adjusted, had risen substantially in the early months of the year, again levelling off in the three months to July. In 1965, however, they continued to rise sharply up to October. This can be seen clearly in Chart A (p. 41), in which movements in the seasonally adjusted net figures for the clearing banks over the second and third periods are plotted, taking July 1961 and November 1964 as 100 respectively. For 1957 seasonally adjusted figures are not available on the official basis and so no curve is given, but deposits were again rising from September until the end of the year, and possibly more swiftly than can be accounted for by seasonal influences alone. In 1965, too, the expansion of deposits was quickly resumed.

In 1957 advances were expanding, although restraints were being applied. Once again seasonally adjusted figures are not available. However, after the restrictions were lifted in 1958 advances surged upwards. In both 1961 and 1964 the rates of growth over the twelve months to the raising of bank rate were fast, increases of 10 and 14 per cent respectively being recorded. As may be seen from Chart B (p. 41), between July and October 1961 net advances of the clearing banks, seasonally adjusted, fell by 5 per cent, and it was not until October 1962 that the total rose above that of July 1961. The movement since November 1964 was less clear. A fairly sharp decline in January and February of 1965 was followed by a re-expansion, leading to the imposition of quantitative and other restrictions as already recorded, and subsequently the seasonally adjusted curve levelled out.

Despite these somewhat disparate movements in the totals, the impact on lending categories that came under particular restraint was broadly similar. This is most clearly seen in the figures for lending to personal and professional borrowers. In each period the total for this category for all reporting banks was rising up to the time that selective restrictions were imposed, though not rapidly in 1957 and 1961 when restrictions were already in force, but in the nine months following the nearest classification date declines were recorded of just over 2 per cent in 1957–8, of nearly 3 per cent in 1961–2, and of over 6 per cent in 1964–5.

The pattern of advances to another 'restricted' category, hire purchase finance companies, was less even. In the earliest period, when bank credit to such borrowers was only £33·5 million, lending was reduced by nearly 8 per cent in the nine months following the nearest classification date to the imposition of restrictions in September. In 1961–2, aggregate lending to hire purchase finance companies rose by over one sixth to £158 million in the six months to August 1961, but then fell sharply, by over one third in the following nine months, and did not regain the August 1961 level for nearly four years. In the 1964–5 period, bank lending to this category continued to rise between November 1964 and May 1965, but by August had fallen back almost to the level of the previous February. The overall increase in such lending in the nine months from November 1964 was about 6½ per cent.

In the early part of 1957 hire purchase transactions were already strictly controlled, but outstanding hire purchase debt was rising and continued to do so after September. In 1961 the direct controls were somewhat less onerous, but after July the total of outstanding hire purchase debt began to fall and did not start to rise again until the following May. In 1964-5, the total outstanding was increasing rapidly in the six months before the imposition of credit restrictions. From the end of November it continued to rise, at first at a slower rate, and over the nine months to August 1965 the total increased by 9 per cent. It was not until June 1965 that the statutory requirements regarding hire purchase transactions, which had been applied unaltered since mid-1962 were tightened.

The other lending activities of the banks that had been subject to restraint were less precisely identifiable with the established classifications of advances. For building and contracting, which to some extent were affected by the periodical requests to the banks to restrict lending, the total declined after August 1957 and 1961, but in 1965 the rise continued, though at a slightly slower pace. For 'other financial' lending, a fairly sharp decline occurred between August and November 1957, and in 1961 and 1964 the upward trend was halted.

Movements in the US dollar–sterling exchange rate are of special interest in comparing the three credit squeezes and their effectiveness, and these are plotted in Chart C (p. 41). It needs to be borne in mind that the rate against the dollar will be subject to two other particular influences, one being the firmness or weakness of the dollar itself in relation to third currencies generally, and the other the operations in the market of the exchange authorities.

Even with these qualifications, the chart makes plain why the measures of the autumn of 1964 had to be followed by further action. The initial response, as reflected in the exchange rate, was much less robust and sustained than in 1957 or 1961. In 1964–5, by contrast with earlier periods, the Bank of England was operating actively in the forward exchange market. The three months' forward rate for US dollars, which had been quoted at a premium of about ½ cent until October 1964, rose sharply to 2 cents in November and remained at around this level until April 1965; by the end of October it had fallen to about 1 cent.

As with the imposition, so with the lifting of restrictions differences can be

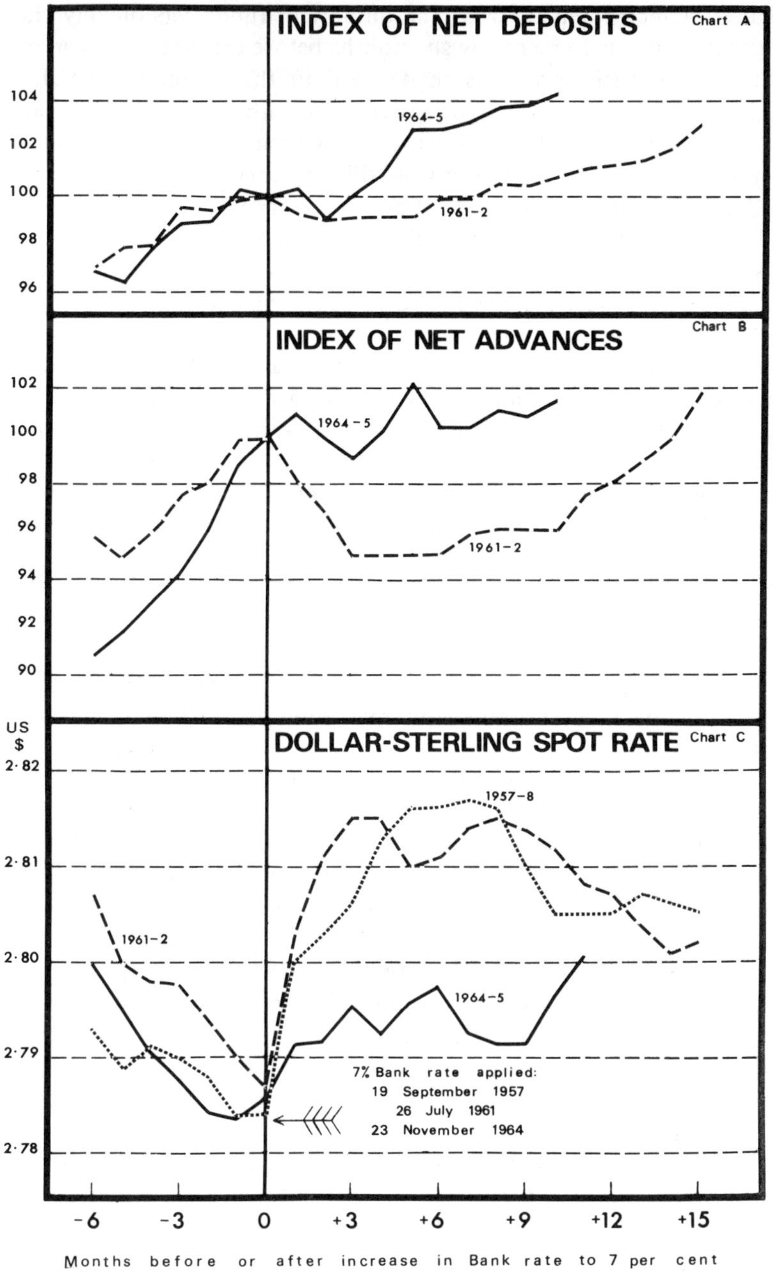

Index numbers of net deposits: gross deposits of London clearing banks, less balances with and cheques in course of collection on other banks, and less items in transit, seasonally adjusted. *Index numbers of net advances:* advances and other accounts of London clearing banks, less items in transit and advances to the nationalized industries, seasonally adjusted. July 1961, November 1964 = 100. *US dollar-sterling rate:* monthly averages of daily middle spot rates.

indicated. After September 1957 the outflow of funds was quickly checked. Nevertheless, it was to be nearly six months before the first reduction in bank rate from the crisis level was made, and in the meantime the domestic situation had begun to show signs of deflation, with unemployment rising and industrial production falling. However, in March and again in May 1958 it was indicated to the banks that it was still necessary for the level of advances to be held down in order to prevent any recurrence of inflationary pressures. But by the middle of the year, official policy had turned clearly towards expansion; in July, that is, ten months after their imposition, all restrictions on bank lending were removed, and at the same time the exemption limit below which applications to raise new capital need not be submitted for approval to the Capital Issues Committee was raised substantially. Bank rate then stood at 5 per cent, and in the following month it was reduced to 4½. Hire purchase controls were lifted in two stages, being eventually removed in October.

In 1961 the first reduction in bank rate from the 7 per cent level came much more quickly than in 1957, and by April 1962 it had been lowered to 4½ per cent, but at that time other credit restrictions were still being maintained. Even when the release of part of the Special Deposits was announced at the end of May 1962, the banks were told that this would only permit of a limited relaxation of credit, and were asked to maintain restraints on advances for speculative purposes, 'especially for building and property development', and to keep within modest limits any relaxation in lending connected with consumption at home.

A second release of Special Deposits, described as 'a natural relaxation in present circumstances', was announced towards the end of September 1962, but a few days later all previous directives to the banks regarding the exercise of 'restraint and discrimination in the granting of credit' were withdrawn. Even so, they were still asked to give priority to export promotion and the overseas earnings of this country, as also were other financial institutions which were similarly freed from restraint. In addition the banks were requested 'to give special consideration to the promotion of business in those areas of the country where resources are not being used to full capacity'. The final stage in the restoration of freedom in lending activities came in December 1962 with the release of the remaining Special Deposits by the Bank of England.

Thus within about eighteen months from the taking of emergency action, against twelve months in 1957–8, all restraints on bank lending had been removed by stages and all Special Deposits had been returned. From start to finish, the dismantling of restrictions extended over a period of six months, against four months in 1958. Movements in bank rate during each of the three periods are plotted in Chart D.

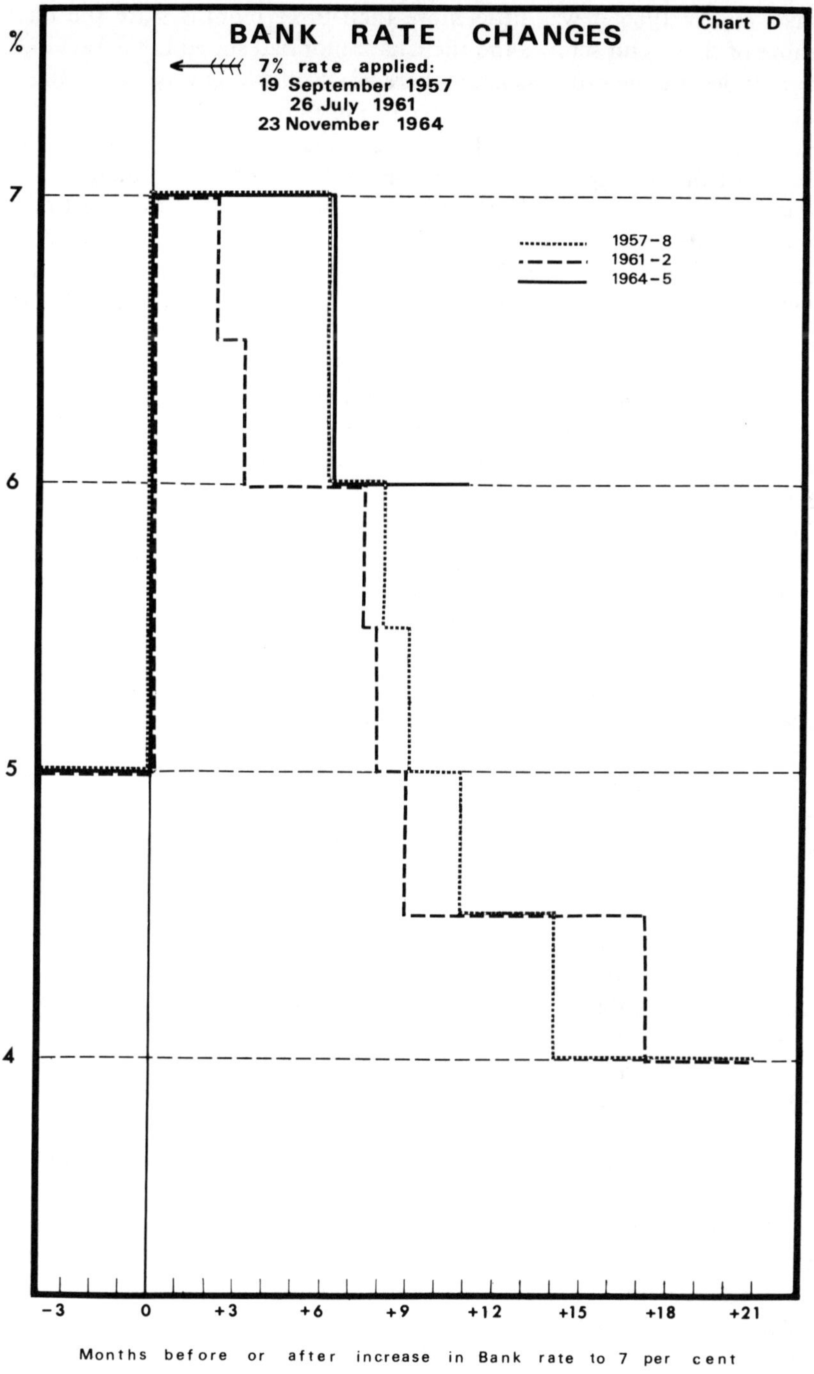

BANK RATE CHANGES
Chart D
%
7% rate applied:
19 September 1957
26 July 1961
23 November 1964
7
6
5
4
1957–8
1961–2
1964–5
–3
0
+3
+6
+9
+12
+15
+18
+21
Months before or after increase in Bank rate to 7 per cent

In November 1965 it was little more than three months since the final tightening of the 'credit screw', and the Chancellor had stated in the previous month that despite the progress made there was 'still a long way to go'. Bank lending was kept within the limit on expansion imposed in May 1965, even allowing for seasonal influences. The nearest figures for net lending to the private sector that can be derived from the monthly published statements of the clearing banks are gross advances less items in transit and less loans to the nationalized industries, but they do not take into account changes in lending to local authorities and other public corporations. The total arrived at in this way fell by £74 million, or by about $1\frac{1}{2}$ per cent over the seven months to mid-October 1965; the 'permitted' rise of 5 per cent for the twelve months to March 1966 would be £232 million. In the Bank of England's *Quarterly Bulletin* for September 1965 it was remarked that 'there seems no doubt that the clearing banks have kept well within the 5 per cent limit'. The quarterly classification of bank advances and the special returns for the intervening months that were being made to the authorities by the clearing banks indicate that the qualitative restraints also were being observed.

A limit was also applied to the rate of increase of acceptances and purchases of commercial bills, and the banks were asked to pursue the same objectives as those applied to advances. The Bank of England reduced the proportion of inland finance bills that it would accept in its sample purchases in the market from 50 to 35 per cent, and some banks were reported to have become more selective in the paper they were prepared to buy. In the seven months to mid-October, the clearing banks' holdings of commercial bills rose, on balance, by over £24 million, or $5\frac{1}{2}$ per cent, but the significance of this relatively rapid increase is not easy to assess in view of seasonal and other factors. On both the question of bill finance and of ordinary bank credit the Bank of England kept in close touch with the individual banks and associations concerned.

In previous credit squeezes the Midland Bank had experienced a marked falling off in the number of applications made by customers for advances, a slackening in demand attributed in part to the high cost of borrowing with bank rate at 7 per cent, to uncertainties about trends in business affairs, and also to the publicity given to the directives. The same slackening was apparent in 1965 but agreed facilities tended to be used more fully, in aggregate, than at times when no restraints were placed on bank lending. Usually the proportion of advances outstanding to agreed facilities is well below two thirds, but in mid-1961 it was already running at over 70 per cent and in 1965 it mounted above 68. Then, too, it is common in times of stringency for those undertakings that are in a position to do so to lean more heavily on trade credit. From reports regularly provided by branch managers of this bank, however, it would seem that resort to non-bank sources of finance was less marked during 1965 than in 1957–8 or 1961–2. One reason for this may have been the widening of the range of financial institutions that were required to exercise restraint in their lending activities in the same way as the deposit banks.

In each of the three crises the immediate impact became more severe, with heavier pressure on sterling and greater recourse to assistance from abroad by way of holding action. The credit squeezes, too, became more penetrating, ranged more widely and lasted over longer periods. In each of the three, bank rate was raised by two full points to 7 per cent, serving both to establish a wide interest rate margin for short-term funds in favour of London and to indicate the determination of the authorities to restore the situation. In 1964, however, the increase came at a later stage in the course of the crisis and whereas in 1957 and 1961 the move quickly brought a sustained favourable reaction, this was not so in 1964.

With bank rate, direct restrictions on bank lending constituted the centrepiece of official action and showed similarities on each occasion, though here again the response was rather different in the figures for 1965. Generally, a slowing down of the previous rate of growth was called for, and qualitative criteria were laid down, with finance for exports given priority and lending for consumption – to personal and professional borrowers and to hire purchase finance companies – marked out for special restraint. Then, too, the use made of direct controls over hire purchase transactions was less uniform.

More significant is the fact that the requests to the banks on lending policy had to be reinforced ever more extensively. In 1961 and again in 1965 direct action on bank liquidity was taken through calls for Special Deposits, with the intimation that the impact should fall on lending. In 1965, too, the restraints on ordinary lending were also applied more specifically than before to purchases and acceptances of commercial bills, and borrowing by companies controlled from outside the sterling area was more strictly regulated. Then again, the range of financial institutions required to comply with the wishes of the authorities was extended in 1961 and it ranged even further in 1965. By then the authorities were exerting moral suasion over virtually the whole range of lending institutions.

In the dismantling of credit controls the pattern was essentially similar in both 1958 and 1962. In each year the process was begun cautiously, but was completed fairly quickly once it had started, within four months and six months respectively. In the 1965 squeeze, bank rate was lowered already, some short-term rates having fallen from exceptionally high levels reached in the critical weeks. But the reduction – to 6 per cent six months after it was raised to 7 – was accompanied by a tightening of hire purchase controls, and it was emphasized that the change did not represent an easing of credit restraint.

So despite the reduction in bank rate, the process of dismantling the restrictive measures inaugurated a year previously had still to begin in November 1965. And the heavy reliance upon monetary regulation continued, with curtailment of bank lending prominent among restrictive measures.

Devaluation – For the Record
February 1968

The decision to devalue sterling was taken by the government following a review of the position and prospects of the United Kingdom economy, including the outlook for the balance of payments during 1968. The purpose was 'to achieve a substantial surplus on the balance of payments consistent with economic growth and full employment'.

Measures taken over the three years prior to the devaluation, and particularly those of July 1966, had succeeded to some degree in reducing the pressure of domestic demand. Exports rose markedly in the second half of 1966, and a surplus of £169 million was achieved on the current balance of payments for the last quarter of the year. Exports continued to rise strongly in the early months of 1967, but thereafter were tending to decline, partly as a result of the dock strikes in London and Liverpool, and the closure of the Suez Canal, but reflecting also the general slowing down in the growth of international trade; the level of imports remained comparatively high. Over the ten months to October 1967, the total for exports was less than 2 per cent above that for the corresponding period of 1966, whereas imports were over 5 per cent greater.

Deficits on the current balance of payments became progressively larger, rising from £28 million in the first quarter of 1967 to £87 million in the second and £116 million in the third. In the first half of the year the deficit had been offset by a positive 'balancing item', but in the third quarter this was negative, probably reflecting adverse changes in the timing of commercial payments or perhaps unrecorded capital outflows (see *Economic Trends*, December 1967, p. xv).

Sterling was weakening from April 1967 onwards, affected by the deteriorating trade position, the rise in short-term interest rates in other markets and uncertainties related to Britain's application to join the European Economic Community. The Middle East crisis exacerbated the decline in confidence in sterling and short-term funds continued to be withdrawn, at varying pace, until devaluation. Over this period, the Bank of England found it necessary to give substantial support to sterling, operating in both the spot and forward markets, and assistance was provided from overseas central banks to an unspecified extent.

International support arrangements for sterling over the previous three years had been substantial. Facilities known to have been available to the United Kingdom from overseas banks and international financial organizations during the months before devaluation included a line of credit of $1000 million from a number of foreign central banks, the US Treasury and the Bank for International Settlements, for offsetting withdrawals of funds but not to cover a balance of payments deficit; and reciprocal swap facilities totalling \$1350 million with the US Federal Reserve. The line of credit of \$1000 million included a facility – reported to be £100 million – concluded independently with the Bank of France in June 1966.

Of the earlier drawings from the IMF, of \$1000 million in December 1964 and \$1400 million in May 1965, the smaller amount fell due for repayment by December 1967, but \$400 million had been repaid in advance by the United Kingdom in May, while a substantial amount of sterling had been withdrawn from the Fund by other countries. The balance was repaid by the due date with the assistance of a loan of \$250 million arranged through the Bank for International Settlements in November; repayment of this loan was to be made in instalments between mid-1968 and mid-1969.

The gold and convertible currency reserves, as published, fell from £1216 million in April to £1003 million at the end of October 1967, despite the inclusion of a loan of £37·5 million made by three Swiss commercial banks in October. Total reserves rose to £1223 million by the end of November, but the figure was based on the new rate of exchange and it included the realized proceeds of the remainder of the Treasury's portfolio of dollar securities – amounting to £204 million at the new rate – which were taken into the reserves during the month.

With the approval of the International Monetary Fund the par value of the pound in terms of gold was lowered on 18 November 1967 from 2·48828 to 2·13281 grammes, equivalent to a reduction in the exchange rate against the US dollar from 2·80 to 2·40, a devaluation of 14·3 per cent – precisely $14\cdot\dot{2}8571\dot{4}$ – or one seventh. As a result, the values of currencies that were not devalued became 16·7 per cent or one sixth greater in terms of sterling. The new spot dealing limits of the pound against the US dollar were 2·38 to 2·42.

Relatively few countries devalued their currencies following the UK move, even in the sterling area; of those that did the most important in terms of UK trade were Denmark, New Zealand and the Republic of Ireland. The devaluing countries, taken as a whole, accounted for about one sixth of both UK imports and exports in 1966.

The new par values against sterling of some of the principal countries that did not devalue are shown in Table A1 (p. 48); in Table A2 (p. 49) are listed the countries that devalued at about the same time.

The Bank of England, in its *Quarterly Bulletin* for December 1967, commented that an 'outstanding feature of the devaluation has been the understanding with which it has been accepted without widespread devaluation of other important currencies, and the great help extended . . . in many countries, both by loyal holders of sterling, and by those who have given support before and after the event.'

In 1949, when the pound was devalued by 30·5 per cent, the United States was the main country to retain its parity. Those that changed their parities, by varying amounts, included all sterling area countries with the exception of Pakistan, all countries in western Europe except Switzerland and Turkey, all countries in central and southern Latin America except Brazil, and Canada, Egypt, Israel and Thailand.

At the same time as the devaluation in November 1967, a number of measures to reduce domestic demand were announced. Bank rate was raised from 6½ to 8 per cent. 'Severe but very selective' restrictions were imposed on bank lending in sterling to the private sector and to borrowers abroad; with some exceptions, lending outside the public sector was to be held down in aggregate to the levels existing at 15 November for the clearing and Scottish banks, and at end-October for other banks, after allowing for normal seasonal movements. Within this ceiling, priority was to be given to production and investment necessary for the expansion of exports and of invisible earnings and for import saving, such as in agriculture. However, medium-term fixed rate finance for exports and shipbuilding, the short-term export finance at

TABLE A1 *Selected non-devaluing countries*

		Par rate of exchange with £	
		Before devaluation	*After devaluation*
N. America			
US	($)	2·800	2·400
Canada	($)	3·027	2·595
Sterling area			
Australia	($)	2·500	2·143
India	(Rupee)	21·000	18·000
Pakistan	(Rupee)	13·333	11·429
S. Africa	(Rand)	2·000	1·714
EEC			
Belgium	(Franc)	140	120
France	(Franc)	13·824	11·849
Germany	(D. Mk)	11·200	9·600
Italy	(Lira)	1750	1500
Netherlands	(Guilder)	10·136	8·688
EFTA			
Austria	(Schilling)	72·800	62·400
Norway	(Krone)	20·000	17·143
Portugal	(Escudo)	80·500	69·000
Sweden	(Krona)	14·485	12·416
Switzerland	(Franc)	12·244	10·495
Other			
Japan	(Yen)	1008	864

bank rate, and 'any other lending specifically identified with the finance of export transactions' were completely excluded from the ceiling. Other financial institutions were subjected to similar restrictions.

Hire purchase regulations on the sale of cars at home were tightened; the minimum deposit payable was raised from 25 to 33⅓ per cent and the maximum repayment period reduced from thirty-six to twenty-seven months. Various cuts in public expenditure were foreshadowed, including the withdrawal, as from 1 April 1968, of the selective employment tax premium,

TABLE A2 *Countries which have devalued*

		New par rate of exchange with £	*Extent of devaluation on previous IMF parity (%)*
Sterling area			
New Zealand	($)	2·143	*19·45*
Ceylon	(Rupee)	14·288	*20·00*
Hong Kong	($)	14·545	*5·70*
Irish Republic	(£)	1·000	*14·29*
Iceland	(Krona)	136·8	*24·60*
Fiji	(£)	1·045	*8·95*
Other*		(unchanged)	*14·29*
EFTA			
Denmark	(Krone)	18·00	*7·90*
Others			
Spain	(Peseta)	168	*14·29*
Israel	(Pound)	8·40	*14·29*
Brazil (from 4.1.68)	(Cruz.)	7·70	*15·70*
Nepal (from 8.12.67)	(Rupee)	24·30	*24·75*
Macao	(Pataca)	15·546	*5·70*

* Bermuda; British Honduras; Cyprus; East Caribbean Currency Authority; Falkland Islands; Gambia; Gibraltar; Guyana; Jamaica; Malawi; Malta; Mauritius; Sierra Leone; South Arabian Currency Authority; Trinidad.

except to manufacturers in development areas, involving a saving estimated at more than £100 million, and the abolition of the export rebate, then costing just under £100 million a year, also from 1 April 1968. It was stated that the rate of Corporation Tax would be raised from 40 to 42½ per cent in the next budget to apply to company profits in 1967–8.

Formal application was made to the International Monetary Fund for an immediate standby credit of $1400 million, and this was agreed shortly afterwards. Additional support was provided by a number of overseas central banks, which agreed to make available a total sum of more than $1500 million of credit facilities. The IMF standby credit was described by the Chancellor of the Exchequer as 'of great importance not only in reinforcing confidence in the new parity of sterling, but also for the stability of the international monetary system as a whole'.

The Letter of Intent, sent to the managing director of the IMF in connection with the application for the standby credit is reproduced in Appendix 4. It sets out the policies the government intended to pursue to ensure 'the achievement and maintenance of a strong balance of payments, together with a high rate of economic growth which will make for full employment'.

The overriding aim was an improvement in the balance of payments of 'at least £500 million a year', at the new rate of exchange; this would produce a surplus in the second half of 1968 at an annual rate of at least £200 million. The measures announced at the time of the devaluation were expected to 'bring about a sufficient shift in resources in the coming months to go a very long way towards' achieving this improvement, through a reduction of home demand by 'about £750 million to £800 million below what would otherwise have been the case'. Further action would be taken if seen to be necessary to 'maintain the momentum' of the improvement, in the light of the next review of the economy, due in February 1968. The IMF would be consulted following this review and the subsequent ones, planned for July and November.

Fiscal policy would 'continue to play the most important role' in making room for the improvement in the balance of payments. The Exchequer's borrowing requirement for the financial year 1968–9 was to be kept under firm control by restricting it to a maximum of £1000 million, unless another figure was judged to be more appropriate at the time of the various reviews. This would be financed 'as far as possible by the sale of debt to the non-bank public', and interest rate policy would be used to this end. The 'growth of money supply' would be less in 1968 than was estimated for 1967, both absolutely and as a proportion of gross national product. The 'actual course of bank credit in relation to the expected course' would be taken into account at the periodic reviews. The prices and incomes policy remained as outlined in the white paper published in March, but the vetting arrangements would be strengthened.

Should these policies, in the opinion of the UK government or the IMF, turn out to be inadequate, the Fund would be consulted 'during the period of the standby arrangement and as long thereafter as Fund holdings of sterling exceed 125 per cent of quota, to find appropriate solutions'.

Further measures to assist the balance of payments, mainly affecting public expenditure, were announced by the Prime Minister on 16 January 1968. The net effect, it was estimated, would be to reduce planned expenditure of the central government and local authorities in the financial year 1968–9 from £15,378 million to £15,078 million against the estimate for 1967–8 of £14,387 million, all amounts being expressed in '1967 survey prices'. The increase in 1968–9 would accordingly be of 4·8 per cent in real terms, instead of 6·9 per cent; for 1969–70, the real rate of increase over the previous year was put at under one per cent, and the average annual rise in the period 1967–8 to 1969–70 at 2·8 per cent. The Prime Minister's statement, and a table showing details in 1967 prices of expenditure as previously forecast for the next two years and the reductions, were published as a white paper (*Public Expenditure in 1968–69 and 1969–70*, Cmnd. 3515).

The largest 'saving' in 1968–9, of £80 million, was to be achieved by halting the planned acceleration of payment of investment grants, leaving the time-lag between investment and payment at twelve months. The other main reductions in projected expenditure in 1969 were for roads (£53 million), education (£39 million), health and welfare (£29 million), housing £27 million), environmental services (£26 million), and home defence (£14 million), In addition, higher National Health and Insurance contributions of employers and employees were expected to increase revenue by £25 million. Substantial savings on the defence budget were expected in later years as a result of cuts in commitments and other changes, but none in 1968–9; the total for 1969–70 was reduced by £110 million.

The Prime Minister stated that these measures represented 'only part of a continuing process which will dominate national financial and economic management for the next two years. Other measures including budgetary decisions will be required.' He emphasized the 'paramount importance' of a successful prices and incomes policy.

During the ensuing debate, the Chancellor of the Exchequer forecast that the next budget, which had been brought forward to 19 March, would be a 'hard' one. He estimated that 'we need to put about £1000 million in the balance of payments to get the turn round we need and to meet the additional calls imposed by the loss in the terms of trade'. The economy could 'safely be allowed' to expand by roughly 4 per cent a year in 1968 and 1969.

3

Debt Management and Credit Control

Government Debt Policy and the Banking System
February 1958

It is common knowledge that among the consequences of two world wars has been a great increase in Britain's national debt. Not so generally appreciated is the fact that this has led to the development of a new technique of debt management, applied to the purposes of monetary policy, which is directed towards exercising calculated effects upon the banking system.

Before the First World War the total debt amounted to only about £700 million, consisting mainly of 'old' Consols; debt management presented no difficulty; bank portfolios contained many investments other than British government securities; and Treasury bills played little or no part in the operations of the money market. The recital of these facts points an immediate and obvious contrast with conditions at later dates. By the close of the First World War the national debt had multiplied ten times over; by the beginning of the Second World War it stood at about £8300 million, and by its end had passed £23,000 million. Early in 1958 the total exceeded £27,000 million, mainly as a consequence of government financing of various official and semi-official bodies. If the government-guaranteed stocks of the nationalized undertakings be added, a figure of more than £31,000 million is reached. The debt comprised securities with periods to redemption ranging from a few days to nearly half a century, together with some having no final, unavoidable date of repayment. Of the total of direct government debt, rather more than one half consisted of securities dealt in on the stock exchanges, and about one fifth of floating debt.

Clearly, then, management of the national debt was by then in itself a far more intricate task than it used to be even in the inter-war period. More important, debt management had to be fitted into the requirements of monetary policy, since it directly influences conditions in the money market and in the banking system as a whole. On occasion, debt management expressed itself in dramatic, broadly pervasive measures, such as the War Loan conversion operation of 1932 and the issue of Serial Funding Stocks in exchange for Treasury bills in 1951. Less conspicuously, it operated almost continuously and with equally significant effects. In the 1950s debt requirements had tended to complicate, if not obstruct, monetary policy. Late in the decade, for example, great importance came to be attached to the desirability of funding a part of the floating debt, but market conditions were by no means consistently favourable to the process. It is therefore of interest to examine the way in which debt management has developed, and to trace some effects of the new technique.

One of the difficulties of debt management arises from irregularities of date. On the one hand, blocks of government securities, amounting perhaps to several hundreds of millions of pounds at a time, fall due for repayment at particular dates or within periods giving only a limited flexibility. On the other hand, the funds made available through the savings of businesses, other corporate bodies and private persons come forward in a continuous, more or less steady flow, seeking opportunities for investment. It had long been a practice for a maturing security to be dealt with by a 'conversion' offer of a new security, with terms adjusted to current market conditions, in exchange for the expiring one. Holders who are thus induced to retain their investment will accept the offer, while others may find it more convenient to require repayment in cash. This practice, however, does not by itself overcome the difficulty arising from a hard-and-fast final date of redemption.

The authorities have therefore developed a new technique, which, though by no means easy to describe, already follows a fairly well-defined pattern. The basis for the operations is the large volume of government securities held by 'public departments'. The total of these securities, which have been described as a 'masse de manœuvre', comes to several thousands of millions of pounds. The largest constituent parts are the securities held in the Issue Department of the Bank of England against the note issue, together with those in the Exchange Equalization Account (which is managed by the Bank of England on behalf of the Treasury), and those held by the National Debt Commissioners as responsible for various official funds, the largest being the National Insurance Funds and the moneys deposited with the Post Office and trustee savings banks. Some years ago the Comptroller-General of the National Debt Office was questioned by a parliamentary committee about the choice of investments for funds under the control of the Commissioners. He stated that, subject to considerations as to suitability (with reference to such matters as actuarial liabilities and varying liquidity requirements), the Treasury had 'a very great voice' in broad policy, at least as regards a large part of the funds. He cited the combating of inflation as one purpose of government policy that it was his duty to further.*

It may be supposed that wide freedom of action is enjoyed in respect of about £2000 million of government securities held as backing for the note issue by the Issue Department of the Bank of England. The composition of this holding is never disclosed, but it is thought to include a variety of gilt-edged securities with a substantial quantity of Treasury bills, issued directly through the 'tap'. By the nature of their function as cover for the note issue, these investments are not subject to stringent selective tests, and the only statutory requirement is that the holding has to be revalued weekly at current market prices. Differences between book and market values are then, in common with any profit on the note issue, transferred in cash or securities to or from the Exchange Equalisation Account. Changes in the portfolio are made without public knowledge, and it is thought that, with these advantages, switches between holdings of different securities are frequently undertaken to assist government debt operations.

In the open market the 'authorities' follow two main courses with the object of promoting the steady absorption of gilt-edged securities into private holdings. First, the government broker acting for public departments is put in a position to offer suitable government securities at prices related to current conditions on the stock exchange. Thus they are ready to take advantage of any opportunity to make net sales to the public. It is in this way that marketable government securities generally reach the investing public, since occasional new issues offered by prospectus for cash are, in practice, largely absorbed by the public departments. Thereafter the process of 'peddling out' the securities to corporate and personal investors may be spread over such times as market conditions determine. The proceeds of net sales are likely to be placed in tap Treasury bills for the time being, and the bills in turn tend to be relinquished, as required, to take up further new issues.

Secondly, the authorities seek systematically to buy up in the market the next maturing government security, so that when the date for repayment is reached the bulk of the outstanding issue will be held by public departments. Thus the probability of a large-scale, if not complete, acceptance of an offer of conversion is increased. If, moreover, no offer of conversion is made, then, in effect, the maturing security will be replaced by tap Treasury bills, firmly held by the public departments. Either way, the amount of actual cash the government will have to provide is limited to the relatively small amounts needed to pay off 'outside' holders. There is no more than a limited addition, if any, to the liquid resources of the public, held in the banking system. Broadly speaking, in all these transactions in securities the authorities generally act in line with underlying market conditions.

* *Reports and Minutes of Evidence of the Committee of Public Accounts*, Session 1951–2.

By the means thus shortly described the masses of government securities that are subject to official management are used, so to speak, as a stabilizer, so that both the issue of new securities to the public and the repayment of those maturing in the hands of the public are spread over a period instead of being concentrated on particular dates. Thus, not only are heavy movements of funds avoided, but the task of the authorities is eased, inasmuch as the terms of issue, whether for conversion or for cash, need not be precisely in accord with the momentary preferences of the market. Indeed, as government debt operations in recent years have shown, new issues may well be made on terms designed primarily to keep public departments appropriately supplied, and no doubt the departments themselves will bear in mind any opportunities they may foresee of selling securities to the investing public.

This description of modern technique should not be read as implying that debt operations are easy to arrange and can always be managed so as to accord with the requirements of monetary policy. In particular, they may entail an expansion in the volume of Treasury bills at a time when the authorities are aiming at a reduction of the floating debt in order to limit the supply of liquid assets available to the banking system. For example, until 1956 several of the nationalized industries needed large sums for capital expenditure, and sought to raise them by issues of government-guaranteed securities. True to the procedure just described, these issues were first taken up largely by public departments, which then proceeded to dispose of them on the market alongside straight government issues. The sums involved tended to put a strain on the absorptive capacity of the market; disposals were slowed down; and it became necessary to finance ordinary government requirements, to a larger extent than was desired, by the issue of Treasury bills by tender – ultimately, that is, by resort to bank credit. This process, as the Chancellor of the Exchequer explained in his 1956 budget speech, 'impedes the whole operation of our monetary control', and 'the necessity of making frequent issues on the basis of government credit . . . prejudices the national programme of borrowing, re-financing and funding'. Accordingly, arrangements were then made for the capital needs of the nationalized industries to be provided, for a period of two years, directly from the Exchequer out of the general resources available from revenue or borrowing. This change did nothing to promote an enlargement of the flow of savings for investment or to diminish the total demand for capital funds, but it did give some assistance in clearing the way for government debt operations in the market.

A further complication has to be noted at this point. It arises from the fact that the operations of the Exchange Equalisation Account are reflected in the volume and distribution of Treasury bills. An outflow from the gold and dollar reserves provides the authorities with a corresponding amount of sterling, and, as this is promptly placed for the time being in tap Treasury bills, the government's need to borrow on bills sold to the market is reduced.

Conversely, with an inflow of gold and dollars, the Account runs down its holding of tap bills – perhaps even selling some of them in the market – and the volume of bills available in the market is thus increased. Subject to qualifications, then, it may be said that a rise in the central reserves of gold and dollars is likely to lead to an increase in the volume of Treasury bills in the market, thereby raising the liquidity of the banks, while a fall in the reserves tends to reduce the liquidity of the banking system. Thus at a time when, because of restrictive monetary measures or for other reasons, the gold and dollar reserves are being replenished, that very process has the incidental effect of raising the liquidity of the banking system and so working contrary to the restrictive measures themselves.

Unlike the well-known seasonal fluctuations in the floating debt, which are foreseeable with some accuracy, the influence exerted by the fluctuations in gold and dollar reserves is irregular and unpredictable in both direction and strength. A further factor has been consistently obstructive to debt funding for a number of years past, namely the structure of the total debt, and in particular its maturity distribution. The relatively large and growing volume of short-term debt has given rise to recurrent difficulty.

To recount the story in outline, the rapid growth of the national debt during the war years was accompanied by an expansion of bank deposits, and against the added liabilities the banks were required to hold a new type of security, the Treasury deposit receipt, which was not marketable and therefore not counted among their liquid assets. After the war, Treasury deposit receipts were gradually replaced by Treasury bills. In addition, during the war the authorities made substantial issues of medium- and long-term government securities, and some of these were taken up by the banks, as well as by insurance companies, other financial institutions and the public. Since the war, the authorities have had to deal with wartime issues as they have approached and reached maturity. As for the more liquid form of debt, in November 1951 a total of £1000 million of Treasury bills, largely in the hands of the banking system, was converted into short-term marketable securities, thus reducing the banks' ratios of liquid assets to deposit liabilities. These serial funding stocks in turn had to be dealt with as they matured, being replaced largely by other fairly short-term issues. With the upward movement in interest rates, the tendency at first was naturally for conversion issues to be of short-term securities, so as to avoid loading the Exchequer with high interest costs for long periods. Meanwhile, some of the medium-term issues made during the war have come to be included among the short-term securities. Hence the amount of short-term government debt outstanding has risen sharply, as may be seen from Table A3 (p. 58).

It is evident from published statements that during the post-war period the banks came to restrict their government investments to dated securities with comparatively short periods to maturity. Securities issued during the war years and held by them matured or were approaching repayment, while monetary conditions led the banks, in replacing or increasing their investments, to avoid long-term issues. During the 1950s, moreover, the authorities sought to limit the liquid assets available to the banking system. Hence the banks leaned towards government securities with fairly near dates of maturity, so arranged as to provide for periodical reinforcement of their liquid assets in case of need.

TABLE A3 *Short-term government debt outstanding (£m.)*

	Government securities maturing within five years		*Treasury bills outstanding*	
	Finally	*Optionally**	*Tender issue*	*Tap issue*
31 March				
1951	2067	1863	3190	1820
1952	3493	2242	2320	1953
1957	4576	2261	2880	1315
31 December				
1957	3772	2602	3460†	2225†

* Excluding securities having no fixed, final date of redemption.
† The amount of Treasury bills outstanding shows a marked seasonal increase, with its peak around the end of December, i.e. prior to the period of heavy tax inflow.

A further effect of the composition of the debt was that the discount houses extended their activities in short-term government bonds, so that collectively they comprised an active market in government securities having not more than five years to run to the final date of maturity. Such bonds were regularly held by the discount houses in substantial quantity, chiefly on the basis of short loans from the banks. In this way a double service was rendered by the discount market in maintaining banking liquidity – first by taking loans from the banks repayable at call, and secondly by providing a ready market for short-term government securities. The discount houses thus act in the capacity of dealers in a limited group of government securities.

Taking all these factors together, it is not surprising that, with the high interest rates ruling in the 1950s, new issues of government securities, with few exceptions, were of relatively short terms to maturity. Yet this procedure was not all that might have been desired in terms of monetary policy as officially defined. The funding that was undertaken amounted, in general, to little more than postponement.

Nevertheless, for a short while at the end of 1956 and the beginning of 1957 the authorities were able to engage in vigorous selling of longer-term securities from official portfolios; and when the bank rate was lowered from 5½ to 5 per cent in 1957, a statement by the Economic Secretary to the Treasury explained the reduction as contributing to efforts to maintain receptive conditions in the gilt-edged market, which had 'been of such benefit in reducing the liquidity ratio of the banks'. It was hoped to continue to 'make progress in reducing the liquidity of the banks', but in fact the hope proved ill founded.

The attempt to curtail liquidity in the banking system was also obstructed by the very scale of the expenditure undertaken or financed by the government. The government encountered difficulty, at least since 1951, in raising sufficient funds from the public, out of current saving, to bridge the gap between revenue and expenditure, including the large sums provided for capital outlays. As a result, notwithstanding the special operations, the issue of Treasury bills by tender to the market has grown until the amount outstanding was back to the high level ruling before the funding transaction of 1951. Moreover, as the investments of the banks were selected to run for shorter periods and with suitably spaced maturity dates, replenishment of liquid assets occurred from time to time. In general, therefore, the banks' liquidity ratios were running comfortably above the conventional minimum, and it is for this reason, among others, that the authorities sought to restrict bank lending by direct measures. The 'credit squeeze' was, so to speak, a confession of failure on the part of the authorities, in face of their own financial needs, to control the liquidity of the monetary system.

Official debt operations during the financial year so far in 1957–8 differed from those of 1956–7, and a change in tactics can be noted. In the year to March 1957 three issues were made, of rather longer date than in the preceding few years, and the floating debt was reduced; in the succeeding financial year, by contrast, maturing issues were repaid in cash, and, although two new issues were made, the floating debt was, nominally at least, expanded. To recall the details, during 1956–7 a conversion offer in respect of the only maturing issue was accepted by holders (by then no doubt largely public departments) of roughly £657 million out of the £824 million of stock outstanding. In addition, two issues were made for cash: the first, at the beginning of the financial year, consisted of a long-dated stock to raise about £200 million, while the second, in February 1957, was an even longer-dated stock to provide about £240 million. It was reported that the bulk of both these issues had been taken up by the public departments, providing them with securities suitable for market operations.

During the period June–November 1957 three issues fell due for repayment; yet no conversion offer was made, even though the total sum involved was larger than in 1956–7. In respect of two issues, together amounting to £401 million and maturing in June 1957, the Treasury explained, by way of a novel interpretative comment, that as a result of market operations in the preceding months the two stocks were held mainly by public departments, having been bought against the sale of longer-dated stocks. At the same time, a cash issue of £100 million of a short-dated stock was made. Similarly, with regard to the £503 million of stock maturing in the following November it was announced that, as over four fifths of it was held by public departments, no conversion offer would be made. The Treasury added that by this means it was left free to pursue a policy of 'reducing the floating debt at all suitable opportunities by the most appropriate methods'. It is in the light of this statement of policy that the next new issue had to be considered. On January 14 the lists were opened and closed for £500 million of $5\frac{1}{2}$ per cent Exchequer Stock at $99\frac{1}{2}$, repayable in 1966. The whole of the amount was allotted, and, from the terms of issue and of the Bank of England's announcement of the result, it may be supposed that the immediate purpose was to replace Treasury bills in the hands of public departments and the banking system. Even so, the combined effect of operations during the financial year to February 1958 was to increase, on balance, the nominal amount of the floating debt.

The bearing of funding policy upon the banking situation, particularly the liquidity of the banks, was authoritatively discussed by the governor of the Bank of England in a speech at Ipswich in October 1957. 'The "authorities"', he said, 'have a twofold objective. We try to avoid any increase in the floating debt, and indeed to reduce it. [Here he was evidently referring to Treasury bills held outside the public departments – that is, mainly to bills issued by tender – rather than to the nominal total of floating debt.] We also try to avoid adding to the heavy maturities over the next few years, which represent, so to speak, the floating debt at one remove. The aim, therefore, has been to sell longer-term securities either against the purchase of this year's maturities or against Treasury bills.' After pointing out that, under arrangements already made in the current financial year, over £900 million of maturing marketable securities was being repaid and only £100 million issued, he said that 'the bulk of the maturities had been covered by the sales of longer-term securities', although there had been some increase in the floating debt. He reaffirmed the intention that the reduction of the floating debt should 'continue by every appropriate method'. In passing it may be noted that, with the running down of the gold and dollar reserves in August and September 1957, the authorities were helped to avoid a substantial increase in the 'active' floating debt; the process becomes more difficult as the flow of gold and dollars is reversed.

The new issue was therefore timely as marking a further step in a consistent policy.

Managing the Gilt-edged Market – A Temporary Change of Emphasis? May 1969

Almost two thirds of the national debt consists of the government and government-guaranteed stocks which are dealt in in the gilt-edged market. Since 1946, the nominal value of these marketable stocks has risen, from about £12,000 million to around £22,000 million by 1969, mainly because of the government's need to borrow to meet the net overall deficits on its transactions. Of the total in May 1969, about £3500 million was in stocks with no final date of redemption, and the remainder consisted of stocks which must be repaid by the final date of redemption as given in the prospectus, which was moving steadily nearer all the time. The average remaining life to maturity of dated stocks in non-official hands was then about twelve and a half years. However, about £7000 million was due for redemption within five years, and about £1100 million before the end of March 1970.

In their operations in the gilt-edged market, therefore, the authorities must take account not only of any need for finance to cover current requirements, but also of the continuing flow of maturities. Other considerations are the effects of operations on the structure of interest rates and monetary policy generally.

The relative importance attached by the authorities to the various factors in their market transactions has been clearly indicated on a number of occasions, notably in evidence given to the Radcliffe Committee ten years ago* and more recently in an article in the Bank of England *Quarterly Bulletin* for June 1966. The chief purpose of management of the gilt-edged market, according to the article, is 'to strengthen the demand for government stocks. . . . The principal concern is to encourage the widest possible variety of investors, other than the banks, to increase their holdings, and to hold longer rather than shorter-dated stocks. These are essentially long-term aims; in the long run success will depend on investors' confidence in the market and this in turn will rest decisively on their experience of dealing in it.' Again, 'the dominant long-term consideration in debt management' is to 'ensure so far as possible that suitable finance for the Exchequer is available, and will continue to be available in the future . . . '

Other aims are to influence the structure of interest rates, credit policy and the liquidity of the banks, but these were explicitly said to be subsidiary to the longer-term objectives. However, if the continued availability of suitable finance to the government is ensured, then 'there need be no excessive recourse to short-term borrowing from the banks on Treasury bills and accompanying

* *Memoranda of Evidence*, vol. I, part II, section 10, paras. 15–27.

increase in the money supply'; while 'policy on interest rates can, and in all the circumstances must, concentrate largely on fostering demand, in the future as well as the present'.

The article explains how the Bank generally allows the broad level of prices to be determined by purchases and sales of investors, but intervenes to keep such movements steady and regular. 'The daily concern of debt management is usually to steady the market without opposing it too rigidly, but always within the context of its aims for interest rate and credit policy and for the maximization of demand for British government debt.' Thus it does not try to stop a downward movement, but bids on successively lower levels so as to secure a drop in market prices of 'broadly the dimensions thought desirable'. If 'signs of demoralization' appear the Bank may have to act more decisively, 'because of their overriding concern for the long-term health of the market'. Thus 'the market is dominated for most of the time by its own expectations of future movements in prices', including its expectations of the Bank's tactics, though this factor is 'not one that in the end carries greater weight than the balance of supply and demand' among the holders of the stock. However, because the Bank is able to intervene, either as buyer or seller, 'variations in demand in the market are . . . likely to lead to variations in supply at unchanged or only slowly changing prices, rather than to immediate variations in prices big enough to bring demand back into balance at nearly the same level of supply.'

In other words, the main concern of the authorities has been to ensure orderly marketing conditions with the overriding object of maximizing sales in the long run. On the tactical level, it was pointed out that 'a decline in prices can build up very rapidly once expectations that it will continue have taken hold', and if such expectations were strengthened by the withdrawal of the Bank from the market, 'to arrest or retard the fall may in the end require a disproportionate amount of official support'. More explicitly, a market in which selling 'is generally left unmoderated and then . . . abruptly halted by official intervention at some predetermined level may come to be viewed by investors as arbitrary and unpredictable in its behaviour; there is then a danger that they would be seriously discouraged from investing their funds in it. The likely consequence would be that the capacity of the market would be permanently reduced and with it the ability of the government to borrow at long term.'

Nevertheless, the course of prices over the past twenty years or so may well have led investors at times to regard the market as 'arbitrary and unpredictable in its behaviour'. Prices of all gilt-edged securities have fallen substantially over the post-war period. Last autumn $2\frac{1}{2}$ per cent Consols, for example, which at the end of 1946 were around par, stood at around 33 to show a yield of roughly $7\frac{1}{2}$ per cent. During the past six months, as may be seen in the chart of interest rates in Appendix 3, gilt-edged prices have fallen to new low levels and yields have reached new heights. Early in April, almost all gilt-edged securities were showing gross redemption yields of between 8 and 9 per cent. Moreover, the movements over the past six months have perhaps been sharper and more rapid than in any other comparable period since the war.

It is stated in the issue for March 1969 of the Bank of England *Quarterly Bulletin* that throughout the period November 1968 to February 1969 'the authorities were, as always, prepared to deal in response to market offers, at prices judged by them both to conform with the underlying trend of interest rates and to be consistent with the underlying long-term objective of preserving market conditions favourable to maximum official sales of government debt – particularly sales to investors outside the banking sector.'

Thus the underlying strategy remained unchanged but the detailed description of official tactics during the period suggests, at the least, some modification of earlier practices. It is said that some selling of medium- and long-dated stocks occurred in the first half of November 1968 and 'the authorities readily allowed this to have its effects on yields'. At the time of the international currency crisis during that month the market became more unsettled and 'the authorities therefore modified their tactics in order to steady the market until the outlook was a little clearer'. Then the authorities 'reverted to a policy of allowing any weakness to be fully reflected in prices', for the reason that 'a rise in UK interest rates other than the very shortest was seen as an appropriate accompaniment to the measures which had been taken to restrain domestic demand . . . ' In December 1968 the market became very unsettled because of the rise in US interest rates and the authorities 'sought to exert a steadying influence by lowering relatively slowly the prices at which they were prepared to deal'. But they 'did little to resist' a burst of selling in mid-January 1969, and again towards the end of January they 'did not resist a tendency for yields to rise'. The story is not taken beyond mid-February, when long rates had risen nearly 1 per cent above their October level, and signs of new buying appeared. Subsequently, however, bank rate was raised by 1 per cent – on 27 February 1969 – and prices for a time fell still further with little sign of official intervention.

This change in tactics has naturally raised the question whether official policy in relation to the market also has changed. In the House of Commons in January a government spokesman stated that it had not. Even so, according to the *Bulletin*, 'changes in the surrounding circumstances led to adjustments in the authorities' tactics regarding the prices at which they were prepared to deal'. It would seem reasonable to expect that changed circumstances might also affect the weights given to the various policy objectives. Two developments may have a particular significance here. First may be noted the Letter of Intent sent to the IMF in connection with the application for a standby credit at the time of devaluation (see Appendix 4). This stated that the

Exchequer's borrowing requirement for the financial year 1968–9 would be financed 'as far as possible by the sale of debt to the non-bank public', and that interest rate policy would be used to this end. The Letter also included an undertaking regarding the growth of the money supply, an aspect of policy to which the Fund gave considerable weight. Certainly if the authorities had always stood ready to buy all securities on offer without allowing the price to fall to a level which might discourage sellers, this would have given them no control over cash in the hands of the private sector and thus loosen the tight grip which the authorities were trying, with some success, to impose upon credit and liquidity generally. The second change in circumstances has been the swing into surplus of the Exchequer accounts on an annual basis. For 1968–9 a surplus of £287 million was achieved, and an even greater surplus was estimated for the next financial year.

As already indicated, at times of particular pressure at this period – and notably during the international currency crisis in November 1968 – the authorities have acted to steady the market, but apparently on no more than a limited scale. According to the *Bulletin*, 'net purchases of medium and long-dated stocks during the fourth calendar quarter totalled no more than £69 million . . . By contrast, their purchases of short-dated stocks, at £336 million, were substantial – though the bulk of these reflected sales by the discount market and by holders outside the banking system of stocks maturing in 1969.' In unsettled conditions towards the end of January 1969, 'once again the authorities did not resist a tendency for yields to rise and their purchases were largely confined to the 1969 maturities'.

The *Bulletin* articles, and the movements in prices of gilt-edged securities themselves, point to the conclusion that in the months prior to May 1969 the authorities have been significantly less willing to intervene in the market as buyers than they would have been in similar circumstances previously. That there had been an adjustment of tactics in the operation of the gilt-edged market was acknowledged. Even if there had been no change in policy, it would seem that for a period at least there was a discernible shift of emphasis, with interest rate considerations in the context of the need to restrain domestic demand assuming more than their customary subsidiary role. In his Budget statement in April 1969, however, the Chancellor of the Exchequer expressed the view that the prospects for the gilt-edged market were 'much better' than they had been a year before, 'primarily because the public sector as a whole will be repaying debt'. In addition, he thought that the abolition of long-term capital gains tax on government and government-guaranteed marketable securities 'should make gilt-edged more attractive to investors and will encourage a more active market in gilts – a necessary condition for a successful selling policy'. So maximization of sales clearly remains the underlying objective, but doubtless subject to changes of emphasis and tactics from time to time.

The Gilt-edged Market and Credit Control August 1971

The Bank of England's proposals on 'Competition and Credit Control' (see Appendix 4), constitute a significant milestone in banking and financial management in the United Kingdom. It is likely to be some time before the effects on competition among the banks become clearly apparent: the new arrangements in this respect have not yet begun to come into operation; during a subsequent transitional period individual institutions will be moving towards the minimum reserve assets requirement; and further adjustments to the new situation may then be expected. The changes in official policy in the gilt-edged market described in the consultative document, however, came into operation in May immediately after its publication. These represent a further stage in the continuing development in monetary management in the United Kingdom.

Taken at their face value, indeed, they mark a decisive shift in the direction in which the authorities have been pointing for several years past. To judge from the open and definitive way in which the new 'rules' were announced in advance of their application – unlike previous changes in policy and tactics, which were unheralded – they can be taken to represent the formal position of the authorities for some time to come. What must remain open to doubt is how they will work out in practice, and whether the authorities will hold to their declared attitude if the market comes under severe strain.

In the document published on 14 May 1971 it was stated that the Bank of England's operations in the gilt-edged market would, with immediate effect, be restricted in extent. The Bank would only be prepared to respond to requests to buy stock outright if it had one year or less to run to maturity, though the right to do so for longer-dated stocks was reserved. It would be prepared to undertake exchanges of stock with more than one year to run at prices of its own choosing provided that these did not 'unduly shorten the life of the debt', and would be prepared to respond to bids for holdings of 'tap' stocks and any other stocks that it might wish to sell. This was said to represent 'a return towards the position in the market which they [the Bank] occupied up to some ten years ago'. This cryptic and somewhat puzzling statement can be related, it seems, to the answer given by the then governor of the Bank of England to Question 1762 put by the Radcliffe Committee in 1957: 'Occasionally, when some new development takes place which might cause uncertainty or fluctuation, the Issue Department intervenes temporarily in the market to give a lead or to steady the market, but it is no part of general Issue Department policy to resist a definite trend of markets in one direction or the other.' Subsequently, however, up to 1968, official intervention to steady the market seems to have become more frequent.

The purpose of the modification that has now been brought into effect is described as being to limit fluctuations in the resources of the banking system arising from official operations in the gilt-edged market, and more generally to 'leave more freedom for prices to be affected by market conditions and for others to operate if they so wish'.

The authorities have been moving in the direction of a more passive role in relation to the level of interest rates, reflecting a reassessment of policy objectives, since late in 1968. This trend was specifically recognized by the governor of the Bank of England in a public lecture in December 1970, when he stated that, apart from the needs of government finance, the 'main end' of official operations in the gilt-edged market was to 'achieve the degree of monetary restraint judged to be appropriate to the economic situation and the overall direction of policy. Any particular degree of restraint in any particular circumstances will involve a certain level and pattern of interest rates which will have to be accepted.' At the same time, he felt it prudent to question the expectations of those who believed that 'a purely tactical change in the relatively arcane sphere of operations in the gilt-edged market can magically and painlessly do wonders for the real economy'.

In a further speech at Munich late in May 1971 the governor explained more fully the thinking behind the new gilt-edged policy, and its relationship to the banking proposals published at the same time. He said that 'basically what we have in mind is a system under which the allocation of credit is primarily determined by its cost'. The structure of interest rates would be influenced through 'a general control over the liquidity of the whole banking system', and the proposed new reserve requirements were 'designed to provide a known firm base on which the Bank of England can operate, both in market operations and by calls for Special Deposits, to neutralize excess liquidity which the banking system might acquire'. He envisaged no limitation on the ability of the authorities to neutralize excess liquidity or to bring about sufficiently strong upward pressure on bank lending rates. He accepted that some gilt-edged holders might prefer to stay shorter than previously, 'but their policies will, no doubt, be influenced by the structure of rates as well as by the extent to which private institutions are stimulated to make a better market in gilt-edged than hitherto'.

It will be seen that the new policy places considerable emphasis upon the banks, a main purpose being to affect liquidity or holdings of reserve assets of the banking system as a whole. It is assumed that changes in interest rates have a wide-ranging effect upon the economy, and that the market can be influenced to a significant degree by inducing purchases or sales of securities by the banks.

The classic role of open market operations by the authorities is to affect the credit base of the banking system. For some years past, however, account has also had to be taken of other objectives of open market policy, to such an extent indeed that the effects on bank liquidity had become of subsidiary importance. Now increased emphasis is being put on this aspect, leaving open the question as to the relative importance to be attached to the other objectives of official policy. Here it may be useful to recapitulate what is known of the importance given to these objectives in the past.

In their operations in the gilt-edged market the authorities must take account not only of any need for finance to cover current requirements, but also of the continuing flow of maturities as well as the effects of these operations on the structure of interest rates and monetary policy generally. Of the outstanding total, as at end-March 1971, of marketable government and government-guaranteed securities, less than £3500 million had no final date of redemption: the remaining £18,000 million moves steadily towards maturity. The overriding objective of the authorities, at least until 1968, was to ensure that the public continued to hold the debt. This had involved selling new debt, preferably long-dated, to offset maturities, and this in turn had been felt to require the prevention of sharp fluctuations in prices in order to foster the health of the market. These considerations were explained in an article in the Bank of England *Bulletin* for June 1966, from which the following quotations are selected.

The chief purpose of management of the gilt-edged market was 'to strengthen the demand for government stocks . . . The principal concern is to encourage the widest possible variety of investors, other than the banks, to increase their holdings, and to hold longer rather than shorter-term stocks. These are essentially long-term aims; in the long run success will depend on investors' confidence in the market and this in turn will rest decisively on their experience of dealing in it.'

Other aims were to influence the structure of interest rates, credit policy and the liquidity of the banks, but these were explicitly stated not to be the 'dominant' long-term considerations.

'The daily concern of debt management is usually to steady the market without opposing it too rigidly, but always within the context of its aims for interest rate and credit policy and for the maximization of demand for British government debt.' Because the Bank intervened, either as buyer or seller, 'variations in demand in the market are . . . likely to lead to variations in supply at unchanged or only slowly changing prices, rather than to immediate variations in prices big enough to bring demand back into balance at nearly the same level of supply'.

A market in which selling 'is generally left unmoderated and then . . . abruptly halted by official intervention at some predetermined level, may come to be viewed by investors as arbitrary and unpredictable in its behaviour; there is then a danger that they would be seriously discouraged from investing their funds in it. The likely consequence would be that the capacity of the market would be permanently reduced and with it the ability of the government to borrow at long term.'

This predominant concern with debt management rather than the monetary implications of open market operations did not pass without questioning, by the International Monetary Fund among others. As a corollary of this concern, when the government applied to the Fund for a standby credit at the time of devaluation in November 1967, the accompanying Letter of Intent (see Appendix 4(a)) included undertakings to reduce the rate of growth of money supply, as far as possible to finance the Exchequer borrowing requirement for 1968–9 by the sale of debt to the non-bank public, and to use interest rate policy to this end. A further Letter of Intent in May 1969 (see Appendix 4(b)) had broadly similar monetary implications, although the underlying criterion was the rate of 'domestic credit expansion' – a concept related to money supply.

Following these undertakings the level of intervention in the gilt-edged market may have been reduced, but that a change in tactics was taking place became apparent – and was subsequently confirmed in the March 1969 issue of the Bank's *Bulletin* – towards the end of 1968 and in the early months of 1969. From late 1968 the authorities were significantly less willing to intervene in the market as buyers than they would have been in similar circumstances previously, and more willing to see larger fluctuations in prices.

This change of stance was given more explicit recognition by the governor of the Bank of England in July 1969. He said then* that 'more recently the objectives of open market policy have become more complex when we have been seeking, while continuing to fulfil the earlier functions of open market policies . . . also to constrain any increase in money supply which might result from open market operations'. He added that 'these two objectives can be very difficult to reconcile'. Again, 'the latter day terms of reference designed to secure that we do not increase the money supply unduly, do of course constrain our day-to-day freedom to operate in the market'. And an article in the Bank's *Bulletin* for June 1969 said that the policy of 'leaning against the wind' in the market had enabled the banks to transfer from one government stock to another in the short term without incurring too great a loss.

Thus the latest development is in line with, and carries further, the evolution of policy since 1968, representing a further limitation of the degree of market intervention and giving greater importance to the level of interest rates and the credit base of the banking system. What is less obvious is how the objective of funding the national debt – previously given first priority – is now regarded. The only explicit public reference to this was in the governor's Munich speech, in which he said: 'This does not mean that we have discontinued our normal operations of selling longer dated gilt-edged against purchases of short-dated stocks as a technically efficient way of refinancing

* *Minutes of Evidence taken before the Select Committee on the Nationalised Industries* (Sub Committee B): Bank of England, Question 727 (published in May 1970).

maturities. But it does mean that we shall not generally be prepared to buy stock outright. Thus we shall not normally be prepared to facilitate movements out of gilt-edged by the banks, even if their sales should cause the market temporarily to weaken quite sharply.'

No policy can be regarded as sacrosanct when the situation in which it is operating is susceptible to change. Thus it might be regarded as unfair, or at least otiose, to quote at length from official explanations of a policy which has subsequently undergone such a marked change in emphasis, the more so since one can only welcome, and would certainly not wish to discourage, the growing practice of disclosure of official purposes and attitudes. However, the extensive quotations have been given from the 1966 *Bulletin* because a fundamental element in the situation at that time – the structure and extent of the national debt – has not substantially changed, although the Exchequer is not now in heavy overall deficit, as it was at that time and for some years previously. It might be argued, therefore, that the new policy runs the risk of weakening the public's willingness to hold the debt, except at what would be regarded as unacceptably high rates of interest. It remains to be seen whether, if this prospect should appear imminent, the authorities will maintain their resolve to stay out of the market, or whether they will invoke their saving clauses to an extent that effectively negates the new policy. In this connection, it is useful to look at the patterns of yields and maturities in the market.

From shortly after the end of the war up to about the middle of 1969 the trend of gilt-edged prices was downwards, with the fall becoming pronounced over the last nine months of the period. At the height of the cheap money era late in 1946, $2\frac{1}{2}$ per cent Consols stood at about par, but by 1969 the price had fallen below 27 and the yield had risen from the nominal $2\frac{1}{2}$ per cent to well over 9 per cent. Over the same period prices and yields of short- and medium-dated maturities tended to follow a similar course. At times of crisis, when bank rate was moved up sharply, short rates rose above long rates, but a fairly close correspondence tended to re-establish itself. Throughout the second half of the 1960s the yields on all maturities, though fluctuating, tended to be closer to one another than previously.

In 1970, however, yields and prices of the various maturities began to show a marked divergence, and the differentials established during that year have persisted since, as may be clearly seen from Chart E (p. 70). This shows the margins by which the gross redemption yields on medium-dated (ten years) and long-dated (twenty years) stocks exceeded those on short-dated (five years) stocks. For the past year the long stocks have consistently been yielding at least 1·6 per cent more than the shorts, and recently the margin has risen to 2 per cent; for the mediums the differential has been around 1 per cent.

It is difficult to establish what is a 'normal' pattern for yields on government securities. In a completely free market, one might expect the yields on longer-dated stocks usually to be somewhat higher than those on short-dated

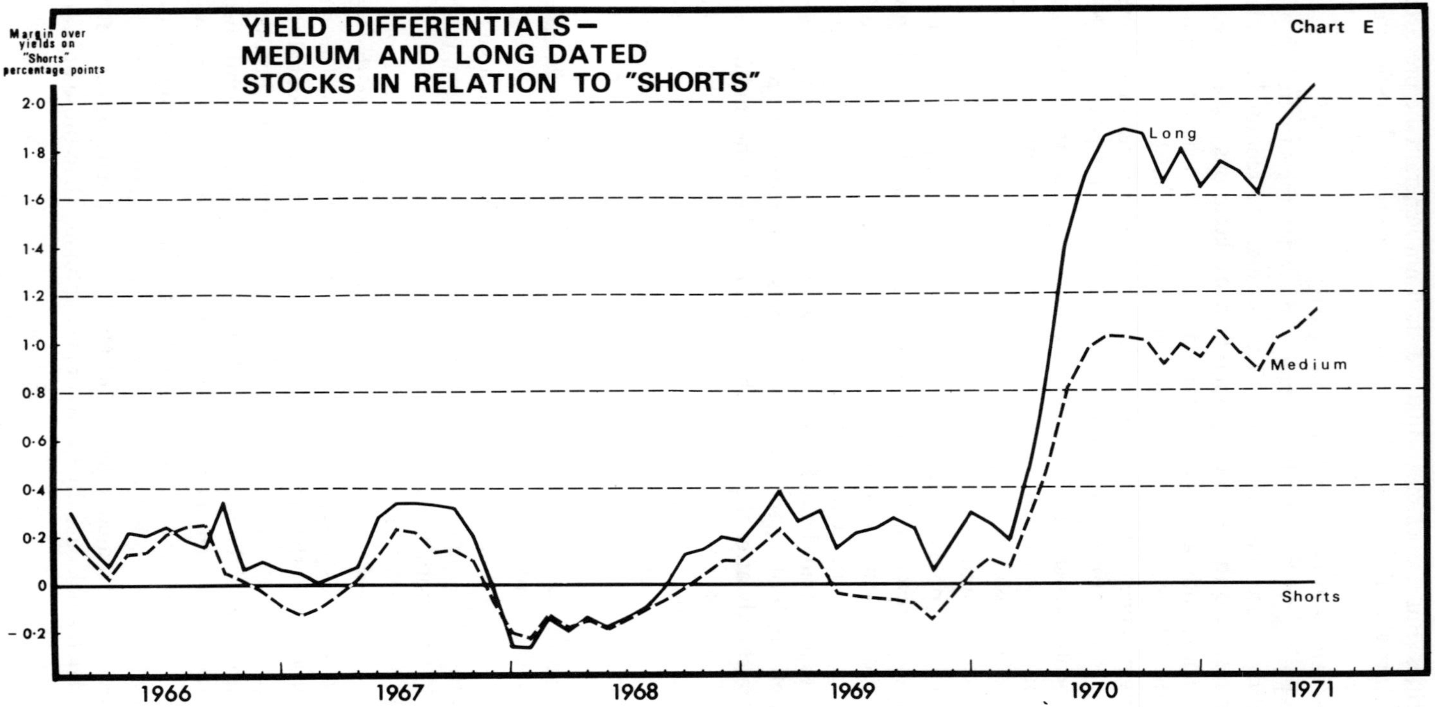

Calculated gross redemption yields on British government securities with five, ten and twenty years to run to maturity, derived by the Bank of England from yield maturity curves fitted by a computer. The figures are plotted monthly, based on averages of Wednesdays.

stocks, since the investor has parted with liquidity for a longer period. In practice, the market has long been influenced by official actions, with changes in bank rate particularly affecting the short end, and official funding policy the yields throughout the range.

Since the middle of 1969 the surplus being earned on the balance of payments has given an underlying strength to the market which had been lacking during the previous five years of payments deficit. Moreover, in 1969 capital gains tax was removed in respect of gilt-edged securities which had been held for one year or more. Again, the world trend of interest rates was generally downwards during this period. A factor operating in the opposite direction, and one that investors have perhaps taken increasingly into account, has been the high rate of inflation, so that an unchanged nominal yield has represented a lower real yield than previously.

In this situation, for domestic reasons the authorities in Britain thought it desirable, at least until April 1971, to maintain the general level of interest rates. Although bank rate had been reduced from 8 to 7 per cent in two stages early in 1970, the authorities thereafter took advantage of the rising trend of the market to make funding sales, thereby moderating the rise, and substantial inflows of funds into Britain early in 1971 were accompanied by renewed and exceptionally heavy funding sales. Only occasionally since early in 1969 has the relative unwillingness of the authorities to support the market been effectively tested, but breaks in the market in April and October 1970 were probably allowed to go further than they would have been previously.

The emergence of the gap between short and long rates from early 1970 onwards may thus be related to an underlying situation in which yields generally might have been expected to fall; at the short end this was allowed by the cuts in bank rate, but at the long end it was frustrated by the deliberate intention of the authorities, given effect by heavy funding sales of long-dated securities, and also by awareness of the modification of official support from late 1968. The relatively high and rising rate of inflation was also an important factor.

Following the announcement of the new policy on 14 May 1971 the differential between the yields on a one-year and a five-year stock widened from about one to 1·35 per cent and it remained at this level. In this way the market adapted itself to the new policy, justifying the governor's surmise in his Munich speech that 'some gilt-edged holders may prefer to stay shorter than hitherto; but their policies will, no doubt, be influenced by the structure of rates.' The investor who seeks the relative security of one-year bonds, which are subject to official support, must be prepared to forgo an interest rate differential which is substantial, and greater than formerly.

Whatever tactics are adopted by the authorities in the gilt-edged market in future, they will continue to be faced with a heavy flow of maturities, involving them in the gradual buying-in of stocks approaching redemption date and the selling of new securities. In the financial year 1969–70, over £1550 million of stocks fell due for redemption; in part they were replaced by conversion issues offered to holders of the maturing stocks, with the remainder – to the extent that it had not already been bought or swapped by the authorities – being repaid in cash. In 1970–1 a further £1331 million, including £758 million of 3 per cent Savings Bonds 1960–70, of which an unusually large proportion was still in the public's hands, fell due and was dealt with similarly.

TABLE A4 *The flow of future maturities* (*years ending 31 March*)

	Nominal amount outstanding of maturing stocks (£m.)	*Number of individual stocks*
1972	1682	4
1973	1794	3
1974	477	2
1975	599	2
1976	1673	2
	6225	13

In the financial year 1971–2, as may be seen from Table A4, around £1700 million nominal of gilt-edged stocks were due for redemption, and in 1972–3 a further £1800 million. Over the next five years more than £6000 million of stocks – over one third of all dated issues – come to maturity. Thus the authorities will have to remain in the market in various ways, including attempting to sell 'tap' stocks, in order to smooth out these operations without causing too much disturbance. As already noted, it is not the Bank of England's intention to preclude itself from carrying out any type of operation which the occasion demands.

This situation is presumably part of the explanation for the apparently arbitrary division in the new policy between stocks of up to one year and those of longer date, whereas, taken by itself and in strict logic, it might seem to call for withdrawal equally from all sections of the market. However, in order to smooth out the periodic maturities the authorities need always to be buying in stocks which are approaching redemption date, and so must encourage holders to sell to them by offering a good price. By concentrating such action upon stocks with one year or less to maturity, they will be taking on as much as they can conveniently handle in this respect.

Of the total marketable debt, excluding holdings of UK official bodies (though not those of local authorities and public corporations), in March 1970 about 13 per cent was held by the banking sector, over one third by other financial institutions, among which the insurance companies are predominant, 14 per cent by overseas holders and over one half of the remainder was in the hands of private funds and trusts.

For stocks with up to five years to maturity, however, the pattern of holdings is markedly different, with the banking sector now accounting for over one quarter of the total. As Table A5 shows, slightly more than one half of the UK banking sector's total holdings have five years or less to run to

TABLE A5 *Holdings of British government securities (£m., March 1971)*

	UK banking sector				
	Deposit banks	*National Giro*	*Discount market*	*Other**	*Total*
By period to maturity					
Up to 5 years	701	4	253	189	1147
Over 5 years and undated	657	4	126	237	1024
Total	1358	8	379	426	2171

* Accepting houses, overseas banks and other banks

maturity; this is a higher proportion than for any other grouping of holders. Even so, the banking sector has been tending to go rather longer in its investments during years in which it has on balance been running down its portfolio, whether by stocks reaching maturity or by sales of short-dated stocks. In the three years from March 1968 to March 1971, total banking sector holdings of government securities of up to five years maturity fell by £840 million, from £1987 million to £1147 million; the reductions were mainly in holdings of the deposit banks and the discount market, which fell by £365 million and £303 million respectively. Total banking sector holdings of bonds of over five years rose over the same period by over £300 million, from £692 million to £1024 million, but all of the increase occurred between December 1970 and March 1971, when strong demand in the gilt-edged market was being met by substantial sales of stock by the authorities and the wide gap was maintained.

Table A6 shows the net transactions in government securities by the main sectors in recent years. The public sector has usually managed to be a net seller, despite heavy maturities, though it was a net purchaser in 1968, when the market was weak following devaluation, and in 1970, when the large and widely held 3 per cent Savings Bond issue matured. Financial institutions other than the banks – particularly insurance companies and building societies – have been consistent and usually large purchasers, and it is to them that the

Bank of England looks effectively to take over, in due course, part of its former role of setting a floor to a falling market.

The banking sector was a net purchaser in the earlier years shown in the table, but a seller thereafter. It should be borne in mind that the clearing banks are particularly affected by the general Exchequer situation; in effect, investments in government securities have come to represent their 'residual' asset, and the fluctuations shown in the table accordingly largely reflect the

TABLE A6 *Transactions in British government securities (£m.)*

	Public sector	*Banking sector*	*Other financial institutions*	*Personal sector*	*Overseas sector*
1965	−221	+ 73	+241	− 91	− 2
1966	−218	+119	+123	− 17	− 7
1967	−520	+233	+514	−237	+ 10
1968	+504	−283	+ 49	−258	− 11
1969	−183	−341	+283	+ 76	+165
1970	+266	−408	+323	−206	+ 25
	−372	−607	+1533	−734	+180

\+ = acquisition of assets
− = sale of assets

fact that the Exchequer was in deficit in the earlier years and in surplus in the later ones. Henceforth, with the new elements of uncertainty introduced into the gilt-edged market with the change of policy, more of the burden of fluctuations in bank assets seems likely, as intended, to be thrown upon advances.

It will be seen that, under the new policy, greater priority is to be given by the authorities to credit control and the liquidity or reserve position of the banking system. This implies that the former main purpose of ensuring the firm holding of the national debt by the public, at least as a primary objective, must correspondingly diminish in importance. Of course, if the new policy helps to bring about an improvement in financial circumstances generally, and a reduction in the rate of inflation, then this will help to strengthen the gilt-edged market and thus indirectly serve the old objective at least as well as previously. However, the disparities that have opened up between yields on 'shorts' and longer-dated stocks seem likely to persist, particularly if inflation continues. Whether they widen further will to a large extent depend on whether the financial institutions that are normally large holders of government securities in due course help to underpin the market, effectively taking the place of the Bank of England by stepping in and buying when they think that a fall in prices has gone far enough.

On earlier pages we have drawn attention to the problem facing the authorities, in that open market operations under the previous arrangements had a rather high degree of uncertainty in their effects upon the credit base of the banking system. The implication of the new policy is some shift in the area of uncertainty, but this does not dispose of the underlying dilemma in this field – that monetary and debt management objectives do not run in harmony.

4

The Supply of Money

Bank Deposits and Currency
November 1957

When the bank rate was raised to 7 per cent on 19 September 1957 the Chancellor of the Exchequer announced a further measure of restriction of bank advances, saying that 'there can be no remedy for inflation and the steadily rising prices which go with it which does not include, and indeed is not founded upon, a control of the money supply'. From this observation, repeated by the Chancellor at the annual meeting of the International Monetary Fund in Washington, it seems clear that in official policy greater emphasis than hitherto is being placed upon the significance of the volume of money. In the previous July, for instance, the Chancellor had commented: 'One does not stop inflation by refusing to print bank notes any more than one cures a fever by trying to hold down the mercury in the thermometer.' In these words he was answering contentions, which he attributed to the 'tranquillizer school', to the effect that inflation could be ended 'quite painlessly' by 'some such device as limiting the note issue'. It would in fact have been difficult to find many adherents of the 'currency school' of 1844, in the sense of advocates of strict control of the note issue as a means of achieving monetary stability. Indeed, most people then as nowadays would argue that nothing more than mere symptomatic significance may be attached to the rapid and continuing growth of the note issue in the preceding ten years, which was in marked contrast to the comparative steadiness of bank deposits – the other main constituent of the active money supply – brought about by official policy.

It can hardly be said that the statutory provisions now operative in respect of the note issue amount to regulation; indeed, they do little more than present opportunities for review. Under emergency legislation introduced at the outbreak of war, and continued thereafter, the Treasury was empowered to alter the fiduciary issue without reference to Parliament. At that time, too, the gold which provided roughly half of the backing for the note issue was transferred to the reserves held in the Exchange Equalization Account, and practically the whole of the note issue became fiduciary. The fiduciary issue rose from £580 million immediately after this operation to £1300 million in May 1945. It moved up to £1575 million by February 1954, when the Royal Assent was given to the Currency and Bank Notes Act, 1954, which re-introduced a semblance of parliamentary control over the fiduciary issue. The Act continued the procedure whereby the fiduciary issue is changed by Treasury minute, issued upon the request of the Bank of England, but it added arrangements for bringing a sustained increase before Parliament. Under the Act, the fiduciary issue was set at £1575 million, subject to variation by Treasury minute; but it was provided that no increase above this figure should 'continue in force after the end of the period of two years beginning with the date on which the fiduciary note issue last stood at or below' £1575 million. However, a procedure was laid down whereby the period for which the basic figure could be continuously exceeded might be repeatedly prolonged, for two years at a time. This can be done by the Treasury's making of an Order which, however, is 'subject to annulment in pursuance of a resolution of either House of Parliament'. Thus, as things have developed, an opportunity for Parliament to challenge a lasting increase in the fiduciary issue arises once every two years.

One month after the passage of the Act the fiduciary issue was raised above the statutory level of £1575 million, to which it has never returned. At its seasonal peak in the summer of 1957 it reached £2075 million. In March 1956, the appropriate Order had been made extending for a further two years the period during which the fiduciary issue might exceed the statutory level, but neither House of Parliament then exercised its right to challenge the lasting increase.

In the days of the gold standard a continued increase in the active note circulation, leading to a fall in the amount of notes held in the Banking Department of the Bank of England, might have been expected to lead to credit restriction along with an increase in bank rate. Since the war years the old signal, provided by 'the proportion' of cash in the Banking Department of the Bank of England to its deposit liabilities, has been ignored as of no practical significance. All that happens when the 'reserve' in the Banking Department threatens to run out in response to public demand for currency is that the Treasury authorizes an increase in the fiduciary issue. The process is repeated at each season of special expansion of demand, notably in the weeks preceding Christmas and August Bank Holiday, but the subsequent seasonal contraction usually leaves the basic issue higher than in the preceding year.

At this period one of the ways in which official policy has latterly sought to hold back inflationary tendencies in the economy has been by limiting that part of the active money supply which consists of bank deposits. Explicitly, the emphasis has usually been on control of bank advances rather than deposits, but the governor of the Bank of England has pointed out that 'the level of bank advances is by no means the whole story. The total level of bank deposits, influenced very greatly by the size and form of government borrowing, is no less important.'

Table A7 indicates some of the changes that have occurred in recent years in the arithmetical relations between liquid bank money and currency in circulation. The figures in the first column are annual averages of the monthly totals of customers' credit balances on current accounts at the clearing banks. These carry no interest and, since current accounts are operated on by the drawing of cheques, they comprise the more liquid, or readily spendable, part of total bank deposits. If, however, the totals were set out it would be seen that broadly the same trends had been recorded. A great expansion of current account balances occurred during the war, and the growth continued at a slackening rate for some years thereafter. In the 1950s, however, largely as a consequence of official actions, changes were slight; the trend was

TABLE A7 *'Liquid' bank money and currency in circulation*

Year	1 *Current account balances with banks* (*£ m.*)	2 *Currency in circulation* (*£ m.*)	3 *Currency as proportion of current accounts* (*%*)	4 *Bank clearings, working-day average* (*£ m.*)	5 *Indices of use made of bank money* *Derived from bank clearings*	6 *Derived from national income*
1938	1244	442	*35·5*	133	*100*	*100*
1946	3377	1332	*39·5*	230	*64*	*63*
1947	3690	1351	*36·6*	244	*62*	*61*
1948	3850	1229	*31·9*	266	*65*	*65*
1949	3940	1238	*31·4*	287	*68*	*68*
1950	3979	1244	*31·2*	315	*74*	*70*
1951	4095	1291	*31·5*	362	*83*	*75*
1952	3961	1370	*34·5*	366	*86*	*85*
1953	3995	1462	*36·6*	410	*96*	*90*
1954	4141	1551	*37·5*	478	*108*	*92*
1955	4113	1657	*40·3*	505	*115*	*98*
1956	3994	1765	*44·2*	532	*125*	*109*

more or less level, with only small fluctuations, for the seven or eight years to 1956.

This trend is in marked contrast with that of the officially estimated amount of currency 'in circulation' with the public, the annual averages for which are given in the second column. The figures include coin as well as notes, but the totals are less than those of the note issue as recorded because they exclude amounts held by the banks in their tills. Currency in circulation reached an early peak in 1947, then fell sharply – largely for special reasons – and ran at a steady level for a few years. Since 1951, however, it increased at the rate of roughly £100 million a year, the figure for 1956 being more than one third higher than that for 1951.

These changes are reflected in the ratio between currency in circulation and current account balances, as shown in the third column of Table A7. In early post-war years the currency circulation bore a somewhat higher proportion to current account balances than in 1938, but the ratio was rapidly reduced, and from 1948 to 1951 it ran at a level considerably lower than that of 1938. From then onwards, with bank balances held down but currency mounting, the proportion has risen sharply each year until by 1956, currency made up nearly one third of the active money supply, as compared with about one quarter in 1938.

Although official policy thus limited the growth of bank deposits, one response was by way of the greater use made of the available quantity of bank money – the velocity of circulation accelerated. No comprehensive figures of turnover on bank accounts are available, but the figures of bank clearings give an indication, admittedly very rough, of changes in turnover. Recorded total bank clearings – as shown in the fourth column of the table – have continued to rise since 1951 at about the same rate as in the preceding five years – and more swiftly, proportionately, than the currency circulation. To judge from figures of the Midland Bank alone, the movement in the aggregate turnover on current accounts has been similar.

A rough measure of changes in the rate of turnover on current accounts as a whole may be obtained by dividing the total for clearings, for each year, by the average of current account balances available in that year, and then converting the resultant figures into index numbers, taking 1938 as 100. On this basis, the rate of turnover immediately after the wartime inflation of deposits was only about two thirds that of 1938. Thereafter, both deposits and clearings continued to expand, but the rate of turnover is seen to have been rising, at first only slowly, but at a gradually accelerating pace. Since 1952, however, with clearings increasing and the amount of deposits held down, the rate of turnover has grown rapidly, so that in 1956 it was 25 per cent higher than in 1938.

The total clearings include a very large amount of purely financial transactions unrelated to the volume of goods and services changing hands in course of yielding and disposing of the national income. These cannot be neatly eliminated, but a closer indication of the course of what may be called trading turnover can perhaps be obtained by adding together the figures for the 'general' clearing at the London clearing house and those for the provincial clearing houses. If this is done it is found that the upward trend in the rate of turnover since 1950 has been substantially slower than that shown in the table, but nevertheless marked. The percentage rise from 1950 to 1956 was 40, as against the 69 shown by the figures in column five of Table A7.

Similar results are obtained by dividing the national income (or, more precisely, the gross national product) by the average of current account balances through the corresponding year. thus relating them to general economic conditions. It is obvious that by no means all the community's transactions are conducted by cheque, but so long as the proportionate uses of bank money and currency are substantially unchanged this calculation – shown in the last column of Table A7 – is valid as indicating broad trends. It too suggests that for a time in post-war years current account balances were high in relation to the community's need for money supply, as compared with the pre-war position, but that this is no longer so. On the national income comparison, however, it was not until 1956 that the pre-war relationship was reached.

During 1957, currency in circulation and bank clearings rose further, following the trends of the previous five years. It would be wrong to place too much emphasis on the 'normality' of the relations existing in 1938, even though in that year business was moderately active and comparatively free from the various hindrances to the free play of market forces which have operated since. The rate of turnover of current account balances, in the period between the wars, used to be sensitive to ups and downs in the state of trade. It fell during the slump of the early 1930s, and rose again with the subsequent recovery, but only slightly, as bank deposits were themselves growing with the somewhat more expansionist monetary policy then being pursued. In 1938, however, turnover was somewhat lower than in the previous year. Currency in circulation rose more sharply during the 1930s than did bank deposits, so that the figure for 1938 shown in column three of Table A7 is higher than for the preceding years.

Thus the present relations cannot be described as 'abnormal' by reference to any 'normal' period in the past. The trends are more important than the comparisons at long range. The figures do, however, suggest that the volume of bank money available may have been favourable to the working out of inflationary pressure in the early post-war years, and that any contrary influence that might have been exerted by checking its growth has been substantially offset by increases in the velocity of circulation. They give no indication of the length of time for which this process can continue before a limitation of the supply of bank money begins to exert a more positive effect.

Money Supply and the Banks
February 1969

Whether or not control of the supply of money should be a major weapon of monetary and economic policy has long been a matter of academic debate, and in Britain it has returned to the forefront in discussions upon practical policy, particularly since the devaluation of sterling in November 1967. The increase in the general level of prices since 1939 has been of the same order of magnitude – about four times – as that of the volume of money. But the relationship is by no means a simple one of cause and effect. However, this may be, in post-war years monetary policy has generally been directed at the volume and direction of bank lending, rather than at the quantity of money. If it should change emphasis and turn to closer regulation of the money supply, the banks will necessarily be just as closely involved.

The only thorough official examination of the monetary system in post-war years has been that by the Committee on the Working of the Monetary System (the Radcliffe Committee) which published its report nearly ten years ago, in August 1959. The Committee endorsed the down-grading of the emphasis upon money supply, in favour of the concept of the liquidity of the economy as a whole. 'Though we do not regard the supply of money as an unimportant quantity, we view it as only part of the wider structure of liquidity in the economy. It is the whole liquidity position that is relevant to spending decisions, and our interest in the supply of money is due to its significance in the whole liquidity picture . . . The authorities thus have to regard the structure of interest rates rather than the supply of money as the centrepiece of the monetary mechanism. This does not mean that the supply of money is unimportant, but that its control is incidental to interest rate policy.'

The Radcliffe analysis has not met with universal acceptance, nor has it been explicitly accepted by the authorities. Indeed, official action affecting interest rates has appeared to follow a variety of expedients. As regards the banks, it has sought to regulate lending rather than deposits. Nonetheless, this attitude was in line with the Radcliffe analysis, which suggested that action affecting the banks should deal with them as 'key lenders in the system' and not as 'creators of money'. 'It is the level of bank advances rather than the level of bank deposits that is the object of this special interest; the behaviour of bank deposits is of interest only because it has some bearing . . . on the behaviour of other lenders.'

Until recently, the supply of money had not been mentioned for ten years in justification of official actions. In 1956 the then Chancellor of the Exchequer raised interest rates on national savings, saying that he had a 'new objective' in doing so: 'The financial critics tell me that I must reduce bank deposits and the floating debt if I am to reduce the money supply. Very well. Let us see bank deposits turned into National Savings. As the National Savings rise the Treasury bills will fall.' At a time of sterling crisis the following year his successor claimed that his measures would strike at 'the root of any inflation – namely the supply of money', and that 'there can be no remedy for inflation . . . which does not include, and indeed is not founded upon, the control of the money supply'. However, his measures were along familiar lines and, taken in context, his statements suggested some confusion between the supply of money and the flow of money incomes.

Thereafter the money supply seemed to drop out of official thinking. For instance, although the short-lived National Plan of 1965 contained a section on the banks, this related only to their capital investment and employment. No comment was thought necessary upon the extent or origin of the rise in bank deposits that would be needed to support the country's proposed economic growth.

The supply of money returned to prominence in November 1967, following the devaluation of sterling. At that time the Chancellor of the Exchequer addressed a Letter of Intent to the International Monetary Fund (see Appendix 4(a)) which included the following undertaking: 'Bank credit expansion will be sufficiently limited to ensure that the growth of money supply will be less in 1968 than the present estimate for 1967, both absolutely and as a proportion of GNP, despite the expected substantial recovery of reserves.' It quickly became apparent that the growth of money supply in the United Kingdom was regarded as a serious weakness in the situation, both in this country and by critics and creditors overseas.

Similarly with public statements by governors of the Bank of England: it is more than ten years since the then governor commented that 'the level of bank advances is by no means the whole story. The total level of bank deposits . . . is no less important.' Then the whole subject seemed to be dropped until last October, when the present governor was more specific: 'The level of internal demand still gives cause for concern', he said. 'I know there are weighty opinions which do not consider that the trend of the money supply has any reliable significance in this context. Maybe it is no foolproof guide, but I for my part believe that we should be more concerned with it, as indeed I know many informed observers overseas feel we should be. The money supply cannot become the be-all and end-all of policy. But when it continues to rise rather fast, and from a level that is high by historical standards, and, above all, when it does this at a time of deficit in overseas payments and when people are uneasily aware that the longer they hold money the less they get for it, then I am sure we must pay attention. I do not accept that controlling the money supply is simply a question of the proper use of central banking techniques, as some appear to believe. Much more fundamental matters are involved.'

In particular, let us add, money supply in Britain has to be considered in the environment of UK financial institutions, especially banks. If the money supply is important, it is presumably because of its relationship to aggregate demand. As the Radcliffe Committee put it, the 'relevance of the availability of funds to the pressure of total demand is what lies behind the supreme importance which is often attached to "the supply of money" '. A clear distinction needs to be drawn between the stock of money and its flow, and until recently attention has been directed almost entirely at the effects of the flow. Today it is being increasingly suggested that attention should be paid to the stock, and in particular to changes in the stock.

In discussing the money supply, however, a satisfactory definition is a first essential. In one sense an appropriate definition depends upon the context in which money supply is to be considered. If related to aggregate demand, the definition has to be concerned with the spendability of money. Thus it should be associated primarily with money in the sense of something that can be spent immediately, as contrasted with near-money, which is moderately liquid but cannot be used directly for spending by the holder. An example of near-money would be funds deposited with a building society or similar undertaking. Much near-money is readily spendable, though not normally directly or immediately as with currency and most bank deposits, but only after some other operation to turn it into one of those forms. Moroever, as we shall see, if it is turned into spendable money it does not increase the total of final means of payment – that is to say, the 'active' money supply.

In *International Financial Statistics*, published by the International Monetary Fund, money is by implication defined as currency and bank deposits, the figures for the United Kingdom including balances on deposit as well as current accounts. 'Quasi-money' – that is, near-money – is defined generally as 'time and savings deposits and other liabilities of the monetary system that the user of the data may or may not wish to consider to be money'. Thus it is clearly indicated that any definition of the money supply is subjective, and depends upon the attitudes of users and their intentions. The figures recorded in *International Financial Statistics* are quite close to those given by the Central Statistical Office in its publication *Financial Statistics*. This, too, admits that 'any definition of the money supply is arbitrary'. The Organisation for Economic Cooperation and Development, by implication, has accepted this point, as it was until recently publishing a series for the United Kingdom on a very narrow basis, but has now changed to one based on the *Financial Statistics* series. This widely accepted definition combines currency in circulation with the public with net deposits by UK residents with the whole of the banking sector,* including both sterling and non-sterling current

* The 'banking sector' comprises the London clearing banks, the Scottish and Northern Ireland banks, accepting houses, overseas and other banks, the discount market, and a number of small banks and the Banking Department of the Bank of England.

and deposit accounts. Table A8 shows the figures on this basis in September 1968, and the comparative figures for September 1964, though, as we shall see, they do not in fact reflect simply the 'active' money supply.

During the year to February 1969, some alarm was expressed at the rapid rise in the UK money supply as indicated by this series, because it is regarded as stimulating aggregate demand. The objection to these statistics as a measure of the 'active money supply' is that they include substantial amounts of near-money. In fact, it is the near-money that has provided the rapidly rising element.

TABLE A8 *Money supply*

	September 1964	*September 1968*	*Increase*	
	£m.	*£m.*	*£m.*	*%*
Net deposits* of UK residents with:				
Deposit banks	8,335	10,072	1737	*21*
Accepting houses, overseas and other banks	841	2,156	1315	*156*
Discount market	62	86	24	*39*
	9,238	12,314	3076	*33*
Currency in circulation	2,336	2,846	510	*22*
Total	11,574	15,160	3586	*31*

* Gross deposits less items in transit, etc., and all inter-bank deposits.

Clearly any definition should include currency in circulation with the public, and balances in sterling on current accounts with the joint stock banks – primarily the clearing banks and their counterparts in Scotland and Northern Ireland. Funds held on ordinary deposit accounts with these banks should also be added, since they can mostly be withdrawn or switched to current account immediately, subject to loss of interest. Deposits with the National Giro should be added when available. But whether the 'active money supply' should extend to other items is open to question.

Nevertheless, the official definition goes much wider than final means of payment. In the first place, it includes deposits with the banks in non-sterling currencies. As, however, these cannot be used for making payments within the United Kingdom, but have to be exchanged into cash or sterling deposits for this purpose, they are clearly 'near' rather than 'active' money. More important, the official total includes all deposits by UK residents with the whole of the banking sector. True the predominant component is balances held with the 'deposit banks' – that is, mainly the London clearing banks and the Scottish and Northern Ireland banks, and, in addition to a number of small banks, the Banking Department of the Bank of England. But the official figures also cover deposits with the discount market, which seem of limited relevance for this purpose, certainly so if they are left for a period.

The main intrusive element, however, is deposits of UK residents with the accepting houses, overseas and other banks. These at present amount to over £2000 million, or about 14 per cent of the total, and as Table A8 shows, they have been rising proportionately much more rapidly than balances with the 'deposit banks'. This figure included £243 million of foreign currency deposits at September 1968 – as against about £77 million only four years earlier – and these, as mentioned above, are not directly relevant to domestic demand.

The largest component of this group was deposits with the accepting houses, followed by those with British overseas and Commonwealth banks. However, more information is available about the deposits of the American banks; a special survey of their business was referred to in the report of the Monopolies Commission on the proposed merger of Barclays Bank, Lloyds and Martins. At the end of 1967, their sterling deposits held for UK residents other than banks amounted to £215 million, of which nearly one half was for British-owned companies and nearly two fifths for subsidiaries or branches in this country of American companies. Over four fifths of the total was interest-bearing, as compared with about two fifths for the deposits of the clearing banks. Thus the great bulk of deposits of American banks was not held in a form immediately available for spending, as on a current account. More important, the arrangements for holding these balances were not comparable with those applying to the deposit accounts of the clearing banks, since American bank offices bid for large deposits of companies, quoting competitive market rates for specified periods. Possibly many American companies would also hold current accounts with them, but the bulk of the British-owned companies would not, and would have to switch the funds back to an account with one of the clearing banks if they wished to spend them. Thus a large proportion of these deposits of American banks should be classified as near-money. This likewise applies, to a greater or lesser extent, to deposits of UK residents with the other overseas banks and accepting houses which are also included in the money supply table.

The statistics show different trends according to the definition employed. Some relevant figures and comparisons with gross national product are set out in Table A9. If the active money supply is regarded as clearing bank net balances, both on current and ordinary deposit account, plus currency in circulation with the public, it will be seen that immediately after the war it was far higher than before, both absolutely and as a proportion of gross national product. However, this proportion fell rapidly until by the early 1950s it was below the 1938 figure, which itself was substantially lower than the average for the 1930s. It continued to fall rapidly until about 1958, but in the past ten years the decline has been slower. If the definition were drawn even more narrowly, to include only currency in circulation and current account balances, the rate of fall would be still more marked, since with the general rise in interest rates an increasing proportion of bank deposits has been held on deposit rather than current accounts (see p. 386). Seen in this context, the statement of the governor of the Bank of England, quoted above, that the present level of the money supply is 'high by historical standards', seems to relate to its absolute level.

TABLE A9 *The growth of money supply*

	Gross national product	*Clearing bank net deposits and currency in circulation*		*Money supply as in* Financial Statistics	
	£m.	*£m.*	*% of g.n.p.*	*£m.*	*% of g.n.p.*
1938	5,175	2,663	*51·5*		
1946	8,855	6,273	*70·7*		
1953	15,062	7,486	*49·7*		
1958	20,396	7,710	*37·8*		
1963	27,163	9,649	*35·6*	10,745	*39·6*
1964	29,313	10,232	*34·9*	11,426	*39·0*
1965	31,310	10,833	*34·6*	12,165	*38·9*
1966	32,858	11,377	*34·6*	12,974	*39·5*
1967	34,292	11,820	*34·5*	13,759	*40·1*

The table also shows money supply on the official presentation; these figures have only been available since 1963. On this basis, the money supply has risen over the past three or four years somewhat faster than GNP and it is to this increase that attention has come to be directed. The swift rise, however, has been in that part which, it is suggested above, is better regarded as near-money, and is only relevant to the level of aggregate demand in so far as the holders regard it as adding to their liquidity. For 'active money', which would seem to be the better basis of comparison, the supply has tended to fall relatively to GNP so that on the face of things it has not been an expansionary force in recent years.

Here, however, another aspect of monetary development has to be taken into account, relating to the flow of money rather than the stock. It is evident from the bank clearing figures, and also from the refinement of them in the Midland Bank Index of Business Turnover, that banking turnover has continued to rise rapidly in recent years, broadly at the same rate as the rise in

GNP. Indeed, the Midland Bank Index has moved very closely with the national income figures for 'final expenditure' on an annual basis – though less so in the quarterly series – and might be considered a useful 'lead indicator'. In other words, an increase in the velocity of circulation has offset the relative decline in the crude quantity of money.

On the velocity of circulation the Radcliffe Committee commented: 'We have not made more use of this concept because we cannot find any reason for supposing, or any experience in monetary history indicating, that there is any limit to the velocity of circulation; it is a statistical concept that tells us nothing directly of the motivation that influences the level of total demand.' Nevertheless, when attention, as at present, is being directed once again at the supply of money, it is perhaps timely to reconsider the relevance of the velocity of circulation, more especially as, in the ten years since the Radcliffe Committee reported, it has ceased to rise as quickly as it had in the previous ten years.

Important changes have taken place over the past ten years or so in the distribution of liquid assets held by the public with, as already indicated, a considerable increase in the volume of near-money in relation to the volume of 'active' money. This has been associated with the growth of non-bank financial intermediaries, a development only briefly noted by the Radcliffe Committee, since the great expansion had then only just begun.

By 'non-bank financial intermediaries' are meant financial institutions other than deposit banks which take money from the public, on deposit or in some other relatively short form, and invest it or lend it out again, generally for slightly longer periods at higher rates of interest. Some of these institutions, such as savings banks and building societies, obtain most of their funds from the personal sector. Others, including discount houses, hire purchase finance houses and local authorities, obtain substantial funds from companies. The growth of some of these institutions and associated markets is discussed in Chapters 6 and 7 in this volume.

Figures that show the rapid growth of near-money are given in Table A10. They illustrate the arbitrary nature of the official definition of money supply, which includes all deposits with institutions which are taken to constitute the banking sector; incidentally, this excludes the savings banks. There seems to be no logical reason why, if a broad definition is required, all the items included in Table A10 should not be included, and maybe others too.

No hard and fast dividing line can be drawn between the various types of near-money, even though some of those shown in the table are probably nearer to being money – in the sense of being held at shorter notice – than are others. In particular, the fact that some of the institutions concerned are called 'banks', whereas others are not, provides no satisfactory basis for drawing distinctions of this kind. Surely it would be better to differentiate between money and near-money, since money can be used for spending in its existing form, whereas near-money has to be turned into money before it can be spent. As the Radcliffe Committee put it: 'There are many highly liquid assets which are close substitutes for money, as good to hold and only inferior when the actual moment for a payment arrives.' To compensate for its relative lack of liquidity, interest has to be paid on near-money.

Although near-money cannot be spent in its existing form, it is nevertheless a significant element in assessing total demand in the economy. The Radcliffe Committee demonstrated that 'the decision to spend . . . depends upon

TABLE A10 *The growth of near-money*

	Deposits of various institutions (£m.) 1958 (December)	1963 (December)	1968 (September)
Accepting houses	100	329	723
British overseas and Commonwealth banks	113	193	394
American banks	59	138	339
Other banks	22	78	700
Total	294	738	2156
Post Office Savings Bank	1646	1791	1784*
Trustee savings banks			
Ordinary departments	815	956	1062
Special investment departments	345	746	1290
Building societies†	2479	4005	7491
Local authorities	404‡	979	1315
Finance houses	128	247	444

Note: Figures for banks, local authorities, and finance houses relate to UK residents other than banks. Figures for 1958 are not directly comparable; that for finance houses is total deposits.
* Includes £171 million in investment accounts.
† Deposits and shares.
‡ Estimated.

liquidity in the broad sense, not upon immediate access to the money. . . . Spending is not limited by the amount of money in existence; but it is related to the amount of money people think they can get hold of, whether by receipts of income (for instance from sales), by disposal of capital assets or by borrowing.' It was for this reason that the Radcliffe Committee recommended action to control the liquidity of the economy as a whole, including near-money, rather than simply the money supply.

Although near-money should not be regarded as part of the money supply, as it expands it influences money supply proper, that is, currency and bank deposits. The amount of currency held by the public is determined by the convenience of the public, the existing statutory control of it being largely nominal – Radcliffe aptly described it as 'otiose'. In fact, currency held by the public remains at a more or less constant proportion of under one tenth of the annual gross national product. The part to which attention should be directed is bank deposits, and in particular to deposits of the London clearing banks.

It is a fallacy to think that additions to the stock of near-money simply represent funds that might otherwise have been deposited in the banks, and would then have increased bank deposits by a corresponding amount. True, if a bank customer transfers funds to a public sector intermediary, which invests its funds with the government in one way or another, then the deposit is lost to the banks. This is because the funds are transferred to the Bank of England, from the account held with it by the clearing bank, thus depleting its 'cash' holding. Indeed, this process also reduces the liquidity of the bank, and if this is already close to the minimum level it may be necessary for the bank to take further action which induces, in addition, a secondary reduction in deposits. However, as Table A10 shows, the intermediaries that place their funds with the government have been gaining funds comparatively slowly in recent years.

Transfers to private sector intermediaries, however, have quite a different effect, since these institutions generally keep their banking accounts with the clearing banks, not with the Bank of England. If a customer transfers funds from his bank account to, say, a building society, the immediate effect is merely to transfer the ownership of the bank deposit from the customer to the building society; in this process one bank may lose but another will gain, so that the total of bank deposits is not affected. Further, when the building society lends this addition to its bank balance to a house purchaser, who pays it to the vendor, these further transactions similarly involve only a shuffling of the ownership of bank deposits. But the amount of near-money – in this case, shares or deposits in building societies – is increased. Similarly when funds are withdrawn from private sector intermediaries for redeposit with a bank, then bank deposits as a whole are not increased correspondingly, since the intermediary has to use its own existing bank deposits or obtain control of others – perhaps by selling an asset – in order to transfer them to the person wishing to withdraw funds. This supports the argument that near-money should not be included in the concept of money supply, since to spend near-money involves a process that reduces the amount of near-money but not the amount of 'active' money.

Even so, the growth of near-money tends as a secondary effect both to limit the willingness of the public to hold deposits, and also the ability of the banks to create new deposits. The public's willingness to hold bank deposits is an indication of its liquidity preference, and this has naturally been affected by the growth of intermediaries offering higher rates of interest than the banks on short-term deposits, even though such deposits cannot be used for making payments. In theory, a situation could arise in which, the public being satisfied with its existing holding of bank deposits, the banks could not create new deposits, even though liquid and prepared to lend. In practice, such a situation has not arisen – at least, not for many years. Indeed, in post-war years the authorities have almost continuously used various methods to restrict bank lending, thus limiting the growth of deposits. Until 1969, at least, lack of borrowers was not a situation which the banks have had to face.

Lack of willingness to hold deposits is most evident as regards companies, many of which are known to keep their clearing bank balances to a minimum. Between the end of 1963 and September 1968, balances of companies with the 'deposit banks' fell by £92 million to £1944 million, whereas those held with accepting houses, overseas and other banks rose from £496 million to £1269 million. This could be looked upon as a movement into near-money. Thus the non-clearing banks receiving these funds will have obtained them in the form of clearing bank deposits, which they will have passed on, so that the deposits are not lost to the clearing banks but merely held by different depositors. Over the same period, the total of balances with deposit banks held by 'other' depositors – largely personal – rose by £2131 million to £8155 million.

Apart from weakening the demand for bank deposits, the growth of deposit-taking intermediaries impairs the ability of the banks to create deposits. Bank deposits are created when the banks either lend money to or acquire securities from the public, but the ability of the banks to expand in this way has been regulated by the observance of the liquidity ratio. Up to 1969 the authorities required the banks to ensure that their liquid assets did not fall below 28 per cent of their gross deposits. Putting it the other way round, the level of deposits was restricted to 3–3½ times the level of liquid assets, and anything which affected the ability of the banks to command liquid assets affected their creation of deposits.

The banks have been adding to some extent to their own liquidity by lending in the form of commercial bills, which may rank as liquid assets, but such lending is now commonly controlled by direct limitation by the authorities in just the same way as advances. In addition, the authorities can affect the liquidity of the banks more or less arbitrarily by calling for Special Deposits, or by releasing them. The main basis of bank liquidity, directly or through the discount market, is short-term government debt, and particularly the Treasury bill. Borrowing on Treasury bills from the banking system tends to be the final balancing item in government finance, when all other items, including borrowing from the public, have been taken into account. Thus any net additional borrowing by the government from the public tends to reduce the supply of Treasury bills to the banks, and conversely.

It is through this mechanism that the growth of intermediaries tends to reduce the ability of the banks to create deposits. For instance, most intermediaries hold a proportion of their assets in the form of government securities. A portion of any increased deposits they obtain will be lent to the government, thus reducing correspondingly the supply of Treasury bills to the banks. More generally, transfers to intermediaries increase their lending power, and their lending stimulates the economy just as much as does bank lending. It thus increases the likelihood of official action to prevent excessive demand on resources developing, and this will commonly include restrictions on the banks; indeed, the banks are usually more effectively controlled than some, at least, of the non-bank financial intermediaries.

To sum up, when a member of the public transfers funds on deposit with a bank to a public sector intermediary which banks with the Bank of England or invests in government securities, the banks suffer a corresponding loss of deposits, and of liquid assets too. With private sector intermediaries, however, the effect is quite different. The primary effect is merely a reshuffling of the ownership of bank deposits, but no reduction of them. As a secondary effect, the banks may be affected adversely, either by a decline in the willingness of the public to hold deposits, or an impairment of the ability of the banks to create them, or both; this, however, is a comparatively minor effect. The National Board for Prices and Incomes, in its report on bank charges (Cmnd. 3292), glossed over this important distinction in a paragraph which concluded that 'either way, whether deposits are transferred to a public sector non-bank or to a private sector non-bank, the reserves and deposits of the clearing banks suffer in the last analysis a decline'.

Over the post-war period as a whole, the course of government finance has been such as to increase the liquid assets available to the banking system, and this has provided part of the basis for the growth of deposits. But the action of the public receiving the increased deposits, in transferring ownership of them to intermediaries offering higher rates of interest, has tended to erode the credit base of the banking system. Even here a contrary effect is traceable. The greatest expansion has been in those intermediaries that keep their accounts with the joint stock banks and their assets mainly in the private sector; if this had not occurred, public sector intermediaries and national savings generally would probably have done better. The effect of such a development would have been more deleterious for the banks, since the whole of the transferred deposits would have been lost to them, and also a corresponding amount of liquid assets. Similarly, company funds which in the 1950s had been put into Treasury bills were withdrawn in the 1960s because of the attraction of the developing outlets with financial intermediaries. In the process, to some extent bank deposits which had been lost were restored, and liquid assets too. Thus the development of these institutions has resulted in the return to the banking system of some part of the deposits previously lost. This argument is supported by the fact that the fall in bank deposits as a proportion of GNP occurred mainly in the period up to the late 1950s, up to which point the growth of the private sector intermediaries was slight. Subsequently their growth has been much more rapid, but bank deposits likewise have been rising faster than before, broadly commensurately with GNP.

A probable explanation of the course of bank deposits since 1946 is that they had been greatly inflated during the war years as a result of government deficit finance; in early post-war years the volume continued to be high relative to demand so their rate of increase was relatively slow. From the late 1950s the growth of bank deposits was more rapid, this time resulting mainly from a great expansion of advances. This suggests that during the first half of the period the growth of bank deposits was restrained by relative lack of demand. By the middle of the period, say ten years ago, GNP had reached a point where the level of bank deposits was no longer high relative to demand, and since then the main influence restricting their growth has been on the side of supply.

Another Look at Money Supply
November 1970

The significance of movements in the money supply in determining the level of economic activity and the pace of inflation remains a matter of unresolved debate and at times acute controversy, in the corridors of power, perhaps, no less than in the groves of Academe. Nevertheless, it is evident from recent official statements that control of the supply of money has been given increased importance in the field of monetary policy, both in this country and in the United States.

Attention was drawn to indications of a change of policy in managing the gilt-edged market in Chapter 3, which noted in particular evidence of an increased reluctance on the part of the authorities to support the gilt-edged market when it was weak. In May 1969 it was seen as a temporary change of emphasis, but it later became apparent that the change – though not necessarily permanent – was rather more fundamental and perhaps less temporary than was realized. It was suggested that restraining the growth of the money supply might have been the motive for the change in tactics followed by the authorities in their market operations over the preceding months.

That this was so has now been confirmed, and most explicitly in the Report from the Select Committee on Nationalised Industries on the Bank of England,* published in May 1970. The governor of the Bank of England,

* HCP 258. The quotations are taken from the answers to Questions 727–56 and 827, and from para. 58 of the Report.

giving verbal evidence on 16 July 1969 on the management of the national debt, said: 'The basic purposes of debt management have been for many years now to ensure the successful issue of new securities, and to ensure the successful redemption of old securities', and he added: 'More recently the objectives of open market policy have become more complex when we have been seeking, while continuing to fulfil the earlier functions of open market policies . . . also to constrain any increase in money supply which might result from open market operations.' He added that 'these two objectives can be very difficult to reconcile'. Again, 'the latter day terms of reference, designed to secure that we do not increase the money supply unduly, do of course constrain our day-to-day freedom to operate in the market'.

He also observed that the Bank of England and the Treasury had agreed a 'memorandum of objectives to be followed' and that the open market operations of the Bank were conducted in accordance with it. As to the preparation of the memorandum, 'We share our consideration of what monetary policy requires and how those objectives are to be achieved and we between us draft a memorandum which gives expression to those objectives. It is one, of course, which has to be approved by the Treasury and the Chancellor himself. Then we work to it.' The change in debt management policy, discussed in Chapter 3, 'resulted from a fresh assessment agreed between the two of us that monetary policy objectives needed to be changed in that area, and they were changed over a period'. It was because of this that a memorandum had been drawn up, for the first time, within the six months before this evidence was given – that is, during the first half of 1969. It may be, however, that it has since been amended or replaced by another; the governor said that he would expect a memorandum 'to be in existence for at least a number of months'.

It was not within his power to let the Committee see the current memorandum, and he seemed to be opposed to publication, because 'those who are operating in the market beside ourselves could be placed in a position to the prejudice of the authorities' and 'the publication of that kind of thing . . . would tie our hands in the future more than we would wish them to be tied'. He pointed out, with justification, that the Bank of England now gives far more information on this and other matters than in the past, particularly in its *Quarterly Bulletin*. He suggested that the change of policy had been explained in the *Bulletin*, although in fact the references therein to open market operations, up to that time and since, are only descriptive and make no mention of memoranda or changes in policy objectives, nor to the supply of money as a criterion of open market policy. In its report the Committee, noting that they were 'not shown the memorandum', commented that they were 'unable to discern the likelihood of any adverse consequences flowing from the publication of that and of more routine policy details after a suitable lapse of time, say three months'.

The Committee had carefully investigated central banking in the United States, where open market policy is determined at regular meetings of the Federal Open Market Committee. An account of the considerations discussed at these meetings, and the text of the resulting policy directives, are published ninety days after the event, and 'without any adverse consequences' observes the UK Select Committee. The American references confirm that the close attention with which variations in the money supply have for some time past been followed in the United States is reflected in policy decisions, and that some conflict arises there also between the monetary objective and stability of financial markets. Thus the directive issued from the 'Fed' in February 1970 said that open market operations should be conducted 'with a view to moving gradually towards somewhat less firm conditions in the money market; provided, however, that operations shall be modified promptly to resist any tendency for money and bank credit to deviate significantly from a moderate growth pattern'. By March the Committee was stating the objective as 'moderate growth in money and bank credit over the months ahead', less stress being given to the state of the money market itself, and this shift of emphasis has been maintained.

Thus it is clear that, in both countries, emphasis in open market operations has been shifting, and deliberately so, towards regulating the money supply, even though it is recognized that this may conflict with other objectives – notably in Britain, that of fostering conditions in financial markets conducive to maintaining the demand for government securities. Indeed the positive likelihood of conflict was suggested by the governor of the Bank of England in a somewhat wry reference to a 'catchword' in the Bank that 'you can fund when you do not want to and you cannot fund when you do want to'.

If the level of the money supply is to be a major element in determining official monetary policy, then it becomes all the more important to ensure that the methods used to measure it are relevant for analytical comparisons of various kinds. On pp. 84–5 it is suggested that an appropriate definition should be 'related to aggregate demand' and thus should include currency in circulation with the public and balances in sterling on both current and deposit account with the joint stock banks and deposits with the National Giro, together constituting the 'active money supply'. It was pointed out that the official definition then in use went much wider than this, and included substantial amounts of 'near-money', in particular deposits with the banks in non-sterling currencies and deposits of UK residents with the accepting houses, overseas and other banks. The question was raised as to whether the inclusion of these items, not representing final means of payment, was appropriate.

Our question has now, in effect, been answered, with the decision to publish in *Financial Statistics* two new series, on narrower definitions, which are designated M_1 and M_2; the existing series will continue to appear as M_3.

The new figures were introduced and explained in articles in the August 1970 issue of *Economic Trends* and the September 1970 issue of the *Bank of England Quarterly Bulletin.* The earlier of these articles explains that the widest definition (M_3) has the advantage of being relatively easily reconcilable with bank balance sheets, 'so that discussion of movements in the total can be given more institutional content'.

It adds that for many purposes it is useful to have figures 'based more firmly on the distinguishing function of money as a medium of exchange', indicating the means of payment in the hands of the private sector and excluding 'those balances which are believed not to be closely related to the level of domestic spending'. The existing definition is 'not entirely suitable' for this purpose, as 'it includes time-deposits with the accepting houses, overseas banks and other banks, which generally have little in common with chequeable current accounts and are not usually regarded as a means of payment. It also includes resident foreign currency deposits, a large proportion of which may at times be balances awaiting opportunities for investment overseas. Changes in these balances seem to be influenced to a considerable extent by the state of capital markets overseas, and thus have no close connection with domestic spending.' The earlier, wide definition also includes public sector deposits, changes in which are related to irregularities in the flow of receipts and payments rather than to public sector spending.

The narrower of the two new definitions (M_1) comprises only notes and coins plus all chequeable current accounts of private sector residents denominated in sterling. This definition, it is suggested, 'can be thought of as representing most closely the function of money as a medium of exchange, and as including the generally acceptable means of payment in the system'. The second new definition (M_2) comprises the items in M_1, plus sterling deposit accounts of private sector UK residents with the deposit banks* and similar deposits with the discount houses. It is pointed out that in practice deposit accounts with the deposit banks 'can generally be withdrawn on demand', and that 'deposits with the discount houses are similar in nature'. The 'degree of substitutability' between these additional items and current account deposits 'would seem sufficient to justify a definition which includes them as well as one which excludes them'.

At present, only M_3 is seasonally adjusted, but M_1 and M_2 will be adjusted in due course. It is also pointed out that quarter-to-quarter movements, particularly in M_1 and M_2, 'should be treated with some reserve'; this is because 'the split between the current and deposit accounts for each of the sectors . . . is not available' and some assumptions have to be made to deal with this and other statistical complications.

* The London clearing banks and their counterparts in Scotland and Northern Ireland, and a few similar but relatively small institutions; plus the National Giro and the Bank of England Banking Department.

The explanation in the *Bank of England Bulletin* refers throughout to the 'stock of money', a term that seems preferable to 'money supply', since the latter contains implicit suggestions of a flow rather than a stock. However, it seems that the official figure will continue to be described as 'money supply'. The different approaches followed by the two articles are of interest; the *Bulletin* starts from basic principles and works its way forward from M_1 to M_3, whereas *Economic Trends* begins with the existing series, M_3, and sheds the items that are thought inappropriate for stated purposes.

The Bank of England justifies the inclusion in M_2 of deposit accounts with the deposit banks, while excluding those with other banks, on the grounds that 'the latter are more commonly of longer maturity' and 'are less easily withdrawn at will'. The more relevant reason for excluding them would seem to be that a deposit balance with one of the 'other banks' can normally only be activated by way of that bank's current account with one of the deposit banks. Accordingly, a withdrawal from such a deposit balance merely involves a transfer of ownership of an existing current account balance; the total of M_1 is not affected. Balances on deposit account with the deposit banks can be transferred to current account, or withdrawn, by a stroke of the pen, thus adding to the money supply as defined in M_1.

Comment by the Bank of England on the use of M_3 perhaps carries with it an uncomfortable implication. The Bank states that 'it is easier to relate analyses of bank lending, and the expansion of domestic credit, to broader, rather than to narrower, definitions of the stock of money, for all deposits can be lent whatever the nature of the initial liability'. This suggests that the choice of series to be used as a guide to policy is to be determined partly by convenience and not simply by its relevance. But which of the three definitions is most appropriate is not easily decided.

Nevertheless, a correct choice may be crucial. On p. 85 it is shown that over the years preceding 1968 money supply on the wide definition had been rising more rapidly than the 'active money supply'. From Table A11 it will be seen that between 1964 and 1969, M_1 rose by about £1000 million, M_2 by about £2600 million, and M_3 by well over £4000 million. The table also relates the series to total domestic expenditure at market prices; the income velocity of money is the inverse of the figures shown in the percentage columns. On the two narrower definitions income velocity rose over the period, whereas on the wider definition it fell.

Finally, it may be noted that all three series still contain some unsatisfactory features, related to compilation rather than to definition. To fit into the official 'flow-of-funds' analysis for the economy as a whole, the figures for money supply are estimated quarterly, at the end of each calendar quarter. Thus they are based upon 'snapshots', at particular dates, of figures which – at least as regards bank deposits, the main component – may fluctuate significantly over a very short period in a way unrelated to their trend. As the Bank of England

Bulletin pointed out in December 1969, 'banking figures at the end of each calendar quarter are especially difficult to interpret, being subject to special end-quarter influences and the effects of the day of the week on which the quarter ends'.

During the second quarter of 1970, the money supply on definition M_3 rose by £870 million, or £700 million after seasonal adjustment, an increase of more than 4 per cent. The *Bulletin* for September 1970 points out, however, that end-quarter influences were particularly marked during this period, and that the increase indicated by mid-month data was smaller. This serves to underline the point, often overlooked, that movements in published data, especially from one quarter to another, may give a misleading impression. It is important that allowance should always be made for the effects of random movements, even if these cannot be quantified or even identified with assurance.

TABLE A11 *Money supply related to total domestic expenditure (annual averages, in £million and as percentage of expenditure)*

	M_1		M_2		M_3	
	£m.	%	*£m.*	%	*£m.*	%
1964	7070	*21·1*	10,508	*31·4*	11,376	*34·0*
1965	7270	*20·4*	11,099	*31·2*	12,100	*34·0*
1966	7508	*19·9*	11,651	*30·8*	12,919	*34·2*
1967	7750	*19·3*	12,194	*30·4*	13,665	*34·1*
1968	8044	*18·7*	12,977	*30·2*	14,978	*34·9*
1969	8075	*18·0*	13,144	*29·2*	15,618	*34·7*

M_1 = Notes and coins in circulation and sterling current accounts held by the private sector.
M_2 = M_1 plus sterling deposit accounts of the private sector with the deposit banks and discount houses only.
M_3 = M_2 plus sterling deposit accounts with other banks, all non-sterling deposits of the private sector and all deposits of the public sector.

5

Regulating Banks and Credit

Banking Regulation in Britain – By 'Suasion' not Statute November 1967

In many countries commercial banks are subject to a formal framework of regulation and inspection laid down by statute, but overseas enquirers are often surprised to learn that this is not so in Britain. It was over a century ago that commercial banks in this country were for the first and only time made subject to a general code governing their formation and conduct, but the act of 1844 (7 and 8 Vict. c. 113) was so oppressive that it was wholly repealed after about a dozen years. No similar legislative restrictions have since been applied, but, nevertheless, the law relating to banking is substantial, as any student for the Institute of Bankers examinations well knows. It is, however, mostly case law relating to particular aspects of banking, and based largely on a few statutes which are also limited in scope, such as the Bills of Exchange Act.

The banks, too, are subject to a number of more general legal provisions, such as the Companies Acts. And they also have to conduct their affairs in accordance with government needs and in harmony with official credit policy as generally conveyed to them through the Bank of England.

This last, the process of 'suasion', as it is called, is quite different from a code of regulation, though, as we shall see, in the background it has some legislative force in the Bank of England Act, 1946. In the main 'suasion' is concerned with monetary controls, which are commonly directed at the economy through the channel of the banks, which otherwise are generally free from comprehensive regulation or inspection of their activities. Even so, various authorities are responsible for somewhat scrappy and piecemeal regulation affecting banking for limited purposes. In this article we indicate in broad terms the principal ways in which the banks are regulated, both by statute and less formally.

A fundamental difficulty that is encountered at the outset is the lack of any statutory definition, of general application, of the terms 'bank', 'banker', or 'banking', even though a special position is often accorded to 'banks' or 'bankers' in legislation. The Bills of Exchange Act, 1882, for example, states merely that '"Banker" includes a body of persons whether incorporated or not who carry on the business of banking', without defining banking. Some legislation has gone a little though not much further by providing administrative machinery for establishing what is a bank for the limited purposes of the specific act. Thus, the Bank of England Act, 1946, provides that: 'In this section [4] the expression "banker" means any such person carrying on a banking undertaking as may be declared by order of the Treasury to be a banker for the purposes of this section.' No such order has ever been made, and the way in which this definition might be interpreted is still unknown.

For particular statutory purposes, however, various authorities are required to prepare their own lists of banks. An important example is that of the Companies Act, 1948, which provides for exemption of a 'banking or discount company' from some of the general requirements relating to accounts as laid down in the Eighth Schedule. The expression 'banking or discount company' here means 'any company which satisfies the Board of Trade that it ought to be treated for the purposes of this Schedule as a banking company or as a discount company'. For many years the names of those exempted were not public knowledge, so that it was not possible to attempt to judge the criteria used by the Board of Trade. More recently, the names have been published, since the list has been adopted for the purposes of the Protection of Depositors Act, 1963, to determine which companies would be exempted from those provisions of the act relating to advertisement for deposits. (A copy of the list current at the end of 1970 is given in Appendix 5.)

Another list, prepared by the Inland Revenue authorities, arises from the Income Tax Act, 1952. Under this, interest on an advance from a 'bank carrying on a *bona fide* banking business' may be paid to the bank without deduction of tax, but the act itself does not define 'bank' or 'banking business'. In a quite different field, the Building Societies Act, 1960, makes the Chief Registrar of Friendly Societies responsible for preparing and maintaining a register of authorized banks with which building societies must keep their accounts; the register is given legal force by way of an order made with the consent of the Treasury. Again, exchange control requirements have led to the preparation of two further lists, this time prepared by the Bank of England, of banks and other institutions that are authorized dealers in foreign exchange and authorized depositories for overseas securities.

Considerable difficulty may arise where no provision is made under a particular piece of legislation for the establishment of some kind of register of bankers, as has been seen in proceedings under the Moneylenders Acts. These acts are not administered by any government authority and no definitions of bank and banking are given. Yet failure to establish that a lender is '*bona fide* carrying on the business of banking' may bring him within the scope of the acts, and result in money lent being irrecoverable and securities taken void. The difficulties to which this can give rise were well illustrated in 1966 in the hearing of the case of the United Dominions Trust *v.* Kirkwood. UDT was able to establish its right to be regarded as a bank, but only on the particular facts of that case, and following the decision some finance houses took steps to make their status more readily demonstrable. Further clarification of the position of particular undertakings has resulted from the Companies Act, 1967, under which the Board of Trade is empowered to certify that a particular body may be regarded as a bank for the purposes of the Moneylenders Acts. (The duties of the Board of Trade have since been taken over by the Department of Trade and Industry.)

The inclusion of the word 'Bank' in the title of an undertaking has never been a sure guide as to its true status, although restrictions on its use have become increasingly stringent. Control is mainly exercised through the Registration of Business Names Act, 1916, and the Companies Act, 1948 (section 17), which prohibit the registration of a firm or company under a name which in the opinion of the Board of Trade is 'undesirable'. In this context, the Registrar of Companies has stated that names which include the words 'Bank' or 'Banking' 'will be allowed only where the circumstances justify it'. Companies registered outside the United Kingdom escape this particular control. The Companies Act, 1967, empowered the Board of Trade to direct any company to change its name if, in the Board's opinion, this is so misleading as to be likely to cause harm to the public.

The importance of this control has been enhanced by regulations made under the Protection of Depositors Act, 1963; in effect these prohibit the use of the words 'bank', 'banker' or 'banking' in advertisements for deposits except where they form part of its name or where the advertisement is by a body recognized for other purposes as a bank. The provisions of the Protection of Depositors Act encompass companies incorporated outside Great Britain, but a loophole may be noted in that regulations in some other countries are less stringent regarding the use of words like 'Bank' in a company's title.

The various lists or registers that have been mentioned are required for defined purposes only, and generally are used not for regulating the activities of the banks but as a means of exempting them from restrictions applied to others. An important exemption that they have long enjoyed is in respect of the legal requirements regarding accounts as applied to companies generally.

It has already been indicated that some of the accounting provisions of the Companies Act, 1948, do not apply to 'any company which satisfies the

Board of Trade that it ought to be treated [for this purpose] as a banking company'. Broadly, these exemptions have allowed the banks to maintain undisclosed sums on contingency accounts – popularly known as hidden reserves – and to transfer unspecified sums between these and their current earnings. The traditional justification for this privilege has been that banks, by the nature of their business, are liable to suffer large inroads into their current earnings because of the need on occasion to make provisions for bad and doubtful debts, and to meet sharp falls in market prices of investments. Although a majority of the Jenkins Committee,* which considered these exemptions a few years ago, favoured their retention, a new situation was established by the Companies Act, 1967.

This gave the Board of Trade power to make orders, subject to approval by resolution of each House of Parliament, reducing or abolishing the exemptions provided under the 1948 act. Such orders may relate to all banks or to 'any class' of them, a class being defined by reference to 'any circumstances whatsoever'.

Like all companies, banks must each year lay before their members in general meeting a profit and loss account and balance sheet drawn up in accordance with the Companies Acts. Every limited banking company must in addition display periodic statements in accordance with section 433 of the 1948 act, set out in accordance with the pattern laid down in the Thirteenth Schedule 'or as near thereto as circumstances admit'. The form of the Schedule can be changed by the Board of Trade by way of a statutory instrument.

The statement, popularly known as the 'frame statement', is required to show the bank's capital and other liabilities and assets as at the end of each half-year, grouped under broad headings as specified, and must be 'put up in a conspicuous place in the registered office of the company, and in every branch office or place where the business of the company is carried on', by the first Monday in February and the first Tuesday in August in respect of the previous half-year. Members of the company and its creditors are entitled to a copy of the statement on payment of a sum not exceeding sixpence (6*d*.). Quite apart from this legal obligation, the clearing banks or their forerunners for half a century and longer have followed the practice of issuing monthly statements of account, which have come to be regarded as important indicators of the current monetary situation.

Although the banks must regularly publish their balance sheets, the make-up and disposition of liabilities and assets are not subject to specific legal controls. Some ratios for the deployment of assets are observed by the clearing banks, in accordance with the wishes of the authorities, but are not embodied in any legislation. Although they originated as conventions based

* *Report of the Company Law Committee*, Cmnd. 1749. In fact, the clearing banks later agreed to disclose inner reserves and 'true' profits commencing with the accounts for the year to end 1969, published in February 1970 (see p. 403).

on banking prudence, today they are applied primarily for monetary purposes; they are considered more fully below.

Similarly in other aspects of their operations, developments are sometimes subject to informal regulation. This is well illustrated by the position in respect of amalgamations. Concentration in the British banking system proceeded largely through amalgamations until the First World War, by which time the clearing banks had emerged in much their present form. A Treasury committee in 1918 recommended legislation to require government approval for further amalgamations, and suggested criteria for judging their desirability. No such legislation was introduced, as the banks undertook voluntarily to submit any further proposals for amalgamations to the authorities for approval.

Since then, amalgamations have been comparatively few, though they have by no means ceased. The general pattern was that a large bank has acquired a smaller undertaking, often one operating in a distinct and separate part of the United Kingdom which for many practical purposes has retained its own identity. A sizeable amalgamation in recent times was the acquisition of District Bank by National Provincial Bank in 1962. Official attitudes have changed. In 1967 the National Board for Prices and Incomes, in its report on Bank Charges (34, Cmnd. 3292) suggested that 'further amalgamations among the banks, carried through to the appropriate point, could permit some rationalization of existing networks'. It also noted that 'the Bank of England and the Treasury have made it plain to us that they would not obstruct some further amalgamations if the banks were willing to contemplate such a development'.

Under the Monopolies and Mergers Act, 1965, amalgamations among banks, as among other undertakings, may be referred by the Board of Trade to the Monopolies Commission. The Board ruled that the arrangement whereby the Midland Bank acquired a one third interest in Montagu Trust constituted a 'merger', but that 'the public interest did not require a reference to the Commission' (see also p. 371).

Although in the conduct of their business the banks in England enjoy a high degree of freedom from legal restraints, one major exception is that they may not borrow by issuing their own bank notes. A century or more ago notes were a main form by which the banks obtained their resources, but the Bank of England is now the sole bank with the right to issue notes in England and Wales. This position came about over a long period of years following the Bank Charter Act of 1844, which laid down strict limitations on the issue of notes. No new banks of issue were allowed; those already issuing notes were permitted to continue to do so, but the maximum for each bank was limited to the 1844 level and this right disappeared with amalgamation. The last note issue of a joint stock bank in England was withdrawn in 1919 and of a private bank in 1921.

However, the banks registered in Scotland and Northern Ireland still have – and use – the power to issue their own notes, though this right is not unlimited. The Radcliffe Committee stated that 'the most obvious peculiarity of the Scottish banks is that they retain and exercise the right of note issue'. Although the legal maximum of the fiduciary issue of the Scottish banks amounted to only £2·7 million late in 1967, some £140 million of their notes were in circulation; for the Northern Ireland banks the corresponding figures were £2 million and £9 million respectively. The amount by which the actual issue exceeds the fiduciary limit must be covered by holdings of Bank of England notes or coins, and the Radcliffe Committee saw 'no reason for interference with existing arrangements. Since the amount is always so far above the permitted fiduciary issue, the banks cannot add to their cash reserves by merely printing notes but, like the English banks, only by attracting balances at the Bank of England or attracting notes from circulation.' However, because of the note issues and the Bank of England notes held as backing, the Scottish and Northern Irish banks did not observe the cash ratio then required of the clearing banks.

The position of two particular classes of bank may conveniently be noted here. For the savings banks, legislative control is comprehensive. The Post Office Savings Bank, indeed, was born of a parliamentary act in 1861, and the trustee savings banks, although unencumbered in the beginning, have been subjected to considerable legislation dating from the first regulatory act in 1817. Even the introduction of new services is dependent upon legislation, as evidenced by the Post Office Savings Bank Act, 1966, which provided the necessary authority for the introduction of investment account facilities, and the Trustee Savings Bank Act, 1964, had to be passed before the trustee banks could offer a current account service. Whereas the commercial banks, in the absence of suspected fraud, are free from outside inspection, the trustee banks are subject to regular inspections on behalf of the Trustee Savings Banks Inspection Committee, a statutory body which submits an annual report to Parliament, and the Post Office Savings Bank is liable to periodical scrutiny by House of Commons committee.

This is in sharp contrast with the position of a foreign-registered bank wishing to open a branch in Britain, which it can do with few formalities. In practice, however, it will be seen that such a branch will be hampered in its operations unless it is recognized by the government departments involved. Moreover, it will be unable to conduct most of the types of business it would wish to unless so authorized by the Bank of England, which may withhold its permission for a probationary period, and will, in any event, also expect its wishes, for example in the lending field, to be observed. A branch of an overseas bank is considered as a UK resident body for exchange control purposes, and so its activities are subject to exchange control in exactly the same way as a domestic bank; in the nature of things, however, this control is likely to apply to a larger proportion of its business than occurs with a British bank. Like any other branch of a foreign undertaking, it is free to remit home its current earnings, and also to repatriate its original investment in this country provided that this has had prior official approval. The number of overseas-registered banks with offices in Britain – almost all of them in London – has been growing steadily in recent years, and at the end of 1967 about one hundred were represented; many, but by no means all, of the newcomers are American.

To return to the indigenous banks, the only piece of general legislation giving wide-ranging power of control is the Bank of England Act, 1946. The purpose of this, as stated in the preamble to the act, was 'to bring the capital stock of the Bank of England into public ownership and bring the Bank under public control, to make provision with respect to the relations between the Treasury, the Bank of England and other banks and for purposes connected with the matters aforesaid'. Under subsection (3) of section 4 the Bank of England may, if it considers such action to be necessary in the public interest, 'request information from and make recommendations to bankers, and may, if so authorized by the Treasury, issue directions to any banker for the purpose of securing that effect is given to any such request or recommendation'. These are wide powers, but they are subject to two provisos. First, 'no such request or recommendations shall be made with respect to the affairs of any particular customer of a banker'. Secondly, before the issue of any directions the Treasury must give the banker, 'an opportunity of making representations.' Since the act also gives the Treasury power to give directions to the Bank of England, this provides an instrument whereby the banks could be brought under detailed control of the government.

In fact, these statutory powers have apparently never been implemented. The position, as the Bank of England saw it in 1957, was expressed in a memorandum submitted to the Radcliffe Committee as follows: 'The Bank have had no formal control over other banks and no duty of inspection; the possibility that the Bank might refuse to continue to maintain an account for another bank has been historically an effective sanction. Since 1946, if the Bank think it necessary in the public interest, they may request information from bankers and make recommendations to them; and, if so authorized by the Treasury, may issue directions to ensure compliance with such a request or recommendation. This power has not been used.'

Indeed, it is arguable that, in this respect, the act made little difference to the pre-existing situation. The habit of the clearing banks of giving every consideration to the monetary policy of the authorities and requirements of the Bank of England had become deep-rooted before 1946, and it has continued to develop since then. It has become the Bank's practice to pass on 'requests' from the authorities to the clearing banks, and the banks invariably do their best to comply. They do, however, let the authorities know their views on such matters as the desirability or feasibility of particular types of control, and commonly are consulted by them beforehand on any proposed development likely to affect the banking system generally or to have implications for the implementation of monetary policy, as, for example, in rates of interest allowed and charged as related to bank rate. In the background, however, is the knowledge that the authorities have statutory powers to enforce their policy requirements even though in the form in which they are expressed – as 'requests' or 'directives' – they have no legislative force.

The clearing and similar domestic banks in the United Kingdom are relatively few in number, engage in the same sort of activities and are accustomed to observing official views in the conduct of their business so as to accord with the national interest. Other banks, such as the accepting houses and the overseas and foreign banks in London, to which the act also applies, are more numerous and also disparate in their nature and activities. For these reasons informal controls are not easy to apply to their businesses, but in recent years 'requests' made by the Bank of England to the ordinary banking system have been extended also to other banking institutions.

It is in the field of lending that 'requests' or 'directives' have been addressed to the banks by the Bank of England, and these have from time to time indicated both quantitative and qualitative criteria to be observed. Qualitative 'directives' have been operative for most of the post-war period, with the emphasis varying from time to time. In general the banks have been asked to give priority to lending for defence purposes and for furthering exports, or for activities that tend to limit imports, such as agriculture. Regional development and productive investment have recently featured in the list of priorities. Commonly, banks have been asked to restrain lending for such purposes as personal expenditure and speculation, for the financing of hire purchase and for property development.

Quantitative 'requests' have been relatively infrequent and of shorter duration. They have, too, often been expressed rather widely; the first such request, in July 1955, was for 'a positive and significant reduction' in advances over the ensuing few months. More recently the requirements of the authorities have been stated with greater precision. In May 1965 the clearing banks were told that their advances to the private sector should not increase at an annual rate of more than about 5 per cent during the year to March 1966, this limitation being applied also to the granting of acceptance facilities and the purchase of commercial bills. These quantitative limits – 105 per cent of March 1965 levels – were renewed for a further period in 1966 but were lifted in April 1967.

In the early years the issue of 'directives' only to the clearing banks among financial institutions was criticized, and nowadays the authorities cast their net much wider to include accepting houses, overseas and foreign banks, discount houses, insurance companies, building societies, and the main associations of finance houses. Some of these bodies would scarcely come within the description 'any banker' to which directions may be given under the 1946 act. The Radcliffe Committee considered whether wider powers of compulsion should be taken, and whether the authorities should compile a 'comprehensive register of financial institutions'. It concluded that this was not immediately needed, though it might be in the future; as yet, no such action has been taken. When the 105 per cent ceiling on advances was lifted as a restriction on the lending activities of the clearing and Scottish banks in April 1967, it was retained for other financial institutions, pending the introduction of fresh arrangements for controlling their lending.

A traditional function of the central bank is to influence the ability of the banking system to create new deposits. Until September 1971 the clearing banks were required to observe two ratios, the cash ratio and the liquidity ratio. Neither was called for by law, but the banks followed them in distinctive ways, and were, in effect, required to do so by the authorities. For this purpose 'cash' comprised holdings of coin and notes, and balances with the Bank of England (excluding Special Deposits), and it was expressed as a percentage of gross deposits. This ratio began to assume importance around the turn of the last century, when, with the growing concentration of banking activity, some of the large banks began publication for the first time of monthly statements of account, and this made it possible to follow the banking situation more closely. Thus, the cash ratio became not only an indicator of strength but also a means of closer regulation of monetary conditions, once it began to be held at an established level. By open market operations the authorities could influence the level of 'cash', and the banks in turn might be constrained to adjust their deposits. If the money market was obliged to turn to the Bank of England, as lender of last resort, to provide more cash, the Bank did so only at its own rate of interest, thus making bank rate effective.

In the inter-war years a cash ratio of 10 to 11 per cent came to be observed, but this was achieved partly by 'window-dressing' the monthly figures. In December 1946, however, the Committee of London Clearing Bankers announced that, 'taking into account the general disposition of bank assets now ruling, it has been agreed in consultation with the Bank of England that the daily ratio of cash balances to deposit liabilities will be maintained on the basis of 8 per cent'. This was treated as a firm requirement until 1971; each bank endeavours to hold its cash ratio at precisely 8 per cent from day to day, though unforeseen movements of funds occasionally resulted in a deviation of a decimal point or two. So long as the Bank of England was prepared to keep a firm hold on the availability of cash, this ratio provided a useful means of regulation, but for many years past the Bank has preferred to furnish cash far more readily, so that it was in practice virtually interchangeable with Treasury bills. The cash ratio, then, served the narrower requirement of helping to regulate short-term interest rates and to preserve, in general, the liquidity of the system. As a prime monetary regulator it was then the liquidity ratio (for changes in 1971 see p. 119 ff.).

This was the ratio to gross deposits of cash and various other liquid assets, principally money at call and short notice (lent mostly to the discount market), Treasury bills, commercial bills and refinanceable export credits, all of which could, if necessary, be exchanged for cash at the Bank of England immediately, and generally without loss. The liquidity ratio assumed a fresh importance in the early 1950s when the authorities returned to the use of interest rates as a means of influencing the monetary situation. During the inter-war years the banks, with no guidance from the authorities, usually maintained a liquidity ratio of around 30 per cent, and historically a ratio of one third was often mentioned. Following the high liquidity of the war years the banks moved back towards former levels, and the authorities took the opportunity of establishing this further means of regulation, once it was clear that the cash ratio had been rendered less effective.

In 1951 the governor of the Bank of England indicated that a liquidity ratio of between 28 and 32 per cent would be expected, although exceptionally a minimum of 25 per cent might be permissible. By 1955, 30 per cent was regarded as the appropriate minimum level and in 1957 the governor of the Bank of England told the Radcliffe Committee that he had 'left the banks in no doubt . . . that they should not allow their liquidity ratios to fall significantly below 30 per cent'.

An important change occurred in 1963. The banks were then experiencing considerable pressure on liquidity, and at the same time the government was anxious to avoid a restriction in bank credit. In the spring the Bank of England indicated that it would take a less rigid view of the newly established minimum level of 30 per cent, and in the autumn the banks were advised that they could 'aim to achieve a liquidity ratio of not less than 28 per cent between now and the make-up date in April 1964'. In practice, 28 per cent continued to be accepted as a suitable minimum until the new system of September 1971.

A suitable minimum, that is, for purposes of monetary control: the banks themselves have said that they would be content to work to a lower figure. In evidence given to the Radcliffe Committee, bankers indicated that they would be comfortable with a somewhat lower liquidity ratio, and later, when it was officially lowered to a minimum of 28 per cent, some banks indicated that they would like to see it lower still. The liquidity ratio was observed in a different way from the fixed cash ratio; it was a floor rather than a rigid line. With marked seasonal fluctuations in the supply of liquid assets, by the end of the calendar year the banks generally built up a substantial margin above the minimum, before the main tax-gathering season ran down their liquidity. By contrast with the clearing banks, other joint stock banks – mainly those in Northern Ireland and Scotland – had no precise and explicit liquidity conventions.

A further and relatively new instrument of regulation had been added to the armoury of the Bank of England in 1958, when all restraints on bank lending were temporarily removed for the first time since the war. The new arrangements, like the directives that preceded them, were introduced without statutory force, but were nonetheless effective. Under the new system the clearing and the Scottish banks may be required by the Bank of England to place with it a deposit equivalent to a stated percentage of their gross deposits, to be held there until released. Such calls for 'Special Deposits' are made with the approval of the Chancellor of the Exchequer, and the amounts earmarked are paid out of liquid assets, but can no longer be treated as such. Hence the banks' liquidity ratio was correspondingly reduced along with their ability to increase their lending. The Special Deposits system was therefore akin to a variable liquidity ratio, and had an effect somewhat similar to that of open market operations.

In 1960 the first call for Special Deposits was made, and by 1961 they were at their highest levels yet recorded – 3 per cent for the clearing banks and 1½ per cent for the Scottish. The banks were free from Special Deposits restraint during the whole of 1963 and 1964, but they were brought into use again in May 1965 and remained until the changes of 1971, when the rates were 3½ per cent for the clearing banks and 1¾ per cent for banks in Scotland. They were then repaid, but the system was kept in being, and Special Deposits were made to apply more widely among financial institutions (see pp. 122-3).

As we have seen, regulation of the banks is in the main effected by 'suasion' rather than by statute, and particularly is this so in matters of monetary regulation. In one sense, we have not told the whole story: no attempt has been made to deal with the broader aspects of monetary management which are of direct consequence to the banks, and especially the day-to-day management of the money market by the authorities, including the influence exerted by them on interest rates, especially at the short end through the level of bank rate. This would bring us into a far wider field than that of the regulation of banks.

Nor have we dealt with actions having their origins in the special circumstances of the war, when the banks were required to immobilize indicated amounts of their resources by taking up Treasury Deposit Receipts. Subsequently, as these were repaid, the banks switched into Treasury bills, until in the early 1950s liquidity generally was considered by the authorities to be excessive for purposes of monetary policy. Accordingly it was decided to 'fund' with short-dated stock a total of £1000 million of Treasury bills and, in the words of the Radcliffe Committee, 'the banks were in effect instructed to take about £500 million out of the total; by this stroke £500 million was switched in the banks' balance sheets from "liquid assets" to "investments", the liquid assets ratio thereby being reduced from 39 to 32 per cent'.

All this, too, was achieved without legislation, illustrating a major advantage of a system of control which is not too formal or too rigid, showing an adaptability to meet changing needs without the delays which might be involved in applying a formal code. Against this, and the virtue of flexibility, is the danger that the wishes of the authorities will lack precision and may not be interpreted in a uniform way, possibly to the disadvantage of those institutions that apply them most zealously. The significance of this aspect was not unduly important when the main concern of the monetary authorities was with the relatively small number of clearing banks and of discount houses with which they were able to maintain close contact. But the risk is heightened when, as in existing conditions, monetary regulation has to be extended more widely to less compact groups of institutions.

Towards an Effective Liquidity Ratio? May 1970

In his budget speech in April 1970 the Chancellor of the Exchequer announced a modest, but still welcome, easing of the quantitative restrictions on lending which have hamstrung banking activities for many years past. Even more significant was his admission that 'though such a control is probably the most direct and effective method of achieving tight short-term restraint, the rigidities and distortions which come from it intensify with the passage of time'. Hence a return to earlier methods of credit regulation was heralded, though by way of Special Deposits superimposed on liquidity ratios.

The liquidity of the banks, said the Chancellor, had now 'come under pressure', and he continued: 'In these circumstances, the use of the Special Deposit mechanism will allow us to exert a continuing influence over the liquidity and lending capacity of the banks. Special Deposits will, therefore, in future be used as freely as is required by the liquidity and actual or prospective lending of these banks. A call for Special Deposits should in no way be regarded as a "crisis" measure, nor, indeed, should a repayment be regarded as a signal of major relaxation.'

This differed little from the announcement of his predecessor in April 1967 that Special Deposits would henceforth be used in 'a new and more flexible way', by 'routine adjustments', made comparatively frequently in accordance with changes in bank liquidity. The stated purpose then was to 'move as rapidly as possible to a less rigid form of overall control' than that of the 'ceiling on advances', which was accordingly to be abandoned in favour of liquidity control operated partly through Special Deposits. But with the devaluation of sterling in the following November ceilings were reimposed on bank lending. Moreover, Special Deposits were maintained and in fact were not altered between the summer of 1966 and April 1970, easily the longest period of fixity since the scheme was introduced.

In Britain, as in other countries, regulation through operations upon the credit base of the banking system was established long before restrictions on advances were introduced, and it has always been accepted by the banks as essential in maintaining orderly monetary conditions. Thus in the management of their assets until September 1971 the clearing banks were required by the authorities to take heed of the ratios to gross deposits of two items – cash (including balances held with the Bank of England), and liquid assets as a whole. Both originated as working ratios, which the banks came to observe for reasons of prudence, but both in course of time were adopted by the authorities for monetary purposes, and it was this aspect that gave them their special significance prior to the advent of the new regulations (see pp. 119 ff.).

As an instrument of monetary regulation (the cash ratio had the longer history, but in this respect was superseded in importance by the liquidity ratio, even though the banks were then still required to maintain a stated proportion of their deposit liabilities in cash. The way in which the cash ratio was used for monetary purposes forty years ago was explained by the 'Macmillan' Committee as follows: 'Since the banks as a whole maintain a cash proportion to deposits of from 10 per cent to 11 per cent, they are, in fact, able to increase their deposits by some ten times the cash created by the Bank of England . . . the opposite process . . . will reduce the cash . . . and entail a reduction of their deposits.'*

Hence by operating on the amount of cash available to the banks, the authorities could influence the level of bank deposits and the ability of the banks to extend credit. The main way of influencing cash holdings was by open market operations. To increase bank cash, the authorities bought securities on the open market, paying for them in Bank of England balances, which are cash. Similarly, to reduce cash they sold securities. It was not the precise level of the ratio that was important but simply the adherence to an established relationship. In fact the development of 'window dressing', to which the Macmillan Committee drew attention, blunted the edge of control.

Since Macmillan, window-dressing was ended, and later the cash ratio requirement was reduced to 8 per cent, but meanwhile cash had in practice become virtually interchangeable with Treasury bills and some other liquid assets. Day-to-day fluctuations in bank cash became so substantial that the authorities would have had little control over short-term interest rates – the

* *Committee on Finance and Industry*, Cmd. 3897 (HMSO, 1931), para. 71.

price of borrowing cash – if they had not carried out their open market operations so as to smooth them out. As the Radcliffe Committee explained, the authorities have consciously and deliberately chosen 'reasonable stability in the Treasury bill rate'.* Accordingly, they operated each day in the discount market in such a way as to mop up any surplus cash or to meet any shortage, and to facilitate maintenance of 8 per cent to the existing volume of deposits. Thus the ratio of all liquid assets – cash, call money, Treasury bills, commercial bills – to gross deposits became the basis of the multiplier process. As we shall see later, the volume of liquid assets was largely within the control of the authorities, who defined them and greatly influenced the quantity available. Since September 1971 the new ratio system has been introduced.

As long ago as 1885, George Rae, then chairman of the North and South Wales Bank, referred in *The Country Banker* to a 'financial reserve' of one third of the amount of liabilities to the public. This was before the heyday of the amalgamation movement in banking that spanned the nineteenth and twentieth centuries, and well before the clearing banks began to publish monthly statements in 1921. As a consequence of these developments the banks became increasingly ratio conscious and, in evidence to the Macmillan Committee, the managing director of the Midland Bank said that the Bank aimed at maintaining, in relation to total assets, 11 per cent in cash, 7 per cent in call money and 15 per cent in bills – a 'liquidity ratio' of 33 per cent, in pre-1971 terms.

The available statistics indicate that the banks had traditionally maintained a liquidity proportion of at least 30 per cent to deposits, and in 1939 this was clearly identified as a conscious working objective (see p. 5). The reliance of the authorities upon the liquidity ratio came even later, at a time – in 1951 – when they were seeking to reintroduce responsive interest rates and closer control over the financial system and banking activities following nearly twenty years of cheap money, during which direct controls and other unorthodox measures had been widely used.

In effect the Bank of England did three things in 1951. For the first time it explicitly made the maintenance of a liquidity ratio a firm requirement; it established, within limits, the level of the ratio; and it applied it for monetary as distinct from banking purposes. It has also defined what may be included among liquid assets, as it did indirectly in earlier times by restricting cover to 'eligible' bills. More recently it has specifically defined what assets may be regarded as liquid, and has at times widened their range, notably by allowing the discount houses to hold a higher proportion of various assets other than bills against money at call, and the banks to include various other quick assets as part of liquidity, such as new forms of money at call other than to the discount houses, and refinanceable export credits.

* *Committee on the Working of the Monetary System*, Cmnd. 827 (HMSO, 1959), para. 376.

In 1951 the Bank indicated that a ratio of from 32 to 28 per cent would be regarded as normal, with an extreme lower limit of 25 per cent. By 1957, however, this degree of tolerance had been removed, with observance of a minimum of 30 per cent being made a specific requirement. In 1963, when an expansion of credit was felt to be desirable, the minimum was lowered to 28 per cent, and at this figure it remained until 1971. Even so, the liquidity ratio was never, like the cash ratio, observed precisely from day to day; instead, it constituted a minimum which would be exceeded when seasonality called for the building of liquidity.

Within a few years of the first indication by the authorities of a specific liquidity ratio requirement, provision was made for its reinforcement should this be considered necessary. In 1958, when it became possible to remove – briefly – all direct controls over bank lending for the first time since the war, it was agreed that, when called upon to do so by the authorities, the banks should place Special Deposits with the Bank of England, at a stated proportion of their total deposits. These Special Deposits would bear interest at a rate related to the Treasury bill discount rate, but they would not be included among liquid assets for the purpose of calculating the ratio.

The introduction of the Special Deposits scheme was an indication that the authorities felt they could not rely solely on open market operations to keep bank liquidity at an appropriate level, but needed in addition an instrument which could be used arbitrarily – or at least independently of market forces. As the Radcliffe Committee put it, the Bank of England 'cannot choose both a rate of interest and the quantity of debt to be held at that rate' (para. 375). Indeed, at times when they desired to restrain bank credit, the authorities were faced with continuing expansion of the supply of liquid assets available to the banking system.

The growth in the volume of Treasury bills, at that time the main component of bank liquidity, arose from continuing deficits on the central government's accounts as well as a weak market for gilts. Although a surplus was often achieved on current revenue and expenditure account, this was never sufficient in any of the eighteen financial years up to 1967–8 to cover capital finance provided from the Exchequer. To the extent that the overall deficit was not met by sales of government debt other than to the banks, or by borrowing abroad because of deficits on the balance of payments, it was financed by the creation of money through the banking system, against the issue of Treasury bills.

Since 1960, however, the availability of liquid assets from the public sector has shrunk. Over the period the reduction of Treasury bills has been due to various factors, including national savings, successful funding sales of government securities, and borrowing from abroad to finance a balance of payments deficit. The contraction in the late 1960s has been particularly striking as, after a long period of deficit financing, budget policy was deliberately designed to show a substantial overall Exchequer surplus. At the end of March 1960, the amount of Treasury bills outstanding which had been issued through the weekly tender amounted to roughly £3500 million, over 12 per cent of the total national debt. Eight years later the figure had fallen to £2090 million, and by the end of March 1970 to only about £1200 million, or about 3·5 per cent of the national debt. The effect of this on the holdings of the clearing banks and the discount market is shown in Table A12.

TABLE A12 *Holdings of Treasury bills by clearing banks and discount market*

	£m.		
	London clearing banks	*Discount market*	*Total*
March			
1960	941	446	1387
1961	790	328	1118
1962	794	371	1165
1963	667	366	1033
1964	667	363	1030
1965	559	215	774
1966	656	400	1056
1967	403	219	622
1968	371	255	626
1969	310	261	571
1970	77	198	275

The Chancellor drew attention to these movements when making his move towards control by Special Deposits. He said: 'As a result of the large government surplus and the substantial sales of government debt to the public over the last year, the liquidity of [the clearing and Scottish] banks has already come under pressure.' Against this may be set the view of the Radcliffe Committee – writing over ten years ago, when the availability of Treasury bills was much higher – that 'funding of Treasury bills beyond a certain (not very remote) point would cause a major upheaval in our financial institutions' (para. 543).

The pressures that these movements might have been expected to exert on the banking situation were relieved from several sources. During the 1960s a recovery in the use of commercial bills of exchange carried holdings of these by the London clearing banks from £166 million at the end of 1960 to £608 million at the end of 1969, and those of the discount market from

£117 million to nearly £600 million over the period. For several years previously the expansion of commercial bills has been controlled by bringing them within the ceilings imposed by the authorities on bank lending and on holdings by the discount houses. Another source of relief, of growing importance in those years, had been the inclusion in the figure of a 'refinanceable' proportion of medium-term export credit advanced against the guarantee of the Export Credits Guarantee Department.

The position was also eased by an increase in the proportion of liquid assets in the form of money at call and short notice lent to the discount market, which holds other assets besides Treasury bills, notably short-dated gilt-edged securities. Then, too, as already noted, other assets were agreed upon for inclusion under money at call other than to the discount market.

The effects of these various movements on the composition of liquid assets can be discerned in Table A13.

An importance economic purpose of fiscal policy has become the need to influence the general level of demand on resources, and in a sense the effect on bank liquidity was incidental. Even more so was the impact of other activites

TABLE A13 *Liquid assets of London clearing banks (yearly averages of monthly figures (£m.)*

	1960	*1966*	*1967*	*1968*	*1969*
Cash	588	767	798	851	879
% of gross deposits	*8·1*	*8·2*	*8·2*	*8·2*	*8·3*
Money at call and short notice to money market	490	731	806	896	981
% of gross deposits	*6·8*	*7·7*	*8·2*	*8·6*	*9·3*
Treasury bills	1007	689	564	468	294
% of gross deposits	*13·9*	*7·3*	*5·8*	*4·5*	*2·8*
Money at call etc. other than to money market	72	275	330	439	469
% of gross deposits	*1·0*	*2·9*	*3·4*	*4·4*	*4·2*
'Other bills'	143	446	492	527	568
% of gross deposits	*2·0*	*4·8*	*5·0*	*5·1*	*5·4*
Total	2300	2908	2990	3182	3191
% of gross deposits	*31·8*	*31·0*	*30·6*	*30·5*	*30·1*

of the authorities, as noted below. Nevertheless the authorities were able to exercise a substantial and increased measure of control over the level of liquidity in the banking system. Hence the growing conviction that the most satisfactory instrument for influencing the level of deposit creation by the banks consists of official pressures on liquidity, to replace direct quantitative and qualitative controls over lending – the direction in which the authorities later moved.

Both before 1951 and subsequently, the authorities had given great weight to direct controls, applied by means of requests or 'directives' to the banks, upon their lending policies. Virtually throughout the post-war period, the banks had been steering their lending to those categories officially accorded highest priority, and restricting it in other directions. For the five years to 1970, except for six months in 1967, bank lending has also been subject to direct quantitative control. This constituted strong medicine indeed. The Radcliffe Committee found justification for such harshness only 'in times of emergency', and on occasion the authorities also accepted the view that directives were undesirable.

Several further factors were relevant when considering some form of control based on liquidity. First, the minimum liquidity ratio of 28 per cent was higher than the figure that the banks themselves wished to work to for purely banking reasons. Bank spokesmen made this point on a number of occasions. Another consideration was that a complete lifting of the ceiling from bank lending would apply to commercial bills as well as to advances, and these were liquid assets for banking purposes which originate independently of the activities of the public sector.

Quite apart from this the authorities, though they have brought the broad level of bank liquidity back into control by orthodox means, were not in a position to adjust it by traditional methods with a fineness appropriate to its use as a means of delicate short-term control. In particular, as the chairman of the Midland Bank has pointed out,* the net outcome of the various forces operating on the liquidity position of the banking system 'is not necessarily in accord with the needs of credit regulation'. For a number of reasons the authorities are inhibited from using open market operations for sensitive control of bank liquidity, since this is not their sole or primary purpose.

The Bank of England operates continually in three financial markets: those in Treasury bills, in marketable government securities (the discount and gilt-edged markets), and in foreign exchange. In the discount market, operations have little relevance to control through liquidity, being mainly directed to securing reasonable stability in the Treasury bill rate; their effect is to make cash and bills virtually interchangeable, without varying the total of liquid assets.

In the gilt-edged market the primary purpose of official operations has been

* *Statement to the Shareholders*, February 1970.

to create conditions appropriate for substantial funding sales, so as to prevent monetization of the national debt. The effect on the credit base of the banking system is also an important consideration.* But because of the difficulties posed by the size and weight of maturing obligations, the underlying objective has to remain the maximization of sales to the public, and the operations considered to be necessary to achieve this will not necessarily affect bank liquidity in the most appropriate way.

The object of official dealings in the foreign exchange market has been to keep the spot rate for sterling steady, usually within specified limits either side of parity, in accordance with the rules of the International Monetary Fund. This involves selling foreign currencies against sterling when sterling is weak, and acting in the reverse direction when it is strong, and in practice the authorities may intervene continuously. Their operations are mainly determined by the balance of payments situation and the strength of sterling and not their effect upon bank liquidity. Much the same considerations applied to operations in the gold market, at least up to the time of the Washington Agreement of March 1968.

In operations in several financial markets, therefore, the authorities are not free to make the regulation of bank liquidity their prime objective. The objectives sought could be conflicting, though in practice, it is true, the net outcome of their operations may be broadly in line with monetary requirements. For instance, when because of the external situation the authorities are buying foreign exchange, the gilt-edged market also is likely to be strong, enabling them to sell government securities. However, the timing and magnitude of these movements seem unlikely to coincide, and the net effect on bank liquidity might be more restrictive or more expansionary than the authorities would wish.

It can be argued nonetheless that a general but flexible policy in relation to bank liquidity is to be preferred to continuing imposition of lending ceilings. As has been noted, less rigidity was clearly the official preference in 1967 when the ceiling on bank lending was removed in favour of the use of Special Deposits in 'a new and more flexible way'. At that time the new road could not be followed, but in 1970 the same signposts were set up.

True, regulation through liquidity pressures, reinforced by Special Deposits, might be marginally less precise in its application than direct limitation of lending, but it is doubtful whether this would be relevant to control of aggregate demand. It should be seen in the context of an annual gross national product of £39,000 million, and an annual requirement by industrial and commercial companies alone for capital purposes of £3000–4000 million, of which a varying proportion, commonly about one tenth, comes from bank lending. Again, companies have aggregate credit balances

* See pp. 53–60 and 'Distribution of the National Debt, March 1969', Bank of England *Quarterly Bulletin*, March 1970.

with the banks of around £3000 million, and trade credit between them – quite beyond official control – is greater than their aggregate bank borrowing of about £5000 million. Besides such figures, any loss of control of bank lending that might occur would be insignificant, and against this would have to be set the 'rigidities and distortions' of the direct method of achieving restraint, referred to by the Chancellor of the Exchequer.

More frequent adjustment of the Special Deposits requirement, as has been proposed, would not be the only way of achieving greater flexibility. A more straightforward and less cumbersome arrangement, having the same effect, would be for the minimum ratio itself to be varied by the authorities in accordance with monetary requirements; Special Deposits would then be superfluous. The reason that they have preferred Special Deposits rather than a variable reserve or liquidity ratio was indicated a few years ago in the Bank of England *Quarterly Bulletin* (December 1962, p. 255), and before that when this novel arrangement was drawn up. The *Bulletin* states that the choice was made because of 'the need to find a general measure of credit restraint that was a specific monetary arrangement between the central bank and the commercial banks and that did not appear to be designed principally as a device for government financing'. The banks were said to have agreed to the Special Deposits scheme in 1958 'after consultation', but the Radcliffe Committee was told that they were only allowed to comment on the proposal for twenty minutes, and that alternatives were not discussed.

The Committee itself, after brief consideration, recorded its preference for a 'straightforward power' to change the minimum liquidity ratio 'in either direction'. In the end, however, whichever system is used the impact may not be all that different. What is desirable is that regulation by ratio should be applied flexibly, taking account both of monetary requirements and of the situation of the banks themselves, and that it should be seen to be a more satisfactory method of establishing the level of bank credit than the imposition of arbitrary ceilings. In 1970 the authorities were once more moving towards monetary regulation by ratio rather than by direct restriction of lending, and it was hoped, emerging from the straitjacket of using both simultaneously.

Banking Regulation and Competition – A Résumé with Commentary of the New Arrangements November 1971

In the document entitled *Competition and Credit Control* (see Appendix 4(e)) it was stated that the Bank of England would, with immediate effect, restrict the extent of its operations in the gilt-edged market, and these aspects are examined in Chapter 3. For the rest, the proposals for major changes in regulation were put forward as 'a basis for discussion' with the banks and finance houses. These discussions have now ended; as expected, they were mainly confined to questions of definition and technique, and the arrangements that began to come into effect in the middle of September 1971 are in essentials the same as those put forward four months previously.

In sum, the changes now made represent a radical alteration in the operation of monetary policy, and more specifically in the methods of control of the banking system. The new policy has three main aspects. Central to it is that all banks should be treated by the authorities in a uniform way for the purposes of credit control. This contrasts with the long-standing special concentration upon the clearing banks. The essence of this policy of uniform application is that identical reserve requirements are now imposed upon all banks; these may be supplemented, as thought necessary, by calls for Special Deposits, again uniformly on the whole banking system.

Under the new arrangements, the authorities will exercise control through interest rate policy and its effect upon the asset preferences and reserve position of the banking system; the objective is to control the money supply or some similar 'monetary aggregate', rather than bank lending as previously. For some years past the main instrument for control of lending had been the form of direct quantitative control generally known as 'ceilings', and this technique is now abandoned.

With the system of control being applied equally to all banks it became desirable, in the eyes of the authorities, that impediments to competition in the banking system should be removed. Accordingly the London and Scottish clearing banks abandoned their collective agreements on interest rates, which applied primarily to the rates allowed on deposits, but also in looser form to those charged on advances.

The changes that have now been effected were foreshadowed by the Chancellor of the Exchequer in his budget speech in March 1971, when he announced that the authorities wished to explore with the banks and finance houses the possible development of new techniques of monetary policy, with the objective of combining an effective measure of control over credit conditions with greater scope for competition and innovation. It may be useful here to indicate briefly some of the main elements in the situation leading up to the initiation of these new techniques.

Many of the problems which the new arrangements were designed to deal with more effectively were of long standing. First was the divergent and uneven development of the banking system over the preceding twenty years. The clearing banks remained the predominant financial intermediaries, but their relative importance had diminished as other banks expanded, were established, or attracted to the United Kingdom from other countries. These other institutions were in the main involved in the expansion of currency and complementary market operations generally, where growth has often been exceptionally rapid. They had also, however, been able to develop sterling banking business, on both traditional and non-traditional lines.

This development had given rise to problems of control for the authorities in relation to the sterling lending of such banks. Quantitative controls came to be applied to the various groups of banks, but some time after they were first imposed on the clearing banks and at different stages of their development. The imposition of cash, liquidity and Special Deposits requirements, such as those applied to the clearing banks, was not felt to be appropriate. It seems fair to say that these other banks had been less susceptible to traditional central bank instruments than the clearers.

More generally, one may cite the recurrent difficulties in the field of official policy, in managing the economy in respect of the balance of payments, growth and price stability. As was stated, with an unusual degree of candour by the Bank of England in a paper prepared in consultation with HM Treasury late in 1969:* 'In one sense economic policy may be said quite simply to have failed', over the preceding ten years, 'in that none of the major economic problems facing the United Kingdom in 1959 can be said to have been solved and some of the most important of them have become more severe'. Hence the frequent resort to direct restraints on bank lending as a matter of expediency, although the disadvantages of this kind of action were becoming increasingly evident and recognized.

Doubts about the course and effectiveness of official policy themselves had resulted, over the previous few years, in increasing attention being given by the authorities to movements in monetary aggregates. This renewed interest in the level of money supply and its possible relevance to economic and monetary management was apparent in discussions with the International Monetary Fund following the devaluation of sterling in November 1967. The subsequent Letter of Intent transmitted to the Fund incorporated undertakings about the growth of money supply and domestic credit expansion.

Then, to an increasing degree during the late 1960s, the clearing banks were coming under criticism for alleged lack of competitiveness, and more especially in relation to their agreements concerning rates of interest paid and allowed. In particular, they received critical scrutiny from two quasi-official bodies – the National Board for Prices and Incomes and the Monopolies Commission. As noted below, however, the strictures offered did not, apparently, reflect views offered in evidence by the Bank of England and the Treasury.

It was often overlooked, moreover, that the clearing banks began to compete – with considerable success – with the other banks through the

* '*The operation of monetary policy since the Radcliffe Report*', *Bank of England Quarterly Bulletin*, December 1969.

formation of special subsidiaries, which were flexible in their operation and could bid for deposits in competition with other banks. The clearing banks were in effect operating a divided structure, the main taking of deposits and relatively traditional forms of lending being done through the parent institutions, with their widespread branch systems, and the competitive taking of large deposits at higher rates for less orthodox and more varied forms of lending being undertaken by subsidiaries, usually operating from a single office.

Thus a varied and diversified banking structure developed and was perpetuated. The desirability of some rationalization and a more balanced response to market influences became increasingly apparent; this called for the removal of discrimination and other hindrances to the full outlet of the potential competitiveness of the clearing banks.

These seem to have been the principal developments which contributed to changing attitudes leading up to the inauguration of the new system. Before commenting on this more fully, it is convenient to note the main features of previous arrangements and the problems to which they gave rise. In the long history of the development of the banking system in this country, and its relationship to the central bank, the Bank of England had come to concentrate its attention, and more particularly its controls, upon the clearing banks, and also upon the traditional discount market which operated as a link between the banks and the central bank.

In November 1951, the authorities began to insist that the London clearing banks should maintain a set minimum liquidity ratio, which soon became clearly recognized as 30 per cent (later lowered to 28 per cent) of gross deposits. They claimed with some justification that this was a ratio which the banks themselves had developed as a working ratio suited to their own needs; certainly this was so before the exigencies of official finance during the Second World War distorted the asset structure of the banks. However, this ratio was now adopted by the authorities for the purposes of monetary control. The cash ratio requirement, the classical basis for regulating the banking system, was still maintained – after the war at 8 per cent – but for various reasons it had become ineffective, and holdings of liquid assets now became the relevant 'credit base'. In 1958 the authorities devised the system of Special Deposits as a way of reducing the liquidity of the clearing banks in much the same way as an increase in the reverse ratio would do in many foreign banking systems.

Monetary control through the liquidity ratio was effective to only a limited degree, generally because the banks had little difficulty in obtaining sufficient liquid assets. The Exchequer was commonly in overall deficit, thus expanding the supply of Treasury bills, an important component of the banks' liquid assets. Again, in their management of the gilt-edged market the authorities were mainly concerned, until relatively recently, with the funding of the national debt, rather than with the effect on the credit base. In the operation of this funding policy, they effectively stood ready to take up gilt-edged securities from the banks. Again, the 1960s saw a great increase in the issue of commercial bills, and of some other items not readily susceptible to official control, which were acceptable liquid assets. In these ways, then, the effectiveness of the liquidity ratio requirement was impaired. Although in principle calls for Special Deposits could be used to reduce bank liquidity to any level regarded as appropriate, in practice they were not pressed so far as to cause the banks acute embarrassment.

However, even though the various requirements imposed on the clearing banks were not operated as exact and sensitive instruments of monetary control, they nevertheless discriminated against these banks and significantly inhibited their development. Other banks were not subject to the same restraints; the only one applied to them was the ceilings placed upon their sterling lending, and these too, in the years up to 1961, were only directed at the clearing banks and were thereafter applied by degrees to the various other kinds of bank. A system of cash deposits, somewhat akin to the Special Deposits scheme, was devised for them, but was never brought into operation; even had it been, it is questionable whether it would have had much effect on the level of lending. The remaining feature of the now superseded arrangements which calls for mention, and on which we comment more fully later in this article, is the various agreements on interest rates which were observed by the clearing banks but not by other groups of bank.

All this is now history, though the effects of such long-standing arrangements on banking structures and practices are likely to persist for some time to come, even if to a diminishing degree. The new system came into effect, nominally at least, on 16 September 1971, with the issue by the Bank of England of a 'Notice to Banks and Finance Houses' carrying the title 'Credit Control – the new approach'. The Notice, reproduced in Appendix 4(g), itself comprises six short paragraphs – some of only one sentence – which among other things stated that previous Bank of England requests about lending would lapse after 15 September 1971. The details of the new arrangements, and in particular definitions of the various items that are now relevant, are set out in an accompanying memorandum 'Reserve ratios and Special Deposits' (see Appendix 4(h)).

The essence of the new system is that each bank – slightly different arrangements apply to finance houses and appreciably different ones to discount houses – is required to observe, day by day, a uniform minimum reserve ratio, and in addition, when called upon to do so, to place Special Deposits with the Bank of England. The basis for determining both the reserve requirements and Special Deposits is the total of 'eligible liabilities'. These consist of sterling deposits, other than those with an original maturity of over two years, and net of inter-bank transactions and sterling certificates of deposit both held and issued. Foreign currency deposits are not included, except to the extent that they are switched into sterling.

'Eligible reserve assets' must be held to the extent of a minimum of $12\frac{1}{2}$ per cent of eligible liabilities. Much of the negotiation since May 1971 was concerned with the composition and precise definition of reserve assets. Broadly, these comprise: balances with the Bank of England, other than Special Deposits; United Kingdom and Northern Ireland Treasury bills; company tax reserve certificates; money at call with the London money market; local authority bills eligible for rediscount at the Bank of England; commercial bills eligible for rediscount at the Bank of England up to a maximum of 2 per cent of eligible liabilities; and British government securities with one year or less to final maturity. It will be seen that this list is similar to the selection of items which the clearing banks were formerly allowed to regard as liquid assets.

It excludes, however, some items which though clearly liquid are too little under the control of the authorities to be appropriate as reserve assets, such as money at call to some other institutions and part of commercial bill portfolios. Two exclusions which are of particular significance to the clearing banks and which they resisted without success are the refinanceable short-term paper arising under the fixed-rate schemes for finance for exports and shipbuilding, previously accepted as liquid assets, and cash in tills. An exclusion of considerable significance for the non-clearing banks is deposits placed with local authorities; for some years previously most groups of these banks, and especially the accepting houses and British overseas and Commonwealth banks, had held substantial sums in this form. A notable inclusion is government securities with one year or less to maturity; some reasons for the inclusion of these are noted on p. 72. In general terms, then, reserve assets comprise short-term government debt, or other assets that the authorities are prepared to turn into cash.

The minimum reserve assets ratio is intended, in the words of the May paper, 'to provide the authorities with a known firm base for the operation of monetary policy'. But it is visualized that something more may be required to make control effective. Previously, the minimum liquidity ratio requirement for the London clearing banks was supplemented as thought necessary by calls for Special Deposits; henceforth the banking system as a whole may be called on from time to time to place Special Deposits with the Bank of England, and as before they will bear interest at a rate equivalent to the Treasury bill rate. Calls will be expressed as a uniform percentage for all banks, as with reserve assets, and normally in relation to each bank's total eligible liabilities. However, at that time further consideration was being given to the possibility of applying a different rate of call to overseas deposits in sterling; there was no suggestion that foreign currency deposits may be brought within the scope of the arrangements.

Meanwhile outstanding Special Deposits made by the London and Scottish clearing banks, equivalent to $3\frac{1}{2}$ and $1\frac{3}{4}$ per cent respectively of gross deposits, were repaid on 15 September. Although some items of substantial size which were previously acceptable as liquid assets do not qualify as reserve assets, nevertheless the effect of the change would have been to leave the London clearing banks with a reserve assets ratio far in excess of the $12\frac{1}{2}$ per cent benchmark, and quite out of proportion, as the Bank of England put it, 'to their present and immediately prospective level of lending'. Accordingly, to assist the transition to the new system, the London clearing banks agreed to subscribe for a total of some £750 million of three new government stocks, that is to say about $6\frac{1}{2}$ per cent of gross deposits and a somewhat higher proportion of 'eligible liabilities' at that date.

Since the basic intention of the new arrangements is that the clearing banks and other banks should be treated similarly in all major respects, it is evident that the issue of gilt-edged securities to the clearing banks only, to absorb 'surplus' liquidity, will not be repeated. Unhappily, there are other significant differences of treatment that will continue. The clearing banks alone are being required to maintain an average balance at the Bank of England of $1\frac{1}{2}$ per cent of eligible liabilities. These balances qualify as reserve assets, but they bear no interest. Cash in tills, previously regarded as a liquid asset, does not qualify as a reserve asset, on the grounds that it is held 'mainly as a stock-in-trade to meet the needs of the banks' customers'. While this ruling applies to all banks, it effectively discriminates against the clearing banks, who as retail bankers with widespread branch systems must hold more cash than other types of bank.

This exclusion is particularly puzzling because, since 1959, member banks of the Federal Reserve System have been allowed to include 'vault cash' – as it is termed in the United States – among their reserve assets. The reason for the change was to correct inequities between banks and to reduce the cost of transporting and handling currency, both considerations which might be thought relevant to Britain. This exception and the Bank of England balance requirement together involve the clearing banks in holding an appreciably larger proportion of unremunerative assets than do other banks.

The banks will wish to hold a 'cushion' of reserve assets in excess of the minimum – as with liquid assets hitherto – to meet seasonal fluctuations and perhaps possible calls for Special Deposits. A curious feature of the new arrangements is that although reserve assets comprise nothing which the Bank of England will not turn into cash, they do not include all assets of this nature, since they exclude rediscountable bills in excess of 2 per cent of eligible liabilities, and also refinanceable credits.

Special arrangements apply to some other groups of institution. The May paper indicated that separate proposals were being made to the members of the London Discount Market Association. These were not published until

July, but formed the basis of the agreement that was brought into operation at the same time as the general scheme. The members of the Association have agreed to maintain at least 50 per cent of their funds in defined categories of public sector debt. The range of eligible assets runs wider than that prescribed for the banks, to take in local authority bonds and stocks and government-guaranteed stocks with up to five years to run to maturity. The discount houses will continue to apply each week for a total amount of Treasury bills sufficient to cover the amount offered at the tender, but from Friday 17 September 1971 discontinued their long-standing practice of tendering at a common, agreed price.

The basic arrangements for banks apply also to members of the Finance Houses Association and some finance houses outside the Association, but with some modifications. For them, the minimum reserve assets ratio is put at 10 per cent, as compared with $12\frac{1}{2}$ generally; calls for Special Deposits will normally be at the same rate as for banks, but in some circumstances could be at a higher rate. Finance houses will be allowed a transitional period of twelve months to build up their holdings of reserve assets. Some houses are understood to be seeking recognition as banks, in which case they will be treated for these purposes as banks. Those with eligible liabilities of less than £5 million will be exempt from the various requirements.

The new arrangements apply in principle to banks in Northern Ireland, but further discussions are to take place with them, in view of difficulties peculiar to the branch banking system in Northern Ireland, notably the fact that it is operated by banking companies which, in varying degrees, operate also in the Republic of Ireland. Moreover, they may in practice be treated differently from banks in Britain for reasons of economic policy.

The third leg of the new arrangements is the abandonment by the London and Scottish clearing banks of their long-standing collective agreements on interest rates. The London deposit rate applying to all 'time' deposits, that is predominantly at seven days' notice, had previously been fixed by agreement between the clearing banks, since 1955 at 2 per cent below bank rate; this has been discontinued and each bank is now quoting its own rate for seven-day money and for other terms. Agreement on rates for advances was much less comprehensive in form, though a minimum rate to be charged to 'blue chip' borrowers was established. This minimum, along with most other lending rates, changed automatically with bank rate. In the new situation, each bank expresses its lending rates in relation to a base rate also determined by itself individually in the light of commercial and market considerations; initially, each bank fixed its base rate at the same level as bank rate, but within weeks one had made a reduction.

The interest rate agreements were undoubtedly monopolistic – or more strictly oligopolistic – in character, and as such were a legitimate subject for questioning. They were, however, unusual or perhaps unique among such arrangements, in that their effect was to keep prices – in this case interest rates – down rather than up. In recent criticism of the agreements it was commonly suggested that the banks were losing deposits by not matching rates quoted in the complementary markets for wholesale funds, which were substantially higher. Without again going into the question as to whether in fact the clearing banks were as a result 'losing' resources (see Chapter 4, p. 90–2), it is pertinent to point out that the comparison is not strictly between like and like, because the ready availability of clearing bank deposits for direct use in spending may enable them to be taken at comparatively low rates and in the case of current account balances at nil rates. Even so, there can be little doubt that the effect of the agreements was to keep interest rates on clearing bank deposits down. This, in turn, enabled the banks to lend more cheaply than otherwise, and at rates demonstrably below those charged by other lenders.

Indeed, following a comment by the then governor of the Bank of England in 1963, the banks put forward some limited proposals for change, but these were not acceptable to the then Chancellor of the Exchequer on the grounds that they would raise the lending rates of the banks. In evidence to the Monopolies Commission in 1968 (HCP 319), enquiring into the proposed merger of Barclays, Lloyds and Martins banks, individual banks suggested that, 'without the agreements, they would end up paying more for the deposits they already receive and would therefore be unable to finance industry and commerce so cheaply'. The governor of the Bank of England was reported to have 'accepted these arguments' and the Treasury representatives 'went further and said that they would wish the present arrangements to survive because they believed that they enabled the major part of the credit requirements of the country's industry and commerce to be satisfied at lower rates than would otherwise be the case'.

This conclusion had been questioned by the National Board for Prices and Incomes in its report on bank charges, published in the previous year (Cmnd. 3292). Even so, the same report noted (para. 54) that 'historically, a case can be made out for an agreement between the banks on the rate of interest to be paid on time deposits so long as the banks remained the predominant financial intermediaries'. With the rapid growth of such other intermediaries over recent years, justification for the agreements has been found in the discriminatory cash and liquidity requirements imposed upon the clearing banks, which restricted their power to generate additional deposits and to compete with other intermediaries. Ceilings on lending have had similar effects.

Some of the criticisms advanced against the agreements have often seemed to give insufficient weight to these and other aspects of practical importance for the banks. Nor was it always made clear whether the clearing banks were expected to compete among themselves or with other intermediaries. If the latter, this would not necessarily involve ending the agreements, only the changing of the level of the uniform deposit rate; moreover, it was often overlooked that the clearing banks, through their subsidiaries, were in fact competing effectively for 'wholesale' deposits and lending.

It would, however, be widely accepted that in a free market situation the distribution of deposits between banks and other intermediaries will be basically determined by the preference of the public, which in turn will be influenced by relative interest rates; in such circumstances the interest rate agreements would not seem to be justifiable. The view of the clearing banks was that no such free market situation existed, because of the special restraints imposed upon them. Now, however, something much more like a uniform market than before has been established.

Some relatively minor respects in which treatment falls short of uniformity have been indicated – the non-acceptance of cash in tills as a reserve asset and the requirement that the clearing banks alone should maintain a specified level of balances with the Bank of England. But some wider grounds for misgiving may be noted.

In the original proposals it was indicated that steps might have to be taken to limit the competition offered by banks – in the context essentially the clearing and other 'deposit' banks – for savings deposits at present invested in public sector debt or with building societies. This reservation seemed inconsistent with the general tenor of the proposals, and in particular with what seemed to be a main justification for the ending of the interest rate agreements. It carried with it the threat that the banks would be inhibited from competing more actively in an area where in any event they operate without some fiscal advantages available to their competitors. The threat remains, though it is possibly a little more remote: following discussions the authorities stated that they saw no need to seek to protect the position of savings banks and building societies, 'at least in present circumstances'.

The quantitative ceiling controls were abandoned, and qualitative guidance withdrawn, although the May paper stated that this last would continue to be provided 'as may be appropriate'. However, no one can be absolutely certain that lending ceilings will never be reimposed, either because the new methods prove generally inadequate in practice, or because ceilings are regarded as necessary in a particular situation. For the clearing banks, however, the abandonment of their interest rate agreements is intended to be lasting.

In the wider context, the generalization of banking control will render more difficult any regional differentiation in policy, to meet the special needs of some parts of the country. In the past, when Special Deposits have been imposed upon the clearing banks, they have been called at only half the rate from the Scottish banks and not at all from the banks in Northern Ireland. It is now intended to impose Special Deposits uniformly across the banking system. However, the application of specific credit policy measures to Northern Ireland – though not Scotland – will in the future, as in the past, take account 'so far as practicable' of 'such special economic conditions as may prevail there'.

Some doubts also remain in the realm of official policy, in addition to those indicated in our previous article in respect of the gilt-edged market. In a speech* in Munich in May 1971 the governor of the Bank of England indicated that basically the new approach to monetary policy implicit in the proposals reflected a change in the official attitude towards two key questions: 'first, what monetary variable should the authorities attempt to influence; and second, by what means should they attempt to influence it?' He stressed the undesirability of confining themselves to any one objective, pointing out that concentration on bank lending had induced distortions in the financial system and in the deployment of real resources. 'For these reasons we have increasingly shifted our emphasis towards broader monetary aggregates – to use the inelegant but apparently unavoidable term: the money supply under one or more of its many definitions, for example, or domestic credit expansion.' It was not made clear, however, how 'monetary aggregates' are thought to influence the economy, nor whether the authorities regard any particular monetary aggregate as being of outstanding significance in this respect.

Presumably 'monetary aggregates' are believed to have a wide-ranging influence, and this is consistent with the generalization of the whole technique of control. The governor described the new system as one in which 'the allocation of credit is primarily determined by its cost. . . . In future the authorities would seek to influence the structure of interest rates through a general control over the liquidity of the whole banking system.' Under the new gilt-edged policy they would 'not normally be prepared to facilitate movements out of gilt-edged by the banks, even if their sales should cause the market to weaken quite sharply'. The reserve ratio and Special Deposits would reinforce their power to 'influence the structure of interest rates. The resulting changes in relative rates of return will then induce shifts in the asset portfolios of both the public and the banks.'

The new policy will, it seems, be based upon open market operations backed up, if necessary, by calls for Special Deposits. It will take effect by shifting the relative terms on the various assets which the banks may hold, thus inducing them to make changes, or to refrain from changes which they may have envisaged. For instance, if interest rates are raised at a time when the banks as a whole have no excess reserve assets, they could then find that they have to sell investments on unfavourable terms if they wish to expand their advances. A single bank, however, would have other ways open to it of

* Published in the *Bank of England Quarterly Bulletin*, June 1971.

acquiring reserve assets, again perhaps on unfavourable terms. Again, it is intended that open market operations should affect the availability of reserve assets, and thus the credit base of the banks. These are the traditional ways in which open market operations were supposed to work; the mechanism of control and the objectives of open market policy have both been adjusted, in the light of previous shortcomings, in the hope of making this policy more effective.

It is difficult to assess what will be the significance of bank rate changes under the new arrangements. Apart from its effect on the Treasury bill discount rate, the influence of bank rate in the past has to a large extent depended on the fixed links maintained between it and clearing bank interest rates, under the now abandoned agreements. It seems likely, therefore, that bank rate will in future exert a more tenuous influence. At the same time, however, its influence may be diffused more widely through the financial system, reflecting the composition and uniform application of reserve assets and possibly Special Deposits requirements.

The credit base of the banking system – apart from the effect of any calls for Special Deposits that may be made – is now 12½ per cent of sterling deposits. In principle, this implies a 'gearing' ratio of eight times – that is, changes in holdings of reserve assets would be matched by changes in deposits of eight times their size. In practice, it may be doubted whether the authorities will be able – or expect – to obtain precise leverage in this way. Although the structure of official control over the banking system has been broadened in its basis and made tighter and more rational in its application, the course of government finance may result in the creation of additional reserve assets, for instance in the form of Treasury bills, thus expanding the credit base of the banking system. Thus the underlying realities have not been changed; deficit financing is still inflationary.

To quote the governor again, 'no limitation is envisaged on the authorities' ability to neutralize excess liquidity or to bring about sufficiently strong upward pressure on the lending rates'. Open market operations, supplemented if necessary by calls for Special Deposits, would be used to offset the effects on the credit base of factors such as the central government's financial position. Indeed, the governor appeared to be suggesting that Special Deposits might be used more vigorously than in the past. The new policy governing official transactions in gilt-edged securities will be a major factor in the exercise of monetary control.

When the new arrangements came into operation in September 1971, the clearing banks stated that 'they support the new arrangements . . . for regulating the monetary system', which they regarded as 'an improvement upon the previous methods of credit control'. They particularly welcomed the uniformity of control over all banks and the abandonment of quantitative ceilings. They still hoped to obtain modifications in respect of the exclusion from reserve assets of cash in tills and the refinanceable part of export and shipbuilding credits. They also expressed their wish 'to see tax concessions similar to those allowed to depositors in building societies and savings banks made available to their own deposit customers'.

Certainly the new arrangements should help to smooth out the distortions that have developed over recent years in response to the differential application of controls. Whether future developments take place through the clearing bank parents or their subsidiaries and whether subsidiaries will continue to engage in their existing activities, will now be determined primarily by the economies or diseconomies of operation. As a pointer to possible trends, the announcement by the banks stated that 'each bank will be free to quote for term deposits', and the Midland and other clearing banks are now doing so.

It is still too early to say what effect the ending of the collective agreements will have on the general level and pattern of rates, but it seems likely that the margins between the banks' deposit and lending rates will come under pressure. The 'squeeze' may be especially severe on the margins of non-clearing banks, who otherwise might find it difficult to retain their share of the market. To begin with, competition emerged most clearly in the field of 'wholesale' deposit business, where the clearing banks had previously been competing through subsidiaries. Initially, the individual base lending rates were at the same level, but one bank soon felt it appropriate to make a reduction.

These particular developments, while perhaps not of great importance in themselves, provide significant confirmation that the banks have moved into a new era. This had already been heralded first, by the removal in the late 1960s of the informal official ban, imposed half a century earlier, upon mergers among the clearing banks, which led to the reduction of their numbers from eleven to six; and secondly, the decision to make full disclosure of the true profits of the clearing banks, beginning with the accounts for the year 1969. Now the methods of control of the banking system also have been radically altered, in a direction that could have a revolutionary impact upon banking practices and structures.

Banking Enters a New Era
Extracts from the Monetary Survey in the *Review* for May 1972

The most immediate and apparent outcome of the changes stemmed from the abandonment of the London and Scottish clearing banks' agreements on interest rates. On the lending side, for most borrowers from 1 October 1971 the banks concerned were quoting rates linked to their own individually fixed base rates instead of bank rate. At first all base rates were established at the same level as bank rate (then 5 per cent) but in mid-October 1971, Barclays Bank lowered its base rate to $4\frac{1}{2}$ per cent, and the other clearing banks made similar reductions late in November. With the withdrawal of the quantitative and qualitative restrictions on lending banks took advantage of their unaccustomed freedom to offer new services to industry, notably loans at medium-term, and to refurbish their schemes for personal loans and other forms of consumer credit.

On the deposit-taking side, each of the clearing banks was now likewise free to fix its own rates and to quote for funds at varying terms, instead of virtually only for balances at seven days' notice at 2 per cent below bank rate as hitherto. Some began to offer a wide range of terms, and some to issue their own negotiable sterling certificates of deposit. Thus to varying degrees they began operating in the complementary money markets directly in their own names, whereas previously, partly because they were then subject to cash and liquidity ratio requirements, all preferred to do so only through special subsidiaries.

The new reserve assets ratio requirement caused no difficulty to any of the groups of banks, as may be seen from Table A14. Of reserve assets, money at call was the largest item, accounting for 67 per cent of the total in March 1972, with government stocks with one year or less to maturity the next largest, at 15 per cent. The proportion for Treasury bills may be expected to fluctuate widely over the year, but in March it was only 4 per cent. Generally, the supply of reserve assets is likely to contract in the tax-gathering season, as 'liquid assets' did previously.

Finance houses began to be treated in almost exactly the same way as banks, the major difference being that the minimum reserve ratio for them is only 10 per cent, not $12\frac{1}{2}$ per cent. Having the status of a bank confers a number of advantages upon finance houses, and some of them evidently regarded these to be worth keeping an additional $2\frac{1}{2}$ per cent in reserve assets. Accordingly some finance houses applied to the Department of Trade and Industry for recognition as banks, and five of them were granted this status. One result of this was a sharp rise in eligible liabilities for all banks, and particularly for 'other banks', in March 1972.

The new series of eligible liabilities and reserve assets dates only from October, so does not cover the whole of the year under review. At the same time the familiar series of monthly clearing bank figures has become distorted since these now include some 'wholesale' deposits and lending. Thus the new situation called for a thorough revision of banking statistics, and provided the opportunity for placing them on a uniform basis for all banks. In March last the Bank of England introduced an interim arrangement, whereby each month, in addition to the 'balance sheet' series, the clearing bank figures are

TABLE A14 *Eligible liabilities and reserve assets (£m.)*

	1971		1972
Eligible liabilities	*October*	*December*	*March*
London clearing banks	10,752	10,946	11,135
Scottish clearing banks	1,021	1,040	1,041
Other deposit banks	257	256	283
Accepting houses	1,085	1,133	1,071
Overseas banks	2,613	2,977	2,967
Other banks	1,418	1,548	2,454
Total	17,147	17,900	18,951
Reserve assets			
London clearing banks	1,777	1,760	1,652
Scottish clearing banks	149	158	145
Other deposit banks	34	36	45
Accepting houses	171	211	186
Overseas banks	451	699	567
Other banks	140	242	321
Total	2,721	3,107	2,916
Reserve ratio (%)			
London clearing banks	*16·5*	*16·1*	*14·8*
Scottish clearing banks	*14·6*	*15·2*	*13·9*
Other deposit banks	*13·1*	*14·1*	*16·0*
Accepting houses	*15·7*	*18·6*	*17·4*
Overseas banks	*17·3*	*23·5*	*19·1*
Other banks	*9·9*	*15·6*	*13·1*
Total	*15·9*	*17·4*	*15·4*

being presented on the same basis as that used hitherto for the accepting houses, overseas and other banks; this has the advantage of permitting some degree of identification of 'wholesale' as distinct from traditional activities. But these figures, too, are available for only part of the past year.

Accordingly, in Appendix 2, Table 5, movements in the main assets and liabilities of the clearing banks are recorded on the usual basis, notwithstanding the impaired comparability after September 1971. It is clear that a large increase in net deposits occurred in the three months to mid-September 1971, before the new arrangements came into force, despite large official sales of government stock to the public. This rise was accounted for partly by the inflow of foreign funds into London, particularly just before the suspension of dollar convertibility in August. The new statistics indicate that thereafter deposits of overseas residents rose by £130 million to £481 million by March

1972, and deposits of UK residents other than banks by £237 million, or 2 per cent, to £10,812 million.

The clearing banks' total holdings of public sector assets again rose, by £351 million, in the year to mid-March 1972, but less sharply than in 1970–1. The large movements in the two component series in the third quarter of 1971 largely reflect the subscription of £750 million to the three new government stocks – $5\frac{1}{4}$ per cent Treasury stock 1973, $5\frac{1}{2}$ per cent Treasury stock 1974, and $6\frac{1}{4}$ per cent Treasury stock 1977 – and the return to the clearing banks of Special Deposits of nearly £400 million, representing $3\frac{1}{2}$ per cent of gross deposits. Throughout the year, official sales of stocks to the public were offsetting to some degree expansionary influences on the banks' deposits.

The removal of all official restraints in September 1971 brought little change in the pattern of lending, owing to the slow recovery of industrial activity. As may be seen from Appendix 2, Table 8a, advances by all banks to manufacturing industry fell by £172 million, or 4 per cent, in the twelve months to February 1972; a decline of £261 million, or 10 per cent in clearing bank lending was partly offset by increased lending to this category by other banks. Personal lending on the other hand rose by £593 million or 57 per cent, and some relatively large increases were recorded for property and construction, financial companies, retail and other distribution and overseas residents. The total of classified advances rose by £2339 million or over 15 per cent during the year.

Over one half of this increase was in lending by the accepting houses, overseas and other banks, reflecting their continued growth generally. As may be seen from Table A15, total sterling deposits of these banks rose from £6454 million to £8582 million during the course of 1971. Of this increase £1012 million was against certificates of deposit. Currency deposits also continued to rise, from the equivalent of £21,087 million at the end of 1970 to £24,026 million in December 1971. The introduction of the new methods of credit control brought these institutions within the scope of formal ratio control for the first time, since they are required to hold specified reserve assets on the same basis as the London and Scottish clearing banks. The greater freedom, however, enabled them to lend more on advances than hitherto; many of the newer established institutions were previously subject to small and arbitrary limits on sterling lending. Advances to United Kingdom residents in sterling rose from just over £1400 million at the end of 1970 to over £2300 million in December 1971 with most of the increase occurring in the final three months.

The new system of credit control necessitated a reconsideration of the long standing arrangements for fixed-rate lending for medium- and long-term exports and for home shipbuilding orders. Under the new monetary arrangements, no part of such lending may be regarded as a reserve asset. However, advances beyond 18 per cent of a bank's current account deposits

TABLE A15 *Selected assets and liabilities in sterling of 'accepting houses and overseas and other banks' (£m. end of period)*

	*Current and deposit accounts**	*Balances with other UK banks*	*Money at call and short notice*	*Loans to local authorities*	*Sterling bills discounted*	*British government securities*	*Advances*	*Other assets †*
1968	4247	1113	255	1104	171	462	1405	301
1969	5108	1567	249	1338	155	430	1466	460
1970	6454	1748	569	1727	170	354	1639	973
1971: June	6926	1693	386	2132	178	410	1723	1200
December	8528	1859	1134	2025	346	497	2612	1387

* Including negotiable sterling certificates of deposit.
† Including coin, notes, and balances with the Bank of England.

are now being refinanced by the Export Credits Guarantee Department for exports and by the Department of Trade and Industry for home shipbuilding. The fixed rate of interest for exports, other than ships, was reduced for new orders from 7 to 6½ per cent on 1 November 1971, and again to 6 per cent from 16 March 1972. The rate for ships, home or export, remained at 7 per cent in conformity with an international agreement. In future, the rate of interest applied to medium-term export finance under the scheme was to be solely a matter for the government. The banks receive an agreed rate of return calculated by reference to market rates with the difference between this rate and the officially determined rates to be effected through the refinance mechanism.

In March 1971 the Chancellor of the Exchequer said that the growth of money supply should be adequate to accommodate the required growth of real demand, but not so large as to give further impetus to the rise in costs and prices, and refrained from giving quantified objectives. In the event, money supply however measured grew at a sharp pace over the year. On the wider definition of money (M_3) the growth between the end of 1970 and the end of 1971 was 13 per cent, against an increase of 10 per cent over the previous year. In his budget speech in March 1972, the Chancellor indicated a significant change of emphasis. He observed that the expansionary monetary policy had been reflected in a faster growth of money supply, and his Budget policy would 'entail a growth of money supply that is also high by the standards of past years'. This was necessary to permit the envisaged growth of real output. Far from expressing concern about possible inflationary consequences, he suggested that his reasoning was now 'generally accepted'.

Some changes were made in the statistics relating to money supply. The old intermediate definition, M_2, drew a distinction between private sector deposit accounts with the deposit banks and discount houses and similar deposits with other banks. Under the new arrangements for credit control, this distinction became invalid as the deposit banks widened the range of terms which they offered on deposits and took 'wholesale' deposits. For this reason, M_2 was discontinued, and deposit accounts appear only in the wide definition, M_3. Movements in M_1 and M_3 are shown in Table A16.

The range of statistics made available by the Bankers' Clearing House was extended in 1971 with the publication of data relating to the banks' own internal clearings. This development had become particularly desirable following the amalgamations of clearing banks.

The value of debit clearings between banks increased by over 9 per cent in 1971, from £772,464 million to £843,626 million, but the number of items cleared only from 727 million to 729 million. Items to the value of £187,471 million were cleared between branches of the same bank in 1971. Inter-bank credit clearings rose by over 29 per cent from £14,391 million to £18,623 million, the latter figure comparing with a total value of £42,983 million for the inter-branch credit clearing. Thus inter-branch clearing, which is used to a considerable extent by companies for passing funds between different parts of their own organizations, accounts for nearly 70 per cent of the total credit clearing, as compared with less than 20 per cent of total debit clearings.

The change in methods of credit control had far-reaching consequences for the discount market, for which special arrangements were agreed. The Bank of England agreed to continue to confine lender of last resort facilities to the market, and the market to continue to cover fully the weekly tender of Treasury bills, though the syndicated bid for Treasury bills which had operated since the 1930s was to be abandoned. The clearing banks, however, continued to abstain from tendering for bills on their own behalf, and to buy them from the market.

TABLE A16 *Money supply (£m. end of period, seasonally adjusted)*

	M_1	M_3
1969	8,620	16,320
1970	9,430	17,900
1971:		
March	9,820	18,400
June	9,900	18,710
September	10,270	19,180
December	10,940*	20,280
1972:		
15 March	(10,624)	20,650

M_1 Notes and coin in circulation and sterling current accounts held by the private sector.
M_3 M_1 plus sterling deposit accounts and non-sterling deposits of the private sector and all deposits of the public sector.
* The figures of M_1 up to September 1971 are not strictly comparable with later figures.

In order to maintain control over the use to which borrowed funds are put, the authorities asked the market to keep a minimum of 50 per cent of their assets in the form of public sector debt, that is Treasury bills, local authority bills and bonds, and government, government-guaranteed and local authority stocks with not more than five years to run to maturity.

Because money lent at call to the market is in eligible reserve assets, following the introduction of the new system, many of the non-clearing banks switched funds to the discount market which had previously been placed outside it. Total borrowed funds rose by £700 million, to almost £3000 million over the year to December 1971. Whereas at the end of 1970 over 62 per cent of the market's borrowed funds came from the London clearing banks, by the end of 1971 the proportion had fallen to 42 per cent; for borrowing from the accepting houses, overseas and other banks the proportion rose from 23 to nearly 38 per cent.

The market's borrowing costs fell during the year along with the general decline in interest rates and the spread of rates quoted widened. From $5\frac{3}{8}$–$6\frac{7}{8}$ per cent in March 1971, the level of call money interest rates to the discount market fell to 1–$4\frac{3}{4}$ per cent at the end of November, but subsequently rates were tending to rise. Despite the fall in borrowing costs, the running yield margins on both Treasury and commercial bills were reduced sharply during the year, since easier money conditions and the abandonment of rates agreements pushed bill rates down. In August 1971 the members of the discount market discontinued the practice of agreeing rates on fine bank bills, and as a result margins became narrower. The market has been able to offset this movement to some extent by a substantially increased turnover of commercial bills, aided by the lifting of the quantitative restrictions on them.

Last year the banks showed greater interest in Treasury bills, and the discount market's holdings were generally lower than in 1970. Nevertheless, the discount houses continued to expand their business and develop their interest and activity in other assets. In particular, their holdings of negotiable certificates of deposit continued to increase rapidly: holdings of sterling certificates rose from £268 million at the end of 1970 to £457 million a year later, and dollar certificates from £39 million to £108 million.

The growth in the market for sterling certificates of deposit continued; the amount outstanding at the end of December 1971 was £2372 million compared with £1089 million a year earlier, and by the end of February 1972 the total had risen further to £2707 million. After the new credit control arrangements came into force, several of the London and Scottish clearing banks began to issue certificates of deposit on their own account, rather than through their subsidiaries as they had done previously, and by March 1972 the amount outstanding was £433 million. Towards the end of 1971 longer-term certificates became more popular; certificates outstanding of three years and over to maturity, which in September totalled only £19 million, had by the end of February 1972 risen to almost £113 million and a similar increase was recorded for certificates with two to three years still to run to maturity. The growth in US dollar certificates of deposit outstanding continued in 1971, rising from the equivalent of £1650 million at the end of 1970 to £1856 million at the end of 1971. Early in 1972 the first dollar CD issue by a London clearing bank was made.

SECTION B

London's Markets for Money

6

Old and New Activities

The Treasury Bill – The Story of an Economist's Invention February 1961

Everyone has heard about Britain's Treasury bills, but few people have ever seen one, even though investment in such bills broadened notably in post-war years. Holdings of Treasury bills are in effect restricted to those prepared to make a minimum outlay of about £5000, and in practice the bills are usually left with the bank or other agent of the investor. The Treasury bill was introduced into the City less than a hundred years ago and was derived, like the cheque, from the centuries-old bill of exchange; yet it is not convincingly portrayed by the statutory definition of its commercial forebear – a definition burnt into the minds of all bank officials from their student days. In appearance and texture a Treasury bill is rather like an old-style five pound note, presenting features – of wording, alternations between italic and other typefaces and so on – which give it an air of an age long past. It bears prominently its title, date of issue and maturity, and amount. The substance of the document reads: 'THIS TREASURY BILL entitles . . . . . . or Order to Payment of [e.g.] ONE HUNDRED THOUSAND POUNDS at the BANK OF ENGLAND out of the Consolidated Fund of the United Kingdom on the 1ST DAY OF FEBRUARY, 1961'. It is signed by the Secretary to the Treasury. An asterisk at the name space leads to a footnote: 'If this blank be not filled in, the bill will be paid to bearer.'

Essentially, a Treasury bill is a document by which the government borrows money at short term, and it is the principal constituent of the 'floating' part of the national debt. Dealings in Treasury bills take place mainly in the discount market and not, as do transactions in most other government securities, on the stock exchange. Nor do transfers have to be recorded in the books of the Bank of England or elsewhere; if the name space is left blank, the bill is a bearer security, and if a name is inserted, then ownership is transferred by endorsement. A Treasury bill has a term of ninety-one days, or occasionally of sixty-three days, the nominal amount of the bill being repayable at these intervals – without days of grace – after the date of issue.

It has the character of a bill also in the manner of rewarding the investor, for the holder of a Treasury bill does not receive interest; instead, the bill is issued at a discount, the holder acquiring it for less than its nominal amount. The rate of discount is arrived at by a weekly sale of new bills. Each Friday the Treasury invites tenders, to be sent to the Bank of England on the following Friday for an amount of bills, in total usually between £100 million and £300 million, the tenders being made 'through a London Banker, Discount House or Broker', and each tender being for not less than £50,000. The tenderer may ask for bills to be dated on any business day of the week following the date of tender, and may choose the denominations of his bills from the available series of £5000, £10,000, £25,000, £50,000 and £100,000. On the afternoon of the Friday to which tenders relate, the Bank of England announces the results, giving the lowest price at which tenders (they have to be expressed as a multiple of one penny per cent) have been accepted, the proportion of applications allotted at this price, the average price for the week's tenders and other information. Some bills are issued to government departments directly, and not through the tender, a process known as issues through the 'tap' which is described later, and some of these bills are issued at a nominal rate of discount.*

Treasury bills, then, are part of the national debt, and until 1961 a total amount of around £5000 million was always outstanding on loan to the Exchequer by regular renewals of these short-dated instruments. Marginally, the total varied, then as now, since the government finds in Treasury bills a convenient means of adjusting the inflow of revenue and other funds to outgoings for expenditure of all kinds. For groups of holders, Treasury bills fulfil particular requirements, above all as providing a ready source of immediate funds. Thus to the discount houses, Treasury bills are the main stock-in-trade, which they can always turn into cash at the Bank of England. For overseas investors, including central and commercial banks abroad, they offer a convenient method of holding sterling in readily realizable form

* Evidence of this differentiation between tap and tender bills is obtainable from government accounts. For example, the total amount of 'interest' paid on Treasury bills in 1959–60 was £140 million; calculating from the amounts and rates at the weekly tenders, the amount paid on tender bills can be put at, say, £123 million; the remainder works out at roughly $\frac{7}{8}$ per cent per annum on the average amount of tap bills outstanding, as against approximately $3\frac{5}{8}$ per cent for the tender bills.

and of obtaining an appropriate return. Similarly, some large commercial undertakings in this country have come to regard Treasury bills as a suitable channel for the temporary investment of surplus cash. The clearing banks are large holders, and Treasury bills occupy a special place among their assets. They constitute, directly and indirectly, the main 'liquid' asset of the banking system, and the only one so regarded that is available in sufficient quantities to maintain their liquidity ratios at the conventional level.* It is through their Treasury bill holdings and money market loans (mainly against Treasury bills) that the banks adjust their cash ratios, and the supply of Treasury bills directly influences the liquidity of the monetary system as a whole. Few of these developments were foreseen when the Treasury bill was introduced in 1877, and these new uses have made the Treasury bill of today quite different from the simple Exchequer version of a bill of exchange.

Prior to 1877 the government's floating debt consisted of loans from the Bank of England and Exchequer bills, these last being clumsy instruments that had fallen out of favour with lenders. In the middle 1870s the government needed funds for the construction by local authorities of schools and sanitary works. The Chancellor of the Exchequer at that time was unwilling to enlarge the permanent debt, then mainly in the form of Consols, and looked for a method of attracting temporary finance that was superior to the unpopular Exchequer bills. He arranged for advice to be sought from Walter Bagehot, at that time editor of the *Economist*.† A prompt and encouraging answer was given: 'The English Treasury has the finest credit in the world, and it must learn to use it to the best advantage. A security resembling as nearly as possible a commercial bill of exchange – that is, a bill issued under discount, and falling due at certain intervals – would probably be received with favour by the money market, and would command good terms.' Acting on Bagehot's advice, the Treasury bill was devised and issued, to gain immediate favour in the market and to hold the field thereafter.

In fact Treasury bills were not extensively issued until the First World War. The legislation by which they were authorized, while not restricting the amount of bills that might be issued, did not extend the powers of the government to borrow, so that in practice bills could be employed only for the financing of Consolidated Fund services, that is, chiefly to cover interest and other transactions relating to the national debt, and here the amounts required were not large. Until the turn of the century issues were made three or four times a year, usually for totals of about £2–3 million at a time, and in these early years bills were offered – on occasion – running for various periods from one to twelve months. A significant development, in 1889, was that, under

* The volume of Treasury bills in issue has been greatly reduced in later years, more commercial bills have become available and the distribution of holdings has changed. Liquidity and cash ratios have been replaced by the reserve assets ratio.

† Lord Welby, in a letter to the *Economist*, 20 November 1909, quoted by several authorities.

permissive legislation, the government began to issue bills directly to the National Debt Commissioners, in addition to those offered for public tender; the 'tap' issue to government departments was thus inaugurated.

In 1902, to meet the financial requirements of the Boer War, the use of Treasury bills was extended to provide temporary finance for the Supply services, and the number of issues rose to about fifteen or twenty a year. The highest amount outstanding at any time before 1914 was recorded during 1910, when it reached £41 million, of which nearly £37 million had been issued by tender. At that time bills issued to finance Supply services had to be repaid by the end of the financial year, and this prevented a sustained growth of the total outstanding. At the outbreak of war in 1914 the amount in issue was £15·5 million, of which £6 million had been issued by tender. Bills then represented only about 2 per cent of the aggregate national debt.

It was again wartime finance that enlarged the total of Treasury bills, this time lastingly. With the outbreak of the First World War in 1914, the rise in government expenditure was met in part by an expansion in the issue of Treasury bills. Then, too, the statutory requirement that bills for Supply purposes had to be repaid by the end of the financial year was withdrawn, so that the main bulwark against the growth of the issue was removed. It was not long before the great bulk of the bill issue no longer represented temporary borrowing in anticipation of revenue, but had in effect become a part of the permanent debt, though still expressed in short-dated securities. The system became, and remains, one in which as bills mature they are repaid from the proceeds of further issues of bills, the funds being largely provided, directly or indirectly, by the holders of the maturing bills. By the end of the First World War the volume of Treasury bills outstanding had risen to roughly £1000 million, out of a total national debt of about £7000 million.

One consequence of raising such large sums by bills was a series of experiments in methods of attracting investment to them. Issues by tender were discontinued for a time after April 1915; following a brief resumption, tenders were again discontinued in June 1917. Instead, bills were made available 'on tap' to all applicants, official or otherwise, at rates of discount announced and varied from time to time. A schedule of rates was published at intervals at which bills for terms of three, six, nine and twelve months were offered, the rates varying in accordance with changes in money market conditions not only in London, but also in New York. Then, as now, some investors in the bills were in the United States, and the government was anxious to encourage an inflow of dollars.

So large a growth in the issue of bills attracted criticism. Mr Reginald McKenna, when Chancellor of the Exchequer, referred to the difficulties arising from the rapid and frequent maturity of bills, and also to the undesirability of borrowing 'bankers' money' rather than 'public money'.*

* *House of Commons Official Report*, 21 June 1915, col. 952.

It was feared, too, that if holders chose not to renew bills as they matured, the Bank of England would be obliged to meet the government's requirements by increasing 'ways and means' advances, in those days regarded as a peculiar danger because it enlarged the credit base of the banking system. In fact, ways and means advances had expanded considerably during the war, and, with the unregulated Treasury bill issue and a growing currency circulation, the level of bank deposits had doubled. Hence various efforts to reduce the outstanding amount of bills, principally by the issue of long-term government loans, some of them with provisions for Treasury bills to be accepted in payment of subscriptions.

For several years the volume of Treasury bills outstanding continued to rise – it reached £1121 million in 1921 – but by then market conditions favoured funding. As trade slackened, interest rates declined, and the volume of bills was reduced by over £500 million in the two years to 31 March 1923, largely from the proceeds of issues of longer-dated securities. The reduction continued, though more slowly, until the bill issue outstanding remained at a level of around £600 million, of which about £150 million consisted of tap bills, issued mainly to provide backing for the enlarged fiduciary note issue.

The issue of bills by regular weekly tender was resumed from April 1921, and other changes were made, including the restriction of the issue to bills of three months' term, the establishment of the minimum figure of £50,000 for any one tender, and the arrangement whereby applicants could choose the day of the week from which their bills were to run. All this helped the money market, particularly by enabling holders to obtain bills maturing at dates on which they would require cash. For a few years the issue of bills to non-official holders through the tap was continued, the 'additional' bills, as they were described, being available at slightly higher rates of discount than at the previous week's tender; but this arrangement was brought to an end in 1925. While regular weekly tenders were necessary in order to refinance what was now an established part of the national debt, the aggregate amount of bills outstanding did not grow, since budgets were generally balanced; thus fluctuations in the total again came to reflect simply temporary unevenness between the flows of money into and out of the Exchequer. But with the government financing commitments on a far higher scale than in earlier years, a marked seasonal pattern had become evident: the government borrowed largely on bills during the first nine months of the financial year, and reduced bills by repayments when tax receipts flowed in during the fourth quarter. Already, however, Treasury bills had come to occupy a central place in Britain's monetary arrangements and constituted a main element in the regulation of banking liquidity.

Bagehot's belief that the Treasury bill 'would probably be received with favour by the money market, and would command good terms' was amply confirmed, the more so as the market itself was changing. From a situation in which the discounting of commercial bills was almost the whole business of the London discount houses, 'the period from 1877 to 1913 witnessed an enormous growth in the importance of the Treasury in the market, especially after 1902.'* The use of the commercial bill of exchange in internal trade had been declining for many years prior to 1914, and then the outbreak of war led to a sharp reduction in the supply of bills for financing international trade. It was at this stage that the government began to borrow heavily on Treasury bills, so that by the end of the war the amount of Treasury bills far exceeded that of commercial bills in the portfolios of the discount houses and the banks. In fact, by means of Treasury bills the gap was filled between government expenditure and inflow from revenue or the issue of securities to the public, a form of deficit financing that helped to bring about a large increase in bank deposits. The risks inherent in this development were realized, as shown in an observation in the report of the Committee on National Debt and Taxation (the Colwyn Committee), issued in 1927. The report has a surprisingly modern ring when it records the view of Lord Bradbury that there were 'potential dangers in that the habit might grow up of using Treasury bills as currency, and the liquid character of the bills might tend to relax the banks' conventional standard of "cash" reserves'. Yet already the essential role of Treasury bills could not be gainsaid. Mr R. H. Brand (later Lord Brand) warned the Committee that if Treasury bills 'were redeemed very rapidly and commercial bills did not as rapidly increase to take their place, the reserves of the money market would be *pro tanto* reduced'. In fact, as has been noted, the funding of Treasury bills was not carried further, while, with the post-war recovery in world trade, the volume of commercial bills recovered to some extent. It has been estimated† – no accurate statistics are available – that the volume of commercial bills coming to the London market did not regain the pre-1914 level, still less reach the high total corresponding to the fall in the value of money, but that at its inter-war peak in 1929 it was roughly equal to the total of outstanding Treasury bills issued through the tender. At this period the clearing banks together held about £100 million of Treasury bills and the same amount of commercial bills, as well as lending £80 million to the discount market, which presumably held bills in roughly similar proportions.

Further contraction in the volume of commercial bills followed the world-wide slump of the early 1930s. It is probable that commercial bills on the London market fell to about one third to one half of the amount to which they had already been reduced in the 1920s; certainly, from then onwards, Treasury bills have predominated in the bill business of the discount market and in the holdings of the clearing banks. This development led to a change

* W. T. C. King, *History of the London Discount Market*, 1936.
† W. T. C. King, *The Banker*, March 1947.

in market arrangements, following the lines described in the Radcliffe report as 'the manifold process of cartelization and "orderly markets" which is believed to have been deliberately fostered by the authorities between 1914 and 1925, when they were anxious to develop the market's appetite for short-term debt and believed that extremely orderly (if not dragooned) short-term markets alone could assure the necessary flow of funds into the Treasury'.

Until the mid-1930s the clearing banks had themsleves tendered for Treasury bills, in competition with the discount houses and other applicants at the weekly tender. With relatively few commercial bills, the competition for Treasury bills was intensified, and discount rates were reduced, the more sharply as the 'cheap money' policy pursued at this time required the authorities to provide a plentiful supply of funds. At this stage, too, the Treasury took advantage of the low level of interest rates to carry further the funding of bills, and the banks found it difficult to buy enough bills to maintain their liquid assets. Meanwhile, the discount market, with its resources, then as now largely borrowed from the clearing banks, found that the rates charged for money at call or short notice from the clearing banks left little margin – at times none at all – in relation to the bill rate. After various experiments, early in 1935 the clearing banks agreed not to tender for bills on their own behalf; instead, they would fulfil their needs from the market. They also undertook not to buy bills in the market at rates lower than the agreed minimum rate at which they lent funds to the market. Shortly afterwards, the banks agreed not to buy bills unless they had been issued at least one week previously – this because the earlier arrangement had led to an increase in tenders from 'outside' sources, these 'stagging' applicants hoping to make a quick profit on the resale of bills.

A further stage in 'cartelization' was the inauguration of the system of concerted tendering by the discount houses. From then onwards – subject to a recent slight modification to be mentioned later – the discount houses have met shortly before each weekly tender and have agreed upon a uniform price at which they would severally tender that week, the amounts of the applications from each house being regulated broadly in proportion to their capital resources. So it was that in 1935 the weekly Treasury bill tender was transformed from one of open competition between discount houses and other applicants – which had reached a cut-throat stage – to one where competition was lessened by the operation of the market syndicate and the policy of the banks. It was a development believed to have the encouragement of the Bank of England, at that time furthering the strengthening of individual discount houses in other ways. Some competition remained for the market 'syndicate', mainly from 'outside' bidders, such as overseas and foreign banks, but also from firms of bill brokers not in the syndicate. The banks, too, have continued to tender on account of their customers.

Another influence on the supply of Treasury bills arose from the establishment of the Exchange Equalization Account, following Britain's departure from the gold standard, with the duty of operating in the exchange market so as to prevent undue fluctuations in the external value of sterling. The Account was set up in 1932 and provided with working funds that over the next year or two amounted to £375 million. In the main these consisted of 'tap' Treasury bills, and from then on the counterpart of its exchange transactions has been reflected in variations in its holding of bills, as largely determined by external circumstances. Hence the volume of bills available in the market is indirectly affected, lessening or increasing the degree to which the Exchequer borrows from the public on Treasury bills. It is not possible to estimate the Account's holdings of bills, as on occasion the government has provided it with further capital in the form of bills, and sometimes its capital has been reduced by cancelling some of its bills. Over the years, too, it has acquired additional resources from profits on its dealings and in other ways. Nevertheless, it is clear that the volume of Treasury bills under the management of the Bank of England was increased by the establishment of the Account, as also by the expansion in the Bank's fiduciary issue when it took over responsibility for the Treasury note issue in 1928, and subsequently as both funds have grown.

It was in the 1930s too that the use of bills under the control of the Bank led to further refinements in debt management. In particular, bills held in the Issue Department came to provide a means of smoothing the repayment and issue of long-dated government securities, as described on pp. 53–60, and in greater detail in the Radcliffe Report. Another development of the 1930s was to change the basis of monetary regulation. The Bank of England enlarged its activities in the market through the services of the 'special buyer', as the discount house that acted as its agent in bill transactions was called. Through this channel temporary stringencies in the market were relieved, the Bank buying bills at market rates instead of requiring discount houses to borrow at bank rate. Thus the way was opened for the cash base of the banking system to be expanded without penalty, at that time in furtherance of the government's cheap money policy and later for finance for war needs.

During the Second World War the government, though seeking to avoid inflationary finance and hold interest rates at a low level, was unable wholly to avoid borrowing from the banking system, with the inevitable expansion in the money supply. At the outset the tender issue of Treasury bills was increased sharply, and an agreement was reached – it has been maintained ever since – whereby the members of the discount market syndicate undertook, as a body, to apply for the whole amount of bills offered week by week. They were able to do so in reliance upon the operations of the 'special buyer', whereby the banking system was furnished with the cash required to provide for the expansion of credit to meet the needs of the Exchequer.* The rise in the bill issue was, however, lessened by the introduction of direct lending by the banks to the Exchequer, by way of Treasury deposit receipts. These were non-marketable securities, running for six months and bearing interest, to which the banks were expected to subscribe in amounts determined by the Treasury from week to week. Even so, the bill issue expanded, from roughly £1100 million at the outbreak of war, of which £650 million had been issued through the tender, to £4200 million at the end of 1945, of which £1800 million was through the tender. In addition, the banks were then holding £1700 million of Treasury deposit receipts.

This diversion of bank funds from the bill market was continued for a few years after the end of the war, but over the period from 1949 to 1952 the use of Treasury bills was resumed, and outstanding Treasury deposit receipts were repaid, the tender Treasury bill issue being increased correspondingly. As the funds were released, the banks bought additional bills and enlarged their loans to the discount market, so that the result of war finance was a great increase in the bill issue and a substantial surplus of liquid assets in the hands of the banks. By October 1951 the total of Treasury bills outstanding was £5550 million and the holdings of the banks, at £1200 million, were the main constituent in liquidity ratios of about 40 per cent.

In post-war years, with the government's part in economic life greatly increased, Exchequer finance absorbed a larger proportion of the national income than before the war, and this affected the Treasury bill issue. At the outbreak of war the government had taken power to borrow in whatever form it might see fit, but, as has been mentioned, it was traditionally reluctant to rely ever more heavily upon the use of Treasury bills. In early post-war years this reluctance was less evident, partly because of the cheap money policy, but also by reason of the new attitude to fiscal arrangements, whereby budgets were seen as providing a means of adjusting the aggregate demand on the economy as a whole. Subsequently, undue reliance on short-term finance again came to be regarded with disfavour. A substantial reduction in the amount of Treasury bills outstanding was made by a special funding operation late in 1951, whereby about £1000 million of Treasury bills were exchanged for Serial Funding Stocks, roughly half this amount coming from bank holdings, as is indicated in Table B1. Thereafter the total for holdings outside the public sector tended to rise, partly reflecting an inflationary trend. The distribution of holdings shows that the proportion in the hands of the discount market has become smaller while that held by others, notably commercial and industrial undertakings, is larger – a development to which

* Under the new arrangements of September 1971 the market is to continue to apply for the whole of the weekly issue and to enjoy 'last resort' facilities. However it will no longer tender at an agreed price.

TABLE B1 *Holdings of Treasury bills outside the public sector*

Mid-March	London clearing banks	Discount market	Scottish banks	Overseas official holdings	Other	Total
	£m.					
1951	1173	738	4	1536	114	3565
1952	678	579	2	972	71	2302
1953	955	596	5	927	214	2697
1954	995	528	9	1086	306	2924
1955	849	452	12	1027	706	3046
1956	946	421	15	921	746	3049
1957	915	283	13	913	583	2707
1958	1082	466	23	765	702	3038
1959	877	351	16	†	†	†
1960	941	446	17	†	†	†

† Not available

we return later. The large part then played by Treasury bills in the liquid assets of the banking system is illustrated in Table B2.

Meanwhile, the processes of more active bill dealing have been eased by two technical improvements: first, in 1950 the term of bills was changed from three calendar months to ninety-one days, thus bringing a regular pattern to issues and maturities over the weeks of the year; secondly, since 1955, some bills have been issued in the later months of some years with a term of sixty-three days so as to swell maturities in the early months of the following year, thus fitting into the Exchequer pattern of inflow of tax payments. Despite the larger holdings of bills outside the market, the regulatory actions of the

TABLE B2 *London clearing banks, liquid assets*

	Treasury bills	Short money	Total liquid assets (including cash and 'other bills')	
Mid-March	£m.	£m.	£m.	% of deposits
1952	678	536	1882	32·0
1953	955	480	2001	33·0
1954	995	475	2065	33·1
1955	849	447	1927	30·1
1956	946	435	2020	33·2
1957	915	455	2017	32·7
1958	1082	447	2169	34·1
1959	877	511	2063	31·1
1960	941	565	2227	31·6

authorities were aided by the still greater holdings of government securities – including Treasury bills – by departments, notably the Issue Department of the Bank of England, the National Debt Commissioners and the Exchange Equalization Account. Meanwhile, the discount houses had developed their dealings in short-dated government bonds, acting as jobbers for this section of the gilt-edged market. Moreover the authorities had developed the practice of 'indirect aid' to the market, whereby on occasion bills are obtained directly from the banks to enable the banks to lend more to the market. On the other hand, the authorities may sell bills to 'mop up' surplus funds. With the larger holdings of bills by government bodies, the issue of tap bills has been about one third of the total for outstanding bills.

During the 'cheap money' period of twenty years to 1951 the 'special buyer' had been active in bill transactions, so providing the cash base required by the banks for the level of deposits resulting largely from the current needs of the government. After 1951 the practice was generally continued, in a market where the scale of government requirements continued to be large and the volume of Treasury bills was about ten times that of commercial bills. Nevertheless, as the authorities restored flexibility in rates of interest, so also the bill market became subject to varying conditions and fresh disciplines. The 'special buyer' at times has left the market short of funds, and some discount houses on occasion have been obliged to borrow at bank rate. Then, too, it has been usual for acceptable bills not to be re-discounted but lodged as security for a loan from the Bank of England, a loan which has to be taken for at least seven days at the penal bank rate. In these conditions competition has become keener at the weekly tender. Again, the Bank of England submits an 'inside tender' on behalf of overseas central banks, while tenders from 'outside' are more aggressive. In particular, as the Radcliffe Committee observed, 'since early in 1955 there has been substantial holding of Treasury bills by industrial and commercial concerns; this interest has continued to a degree having no parallel at any earlier time. The phenomenon is to be associated . . . both with the absolute height of the Treasury bill rate and with the margin between Treasury bill rate and bank deposit rates. . . . There is some ground for asserting that in the last four years industrial and commercial concerns as a group have been willing to hold up to £400 million or more of Treasury bills at any one time, and the habit may be expected to spread.' The Committee suggested that the spread of competition in various directions might 'break down the cartelization and orderliness of the short market'; though it saw 'no cause for alarm' at this prospect. In fact, in 1957, a slight modification of the syndicate arrangement had been made; since then, each discount house had been free to tender for a small part of its requirements at a price other than the agreed price, if it wished to do so.*

A consequence of the higher level of interest rates has been the growth of

* See footnotes on pp. 143, 147 and 149.

the interest charge in the nation's accounts. In the year to March 1952 the amount for 'interest' on Treasury bills was less than £30 million; since then it has ranged from £77 million (1954–5) to nearly £178 million (1957–8), and in the year to March 1960 it was £140 million. The tender bill issue rose on balance over these years by one half and the total for all Treasury bills by about one fifth. The funding of Treasury bills continued to be pressed, not, as in earlier times, simply because a growth in the floating debt was regarded as undesirable, but also as a method of regulating the liquid assets of the banking system. It was pursued even though the interest charge to the government was thereby increased, in part burdening the balance of payments.* When in 1960 it was thought necessary to apply a further check to the rise in bank advances, the method used was to call for Special Deposits by the commercial banks with the Bank of England. The Chancellor of the Exchequer said that this method was preferred to an alternative – the introduction of an explicit and variable liquidity ratio – because it was better suited to practices of the banking system and was more flexible. If we are to judge from the evidence of the Bank of England to the Radcliffe Committee, a further reason was that a rise in liquidity ratios 'effectively required the banks directly to hold additional amounts of government debt [i.e. Treasury bills]'.

Thus the Treasury bill moved to the centre of monetary regulation, a role far different from the straightforward borrowing instrument of Bagehot's invention. As the Radcliffe Report puts it: 'Cash and Treasury bills have come to be practically interchangeable and . . . the supply of Treasury bills and not the supply of cash has come to be the effective regulatory base of the domestic banking system. . . .' But methods of monetary regulation and the part played by the Treasury bill have been changed under the arrangements introduced in September 1971 (see Chapters 3 and 5).

Long-term trends reversed May 1966

A distinctive characteristic of the London money market has long comprised the operations of the discount houses, with their traditional formalized relationships, on the one hand with the Bank of England and on the other hand with the clearing banks. A century ago these singular arrangements were

* In answer to a question in Parliament in May 1957, an estimate was given, and this was repeated by the Radcliffe Committee, as follows: 'It has been estimated that the cost to the balance of payments of an increase in bank rate by one per cent is at the rate of about £15 million a year, on the assumption that other short-term rates also rise by one per cent.'

described in Bagehot's *Lombard Street* and they continue in operation today. True, during the inter-war years Treasury bills replaced commercial bills as the main trading instrument, but the essential activities remain, with the discount houses providing employment for the short-term funds of the banks, and the channel for the smooth and swift interchange of banking funds and for access to the Bank of England as lender of last resort. A major development in post-war years was the extension of dealing in short-term government bonds, the discount houses becoming in effect the jobbers for these securities, so that in 1957 the manager of a leading discount house could tell the Bank Rate Tribunal, 'I am the market in certain short bonds' (Minutes of Evidence, Question 8979).

Such was and remains the classical market, but in the attraction and handling of short-term funds, sweeping changes have occurred. From about the time of the Radcliffe Committee's report in 1959, what were small secondary markets have grown in stature and funds have flooded through them in great tides, notably for local authorities and hire purchase finance houses. Resources have been attracted by high rates, running well above the long-established orthodox market pattern, and activity has been stimulated as an unexpected byproduct of official action, when, for example, the availability of Exchequer funds for local authority borrowing has been curtailed and when credit restrictions have diminished lending by the banks and other institutions. Such funds have often come from interest-conscious undertakings and have sometimes moved in from abroad, particularly by way of overseas and merchant banks and as part of Euro-currency flows.

The movement has represented a response to interest rate levels and a consequence of official action overseas as well as at home, notably by the United States government. And as so often in post-war years the clamour for funds has sometimes made availability more important than cost. In the main these 'new' markets have represented a development of small existing activities, but the funds they handle commonly bypass traditional market routes. But in the classical market, too, some striking changes have occurred, and these are described below.

On pp. 149 ff. we described the rise of the Treasury bill to a dominant position in the short-term money market, with the simultaneous decline in the use of commercial bills. The Radcliffe report (para. 584) spoke of 'the irreversible shrinkage in the relative supply of commercial bills', but, in fact, in the 1960s the long-term trend was sharply reversed; the Treasury bill has declined in importance, and a considerable revival occurred in the use of the commercial bill.

The post-war growth of the national debt, and the maturing of existing securities with the passage of time, have tended to pile up government debt at the liquid end in the form of Treasury bills, but official funding policy, as described in Chapter 3, has helped to swing the weight of borrowing to marketable securities. Table B3 shows changes in the broad composition of the national debt over the six years to 1966. Of the rise in the total, over £1400 million represents existing British Transport stocks taken into the figures, so that the true increase is in fact just over £2000 million. Within the total, Treasury bills issued through the tender have fallen by nearly £1300 million, or by more than one third, to £2180 million. In the earlier years reliance on Treasury bills was lessened by the response to improved terms for national savings securities, an example of the growing sensitivity of the public to interest rate opportunities. Since 1964, Treasury bills have been absorbed by official departments on a considerable scale and tap issues have expanded,

TABLE B3 *Composition of the natio nal debt (£m.)*

	31 March			
	1960	*1964*	*1965*	*1966*
Treasury bills				
Tender	3,480	2,790	2,290	2,180
Tap	1,722	1,628	2,382	2,942
Total	5,202	4,418	4,672	5,122
Marketable securities	14,946	18,162*	17,792*	17,846*
National savings	3,293	3,720	3,823	3,650
Other	4,292	3,926	4,154	4,636†
Total	27,733	30,226	30,441	31,254

* Including £1443 million of British Transport stocks taken over on 1 January 1963.
† Including 'other debt in sterling' which rose by £594 million during the year, mainly because of borrowing from the International Monetary Fund and the United Kingdom's additional subscription to the Fund.

partly a result of the inflow of sterling into the Exchange Equalization Account. Similarly, other debt has risen as a result of borrowing from the International Monetary Fund. Moreover, the National Debt Commissioners have acquired government debt and, as a result of the rise in the fiduciary note issue, the Bank of England has absorbed additional government securities to the extent of £650 million.

In Table B4 holdings of Treasury bills outside the public sector are shown as at the end of each calendar year since 1951. Though the figures do not correspond precisely with those of Table B3 (the dates differ and bills move between the public and private sectors), they show the marked rise up to the late 1950s, and the sharp decline thereafter, The holdings of the clearing banks followed a similar course, while those of the discount market have remained fairly steady, though also tending to fall in recent years. The most striking movement, however, is that for 'other' holders, where the total multiplied nine times over in the ten years to 1960, then reaching £975 million, and subsequently fell to £357 million by 1965. This is traceable very largely to holdings of industrial and commercial companies, for which the total fell in the five years to 1965 by £602 million. Here is further evidence of the movement of funds in response to interest rate differentials. For several years prior to November 1951, bank deposit rate and the yield on Treasury bills had both been ½ per cent. With the return to an interest rate policy, the general level of short-term market rates increased, and a gap opened between the rate for bank deposits and that for Treasury bills. Holders of large

TABLE B4 *Holdings of Treasury bills outside the public sector (£m.)*

End of	*London clearing banks*	*Discount market*	*Overseas official holdings**	*Other*	*Total*
1951	791	628	1171	112	2702
1952	1182	705	861	241	2989
1953	1338	607	1069	282	3296
1954	1199	615	1021	541	3376
1955	1271	652	961	679	3563
1956	1275	523	927	643	3368
1957	1403	585	821	579	3388
1958	1185	594	891	764	3434
1959	1215	635	958	722	3530
1960	1017	574	923	975	3489
1961	1106	533	1076	596	3311
1962	1067	502	1023	450	3042
1963	996	529	1045	496	3066
1964	764	453	1100	374	2691
1965	784	484	1027	357	2652

* Central monetary institutions from 1963.

balances on deposit with the banks presumably found that the higher yield on bills outweighed the greater liquidity and convenience of bank deposits. The subsequent decline in such outside bill holdings is generally associated with still higher rates offered elsewhere with the development of the new markets for money.

The threatened Treasury bill starvation, with its possible consequences for banking liquidity, was relieved by the simultaneous increase in commercial bills. As Table B5 shows, the commercial bill holdings of the clearing banks and discount houses rose by over £500 million, or nearly threefold, between 1960 and 1965. To some extent this was due to the inclusion in the figures of refinanceable export credits from 1961 onwards, but it is also related to the increase in both the volume and value of international trade. Then again, the use of bills to finance hire purchase transactions was growing, while prices generally continued to rise. A further encouragement for the expansion in bill finance was the reduction in stamp duty in 1961, when an *ad valorem* rate, of one shilling per cent on all bills payable more than three days after sight or date, was replaced by a flat duty of 2*d.* per bill.

TABLE B5 *Holdings of commercial bills (£m.)*

End of	*London clearing banks**	*Discount market*	*Total*
1960	166	117	283
1961	250	183	433
1962	269	189	458
1963	311	249	560
1964	420	302	722
1965	451	339	790

* Including refinanceable export credits from 1961.

On occasion bill finance may have been available more cheaply than bank borrowing, and for a time restrictions on bank lending no doubt encouraged resort to bills. An added advantage for banks was that, when with directives went pressures on liquidity, commercial bills could reinforce liquid assets. Nevertheless, if in fact bills replaced advances, the process thwarted credit restraints, and official action has been taken. In 1961, for example, when it seemed that the increasing use of commercial bills might be blunting the edge of restrictions on advances, the banks were asked not to encourage resort to bill finance.

In 1965, too, when bank advances were restricted both quantitatively and selectively, the attention of the banks was drawn to the rise in the figures for commercial bills, and they were requested to limit the provision of acceptance facilities and purchases of commercial bills to the same extent and towards the same objectives as were applied to bank advances. The accepting and discount houses, too, were asked to observe a comparable degree of restraint, and these restrictions, thus widely applied, were continued. With restrictions went selectivity by the Bank of England in its sampling purchases as well as by the clearing banks.

For the clearing banks the supply of bills constitutes the mainstay of their liquid assets, representing the credit base of the system. Prior to 1963 the minimum liquidity ratio, to which increasing attention was paid by the authorities, was 30 per cent, but then it was reduced to 28 per cent. But in

1958, with the introduction of the system of Special Deposits to be made by the banks with the Bank of England, a means had been provided for effectively varying the liquidity ratio for the purposes of monetary regulation. The call for Special Deposits has run as high as 3 per cent of gross deposits of the clearing banks.*

TABLE B6 *Main assets of London clearing banks (yearly averages of monthly figures – £m.)*

	1958	*1959*	*1964*	*1965*
Money at call and short notice to:				
money market	n.a.	425	533	675
other	n.a.	64	205	235
Total	434	489	738	910
% of gross deposits	*6·5*	*7·1*	*8·6*	*10·1*
Private sector				
Advances*	1923	2522	4328	4653
Commercial bills†	110	135	365	461
	2033	2657	4693	5114
% of gross deposits	*30·6*	*38·3*	*54·9*	*56·9*
Public sector				
Treasury bills	1167	1089	790	653
Government stocks	2049	1718	1098	956
	3216	2807	1888	1609
% of gross deposits	*48·5*	*40·5*	*22·1*	*17·9*

* Including advances to nationalized industries and local authorities.
† Including refinanceable export credits after 1961.

Meanwhile, the commercial banks were rapidly switching from public to private sector assets and reversing yet another long-term trend. On the one hand, as we have seen, commercial bills were replacing Treasury bills, while on the other, the expansion of advances from 1958 onwards led to heavy realizations of investments in government securities. Table B6 shows the great redistribution of assets.

Lending to the private sector – advances plus commercial bills – represented just over three tenths of gross deposits in the years up to 1958 and this included public sector items such as nationalized industries and local

* In September 1971 the liquidity ratio was replaced by the reserve assets ratio and the system of Special Deposits extended (see Chapter 5).

authorities. By 1965 this proportion had reached nearly three fifths, reflecting a substantial rise in advances, with an even larger proportional increase in holdings of commercial bills. At the same time finance for the central government by way of Treasury bills and investments in official stocks fell from about one half of deposits in the years up to 1958 to less than one fifth by 1965, the lowest proportion since the early 1930s. Then again, the clearing banks have lent a growing proportion of their funds by way of money at call, and from 1960 the share provided for borrowers outside the discount market has risen. And of the sums lent to the discount market a larger proportion has been used to finance holdings of commercial bills.

TABLE B7 *Discount market assets*

End of	Treasury bills		Government securities		Commercial bills		Total including other assets
	£m.	% of total assets	£m.	% of total assets	£m.	% of total assets	£m.
1955	652	*61·0*	307	*28·7*	45	*4·2*	1068
1956	523	*54·8*	294	*30·8*	85	*8·9*	954
1957	585	*61·2*	223	*23·3*	84	*8·8*	956
1958	594	*56·4*	321	*30·5*	70	*6·6*	1053
1959	635	*56·2*	322	*28·5*	118	*10·4*	1130
1960	574	*48·0*	440	*36·8*	117	*9·8*	1197
1961	533	*43·8*	449	*36·9*	183	*15·0*	1216
1962	502	*40·1*	488	*39·0*	189	*15·1*	1251
1963	529	*40·5*	442	*33·9*	250	*19·1*	1305
1964	453	*35·3*	438	*34·1*	301	*23·5*	1283
1965	484	*33·3*	500	*34·4*	339	*23·3*	1455

In the discount market, too, the weight of public sector lending has diminished, though to a lesser extent. The dominance of the Treasury bill had been enhanced by wartime finance, while dealings had made headway in short-dated bonds, that is, government securities with less than five years to maturity. Indeed, such bonds became an eligible security at the Bank of England for loans at bank rate. These are quite distinct from local authority bonds, issued under statutory authority, given in 1964, which are not eligible.

The recent changes in the discount market's asset structure are shown in Table B7. It will be noticed that after 1959 the decline in the proportion of Treasury bills to all assets became persistent, falling to one third by the end of 1965. In 1960 a substantial rise was recorded in holdings of government securities, the total of £440 million being almost double the low level reached in 1957, when the sharp rise in bank rate had brought losses to bond holders.

Thereafter, bond holdings continued to expand, despite other periods of high short-term rates, and the decline in Treasury bills went on, until in 1965 the total of bonds was above that of Treasury bills, and the proportion of resources in public sector assets was below 70 per cent as against almost 90 per cent ten years before.

Part of the explanation may be seen in the figures for commercial bills. These rose more than sevenfold, to reach £339 million at the end of 1965, while the proportion to all assets increased from less than one twentieth to nearly one quarter. The move to private sector lending by way of commercial bills is greater than the figures in the table suggest, since these are at the end of the calendar year, when Treasury bill holdings are at their seasonal peak. In June 1965, Treasury bill holdings of the discount market amounted to only £201 million, or under one fifth of total assets. This was well below the figure of £317 million for commercial bills, while bond holdings, at £571 million, exceeded those of both types of bill taken together.

Over the ten years to mid-1965, then, the Treasury bill has shifted from first to second – and sometimes to third – place among the three main types of asset held by the discount houses, both because of the contraction in the issue, increased holdings of marketable government securities and the growing volume of commercial bills. For the clearing banks likewise, holdings of Treasury bills have fallen sharply, but so, too, have those of government stocks, as lending to the private sector, both by way of advances and purchases of commercial bills, has grown.

The Radcliffe Committee noted the arrangements, instituted in the 1930s, whereby the banks do not tender for Treasury bills on their own behalf, but buy them from the discount houses, who tender each week for the whole of the bills offered at a uniform price agreed among themselves. The Committee said (para. 589) that it would 'find no cause for alarm if developments within the banking system threatened to break down the cartelization and orderliness of the short market'. In the event, the significance of these arrangements was lessened with the decline in the importance of Treasury bills in the business of the banks and discount houses. However, considerable further developments have occurred and will be discussed on later pages, while the new arrangements for regulating monetary conditions and discount market activities are discussed in Chapters 3 and 4.

London's new markets for money
August 1966

In previous pages we examined the considerable changes that had occurred in recent years in the activities of the London money market, including the fall in holdings of Treasury bills, some recovery in those of commercial bills, and the extension of dealings in short-term government bonds. In essence, however, the classical market remained as a centrepiece of the financial structure, with the discount houses as leading operators, trading in traditional fashion with the Bank of England and the commercial banks. But side by side 'new' markets were developing, in which the volume of short-term funds employed now exceeds that in the long-established markets. They came to be known as 'parallel' or 'secondary' markets, and some as 'unsecured', to distinguish their activities from the secured borrowing of the discount houses in the 'primary' market. It is the new markets we now propose to survey briefly, as far as practice has developed by mid-1966 and information is available.

The task is by no means a simple one, since for some markets a fluid situation means that techniques are still developing, and for most of them statistics are not available or are far from comprehensive. Often existing institutions have grafted fresh activities onto old ones, following time-honoured practice in the financial centre, so that boundaries between the new markets are not clear cut. Broadly, all deal in short-term funds, at rates of interest above the levels obtaining in the traditional market, the traders in the new fields competing keenly as 'takers of funds' and being active as lenders. To aid understanding, however, three main markets may perhaps be distinguished: one in short-term deposits where the principal borrowers are local authorities and hire purchase finance houses; the second dealing in funds generally described as Eurodollars; and the third handling inter-bank transactions in sterling.

All gained impetus during the last decade as official restrictions on the flow of short-term funds were removed, both internally and internationally. Then, too, when credit restrictions hampered other financial activities, including those of the primary market, the new markets gained ground. Above all, the maintenance until 1971 in the primary market generally and by the clearing banks of long-established arrangements on interest rates, following a rigid pattern, left wide open opportunities which the new markets, with their uninhibited flexibility, were not slow to fill.

The prime mover in the new markets is competition in rates of interest, and the springboard for later developments was the change in monetary policy from cheap money to the use of interest rates towards the close of 1951. Bank rate returned to the monetary scene after twenty years of disuse, and the discount rate for Treasury bills once more began to fluctuate week by week. In 1955 bank rate rose to $4\frac{1}{2}$ per cent, and the margin between the clearing banks' deposit rate, changing only with bank rate, and the varying Treasury bill rate, widened to exceed 1 per cent; except for short periods it has remained so. Up to that time most merchant banks and overseas and foreign banks in London had followed the clearing bank interest rate structure, but thereafter for the most part they offered and charged higher rates than the clearing banks for short money. Meanwhile, the deposit rate of the clearing banks continued to be maintained at 2 per cent below bank rate on deposit accounts, though the period of notice for these was reduced to seven days, no interest being allowed on balances on current account. Lending rates to the money market also continued to be directly related to bank rate, the agreed minimum being raised in 1958 from $1\frac{3}{4}$ to $1\frac{5}{8}$ per cent below bank rate. As the clearing banks were thus withholding from competition on rates, either between themselves or with other institutions, opportunities were presented to others and the wide range of rates which became usual can be seen in Appendix 2, Table 9.*

Of particular importance in the development of the new markets have been official changes in arrangements for borrowing by local authorities. For some years these had borrowed largely from the Public Works Loan Board on favourable terms, but in 1955 they were required to meet their needs primarily from the capital market on current terms. Other changes were made from time to time, and in the outcome local authorities developed facilities for borrowing increasing amounts of short-term funds in the market and directly from the public, in ways described below (see pp. 162–3).

In 1958, when for a time hire purchase undertakings and the banks were released from restriction on lending, a swift expansion in their activities followed. Several hire purchase finance houses became associated with the large banks, and, despite the reimposition of restrictions, growth has continued. They too have obtained a substantial part of their resources by borrowing funds at short term, though not generally for such short periods as have local authorities.

Another influence has been the international movement of short-term funds, which is largely free from the restrictions, whether by way of exchange controls or by tax considerations, that affect longer-term international investment. Transactions involving funds of this type were encouraged by the granting of convertibility to external holders of current sterling in December 1958. Such funds were then able to move fairly freely from abroad into the various United Kingdom short-term money markets, or out again, partly in response to levels of interest rates at home and abroad.

All these developments helped to make business undertakings and the public generally more keenly aware of yields, and interest-rate consciousness developed, while the amalgamation and grouping of companies, which continued to make headway, encouraged the better and more profitable employment of their liquid resources. With company officials charged with the duty of seeking suitable outlets, City undertakings themselves found new opportunities for jobbing in short-term funds, borrowing and re-lending them with a small rate margin. In some of the newly emerging markets, funds might

* See pp. 118 ff. for new monetary arrangements of September 1971.

change hands several times before reaching the eventual user of them, and transactions would often be arranged through brokers acting as intermediaries and remunerated by way of commission. So it came about that outside lenders and borrowers were able to use new markets conducted with an altogether higher spectrum of rates. 'Takers of funds', the term embracing overseas banks, merchant banks and various specialized institutions, offered comparatively high rates for deposits which they were able to lend on a remunerative basis, perhaps to local authorities, possibly to hire purchase finance undertakings, and generally in ways not regarded as appropriate for clearing bank advances.

Local authorities comprise one of the main outlets for funds from the new markets. Borrowing by these bodies is subject to strict official regulation and several changes in policy have occurred in post-war years. In particular, access to the Exchequer through the Public Works Loan Board has been varied, as when late in 1955 local authorities were required to meet their needs in the capital market as far as practicable, the PWLB then becoming, as it were, the 'lender of last resort'. Thereafter, local treasurers displayed considerable ingenuity in devising ways of borrowing directly from the public. With stock issues also controlled, they turned to short-term, temporary borrowing – mainly by way of deposits – partly because this promised safeguards against a possible fall in long-term rates, but also because it suited lenders, and the market quickly responded. Later, easier access to PWLB funds was allowed, and official restrictions were imposed on the extent of temporary borrowing, defined as for periods of less than one year, so that its growth was checked (see p. 307).

At the end of 1965, outstanding temporary borrowing amounted to £1798 million, compared with £1116 million four years earlier. Of the total, £1257 million, or nearly three quarters, was repayable within seven days. In fact, deposits were accepted for as short a period as overnight. They were not, however – as in the inter-bank and Eurodollar markets – normally taken for 'broken' periods, but for a stated range of periods of notice, such as two days or seven days. Alternatively they might be for stated minimum periods – for instance, an arrangement for one month fixed, and then at seven days' notice. Deposits were also taken for a fixed period of 364 days. The minimum sum taken on deposit in these ways was usually £50,000, though smaller amounts could be negotiated. Sums of £500,000 to £1 million were often seen, and larger amounts occasionally. As will be realized, to provide and maintain this large flow of funds involved substantial market activity.

In competing for funds, especially with finance houses, local authorities have advantages in that their borrowing is secured on the local rate revenue and has trustee status. Existing deposits came in roughly equal proportions from banks, other financial institutions, industrial and commercial companies, and other lenders. A considerable part of the funds employed clearly came from abroad. Thus at the end of 1965, loans to local authorities – presumably mainly temporary – by accepting houses amounted to £242 million and those by overseas and foreign banks to £323 million. In so far as this reflects overseas funds, difficulties might arise when sterling is under pressure. As elsewhere in the new markets, brokers were active in handling funds for placing with local authorities, with several firms specializing in this field. A few firms of stockbrokers and foreign exchange brokers also participated in this market. Though we are here concerned only with temporary borrowing, mainly by way of deposits, local authorities also borrow for periods of one or more years on mortgages, and these are commonly arranged by the same brokers who handle municipal business, who quote rates for a wide range of periods, from short to long.

A further development in recent times has been the issue of local authority bonds, under a statutory authority given in 1964. In the two years since then the amount outstanding has risen to about £180 million, generally in the form of one year bonds – hence the name 'yearlings' – although, as a result of a change in borrowing controls, many new bonds are for periods of two years. Maturities were usually refinanced by the issue of further bonds. Most of these bonds received a Stock Exchange quotation, and were placed in the market by stockbrokers, but a few were issued without quotation. Some were distributed by merchant banks among discount houses, thus providing them with a new form of asset, but the Bank of England did not accept local authority bonds as security for loans, and the clearing banks did so only to a limited extent. However, both for quoted and unquoted bonds of local authorities an active market existed among a narrow range of institutions, and one distinct from the market for deposits.

As has been mentioned, the growth of hire purchase finance houses was supported by attracting funds on deposit; this was the other main outlet of the new market in short-term funds, and one that competed directly with local authorities. At the end of 1957, deposits held by the members of the Finance Houses Association, comprising about four fifths of all finance house business, amounted to less than £100 million but by early 1961 they had risen above £300 million. Published statistics have since become more comprehensive and detailed, and a selection of the figures for the three years to March 1966 is given in Table B8. This shows the continued rapid rise in deposits, which comprise nearly two thirds of total resources. The largest source of them – and one which had been growing swiftly – comprises industrial and commercial companies in the United Kingdom; substantial sums were also deposited by banks and other financial institutions, and – of particular significance – by overseas residents.

Finance houses usually obtained funds for comparatively short periods, largely because such balances were more readily attracted. Thus deposits were commonly arranged for three or six months, though they were sometimes renewed on maturity. In general, the rates of interest offered to private individuals were expressed in relation to bank rate and vary with it, but for the larger sums commonly available from institutional and other corporate lenders rates were often fixed throughout the period of the deposit, after negotiation with the finance house. Rates on offer differed somewhat between finance houses, because deposits with them were unsecured, and houses vary in size and standing, while some had close connections with banks. Most large houses obtain their deposits, either directly or through brokers, without advertising. Occasionally finance houses might themselves have surplus funds, and then brokers would find remunerative temporary employment for them elsewhere in the secondary market.

TABLE B8 *Deposits with hire purchase finance companies (£m.)*

	Total	*United Kingdom*				*Overseas residents*
End of March		*Banks*	*Other financial institutions*	*Industrial and commercial companies*	*Other residents*	
1963	332	52	40	122	36	82
1964	412	85	43	164	48	72
1965	536	127	47	197	76	89
1966	664	109	74	241	99	141

Resources were also obtained through open acceptance facilities with non-clearing banks; bills drawn under them by finance houses were usually discounted by the acceptor and might then be sold to the discount market. In the comprehensive figures for March 1966 discounts provided £116 million, other borrowing £123 million and deposits £664 million.

For finance houses and local authorities we know the extent of the funds they collected though their movement through the market was by no means closely recorded, but for other newly developed markets not even the figures of receipts by users were available. Indeed, it might be virtually impossible to obtain worthwhile statistics, for in both the Eurodollar and inter-bank markets the same institutions may act as sources of funds, as dealers and as borrowers. As with other new markets, growth and development has been determined largely by competitive interest rates. For some years to 1966 short-term rates in London were higher than those in overseas financial centres. Other reasons for the rapid development included the specialization and advanced organization of financial markets in London, and particularly the foreign exchange market, as well as the availability of remunerative outlets for funds in the market for short-term deposits.

The inter-bank market in sterling deposits and the Eurodollar market in currencies overlap, so that related aspects and activities in common must first be noted. In both, the main dealers, operating as principals, are the merchant banks, foreign banks in London and British banks operating abroad, and include some banks that are subsidiaries of, or associated with, clearing banks; the clearing banks themselves do not take part in the inter-bank market, but they may be active in Eurodollars. As will be appreciated, funds from abroad play a part in both markets, though notably in that for Eurodollars. For instance, funds from overseas may come into the country through the London branch of an overseas bank for lending to British local authorities, that is, into the market for short-term deposits, or they may originate in the form of Eurodollars and be swapped into sterling, with forward cover, for lending to other secondary markets. The particular course which funds follow is influenced by ever-moving interest rates and exchange rates, with operators bearing in mind the total cost of transactions, including forward cover; and jobbing and arbitrage dealings take place in response to changing market conditions. The clearing banks and discount houses, at that time observing their undertakings on interest rates, were involved to a small extent only.

In both markets transactions commonly take the form of deposits, placed by one institution with another for a specified period at an agreed rate. The restrictions imposed by exchange control on borrowing and lending then bore less heavily upon transactions in deposits, and funds redeposited could constitute a useful reinforcement of bank liquidity. Dealings are commonly conducted through the intermediary of brokers in an informal way, in large round amounts. The deposits, i.e. loans, are unsecured, and each institution commonly observes limits regarding the extent to which it will place deposits with other individual institutions in the market. Occasionally, interest rates are varied in accordance with the standing of the borrowing institution.

Some idea of the complexity of operations in the secondary markets may be gathered from simply listing the categories of providers of funds and dealers. Among the main lenders are: British banks operating abroad; merchant banks, using funds which are both domestic and overseas in origin; foreign banks with offices in London; and, indeed, those not directly represented in London, including central banks and supranational institutions. Many of these institutions also act as dealers in the various markets. But other lenders may include: insurance companies, pension funds and similar institutions; large commercial and industrial companies; and perhaps discount houses, savings banks, and finance companies when, exceptionally, they hold surplus funds. Probably about a hundred institutions take part at times in the inter-bank market, and more in that for Eurodollars, with perhaps a dozen brokers, some specializing in particular sides of secondary market activities.

For lending institutions, the practice has grown up for funds from non-bank lenders to enter the market in the first instance by being placed on deposit with a non-clearing bank, rather than with the user directly. Even if all lenders and eventual borrowers in these markets could be identified, this would not give a complete picture, since funds may change hands a number of times, constructing a chain of borrowers and lenders.

The involved course of transactions and the limitations of the available statistics make estimates of the size of these markets difficult. Figures of accepting houses and overseas banks in the United Kingdom show that money lent by them to the discount market remained almost unchanged over the three years to mid-1966, whereas direct loans to local authorities rose sharply. Steep increases were also recorded for deposits and advances, both as regards United Kingdom and overseas residents, and in both sterling and other currencies; deposits and balances with other United Kingdom banks similarly rose sharply. However, the items distinguished cannot be definitely attributed to particular markets or activities, and as the banks and other institutions deal with one another the likelihood of multiple counting is evident.

Some London banks accepted foreign currency deposits between the wars, but it is only since late in the 1950s that transactions have grown to large proportions. Then a number of banks became engaged in currency transactions of this kind and an active market resulted. It was at that time, too, that the name 'Eurodollars' began to be used, although other currencies were also involved, if by no means as extensively as United States dollars. Eurodollars are traded in the principal financial centres outside the United States, but here we are describing only the London situation. Eurodollars are simply dollars which have been deposited with a bank outside the United States, and are still denominated in dollars. A main attraction has been the generally higher level of interest rates in countries outside the United States, where rates were held down by official regulation, and the large volume of Eurodollars has also been associated with the continuing outflow of funds from the United States for capital development and government purposes, resulting in a persistent deficit on her balance of payments. Some of the attempts by the United States government to deal with this deficit, as by the interest equalization tax and by voluntary restraint on lending, have tended to induce borrowers, shut out from the United States, to turn to the Eurodollar market. An active market in lending and relending has developed with the principal centre in London, where a highly developed foreign exchange market operates and where it is easy to find remunerative outlets for investment.

Reference has been made to the various groups of banks in London that participate, which include the clearing banks, and these handle Eurodollar deposits that have, for the most part, come from continental banks. Dealings take place largely between members of the foreign exchange market, and are commonly arranged in much the same way as purchases and sales of currencies

– that is, through the intermediary of foreign exchange brokers, who act as agents in bringing the principals together for a commission. Transactions are in large round amounts, typically in units of $1 million, though they may occasionally be for sums as small as $100,000. Deposits may be accepted at call, and for some the term may run for up to two years or occasionally longer, though the bulk are probably arranged for periods running between two days and three months. Sometimes deposits may be renewed upon maturity, this being arranged at the current market rate at the time of renewal. Dealers relend with a margin of perhaps one sixteenth or one eighth per cent in the rate of interest on transactions with other dealers, but if the funds are lent outside the market a larger margin is required.

Numerous users are ready to meet interest charges at the higher levels. Borrowers may require Eurodollars as an alternative to other forms of financing, as when development is made by large companies operating internationally, or by European subsidiaries of United States undertakings. They may be required to finance trade or investment projects. When market circumstances are propitious they may be sold for sterling, commonly with forward cover, for lending in the inter-bank market, or to local authorities or, less commonly, to finance houses. Eurodollars are also used for subscription to new capital issues denominated in US dollars, arranged in London or elsewhere, but this is distinct from the short-term market, with which we are here concerned.

An indication of the size of Eurodollar funds outstanding at any one time in the London market is given by figures issued by the Bank of England of 'external liabilities and claims of UK banks in foreign currencies'; these are shown in Table B9. They include foreign currency balances of banks with their correspondents abroad – and vice versa – in order to carry on their day-to-day foreign business, and balances held on behalf of UK customers who have official permission to retain foreign currency. But a large and growing part of the total represents on-lending of Eurocurrencies. At the end of 1957 the total of external liabilities of UK banks in foreign currencies amounted to about £70 million and by 1962 it had reached just over £1000 million. Since then the figure has again doubled, and at the end of March 1966 it was nearly £2200 million. The excess of external liabilities over claims, or the net liability in foreign currencies, at the end of March 1966 was £75 million. This gives an idea of the extent to which currency deposits have been switched into sterling, but it understates the amount somewhat because of slight differences in the coverage of the figures as regards items other than currency deposits. The amount switched into sterling is small in relation to the total of external liabilities; in 1964 the proportion was officially estimated to be about one tenth.

An analysis by countries of external liabilities and claims by British banks in United States dollars, which represent about nine tenths of the total, is set out in Table B10. It shows that more than half of the dollar funds passing through London came from western Europe, though it is not possible to say how much of the funds were first placed in European centres from elsewhere and then attracted to London. More deposits are on-lent to North America than to western Europe.

A development of the past few months has been the issue in London of negotiable certificates of deposit denominated in US dollars, thus providing a market instrument for dealing in Eurodollars. The London offices of United States banks were the first to issue these certificates, which initially are for periods of 30, 60, 90, 120, 150 and 180 days, in multiples of $1000, or sometimes of $5000, but for not less than $25,000, a far smaller figure than has been usual in Eurodollar dealings hitherto. Some international broking houses and others have undertaken to make a market in these 'London dollar CDs,' which, because of their convenience, provide a yield of about one eighth per cent below the corresponding rate of interest for Eurodollar deposits.

TABLE B9 *External liabilities and claims of UK banks in currencies other than sterling (£m.)*

	U.S. dollars	*Swiss francs*	*Deutsch marks*	*Other currencies*	*Total*
End of period					
UK liabilities					
1962	884	62	38	54	1038
1963	1072	76	65	67	1280
1964	1564	83	83	54	1784
1965	1879	72	96	61	2108
1966 March	1945	98	101	54	2198
UK claims					
1962	803	n.a.	n.a.	n.a.	1010
1963	1024	71	68	105	1268
1964	1312	85	119	110	1626
1965	1624	81	162	113	1980
1966 March	1743	97	166	117	2123

A main function of the inter-bank market is to enable the institutions taking part in it – possibly a hundred or so of the non-clearing banks – to adjust their liquidity position from day to day, and indeed throughout the day. In the classical market the clearing banks have accounts with the Bank of England and adjust their cash position – cash comprising liabilities of the central bank and coin – through the discount market as may be required in the course of each day. In the inter-bank market, the banks involved generally keep accounts with the clearing banks and settle their transactions through them, maintaining the requisite balances nowadays largely by inter-bank dealings. Thus, whereas in earlier times they might have adjusted balances with the clearing banks by selling bills, by calling in funds lent to the discount market against security, or in other ways, nowadays they may lend and borrow between themselves on an unsecured basis. This, with brokers as go-betweens, provides a convenient and expeditious means of achieving the same purpose. But the discount houses thereby miss a considerable turnover of business even though some of the funds may become available to them later through the clearing banks.

TABLE B10 *External liabilities and claims of UK banks in US dollars Country of borrower or lender (£m.)*

	Overseas sterling area	*North America*	*Western Europe*	*Other*	*Total*
End of period					
UK liabilities					
1962	18	263	449	154	884
1963	37	264	520	251	1072
1964	76	455	716	317	1564
1965	116	356	1019	388	1879
1966 March	129	382	1035	399	1945
UK claims					
1962	2	332	336	133	803
1963	3	309	519	193	1024
1964	4	447	600	261	1312
1965	23	610	641	350	1624
1966 March	25	812	545	361	1743

Thus an active market has developed since 1960 in sterling funds, which may include, when market circumstances permit, Eurodollars that have been swapped into sterling. As with Eurodollars, transactions are in large, round amounts that are borrowed and lent unsecured, so again the standing of the taker is important. Deals are generally arranged through brokers, who approach institutions to see what business is likely to be forthcoming and to obtain an indication of rates. Most of these are foreign exchange brokers, but they also include one or two specialized houses formed since the business began to develop. Transactions are usually for short periods; they range from overnight up to about six months, but the great bulk of funds is lent for periods of fourteen days or less. Short transactions are rarely renewed; long ones rather more often. The minimum sums which are lent are commonly £50,000 or £100,000, and round sums up to £500,000 are typical, but amounts of over £1 million are not often seen as big sums on offer are split.

Here again, statistics are lacking and the course followed by funds moving through the market cannot be established with precision. It has been suggested that in 1966 a fund of possibly £1000 million was involved, and that the daily turnover rested between £50 million and £100 million.

Although aggregates of the funds employed in the several short-term markets, including the discount market, can only be estimated, for some with no claim to precision, it may be useful to bring together, as in Table B11 below, various totals that are on record or have been suggested, so as to indicate broad orders of magnitude at the end of 1965. These are not, of course, separate funds, as money often passes from one market to another. Then again, no estimate can be given of the volume of turnover, although it must be large, if only because of the short-term nature of most transactions. However, it may be noted that the amounts passing through the 'Town Clearing' of the clearing banks – through which transactions of the secondary markets, as of the primary market, generally pass – increased between the years 1960 and 1965 by £168,000 million to reach £347,000 million.

TABLE B11 *Order of magnitude of resources of short-term markets (end of 1965)*

	£m.
Discount houses	1400 (total resources)
Finance houses	600 (deposits)
Local authorities	1700 (temporary borrowing)
Eurodollars	2000 (see tables B9 and B10)
Inter-bank market	1000 (estimate—see above)

The rates of interest obtaining in the various secondary markets fluctuate in response to changes in supply and demand, and they are not always in regular relationship, as may be seen from Appendix 2, Table 9. Nevertheless some patterns could be traced and regarded as typical. Rates for periods of up to one week were commonly related to those for lending to the discount market, and might be $\frac{1}{4}$ to $\frac{3}{8}$ per cent above them in the inter-bank market, and slightly higher still – by a further $\frac{1}{8}$ to $\frac{1}{4}$ per cent – in the local authority market. Rates for one month or more were usually related to bank rate, running at a margin above it that increases slightly with the length of the period, and varies with particular markets. Thus for three months the margin above bank rate might be $\frac{1}{2}$ to $\frac{5}{8}$ per cent in the inter-bank market, $\frac{1}{4}$ to $\frac{1}{2}$ per cent for local authorities and $\frac{3}{4}$ to 1 per cent for finance houses. As Eurodollars are essentially an international market the rates ruling do not always follow those in the other secondary markets closely, particularly as the cost of forward cover – which itself may vary – has to be taken into account.

As the new markets for short-term money develop, the contrasts with orthodox procedures become more evident, but established connections are maintained and occasional new bridges are built. In 1966 the clearing banks and discount houses continued to stand aside from the rates battle, though the banks participated, if not very extensively, in the new activities, both directly as in the Eurodollar market, and indirectly through their subsidiaries or associated banks. Even this small comfort was denied to the discount houses; they saw new active markets in short-term funds spring up, with considerable turnover in which they did not share. But most of the banks operating in the inter-bank and Eurodollar markets continued to lend funds to discount houses, so maintaining connections and facilities for their bill business. Then again, a few discount houses took steps to associate themselves with firms of brokers active in the local authority and inter-bank markets, and at least one helped to provide a market in London dollar certificates of deposit by acting as a broker itself.

Of particular consequence was the emergence of a new level of market rates. A relatively high level would be expected in the new markets, since lending there, except to local authorities, is all unsecured, whereas in the discount market it is secured. Again, since the operations of the discount market were regulated from day to day by the Bank of England, the rates obtaining were, as for previous generations, likely to be strongly influenced by the authorities. The position is different in the new markets, where much of the money flowing through is on its way to financing consumer goods, or the expenditure of local authorities, all representing spheres at one remove or further from bank rate and the complex of rates associated with it.

Rates in the new markets have run well above those in the primary money market, including the Treasury bill rate. Then, too, the new market rates fluctuated more widely and more frequently and were readily adapted for particular needs. Indeed, it was the rates in the new markets that attracted overseas funds as well as home balances; it was these rates that were responsive to the daily market situation for short-term funds. London had not only new markets for money, but also a new basis for rates. And in important directions the going rates in the new markets have come to represent the gauge for the employment of short-term funds. They are the new key to London rates, with far-reaching consequences in the daily distribution of funds and implications for monetary policy.

7

Further Developments in London's Money Markets

Clearing Banks and Discount Houses August 1969

Developments in the London money markets over a considerable period to 1966 were examined in the previous chapter. Important changes in the activities and assets structure of the traditional discount market were noted, in particular the revival of the commercial bill and the decline of the Treasury bill from the dominant position it had held for so long. Further, and quite separate from the traditional market, were dealings in short-term funds that largely bypassed it, and a number of 'new' markets had developed since the late 1950s. These new markets, also designated as 'secondary', or more often – and more accurately – as 'parallel', were in short-term deposits with local authorities and finance houses, Eurodollars, and inter-bank balances; the principal operators were accepting houses and overseas and foreign banks. The picture there presented in all important respects remains a true one in 1969. But some significant changes have taken place over the past three years, and these are now recorded.

Since 1966 the two sets of markets have moved somewhat closer together, largely because of moves by the clearing banks and the discount houses, the traditional market bodies, towards greater participation in the new fields of activity. Despite criticism from official and other sources, the clearing banks in 1969 were still maintaining their traditional structure of interest rates allowed, related to bank rate and agreed among themselves. The setting up of special subsidiaries had continued, however, and because official restrictions inhibited development of more orthodox types of lending business, these have participated actively in the new markets. Some particulars of the principal banking subsidiary and affiliated companies of the clearing banks which do so are given in Table B12 below. All these companies operated in the 'new' markets for sterling and/or currency deposits. All have issued certificates of deposit denominated in sterling and some have offered also dollar CDs.

TABLE B12 *Principal deposit-taking subsidiaries and affiliates of the clearing banks**

Bank	*Subsidiary or affiliate*	*Deposits (£m.)*
Midland	Midland and International Banks (45% participation)	467 (March 1971)
	Midland Bank Finance Corporation (wholly owned)	529 (March 1971)
Barclays	Barclays Bank (London and International)†	542 (Sept. 1970)
Lloyds	Lloyds Bank Europe (wholly owned)	541 (Sept. 1970)
Williams & Glyn's	Williams, Glyn	183 (Sept. 1970)
National Westminster	Westminster Foreign Bank (wholly owned)	884 (Dec. 1970)
	County Bank (wholly owned)	246 (Dec. 1970)
	Coutts Finance (wholly owned)	230 (Dec. 1970)
	International Commercial Bank (22% participation)	295 (Dec. 1970)

* A more extensive list of major subsidiaries and affiliates appears in Appendix 5(b).
† Amalgamated with Martins Bank Finance as from 1 May 1969.

The discount houses have continued to make shifts in the disposition of their assets, according to the availabliltiy and profitability of the various types of paper in which they deal. They, too, have participated in the new markets in various ways, as principals, brokers or agents, sometimes directly and sometimes through subsidiaries or participations.

Activity in the new markets, which remain closely interrelated, has continued to run at a high level. The inter-bank market has grown appreciably in size, but the expansion of that in Eurodollars has been little short of phenomenal. The working of the markets has been assisted by a number of technical changes, and some regroupings have taken place among the various brokers and dealers. Transactions continue to be distinguished from those in the traditional market by being largely unsecured, with funds often placed for stated fixed periods, mainly short. Dealings have meanwhile begun in certificates of deposit, denominated both in dollars and sterling, and issued by non-clearing banks, and the discount houses have established secondary markets in these instruments.

Monetary policy has remained active and restrictive. Throughout most of the period qualitative and quantitative controls have been applied to bank lending, and ceilings have also been established for commercial bills, including those of the discount market. Some of the activities of the accepting houses, overseas and foreign banks have been subject to similar restraints. These have not ordinarily affected their operations in the various money markets, although the growth of short-term borrowing by both local authorities and hire purchase finance houses has been curbed in other ways. Monetary action has been strongly reinforced by other measures, in particular the swing-round in the Exchequer accounts from overall deficit to overall surplus, and a change of emphasis in the operations of the authorities in the gilt-edged market (see Chapter 3). As a consequence, rates of interest have been high and generally rising throughout the period, with movements in other financial centres and in the Eurodollar market also contributing to the upward pressures.

The combined ratio of liquid assets of the clearing banks to deposits was then being maintained at or a little above the indicated minimum level of 28 per cent, and between July 1966 and August 1969 Special Deposits at 2 per cent of gross deposits had been required to be held at the Bank of England. In the composition of the total of liquid assets, trends that had earlier become apparent had persisted. Commercial bill holdings were broadly maintained, thanks partly to the growth of refinanceable export credits. Treasury bills continued to fall, and the banks had tended to favour call money rather than Treasury bills. The figures are summarized in Table B13 and may be followed in Chart (h) in Appendix 3.

Within the rising proportion of call money, from 6·5 per cent in 1958 to 12·8 per cent in 1968, about two thirds continued to be lent to the discount market, with part of the remainder consisting of the on-lending of foreign currency deposits, particularly Eurodollars. Balances with other banks, both in sterling and in foreign currencies, were classed as liquid assets, whereas short-term lending to finance houses and local authorities had to be taken within the officially restricted total of advances, and so the clearing banks did not participate substantially in these markets.

Several mergers took place in the two or three years to 1969, not only between clearing banks, but also among Scottish banks and British overseas banks, and as integration arrangements are completed the number of large lenders to the discount market will be appreciably reduced. The mergers have also raised the possibility of changes in the attitude of the banks to the market.

In evidence to the Monopolies Commission on the proposed merger between Barclays, Lloyds and Martins banks (H.C.P. 319), which was eventually disallowed, the London Discount Market Association expressed

TABLE B13 *Liquid assets of London clearing banks yearly (averages of monthly figures) (£m.)*

	1965	*1966*	*1967*	*1968*
Cash	739	767	798	851
% of gross deposits	*8·2*	*8·2*	*8·2*	*8·2*
Money at call and short notice to:				
Money market	675	731	806	896
Other	235	275	330	439
% of gross deposits	*10·1*	*10·7*	*11·6*	*12·8*
Treasury bills	653	689	564	468
% of gross deposits	*7·3*	*7·3*	*5·8*	*4·5*
Other bills	461	446	492	527
% of gross deposits	*5·1*	*4·8*	*5·0*	*5·1*
Total	2763	2908	2990	3182
% of gross deposits	*30·7*	*31·0*	*30·6*	*30·5*

fears that the combined bank would be 'too dominant in the London money market', leading to various types of rigidity in the market. It also feared that 'the decline in settlements between the clearing banks which would result from the mergers might lead to a reduction in turnover in the money market and to a reduction in the volume of money lent to the market by the clearing banks'.

The Treasury and the Bank of England thought that if the merger took place some rigidity might from time to time develop, both as to the acceptability of some classes of paper and to rate structure on call money, but that this would be no more than a question of degree. They did not expect that the discount market would be bypassed in favour of direct inter-clearing bank settlements on the lines of the inter-bank market operated by the non-clearing banks. Lending to the discount market might be marginally smaller. The majority of the Commission accepted the market's views in the main but, by contrast with the authorities, thought it possible that 'with the passage of time the clearing banks, if there were only three large ones, might start bypassing the discount market and dealing direct with one another and with the Bank of England in settling their daily cash surpluses and deficits and in transactions in Treasury bills'.

The structure of the discount market itself has shown little change since some reorganization occurred in the early post-war years. Since then, two members of the London Discount Market Association, Cater, Brightwen and

Ryders Discount, have merged to form Cater Ryder, and Gerrard & Reid, which was formerly outside the Association, has been admitted to it. In July 1969 it was announced that National Discount Co., one of the largest houses, had agreed proposals for an amalgamation with Gerrard & Reid. As a result the number of houses in the Association was reduced from twelve to eleven.

Little change took place over the three years to 1969 in the composition of the discount market's borrowed funds, apart from the tendency noted above for call money from the clearing banks – always the predominant source – to rise. The amount borrowed from the accepting houses and overseas and foreign banks – previously over £200 million – fell to around £150 million, even though the total liabilities and assets of these banks had grown very rapidly. They continued to develop the inter-bank market as a means of maintaining and adjusting their liquidity, but found it convenient to continue to lend to the discount houses, whose existence ensured a market for their acceptances.

As noted in Chapter 6, the most striking trends up to 1966 in the discount market's portfolio were the continued rise in total assets, a sharp fall in holdings of Treasury bills, the revival of commercial bills, and the maintenance of bond holdings, despite short-term fluctuations, at a broadly steady proportion of total assets. Subsequent changes can be traced in Table B14.

It will be seen that although the growth in total holdings continued until

TABLE B14 *Discount market assets*

End of	*Government securities*		*Treasury bills*		*Commercial and other sterling bills*		*Other assets*		*Total*
	£m.	*% of total*	*£m.*	*% of total*	*£m.*	*% of total*	*£m.*	*% of total*	
1958	321	*30*	594	*56*	70	*7*	68	*6*	1053
1963	442	*34*	529	*41*	249	*19*	84	*6*	1305
1964	438	*34*	453	*35*	302	*24*	90	*7*	1283
1965	500	*34*	484	*33*	339	*23*	132	*9*	1455
1966	542	*35*	424	*27*	404	*26*	195	*12*	1565
1967	544	*31*	548	*31*	437	*25*	218	*12*	1747
1968	306	*18*	471	*28*	560	*34*	326	*20*	1663
March									
1967	678	*47*	219	*15*	379	*26*	168	*12*	1444
1968	573	*39*	255	*17*	414	*28*	217	*15*	1459
1969	254	*19*	261	*19*	520	*38*	323	*24*	1357

1967 it has since been reversed, a movement associated with the swing from deficit into surplus in the Exchequer accounts as well as the growth of the new markets. Nevertheless, Treasury bill holdings at the end of 1968 were at roughly the same level as three and four years before; the totals for commercial bills and other assets had continued to rise sharply, but bond holdings had been substantially reduced over the following year. Accordingly the combined proportion for government bonds and Treasury bills had continued to fall; until ten years before it was around 80–90 per cent, depending upon the time of year, but well below 50 per cent. Seasonal movements affect particularly Treasury bills, holdings of which fall sharply in the first quarter of each year, as the figures for end-March in Table B14 indicate.

Interest rates, an important influence on the level and composition of the market's portfolio of bonds, have generally been high in the 1960s. The losses that can be incurred when rates are rising are greater and more persistent on bonds than on the other types of asset that the market holds, which are mainly much shorter dated. Losses have been experienced in this way within the year to May 1969, as they invariably are when interest rates are rising. Until these years, the houses had considered that bond holdings might be as much as about eight times true capital resources, but then they were inclined to take a more conservative view and also to hold a higher proportion of relatively short-dated bonds. Although holdings of government securities with more than five years to run to maturity have never been large, they accounted for £51 million of the peak holding of government securities of £678 million in March 1967 but had fallen to only £2 million by March 1969.

As for total bond holdings, short-term movements are commonly quite large, the five end-quarter figures for the period up to March 1969 being £573 million, £378 million, £521 million, £306 million and £254 million. Thus the net movement over the twelve months was a reduction of more than one half. Turnover in bonds also has fallen, though remaining considerable. In 1967, it was ten to twelve times the average level of the discount market's holdings, and represented over one-third of total short-term bond dealings. In 1968 the turnover rate fell to less than nine times and to just over one quarter of total dealings. The reduction was most marked in the second half of the year.

Holdings of Treasury bills might have been expected to fall in view of their reduced availability. The outstanding volume of bills issued through the tender declined from £3480 million to £2180 million over the six years to March 1966, and over the next three contracted further, to only £1390 million. This decline has arisen not only because of the adverse balance of payments, which in effect has been providing the Exchequer with resources from overseas, but also because of the surplus on the Exchequer accounts. The brunt of the reduction in the government's need to borrow in the domestic market has fallen upon the Treasury bill issue, the residual element.

The average amount of bills issued at the weekly tender fell from £232 million in 1964 to £145 million in 1968, and for the first ten weeks of 1969 – admittedly the seasonal low point – it was only £100 million.

The same trends are shown by the figures for Treasury bills held outside the public sector, as given in Table B15. The total has risen since 1965, but this is more than accounted for by holdings of overseas central monetary institutions, arising from operations to support sterling. Considering the trend in availability, the discount market's holdings of Treasury bills were well maintained in the three years to 1968, but those of the clearing banks, which buy them from the discount houses, fell substantially. Even so, the figure for the discount market for end-1968 seems to have been not quite typical of that year; the holdings at the end of each of the three previous quarters were less than £300 million.

TABLE B15 *Holdings of Treasury bills outside the public sector* (*£m.*)

End of	*London clearing banks*	*Discount market*	*Overseas central monetary institutions**	*Other*	*Total*
1958	1185	594	891	764	3434
1963	996	529	1045	496	3066
1964	764	453	1100	374	2691
1965	784	484	1027	357	2652
1966	650	424	1238	330	2642
1967	508	548	1753	347	3156
1968	518†	471	2466	249	3704

* Overseas official holdings for 1958.
† Includes estimates for two small clearing banks which no longer publish balance sheets at the end of the calendar year.

The proportion of the bills allotted at the syndicate's tender price has varied substantially, from the extremes of nil to 100 per cent for ninety-one-day bills during the past year. With the syndicate committed to tendering for all the bills offered, and outside competition sometimes reduced owing to the general expectation of rising rather than falling interest rates, it has sometimes found itself obliged to take up rather more bills than it might have wished, despite adjustments in its tender price; it is partly for this reason perhaps that the market's Treasury bill holdings did not fall quite as much as might have been expected.

In 1968 the commercial bill once more provided the largest single asset in the discount market's holdings, a position not seen for many years past; even as recently as 1959 the Radcliffe Report spoke of 'the irreversible shrinkage in the relative supply of commercial bills'. As Table B16 shows, holdings of commercial bills, by the clearing banks as well as the discount market, continued to grow during the years to 1968, despite the official limitations applying to both types of institution that have been in force for most of the period since 1965. The figures for the banks include refinanceable export credits, which have been rising rapidly and are outside the control of credit restrictions. For the discount market, the application of the control is complex, and houses are required to take into account changes in their portfolios and their rediscounts; thus the continued rise in their holdings has been possible because bills under rediscount have been falling. Moreover, their holdings under this heading included some public sector bills, which were outside the control.

TABLE B16 *Holdings of commercial and other bills* (£m.)*

End of	*London clearing banks*	*Discount market*	*Total*
1960	166	117	283
1961	250	183	433
1962	269	189	458
1963	311	249	560
1964	420	302	722
1965	451	339	790
1966	453	404	857
1967	472	437	909
1968	525†	560	1085

* Holdings of commercial bills and public sector bills other than UK Treasury bills. For the clearing banks, including refinanceable export credits from 1961; for the discount houses, excluding foreign currency bills.
† 11 December.

Among the public sector bills are those issued by local authorities, a form of finance that has been tending to gain favour with some of them in these years. Power to issue bills requires a special local act, and none was passed between 1935 and 1965, although some authorities were then issuing such bills under powers previously obtained. In 1965 Manchester Corporation was authorized to increase the maximum amount of its bills in issue from £1 million to £3 million. Other authorities have since been granted powers of issue, among them the Greater London Council for bills up to a total of £25 million and the Greater London boroughs up to an aggregate total of £30 million. Despite some official restrictions on their issue, local authority bills are rediscountable at the Bank of England and stand outside the official ceiling, and accordingly they are an acceptable form of investment for the discount houses. The banks also are willing to discount them, or to take them as collateral. The yield on them is slightly higher than on Treasury bills.

The discount houses have likewise been investing or acting as jobbers in local authority marketable bonds, included with their 'other assets' which have been rising rapidly in recent years. Under statutory authority given in 1963, local authorities have been issuing bonds with a life of between one and five years, most issues having been for one or two years. Some have gone direct to a discount house or other institution but others have been marketed through the Stock Exchange, in which event they are quoted. Unlike local authority bills, however, bonds are not eligible as security for loans from the Bank of England; accordingly the clearing banks accept them as collateral only to a limited extent and the discount market's holdings are thus restricted.

The Bank of England has become increasingly flexible in the techniques it uses for regulating the day-to-day flow of funds in the discount market. Previously it had bought and sold Treasury bills in the market at market rates, but when lending at last resort it had confined itself to minimum periods of seven days against the security of eligible paper. In mid-1969, apart from a short period just before devaluation of sterling, it has not lent at bank rate for seven days since May 1967. However, in September 1966 it had begun to lend overnight at market rates, and since then it adopted a variety of techniques so as to lend at either current market rates or at bank rate for periods of anything between overnight and seven days, and sometimes to use a mixture of these various techniques on the same day. Exceptionally, in July 1969 the Bank lent at market rates for a period of eighteen days, to bridge the gap between the issue of a new government security and the repayment of two maturing ones.

As a result of such developments, the proportion of the discount market's funds which is shown in the official statistics as being borrowed from the Bank of England was rising until March 1968, but this did not necessarily imply an increase in the amount of assistance given, since lending had to some extent replaced the buying of bills to relieve a shortage of funds. Subsequently such borrowing fell away, but the Bank found that its new techniques gave it closer day-to-day control over money flows.

The Bank of England again broke new ground in February 1969 by buying commercial bills at market rates for the purpose of easing a shortage of funds in the market, and further purchases were made from time to time. Previously the Bank had purchased commercial bills only on a regular sampling basis so as to check the quality of the bills in the market. This development is to be explained by the fall in holdings of Treasury bills.

The various developments so far recorded for the discount houses have in the main related to their traditional lines of business. But possibly of greater significance for the long term have been the moves taken over the past few years towards participation, within the limits imposed by the authorities, in the new money markets. The discount houses have traditionally borrowed from the non-clearing banks, but on a somewhat smaller scale in recent years, as these banks have tended to adjust their liquidity among themselves in the inter-bank market. The discount houses have indeed become occasional lenders to some of the non-clearing banks for very short periods, thus in effect lending in the inter-bank market. Their scope for expanding this activity is limited, however, since the lending is unsecured and generates no paper which can be used for borrowing from the Bank of England.

In 1968 some houses began to operate a market in foreign currency bills of exchange, financing their portfolios by borrowing in the Eurocurrency market. Not all houses were able to participate directly, however, since it was against official policy for those houses with interests in foreign currency broking to act as principals in foreign currency bills. Earlier, several houses had acquired interests in firms of brokers which acted as intermediaries in other new markets. The 'secondary' market in the relatively new certificates of deposit was largely provided by the discount houses. They deal directly in sterling CDs but for dollar CDs those with broking interests deal through these subsidiaries, the others acting directly as principals.

Among those which act through brokers, Cater Ryder has formed Cater (Brokers) Ltd, which acts as brokers in the markets for local authority, finance house, and inter-bank deposits. The same house has acquired M. W. Marshall & Co. Ltd, foreign exchange and currency deposit brokers and has a subsidiary engaged in currency deposit broking in Switzerland. Clive Discount has acquired a 75 per cent shareholding in Guy Butler & Co. Ltd, currency deposit brokers, and a $66\frac{2}{3}$ per cent shareholding in Long, Till & Colvin Ltd, local authority deposit brokers. Union Discount has a 51 per cent share in Roberts Union Co. Ltd, brokers in local authority, finance house and inter-bank deposits. Jessel, Toynbee has acquired a 40 per cent holding in Charles Fulton & Co. Ltd, brokers in the inter-bank and local authority markets and also in the foreign exchange and currency deposit markets. Gerrard & Reid has acquired a 10 per cent holding in P. Murray-Jones Ltd. brokers in the foreign exchange, inter-bank and local authority markets.

No figures of discount market holdings or turnover in the new markets are available, though the growth of their 'other assets', shown in Table B14, relates largely to these activities. Such developments are important, at least potentially, as providing links between the old and the new money markets, and a means by which the discount houses may participate in the activity and growth of the latter. Meanwhile the new arrangements of September 1971 have called for adjustments in practice and techniques (see Chapters 3 and 5).

Continued Expansion in 'Complementary' Markets November 1969

Developments over the three years to August 1969 in the traditional money market – the clearing banks and the discount houses – were examined in the previous section of this chapter. It was noted that the clearing banks had continued to place funds at call and short notice on a secured basis with the discount houses, but that both types of institution had increasingly moved towards greater participation in the other interconnected markets. The clearing banks had done so through subsidiary or affiliated companies, and the discount houses either directly or through interests in brokers.

It is with developments in these other markets that we are now principally concerned, in order to bring up to date the account given in Chapter 6 of the position in 1966. First, however, we revert to the problem of nomenclature. These markets have been variously designated as new, secondary and parallel, but none of these adjectives provides an accurate description and in important respects all of them might be thought misleading. The markets are no longer 'new'. In size they are certainly not secondary and this word is now used – more appropriately – for markets, such as those in certificates of deposits, which deal in paper which has been issued elsewhere. Since so many points of contact with the traditional market are developing, 'parallel' also is becoming a misnomer. But in conjunction with the traditional market they in effect constitute virtually the whole range of outlets for short-term funds, and we propose to call them collectively the 'complementary' markets.

Four of them can be distinguished, though they are closely interconnected, dealing in short-term deposits with local authorities and with instalment finance houses, Eurodollars, and inter-bank sterling balances. Funds may flow between the sterling markets if interest rate differentials arise, though each preserves its special characteristics and funds taken by local authorities and instalment finance companies are employed in their distinctive domestic activities. The eventual borrowers of Eurodollars are largely to be found overseas, since use of this market by domestic borrowers is sometimes restricted. The inter-bank market operates in the liquid balances of the non-clearing banks.

The growth of all the complementary markets has been associated with the development of the accepting houses, overseas and other banks in London. Deposits with these banks were increasing rapidly up to 1966, and expansion since then has been even faster. The total rose by more than three times between the end of 1965 and June 1969 when it exceeded £19,000 million. The contribution of the differing types of banks to be found in this group to the increase has varied, as may be seen from Table B17. Comparison of the figures over the three-year period to June 1969 is complicated by improvements made to the official statistics, by the inclusion of new contributors during the fourth quarter of 1967, and the occasional transfer of individual banks from one category to another. In addition the statistics for foreign currency deposits, being expressed in terms of sterling, are swollen by one sixth at the later of the two dates as a result of the devaluation of sterling in November 1967. Nevertheless, the figures in Table B17 provide broad indications of relative rates of growth.

Although total sterling deposits rose by over 50 per cent over the three years – hardly a slow rate of growth – the expansion of foreign currency deposits by nearly three and a half times was far more striking. Each group of banks increased its foreign currency deposits, the largest sums being taken by the American banks in London, which now hold well over one half of the total non-sterling deposits, an appreciably higher proportion than three years earlier. However, the 'other banks' are able to claim the most rapid percentage rate of growth over the period, both for sterling and non-sterling currencies. This category includes some of the smaller merchant banks, but mainly comprises the special subsidiaries of the clearing banks, mentioned in our previous article. The growth of their sterling deposits, both absolutely and proportionately, answers in part at least the criticisms made at that time of the clearing banks concerning 'competition for deposits'.

The assets and liabilities of the various categories of banks are regularly analysed in considerable detail in *Financial Statistics*, and selected figures for the group as a whole are given in Table B18. This indicates, like the preceding table, that the predominant element of growth over the past three years has been in borrowing and lending in foreign currencies on account of both non-residents and UK banks, reflecting the phenomenal development of the Eurocurrency market. In total, foreign currency liabilities have multiplied more than four times to a sterling equivalent of about £14,500 million. For the rest, loans to local authorities have more than doubled to reach over £1300 million, and sterling deposits of and with UK banks, giving an indication of the size of the inter-bank market, have roughly trebled and are now both in the region of £1200 million. Separate figures for lending to instalment finance companies by the banks covered in the table are not given, but it is clear from other sources that this outlet is quite small relatively, and growth has been inhibited by restrictions on bank lending. Lending to the discount market is also relatively small and has been declining, and in June 1968 was below £150 million.

In general, changes in the assets structures of the various categories of banks have tended to follow the overall pattern indicated in Table B18 fairly closely over the three years to 1969. However, the growth of 'balances with other banks', both in sterling and other currencies, was particularly marked for 'other banks'. The 'other banks' accounted for around one

TABLE B17 *Deposits of accepting houses, overseas and other banks*

	Sterling			*Other currencies*			*Total*		
	June 1966 (£m.)	*June 1969 (£m.)*	*Change %*	*June 1966 (£m.)*	*June 1969 (£m.)*	*Change %*	*June 1966 (£m.)*	*June 1969 (£m.)*	*Change %*
Accepting houses	716	1063	+ *48*	382	1,197	+*213*	1098	2,260	+*106*
British overseas and Commonwealth	1083	1279	+ *18*	766	2,189	+*186*	1849	3,468	+ *88*
American	423	600	+ *42*	1457	8,400	+*477*	1879	9,001	+*379*
Foreign banks and affiliates	261	317	+ *21*	218	908	+*317*	479	1,225	+*156*
Other overseas banks	212	183	− *14*	372	925	+*149*	584	1,108	+ *90*
Other banks	235	1159	+*393*	99	872	+*778*	334	2,032	+*508*
Total	2930	4601	+ *57*	3295	14,492	+*340*	6225	19,093	+*207*

TABLE B18 *Accepting houses, overseas and other banks, selected liabilities and assets (£m.)*

	Dec. 1965	*Dec. 1966*	*Dec. 1967*	*Dec. 1968*	*June 1969*
Liabilities					
Deposits:					
UK banks					
Sterling	366	484	736	1,059	1,190
Other currencies	684	920	1575	1,947	3,641
Other UK residents					
Sterling	1046	1159	1571	1,939	2,062
Other currencies	90	122	219	277	371
Overseas residents					
Sterling	1356	1250	1186	1,084	1,069
Other currencies	2042	2793	4061	6,523	9,454
Negotiable certificates of deposit:					
Sterling	—	—	—	165	281
Dollars	—	81	249	597	1,026
Total	5584	6807	9597	13,591	19,093
Assets					
Balances with other banks:					
Sterling	421	510	760	1123	1,281
Other currencies	629	835	1475	1848	3,520
Call money to discount market	248	198	210	182	143
Treasury bills	80	61	80	47	47
Loans to local authorities	565	527	796	1104	1,308
Government securities	512	557	558	461	243
Advances:					
to UK residents					
Sterling	912	934	1040	1164	1,186
Other currencies	136	154	280	476	536
to Overseas residents					
Sterling	377	278	258	241	206
Other currencies	1786	2771	4055	6738	10,140

half of the large increase in lending to local authorities; by contrast, lending for this purpose by 'other overseas banks' and by 'foreign banks and affiliates' showed little net change. Nearly two thirds of total advances were accounted for by the American banks, against less than one half in 1966; the bulk of this was non-sterling lending to overseas residents, indicated the predominance of these banks in the Eurodollar market.

The accepting houses and other banks do not as a rule seek the funds of small customers, but offer competitive rates in order to attract sums in large amounts, thus establishing the pattern for the four markets considered separately. Deposits are taken for varying periods both to suit the needs of the depositor and to meet lending commitments, and the accounts on which such deposits were held were accordingly not strictly comparable with those maintained with clearing banks. They had, however, proved competitive with the deposit accounts of the clearing banks, particularly in respect of fluctuating cash balances of large companies. Deposits of all kinds by UK resident companies with the deposit banks – mainly the clearing banks and their counterparts in Scotland and Northern Ireland – fell on balance from £1784 million in June 1966 to £1679 million in June 1969, while those with the accepting houses, overseas and other banks rose from £713 million to £1307 million, continuing their earlier growth.

In 1966 some of these banks began to issue negotiable certificates of deposit denominated in dollars, a convenient way of raising funds for periods of up to five years. The amount outstanding rose rapidly, in the first half of 1969 from nearly £600 million to over £1000 million. A secondary market in them had been developed, although its growth was inhibited by rising interest rates which have depressed prices. Certificates were issued by some of the subsidiaries and associates of the clearing banks, but not the clearing banks themselves, and also by many overseas banks particularly the US banks.

Since October 1968 a number of non-clearing banks had also been making available negotiable certificates of deposit denominated in sterling. These have no special advantages for the issuing banks, but companies and others can thereby receive the current rate of interest for months or years to come, while maintaining a higher degree of liquidity than is afforded by fixed deposits. Negotiability of the new instrument, like the dollar CD, depends on the development of a 'secondary' market in which certificates can readily be bought and sold, and this has been provided by discount houses, thus making a further link between them and the complementary markets. Five of them are operating as brokers through subsidiary companies and the other seven deal directly on their own account. The certificates are similar to those issued in the dollar market in that they are unsecured and are in bearer form, but the minimum amount is £50,000. In order to prevent unauthorized switching out of sterling by sterling area resident holders they must be held by an Authorized Depositary. Certificates may be issued for periods of from three months up to five years, though by 1969 most had been for up to one year.

Since they were first made available interest rates have been tending to rise, so that potential purchasers have been reluctant to commit their funds at a fixed rate for a fixed period ahead, but even so the amount of certificates outstanding rose from £165 million in December 1968 to £323 million in

September 1969. Part of this was no doubt held by the discount houses so as to ensure their ability to operate the secondary market activities, but otherwise holdings were thought to be largely confined to financial institutions and companies; those of overseas residents amounted to only £37 million in June 1969.

The introduction of sterling CDs was facilitated and indeed encouraged by the authorities, but some of their rulings did not help the development of the market. Thus CDs were not eligible security for last resort borrowing by the discount market, and holdings of clearing banks could not be regarded as liquid assets in calculating liquidity ratios. As for the issuing banks themselves, certificates will be treated as ordinary deposit liabilities for the purposes of the Cash Deposits Scheme if this is brought into operation for non-clearing banks. Should the clearing banks decide to issue them then they would be subject to the Special Deposits requirements, and presumably to cash and liquidity ratios. To mitigate these drawbacks, some issuers of sterling CDs have agreed to provide limited standby facilities, for use in exceptional circumstances, to the secondary market in respect of their own issues, thus in effect undertaking to act to some extent as lenders of last resort. The clearing banks undertook to accept from the discount market limited quantities of certificates, other than issues of their own subsidiaries or affiliates, in substitution for other 'eligible' securities held against call money.

Local authorities represent one of the main outlets for funds raised in the complementary markets. In competing for deposits, they have an advantage in that their borrowing is secured on the local rate revenue and has trustee status. Since early in 1969 they have been permitted to pay interest gross to depositors before deduction of tax where the deposit is for less than one year, thereby bringing the local authority market into line with practice in the other money markets. Brokers were active in handling funds for placing with local authorities.

At the short end of the local authority market the terms might be overnight, repayment at call, or at two or seven days' notice on either side. For longer-term funds raised against deposit receipts, terms were usually for a minimum stated period of say one, three or six months and thereafter at seven days' notice, or alternatively for fixed periods of up to 364 days. The minimum sum taken on deposit was usually £50,000 although smaller amounts could be negotiated. At the other end of the scale sums of £500,000 to £1 million were frequently seen, while much larger amounts were sometimes arranged. With sums of this magnitude being borrowed and lent for short periods, so as to sustain a large outstanding total, the turnover of funds in this market is great.

The development of this market has largely reflected changes in official policy towards local authority borrowing, which at first stimulated its growth but for several years to 1969 has been attempting to limit it. In the years following 1955, when the role of the Public Works Loan Board was reduced to virtually that of lender of last resort, the market grew rapidly but subsequently it slowed down considerably; since 1964 the authorities have enjoyed access to borrowing from the Exchequer through the PWLB within quota limits and to a further extent at higher rates of interest. Since 1967 the Board's rates for borrowing have reflected the appropriate government lending rates; for some time previously quota rates had been a little below market levels.

Local authorities continued to raise funds in the new capital issues market, though few issues came forward during 1969. Issues of negotiable bonds became popular after general statutory consent was given to this type of borrowing in 1963, but the flow of such issues remained controlled by the Bank of England, and increasingly the funds raised were used to repay earlier maturing issues, these mostly having been made for only one- or two-year periods. The government indicated in 1969 that it wished to encourage local authorities to meet some of their capital requirements by borrowing abroad, thus opening up a new channel of finance. So far only one authority – Derbyshire County Council – has raised a foreign currency loan, for Deutschmarks 50 million, or the equivalent of a little over £5 million.

Despite these developments local authorities continued to rely heavily upon temporary borrowing–that is for periods up to one year–although the central government had been bringing such borrowing under restriction for several years past. Each authority was expected to bring its total of temporary debt to not more than 20 per cent of total outstanding loan debt, and the amount repayable in three months or less to not more than 15 per cent. These requirements were to have been met by March 1968, but the period was extended until March 1969. As at 31 March 1968 local authorities in aggregate were already meeting the 20 per cent requirement but it was thought that about 300 were still in excess of the limit, and that about £250 million of funding was necessary to bring them all into line.

Early in 1966, following several years of rapid growth, outstanding temporary debt of local authorities amounted to about £1700 million, of which around 70 per cent was repayable within seven days. As may be seen from Table B19 the total has subsequently fluctuated, but at the end of June 1969 it was £2122 million, of which £1649 million, or nearly four fifths, was repayable in up to seven days. Bank overdrafts, which fluctuated rather more than sums from other sources, accounted for only £169 million against £141 million a year earlier and £56 million recorded in March 1966. The total for temporary debt included £527 million of 'other loans' from banks in June 1969, when the accepting houses, overseas and other banks are shown as lending £1308 million to local authorities, suggesting that much of their borrowing from these banks is for periods of more than one year. For shorter periods, financial institutions other than banks were providing £474 million in June 1969, industrial and commercial companies £315 million, and the

TABLE B19 *Local authority temporary debt (£m.)*

	Banks		*Other financial institutions*	*Industrial and commercial companies*	*Personal sector*	*Other (inc. inter-authority debt)*	*Total*
	Over-drafts	*Other loans*					
1965							
March	147	404	212	506	314	264	1847
1966							
March	56	332	372	384	325	259	1728
1967							
March	54	382	326	334	303	321	1720
1968							
March	174	491	353	410	334	311	2073
1969							
March	133	501	438	312	330	309	2023
June	169	527	474	315	343	294	2122

personal sector £343 million; as compared with three years previously, borrowing from other financial institutions tended to rise slightly and that from industrial and commercial companies to fall slightly.

In general the instalment finance houses seek to attract relatively large amounts from institutional and other corporate lenders. Deposits are commonly arranged for three or six months, with the rate of interest for the period of the deposit fixed at the outset and not linked to bank rate. The rates offered vary according to the term and size of the deposit, and also, since deposits are unsecured, according to the size and standing of the house; those with clearing bank connections will generally be in a position to offer the finest rates. Most large houses obtain their deposits through brokers or otherwise without advertising. Occasionally finance houses may themselves have surplus funds but these may then be on-lent elsewhere in other markets.

In 1966 the market for deposits with instalment finance houses was probably the smallest of the four – precise comparison is difficult – and it was more clearly so in 1969. Indeed, total funds employed there had tended to fall slightly on balance from around £1000 million to a little more than £900 million, probably because this market suffered from official restraints more than any of the others. Lending by finance houses had been restricted throughout the period; by late in 1969 it was still not allowed to rise above 98 per cent of the level at end-October 1967. Moreover, the terms of hire purchase contracts for consumer durable goods – the main outlet for their funds – had been generally tightened by increasing the minimum deposit and shortening the maximum repayment period. Having no scope for developing outlets for their resources, finance houses were not concerned to increase their borrowing. Moreover, one of their means of borrowing is through bills drawn under acceptance credits with non-clearing banks, which are usually discounted by the acceptor and may then be sold to the discount market. These bills were affected by the ceiling placed by the authorities on bill discounting, and so their total remained virtually unchanged, on balance, at a little over £100 million.

About two thirds of the resources of instalment finance companies comprise deposits, the total of which rose to a peak of over £700 million in 1966, but has since fallen on balance to £638 million in June 1969, having been below £600 million at times. A breakdown of deposits with finance companies is given in Table B20, which shows that of the total at end-June 1969, £293 million had come from industrial and commercial companies, £205 million

TABLE B20 *Deposits with hire purchase finance companies (£m.)*

End of June	*United Kingdom*					
	Banks	*Other financial institutions*	*Industrial and commercial companies*	*Other residents*	*Overseas residents*	*Total*
1965	135	64	228	96	111	634
1966	109	81	257	105	152	704
1967	103	65	219	104	130	621
1968	104	63	254	106	71	598
1969	107	98	293	107	33	638

from banks and other financial institutions and £107 million from other UK residents. This pattern had not changed greatly over the years, but deposits of overseas residents had fallen sharply, to only £33 million in June 1969 from a peak of £152 million in mid-1966.

The Eurocurrency market – predominantly in Eurodollars – by 1969 was by far the largest of the four complementary markets, and also the most complex in its ramifications, since it was and is part of an international market in foreign currency deposits. Its interaction with the various sterling markets involves switching between Eurodollars and sterling. However, the basis of the market is the taking of deposits denominated in foreign currencies and the on-lending of them in the same form. Such business is conducted to some extent by most of the various banks in London, including the clearing banks, although they tend to operate through their special subsidiaries rather than directly.

As in the other markets, dealings are commonly arranged through brokers, some of them foreign exchange brokers. Transactions are in large round amounts, typically in units of $1 million, though they may occasionally be for sums as small as $100,000. Deposits may be placed for periods ranging from call, up to two years, or occasionally longer, though the bulk are probably for between two days and three months. They may be renewed on maturity, at the then current rate. Banks relend to other banks with a fairly fine margin; if the funds are lent outside the market a larger margin is required.

The available statistics are more difficult to interpret than those for local authorities and finance houses, in particular because resources are often on-lent a number of times between banks. It is apparent, however, that it is this market which has shown by far the most rapid growth over the three years to 1969. Moreover, the market in London is only the major part of an international market in foreign currency holdings, predominantly but not exclusively dollars, and dealings also take place in a number of other European centres. Apart from US dollars, the currencies most commonly handled on the London market are Deutschmarks and Swiss francs.

The Bank for International Settlements in its annual report for 1968–9 estimated that at the end of 1968 the volume of Eurocurrencies had already expanded to $30,000 million; at the corresponding point in time the external liabilities and claims of UK banks in foreign currencies, as published by the Bank of England, both amounted to the equivalent of about £7000 million or $18–19,000 million. At the end of June 1969 the UK figures were over £10,500 million or $25,000 million – against £2100 million or so at the end of 1965 – with £9441 million denominated in US dollars. However, the UK totals cannot be directly related to the BIS aggregates because of differences in the computation of the statistics. In particular, the UK figures include working balances of foreign currencies held by the banks for normal exchange operations.

The Bank of England series also differ substantially from those given to illustrate the activities of the accepting houses and other banks in Table B18. The principal difference is in the treatment of liabilities and claims denominated in currencies of overseas sterling area countries; they are not included in Tables B21 and B22. These show the external liabilities and claims in non-sterling currencies of UK banks, these including all the non-clearing banks as well as the offices in London of foreign banks. They provide some indication of the size, growth and nature of the Eurocurrency market in London at that time.

Broadly speaking, the figures in the tables for UK liabilities represent Eurocurrency deposits and UK claims are Eurocurrencies that have been on-lent. The totals for claims also include the floats of foreign currencies that are normally held by British banks, so that if all Eurocurrency deposits were on-lent, the total of claims would exceed that of liabilities. In practice, some

TABLE B 21 *External liabilities and claims of UK banks in non-sterling currencies (analysis by currencies) (£m.)*

End of period	*US dollars*	*Other non-sterling currencies*	*Total*
UK liabilities			
1965	1893	229	2,122
1966	2727	275	3 002
1967	4037	345	4,382
1968	6402	729	7,131
1969			
March	7457	769	8,226
June	9441	1066	10,507
UK claims			
1965	1624	356	1,980
1966	2611	409	3,020
1967	3836	538	4,374
1968	6242	867	7,109
1969			
March	7340	878	8,218
June	9332	1205	10,537
Net liabilities (+) *or claims* (−)			
1965	+269	−127	+142
1966	+116	−134	− 18
1967	+201	−193	+ 8
1968	+160	−138	+ 22
1969			
March	+117	−109	+ 8
June	+109	−139	− 30

Eurocurrencies will be switched into sterling, rather than on-lent, thus resulting in a net liability position. It will be seen that net liabilities have generally been small, and in June 1969 they gave way to a net claim position, although for US dollars liabilities exceed claims by £109 million. The figures suggest that switching into sterling – never substantial – had been largely eliminated by 1969, a development attributable in part to uncertainties about the exchange parities but perhaps more to interest rate differentials. Eurodollars may be switched into sterling when short-term sterling interest rates – particularly on deposits with local authorities – exceed those on Eurodollars, allowing for the cost of covering the foreign exchange risk in the forward market. At least since the devaluation of sterling in November 1967, a covered switch out of Eurodollars into sterling would have been unprofitable by a varying and occasionally wide margin.

TABLE B22 *External liabilities and claims of UK banks in non-sterling currencies (analysis by area of holder) (£m.)*

End of period	*Overseas sterling area*	*North America*	*Western Europe*	*Other*	*Total*
UK liabilities					
1965	125	365	1165	467	2,122
1966	200	549	1692	561	3,002
1967	298	912	2413	759	4,382
1968	543	1624	3917	1053	7,137
1969					
March	662	1864	4321	1379	8,226
June	839	2396	5678	1594	10,507
UK claims					
1965	24	630	916	410	1,980
1966	39	1337	1161	483	3,020
1967	99	1854	1452	969	4,374
1968	177	3260	2161	1511	7,109
1969					
March	250	4348	2082	1538	8,218
June	313	6032	2649	1543	10,537
Net liabilities (+) *or claims* (−)					
1965	+101	−265	+249	+ 57	+142
1966	+161	−788	+531	+ 78	− 18
1967	+199	−942	+961	−210	+ 8
1968	+366	−1636	+1756	+458	+ 28
1969					
March	+412	−2484	+2239	−159	+ 8
June	+526	−3636	+3029	+ 51	− 30

Until a few years prior to 1969, UK residents other than banks were not allowed to borrow foreign currencies. Banks could switch Eurocurrencies into sterling, but the total of their sterling lending was restricted, so effectively British borrowers had no access to the pool of Eurocurrencies. Thereafter, the restrictions on the borrowing of currencies, other than by authorized banks, were progressively eased by administrative action. At first, borrowing in the Eurodollar market was sometimes permitted in order to finance direct capital investment overseas (this amounted to £35 million in the first quarter of 1969 and £15 million in the second). Later, it was permitted to borrow Eurodollars and switch them into sterling for financing domestic capital investment. By November 1969 this could be done for almost any domestic purpose for which sterling lending by banks might be used if its total were not restricted. Switching into sterling leaves the borrower with an exchange risk, which he could cover in the forward market only for the last quarter of the period of the loan and then only up to a maximum of six months. Although this development is important in principle, the total sums involved were still comparatively small, to judge from the figures of switching quoted above.

In Table B22 net liabilities and claims are analysed according to the area of the holder. This shows the extent to which foreign currencies had been borrowed from various countries and on-lent to others, in particular the great growth in the on-lending of Eurodollars, coming from western European countries, back to the United States from 1965 to 1969.

During 1969 some concern was expressed about the implications of the rapid growth of the Eurodollar market, associated with the continuing deficits in the United States balance of payments, while the high and generally rising rates in the Eurodollar market attracted to it an increasing proportion of dollars held outside the United States. Although there is no lender of last resort to the market, a number of central banks have at times used various techniques which have had the effect of making some of their dollar holdings available to it. Although they have done this partly for their own domestic reasons, it has seemed at times as if they, along with the Bank of International Settlements, have come to accept some responsibility for the orderliness of the market, conducting open market operations there if not formally undertaking to act as lender of last resort.

Perhaps of wider concern was the effect on interest rates on Eurodollars of their repatriation to the United States, mainly through the London offices of United States banks. Because of the continuing control of some domestic interest rates under Regulation Q, at a time when others have been rising sharply, US banks were unable to prevent a reduction in their domestic borrowings, particularly against certificates of deposit, and they have sought to maintain their resources by the repatriation of Eurodollars. This process was facilitated because at that time borrowings from their London offices carried no reserve obligation; since October 1969, however, the US Federal Reserve has imposed a 10 per cent reserve requirement on the amount by which such Eurodollar borrowing exceeds the May 1969 level. The amount repatriated rose sharply from a little over $5000 million at the end of 1968 to about $14,000 million in June 1969, at about which level it has since remained. Interest rates on three-month Eurodollars rose to well over 11 per cent in June 1969, though they later fell to rather more than 9 per cent.

Pressures in the Eurodollar market have affected interest rates in other centres, and especially in those countries where holders of domestic currencies have been permitted to switch into Eurodollars. As a result some countries placed limits on Eurocurrency activities across their borders. The central bank in the Netherlands in July 1969 imposed controls over the level of banks' net foreign exchange positions, a reduction of 10 per cent being called for in the second half of that year. Earlier in 1969 similar measures were introduced in Belgium, and in Italy banks were instructed to liquidate their foreign currency positions by end-June.

The development of the other markets in short-term funds, and the comparatively high rates of interest established in them, provided the main impetus for the progress of the sterling inter-bank market, as used by the non-clearing banks to adjust their liquidity positions from day to day and indeed throughout the day.

For these banks, numbering perhaps well over 150 against a hundred or so in 1966, cash includes balances with the clearing banks. Previously they had adjusted their positions by selling and buying bills and by calling in funds from, or lending to, the discount market against security, as the clearers do. As the other short-term markets grew, their cash positions became increasingly liable to rapid and substantial fluctuations, and correspondingly they sought speedier and more flexible methods of adjustment. Moreover, the volume of funds placed in the traditional market, where rates are lower than elsewhere, declined, thus reducing the scope for adjustment through this channel.

In 1969 the main way in which the non-clearing banks adjusted their liquidity positions was by lending and borrowing clearing bank balances between themselves on an unsecured basis, in other words in the inter-bank market. They placed there short-term funds for which no immediate or suitable outlet was seen elsewhere thus providing a cushion of liquidity for the other money markets.

Deals in the inter-bank market were generally arranged through brokers, including foreign exchange brokers and some specialized houses set up since the business began to develop. Most of the transactions were for short periods, the great bulk of funds being lent for periods of fourteen days or less, including substantial sums which were lent on an overnight basis, although some lending was for up to about six months. In the inter-bank market the minimum sums which are lent are commonly £50,000 or £100,000 and round sums up to £1 million are typical; amounts of £2 million or over are not often seen as large sums on offer are spread.

As with the Eurodollar market, no statistics are available which relate solely and comprehensively to the inter-bank market. However, a rough indication of its size is provided by the sterling deposits held by the non-clearing banks for other UK banks as recorded in Table B18. Such deposits used to consist entirely of working balances, held mainly with the clearing banks, but by 1969 they mainly reflected operations in the inter-bank market, although some multiple counting may occur when funds are on-lent several times. At the end of 1965, when the inter-bank market was already well under way, the total was under £400 million, but by 1969 it was in the region of £1200 million.

An important respect in which the complementary markets and the traditional market differed is the way in which interest rates were determined. In the traditional market they continued to be closely related to bank rate until 1971, but the operations of the Bank of England had only a limited effect on the complementary markets, where the links with bank rate were becoming increasingly tenuous. In 1966 it was possible to indicate a typical – though by no means invariable – structure of rates in the complementary markets, which was generally based upon bank rate. By 1969, it was no longer possible to discern such a pattern, and the direct influence of bank rate seemed to have diminished. Factors that have grown in importance – apart from technical ones depending upon the day of the month – are the rates obtainable day by day on other short-dated fixed-interest investments, such as government securities, sterling CDs and yearling bonds, the yields on which are mainly determined by market circumstances.

It is the general practice for a rate in the complementary markets to be quoted and fixed for the period of the deposit, so that if bank rate changes during the period, the rates on outstanding transactions are not altered. Even so, at that time some account had still to be taken of bank rate in arranging new transactions, because of competition with the traditional market, where it was then the dominating influence. Accordingly operators in the complementary markets tended to take a view as to the next change in bank rate and go shorter or longer – as the case may be – thus affecting the spread between longer and shorter rates there. More generally, with the increasing tightness of money during 1969, the margin between rates in the complementary markets and those in the traditional market widened.

Even in the local authority market – the one in which bank rate has probably the most influence – the difference between bank rate and rates offered on say three-month deposits has ranged from around nil to over 2 per cent, and in the market for finance house deposits the margins over bank rate tended to be greater still, as may be seen from Table B23.

Rates in the inter-bank market became particularly volatile, varying greatly from day to day and during the course of each day. During 1968–9 fluctuations became greater, with some particularly high rates – 20 per cent and even much higher for overnight money – having been recorded at times of international currency crisis, and over the half-year ends when funds for 'window-dressing' purposes were in strong demand. At the other extreme, the overnight rate was as low as 1 per cent on one occasion earlier in 1969 and it has become impossible to trace any direct relationship with bank rate.

In the Eurodollar market the rates have been determined by international influences. As already noted, rates have been forced up considerably during 1968–9, and tended to exert upward pressure on domestic interest rates in leading industrial countries. Until late in 1968 the three-month Eurodollar rate remained below the United Kingdom bank rate but the position thereafter

TABLE B23 *Interest rates per cent per annum (end of period)*

	1964	1965	1966	1967	1968				1969		
					Mar.	*June*	*Sept.*	*Dec.*	*Mar.*	*June*	*Oct.*
Bank rate	7·00	6·00	7·00	8·00	7·50	7·50	7·00	7·00	8·00	8·00	8·00
Clearing banks											
deposit rate	5·00	4·00	5·00	6·00	5·50	5·50	5·00	5·00	6·00	6·00	6·00
call money rate*	5·375	4·375	5·375	6·25	5·875	5·875	5·375	5·375	6·25	6·375	6·375
Treasury bills (yield)	6·74	5·60	6·64	7·62	7·24	7·37	6·69	6·90	7·93	8·04	7·90
Bank bills (3 months)	6·84	5·91	6·91	7·78	7·41	7·66	6·97	7·28	8·41	8·88	8·88
Deposits with local authorities											
(7 days)	8·00	6·25	7·38	8·44	9·00	8·13	7·44	7·25	8·69	8·69	8·75
(3 months)	7·69	6·38	7·28	7·63	8·06	8·13	7·40	7·75	8·88	9·38	9·06
Deposits with finance houses											
(3 months)	7·69	6·56	7·38	8·19	8·75	8·50	7·56	8·00	9·13	9·81	9·81
(6 months)	7·63	6·75	7·44	8·25	8·00	8·50	7·56	8·13	9·19	9·94	9·88
Eurodollar deposits											
(3 months)	4·50	5·25	7·75	6·31	6·38	6·88	6·25	7·13	8·53	10·56	10·00

* Minimum.

was reversed and during 1969 it has risen above most of the prevailing rates in the other short-term markets. Direct comparisons are of little value without taking into account the fluctuating cost of forward exchange cover.

With the sharp upward trend in interest rates generally during the first half of 1969, the margin between rates in the traditional and other markets tended to widen. One consequence was that the clearing banks' 'blue chip' rate – until then ½ per cent above bank rate – moved increasingly out of line with the rates at which funds could be placed elsewhere at short term. This margin was one reason given by the authorities for increasing bank rate from 7 to 8 per cent in February 1969. However, rates in the complementary markets also rose, and the previous margins were broadly maintained. In October 1969, the clearing banks raised their lending rates by ½ per cent, while still keeping them linked to bank rate, which was not altered.

The size of the various short-term markets can be estimated only with varying degrees of precision and no indication of the volume of turnover can be given, although it must be large because of the short-term nature of the transactions. However, it may be noted that the amounts passing through the 'Town Clearing' of the clearing banks – through which most of the transactions of these markets pass – rose from £168,000 million in 1960 to £347,000 million in 1965 and £516,000 million in 1968 – a faster rate of expansion than other clearings. An attempt to indicate the growth of the resources employed in each of the markets is given in Table B24.

TABLE B24 *Order of magnitude of resources of short-term markets (£m.)*

		end-1965	*June 1969*
Discount houses	(total resources)	1400	1,600
Local authorities	(see Table B19)	1700	2,100
Finance houses	(see Table B20)	600	600
Eurocurrencies	(see Tables B21 and B22)	2000	10,500
Inter-bank market	(see Table B18)	350	1,200

From the foregoing account, it will be apparent that the various complementary markets, though differing somewhat in origin and purpose, are in a number of respects similar. Each deals in short-term deposits – mainly very short, except for finance houses. Transactions are specially arranged through brokers, mainly on an unsecured basis. Rates of interest fluctuate throughout each day, in accordance with supply and demand. Funds may flow between them if interest rate differentials arise.

Some of them grew rapidly in the years to 1969, but temporary borrowing by local authorities by then was restricted to a proportion of their total borrowing, and so could not expand at a more rapid rate, though a steady upward movement could be maintained. Development of finance house business was held in check by the limitation on lending, though the prospects seemed to favour long-term growth. A return of US interest rates to more normal levels, coupled with the recent imposition of reserve requirements upon Eurodollar borrowings, might moderate the remarkable rate of expansion of the Eurodollar market. The inter-bank market, which facilitates operations in the other markets, and presumably its rate of growth, could be influenced by that of the others.

However, all four markets were firmly established, and settling down to a steadier rate of long-term growth, with the development of further links of various kinds with the traditional market. The next stage in their development would be in the setting of the new arrangements for regulating monetary conditions, as recorded in Chapter 5.

SECTION C

The Annual Monetary Surveys

(The years are for the twelve months to April)

8

Stimulation and Expansion

1959 – Stimulation

The outstanding feature of the story of monetary developments during the year to April 1959 was to be seen in a definite change in the condition of Britain's economy and a corresponding change in government policy. Broadly speaking, until the middle of 1958 the efforts of the authorities were still mainly directed to restraining inflationary trends, with a close watch on movements in the exchange value of sterling. Thereafter, the slackening in trade at home, with a rising trend in the figures of unemployment and other signs of incipient recession, called for measures to stimulate business activity – measures which were rendered possible by the sustained strength of sterling abroad. In the early part of 1959 further measures of stimulation were applied, not least among them being those announced in the budget. Even in April 1958, however, it was becoming clear that the level of business activity was declining and that the outlook was far from promising. In fact conditions worsened, and as a result the direction of the government's financial policy radically altered, and many of the controls imposed during the previous four years were relaxed or abolished.

Two aspects of the situation were generally felt to be disturbing: first, the rise in unemployment and under-employment, and secondly, the evidence that the utilization of plant and equipment was well below capacity. The number of registered unemployed increased from 444,000 in April 1958 to 621,000 in January 1959, and a marked rise occurred in the number out of work for more than eight weeks. Some improvement took place in February and March, when the number out of work fell to 550,000 or 2½ per cent of the working population, but overtime working had diminished and short-time working increased. Meanwhile, references to plants running below capacity increased; as a general indication of the position, new investment in industrial equipment was estimated to have added about 15 per cent to capacity since 1955, but the volume of output was virtually unchanged. Again, the number of unfilled vacancies, which had not exceeded the number of unemployed since October 1957, continued to fall, to as low as 154,000 in February 1959, though here some rise was recorded in March.

By the spring of 1959 it seemed that the downward trend in business activity had been prevented from merging into a sharp recession, but that a definite upward trend had failed to develop. The Council on Prices, Productivity and Incomes, in its second report issued in August, had noted that a slackening in demand had been required in order to strengthen the balance of payments and bring about greater stability in prices, and suggested that official policies had justified themselves on these tests. It was plain, however, as the Council had in mind, that a change in policy was now required, particularly as in a number of areas the proportion of unemployed was well above the national average. Some of the government's measures to restore activity were designed to provide direct aid for districts where unemployment persisted at a relatively high level.

Although from the middle of 1958 official policy turned towards expansion, it did so cautiously, always with an eye on the possibility of a recurrence of inflationary trends. In November, for example, the Chancellor of the Exchequer stressed the care that was being taken to avoid setting in motion another inflationary movement, adding: 'If I were to see signs of that danger at any time I should not hesitate to take what counter action was necessary.' The governor of the Bank of England was equally firm. Speaking in October, he declared his conviction that over the longer term, 'the next decade or so', the monetary authorities, 'in their task of helping to create conditions for sound and steady development . . . will be more often required to restrain than to force the pace'. At times, therefore, there might be 'something of a dilemma between short-term and longer-term aims. In the short-term we must try to prevent the economy, only recently recovering from long years of overstrain, from running down fast or far: but in meeting this threat we must not build in new hostages to inflation in later years.' Again in March 1959 he said that he thought the main future preoccupation would be the moderation of inflationary pressures.

The authorities sought to promote business activity mainly by stimulating demand for consumer goods and by enlarging public capital expenditures. The government, anxious to avoid any risk of renewed inflation, applied its measures tentatively. As is noted below (p. 206), the reductions in bank rate were described as 'technical adjustments' or as following the market, and not as measures of expansion. Hire purchase controls were lifted in two stages, the end of controls coming barely six weeks after the first relaxation. Restrictions on new issues of capital were eased and then, some months later, largely removed, but the Capital Issues Committee was kept in being. In July bank lending was released from quantitative controls, but this step was accompanied by the announcement of a quite new form of regulation to be held in reserve.

It was the removing of quantitative controls over bank advances that was widely interpreted as marking unmistakably the change in direction in official policy. A number of small relaxations had been announced earlier, but on 3 July the new course was made clear when the Chancellor of the Exchequer announced the withdrawal, as from the end of that month, of the limitation on the total of bank advances that had been imposed in the previous September. He said that he hoped in future to dispense with the use of quantitative requests of this kind to banks as an instrument of monetary control, but that a new system of Special Deposits with the Bank of England would be made available temporarily to supplement other controls, pending consideration of any recommendations that might be forthcoming from the Radcliffe Committee.

At the same time, a new order restored to £50,000 the limit on borrowing that could be undertaken without reference to the Capital Issues Committee; it had been reduced to £10,000 in March 1956. Some loopholes in the regulations were blocked and bonus issues exempted from control, except where the issue of redeemable securities was involved. A new memorandum of guidance to the Committee left it free to take 'a longer view of proposals' and released it from the obligation to concern itself with the appropriateness of bank finance, where this was proposed, for capital purposes. Applications from hire purchase companies should be 'critically scrutinized', but could now be approved if they were considered 'desirable as a means of improving the stability of the hire purchase financial system'.

The relaxation proved to be only a step towards, in effect, decontrol. In February 1959 the control of borrowing and the issue of securities was lifted by a general consent given under the Control of Borrowing Order, 1958 (an order which consolidated all previous orders). Specific consent continued to be required for bonus issues of redeemable securities (and, in March, control over the issue of redeemable securities for capitalization of reserves was extended to include operations with a nominal value below £50,000), for borrowing by local authorities and for any transactions by undertakings resident outside Britain. The timing of larger issues was still to be arranged with the Bank of England so as to preserve an orderly market. With this wholesale removal of restrictions, bank advances also were released from qualitative as well as quantitative controls.

Passing from capital and credit controls, in September 1958 a wide range of goods was exempted from regulations concerning the minimum cash payment and maximum credit period in hire purchase transactions. It ncluded industrial plant, agricultural machinery, heavy commercial vehicles, and domestic or personal equipment such as furniture, carpets, cookers, bicycles and motorcycles. For the other goods, principally cars, radio and television sets, washing machines, refrigerators, shop and office furniture, aircraft and ships, the statutory minimum deposit was fixed at $33\frac{1}{3}$ per cent of the price – a reduction for all items except cars – the maximum period of repayment remaining at twenty-four months. For rental arrangements, goods still controlled were to be available on payment of four months rent in advance instead of nine months as previously, and all goods more than three years old were exempted from control. Again the relaxation was followed quickly by decontrol. At the end of October 1958 the restrictions on the terms of hire purchase transactions and rental agreements were lifted.

The bank rate had been reduced in March 1958 from the 'crisis' level of 7 per cent to 6, and the next fall, on 22 May, was by only one half per cent to $5\frac{1}{2}$. The shallow step down indicated official caution, which was emphasized by the fact that the reduction could have been justified on market grounds for some time previously and that it should not be taken as a 'green light' or measure against depression. No explanation at all was made on 19 June when a further fall to 5 per cent – already discounted in the market – was announced. This was the level at which bank rate had stood before the steep rise in September 1957, and it was inferred that the authorities did not expect lower interest rates to contribute largely to economic expansion, the reduction merely expressing the thought that high rates were no longer necessary to defend sterling. When a further one half per cent reduction was announced on 14 August it was semi-officially described as in line with the credit relaxation announced in the previous month, although again it was stressed that the change could be justified on technical grounds. The last change, to 4 per cent – the lowest level since early in 1955 – was made on 20 November, and once more this was explained as a technical adjustment which should not be interpreted as a further step towards expansion.

By now, however, it had become widely accepted that the lowering of bank rate had some part in the general tactics of re-expansion. In addition, with bank rate at 4 per cent the gilt-edged market was strengthened in preparation for the conversion of 2 per cent Conversion Stock due in January. Throughout the seven-to-four period the authorities continued to 'fund' government securities by sales from official holdings to investors. These tended to sustain the long-term rate of interest at a relatively high level, as did the sales which some banks undertook, in the last month or two of the period, in order to make room for growing advances. The widening margin between short- and long-term rates in turn brought difficulties (see p. 214), and expectations of a still lower bank rate were falsified. In January the governor of the Bank of England said, in reference to bank rate: 'We are now more comfortably poised at a level from which we can move in either direction, upwards or downwards, as circumstances may require.'

If the purpose of lowering bank rate was not clearly expansionary, at any rate on the literal reading of semi-official utterances, the enlargement of public outlays was expressly directed to this end, as had been the relaxations in controls. During the summer and autumn of 1958, upward revisions were announced in the rate of expenditure on capital investment programmes under the influence of the government. For example, the railway modernization programme was speeded up; spending on roads and electricity development was accelerated; and plans for increased school building and enlarged investment by the Post Office were published. In addition, the Minister of Housing and Local Government advised local authorities that capital projects, including schemes for water supply and sewerage as well as housing, that could be completed by the end of 1959 would be sympathetically considered, especially for areas of high unemployment. The Chancellor of the Exchequer explained that the intention was to take advantage of easier economic conditions to bring forward some expenditure that would otherwise have had to be incurred later. Thus the increase in public investment was regarded as filling a gap at that time expected to result from a diminution in private capital expenditure in 1959. In February he said that plans for increased public capital expenditure were being carried out, and that it looked as if total outlays might prove to be higher than had been forecast; in his budget speech he spoke of an increase by nearly £200 million.

Other measures also involved increased public outlays. Fresh legislation provided government assistance for 'small farmers'; and finance was proposed for building societies, conforming with stated requirements, to assist them in granting mortgages on older properties. The Distribution of Industry (Industrial Finance) Act gave the Treasury power to make loans and grants 'for purposes likely to provide more work in places where a high rate of unemployment would otherwise be likely to continue'. Apart from the new legislation, it was also agreed that the government would provide a loan of £50 million towards the building of a steel strip mill in Scotland and £60 million for one in Monmouthshire.

As to fiscal measures, the increases in the 'initial allowances' in the 1958 budget proposals were doubled, the rates then becoming 30 per cent for plant and machinery, and 15 per cent for industrial buildings. In the 1959 budget the Chancellor announced a reduction in the standard rate of income tax by 9*d.* to 7*s.* 9*d.* and a reduction in the other rates by 6*d.*; a cut, by one sixth, in the three highest rates of purchase tax; changes in beer and liquor licensing duties giving a price reduction to the consumer of 2*d.* a pint; the replacement of initial allowances by a combination of investment allowances and initial allowances for most items of capital expenditure; a reduction in licence duty for passenger vehicles; and a speeding up of the payment of post-war credits.

Over the year to May 1959, the direct additions to spending power resulting from government action were comparatively small, but a main support for demand developed from the removal of controls holding down the volume of credit. The additional capital expenditure in the public sector may have further enlarged the total for 1959–60 by £158 million, or by about 11 per cent. About as much, however, was added since August 1958 to the total volume of private debt outstanding on account of hire purchase and other credit sales, while bank advances rose by £460 million, or 23 per cent, since July 1958. The budget proposals involved further additions to public outlays and a considerable increase in sums left in taxpayers' hands. Tax reliefs were expected to amount to £295 million during the year to March 1960, and added repayments of post-war credits to a further £71 million. On Exchequer accounting, the net total for payments below the line was to rise to £823 million, or £264 million above the figure for 1958–9, and the overall sum to be met by borrowing increased to £721 million, as compared with £182 million.

Before the budget announcement, evidence of a check to the drift in the level of business activity had been found in the reduced unemployment figures and in the answers to the questionnaire circulated by the Federation of British industries in February 1959. The replies indicated, it is true, that the decline in manufacturing investment had continued, but they also showed a general expectation of rather better business, as compared with views expressed in October. On balance, the rate of inflow of new orders had risen, and so had the level of output. Significantly, the increased orders were wholly for the home market, a further decline being recorded in new orders for export. As to the general outlook, more than one third of the members replying felt more optimistic about the future than they had four months previously, and nearly one half felt about the same. Some replies confirmed the view that increased production would be achieved without an expansion of the labour force, and about four fifths of the companies replying were still working below capacity in February.

As was confirmed by other investigations, particularly those of the National Institute of Economic and Social Research as published in the second issue of its *Review*, the small recovery so far had been largely in the home market, and it was not easy to see grounds for an early and marked improvement in export sales. Meanwhile, imports were growing, not only to provide for enlarged requirements of raw materials, but also to satisfy direct demands of consumers.

Sterling in demand

Almost throughout the fiscal year 1968–9 sterling had been everywhere in demand. On only two or three days had the spot rate fallen below the parity with the United States dollar, and at the end, as at the beginning, of the financial year it stood close to the upper limit of $2·82. Forward rates too were steady, at ½-cent premium for one month and 2 cents for three months until

August, when a narrowing of the forward margins became noticeable; and in March they were only ¼-cent for a month and ½-cent for three months. The rate for transferable account sterling, which had been running generally at 2–2½ cents below spot, began to rise steadily in late September, encouraged by expectations of further steps towards the convertibility of sterling. In fact, the spot and transferable rates were merged at the end of the year. The rate for security sterling was also well maintained.

To some extent the favourable trend of sterling reflected the lessened demand for dollars. Thus, on occasions in the middle of 1958 the rates of sterling fell to the support points for a number of European currencies, though by the end of September sterling rates were well above the minima for all currencies except the Dutch guilder, and even that rate had recovered by November. It was thus in conditions of strength that Britain formally merged the transferable and spot rates for sterling, acting in consultation with Commonwealth and other countries, in particular with France and Germany. As from 29 December 1958 practically all sterling – henceforth known as 'external account sterling' – held or acquired by non-residents of the sterling area became freely convertible throughout the world at the official rates, the margin for United States dollars remaining at $2·78–2·82. Similar convertibility was not extended to sterling area residents or to blocked sterling accounts (including 'security sterling') or to other accounts subject to special restriction – a category at that time including Egyptian accounts, which became convertible under the Anglo-Egyptian financial agreement early in 1959. For sterling area residents, the list of 'specified currencies' which must be offered for sale to authorized dealers was reduced in March 1959 to include only the United States and Canadian dollars, along with the eleven European currencies that were convertible.

The merger did, in effect, little more than rationalize a situation that had generally obtained since the rates for transferable sterling in overseas centres became officially supported, in February 1955. Nevertheless, it could properly be regarded, abroad as well as at home, as a sign of strength and confidence. In the words of the deputy governor of the Bank of England, it was mainly a 'technical' change that attracted 'more than its proper share, it might seem, of world attention' because 'the rest of the world is interested in sterling as a convenient means of international payment'. Attention was also aroused because it formed part of a coordinated development whereby several other European countries simultaneously announced steps to complete, more or less, convertibility of their currencies at least for non-residents. At the same time the French franc was formally devalued by approximately 17½ per cent, and the 'heavy' franc introduced for old francs at one new to a hundred old.

With this widening of convertibility, the European Payments Union came to an end and was replaced by the European Monetary Agreement, which had been negotiated with this purpose in view as long ago as August 1955. When the Union was dissolved, the United Kingdom debt to it amounted to £135 million, and this has since been funded. The Monetary Agreement, like the Payments Union, provided for a multilateral system of settlements at monthly intervals, but at less favourable rates of exchange than through financial markets, and with payment of balances in full in gold or dollars. Restricted credit facilities would be available from a working fund, at the discretion of OEEC, to be maintained at about $100 million, the purpose thereof being to assist members to overcome temporary balance of payments difficulties without reimposing trade restrictions. In the ordinary way, then, settlements among members would be made through the foreign exchange markets; and so far only small use has been made of clearing arrangements under the Monetary Agreement.

The position of sterling made possible a number of further, minor relaxations in exchange control arrangements. Thus in January 1959, authorized banks were permitted to export sterling notes to non-residents of the sterling area against payment in sterling from an external account, or in any foreign currency; and in March the amount of sterling notes which travellers were permitted to carry abroad was raised from £10 to £20. Restrictions on the transfer of legacies to Canada and former 'American Account' countries were removed in February, while in March the purposes for which banks were allowed to authorize forward cover for foreign exchange dealings were extended to include 'invisible' transactions and funds for approved capital investment, as well as goods and freight, though cover for speculative purposes remained banned. Forward dealings in gold were also made permissible without Bank of England authorization. In February the ban on usance credits for financing trade between countries outside the sterling area was lifted, though two other restrictions which also had been imposed or reinforced in September 1957 – the prohibition of refinance arrangements and of overdrafts for non-residents except with specific sanction – remained in force as a safeguard against speculation in sterling.

During the first quarter of 1959, with the rate for sterling above $2·81 and tending upward, the authorities are reported to have added to Britain's reserves by supplying the market with sterling, while allowing the rate to improve slightly. The rate for security sterling also rose above $2·81, indicating an inflow of investment funds.

A firm basis for the strength of sterling was provided by unusually favourable movements in Britain's external trade. Even in 1957, when the pressure on sterling was heavy, the current balance of payments had been sound, and subsequently it improved still further. For the first half of 1958 the surplus on current account of £327 million was greater than in any whole year since the end of the war. In the second half the surplus was sharply reduced, in accord with the seasonal pattern, but, even so, the surplus on current account for the year reached £455 million, as compared with £263 million in 1957.

During 1958 a further marked improvement had occurred in the terms of trade. The aggregate values of both imports and exports fell as compared with 1957, but for imports the decline was sharp and entirely due to lower prices, particularly of basic materials; while for exports the fall was less marked and mainly attributable to a rather smaller volume of shipments. Then, too, net receipts from invisible items on commercial account were substantially higher than in the previous year, though this rise was largely offset by a net increase in government expenditure abroad. The Chancellor of the Exchequer noted that Britain maintained her share of world trade in 1958 for the first time since 1950, and that exports were being sustained 'mainly because of the excellent progress made in sales to the United States'.

The improved balance of current payments, along with increased confidence in sterling, contributed to a rise in the central reserves – comprising gold and other convertible currencies besides dollars – while permitting repayments of external debt and large investment overseas. Over the year 1958 the reserves showed a net rise of £284 million, to £1096 million. The whole of the net increase took place in the first half of the year; at the end of the second half the service of the loans from the United States and Canadian governments was resumed, absorbing the smaller additions to the reserves over the preceding six months. The reserves rose again in January and February, but in March Britain repaid £71 million of the £200 million drawn in dollars from the International Monetary Fund in December 1956. These government debt payments were partly offset by special receipts from Germany for support costs and advance payments for arms. As for the positive capital outflow, the United Kingdom's net long-term overseas investment in 1958 was estimated at £236 million; nearly all of this went to the rest of the sterling area, the outward movement to other countries being almost wholly offset by an inward flow. Reflecting all these movements and the fluctuations in short-term assets and liabilities, by the end of March the central reserves, at £1121 million, showed an increase of £132 million on the year.

During 1958 the total of 'sterling balances' rose by £54 million to £3969 million, and, if the small holdings by non-territorial organizations are excluded, those identifiable with particular countries increased, more especially in the last quarter of the year, by £76 million. Throughout the period the balances of non-sterling countries, particularly in Europe, grew steadily with the strengthening of confidence in sterling, but the holdings of countries within the sterling area were declining until September, as the balances were drawn upon to finance trading deficits. Primary producing countries were able, by using their sterling balances, to maintain purchases from abroad, particularly from Britain, despite the fall in commodity prices. The change in the December quarter, when sterling area countries were able to increase their United Kingdom sterling holdings by £38 million, occurred partly for seasonal reasons and partly as a result of the raising of loans outside London. Taking the year as a whole, holdings of sterling area countries fell by £82 million, while those of other countries rose by £158 million. Sterling area countries accounted for 78 per cent of the total for sterling balances held by countries at the end of 1958, as compared with 83 per cent a year earlier.

The strengthening of the reserve position has to be related to the fact that the calls thereon during 1959–60 were enlarged by arrangements entered into during the year. At the end of December a further instalment of principal and interest on United States and Canadian loans, amounting to £70 million, was due to be paid; and from the beginning of 1960 Britain has undertaken to repay, by monthly instalments of £5 million, the balance of the IMF credit. As a result of the decision to increase the quotas of the International Monetary Fund by 50 per cent, one quarter of the increased quotas – that is £58 million for the United Kingdom and about £40 million for other sterling area countries – would have to be found from the reserves in 1959, the balance being held by the Fund as interest-free notes or balances in Britain.

Substantial commitments were accepted also for increased investment overseas. In 1958, independent Commonwealth governments raised £45 million in the London market, Colonial governments borrowed a further £5 million, and net private investment in the sterling Commonwealth countries was considerably higher than in earlier years. At the Commonwealth Trade and Economic Conference held in Montreal in September 1958 it was agreed that further funds should be provided particularly for under-developed areas. The Chancellor of the Exchequer announced that the United Kingdom government would make available 'Commonwealth Assistance Loans', on a government to government basis, to independent Commonwealth countries, through the Export Credits Guarantee Department. Assistance to a total of £50 million had already been arranged for India and Pakistan, and other proposals were being considered. Arrangements were also being made for increased funds for colonial territories from government sources. As for non-government lending, steps were being taken towards the provision of further resources for the Commonwealth Development Finance Company. And finally, subordinate overseas authorities (more particularly local governments and public utilities) of the less developed overseas Commonwealth countries were to have direct access to the London Market.

As to the general trading outlook, the *Economic Survey* noted that the gradual increase in the volume of imports, which began in the last quarter of 1958, was expected to continue, but no increase had been recorded thus far in the average level of import prices, though the downward trend in commodity prices appeared to have ended. These countries might again choose to run down their sterling balances, and were expected to receive loans from international organizations and from other countries, including Britain.

Monetary developments at home

The year's fiscal operations were on the whole restrictive. The budget surplus 'above the line' was £377 million in the financial year to 31 March and with net expenditure 'below the line' amounting to £559 million – the great bulk of which consisted of the provision of money for capital expenditure in developing power and transport services – the deficit overall was £182 million, as compared with £212 million in the previous year. This overall deficit made but a small demand upon a well-maintained flow of savings, which in the aggregate amounted to about one fifth of the national product, or nearly £4100 million. Of this amount, savings by persons, as against companies and other corporate bodies, were estimated at about £1470 million, and a much larger share of this sum than in previous years was attracted into government securities by reason of the maintenance of terms established when interest rates generally were at their highest level. Thus the year was remarkable for a substantial inflow into 'national savings': savings certificates and defence bonds, after small net falls in the preceding year, showed a net increase by £132 million and £108 million respectively in the financial year to March 1959, while net receipts from premium bonds, at £66 million, were lower than in the year before. Doubtless the inflow was due in part to the raising, a year before, of the limit on individual holdings of the current issue of savings certificates, from 600 to 1000 units, and the offer at the same time of the new series of defence bonds bearing interest at 5 per cent per annum and repayable after seven years at £103 per £100. With the fall in the level of interest rates generally, the pulling power of these terms was demonstrated by the fact that over the same year a fall occurred in balances with the Post Office Savings Bank and in ordinary accounts with the trustee savings banks, which yielded, as ever, 2½ per cent.

Meanwhile the authorities continued, at any rate in the earlier part of the year, to carry out funding operations by way of sales of securities by public departments, and the substantial unloading of stock, to quote the *Economic Survey*, 'increased the authorities' control over the liquidity of the monetary system'. One way in which it did so was by facilitating the operations necessitated by stock maturities. Holders of the £676 million of 4 per cent Conversion Stock maturing in June 1958 were offered conversion into equal nominal amounts of either of two new securities, 4¾ per cent Conversion Stock 1963 and 5¼ per cent Conversion Stock 1974, those accepting the longer-dated security receiving a bonus of £2 10*s*. per cent. Only £26 million had to be repaid in cash. Later on, when some of the banks found it necessary to sell investments in order to meet the rising demand for advances, conditions in the gilt-edged market became less favourable for official funding operations. The January 1959 maturity of £592 million of 2 per cent Conversion Stock was dealt with by a limited offer of only £250 million of 4½ per cent Conversion Stock 1964. The list remained open for a fortnight, and it was generally supposed that acceptances of the conversion offer were almost wholly in respect of official holdings of the maturing security. The Chancellor of the Exchequer had explained that the rise in the floating debt, resulting from the cash portion of repayments of maturing securities during the year, occurred in the holdings of departments, floating debt in the hands of the market having decreased.

The net result of these and other factors was that, at a time when short-term interest rates were being reduced, step by step, the longer-term rates remained relatively steady over the year. While bank rate had come down from 7 to 4 per cent the yields on government stocks, ranging from 'shorts' to 'irredeemables', had declined by no more than one half to three quarters per cent.

With long-term rates relatively high, uncertainties in the business outlook and, for the greater part of the year, official restraints on borrowing, the total of new capital issues in 1958 was lower than for 1957, while issues on behalf of companies fell even more markedly. Nevertheless, the demand in the market for equity investments remained strong. Offers of convertible loan stock were far less general than a year before, and securities with fixed interest terms made up a somewhat smaller proportion of the total. During the second half of the year several issues by local authorities or public boards were made, all of them being for periods of fifteen to twenty years and offering interest at 5½ per cent, the issue price rising from £97½ in June to £99½ in January. Meanwhile a few companies, and governments of overseas territories, continued to borrow at 6 per cent. The acceptability of these issues at fixed rates varied from time to time, some being over-subscribed while substantial parts of others were left with the underwriters. Following the almost complete removal of controls over new capital issues, early in 1959, the amount of new money raised in the first three months was somewhat above that for the corresponding period of 1958, when an unusually large issue for an oil undertaking was made. For investment in unit trusts, a marked expansion took place in 1958.

Between 20 March and 20 November 1958, the bank rate was reduced on five occasions, starting at 7 per cent and ending at 4. As has been noted already, reductions were generally semi-officially explained as having been made to follow, rather than to direct, market conditions; and indeed, each had been anticipated in market rates. Thus the discount rate for Treasury bills was falling almost continuously until February 1959, when expectations of a further reduction in bank rate were moderated by the rise in interest rates in the United States. One factor contributing to the downward trend was the growth in the volume of tenders for Treasury bills from outside the discount market applicants. On several occasions during the year new high records for applications were reached, for example the total of £490 million on the first Friday in December 1958 was nearly double the amount for which tenders were invited. In February 1959 the tender rate for Treasury bills actually fell slightly below 3 per cent, but thereafter, with the change of outlook, it recovered to just over $3\frac{1}{4}$.

Right down to October 1958 the authorities were in firm control of the market, discount houses being obliged to borrow at bank rate on a few days in each month. Thereafter rather easier conditions prevailed, apart from a renewed tightening of control early in 1959. The chairman of one of the discount houses has noted that during 1958 one or more of them were forced to borrow at bank rate on ninety-six days, as compared with seventy-eight days in 1957, and that, taking all twelve houses together, the market was 'out of the Bank' on only thirty-three days, as against forty-three days in 1957. He added that 'this pressure of short money may have been necesasry [in the view of the authorities] to prevent money and bill rates coming down faster than was required'. As was customary, the banks reduced the rate of interest allowed on deposit accounts strictly in accordance with the changes in bank rate. As for the facilities provided to the discount market, in October the average rate earned on these short-term loans was raised, in some instances by reducing the proportion lent to a particular house at the minimum rate and in other instances by raising the rate on the 'further amount' by one quarter per cent. Again, when bank rate fell by one half to 4 per cent in November, the average rate on loans to the discount market was reduced by only $\frac{3}{8}$ of 1 per cent.

Other rates also were declining over 1958–9. The rate of tax-free interest on tax reserve certificates was lowered in stages from $3\frac{1}{4}$ per cent at the beginning of April 1958 to $2\frac{1}{4}$ in November; nevertheless, the inflow of funds to the Exchequer on account of net subscriptions to tax reserve certificates during the period 1 April to 31 December 1958 was substantially above the level of the previous year. The rates charged on loans to local authorities from the Public Works Loan Board were lowered in several steps, irregularly according to term, and by the end of March the range had become 5 per cent for loans up to five years and $5\frac{3}{4}$ per cent for loans of longer term. Similarly, market rates on local authority mortgages declined, from about $6\frac{1}{4}$ per cent in March 1958 to $5\frac{1}{4}$ or $5\frac{1}{2}$ per cent a year later for mortgages running for periods of two to eight years. The Agricultural Mortgage Corporation reduced its lending rate from 7 to 6 per cent in July 1958, and to $5\frac{1}{2}$ per cent in April 1959.

An exception to the general downward movement in rates was provided by most building societies, who felt it impracticable to lower rates charged on mortgages, since they could hardly reduce the rates allowed on money placed with them while the high yields already noted were obtainable on 'national savings'. The Building Societies Association continued to recommend a mortgage rate of 6 per cent to its members, though a few societies, including the largest of all, did in fact reduce their mortgage rate for owner occupiers to $5\frac{1}{2}$ per cent for new loans immediately, and for old borrowing after some delay, and also lowered the rates allowed to investors.

The position of the banks underwent marked changes during the year, largely as a result of the redirection of government policy. Early in July 1958 the Chancellor of the Exchequer announced the removal, from the end of that month, of the 'ceiling' on bank lending, which had been imposed as one of the restraining measures taken in the autumn of 1957. The lifting of 'quantitative' control was followed, in February 1959, by that of 'qualitative' control exercised by the authorities over many years through 'requests' varying from time to time in stringency. The easing and removal of externally imposed restraints on bank lending led to a swift growth of lending at a time when the demand for bank advances might have been expected to slacken, with business lagging, prices steady and stocks declining in some trades. Meanwhile, net deposits increased over the year to March 1959, and the rise was marked, particularly after October, in current accounts. Moreover, the amount of notes in circulation rose, though only by one half as much as during the preceding year. The additions to the money supply, of about £250 million, in these forms took place entirely after October 1958.

It was the rapid growth of advances that clearly reflected the new official policy and brought other changes in banking figures. The increase during the seven months to March 1959 amounted to nearly £450 million, or more than one fifth. By the end of 1958, advances had passed the previous high record, reached in mid-1955, and by March the proportion of advances to gross deposits had risen to nearly 37 per cent. Bearing in mind the influences tending to depress requirements of bank credit, the sharp upward movement suggests that the withdrawal of controls had released a long-suppressed demand. Thus the quarterly classification of bank advances shows that over the six months to February 1959 the aggregate for all banks rose by £375 million, or by 18 per cent, more than one half of the increase being recorded in the groups for personal and professional advances and for lending to farmers, shopkeepers and builders and contractors. Inferentially, it seems to have been the borrowers of relatively small sums, in their personal capacities or as operating private businesses, who had felt the pinch of restrictions on bank lending.

Continuing with the February analysis some expansion occurred also in most other groups, particularly the heavy industries, food, drink and tobacco, public utilities, and local government; but the largest proportionate increase was recorded for loans to hire purchase finance companies. In January the governor of the Bank of England remarked that the rate of growth in bank advances would 'need to be carefully watched', though he felt that so far it had helped to maintain activity over a period that might otherwise have shown more signs of recession.

The lifting of controls was followed by a prompt resumption of initiative in banking. In mid-1958 only one bank in the United Kingdom, and that in Scotland, was associated with a hire purchase finance undertaking. By the end of August, nine further schemes linking banks with hire purchase finance undertakings had been announced, and others followed. The extent of the individual banks' interests in hire purchase finance undertakings varied, some having acquired the whole of the share capital and others a holding of less than one half of the equity. The movement involved a total investment of nearly £40 million, over one third of which comprised additions to the capital resources of the finance companies. The governor of the Bank of England expressed his belief that this 'closer connection between the banking system and the hire purchase industry [was] in the public interest', and said he was sure that the banks had been 'wise to participate indirectly through specialist companies rather than attempt direct management of two quite different types of lending'.

Almost immediately after the beginning of the entry into hire purchase, several banks in succession announced 'Personal Loans' schemes, by which advances were offered, without security, for sums generally up to £500 and repayable with interest, calculated at the rate of 5 per cent per annum on the original loan, in equal monthly instalments over periods of up to two years. One special attraction of such loans lay in the fact that interest payments ranked for income tax relief, whereas hire purchase charges did not. Another advantage offered by some banks under the scheme was the cancellation of any part of the debt that might be outstanding on the death of the borrower. The pioneer bank in these activities – the Midland – stated that during the first four months more than 45,000 Personal Loans had been arranged for sums averaging £160, over one half by value of the loans being for the purchase of motor vehicles and most of the rest for furniture, fittings and equipment and repair or improvement of premises. The amount outstanding, for this one bank, was then nearly £7 million. The Chancellor of the Exchequer had earlier said that he was 'glad to note the initiative of the banks in Personal Loans'.

The lending developments noted altered the proportions of bank assets. First, the proportion of liquid assets, comprising cash, bills and money market loans, from being comfortably above the conventional minimum 'liquidity ratio' of 30 per cent of gross deposits, declined, until by March 1959 the average for the clearing banks was only a little above the customary standard, while the figures for some banks were slightly below it. Secondly, between September 1958 and March 1959 the investments held by the clearing banks were reduced by £275 million in the process of making room for advances; and the proportion of investments to deposits, at 29·1 per cent, was the lowest reached for a number of years.

No occasion had arisen for the exercise of powers newly acquired by the authorities when the 'ceiling' on bank advances was removed in July 1958. It was then arranged that, as a restraining measure in case of need, the Bank of England might call on the commercial banks to place with it stated amounts of 'Special Deposits', which would not rank as liquid assets. While, therefore, the 'Special Deposits' would earn interest, at a level based on the Treasury bill rate, they would have the effect of freezing a part of the banks' lending power. The system was stated to be a provisional arrangement pending any recommendations that might be made by the Radcliffe Committee.

The year brought yet another adjustment to the balance sheets of the banks through a general increase in capital, and by March the aggregate of the paid-up capital and reserve funds of the clearing banks, at £218 million, was higher by £24 million than a year before.

During the year the Committee on the Working of the Monetary System, generally known as the Radcliffe Committee, had been continuing its investigations; and its inquiries had led to the publication of improved banking statistics. The combined monthly statements of the clearing banks provided additional figures, breaking down several items. Thus totals for the clearing banks as a whole were given for current account balances, for deposit accounts and for 'other accounts', defined as 'credits in course of transmission, suspense accounts and internal funds of the banks'. Again, the banks' aggregate holdings of notes and coin were distinguished from their balances with the Bank of England, both being components of their cash holdings, and items in transit could be excluded from the figure for advances.

The report of the Radcliffe Committee is eagerly awaited, and no doubt a major byproduct of its work will be a substantial volume of new material concerning the operation of the monetary system. Thus the Bank of England, in its last annual report, published in August 1958, records that it had been engaged 'almost throughout the year' in preparation and submission of evidence to the Committee. It included 'a survey of monetary experience in the United Kingdom over recent years', and the hope was expressed that this survey would, when published, 'form a basis for a more detailed annual review of the monetary situation in future years' than it had been the practice to issue hitherto. In our Monetary Survey for 1958 note was taken of the central bank's more frequent comments upon monetary conditions, and in the present Survey we have been able to site statements, emanating from the Bank, on a variety of matters.

It has become more and more widely accepted that a full-scale, authoritative annual review of monetary affairs could be of great help to those who are concerned to understand and interpret official policy on the background of current economic developments. In the ten years over which this Monetary Survey has appeared we have been conscious of how much more information is needed, particularly about official operations, if widespread appreciation and truly objective criticism are to be fostered in the interests of healthy management of the nation's monetary system. Private surveys can, at the best, be only inadequate contributions to public education in these matters by comparison with fully documented reports having all the authority of complete knowledge of the facts and of the considerations entering in to the determination of policy.

1960 – Expansion: The best post-war year

On the whole, the year to April 1960 must be accounted one of the most satisfactory – perhaps, indeed, the best – of the post-war period. At home, stability in consumers' prices had been maintained, side by side with substantial expansion in output, while the enlarged demand for labour had restored full employment in most areas. Internationally, sterling had remained strong, with external convertibility for current transactions firmly re-established. Towards the end of the year the expansion was officially judged to have reached a point at which overstrain and inflationary pressure might shortly re-assert themselves. In September the managing director of the International Monetary Fund had expressed the view that the era of post-war inflation was at an end internationally; and in November the governor of the Bank of England, referring to Britain alone, said that 'we are entering into a new phase. After the distortions and controls of the war and post-war periods, we seem now to have come, both domestically and internationally, to a position of more stability, with the freedom of markets largely restored.' On that occasion the Chancellor of the Exchequer, rather more cautiously, described 1959 as 'a year of achievement' and 1960 as 'a year of opportunity'.

The expansion of production and employment was called forth by a rising level of demand, in both home and export markets. At home, the expansion in consumption, particularly of durable goods, had been encouraged by reductions in taxation, and was financed partly by a sustained increase in hire purchase debt. For several months the capital goods industries seemed to be lagging behind, with little sign of revival in private capital investment, but later in the year – and particularly after the uncertainties of the general election had been resolved – it became plain that the home demand for capital goods, too, was substantially enlarged. Stocks held by manufacturing industry, which had been run down during the previous twelve months, were being rebuilt from about the middle of 1959. Only a few industries, notably coal and shipbuilding, were untouched by the general trend. The growth in business activity was accompanied by a rapid increase in bank advances, again widely spread, both geographically and by industries, with a marked rise in lending to retail traders, hire purchase finance companies, and personal and professional borrowers.

With home demand expanding, a substantial increase occurred in imports, and, although exports also rose, the achievement of 1958, when a surplus was earned on visible trade, was not repeated. Nevertheless, last year's deficit on merchandise trade was relatively small. The 1959 current account surplus, including invisible items, was lower, amounting to no more than £145 million. The year's results were aided by recovery in international trade; in addition, the terms of trade, which had turned in Britain's favour with the fall in world commodity prices during 1957 and 1958, remained so throughout 1959. With Britain's satisfactory trading situation and general confidence in the course of her home conditions, sterling remained strong on foreign exchange markets abroad, and various large capital payments were made from the central reserves. Apart from these special items, the total for reserves grew month by month up to November 1959; it then fell with a worsening in the balance of payments position and possibly a net outflow of short-term capital, to take advantage of higher levels of interest rates in other financial centres. Subsequently, with a change in interest-relations, some rise in the reserves was recorded.

During the year, wholesale prices of basic materials used in manufacturing industry showed a slight tendency to rise, but, as already noted, prices at later stages in the chain of manufacture and marketing – and particularly retail prices of consumers' goods – were steady throughout the year. This record was described officially as based to some extent on the stability of import prices at their reduced level, and on reductions in indirect taxation. Thus it was 'impossible to say that the underlying upward trend has been entirely eliminated; it has certainly, however, been much more moderate than in any period since the war'. In these conditions, the Chancellor of the Exchequer repeatedly urged upon industry the desirability of ensuring that the rise in productivity associated with economic recovery should be reflected in price reductions, rather than in increases in profits or wages; but the Federation of British Industries declined to make any definite recommendation on these lines to its members. The official policy was supported by the Council on Prices, Productivity and Incomes, in its third report issued in August, but, despite a number of price reductions, no decline in the official index number could be reported.

Along with the steadiness of prices went a slowing down of the pace of the rise in wage rates; the official index of weekly rates rose by little more than 1 per cent in the twelve months to February 1960. Trade union claims tended to stress reductions in hours in the standard working week, though also pressing for wage increases in later months. The employment situation improved fairly steadily, but by early 1960 it was evident that the recovery was uneven. In the Midlands and south, labour shortages were appearing in some industries and occupations, whereas less than full employment obtained in districts in Wales, in Scotland and in the north of England. Accordingly the government vigorously applied its powers to influence the distribution of industry, both by the Local Employment Act 1960 which extended the scope and availability of financial inducements to undertakings to develop in areas of comparatively high unemployment, and by directly pressing such locations upon manufacturers, notably in the motor industry.

Apart from these and other measures to ease the difficulties of particular areas and industries – such as the cotton industry reorganization scheme – economic recovery made headway under the impetus of measures introduced in the previous year. Indeed, early in 1960 the authorities were beginning to express anxiety about the recurrence of inflationary pressures. For one thing, it became plain that government expenditure was likely to increase substantially during the ensuing year, not only for defence, but also on account of industry and other purposes, and that this would come at a time when – if existing trends continued – inflationary pressure might be developing. Then, too, full employment had been reached in some parts of the country, and demands for wage increases were under negotiation. In January the official figures indicated a substantial prospective increase in capital expenditure by private business during 1960 and meanwhile the balance of payments situation had moved less favourably for Britain. As the Chancellor described the position on 26 January: 'The economy has been expanding rapidly since the middle of last year. This is a welcome development which has accorded with the needs of the situation. But in recent weeks there have been a number of indications that some strains may be developing.'

It was in these circumstances that bank rate was raised, on 21 January 1960, to 5 per cent, after having been unchanged at 4 for fourteen months. The rise had been expected because of upward movements in rates in financial centres abroad, but it was a surprise to learn, from official pronouncements, that it had been primarily directed to steadying domestic conditions, as a warning signal against an incipient boom. In the following month a further step, again in the field of interest rates, consisted of a lowering of the prices at which the authorities were prepared to buy government securities, this being presumably aimed at discouraging the rate of growth in lending, particularly by the banks. These measures are referred to in the third section below, but here it has to be said that the changes were not accompanied by other controls: this was no 'package deal', as so often presented in post-war years to put to rights an economy running off balance. It would be truer to describe them as mildly restraining monetary measures applied in accordance with the new orthodoxy of action on interest rates.

Sterling strong and convertible

Since the establishment, at the end of 1958, of almost complete convertibility of sterling held by non-residents of the sterling area, the pound had remained strong on the foreign exchange markets of the world. Indeed, during 1959, with an adverse position on the United States balance of payments, uncertainties were sometimes expressed as to the stability of the dollar, so that sterling was all the more widely in demand. As in domestic monetary conditions in Britain, so in external developments the situation became rather less favourable, with the balance of payments moving into deficit in the last quarter of 1959. For the greater part of the year, however, Britain was able to make further relaxations in trade and currency controls, then relatively minor in scope after the substantial moves towards greater freedom a year previously.

At the annual meeting of the International Monetary Fund in September 1959, the United States representative had urged the reduction or removal of discrimination against dollar trade. In the following November, Britain lifted most of the remaining quantitative restrictions on imports, affecting particularly the dollar countries. The Chancellor described this as 'part of a steady process which the government has been carrying out over recent years', but he also related it to the balance of payments problem of the United States authorities, who 'look to other countries for cooperation in putting the matter right'. From 1 February, some of the remaining quota restrictions on imports from the dollar area were removed, and the agreement which had limited remittances to the United States of earnings from films exhibited in Britain was ended.

A more general measure of liberalization was the virtual abolition, as from 1 November, of restrictions on currency, including dollars, made available to United Kingdom residents for purposes of travel abroad. Banks and travel agents were then allowed to supply up to the equivalent of £250 a year per person and permission for larger sums was usually granted where the Bank of England is satisfied that the funds are in fact required for travel purposes, and not for export of capital. Corresponding adjustments were made in other travel allowances, including those for business and health purposes. Shortly afterwards it was announced that travellers from Britain would be permitted to take with them up to £50 in sterling notes and £250 in foreign currency notes, the previous limits having been £20 and £100 respectively. Other amendments in exchange control regulations included the extension of the powers of the banks to approve applications for miscellaneous commercial and other purposes. Forms were no longer required for imports from outside the sterling area up to a value of £500, or for private gifts in kind of up to £100 in value sent to recipients outside the sterling area. The export of gold in manufactured or semi-manufactured form was no longer regulated, though export of bullion or coin remains controlled. In these ways, the remaining trade and exchange controls were further diminished, and the Chancellor was able to assert that, while 'in formal terms, the pound is convertible only for non-residents . . . in view of the ending of currency restrictions on travel and on most of our imports from dollar and non-dollar countries, it is in effect convertible also for residents, except for capital movements'.

Although Britain's balance of payments position continued to be satisfactory for most of 1959, the current surplus was substantially lower than that recorded for the exceptionally good year of 1958, and a small deficit occurred in the closing quarter of the year. Meanwhile, the 1958 surplus was revised downwards to an unusually large extent; it was estimated to have been £349 million, as compared with the original figure – recorded in our Survey for 1959 – of £455 million. (It appears that the estimated gross earnings of British shipping were much lower than had been supposed, the new information following upon a direct inquiry into the industry's earnings.) Only on the second quarter's figures did the 1959 surplus exceed that of 1958, and for the year as a whole the surplus was reduced by £204 million to £145 million. A favourable balance of £219 million with the rest of the sterling area was partly offset by a deficit of £74 million with the rest of the world, although a surplus of £143 million with North America was recorded.

Overseas sterling holdings rose during 1959 by £227 million to £4203 million, the highest total then recorded. Part of the increase was in the holdings of 'non-territorial organizations', following Britain's increased subscription to the International Monetary Fund. Moreover, holdings by countries rose by £143 million to £3498 million, also a record high figure, but this was more than accounted for by the larger holdings of overseas sterling area countries, possibly because of increased earnings from sales of raw materials. Iraq left the sterling area in June.

The central gold and currency reserves were rising until towards the end of 1959, but were thereafter subjected to less favourable movements in trade and finance, as well as to some large outgoings on capital account. In addition to the transfer of the regular instalments of capital and interest on the United States and Canadian loans at the end of December, amounting to roughly £70 million, the gold portion of Britain's increased subscription to the IMF involved a payment of £58 million in May 1959. Some other countries in the sterling area also drew on the central reserves to provide gold for their IMF subscriptions. In October, Britain repaid, in advance of the due date, the $250 million drawn in October 1957 from the line of credit arranged with the US Export-Import Bank. This prepayment, besides reflecting confidence in Britain's external financial position, was described by the Chancellor as a measure of cooperation with the United States in dealing with her external payments problems. Another demonstration of strength was the announcement in December that Britain would not seek to renew the standby credit of $738·5 million which had been arranged three years earlier with the IMF. Since January 1960, moreover, Britain had been repaying, in monthly instalments of roughly £5 million each, the balance of the $561 million drawn from the IMF towards the end of 1956; $200 million had been repaid in March 1959.

Other capital transactions were also large, including £39 million in repayment of debts outstanding to members of the European Payments Union at the time of its dissolution.

Had it not been for these various payments the rise in the reserves would have continued until November 1959. The small fall in that month was the first net decline for over two years that was attributable to ordinary financial and commercial transactions. The decline in the reserves, after adjustment for special items, continued during December and January, but a rise was recorded in February 1960 and again in March. In the budget speech the Chancellor said: 'There is likely to be a continuing rise in overseas investment, both public and private', so that 'we must increase our export earnings. That is the central challenge.'

Foreign exchange rates for sterling followed a course similar to those of the balance of payments and movements in the reserves: for most of the year rates remained firm; then some weakening was noticeable in November and December, followed by a recovery. With the disappearance of the 'dollar gap', sterling remained above par against the US dollar throughout most of the year, though it had fallen fractionally below par during December and early January. The rate for security sterling – still under restrictions – fluctuated more widely, but remained within about 1 per cent of the spot rate and was often well within this margin. The 'dollar premium' – paid on purchases of dollar securities in Britain – had disappeared just before the extension of convertibility in December 1958; it reappeared in July, a development attributed at the time to hedging activities with Britain's general election in mind. After the election it again fell to nothing in October, only to re-emerge a week later, thereafter rising slowly to touch 4 per cent in January and February. It then fell, and stood at 1¼ per cent early in April 1960, the fluctuations possibly reflecting the views of investors as to the relative advantages, day by day, of stock exchange opportunities in London and New York. Two technical changes occurred in the foreign exchange market. One was an agreement by dealers, as from May 1959, no longer to be obliged to quote rates for trading in North American and continental currencies in fractions of the currencies concerned; they could, if they wished, quote in decimals, though in practice few seem to have done so. Secondly, from January 1960 the Bank of England ceased to quote official buying and selling rates for currencies other than the United States dollar, thus adopting the practice followed in other west European countries since the end of 1958. As these countries also quote limits in respect of the United States dollar, limits for the other currencies were maintained by international arbitrage dealings.

A divergence in monetary policies pursued in Britain and in overseas countries during the year influenced the flow of international funds. In Britain, the Treasury bill rate remained fairly steady, between 3¼ and 3½ per cent, from the end of 1958 until December 1959. By contrast, the United

States Treasury bill rate, after remaining fractionally below this level until August, rose well above the United Kingdom rate, to over 4½ per cent in December and early January; after then it fell. As a consequence, the discount on forward sterling narrowed, and in August forward sterling was at a premium against the dollar for the first time since December 1954. The premium increased later in the year, with the widening of the gap between the bill rates in the two countries, but in January 1960, when bank rate in Britain was raised while the United States bill rate fell, forward sterling declined to a slight discount.

It was also reported that a net outflow of short-term capital from Britain had resulted, not from speculative activity, but from the higher level of rates abroad, and this probably continued until bank rate was raised on 21 January. Funds were attracted to Frankfurt as well as New York, because developments in West Germany had led the central bank to raise its discount rate in September and again in October, and to follow this with increases in commercial bank reserve requirements. It was to these influences that the Chancellor referred in his comments on the weakening of the sterling rate in November and December and the outflow from the reserves. Figures subsequently published showed that by the end of December 1960 sterling holdings of the dollar area and of OEEC countries were substantially higher, on balance, than three months earlier.

As has been noted, the rise in bank rate on 21 January was officially said to have been made primarily for domestic reasons, but the external situation was also in mind, as official statements later made clear. Thus on 12 February the governor of the Bank of England pointed to the greater responsiveness of funds to interest rate considerations, and said: 'Arguments in the overseas field were pointing the same way [as domestic considerations]: interest rates in several of the main financial markets having for some months been higher than London rates, and monetary conditions tighter. In this respect the position has changed noticeably in the past two years. . . . With the much greater stability of the exchanges in the past year or two, and with increasing freedom of trade and currency movements, comparative interest rates have become somewhat more decisive, both in shifting short-term investment from one country to another, and, perhaps even more important, in making borrowing cheaper in one market than another. It seems to me that we should learn to live with movements of this sort without taking them too tragically. . . . Where there is a conflict between these "overseas" arguments, and the "domestic" arguments for interest rate changes, I would rather see some resort to the use of reserves than a slavish following of interest rate movements made by other countries for their own reasons. On 21 January, however, there was no such conflict.'

Capital for long-term investment also moved more readily, particularly in the form of portfolio investment. In many countries investment trusts or unit trusts have been formed to hold securities of companies operating in other countries, and facilities have been developed to allow for international dealings in such securities, partly encouraged by the progress of the European Common Market. Then, too, arrangements were made by some banks and financial undertakings to enable private investors to buy, hold or sell gold by means of gold certificates. These facilities were made available chiefly in Canada, South Africa and Germany.

Monetary policy and the banks

An outstanding development of 1959–60 was the sustained rise in bank advances, which had started with the removal of direct restrictions on bank lending in July 1958. On the returns for mid-March 1960, advances of the clearing banks amounted to £3121 million, as compared with £2446 million a year earlier and £2000 million in July 1958. Each quarter of the year showed an increase, and the added borrowing was spread over the various groups, though somewhat less marked for industry than for trade (especially retail trade) and for personal and professional borrowers. It comprised, in the main, an expansion in ordinary borrowing, supplemented by the initiative of the banks in extending facilities, particularly by way of Personal Loans introduced towards the end of 1958. For most of the year the resources of the banking system were being enlarged, following the expansive budget of 1959. With somewhat increased offerings of Treasury bills at the weekly tender, side by side with official debt operations, the liquid assets of the banks were augmented while net deposits rose from £6328 million in March 1959 to £6684 million a year later. It will be noted that the growth of deposits covered little more than one half of the expansion in advances; for the rest, the demand was met by reductions in investment holdings. Other institutions besides the banks were also lending more, especially through hire purchase facilities, the outstanding total of hire purchase debt rising from £642 million in April 1959 to £889 million in February 1960.

Until the beginning of 1960 no official concern was expressed with the course of the figures. In November the Chancellor said that 'the expansion of bank credit is, of course, to be expected with the revival of the economy, and I do not find the monetary situation out of balance, though I shall continue to watch it carefully'. At that time, too, the governor of the Bank of England said: 'I judge the increase in bank advances to have been helpful to industry and commerce as far as it has gone, but to need watching if it should continue much longer at the same pace.'

Even when some restraint was thought to be advisable, it was applied lightly and with carefully qualified observations. Thus in February the governor of the Bank of England explained the rise in the bank rate as having been made because 'we felt that, on balance, the domestic scene called for a first step, or at least a signal, in the direction of caution. . . . We had to convince ourselves that we should not do more damage by risking some check to incipient, and desirable, new investment than good by changing the general monetary emphasis towards restraint. The decision went on balance in favour of an increase in bank rate.' He also spoke of the benefits to be secured by taking 'preventative action in good time' and of a readiness 'to take further restraining measures if they seem necessary'. A further comment was in similar tone: 'Advances have gone on rising sharply: the trend is likely to continue upwards, if only because of commitments entered into earlier, but there seem to be some signs that the increase in new facilities granted may be flattening out a little – I should certainly regard that as welcome.' Two months later the authorities had moved nearer to further action, as indicated by the Chancellor in his budget speech. He then said: 'Last year, we were glad to see an expansion of credit, which made a notable contribution to our policy of stimulating the economy. Now, however, I judge that we have reached the stage where we should be cautious about further expansion of credit. . . . Steps in changing the climate for private lending have already been taken by the increase in bank rate in January and in open market transactions. . . . I think it likely that the time may soon arrive when it would be right that we should take other steps to restrain further expansion of private credit; and we stand ready to do so.'

Thus for the first three quarters of the year to April 1960, the monetary policy of the authorities sought simply to facilitate the measures for stimulation applied in the previous year and through the 1959 budget. The swift response in bank and other lending has been noted, but the contribution from fiscal action proved to be less than had been expected, partly through the secondary effect of the rise in incomes. The budget had been designed 'to give a further limited but effective impetus to the expansion of our economic activity', with an overall deficit of £721 million, compared with £182 million in the previous financial year. In fact, the pace of economic recovery during the year led to enlarged revenue, while expenditure, particularly below the line, fell short of estimates, and the overall deficit was no more than £314 million, so that net borrowing was less than had been foreseen.

At the same time, receipts from national savings exceeded expectations, the rapid growth of the previous financial year continuing throughout 1959–60. The previous year's total, of £327 million, was the largest then recorded, and a 'target' of £250 million was set for 1959–60, though thought at the time to be 'taxing optimism to the limits'. In the event, the figure was reached after thirty-two weeks, and the target was raised to £400 million, the eventual net increase in investment being £389 million. In May 1959 the Chancellor gave a warning that he could not allow 'the terms of national savings securities to get out of line with terms of borrowing generally' – a warning which perhaps helped to maintain sales thereafter. On balance, net sales of savings certificates were lower, while net sales of defence bonds rose; and a 'remarkable improvement' occurred in deposits with the Post Office and trustee savings banks. For these* the rate of interest remained – as ever – at 2½ per cent, the recovery being attributed to growing appreciation by the public of the advantages of the tax concession granted in 1956, and to the 'generally stable price level'.

As from 2 May 1960, the limit on the aggregate amount which a person might deposit in the Post Office or the ordinary department of a trustee savings bank was increased from £3000 to £5000, and the annual limit abolished. Other adjustments to encourage national savings were announced in the budget speech. The limit on individual holdings of the current issue of savings certificates was increased from 1000 to 1200 units; a new issue of defence bonds was to be made in June, with the same terms as the existing issue but with a limit on holdings of £5000 in addition to any previous issues; and the terms of premium bonds were being made more attractive in various ways.

As for marketable gilt-edged securities, new issues for cash or conversion almost exactly offset maturities during the financial year, though with rates generally at higher levels. In August, holders (including official bodies) of £302 million of 3 per cent War Loan 1955–9 were offered conversion into a further tranche of 4½ per cent Conversion Stock 1964 or a new 5 per cent Treasury Stock 1986–9; holders of £54 million of the old stock switched into the shorter-dated and of £144 million into the longer-dated stock. At the same time, cash applications were invited for the new stock, and applications amounting to £157 million were allotted in full. At the end of December, holders (again official as well as private) of 2 per cent Exchequer Stock 1960 and 3 per cent Exchequer Stock 1960 were offered conversion into a new 5 per cent Conversion Stock 1971; the offer was accepted by holders of £309 million of the £448 million of the former stock and £103 million of the £200 million of the latter, the balances being repaid in cash before the end of the financial year. In January, a further £200 million of 4½ per cent Conversion Stock 1964 was issued for cash, and on this occasion the result was given in a new form: 'the full amount of stock offered has been allotted, all applications from the public being allotted in full'. This followed upon the Radcliffe Committee's criticism (para. 580) of the former method of recording results of government issues, and the Chancellor's undertaking† to 'find a more dignified form' of statement, though he had added his doubts as to 'whether it would be right to announce the sales of stock to the public [as distinct from public departments] on the first day of issue'.

Thus the official figures as immediately available of nominal issues, conversions and maturities continued to be unhelpful as a guide to net

* Excluding deposits in the special investment departments of the trustee savings banks.
† *Hansard*, 26 November, col. 588.

government borrowing on gilt-edged securities, since they did not take into account the transactions of government departments, chiefly the Issue Department of the Bank of England. After an interval, however, it became possible to see the weight of these and other 'departmental' transactions. The Radcliffe Committee published for the first time a table indicating the sources of net government borrowing, and the figures were issued, with further detail, on a quarterly basis. Changes in the holdings of the departments and net sales to the public were distinguished, but unfortunately publication was subject to delay: thus the figures for the third quarter of 1959 appeared in the press on 9 April 1960. Similarly, the new information recorded changes in the holdings of Treasury bills outside the government departments, which took into account not only the bills issued through the weekly tender, but also net official purchases or sales of bills, though again subject to delay and so giving no indication of recent transactions. During 1959–60 the total floating debt rose rather less than in the previous year, when the tap issue was swollen by net maturities of gilt-edged; in the latest year, however, the volume of tender bills outstanding rose by £560 million, as compared with a fall of £200 million in the preceding year. As the Chancellor explained in course of the survey of 1959–60 in the budget speech: 'Unlike the previous year, we had no long periods of sustained demand for gilt-edged stocks, and we were only occasionally able to sell on any scale.... The market also needed a good deal of help from the authorities to absorb the heavy sales of securities by the banks throughout the year. . . . As a result of these and all the other transcations of the Exchequer, there has been a substantial rise in the amount of Treasury bills in the market. Some of the additional bills were taken up by the clearing banks, but far more by others; much of this probably resulted from the rise in overseas holdings of sterling.' Hence the sustained liquidity of the banking system.

In these conditions, the discount rate on Treasury bills was fairly steady throughout most of 1959–60, with bank rate unchanged at 4 per cent. From about 3¼ per cent in April 1959, the Treasury bill rate rose gently to nearly 3½ in June, remaining at about that level until December. Over the period, the Bank of England rarely enforced the penal rate; indeed, for eight weeks in the early autumn no discount house was 'in the Bank'. At this stage the United States Treasury bill rate was high and still rising, and the prospect of an increase in bank rate in Britain was coming into discussion. In December the market had to borrow from the Bank of England at bank rate on ten occasions, and accordingly the Treasury bill rate began to rise week by week, reaching over 3¾ per cent on 15 January 1960, the Friday before bank rate was lifted to 5 per cent. In the following week it rose by about three quarters per cent to just over 4½, at which level it remained, notwithstanding the fall in the United States Treasury bill rate and some lessening of pressure on the market by the Bank of England.

During the year two discount houses were amalgamated, and a firm of brokers previously outside the 'syndicate' was granted discounting facilities with the Bank of England and admitted to membership of the London Discount Market Association.

With the economy steadily expanding, gilt-edged prices remained relatively steady until December, when a decline took place. Following the increase in bank rate, the market steadied for about a month; meanwhile, however, bank advances had continued to grow at a rate which involved further large reductions in the banks' holdings of gilt-edged securities. For a time these were absorbed largely or wholly by the authorities at the prevailing prices but on 24 February 1960 the government broker suddenly reduced his buying prices. No official explanation was then given of the change, but in the following week a government spokesman, answering a question in the House of Lords, said: 'The government does not believe that the market ought to be insulated by official action from the effects of decisions by holders of gilt-edged stock to buy or sell, though at times it may be desirable to assist in maintaining orderly market conditions.... All that happened last week was that the weight of selling mainly from the banks was so great that the authorities decided to make a larger reduction than normal in the prices at which they were prepared to buy.... We do not think it is right that the government should be a kind of sink for unwanted government stock at an artificially high price.' This statement of policy was related more closely to the banking situation by the answer to a further question in the Lords, the official view being that as a rule the banks sell short-term dated securities, and 'they offered an exceptionally large quantity . . . to the government broker who accordingly marked down the price by one point, because he felt it was undesirable that an artificially high price should be maintained by the government when so many securities were being offered'.

The immediate object of the lowering of prices was presumably to discourage sales of gilt-edged securities, and thus to exert a restraining influence upon bank lending policies. One incidental consequence, however, was the provocation of further complaints – they had been made on various occasions during the year – as to the 'loss' of capital values brought about largely as a result of official policy. A number of questions were asked in Parliament, particularly representing the grievances of investors who had accepted the War Loan conversion offer in 1932 – partly, it was suggested, on patriotic grounds – and had retained their holdings, but the Chancellor declined to vary the terms of outstanding stocks, as by fixing definite redemption dates for 'irredeemables'.

On a wider view, the operation lifted the level of rates generally. The yield on Consols, after running for some months at about $4\frac{3}{4}$ per cent, in December moved to over 5, and at the end of February 1960 to $5\frac{1}{4}$, with yields on short-dated securities moving more sharply, both after the increase in bank rate and following the lowering of the authorities' buying prices in February. Shortly after the rise in bank rate, the tax-free rate of interest paid on tax reserve certificates was increased from $2\frac{1}{4}$ to $2\frac{1}{2}$ per cent, and slight increases were made in the lending rates of the Public Works Loan Board.

At this stage equity prices tended to move along with those of gilt-edged securities. For most of the year, equities, by contrast with gilt-edged, had continued the rapid upward movement which had begun early in 1958, and they gained impetus after the general election, the volume of transactions being unusually large. The Actuaries' Investment Index of industrial ordinary share prices, which had risen from below 93 (December 1957 = 100) in February 1958 to nearly 141 in April 1959 – the starting point of this Survey – reached new record high levels, with a peak of 191 in December 1959. Thereafter prices fell back, despite increased company profits and dividends. Monetary developments were generating uncertainties as to the future trend of the economy, and leading to fears of possible re-institution of more direct restraints. A contribution to a more cautious attitude had already come from the governor of the Bank of England, when in November he spoke of 'a marked and sometimes slightly disquieting boom in equity prices'. In February again he said that he still felt 'some disquiet', though he would not 'hazard a view whether prices will rise or fall, or whether the present yield basis is justified. I do, however, see some danger, particularly to the small investor, in the prevalent mood that one only has to buy a few equities and one is certain to make money.' In his opinion, 'the great problem is that there is too much money chasing too few first-class shares'.

Throughout the year the market was absorbing a substantial flow of new issues of shares, new money raised in this way during 1959 amounting to £274 million, or three times as much as in 1958 and not far short of twice the high figure recorded for 1957. Companies also raised over £100 million by way of marketing of fixed-interest-bearing securities, or rather more than had been so borrowed in the previous year. New issues of ordinary shares have continued to run at a high level during the early months of 1960. Apart from the trend of both corporate and individual investment in favour of ordinary shares, further demand arose from the activities of unit trusts, for which the marked expansion noted a year ago was continued. A new series of monthly figures gave the total for the value of units outstanding, at market prices, as nearly £200 million in December and £206 million in March. Estimates for the Radcliffe Committee had put the total at about £60 million in June 1958 and about £120 million a year later. Despite increases in dividend distributions, the swift rise in share prices led to a reduction in 'yields', and during the summer of 1959 the average yield on shares included in various indices fell below the yield on Consols.

The policy pursued by the authorities in seeking to contain the expansive movement in the economy materially changed the banking situation. The rise in bank rate in January was at once carried through, as usual, into the rates allowed by the banks on deposit accounts and charged for lending, while the lowering of the level of gilt-edged prices came at a time when the banks were selling government securities to make way for a sustained and rapid rise in advances. With the increase in advances and seasonal pressures, the liquidity ratio for the banks as a whole was only just above the conventional minimum of 30 per cent. Even though it had not been made 'explicit', as recommended by the Radcliffe Committee, the Committee's confirmation of the liquidity ratio as effectively governing the level of deposits reaffirmed its importance. Moreover, after the heavy reductions in investments during the preceding months it was reasonable to suppose that the banks' holdings of bonds with near maturities had become attenuated. Thus the banking situation became more sensitive to monetary measures, in line with the Radcliffe Committee's insistence upon debt management as the main instrument of monetary policy. Meanwhile, the growth in advances had carried them to a level, for the clearing banks as a whole, of over 44 per cent of deposits in March 1960, or roughly the same as in the late 1930s. At that period, however, advances of the banks as a whole represented about 22 per cent of the national income for the year, whereas at the end of 1959 the proportion was no more than 18 per cent.

The Radcliffe Committee's principal observations and recommendations relating to the joint stock banks are noted in Chapter 1. Subsequently some changes in practice were announced and official views made known* upon various recommendations. Following the debate, the fact that bank rate was unchanged was announced specifically (though in somewhat out-moded terms†) as having the approval of the Chancellor of the Exchequer, thus following, though by no means closely, a recommendation of the Radcliffe Report. In course of the debate the Chancellor had said he did not accept the recommendation of the Radcliffe Committee calling for a standing committee of representatives of the Bank and the government to 'advise the authorities on all matters relating to the coordination of monetary policy as a whole'; he had, however, made arrangements for the Bank of England to be 'permanently represented on the various official committees by which economic policy is already formulated and advice to Ministers on it is coordinated'. Upon the proposal that in some circumstances a variable liquidity ratio might be used, rather than the Special Deposits scheme, for restraining bank lending, it was stated that the government would 're-examine this question'; but the results of that re-examination remain to be disclosed. The recommendation that direct control of bank advances should be used only in an 'emergency' was obliquely rejected by the Chancellor, who said that 'a government must be free to make any change in the economic circumstances with which-

* Particularly in a debate in the House of Commons, 26 November 1959.

† 'The Bank of England have decided, with the approval of the Chancellor of the Exchequer, that there shall be no alteration in the rate of discount this day.'

ever of the available measures they judge likely to be most effective in those particular conditions without any implication that the situation which is being dealt with is of an emergency order'.

Two suggestions made by the Committee for extension of bank lending practices were adopted by the Midland Bank, with the introduction of specifically long-term loans to farmers and term loans for small businesses. Then, too, the banks have gone some way towards extending more widely the use of their long-established system of credit transfers, the first stage in the process being the establishment of a general credit clearing. The Radcliffe Committee had referred to the possibility of establishing a transfer system in this country on lines comparable to those of the 'giros' operating in several continental countries.

In addition the year 1959–60 was notable for improvements in information and statistics on monetary conditions, resulting largely from the proceedings and proposals of the Radcliffe Committee. To assist the Committee in its investigations a comprehensive survey of past monetary policy was submitted by the Bank of England, and, if the Committee's recommendations were adopted, something of this kind would be continued indefinitely. Improved banking statistics had been introduced before the publication of the Committee's Report, and these had been regularly issued. The Report contained new statistics of the financing of the public sector, in which net borrowing in various forms from internal sources and from the public were set out, and publication of these figures has been continued in even greater detail. Another improvement has been the introduction of quarterly balance of payments statistics in summary form, as an addition to the regular half-yearly white papers. Then, too, a greater readiness to offer official comment on developments in monetary policy has become evident: shortly after the rise in bank rate in January 1960 the Chancellor of the Exchequer made three statements, within little more than twenty-four hours, explaining why that particular step had been taken. These and other additions to the stock of knowledge on, and contributions to understanding of, current monetary affairs are of first importance in establishing a more informed awareness among the public generally of the trend of monetary policy.

9

Years of Disappointment

1961 – Uncertainty and paradox

A period of uncertainty in economic conditions rendered interpretation and analysis even more difficult than usual during the twelve months to April 1961. Following a rise in bank rate in January 1960, further measures were applied in April to restrain demand – the reimposition of hire purchase controls and the first call on the banks for Special Deposits – and within two months a second call for Special Deposits had been made and bank rate had been raised again, from 5 to 6 per cent. Since the end of June, however, no additional restrictions have been introduced; indeed, two small reductions in bank rate have been made for external reasons, and hire purchase restrictions have been eased to assist the industries directly affected. To quote the governor of the Bank of England, the 'rising boom' had gone 'off the boil' by last autumn. In fact, industrial production in aggregate ceased to rise, and some industries, especially those making durable consumer goods, experienced a sharp fall in demand. Yet the levels of employment and consumption remained high. A second paradox was shown in the external situation. Although the current balance of payments moved heavily into deficit – a development that seems to have influenced the authorities against measures to re-expand home demand – sterling was strong in overseas markets and the gold and currency reserves continued to rise each month until February 1961.

In the early months of 1960 the monetary authorities had been moving towards a policy of restraint, directed primarily to steadying domestic conditions, and as a safeguard against inflation. Bank rate had been increased from 4 to 5 per cent in January and, in the following month, an increase in long-term interest rates had been encouraged by a lowering of the prices at which the authorities were prepared to buy government securities. At the end of April further restraints were announced, and two months later other restrictive action was taken. Together these measures might be said to amount to a spread-over 'package deal' in that they included a further increase in bank rate and the controls over banking and hire purchase transactions. The Bank of England made an initial call on 28 April 1960 for Special Deposits, to be made on or before 15 June, at the rate of 1 per cent of gross deposits for the clearing banks and ½ per cent for Scottish banks, thus introducing a quite new method of regulation to which further reference is made below. Controls over hire purchase transactions were imposed on 29 April, comprising a minimum deposit of 20 per cent on a wide range of goods including cars and domestic appliances, and 10 per cent on others, such as furniture, cookers and bicycles. The maximum period of repayment was fixed at two years for all controlled goods except cookers, wash boilers and water heaters, for which it was four.

On 23 June bank rate was raised again, to 6 per cent, and a further call was made for Special Deposits at the same rates as before bringing the proportion of deposits to 2 per cent for the clearing banks and 1 per cent for the Scottish banks. One half of the further requirement by way of Special Deposits had to be made by 20 July and the balance by 17 August. On this occasion a spokesman for the Bank of England said that official action was 'directed to the domestic situation, but bearing in mind the effect which the domestic situation has on the external situation', and the Chancellor of the Exchequer described the object of policy as to 'maintain the economy in balance and to keep off inflation'. He also undertook to hold the level of public sector investment in 1961–2 at the estimated level for 1960–1.

According to the *Economic Survey 1961* (Cmnd. 1334), the measures 'checked total home demand; consumption fell slightly and investment rose strongly; the rate of stockbuilding stopped rising after the middle of the year'. As the records showed, imports rose throughout 1960, while exports declined after the first quarter. Industrial output, which had increased in aggregate by more than 10 per cent during the year to March 1960, ceased to rise after April, and from November onwards the seasonally adjusted index tended to fall; by January 1961 it was no higher than the year before. By contrast, the total for employment rose to record high levels, and the percentage of unemployed remained low. Meanwhile, prices and wage rates edged upwards, retail prices increasing by nearly 3 per cent, and the wholesale prices of finished goods by 2½ per cent, in the year to March 1961.

Some unevenness in the business situation reflected the 'directional effects' of the restrictions. The controls over hire purchase quickly lessened the demand for durable consumer goods, and the rise in bank advances to personal borrowers, partly for the purchase of such goods, was checked when restrictions on the banks came into effect. For example, the demand for motor cars – also suffering from a fall in exports – sharply declined, and it was likewise reduced for domestic appliances and furniture. As output was curtailed, short-time working and some dismissals of workpeople were recorded in these industries, as well as in a few others, such as shipbuilding, where activity slackened for different reasons. By contrast, production in most other industries continued to expand, though less rapidly than in the previous year. A substantial fall in industrial output as a whole was avoided, mainly because of buoyancy in the volume of fixed investment and a remarkable increase in stocks. It was estimated that during 1960 the expansion in stocks, mainly by industry, was greater than in any year since 1951; to some extent the rise was involuntary, consisting of stocks of unsold manufactured goods, but it was also due to greater stockbuilding at all stages of production and it included large accumulations of imported raw materials.

In the industries experiencing a setback in activity, both the employers and the trade unions were anxious to avoid the dismissal of workpeople, so that short-time working became widespread in several undertakings, particularly in the motor industry. Elsewhere a shortage of skilled employees persisted and overtime working remained at a high level. Indeed, taking the country as a whole, from June to September 1960 the number of unfilled vacancies exceeded the total unemployed for the first time since the autumn of 1957.

By the autumn of 1960 it was being suggested that the restrictions should be relaxed, but with indications of inflationary pressure still appearing in the economy, and with a continuing worsening in the balance of payments position, the Chancellor of the Exchequer rejected these suggestions 'in the interests of the economy as a whole'. Speaking at the annual 'bankers' dinner' at the Mansion House in October he said that it was 'too soon to talk of demand becoming insufficient', but that credit restrictions would be eased as soon as it was safe to do so – that is, 'as soon as we judge that the rate of investment and the growth of exports will not suffer'. On the same occasion, the governor of the Bank of England expressed the view that it would be unwise to remove restraints while there was a risk of 'starting the pot boiling again', but that it would be just as unwise to keep too much rigidity too long merely for fear that minor adjustments might be misinterpreted as a change of direction'.

In the event bank rate was reduced from 6 to $5\frac{1}{2}$ per cent on 27 October 960 and to 5 per cent on 8 December, but it was officially stated that neither of these adjustments implied a change in the policy of restraint at home; they had been made for external reasons, the previous rate having been 'unnecessarily high in relation to rates in other financial centres'. A further measure of relaxation took place towards the end of January 1961, when control over hire purchase was eased by extending the maximum period of repayment to three years in respect of goods for which it had previously been two. This mainly affected the motor industry and, as the seasonal recovery in demand took effect, activity in the industry improved in the early months of 1961.

Sterling withstands speculation

The difficulties in Britain's domestic conditions were complicated by the swift deterioration in her external situation, the authorities having less room for manoeuvre as the balance of payments position moved more and more unfavourably. A deficit was recorded on the balance of payments on current account in each of the three quarters from April to December, and probably also in the first quarter of 1961. The current deficit for the calendar year 1960 – as calculated on a new basis – amounted to £344 million, and was the first since 1955 and only the third recorded in the past thirteen years; it compared with a surplus for 1959, on the revised basis, of £51 million and of £291 million for 1958. The value of imports, seasonally adjusted, continued to expand in 1960, a rise stimulated by the high level of home demand, the rebuilding of stocks and trade liberalization measures, though the rate of increase slackened after the middle of the year, when home demand became less pressing. By contrast, exports reached a peak in the first quarter of 1960 and thereafter they tended to fall, though recovering slightly in the fourth quarter. A conspicuous reduction in 1960 was the sharp fall in shipments of cars to North America, but other exports to this area also fell, and towards the end of the calendar year exports to all areas were stable or declining, except to western Europe where some increase occurred, despite the difficulties for particular exporters arising from the development of the Common Market.

As recorded in the balance of payments figures, imports rose during 1960 by £499 million and exports, including re-exports, by £202 million, the excess of imports increasing to £366 million as compared with £69 million a year before. This was accompanied by a continuation of the decline in net income from 'invisibles' from £229 million in 1958 to £120 million in 1959 and only £22 million in 1960. In these items the deterioration in 1960 resulted mainly from higher government current expenditure abroad, chiefly on defence, adding £57 million, and increased payments of interest, profits and dividends amounting to £35 million, largely on account of higher interest payments on sterling holdings.

Efforts to combat the unsatisfactory trend in exports included a government campaign, with ministers visiting many industrial centres to give encouragement to exporters. An additional incentive comprised the decision to reduce form-filling by abolishing, from the beginning of September, the need for exchange control declarations for export shipments valued at up to

£2000; the previous limit had been £500. Next, improvement was made in export credit facilities. In October the Export Credits Guarantee Department was authorized to insure credit on longer terms than the ordinary maximum of five years, in circumstances where this was 'necessary to allow a United Kingdom exporter to match terms offered by a foreign competitor with the backing of an export credit guarantee institution or equivalent official support'. Each application was to be considered on its merits, and longer-term credit would only be insured where there were strong commercial grounds for winning the contract. It was emphasized that it was not intended to take the initiative in lengthening the terms of credit in competition with other countries. Arrangements were also announced for special assistance where the ECGD was 'reasonably sure' that the British exporter was encountering longer terms offered by foreign suppliers, even though it was not established that the competitor was backed by a credit insurance institution. In particular circumstances, the ECGD was also authorized to give part period cover. In April further improvements in facilities were announced, comprising reduced charges for medium-term insurance; more general guarantees for longer periods than five years, and loans in exceptional circumstances; and a simplified service for small-scale exporters. In August, the *ad valorem* scale of stamp duty on bills of exchange is to be replaced by a flat rate duty of 2*d.* in order to help exporters.

Meanwhile, the Bank of England announced in February that where the clearing, Scottish and Northern Irish banks had given export credit for a term of more than three years, repayable by instalments and covered by the ECGD, the Bank would stand ready to refinance that part of such credits which was within eighteen months of maturity (see p. 247).

To complete the record of developments in the balance of payments situation during 1960, the deficit of £344 million on current account was accompanied by net outgoings of £201 million on long-term capital account. If the payment made to the International Monetary Fund in 1959 in respect of the increase in subscriptions be excluded, this indicates a slight fall in long-term overseas investment both on government and private accounts. With the new official statistics of private investment moving into this country as well as out, it has been revealed that the inflow last year amounted to £173 million, or only £101 million less than private British investment overseas. A substantial part of this investment in Britain comprised profits retained in the country by overseas companies operating here, and it is the upward movement in the estimates of retained profits which accounts for the revision in the figures of the current balance of payments. It might have been expected that the heavy outgoings in respect of the current deficit and long-term investment, together amounting to £545 million, would have led to a severe drain on the gold and convertible currency reserves. In fact, the reserves rose by £177 million during 1960 and the sterling holdings of 'international organizations' were reduced by £156 million (see Appendix 2, Table 2). This was accounted for by a rise of £380 million in sterling holdings of overseas countries, an inflow of identified short-term capital of £119 million, and by an unprecedentedly large 'balancing item' of £377 million, which in the official view was 'probably associated with an unrecorded capital inflow into the United Kingdom'.

Here, then, is part of the explanation of the strength of sterling and growth in central reserves while the balance of payments was moving adversely; another aspect was the weakness of the dollar and outflow of gold from the United States where, to add to the paradox, the current balance of payments was improving. In the autumn Britain made prepayments of debts and other transfers, including the paying off of the whole of her outstanding liability to the International Monetary Fund. Of the \$561·5 million drawn in December 1956, \$200 million had been repaid in March 1959, and the balance was to be settled by monthly instalments in 1960 and 1961. By October 1960, however, various prepayments had cleared the liability. The annual payments amounting to \$187 million, for the service of the United States and the Canadian debts were made as usual in December and at that time a special transaction was arranged whereby the United Kingdom sold US \$47·4 million to the International Monetary Fund for sterling. This reduced the Fund's holding of sterling to 75 per cent of Britain's quota, the percentage below which a member may not withdraw its own currency from the Fund. Because of the low level of its reserves at the time of joining the Fund in 1946, the United Kingdom had been permitted to subscribe more than 75 per cent of its quota in sterling.

Even so the gold and foreign exchange reserves rose to £1154 million by the end of 1960, while overseas holdings of sterling increased to £4436 million. It is worth noting that the overseas sterling countries actually drew upon their sterling balances to the extent of £224 million, mainly in the second half of the year; the net increase resulted from the rise in balances of non-sterling countries, by £604 million, to reach £1407 million in December, the highest level ever recorded. The figures have since been revised somewhat (see Appendix 2, Table 2). This flood tide was attributed mainly to the relatively high level of interest rates – both long- and short-term – in London as compared with other financial centres, besides uncertainties as to the position of the United States dollar and some other currencies; but it was also prompted by measures introduced in Switzerland and West Germany to discourage the inflow of short-term funds. Almost all of the increase was for the accounts of holders in North America and western Europe. A special transaction whereby Ford Motor of Detroit provided sterling to buy the shares of minority holders – largely British residents – in Ford Motor of Dagenham temporarily added £131 million to North American holdings of sterling. The transfer strengthened the United Kingdom's external liquid position by bringing an increase in the gold and currency reserves, offset by an increase in American long-term investment in equity capital in Britain.

Another aspect of the inflow of funds into Britain is to be seen in the figures for the United Kingdom business of overseas banking offices and accepting houses, published regularly for the first time for 1960 as a half-yearly series. As may be seen in Table C1, during 1960 the aggregate for deposits of overseas banking offices with the four groups for which figures are available rose by £283 million and those of other overseas residents by £141 million. Most of the rise occurred in the first half of the year, and, although the authorities on a number of occasions indicated that by no means all of the inflow of capital into Britain was for short-term investment, it seems that it was attracted in the main by passing influences. With the two reductions in

TABLE C1 *Overseas banks in Britain* (*changes in deposits and advances in 1960*) (*£m.*)

	British overseas banks	*American banks*	*Other foreign banks*	*Accepting houses*
Deposits				
UK residents	+ 37	+ 22	+ 20	+ 60
Overseas banking offices	+ 10	+128	+ 79	+ 66
Other overseas residents	+ 60	+ 33	+ 10	+ 38
Total	+108	+183	+108	+164
Advances				
UK residents	+ 27	+ 12	+ 12	+ 52
Overseas banking offices	+ 37	+166	+ 28	+ 30
Other overseas residents	+ 20	—	+ 4	+ 15
Total	+ 84	+178	+ 44	+ 97

bank rate in October and December, designed to lessen the interest advantage of London, along with the less favourable external position of the United Kingdom and the restoration of confidence in the United States dollar, the inflow into Britain was diminished and some withdrawal took place. The gold and foreign exchange reserves, after rising for more than twelve months, fell by £18 million in February 1961.

Early in March 1961 the Deutschmark and the Dutch guilder were revalued by 5 per cent, a move that gave rise to expectations of other currency changes. Considerable speculation in currencies developed, partly directed against sterling, leading to a heavy outflow of funds from the United Kingdom as the authorities operated to support the pound. The Chancellor of the Exchequer reaffirmed on several occasions that there was no intention of devaluing sterling, stating on 8 March that the government did not 'consider that the pound [was] overvalued in terms of other currencies'. Subsequently the pressure on sterling eased, and further help came in the following week from a statement issued jointly by the governors of eight European central banks that 'rumours . . . of possible further currency adjustments' had 'no foundation'. The governors also stated that they were 'cooperating closely in the exchange markets', but did not say how they were doing so. It has been suggested that the central banks of countries receiving an inflow of capital would hold, temporarily at least, balances in the currencies of countries suffering an outflow of capital, to a larger extent than was usual. Hence the effects of speculation against sterling may not be reflected to the full in the fall of Britain's reserves, amounting to £62 million in 1961.

For the thirteen months from mid-January 1960 the rate for sterling generally stood above parity against the United States dollar (see Appendix 3, Chart (e)). It was, however, frequently quoted below par against some other currencies. The Bank of England *Quarterly Bulletin,* referring to the position after mid-August 1960, said that 'such fluctuations as there were . . . could usually be attributed to changes, actual or expected, in comparative interest rates. For example, a relatively sharp, but short-lived, fall during the latter part of September was associated with continental rumours of a reduction in bank rate, which coincided with a renewed movement of funds to West Germany stimulated by discussion of that country's creditor position at the annual meeting of the International Monetary Fund.' Two weeks after the reduction in bank rate to 5½ per cent in October the external value of sterling began to decline, and when bank rate was again lowered in December 1960 the rate fell below \$2·81. In February 1961 the rate moved below the par value of \$2·80, and following the revaluation of the Deutschmark it declined to little more than \$2·79¼ at one point in March and to under par against other major currencies. As currency speculation abated, the rate tended to recover, and in April sterling was running slightly below par against the dollar.

The premium for forward dollars was about ¼ cent for one month and ½ cent for three months in April 1960, and in the summer, when bank rate in the United Kingdom was increased and Federal Reserve discount rates lowered, these margins increased to over ½ cent and over 1½ cents, respectively. After Britain's short-term interest rates had been adjusted the one-month premium reverted to ¼ – ⅝ cent and that for three months fell to ¾ – ⅞ cent. The margins did not widen when speculation followed the revaluation of the Deutschmark, but after the spot rate for sterling recovered the forward rates again declined and the margins increased to about ¾ cent and 1¼ cents respectively; these narrowed again in April 1961 to ½ and 1⅛ cents.

For several months prior to mid-June 1960 the rate for security sterling had been fluctuating, mainly below US \$2·78, but thereafter it rose sharply to reach, in mid-August, virtual parity with the current market rate for external sterling, which then stood at \$2·81. Thereafter, for about four months, in the words of the Bank of England, there 'ceased to be any advantage in using security sterling compared with external sterling for portfolio investment in the United Kingdom' and the 'weight of funds seeking such investment was felt directly in the market for external sterling'. In mid-September when demand for sterling was strong, security sterling was quoted at \$2·81$\frac{9}{16}$. From about 16 December 1960, however, it fell sharply, perhaps because of the increasing tendency to withdraw funds from Britain, and a margin was established below external sterling, of about 1½ cents. Thereafter, the value of security sterling fluctuated, mainly between \$2·78 and \$2·79, though it fell sharply in March 1961 to \$2·75, the lowest level for over three years.

Short-term investment, with forward exchange cover, was more remunerative in London as compared with New York throughout 1960 because of the relatively high rates for Treasury bills. In establishing forward margins, however, an important influence was exercised by 'swap' transactions arising from dealings in 'Eurodollars' or, more recently, in 'Eurosterling'. Eurodollars consist of balances in United States banks, owned outside the dollar area, which are lent to obtain a higher rate of interest. They may be borrowed, for example, by an overseas resident requiring dollars, if he is able to obtain finance in this way more cheaply than by borrowing in New York, or by a trader requiring sterling for three months, whenever the rate of interest, plus the cost of converting into sterling temporarily by means of a three months 'swap', is less than that for borrowing sterling direct. In the market for Eurodollars in London and other European centres, countries with high domestic rates of interest had been keen borrowers; it was suggested that, of about \$1000 million of 'Eurodollars' being lent through London at the end of 1960, about one half was borrowed by Japan. Similarly in centres on the continent a market had developed for Eurosterling, dealing in external account sterling which was used to make short-term loans to other non-residents of the sterling area.

An unusual development took place in the London gold market. In August 1960, with a number of countries adding to their reserves, and preferring to hold gold rather than dollars, the demand for gold in the London market was growing. Under this and other influences, the price rose to the equivalent of \$35·26 per fine ounce, although monetary authorities were able to purchase gold from the Federal Reserve Bank of New York at the statutory price plus handling charges, and even after payment of shipment and other expenses the cost in Europe was only about \$35·20 an ounce. It is possible that central banks were unwilling to add to the difficulties of the United States authorities by increasing the outflow of gold from that country. When in September the meeting of the International Monetary Fund passed without any adjustment of parities, the demand for gold slackened, and the price fell. Then, on 20 October 1960, the price suddenly leapt upwards, dealings taking place at the equivalent of $40 per fine ounce. The United States Treasury promptly reaffirmed the intention to continue to deal at the official rate of $35 per fine ounce, exclusive of handling charges, and to sell only to monetary authorities for 'legitimate monetary purposes'. On 21 October the price fell to the equivalent of $37, and in the following weeks it continued to decline. The Bank of England *Bulletin* explains, however, that on several occasions 'the scale of the Bank's operations had . . . to be increased to prevent conditions in the market from getting out of hand'. Early in January 1961 the United States prohibited its residents, as from 1 June, from holding gold outside the country. (They were already forbidden to hold it within the United States.) Later that month the new United States President firmly reasserted the intention to maintain unchanged the gold parity of the dollar, and shortly afterwards the London price fell below $35·20.

Since the end of 1958 sterling has been fully convertible for the current account transactions of non-residents, but, under the 'transitional period' arrangements of Article XIV of the International Monetary Fund Agreement, it would have been possible to reimpose exchange restrictions. A formal move was made in February 1961, when Britain and nine other countries, mostly west European and including West Germany and France, accepted the provisions of Article VIII whereby restrictions on current payments, multiple exchange rates and discriminatory currency practices cannot be introduced without the consent of the Fund, which may be given only in exceptional circumstances. One consequence of the adoption of Article VIII was that sterling and the other currencies involved could be used to make repayments to the Fund. Previously, repayments had to be made, in effect, in gold or in United States or Canadian dollars, the only major convertible currencies of member countries. It is expected that members would be prepared to sue the facilities of the Fund more readily, and the United States President stated his country's willingness to use the resources of the Fund if it became expedient to do so. The governor of the Bank of England said that he would 'like to see countries draw on [the Fund's] facilities as a matter of ordinary business when they need to reinforce reserves and repay when reserves are rising'. Advance repayments made by Britain in 1960 were 'an instance of this policy'.

The banks and liquidity pressures

On 28 April 1960, when the Chancellor of the Exchequer announced the first call for Special Deposits and the reimposition of hire purchase controls he said that 'these measures, together with the budget, will act as a check on the tendencies making for overstrain on the economy while not preventing the continuance of sound and steady expansion within our resources'. In answering questions, he added that they were 'fully in line with the objective . . . of not halting expansion, but of putting a slight brake on its rate to ensure that the rate of continued advance would be within our resources'. Referring to the call for Special Deposits, the Chancellor expressed the view that the 'reasonable time' that the banks had been given to adjust their existing commitments and the 'deliberately moderate' size of the initial call, would 'influence them in the direction of moderating their advances rather than selling gilt-edged stocks'. The Bank of England subsequently noted that 'other groups of banks were officially informed of the call being made upon the clearing banks and Scottish banks and were made aware of the authorities' desire to encourage restraint in bank lending'. As to the reintroduction of hire purchase controls, the Bank said that there 'appeared to be a clear case for a selective control of this kind', and also that 'it was desirable that restraint should be applied not only to the banks, but as widely as possible over the whole field of short-term lending'. In June a second call for Special Deposits, with an increase in bank rate to 6 per cent, reinforced the earlier measures. In the words of the Bank of England, 'it was decided to take a further series of measures to make private credit more expensive and difficult to obtain; and to discourage any impression that the authorities were ready to acquiesce in a resumption of inflation'.

When, for reasons related to the external situation, bank rate was reduced in October and December 1960, and to help particular industries a slight relaxation of hire purchase controls was made in January 1961, it was stated that the policy of restraint was to continue; 'the economic prospect as a whole, including the outlook for costs and prices, still did not warrant any general relaxation of credit policy'. No further changes in Special Deposits were made. The governor of the Bank of England described the system in October as one that had 'proved a useful addition to our monetary armoury', though he had the feeling 'that any prolonged or frequent use of this system (or indeed of any form of credit squeeze on the banks, voluntary or compulsory) is both unfair to the organized banking community, and in the long run liable to be ineffective'. Four months later he said that he thought that monetary policy had achieved a considerable part of its objective. The restrictions had contributed to preventing an 'overboiling' of the economy in the spring of 1960, had 'helped to maintain confidence in sterling over a period when weakness would have been a danger both nationally and internationally' and had had some influence in diverting bank credit away from consumption towards investment.

The Chancellor, in his budget speech on 17 April 1961, proposed two 'new economic regulators' which would 'very much improve the government's capacity to adjust trends in the economy without violent movements', and so would lessen the burden to be borne by monetary policy. He said that there had been 'much complaint about the jerkiness of government action in controlling the economy; what has been referred to as a policy of stop and start. . . . Monetary methods, the bank rate, the Special Deposits scheme, and the hire purchase restrictions . . . have their disadvantages. It is not always possible to arrange that the same level of bank rate suits us domestically and internationally. A high rate may be prudent at home if demand is too high, but it may attract at some cost to us short-term funds from overseas which are not really wanted. . . . Regulation by means of the budget . . . should remain the chief instrument, but it is not always possible to arrange that conditions will remain precisely the same over the following twelve months. . . . While not dispensing with any of these monetary methods, we do need further means of stimulating or restricting the economy, by measures which can be brought into operation quickly at any time of the year, and the effect of which will be reasonably rapid and widespread.'

Accordingly he proposed that the government should be given power to direct, at any time of the year, that 'either a special surcharge or a special rebate should be applied to all the main Customs and Excise revenue duties and to purchase tax', at any rate up to 10 per cent of the existing charges; in this way consumers' purchasing power could be stimulated or restrained 'by a maximum annual rate of over £200 million a year each way'. He also proposed similar power to impose 'a special surcharge on employers analogous to a payroll tax', at a rate of up to 4*s*. per employee per week; this could 'withdraw from the economy about £200 million in a full year'. Action under either or both of these powers would be subject to confirmation by the House of Commons. Both powers would be sought for a period of one year and be subject to annual renewal. By using 'these two new fiscal powers . . . either together or separately' the government would be 'able to act by quick and flexible fiscal means in the interval between this and the next budget, thus reducing during that period dependence on regulation by monetary and credit restrictions'.

In the year under review the credit squeeze in its new form, reinforced by a vigorous funding policy, had in fact slowed down the growth of bank activity. Gross deposits of the clearing banks rose by about £140 million to £7189 million, whereas in the previous twelve months the increase had been by more than £400 million. A renewal of the shift from current to deposit accounts was evident during the year, presumably encouraged by the higher level of deposit rate; credit balances on current accounts fell by £54 million, while those on deposit accounts increased by £128 million. About one half of the rise in total deposits over the year was in respect of 'other accounts', and this was partly due to the operation of the credit clearing. The comparison with a year earlier is also affected by the transfer, at the close of business on 31 December 1960, of Lloyds Bank branches in India, Pakistan and Burma, to National and Grindlays Bank, a non-clearing institution; their deposits were possibly about £50 million.

Advances of the clearing banks rose over the year to March 1961 by £347 million to £3468 million, as compared with an increase of £674 million in the preceding year. After a sharp rise in the first month, the increase was spread fairly evenly throughout the year. By March advances accounted for 48·2 per cent of deposits of the clearing banks, the highest proportion recorded since the middle of 1932, and comparing with 44·3 per cent in March 1960. Again the figures are slightly affected by the transfer of Lloyds Bank eastern branches. Another special influence, from February 1961 onwards, has been the treatment in bank statements of the refinanceable portions of export credits.

Under new arrangements announced on 6 February, the Bank of England stood ready to refinance a part of medium-term export credits granted by a clearing bank, a Scottish bank, a Northern Irish bank, or by special arrangement, any other bank on similar lines, provided the credit was for more than three years, repayable by instalments and covered by the Export Credits Guarantee Department. The refinanceable part consists of instalments due within eighteen months, and, since these could be turned into cash at any time, they were regarded by the banks as liquid assets. Thus from February onwards the amounts refinanceable were transferred from advances and included with bills in the clearing banks' monthly statements. The advantage to a clearing bank is therefore not an addition to cash, unless it were to refinance the credit, but an addition to liquid assets. With a credit repayable in equal instalments spread over a period of five years, the refinanceable proportion works out at 30 per cent of the total credit, so corresponding with the then conventional liquidity ratio, and therefore export credits in this category were not subject to the general restraints as operating on bank liquidity.

It is evident from the quarterly classifications of bank advances that the distribution of lending over groups of borrowers was influenced by the restrictions. About one third of the increase in advances during the year to February 1961 went to the engineering and other heavy industries, where borrowing rose by nearly one half. Later in the year some recovery in lending to the consumer goods industries and to services was apparent. Advances to personal and professional borrowers, after rising rapidly in the previous year, have remained almost unchanged since May 1960.

With the impetus towards rising advances still evident, the authorities maintained the full rigour of the Special Deposits arrangements. Each clearing bank was required to hold funds in a special account with the Bank of England, since last August to the extent of 2 per cent of its gross deposits. With gross deposits fluctuating, the amounts of Special Deposits were adjusted, usually three weeks after the date of each mid-monthly statement. Interest is allowed on Special Deposits week by week at a rate calculated as the multiple of one sixteenth per cent nearest to the average Treasury bill rate at the previous weekly tender. Special Deposits may not be counted as part of the liquid assets of a bank, and as the convention of maintaining liquidity ratios at a minimum of 30 per cent was then closely watched, the effect was to curtail funds for lending. In fact during most of the year the liquidity ratios of the banks were running closer to 30 per cent than is usual and it was plain that, at the time of seasonal strain in the early months of 1961, it would not be easy to observe the conventional proportion.

The Bank of England took the view that 'there were two factors which . . . might in some degree offset the usual seasonal pressures; . . . first, the receipt of money by UK shareholders of Fords and secondly, the possibility that funds required for the payment of taxes might be found to a lesser extent than usual by the running down of deposits or the taking of advances. . . . These possibilities and, of greater importance, the feeling that the economic outlook did not warrant any further relaxations caused the authorities to leave the level of special deposits unchanged.' In the event, the liquidity ratio for the clearing banks combined was reduced to 30·5 per cent in March, and for three of the big banks it had on occasion fallen slightly below 30 per cent.

As was to be expected the banks continued to reduce their holdings of investments to provide for the growth in borrowing by customers, following the tradition of regarding investments as the residual item in the distribution of bank assets. In the year to March 1961 investments of the clearing banks in government securities fell by £294 million equal to more than three quarters of the rise in advances over the period. In the previous year, the reduction in investments had been larger still at £448 million. In March 1961 the total for investments of the clearing banks was £1187 million, the lowest figure recorded since 1945, and representing less than 17 per cent of deposits, a proportion lower than at any time since the spring of 1932. As is noted below investments sold by the banks in the nine months to December 1960 were absorbed by private investors at home and overseas. Sales by the banks are often of such a size that they are taken up by the government broker in the first place but in this period – by contrast with the previous financial year – such official support was 'purely temporary'.

During the year two banking developments occurred that may bring extensive changes in British banking activity. The first was the inauguration of the general credit clearing by the banking community itself, and the second legislation permitting the payment of wages through banks. The clearing banks introduced a General Credit Clearing on 20 April 1960, through which credit transfers between banks are passed for settlement, on broadly the lines recommended by the Radcliffe Committee, although a preliminary investigation of the scheme had been announced before its report was published. It represented a development of the long-established 'traders' credits' system, with all credit payments passing through clearing arrangements as with cheques. It is thus similar to the giro transfer systems familiar in continental countries and elsewhere, but hitherto not generally applied in this country, where the cheque system is highly developed. The first stage applied credit clearing to traders' credit transfers, including salary and pensions payments so distributed and standing orders; six months later the scheme was extended to include credits paid in over branch counters, by customers, for transmission to accounts at other branch banks. Somewhat later the Scottish banks introduced similar facilities. On 6 March 1961 both groups of banks brought into operation the third and final stage, whereby the facilities for credit transfers were made available to all members of the public whether they were customers of a bank or not. Payment may now be made by anybody at the counter of any branch of a clearing or Scottish bank for transmission to an account anywhere in the United Kingdom. A small charge is made for each credit received from a non-customer. Similar arrangements were introduced in Ireland in April 1961. Between 1 May 1960 and 31 March 1961, items valued at £3497 million passed through the clearing banks' credit clearing, as compared with £214,624 million for the cheque clearing for the same period.

The Payment of Wages Act was passed in 1960. It authorized the payment of wages by direct transfer to a bank account or by cheque, or in other defined ways, provided the employee requested payment through such channels. The legislation authorized payment of wages by direct transfer to be made from 2 December onwards, but payment by cheque was to await a day still to be appointed by the Minister of Labour. He has undertaken to consult interested parties, such as banks and shopkeepers, before making the necessary Order.

The 1960 budget was designed to be more or less neutral in its effect on demand in the economy and left £318 million to be covered by borrowing, taking below-the-line items into account, or about the same amount as in the preceding year. In the event, net borrowing amounted to £394 million. As will be seen from Appendix 2, Table 3, on government finance, with sinking fund provisions excluded from ordinary expenditure, and transactions affecting the Civil Contingencies Fund included among below-the-line items, the overall deficit was £349 million in 1960–1 as compared with £275 million in 1959–60.

In the budget speech in April 1961, the Chancellor said: 'The broad effect of the budget must be counter-inflationary; there must be a larger surplus above the line than last year and a smaller overall deficit.' This would result largely from the natural buoyancy of the revenue without substantial addition to taxation. Nevertheless, he estimated that the net effect of proposed tax changes would be to increase revenue by £68 million in 1961–2. With this addition he budgeted for a surplus above the line of £506 million, as compared with an out-turn of £147 million in 1960–1; and a net borrowing requirement of £69 million as compared with £394 million. 'This amount', he added, 'is well within what I may reasonably expect to raise from national savings and other forms of non-marketable debt. . . .While we shall not lose sight of our longer-term aim of lengthening the debt already in market hands . . . we shall not, if things go as we expect, be looking for new money from the gilt-edged market in 1961–2. This will give us additional room for manoeuvre in our monetary policy from now on.'

He described the situation in the previous year as one in which 'the borrowing problem set by [the] overall deficit was substantially increased by the need to finance both the rise in the gold and foreign currency reserves and our other external transactions. Over the year our total requirement, after employing receipts from extra-budgetary funds, was £560 million. £115 million of this came from the increase in the note circulation, £300 million was raised by borrowing from the public, and a further £145 million was provided by Treasury bills held by the Bank of England against the Special Deposits called from the banks.'

Net receipts from national savings fell from £389 million in the financial year to March 1960 to £341 million in 1961 but, even so, this was the second highest figure ever recorded. The limit on individual holdings of the current series of savings certificates had been raised from 1000 to 1200 units in April 1960, but net investment in the year to 31 March 1961, fell by £10 million to £57 million. Similarly net investment in defence bonds declined by £37 million to £107 million, despite the introduction in June of a new series, on the same terms as for the previous issue, but with a limit on individual holdings of £5000 in addition to any previous issues held. By contrast, the new terms for premium savings bonds which took effect during the year – an increase in the maximum permitted holding from £500 to £800, a reduction in the period of qualification before participation in the monthly draw from six to three months and an increase in the maximum prize from £1000 to £5000 – increased their popularity, and net receipts rose by £15 million to £56 million. For other items included in national savings, the improvement in the experience of the Post Office Savings Bank recorded a year earlier continued, net withdrawals again being comparatively small, amounting to £14 million. For the ordinary departments of trustee savings banks, the excess of new deposits over withdrawals was not maintained, the two being roughly in balance, but amounts held in special investment departments again rose rapidly. From 2 May 1960, the limit on the aggregate deposit which any one customer may hold in the Post Office Savings Bank or in the ordinary department of a trustee savings bank was raised from £3000 to £5000, and the limit on the amount deposited during one year was abolished.

The Exchequer was well placed for transactions in marketable securities. No government stocks were due for repayment during the fiscal year, and £1070 million was raised by three cash issues. In July, £300 million of $5\frac{1}{2}$ per cent Treasury Bonds 1962 were issued at £99, offering a yield rather higher than that current in the market and so marching with the upward trend then evident in interest rates and bringing appropriate adjustments in market prices of other short-term issues. As usual, no figures of private as compared with official applications were revealed, but it was suggested that substantial amounts of this issue were taken up by the market. An issue of £500 million of 5½ per cent Treasury Stock 2008–12 was made at £95 in October 1960, the terms including special provisions for tax exemption for non-resident holders, perhaps to attract into long-term investment the foreign funds flowing into London at that time. The issue was also thought to be designed to replenish official holdings of long-dated stock, which seemed to be running short. In February 1961, a further £300 million of an existing security – 4¾ per cent Conversion Stock 1963 – was issued at £99⅜. At the same time holders of the £796 million of 2½ per cent Funding Loan, due for repayment on 15 April, were offered conversion into a new tranche of 5½ per cent Exchequer Stock 1966; holders of about £482 million of the maturing stock accepted the conversion, but the transaction is not included in the figures for 1960–1.

Of the £1070 million provided in these ways for the Exchequer during the financial year 1960–1 a proportion – the amount is not disclosed – was taken up by government departments, and departmental holdings of tap bills were reduced accordingly. During the year, the government provided £56 million for reduction of external debt, and among repayments of internal debt, £145 million for interest-free sterling notes held by the International Monetary Fund, that were redeemed as noted in the previous section. A further £150 million of Treasury bills was issued to the Exchange Equalization Account, to assist it in financing the inflow of gold and foreign exchange to the reserves. Even so, it was possible to reduce the outstanding total of Treasury bills by £554 million of which £380 million represented tender bills, and this added another twist to the screw pressing on bank liquidity. Over the year, Treasury bill holdings of the clearing banks fell by about £151 million, only a little above the £143 million transferred to the Bank of England as Special Deposits; these Special Deposits were used to increase the Bank of England's own holdings of Treasury bills.

To judge from changes in government debt held by the public for the three quarters to December 1960 – more recent figures are not yet available – the control of bank liquidity was greatly helped by the success of official 'funding policy'. The *Economic Survey* records that, in the quarter to June, 'the banks were . . . considerable sellers of securities, but the appetite of non-banking holders for gilt-edged securities revived sufficiently to enable the market to absorb these sales without other than purely temporary official assistance. . . . During the second half of the year the banks continued to be net sellers of gilt-edged securities, though on a considerably smaller scale than in the first half of the year. But there was a strong resurgence of demand for gilt-edged securities . . . both by domestic non-bank investors and non-official overseas buyers.'

In the three months to June 1960, holdings of marketable government debt by the public were little changed on balance. In the second half of 1960, however, they rose by £558 million, of which £158 million was for bills and £400 million for stocks. Taking the clearing and Scottish banks and discount houses together, no substantial net movement was recorded for this period; holdings of bills rose by £48 million, but those of stocks fell by only £22 million, the substantial sales by banks being largely offset by discount market purchases. Overseas central banks and other official bodies added to their investments in stocks and reduced their holdings of bills; but other home and overseas non-official holders made net purchases of stocks to the extent of £382 million, and of bills amounting to £181 million, of which £131 million was accounted for by the arrangements for financing the Ford Motor take-over bid. It seems probable that a substantial proportion of the funds flowing into Britain from abroad – estimated by the Bank of England at £350 million in the second half of the year – was used to purchase government stocks.

While over the financial year short-term interest rates, after rising, began to fall, long-term rates crept upwards throughout the year. In mid-April 1960, with bank rate at 5 per cent, the average rate of discount on Treasury bills was about $4\frac{5}{8}$ per cent. The margin of $\frac{3}{8}$ to $\frac{1}{2}$ per cent persisted, with the raising of bank rate, until October. Thereafter the bill rate fell; bidding from outside the discount market syndicate was competitive and it included investment of liquid funds from abroad; and little resistance to the movement came from the authorities. Hence the two reductions in bank rate were anticipated in market developments, although an earlier downward trend had encountered opposition from the authorities. The average rate of discount at the weekly tender fell from about £5 11*s*. 9*d*. per cent per annum on 2 September to £5 10*s*. 2*d*. a week later, but on 10 September 1960 several discount houses were forced to borrow from the Bank of England at bank rate, this being the first such borrowing at a penal rate since the end of June and the first on a Saturday for more than eight years.

Since October the margin between bill rate and bank rate usually exceeded $\frac{5}{8}$ per cent, sometimes reaching $\frac{7}{8}$. The average tender rate for bills continued to decline until the beginning of February 1961, when it was little more than $4\frac{1}{8}$ per cent, but with expectations of a further reduction in bank rate then receding it later rose to about $4\frac{1}{2}$.

Since December 1960, bank rate has stood at 5 per cent, the same level as in April 1960, but over the year the process of debt management resulted in an upward trend in the yields on government securities, with sales from official portfolios taking place when opportunity offered. Among the 'shorts', the yield on $4\frac{1}{2}$ per cent Conversion Stock 1964 was 5 at the beginning of April 1960, but $5\frac{1}{2}$ per cent by the third week in June. It rose well above 6 per cent when bank rate was increased to that level, but fell for a few weeks prior to mid-November under the influence of the declining Treasury bill rate. Yet, although the Treasury bill rate continued to fall, and bank rate was lowered in December, the yield on $4\frac{1}{2}$ per cent Conversion remained at about $5\frac{1}{2}$ per cent. In March it was still at this level, a rise of $\frac{1}{2}$ per cent over the year.

For much of the year to April 1960 yields on most medium- and long-dated government stocks stood above 6 per cent. On $2\frac{1}{2}$ per cent Consols it rose from about $5\frac{3}{8}$ in April 1960 to over $5\frac{5}{8}$ in June, but fell towards the end of August to under $5\frac{1}{2}$, fluctuating at about that level for about three months. Since the end of November it has again shown an upward trend, reaching nearly 6 per cent early in April 1961. In June 1960, the prices of all 'irredeemables' and some 'longs' fell, and by the end of January still lower levels had been recorded for all securities having twenty-four or more years to run; their previous low record had been set in September 1957, when bank rate was raised to 7 per cent. Prices have continued to decline and new low points for $2\frac{1}{2}$ per cent and 4 per cent Consols were established in April 1961.

The deposit rate of the London clearing banks continued to run at 2 per cent below bank rate, and lending rates have fluctuated with bank rate changes. The Agricultural Mortgage Corporation twice increased its lending rate, which now stands at $6\frac{1}{2}$ per cent. The minimum mortgage rate recommended by the Building Societies Association was raised from $5\frac{1}{2}$ to 6 per cent in the summer of 1960, and recently spokesmen for the movement have suggested that another rise is in prospect. The rates at which local authorities borrow from the Local Loans Fund were raised twice; since August 1960 they were $6\frac{1}{8}$ per cent for loans of over thirty years and $6\frac{1}{4}$ per cent for shorter loans. The tax-free rate of interest on tax reserve certificates was twice raised and once lowered, the net rise over the year being from $2\frac{1}{2}$ to 3 per cent; a new series of certificates, with further attractions for investors was introduced in March 1961.

Since access to the Local Loans Fund and the new issue market continued to be restricted, local authorities maintained their efforts to borrow on mortgage and at short-term. Over the year the rate of interest on local authority mortgages for two to three-year terms hardened from $5\frac{3}{4}$ to $6\frac{1}{4}$ per cent, and the rate for loans at seven days' notice increased from $4\frac{7}{8} - 5$ per cent to $5\frac{1}{4} - 5\frac{1}{2}$ per cent. Although this rate usually reflects changes in short-term interest rates and moves with bank rate, it rose sharply in March 1961, possibly as a result of the withdrawal of a substantial volume of foreign funds.

Following the marked rise in 1959, prices of ordinary shares fluctuated during 1960 at a somewhat lower level than that recorded at the beginning of the year. Since December, however, prices have risen substantially; the various indices all suggest that they have risen to a higher level than ever before. In brief, during the twelve months to April 1961 the trends established in previous years continued: equity prices rose still higher and gilts fell still lower. The buoyant market for ordinary shares persisted despite the large volume of new issues of equity capital. The amount of new money raised in

1960 by the issue of all classes of security was £557 million, a figure only once previously exceeded – in 1955, when out of a total of £567 million, £295 million was borrowed by the nationalized industries. These then obtained their long-term capital from the Exchequer. Issues of ordinary shares accounted for about two thirds of the total raised by companies in 1960, and amounted to £346 million, as compared with £274 million in 1959 and £93 million in 1958. The high level of activity continued; in the first three months of 1961 £127 million of new money was raised by issues, as compared with £132 million in the corresponding period of 1960.

Notwithstanding the further increase in dividend distributions, yields on ordinary shares remained relatively low and tended to fall. The yield on the Actuaries' Investment Index has been below 5 per cent throughout the period, and in March 1961 it was $4\frac{1}{2}$ per cent; the yield on the *Financial Times* index was somewhat lower. Thus the 'reverse gap' has persisted; for most of the period the yield on the Actuaries' Index was $\frac{3}{4}$ per cent below that on $2\frac{1}{2}$ per cent Consols and more than one per cent below that on most long-dated gilt-edged stocks.

During 1961 the Bank of England, upon advice from the Radcliffe Committee and others, issued a far more extensive annual report, and began the publication of a *Quarterly Bulletin,* providing further statistics and articles discussing monetary developments. These new publications, prepared with the knowledge and authority of those directly responsible for many of the developments, are to be warmly welcomed and we acknowledge the great help they have provided in the compilation of this Survey.

Because the *Midland Bank Review* reaches a large, growing and varied readership in Britain and throughout the world, and many of our readers have expressed a particular interest in the annual Monetary Survey, we are continuing the series. It presents an independent, unofficial account of monetary conditions which is intended to be entirely objective and should be all the better for the added material that can now be drawn upon.

1962 – Inflation: The 'Little Budget' and the 'Pay Pause'

During the year to April 1962 inflationary developments were gathering strength in the early months, and later, following remedial action, a setback to growth was evident. Externally, the position became so adverse as to lead to a sharp outflow of funds and borrowing abroad on an unprecedented scale. In the 'little budget' of July last, severe credit restrictions were imposed, after a pattern made familiar in previous periods of strain, but this time with the addition of fresh measures. One of the new fiscal 'regulators' was brought into operation by the application of the 10 per cent surcharge on taxes on most consumer goods, and efforts were made to establish a better relationship between the growth of incomes and of output, particularly by means of the 'pay pause'.

This firm treatment of Britain's disorders, with support from abroad, restored confidence in sterling. Interest rates were held at high levels – bank rate was raised from 5 to 7 per cent late in July; it was still as high as 6 at the turn of the year, and was not back at 5 until late in March 1962 – and funds flowed back to London.

A further disappointment came from the development of the budget situation. It had been supposed that the counter-inflationary budget of April 1961, with revenue again increased by the additions to taxation in the following July, would result in an overall surplus. In fact, large supplementaries involved additional outlays, and an overall deficit was recorded.

In the early months of 1961 industrial production in Britain was rising and exports were moving upwards slowly. Home consumption, however, continued to expand and imports were running at high levels. In his budget in April 1961, the Chancellor of the Exchequer was plainly disturbed by the possibility of inflationary developments: some increases in taxation were imposed and he took powers to vary indirect taxes and to make a surcharge on employers 'analogous to a payroll tax'. These were intended to provide economic regulators, for use during the year if required, and it was hoped that they would lessen the need to rely as heavily as in the past on monetary measures for adjusting the economy. It was not long before one of the new regulators was brought into operation, accompanied by monetary restraints of noteworthy severity.

By the summer the economic situation had worsened. With the growth in consumption, fixed investment had risen rapidly, particularly on account of government, local authorities and the nationalized industries. In construction and capital goods industries it was becoming more difficult to meet demand and order books were extending. Unemployment fell to only 1·2 per cent of the working population, and shortages of labour, especially in skilled trades, became marked in some areas. Wage and salary increases, with rises in other incomes, led to a sharp expansion in personal incomes, and prices moved upwards. In the words of the Bank of England *Bulletin* for September, it 'seemed likely that over the year to June 1962 the pressure of home demand, which was already excessive, would rise still further and that the rise in home prices and costs would continue'. At the same time, the slight upward trend in exports lost impetus, though some improvement in the balance of trade followed a reduction in imports, associated with a diminished rate of stockbuilding, and a continuation of the downward drift in import prices.

In March 1961, a difficult situation was brought to a head by the revaluations of the Deutschmark and guilder, leading to uneasiness in financial centres as to the par values of other currencies. These developments are discussed below and here we simply note that a massive outflow of funds from London brought a heavy strain on sterling that called for immediate relief, by substantial credits from abroad and a sharp application of credit restraints.

The measures introduced on 25 July became known as the 'little budget' because the Chancellor of the Exchequer announced, among steps designed to relieve immediate pressures and give time to work out long-term policy, the first application of a new economic regulator. This comprised a surcharge of one tenth (the maximum amount permitted under the Finance Act, 1961) on the existing rates of most customs and excise duties and of purchase tax. It was also stated that the growth of public expenditure was to be checked in several ways, including the suspension of the arrangements for assisting building societies to make loans for buying old houses. Then, too, the Chancellor called for a 'pause' in increases in wages and salaries and promised to set up the National Economic Development Council.

Besides these steps to restrain consumer expenditure and to improve long-term planning, further restraints on credit were imposed. Bank rate was raised from 5 to 7 per cent, and additional calls for Special Deposits were made upon the banks. These are described in detail on pp. 263–4, as also are the requests to check the growth in bank advances in particular directions and other restraints on lending.

Of immediate assistance to the balance of payments position were proposals to reduce government expenditure overseas, and to examine more stringently applications for private investment outside the sterling area. British firms operating abroad were encouraged to remit home a higher proportion of their overseas earnings. Meanwhile, sterling had been supported by the Basle arrangements between central banks (see p. 259), and this aid was reinforced – and quickly replaced – by credits from the International Monetary Fund. In August, Britain drew the equivalent of $1500 million in a number of currencies and arranged a standby credit for $500 million.

In one major aspect of Britain's difficulties, the July measures achieved their aim. The pressure on sterling was relieved, short-term funds began to flow back to London and the central reserves were strengthened. Bank rate was reduced by ½ per cent at the beginning of October 1961; again four weeks later, and with two further reductions in March 1962 it was restored to 5 per cent. On 26 April it fell to 4½ per cent. Repayments were also made to the IMF, in advance of the due date, in October and November 1961 and again in February 1962. In home conditions, the effects of the measures were also apparent. Consumers' expenditure, measured at constant prices, declined, and the value of retail sales fell until a more than seasonal recovery in December. Stock-building was reduced substantially. Capital expenditure continued to rise, until the fourth quarter of the year, but then a decline was recorded. An investigation undertaken by the Board of Trade at the end of 1961 indicated that private capital expenditure in 1962 would run at about the same level as during the previous year, a reduction in outlays by manufacturing industry being offset by increases expected elsewhere. Meanwhile, expenditure by government and nationalized industries, both on capital and on current account, continued to rise.

The purpose of deliberately slackening home demand was to leave room for an expansion in exports. Yet, although spare capacity became available, little further increase in overseas shipments took place, and output continued to decline. The index of industrial production (1958 = 100), which had risen from 112 in January to 116 in June (seasonally adjusted), remained at this figure until August, but fell thereafter, to stand at 112 from October onwards, and to sink to 111 in January 1962. The decline in activity was slightly more noticeable in manufacturing industry than in other groups; in particular, the fall in steel output quickened, and a sharp contraction occurred in the production of clothing. In these conditions, the labour shortage was eased, and by October the number of persons recorded as unemployed exceeded the number of vacancies notified, while by the early months of 1962, unemployment was standing at 2 per cent of the working population.

The Federation of British Industries noted that over each of the four-monthly periods at which its regular survey of industrial trends is conducted, business men had become less optimistic than during the previous year, with more firms reporting work as below capacity, costs rising and profit margins reduced. In October and again in February 1962 it was found that the shortage of labour was no longer the main influence limiting production. It was then being restrained by a lack of orders.

With the contraction in demand, prices of some goods, especially among consumer durable goods, were reduced; but, taken as a whole, retail prices, as measured by the official index, rose by nearly 5 per cent during the year to March 1962, about two thirds of the rise occurring after July; after November, however, the rise in the index was comparatively slight. Wholesale prices of basic materials rose by only 1 per cent and wage rates by about 2½ per cent.

In part this was due to the July measures themselves, the surcharge on existing taxes being estimated as adding possibly as much as 1½ per cent to the official index of retail prices. Industrial costs were higher as taxation on fuel oils had been increased. In addition, wage rates rose, partly because of the implementation of negotiations completed before the 'pay pause', partly by reason of sliding scale cost-of-living increases, and partly because awards were negotiated under pressure from workpeople and salary earners. Nevertheless, the influence of the 'pay pause' was clear in the slow rate of rise in wage rates. Selective increases in industrial coal prices were made, and steel prices were raised in February 1962, partly to maintain profitability when output was running below capacity.

As the 'pause' ended on 31 March 1962, a number of wage increases, agreed but deferred during its term, became payable in April. In February, the government white paper on *Incomes policy: the next step* (Cmnd. 1626), suggested 'strictly limited' pay increases in 1962, related to the likely expansion in production per head of 2 to 2½ per cent.

The Chancellors' proposals for the establishment of the National Economic Development Council were discussed during the summer months, but the cooperation of trade unions was not secured until early in 1962. The Chancellor originally envisaged the Council's duties as 'the joint examination of the economic prospects of the country stretching five or more years into the future'. This was amplified at the first meeting of the Council early in March 1962, when he said it was 'to examine the economic performance of the nation with particular concern for plans for the future in both the private and the public sectors of industry . . . to consider together what are the obstacles to quicker growth, what can be done to improve efficiency and whether the best use is being made of our resources . . . to seek agreement upon ways of improving economic performance, competitive power and efficiency, in other words to increase the rate of sound growth'. He went on to emphasize his wish for the Council to be an independent influence in the country's affairs. 'I do not want this to be a body which just listens to government decisions, and is merely asked for comment. I want it to have an important impact on government policy during the formative stages, and upon the economic life of the nation.'

Sterling given strength

Taking 1961 as a whole, the external situation of Britain turned out to be better than in the previous year, despite a further sharp fall in the contribution from 'invisible' items. On visible trade account the adverse balance of £135 million was little more than one third of that of a year before, and, after bringing 'invisibles' into account, the deficit on current account of £70 million was barely one quarter of the figure for 1960. A surprising change consisted of the swing from debit to credit on long-term capital account; the balance for 1961 was favourable by £8 million, by contrast with the customary outflow, in 1960 amounting to £202 million. The swing was due to a number of special receipts, including £221 million by way of advance repayments of debt from France and West Germany, the loan from Switzerland and repatriation of ownership of the Ford Motor Company.

It is, however, the table for the monetary counterpart in the white paper *United Kingdom Balance of Payments 1959 to 1961** that tells the disturbing story of external developments during the year. It shows a withdrawal of funds

* Cmnd. 1671. Revised figures are given in Appendix 2, Tables 1 and 1a (UK Balance of Payments) and Table 3 (Assistance for Sterling).

during the first half of 1961 of £427 million, notwithstanding the safeguarding of reserves by the Basle arrangements. The outflow continued during July, but thereafter the movement was reversed. Large-scale currency withdrawals from the International Monetary Fund were arranged; the Basle credits were repaid and the central reserves, having been reduced by £164 million in the first half of 1961, increased by £195 million in the second. Some part of the fluctuations in monetary transactions escapes record, as for instance, the 'leads and lags' in trade payments. These form part of the 'balancing item' which for 1961 was positive at £81 million as compared with the positive figure, as revised, of £306 million for 1960.

Here, then, in barest outline is the story of the sudden withdrawal of funds from Britain, an outflow, in the words of the Bank of England *Bulletin*, 'of a magnitude which had not been seen in the post-war years'. The movement began before publication of the unsatisfactory figures for the balance of payments in 1960, and followed upon the revaluations of the Deutschmark and guilder early in March, which led to widespread expectations of other changes in exchange parities. At that time international short-term fund were held in London to a large extent, so that, as the Bank of England *Bulletin* explained: 'sales of sterling were as much due to the wish to acquire currencies which might be revalued upward as to lack of confidence in sterling'. Once the outflow had begun, however, 'overseas holders of sterling immediately began to look much more closely at the United Kingdom's prospects and their implications for sterling and to contrast them with the improved outlook for the US dollar'.

The governors of the central banks of Britain, France, West Germany, Italy, Belgium, Holland, Sweden and Switzerland, meeting at the Bank for International Settlements in Basle, issued a communiqué on 13 March 1961 stating that they were satisfied that rumours about further currency adjustments had no foundation, and adding that they were taking steps to cooperate closely in foreign exchange markets. This emerged in the Basle arrangements to support sterling over the next few months. At the end of June assistance amounted to £323 million, of which £112 million consisted of direct holdings of sterling by overseas central banks in excess of their ordinary requirements, £85 million of sterling held indirectly through foreign commercial banks, and £126 million of aid provided in the form of currencies other than sterling. The Bank of England described it as 'clear in the minds of all concerned that this was essentially an essay in short-term banking accommodation which would be reversed in a reasonably short space of time, either by a reflux of short-term funds or recourse in due time, if this reflux did not occur, to one of the international sources of longer-term financial accommodation'.

In July, sterling was again under heavy pressure, and early in the following month arrangements were made for assistance for Britain from the International Monetary Fund (see Appendix 2, Table 3). The facilities amounted to the equivalent of US \$2000 million in all, of which \$1500 million (approximately £536 million) was made available at once, the remainder comprising a standby credit. In the immediate drawings by Britain, United States dollars accounted for \$450 million, the equivalent of \$270 million being taken in Deutschmarks, \$270 million in French francs, \$120 million in lire, \$120 million in guilders, and smaller amounts in Belgian francs, yen, Canadian dollars and Swedish krona. These funds were used to reimburse, over the ensuing few weeks, most of the central banks' credits extended under the Basle arrangements. Switzerland is not a member of the IMF, and during October an inter-governmental loan of Swiss frs. 215 million (£17·5 million) was arranged to fund the balance of the liability.

Britain's large drawing in foreign currencies from the Fund reinforced her reserves, but also resulted in the proportion held in gold being reduced to a low level. For a time, the dollars provided were in the form of special non-marketable 'certificates of indebtedness', in order to avoid disturbing the New York money market, but in November 1961 Britain purchased gold for dollars to the extent of \$300 million so as to bring about a better distribution of her reserves.

A second consequence was to deprive the Fund of supplies of various currencies and to emphasize the need for an enlargement of the resources available for supporting international liquidity. In December 1961, ten western countries agreed to make funds available, in their own currencies, for re-lending by the Fund. Each application to the Fund for assistance from these further resources requires the approval of countries providing them, as well as of the Fund. The 'club', as it is known, comprises the United States, furnishing \$2000 million out of the agreed total of \$6000 million, the United Kingdom and West Germany, each making available the equivalent of \$1000 million, and Italy, France, Belgium, Holland, Sweden, Canada and Japan.

The Bank of England has observed that these 'important additional resources will enable the Fund to fulfil more effectively its role in promoting the stability of the international payments system, with benefit to all countries'; it was added that they do not preclude 'the possibility that any future major disturbance in the exchange markets may be met initially by cooperation between central banks'. In the view of the IMF the 'new general borrowing arrangements are designed to provide the Fund with additional resources of [currencies of countries with strong balance of payments and reserve positions] when they are needed for the purpose of forestalling or coping with an impairment of the international monetary system. In this way, both the liquidity of the Fund and the resilience of the monetary system will be enhanced, to the benefit of all members.'

As confidence in sterling was restored balances returned to London. At the end of November, rumours of a possible revaluation of the lira led to some withdrawals, and at the end of December repatriations of funds were made by overseas financial institutions for balance sheet purposes, but by the early months of 1962, the inflow was again noticeable. Hence it was possible to repay in advance £225 million of the IMF credit, £100 million in October, £50 million in November and £75 million in February. The debt outstanding has been reduced further by withdrawals of sterling by other countries, and at the end of February 1962 it stood at £282 million.

These and other special transactions gave rise to large movements in Britain's gold and foreign currency reserves and in overseas sterling holdings, which were thus still further removed from a simple reflection of trends in overseas payments (See Appendix 2, Table 2). The reserves fell in the first half of 1961, when the speculative movement against sterling was in full swing, but they were restored following the IMF borrowing. Thereafter, notwithstanding repayments under the Basle arrangements, as well as to the IMF and to the United States and Canada on account of the annual instalments on the post-war lines of credit, the reserves have remained generally around £1200 million.

Overseas holdings of sterling increased over the year, largely because of the increase in sterling holdings of the IMF. Holdings by sterling area countries were also somewhat higher, but those of other countries were reduced. In particular, holdings by residents of North America fell by £210 million and of western Europe by £121 million, though at the end of June 1961 £197 million was held in sterling under the Basle arrangements, mainly in Europe.

The weakness of sterling that had developed in the spring of 1961 was overcome by the July measures. The spot rate rose above parity with the dollar in the first week in August, and was as high as \$2·81 a month later. Apart from a small setback in December, sterling remained strong in world markets, on occasion well above \$2·81½. This situation was, to some extent, associated with weakness in the dollar, but in recent months sterling has often stood above parity with other currencies also, including the Deutschmark, guilder and Swedish krona.

Broadly speaking, the forward rate followed the trend of spot quotations for sterling, and at the beginning of July 1961 the forward discounts were 1 cent for one month and 3 cents for three months. Then, to quote the Bank of England, 'sentiment changed abruptly. It came to be felt that measures to restore the exchange position would be taken' and forward margins narrowed. A first effect of the July measures was to widen the forward margins again, as short-term interest rates in London were raised well above those ruling in New York. The margins were reduced in October 1961, and narrowed further to about ½ cent and 1¼ cents respectively, after bank rate had been reduced to 5 per cent in March 1962.

When comparing yields on investments in short-term government debt in the two centres, and allowing for forward exchange cover, the advantage had been with London during the year to March 1961. In the next year, however, investment of this kind was sometimes more remunerative in New York, as in the summer of 1961, and sometimes in London, as during the autumn. In the previous survey reference was made to the growth of dealings in Eurodollars and Eurosterling, mainly as a consequence of differences in borrowing and lending rates between financial centres (see p. 243). For example, it has sometimes been profitable for merchant and overseas banks in London to accept deposits in United States dollars, switch them into sterling and arrange forward cover, and then employ the sterling in various ways, such as in temporary lending to local authorities. Rates of interest offered for dollar deposits at three months' notice in London have moved around 3½ per cent during the past year, but last December they rose for a time to well above 4 per cent.

The rate for security sterling, for which the market is narrow, fell to \$2·74⅞ at one time in July, or 3⅝ cents below the spot rate. Thereafter a sharp recovery occurred to within 1¼ cents of the spot rate. In October 1961, however, it rose as investment funds flowed back to London, until security sterling was only slightly cheaper than external sterling, a situation that prevailed.

In the year to May 1962 in the London gold market, the wide fluctuations in price that had occurred in the autumn of 1960 were not repeated. In the spring and early summer, the price was slightly above the par value of \$35 per fine ounce, with supplies coming forward from Russia, from United States citizens who had to dispose of their holdings by mid-year, and from the Exchange Equalisation Account, then needing to replenish its holdings of convertible currencies. The demand increased from central banks and by reason of monetary disturbances, and the price rose to reach nearly \$35·20 in August. The Bank of England provided 'moderate amounts' of gold for the London Market to bring the price below \$35·20, and from about the middle of November it declined, to stand at about \$35·08½ in March 1962.

An interesting development in the background to the gold market was disclosed by press reports that central banks had provided supplies of gold to steady the London price towards the end of 1961, and that further co-operation between central banks was under discussion to establish an international 'gold pool'.

Despite the general improvement in the balance of visible trade, exports did not recover after the spring of 1961. Nevertheless the value of exports, as recorded in the balance of payments white paper, was £3863 million in 1961, or £156 million more than in 1960.

Apart from relieving the pressure of home demand, which in the view of the Chancellor of the Exchequer* would 'make it easier for industry to meet

* Speech to Birmingham Chamber of Commerce, 18 January 1962.

the increased overseas demand we expect to develop', the government relied mainly on exhortation in its attempts to encourage exports. However, in the early months of 1962 improvements in financial facilities were announced, including those provided by the Export Credits Guarantee Department and by the banking system.

Although the higher level of exports made the larger contribution to the reduction in the visible trade deficit in 1961, the value of imports also fell by £100 million to £3998 million. The decline occurred mainly in the first half of the year, the trend thereafter being steady or perhaps slightly upwards. The changes were shared unevenly between the main groups of products. The cost of imports of food, drink and tobacco fell by about 3½ per cent, mainly because of lower prices, but for imports of fuels lower prices offset a higher volume. Imports of manufactured products rose by 4 per cent, but those of raw materials fell by 7 per cent, despite stability of prices, reflecting a decline from the rate of stockpiling in 1960 and the restraints on demand.

As to export prospects, the President of the Board of Trade in March said that it would be 'a year of great opportunity for our exporters'. In sharp contrast to 1961, all the main markets should be expanding. This had not happened since 1959, at the end of which 'exports were 12 per cent higher than they were a year earlier'. The basis for this view was that 'the United States economy [had] come fast out of its recession', and 'in western Europe the rate of expansion may well be higher this year than last'. Then, too, the 'continuing rapid rate of activity in industrial countries will benefit primary-producing countries which were doing badly last year', and would lead 'to a considerable growth in the export earnings of primary producers and consequently in their ability to import'.

Monetary and fiscal pressures

When the new fiscal regulators were announced a year before, the Chancellor believed that use of them would reduce 'dependence on regulation by monetary and credit restrictions'; still earlier, when the Special Deposits scheme was introduced in mid-1958, it was hoped that this would replace government 'directives' on bank advances. In the event, both expectations failed. In July 1961, when the new surcharge was first applied, it was accompanied by steps to bring bank credit under restrictions that together were more severe than had been experienced at any other critical period since the end of the war. Bank rate was raised to 7 per cent, further Special Deposits were called from the banking system, raising the proportion to 3 per cent of gross deposits for the clearing banks and 1½ per cent for the Scottish banks, and it was made plain that the impact of these measures was to fall on the level of bank advances.

The 'directives' reappeared by requests to the banks to be 'particularly severe towards proposals for new advances, or the renewal of existing commitments, for purposes of personal consumption, including hire purchase, and for speculative building, property development and other speculative purposes'. The idea was that by reduction of advances in these directions, lending to aid exports could be increased without a marked rise in the total for advances.

Statements from official sources indicated that the aim was to check the rate of rise in bank advances, and this came to be interpreted as a request that the level of advances at the end of the year should be no higher than in June. At the same time the banks were not to encourage an increase in the volume of commercial bills. In fact, the banks were able to reduce advances well below the June figure by the end of 1961, partly because of steps taken some time before the July directives were issued. The upward movement in advances had gathered speed in the first half of 1961 – it had not been marked in the preceding half-year – and further reductions in holdings of investments had occurred. The high record of £3540 million in advances for the clearing banks was reached in July, but thereafter the trend was reversed sharply. By mid-September, the aggregate had been reduced by £232 million and the fall continued until the end of the year.

In mid-1961, with deposits growing somewhat, allowing for seasonal movements, the proportion of advances had risen to about 47 per cent of gross deposits for the clearing banks, and investments had been reduced to 14 per cent. It was a situation in which the banks were already conscious of the need to steady the rate of rise in advances. In the Midland Bank, branch managers had been advised several months earlier that new lending should be confined to facilities urgently needed 'in connection with the day-to-day business requirements of our trading customers in the ordinary course of their business'. After the further restraints in July, these warnings to branch managers were made more explicit, and at Head Office, when considering requests for advances, every care was taken to see that the official restrictions were closely observed. In accordance with the government policy statements, facilities for hire purchase were curtailed, while advances to local authorities were less readily provided.

In so far as the 'directives' proscribed lending for property development, the first effect of restrictions became evident among applications from relatively large borrowers, a direction in which a substantial influence on the aggregate figures could be brought to bear quickly. Subsequently, the curtailment of facilities for personal consumption spread the effects throughout the whole range of borrowers, including those for relatively small amounts. In particular, the growth was arrested of the various special forms of lending, introduced by the banks when the restrictions on advances were removed in mid-1958. For example, during 1961 the amount outstanding under the Midland Bank's personal loans scheme was reduced to little more than one half of the highest figure recorded.

To some extent the movement in bank advances at home may be associated with changes in 'leads and lags' in overseas settlements as sterling moved in or out of favour with traders abroad, since exporters might need to borrow larger amounts if overseas buyers were slow to pay, and importers hastening payments might likewise lean more heavily on banking facilities. This influence, it may be supposed, tended to swell advances in the first half of 1961 and to diminish them in the later months. In general, however, facilities for exporters continued to be provided readily, notwithstanding the pressure to slacken the rate of lending in other directions. For special facilities covering terms of up to seven years, including the pre-shipment period, no customer in the Midland Bank was refused an advance where his application was supported by the appropriate guarantee from the Export Credits Guarantee Department. In earlier pages we mention the facilities whereby the Bank of England arranged to refinance a part of medium-term export credits in such a way as to prevent such advances from pressing upon the liquidity positions of the banks, and also the further facilities for export finance (see p. 243).

The consequences of the restrictions on the distribution of advances between industries can be followed in the regular quarterly classification of advances for the banks as a whole, summarized in Table C2 on p. 266. Between August and November 1961 nearly two thirds of the decline in the aggregate for classified advances was accounted for by groups other than industry and trade, including personal and professional, and more than one quarter by financial groups alone. Lending to the service trades – including retail trade – declined over that quarter, contrary to the usual seasonal movement in borrowing by shopkeepers. In the three months to February 1962, when advances rose again largely to provide for tax payments and for seasonal reasons, advances to agriculture and to hire purchase finance companies fell still further. Over the year to February, classified advances rose in aggregate by £132 million, or by more than 3 per cent, but the change in emphasis was evident. Increases were recorded for engineering, chemicals and a few other groups, but lending to agriculture, the food, drink and tobacco industries, local government, hire purchase companies and for the personal and professional groups was lower on the year. Annual figures are given in Appendix 2, Tables 8 and 8a.

Other banks besides the clearing banks, and financial institutions generally, were likewise asked to observe the restrictions on lending, and advances of the Scottish banks fell until October. So also lending by the Northern Irish banks was reduced in the second half of 1961, and advances to British residents by British overseas banks, foreign banks and accepting houses contracted, mainly late in the year. Hire purchase finance companies, with banking facilities reduced, were requested not to seek to attract funds from the public beyond those needed to provide for existing commitments, and the amount outstanding on hire purchase contracts began to fall in August.

With the rapid contraction in advances the clearing banks were able both to provide the additional call for Special Deposits, absorbing about £75 million, and to build up liquidity positions, until by mid-December 1961 the liquidity ratio for the clearing banks as a whole was over 35 per cent of gross deposits, as compared with 32 per cent a year earlier. Thus increased funds were made available at call and short notice, while Treasury bill holdings rose by £227 million between August and January, or by about twice as much

TABLE C2 *Classified advances in Great Britain of members of the British Bankers' Association* (*£m.*)

	1961				*1962*
	Feb.	*May*	*Aug.*	*Nov.*	*Feb.*
Agriculture and fishing	371	388	397	376	367
Heavy industry	583	591	603	599	645
Textiles	151	166	165	155	165
Food, drink and tobacco	213	227	215	205	207
Other industry and manufacture	612	664	668	632	702
Services (including retail trade)	442	452	434	429	452
Total industry and trade	2371	2488	2483	2397	2538
Public utilities	78	73	86	73	85
Local government	91	99	99	77	79
Personal and professional	691	705	705	664	672
Financial and other	487	522	543	480	476
	3717	3886	3917	3691	3850

as in the corresponding period of the preceding year. Holdings of 'other bills' were rising sharply in the early part of the year, the figures including that part of medium-term export credits available for refinance at the Bank of England. After the July measures, however, the rise was checked. It should be noted that in October 1961 an adjustment in balance sheet entries, so as to establish uniformity of definition between the banks, resulted in a reduction in the published total for advances of the clearing banks by about £30 million and a corresponding increase in the item for 'money at call and short notice'.

In addition to strengthening liquidity ratios, some of the clearing banks began to restore their holdings of government securities. In August 1958 investments of the clearing banks had stood at £2199 million, or over 33 per cent of deposits; three years later the total had fallen to £1047 million or 14 per cent of deposits. The subsequent reversal of this movement was noteworthy, though small in amount, the additions to investments reaching £75 million by January 1962. As investments constitute a residual item among bank assets, this change in direction was to be expected when advances were reduced, but it may also have been prompted by the improvement in the liquidity positions of some banks that followed the reclassification mentioned above, and also by preparations for the maturity of holdings of 4½ per cent Conversion Stock 1962 in February 1962. Even so, as compared with a year earlier, investment holdings in March were lower by £90 million. The changes by quarters and financial years are summarized in Appendix 2, Table 5. For the Scottish banks, the decline in investments continued, but the ratio to gross deposits remained higher than that for the clearing banks. Investments of the Northern Irish banks reached a low point in October.

As Appendix 2, Table 5 shows, the net deposits of the clearing banks grew rather more rapidly in the latest financial year than in 1960–1. Allowing for seasonal influences, an upswing in the spring of 1961 was followed by several months when the tendency was downward and then by a renewed expansion in the early months of this year, the seasonal outflow being less marked than usual. The shift in favour of interest-earning deposit accounts persisted; the total for current accounts actually fell slightly during the financial year.

The *Economic Survey 1962* (Cmnd. 1678), in examining changes in savings in 1961 compared with the previous year, refers to the rise in 'net personal bank deposits', that is, current and deposit accounts of persons less advances to them, as the 'largest single identified change. . . . The growth in 1961, at £271 million, was the largest absolutely and in relation to the level of deposits, in any of the last fifteen years.' When set beside the diminished rate of growth in national savings, and other changes in personal investment, this is suggested as indicating that 'there was a significant move towards more liquid forms of personal asset-holding in 1961'.

During the year, however, bank rate was running at high levels, so that rates allowed on bank deposits were relatively attractive, the more so as the search for funds by hire purchase undertakings was officially discouraged. Then, too, the squeeze on personal lending will have lessened the deduction from personal deposits and so augmented the net figure, though the same influence may also have called into active use balances hitherto left as savings.

In the monthly clearing banks figures, some part of the rise over the year in gross deposits is traceable to 'other accounts', and this in turn results from the continued growth of the credit clearing. The value of items passing through the credit clearing rose from £15·7 million per working day in the first quarter of 1961 to £18·1 million in the corresponding period of 1962; for the month of December it was above £20 million. For most months, the credit clearing has represented about 2 per cent of the value of items passing through all cheque clearings, and about 12 per cent of the total less the town clearing. Whether by cheques or transfers, it is plain that activity on bank accounts has continued to increase; in the Midland Bank the annual turnover on ordinary current accounts rose by one twelfth in 1961 as compared with the preceding year, and was then over fifty times the aggregate for balances on these accounts, or approximately twice the rate of ten years ago.

In the use of notes and coins further growth was recorded during 1961, though the expansion in estimated circulation with the public of 4 per cent was rather less than in the immediately preceding years. Cash passing over the Midland Bank's counters was 8 per cent higher on the year, at an average of £16·7 million a day.

In December 1961 the Chancellor of the Exchequer announced that the government had agreed, in principle, that Britain should change to a decimal currency, but that the decision to proceed was delayed pending the report of a committee appointed to examine the cost of doing so, and other aspects of the change, including the particular system to be adopted.

The budget of April 1961 was designed to be 'counter-inflationary', and, when the 'little budget' in July increased revenue by the 'surcharge', a small overall surplus was expected. During the year, however, ordinary expenditure substantially exceeded the estimates, and net below-the-line outlays were above those forecast, despite the suspension of the scheme for loans to building societies. If transactions involving the civil contingencies fund are included, the below-the-line deficit amounted to £626 million, and the deficit overall was £176 million, that is, about one half that of 1960–1. After allowing for special items, the Exchequer's borrowing requirement was £257 million (See Appendix 2, Table 4).

The deficit occurred although the government had intensified efforts to restrain the growth in its own expenditure. An official committee of inquiry into the control of public expenditure reported in July that attempts to expand or contract expenditure quickly, as a means of economic regulation, might have damaging effects, and suggested that regular surveys of expenditure covering a period of years ahead should be undertaken. The government accepted these proposals and created a new post, that of Chief Secretary to the Treasury and Paymaster General, to which a senior minister was appointed, with special responsibility for supervising government expenditure. Even so, it became clear early in 1962 that the Chancellor's intention, expressed six months earlier, to keep the increase in supply expenditure in 1962–3 to 'a level not more than 2½ per cent in real terms . . . above the estimates for 1961–2' could not be fulfilled without substantial changes in policy.

The Chancellor said that the 'theme' of the budget introduced in April 1962 was 'the maintenance of a firm base for sound expansion'. The estimated net effect of various changes in taxation was to reduce revenue by £10 million in 1962–3. It was expected that the surplus above the line would be little changed, but that net below-the-line payments would fall, thus reducing the overall deficit by £137 million. He judged the resultant borrowing requirement 'to be about right from the general economic point of view', and well within the estimated yield from non-market sources. The surcharge on customs and excise duties and purchase tax was removed, but the basic tax rates were raised correspondingly to preserve aggregate revenue; power to use this regulator, but not that related to a levy on employment, was sought for 1962–3.

Over the financial year 1961–2 receipts from national savings and other non-marketable debt were reduced, and by no means provided for the Exchequer's deficit, as had been expected at the time of the April budget. Net receipts from national savings fell from £341 million in 1960–1 to £176 million, with a net repayment of national savings certificates and smaller net inflows from defence bonds and premium savings bonds. In all, these movements in national savings and some changes in accounting procedure added £164 million to Exchequer liabilities. Holdings of tax reserve certificates, the other form of non-marketable debt that helps to provide funds for the Exchequer, rose by only £19 million during the past financial year, although these had furnished over £200 million towards the finance of the Exchequer's seasonal deficit up to the end of December.

Despite these unfavourable developments, the Chancellor was able to fulfil his hope that 'he would not be looking for new money from the gilt-edged market'. In fact, with maturities and the application of sinking funds, the amount of government marketable securities outstanding fell by £626 million to £15,263 million. In April 1961, £313 million of 2½ per cent Funding Loan 1956–61 was repaid, the balance of the total issue of £796 million having been converted into 5½ per cent Exchequer Stock 1966; in February and March 1962, £275 million of 4½ per cent Conversion Stock 1962 was repaid at maturity, the remainder of £473 million having been converted into 6 per cent Conversion Stock 1972 or into a new tranche of 5½ per cent Funding Stock 1982–4. In this general lengthening of the term of the marketable national debt, presumably the bulk of the new securites was taken up, in the first instance, by government departments (see Chapter 3); the extent of private application for issues of gilt-edged securities is not disclosed. Until the later months the banks were not increasing their holdings of government securities.

With the reduction in the volume of marketable government securites went a decline in market Treasury bills, the amount of bills outstanding issued by tender falling slightly over the year to £3000 million. In mid-March 1962, clearing bank holdings of Treasury bills were little changed as compared with a year earlier. Some other forms of debt were reduced, and the diminution as a whole was offset partly by borrowing from the International Monetary Fund, of which £281 million was outstanding in February, but mainly by a sharp rise in Treasury bills issued through the tap. These rose by £783 million to £2330 million in the year to 31 March 1962.

It seems probable that most of the increase was associated with operations in the gilt-edged market. Part of the stock repaid at maturity during the year will have been held by departments, and proceeds of sales of marketable government securities may have led likewise to a rise in their holdings of tap bills. In the nine months to mid-December 1961 holdings of government stocks by the public, including the banking system, recorded a net fall of £104 million, but they had been reduced by £260 million in the June quarter and by £27 million in the three months to September, and had risen by £183 million in the December quarter. It has been stated that the authorities supported the gilt-edged market in July, but that funding sales of gilts were made in August and September. Moreover, the gilt-edged market had been firm since October, with a strong demand reported from overseas buyers, and in the early months of 1962 it was reported that official holdings of 5½ per cent Treasury Stock 2008–12 and 5½ per cent Exchequer Stock 1966 had been exhausted. In mid-March, it was suggested that supplies were running out of 5½ per cent Funding Stock 1982–4, the only long-dated stock still available on tap.

With supplies of tender Treasury bills restricted and a firm credit policy, the discount market has experienced periods of stringency. Total assets of discount houses rose by £23 million to £1077 million in the year to mid-December 1961, and of this sum £545 million was then held in government bonds, £428 million in Treasury bills and £156 million in commercial bills. It seems that throughout the year holdings of bonds were rather higher than those of Treasury bills, a situation that has not obtained since the aggregate figures were first made available in 1951. Borrowed funds rose slightly in 1961 to £1016 million, of which the clearing banks provided rather more than one half.

During the year assistance to the discount market had been given by the authorities on many occasions, but in the months from September to January, when interest rates were tending to fall, a sterner attitude was evident, and substantial sums had to be borrowed from the Bank of England at bank rate. In those five months, on a few days only were such advances not outstanding.

Over the year, short-term rates of interest fluctuated, generally speaking following bank rate, while long-term rates, though declining from a peak reached in the previous summer, remained higher on a yearly comparison. The average rate of discount at the tender for Treasury bills in mid-April 1961 was just under 4½ per cent, with bank rate at 5 per cent, and when it rose to 7 per cent, bill rate followed, increasing by just over 2 per cent. Throughout August, at nearly 6¾ per cent, the bill rate was little more than ¼ per cent below bank rate, but in September the margin widened to nearly ½ per cent. It continued to fall as bank rate was reduced in October and November, to under 5¼ in the first week in February 1962. Thus the margin below bank rate grew to over ¾ per cent, partly in expectation of a further early reduction in bank rate, and partly because of the high demand for a smaller issue of bills, especially from overseas sources. As bank rate did not then fall, the syndicate reduced its tender price, and the bill rate rose to over 5½ per cent in March. When the bank rate was reduced to 5½, and quickly to 5 per cent, the bill rate fell by the full 1 per cent and the downward trend has continued.

Yields on short-term bonds have moved in a somewhat similar way. For example, the redemption yield on 4½ per cent Conversion Stock 1964 was about 5¼ per cent in April 1961; it fell slightly during the next month but thereafter rose to reach 6 per cent just before, and 6½ per cent just after, the increase in bank rate in July 1961. It remained at about this level until bank rate was reduced in October when it fell sharply and continued to decline until the next change in bank rate, when it stood at 5¾ per cent. It then fell to 5 per cent, a net reduction of ¼ per cent over the year.

A year earlier yields on medium- and long-term gilt-edged securities were around 6 per cent, but by August they ranged from 6½ to 6¾. Besides the increase in bank rate and general economic uncertainties, sales by trustees were reported to have been taking place in order to rearrange portfolios following the liberalization in investment rules brought about by the Trustee Investments Act, 1961. During the summer of 1961, most gilt-edged stocks having five or more years to run to maturity touched the lowest prices ever recorded. From October onwards, the demand for gilt-edged recovered, partly because of obscurities in the outlook for ordinary shares, and partly because of buying from abroad, attracted by the high yields. In these conditions, yields fell to below 6¼ per cent, and possibly the movement would have been sharper had it not been for the ready supply of stocks from official portfolios.

The deposit and lending rates of the London clearing banks have, as usual, moved strictly in conformity with changes in bank rate. In June the Building Societies Association announced that it was recommending members to raise minimum mortgage rates of interest from 6 to 6½ per cent, and rates allowed on shares from 3½ to 3¾ per cent, with tax paid by the society. The tax-free rate on tax reserve certificates was increased from 3 to 3½ per cent in August, lowered to 3¼ per cent in November and was back again at 3 per cent in March. The Agricultural Mortgage Corporation raised its lending rate in two stages, from 6½ to 7½ per cent. The rate charged to local authorities by the Public Works Loan Board was altered on five occasions, the net effect being to raise rates on loans of not more than thirty years from 6¼ to 6¾ per cent, and for loans of over thirty years from 6⅛ to 6¾ per cent also.

For local authorities with access to the funds of the Public Works Loan Board narrowly restricted and issues on the market strictly regulated, the cost of borrowing was reflected in rates offered in the market.* These have fluctuated, mainly following other rates, although at the short end they were influenced by movements of funds from abroad. For example, a sharp increase took place in the rate offered for temporary borrowing when foreign funds were being withdrawn in December. Nevertheless, the rate for money at seven days' notice was unchanged over the year, at 5¼ per cent, and that for

* The development of this market was discussed in the *Midland Bank Review* for November 1961: 'Borrowing by local authorities—further sources of funds.'

mortgages of large amounts was about $\frac{1}{2}$ per cent higher at $6\frac{5}{8}$ to $6\frac{3}{4}$ per cent.

In the equity market a sharp change in trend was recorded rather less than a year ago. The upward movement in prices came to an end in the middle of May when, as measured by the daily indices, new record levels were reached. Thereafter prices fell sharply until October, apart from a small resumption of buying in July and August, possibly mainly on account of trustees. Since October, prices have moved irregularly. The yield on *The Financial Times* ordinary share index rose from $4\frac{1}{4}$ per cent in May 1961 to 5 per cent in July, later fluctuating between 5 and $5\frac{1}{2}$ per cent. The yield on the Actuaries' Investment Index, though generally higher, showed a similar trend.

In new capital issues, too, a change in trend was evident during the year. In each of the six months from April to September, issues were higher than in the corresponding month of 1960, the aggregate for the six months reaching £400 million; in each of the next six months issues were lower than a year before, with the exception of March, when a number of large issues were made, and the total for the previous six months fell to £220 million.

1963 – Awaiting Improvement

In economic matters the year to April 1963 was, like its predecessor, a disappointing one. True, for most of the year the external situation gave rise to little anxiety, with the value of sterling well maintained on markets abroad and an improvement in the balance of payments situation. Even here, however, the trend of exports was far from satisfactory, particularly in the second half of 1962. In home conditions the situation was marked by disturbing developments: the lack of growth in industrial output; the continued fall in new industrial investment; the increase in the extent of unused productive capacity, and, not least among discouraging items, the rise in the numbers unemployed, more especially in the north and in Scotland.

Throughout the year major uncertainties persisted. Until January manufacturers awaited the outcome of long-drawn-out negotiations on Britain's application for membership of the European Economic Community. When these were broken off, fresh uncertainties became apparent and prospects remained clouded, even though for some months previously the emphasis in official policy had been on measures to stimulate the economy. In October, the Chancellor of the Exchequer had said 'Our major objective now . . . is to achieve a higher and more stable rate of economic growth', and by January 1963, many of the restrictive measures that had been introduced in July 1961 had been withdrawn and other steps had been taken to encourage consumer demand and investment. Even then the economy remained sluggish and unusually severe weather added to Britain's difficulties.

In its study of obstacles to quicker growth the National Economic Development Council has adopted, as a 'target', an annual growth rate of 4 per cent for the period 1961–6, and this was accepted as feasible by the government; indeed, the 1963 budget proposals were specifically designed to match it. A further development in 1962 was the setting up of a National Incomes Commission, to report upon the economic effects of important pay and similar awards.

Although during the year a number of measures were taken to encourage expansion, most of these came in the second half of the period and were slow to take effect. In May 1962 all the restrictive measures, imposed in mid-1961 to meet external strains, were still in force, except that bank rate had by then been reduced from 7 to 4½ per cent. In the 1962 budget little net change in taxation had been made, even though productive capacity was not fully employed and the current balance of payments had moved into surplus, because the Chancellor of the Exchequer thought that in total 'the increase in home demand over the next twelve months looks like being substantial'.

Even so, by June the easement of official restrictions had begun. The first return to the banks of the Special Deposits they held at the Bank of England was announced, official restraints on bank lending were modified, and the minimum statutory deposit for hire purchase transactions was reduced for a wide range of goods. Later in the year, it became clear that expectations of a substantial expansion in the economy, and more particularly in consumers' expenditure, were not to be fulfilled, and the relatively high level of unemployment and the continuing fall in industrial investment were special reasons for uneasiness. At the same time the improvement in the external situation remained no more than moderate, and the growth in exports lost headway. The dilemma in which the authorities believed themselves to be was expressed in the Bank of England's *Quarterly Bulletin* for September as one where the 'stimulation of home demand would do more harm than good if it led to an excessive rise in personal incomes, a fresh weakness in the balance of payments and an ebbing of foreign confidence in sterling'.

Nevertheless, thereafter further measures were plainly required. Within three months, all restrictions on bank lending were withdrawn and the remaining Special Deposits of the banks released; bank rate was reduced from 4½ to 4 per cent; an additional £42 million of post-war credits was made immediately repayable; the highest rate of purchase tax was reduced from 45 to 25 per cent; increases were announced in public investment; and taxation allowances in respect of capital investment were improved.

Yet demand failed to recover and output to respond, and the situation generally continued to deteriorate, partly because of a prolonged spell of severe weather. Thus an expansionary budget was widely expected; in the event the Chancellor of the Exchequer announced proposals for reliefs from taxation equivalent in aggregate to over £250 million.

The gross domestic product in 1962 was virtually unchanged as compared with 1961, if calculated at constant prices, though at current prices it rose by about 3½ per cent. On the latter basis, consumers' expenditure rose by 5 per cent and public authorities' current expenditure by 6, but fixed capital investment by no more than 1 per cent (this meant that in 'real' terms it declined). Then, too, investment in stocks, at 1958 prices, rose by only £99 million, as compared with £292 million a year before, and exports failed to rise at all after the first half of the year. The index of consumers' prices (1958 = 100) increased from 104·2 in 1961 to 107·8 in 1962, retail prices having risen sharply until June 1962, and thereafter steadied. For the year 1962, the index of industrial production—embracing industries responsible for nearly one half of the gross domestic product—was less than 1 per cent higher than in 1961. On a seasonally adjusted basis (average of 1958 = 100), it rose from the low level of 111 in January to 115 in April and 117 in June, but thereafter not only failed to rise further but showed a tendency to decline. The estimate for December was 111; an appreciable dip occurred in January 1963 but preliminary figures indicate some recovery in February.

Unemployment rose throughout the second half of 1962, and the further marked deterioration that occurred at the beginning of 1963 was only partly to be explained by adverse weather. In February the total number unemployed was 878,000, representing 3·9 per cent of the working population, the highest level since the fuel crisis of 1947; the number wholly without jobs, as distinct from those temporarily unemployed, was the largest since 1940. Although unemployment fell in March to 702,000, or 3·1 per cent, and again in April to 605,000, or 2·7 per cent, the regional incidence remained disturbingly uneven; in March the rate in Northern Ireland was 9·3 per cent, in the Northern region of England 6·0 per cent, in Scotland 5·7 per cent, and in Wales 4·5 per cent. In spite of rising unemployment and official adherence to the policy of incomes restraint, hourly wage rates rose by over 4 per cent during 1962, partly because of increases deferred until the 'pay pause', which had been introduced in July 1961, ended in March 1962. Even so, the tendency for earnings to rise faster than wage rates diminished.

In 1962 the total for public and private capital investment measured at constant prices was slightly lower than in 1961, outlays by manufacturing industry and the distributive and service industries having fallen sharply. It was public development that supported the total for investment, particularly in dwellings. On a seasonally adjusted basis some destocking was recorded in the first quarter of 1962, followed by stockbuilding at only a moderate rate during the rest of the year. The regular inquiry into industrial and export trends undertaken by the Federation of British Industries in January indicated that about two thirds of the respondent companies were then working below capacity, and that the amount of spare capacity had further increased over the eight months to January. More firms were becoming less optimistic about the general business situation, with lack of demand then thought to be the primary factor limiting output.

In the *Economic Report 1962*, issued in place of the customary *Economic Survey*, the failure of activity to quicken, as expected, in the second half of 1962 was attributed mainly to the fact that exports did not rise after the middle of the year; another, though 'less important', reason was the change in private investment intentions. Following these adverse developments came the failure of the negotiations for entry into the European Economic Community, and the whole situation added to the interest in the studies being undertaken by the National Economic Development Council. The 'office' of the Council adopted as a basis for discussion an annual rate of growth of 4 per cent in the economy for the five years to 1966, and an outline model suggested that to achieve this rate, increases of 5·0 per cent a year in exports and of 5·3 per cent in investment would be required. Early in 1963, the Council itself agreed that a 4 per cent rate of growth during the period 1961–6 should be regarded as a 'firm objective' and it was stated that the government accepted this aim 'wholeheartedly'.

A new development was the setting up in November of a National Incomes Commission. The Prime Minister stated that it would be a permanent body, to consider, and report on, wage, salary or other claims and awards 'of special importance', taking into account the particular circumstances in the industry concerned and 'the wider considerations of national interest such as the need for increases in incomes to be matched by increases in production', the terms of reference authorizing the Commission to consider restraint of profits. The Trades Union Congress decided not to cooperate with the Commission. Several awards have already been referred to the Commission; at a meeting held in February 1963, it was indicated that 2–2½ per cent was still officially regarded as the 'guiding light' for annual increases in personal incomes, but in the budget statement the Chancellor of the Exchequer said that 'the figure appropriate to a 4 per cent growth rate . . . is about 3 to 3½ per cent on the average'.

External situation better

A distinct improvement in the external situation of the United Kingdom, which followed the measures of July 1961, continued during the first half of 1962 but it was barely maintained in the second. Taking the year as a whole, the current account of the balance of payments is estimated to have shown a surplus of £67 million, as compared with deficits of £72 million and £308 million in 1961 and 1960 respectively. On long-term capital account further substantial overseas portfolio investment in the United Kingdom contributed to a small net inflow in the first quarter, but this was more than offset in the second quarter by the customary outflow, which continued throughout the remainder of the year. The balance on current transactions and long-term capital account combined was a deficit for 1962 of £25 million, about the same as in the previous year, but the residual 'balancing item' was much larger for 1962, with a positive figure of £128 million which, to quote HM Treasury, 'can probably be attributed to net unrecorded receipts on current account'.

Overseas trade, like the balance of payments as a whole, was more favourable in the first half of 1962 than in the second. For the year, the value of exports and re-exports as recorded in the balance of payments figures was £3988 million, or 3·2 per cent more than in 1961, and imports, at £4059 million, were 1·1 per cent higher. Import prices again fell slightly, and those of exports rose for the third successive year. The adverse visible trade balance was £71 million, about one half that of 1961. The trade returns for the first quarter of 1963 show that exports were 3 per cent higher, on a seasonally adjusted basis, than in the previous quarter, but that the level of imports was little changed.

The increase in the export total for 1962 was mainly attributable to a rise of 17 per cent in shipments to EEC countries, particularly of machine tools and cars, while to other members of European Free Trade Association exports as a whole rose by 7 per cent. Sales to North America increased and to sterling area countries they fell slightly, increased sales to Australia being offset by smaller trade with New Zealand, India and West Africa. The outcome of these movements was that, for the first time on record, exports to western Europe just exceeded those to sterling area countries, accounting for 36 per cent of the total for Britain's shipments abroad (19 per cent to EEC countries) against 35.

The somewhat higher level of imports was due to increased purchases in the second half of the year of industrial raw materials, possibly as a result of resumed stock-building. Imports from EFTA countries fell slightly but the total for EEC countries rose by 5 per cent, and from sterling area countries by 2 per cent. Purchases from North America showed little change.

With the improvement in the balance of payments went a strengthening of the external situation, although the gold and currency reserves at end-March last, at £1005 million, were £228 million lower than a year before. This decline was more than accounted for by special transactions, and in particular by further repayments of borrowing from the International Monetary Fund. By contrast with 1961, speculative movements of capital were relatively unimportant up to the end of 1962, a substantial inflow in the early part of the year tending to fall away later, partly, it seems, because with bank rate at or below 5 per cent from 22 March onwards interest rates in Britain were brought closer into line with those in other countries, and partly because the sterling area as a whole moved into deficit with the rest of the world. At the end of January 1963, however, and again in February and March, the pound came under pressure, and, as recorded later, special action was taken to restore the reserves as shown in the monthly figures.

Overseas holdings of sterling declined by almost £400 million over the calendar year, as compared with a fall of less than £200 million in reserves, and the balance of external monetary movements was favourable to the extent of £103 million, after allowing for miscellaneous short-term capital movements. In detail the sterling holdings of the International Monetary Fund declined by over £350 million, mainly on account of debt repayments, while holdings of the sterling area countries again rose slightly. The decline of £89 million in the total for holdings of non-sterling countries was fairly evenly spread, and movements in the North American figures were affected by a reciprocal exchange arrangement, announced at the end of May and running for three months, between the Bank of England and the Federal Reserve Bank of New York. The Bank of England made available in London £18 million for account of the Federal Reserve Bank of New York, which made a corresponding deposit in New York of $50 million in favour of the Bank of England. The transaction was reversed at the end of August, but the facility was continued thereafter on a standby basis. This arrangement was one of several measures taken by the United States to protect the external value of the dollar.

Of the credit amounting to £536 million made available to the United Kingdom by the International Monetary Fund in 1961, £225 million had been repaid by February 1962. Further advance repayments, of £25 million each, were made in April and May, and in July a payment of £183 million extinguished the outstanding liability, that in the meantime had been reduced by sales of sterling from the Fund to other countries. At the same time new standby facilities were made available by the Fund to the United Kingdom for $1000 million (the equivalent of £357 million), to run for one year from 8 August 1962. Meanwhile, Britain had played a part in arrangements in support of the Canadian dollar; foreign currencies lent to Canada by the Fund in June had included the equivalent of US $100 million in sterling, and the Bank of England itself lent US $100 million to the Bank of Canada, this being repaid towards the end of 1962.

The external rate for sterling remained fairly steady over the year to May 1963 with spot rate against the US dollar generally standing above $2·80. From a high level of about $2·81¼ prevailing early in May 1962, the rate declined slightly towards the end of that month reflecting some doubts about both key currencies. A further slight falling away in August and September was made good by the end of the year. During 1963 sterling fell sharply at the end of January, following the breakdown of the negotiations for Britain's entry into EEC, and fairly substantial official support seems to have been required. Renewed weakness about a month later, when sterling dipped below dollar parity, appears to have been associated with unofficial assessments of the United Kingdom situation that included suggestions that it might be advisable for sterling to be devalued. It was not shown that sterling was overvalued in relation to any other major currency and the official attitude did not change from unequivocal support for the external value of the currency.

The Chancellor of the Exchequer, in his budget statement, disclosed that in order to meet 'speculative pressure' in February and March, the United Kingdom had 'called upon the support available to us from other central banks, which has been willingly given'. In all, $250 million had been borrowed, and the effect had been 'that we have temporarily exchanged obligations to central banks for obligations to a wide variety of other holders of sterling'. Incidentally, while sterling for most of the year had stood above parity with the United States dollar, the dollar was also quoted below parity against most European currencies, except the Deutschmark and those of Scandinavian countries.

Forward market rates for sterling followed the spot rate closely, with only a small margin. Security sterling also moved generally within narrower limits than for some time, though a marked fluctuation occurred around the beginning of June 1962, when the rate fell from $2·81 to little more than $2·79½, at the time of a sharp decline in Stock Exchange prices. Subsequently the rate for security sterling again tended to fall, with a widening of the margin against the spot rate, but these trends were later reversed.

In the markets for Eurosterling and Eurodollars, the demand for Eurodollars tended to slacken in early 1963, possibly because of amendments to Regulation Q in the United States. Nevertheless rates on Eurodollar deposits in London at three months' notice were slightly higher than in the previous twelve months, but even so they rarely exceeded 4 per cent. By contrast, interest rates on Eurosterling deposits in Paris at three months' notice were generally at or near 4½ per cent, that is, a good deal lower than in the previous year, when for some time the rate was well over 7 per cent.

United Kingdom exchange control restrictions were relaxed further in May 1962, when holders of dollar securities were permitted to switch into other foreign securities and vice versa, and residents of the scheduled territories other than the United Kingdom were allowed to buy dollar securities in the United Kingdom. The effect was to amalgamate 'hard' and 'soft' dollars into one type, known as 'investment' dollars. At the same time the restrictions were eased by permitting direct investment in non-sterling countries by United Kingdom residents, of the same kind as would have been allowed before July 1961, through the investment dollar market or by 'suitable' borrowing abroad, even if no clear and commensurate benefit to the balance of payments was in prospect in the short term.

Subsequently, the premium for investment dollars widened, from 2½ per cent at the beginning of September to 10 per cent at the end of January, partly, it is thought, because businessmen were seeking to extend their interests in Europe in anticipation of British entry into EEC. This high rate, in a market which is narrow, was not consistently maintained, but premiums of 10 and 11 per cent were again being quoted at times in March and April 1963.

In his budget speech, the Chancellor noted the 'substantial resources' available to withstand temporary fluctuations of confidence in sterling—the reserves themselves, the standby credit with the IMF, the further drawing rights on the Fund, and Britain's official holdings of dollar securities averaging around one billion dollars in value. He went on to refer to 'the intangible asset of the developing cooperation between countries of the free world in tackling monetary problems', and later said that he would 'continue to pursue international agreement on further additions to world liquidity that would not throw undue strain on the key currencies'.

At the annual meeting of the International Monetary Fund in September 1962 the Chancellor had himself put forward a suggestion for improving international liquidity by way of 'an arrangement of a multilateral character'. Under such a scheme 'countries could continue to acquire the currency of another country which was temporarily surplus in the markets and use it to establish claims on a mutual currency account which they could themselves use when their situations were reversed. Such claims on the account would attract the guarantee that attaches to holdings in the Fund.' On this proposal no further action was taken.

A particular development in cooperation between countries was the formal coming into operation, in October 1962, of the arrangements which were agreed at the end of 1961, whereby ten industrial countries undertook to make supplementary resources, amounting in aggregate to the equivalent of $6000 million, available to each other in case of need through the IMF. The United Kingdom commitment is to supply, if required, £357 million under the stipulated terms, which include a 'gold clause' to cover reimbursement in terms of the equivalent in gold of the amount lent.

A withdrawal of 'gold clause' guarantees occurred when the European Monetary Agreement was renewed with effect from March 1963. The dollar exchange guarantee arrangements covering European currencies held by European central banks, which previously applied to total balances, under the new Agreement relate only to nominal amounts, the so-called 'working balances'; for sterling the guarantee covers an aggregate of £11·25 million.

During the year, too, more became known of the 'gold pool' which was established towards the end of 1961 to help to steady the London gold price. Under this arrangement, when demand is heavy other central banks supply gold to the Bank of England for the pool according to agreed quotas, sales by the pool being later replenished from market and other sources, and the contributing central banks reimbursed as opportunity arises. In this way the burden of keeping the gold price near to the par value of $35 per fine ounce no longer falls primarily on the United States gold stock.

During 1962 the buying of gold on private account, in total representing two thirds of gold becoming available from all sources, was probably greater than in any other post-war year, but despite some pronounced fluctuations in demand, the price moved within narrow limits. 'Substantial intervention' by the Bank of England, acting as agent for the gold pool, was reported both in the early summer months, when the possibility of a change in the dollar price of gold came under discussion, and again in October, at the time of the crisis over Cuba. On both occasions a large increase in the demand for gold was accompanied by only a slight rise in the price. The buying pressure in October, which appeared to arise largely in continental Europe, 'was the heaviest experienced since the London market was reopened in 1954'. Even so, it has been suggested that at the end of 1962 the pool may have had a surplus of $50 million in gold over the original figure of $270 million. From time to time consignments of gold from Russia had reached the market without having any marked effect on prices (see Appendix 2, Table 11).

Monetary restraints removed

In April 1962 bank rate was lowered to 4½ per cent in view of the continued strength of sterling. At this level it remained until last January, but meanwhile other steps to encourage expansion of the economy were taken in the monetary field. At the end of May it was announced that Special Deposits of the clearing banks were to be reduced from 3 to 2 per cent, and of the Scottish banks from 1½ to 1 per cent, in two stages on 12 and 18 June. It was officially stated that the release, the first since this new instrument of monetary control had been brought into effect in April 1960, was due to the United Kingdom's 'economic improvement'. Concurrently, the governor of the Bank of England wrote to the banks informing them that they need no longer adopt quite so severe an attitude towards applications for advances, though they were still requested to be selective in their lending. Thus they were to 'continue to pay primary regard in their advances policy to the requirements of exports and of production which would aid exports', to maintain restraints on advances for speculative purposes, 'especially for building and property development', and to keep within 'modest limits' any relaxation in lending connected with consumption at home.

A second release of Special Deposits, again of 1 per cent for the clearing banks and ½ of 1 per cent for the Scottish, was announced on 27 September, the reduction to be made in two stages on 8 and 15 October, and being described as 'a natural relaxation in present circumstances'. This was accompanied, a few days later, by the withdrawal of previous requests made to the clearing banks, in July 1961 and May 1962, regarding the exercise of 'restraint and discrimination in the granting of credit'. The Bank of England also informed other banks in the United Kingdom, including members of the associations of the overseas and foreign banks and the Accepting Houses Committee, that similar requests made to them for restraint in lending had been withdrawn. Similar letters were sent by the Bank to the British Insurance Association, the Finance Houses Association and the Industrial Bankers Association. The governor also said: 'I am sure that I can rely on banks and other financial institutions, who have been so helpful in their cooperation, to continue to give priority where necessary, and encouragement always to activities which promote exports and the overseas earnings of this country. I would also ask them, in so far as it is within their power, to give special consideration to the promotion of business in those areas of the country where resources are not being used to full capacity.'

The final stage in the restoration of freedom in lending activities, such as existed between July 1958 and early 1960, was the release of the remaining Special Deposits of the clearing and Scottish banks – by now reduced to 1 per cent and ½ of 1 per cent of gross deposits respectively – on 10 and 17 December. As with the previous releases this step was officially described as justified by the 'general economic position'. Thus within a period of about six months, all the restraints on bank lending had been removed, and all Special Deposits with the Bank of England, which at one time had exceeded £230 million, had been returned to them. 'By removing all restrictions on credit', the Chancellor of the Exchequer said, 'we have ensured that adequate finance will be available for expansion'. It also marked the end of the first use of the system of Special Deposits (see Appendix 2, Table 7).

The next step, long anticipated, was a further reduction in bank rate, on 3 January, from 4½ to 4 per cent, when it was stated that the change reflected the domestic economic situation and was consistent with the current strength of sterling in the exchange market. At the same time the Bank of England informed discount houses that it reserved the right in future to charge ½ or 1 per cent over bank rate for loans for a minimum of seven days at its discretion, thus reintroducing a practice which had been followed up to 1939. The Bank itself has described this change in policy as strengthening its 'ability to influence the Treasury bill rate, directly and by implication'.

Other measures of stimulation during 1962 were less closely related to banking activities. In June the minimum initial deposit on hire purchase contracts on all goods for which it was 20 per cent, except motor vehicles, was reduced to 10 per cent, and this concession was extended to motor-assisted cycles in October. In October and November fresh measures of encouragement included an immediate reduction in the qualifying ages at which post-war credits were repayable, at an estimated cost to the Exchequer of £42 million; an increase in public investment; a reduction of the rate of purchase tax charged on motor cars from 45 to 25 per cent; and an increase in investment and depreciation allowances, and improved write-off arrangements for scientific research assets, to be authorized in the 1963

Finance Act but to be back-dated to 6 November 1962. From 1 January 1963 the rate of purchase tax on all goods still chargeable at 45 per cent, the highest rate, was reduced to 25 per cent.

The process of stimulation was carried forward in the budget speech last April (see p. 285 below). Among the measures, income tax reliefs were designed to benefit especially those with smaller incomes; the improvements in capital investment allowances, announced in November, were confirmed and extended, and special assistance was announced as available to firms setting up or expanding in development districts.

The restoration of freedom in lending operations to the banks was not at first accompanied by marked expansion in advances, the net total for the London clearing banks rising by only £173 million, from £3375 million to £3547 million, over the ten months to January 1963. In the two following months, however, an upward surge took place in the demand for bank advances, carrying the figures forward far more rapidly than might have been expected from the customary expansion as tax payments were made by customers. In February, the total rose by £186 million, then the largest monthly increase in advances on record, and in March by £105 million, bringing it to £3839 million.

In fact, though a small rise in advances took place in the early months of 1962, thereafter the trend had been indeterminate, until the lifting of all restrictions and the release of remaining Special Deposits led to some re-expansion. Even so, by January of 1963 net advances of the clearing banks had recovered only to the level recorded just before the 'little budget' of 1961. In its December *Bulletin* the Bank of England said that 'it was doubtful whether total demand for bank advances would prove as strong as in the year following the removal of credit restrictions in July 1958' as the banks were 'not so well placed to meet a strong and sustained rise as they had been in 1958'. Indeed, by March 1963 the ratio of gross advances to gross deposits for the London clearing banks combined had risen to 51·6 per cent, the highest level since the early 1930s.

As restrictions were withdrawn, the pattern of lending changed. The quarterly analyses of advances in Great Britain of members of the British Bankers' Association are summarized in Appendix 2, Table 8, and of the increase of £476 million in total lending over the year to February 1963, £290 million occurred in the three months from November. Over the year a rise of £120 million was recorded for the personal and professional category, where previously credit restrictions had curtailed personal borrowing. But for another category under particular restraint, the hire purchase finance companies, bank advances in February last, at £99·3 million, were in fact slightly less than a year before, the rise in the section 'financial and other' being due mainly to borrowing by other financial institutions. Lending to the industry and trade groups in aggregate rose over the six months to August and fell in the following three months, but a widespread expansion occurred between November 1962 and February 1963.

When the releases of Special Deposits were made, the pressure for advances was slight, and the banks began to rebuild their holdings of government securities. Following the return to the clearing banks of about £72 million in June, their investment holdings rose by £73 million, the largest increase over one month to be recorded for eight years, and the return of £76 million in October was associated with a further rise in investments of £88 million. However, between 21 November and 16 January the balance of Special Deposits, amounting to £77 million, was returned, but investments rose by only £35 million. With the period of seasonal pressures approaching, it was clearly desirable to provide some reinforcement to liquid assets, and during February and March some sales of investments were made by the banks. Nevertheless, at mid-March investments stood £137 million higher than twelve months previously, the total of £1234 million representing 16·0 per cent of gross deposits, as compared with 14·8.

Following the marked contraction over the year in the volume of Treasury bills issued through the tender, the clearing banks' holdings fell by £127 million in the year to March, and at £667 million reached the lowest level on record in the post-war period. In the early months of 1963 the pressure on banking liquidity was evident, and in March the combined liquidity ratio for the clearing banks was only 30·5 per cent as compared with 32·6 per cent a year before, and for three of them it fell slightly below the minimum of 30 per cent. These 'deviations' were reported to be acceptable to the authorities, as a temporary measure to meet seasonal needs, at a time when it was clearly not advisable to bring pressure to bear on the growth in advances.

The rise of £259 million in net deposits of the clearing banks over the twelve months to March 1963 was greater than in any previous financial year. From October 1962 onwards, in each month they had exceeded the level recorded in the corresponding month of 1961–2 by at least £200 million, partly because of the decline in deposits that had occurred with the severe restrictions in the second half of 1961. Even so the percentage increase was little faster than the rate of rise in retail prices, and a contribution to last year's growth may have come from the recall of the old series of £1 notes which ceased to be legal tender on 28 May 1962. It was estimated that of the £210 million paid in, perhaps £40–50 million was left on deposit with the clearing banks, and that about the same amount was invested in various ways. Meanwhile, the volume of currency in circulation with the public showed little change over the year, and as a percentage of gross domestic product it actually fell from 9·1 per cent in 1961 to 8·8 in 1962. The proportion to gross domestic product of gross deposits of the clearing and Scottish banks combined was 34·4 per cent, as compared with 34·6 per cent a year earlier, but the fall seems to have been checked in the later part of the year.

The shift towards interest-earning deposits in 1961–2 was reversed in the latest financial year, probably because of the lower average level of interest allowed after reductions in bank rate. The total of balances held on current accounts increased sharply, especially in the last six months of the period, and 'other accounts' continued to expand, to some extent reflecting the steady growth of the clearings.

The value of items passing through the credit clearing was £20·7 million per working day in the first quarter of 1963 as compared with £18·1 million and £15·7 million in the corresponding periods in 1962 and 1961 respectively. The debit clearing also continued to expand, the town and general together handling items valued at £951·6 million per working day on average in the first quarter of 1963, against £861·8 million in the corresponding quarter of 1962; the figure had exceeded £1000 million for the first time in October. Credit clearing now represents about 2¼ per cent of the value of all debit clearing. The Midland Bank Index of Business Turnover, which is derived from figures of total drawings on current accounts, was 7 per cent higher in 1962 than in 1961.

In May 1962 the credit clearing system was extended to enable transfers to be made through trustee savings banks by their customers, and in February 1962 the Financial Secretary to the Treasury stated that the government would not oppose a private member's bill sponsored by the trustee savings banks to allow them to operate a cheque system, provided that the arrangements did not impose 'any financial burden on the Exchequer'.

No change on balance was recorded in net deposits with the Scottish banks in the year to March, the total being £646 million. Lending increased by £48 million to £431 million, and liquid assets were reduced, despite the release of Special Deposits, and so also were investments. A small fall in the issue of notes by Scottish banks was recorded. Gross deposits and advances of the Northern Irish banks both rose moderately in 1962–3. Generally speaking, the resources of the accepting houses and of British overseas and foreign banks continued to increase more rapidly than those of the clearing banks.

An order under the Payment of Wages Act, 1960, was made by the Minister of Labour, authorizing the payment of wages by cheque, if requested by the employee, as from 1 March 1963. Payment of wages by direct transfer to a bank account had been permitted under similar conditions since 2 December 1960.

The budget for 1962–3 was intended to be counter-inflationary, being designed to produce an above-the-line surplus of £433 million and to leave an overall deficit to be covered by borrowing of £74 million. Despite supplementary estimates, the eventual above-the-line surplus was only £80 million less than forecast. Net payments below the line, however, fell short of the expected figure by almost £90 million.

The annual Exchequer figures in recent years are summarized in Appendix 2, Table 4; transactions affecting the Civil Contingencies Fund are included in the below-the-line items and sinking fund provisions are excluded from ordinary expenditure. The below-the-line deficit in 1962–3 amounted to £416 million and the overall deficit to £24 million, as compared with £176 million in 1961–2.

In presenting his budget proposals for 1963–4, the new Chancellor of the Exchequer – Mr Reginald Maudling had succeeded Mr Selwyn Lloyd in July 1962 – said that his main theme was 'expansion without inflation, and the achievement of the 4 per cent growth target'. Britain had reached the position where there was 'substantial under-employment of resources, but where costs [had] been held stable in relation to those of our competitors'. Estimates based on the then current level of taxation suggested that there would be 'a rise in national output this year, but it would be unlikely to reach 4 per cent over the whole year, nor would it be as vigorous as our economy [could] sustain'. The Chancellor, therefore, reached the conclusion that 'tax concessions in the current year of the order of about £250 million [were] required to stimulate the economy'.

Income tax reliefs and the abolition of Schedule A tax on owner-occupied dwellings, were expected to amount to £221 million in 1963–4 and £294 million in a full year. Stamp duty on a number of transactions was halved, at a cost to the revenue of £27 million in 1963–4 and £40 million in a full year. The improvements in capital investment allowances were expected to amount to £12 million in the current year but nearly £250 million a year in due course. Other changes in taxation included amendments to estate duty and reduced import duties on some shipments from EFTA countries.

As a result of these changes in taxation and increased government expenditure, the budget estimate was for a deficit above the line of £90 million, the first such deficit forecast at the time of the budget since 1946, and an overall deficit of £687 million. If sinking fund provisions were excluded from ordinary expenditure, the above-the-line deficit was expected to be £48 million and the overall deficit £645 million.

During the year the national debt was slightly reduced, excluding £1443 million of British Transport Stock for which the Exchequer took over liability as from 1 January 1963, under the Transport Act, 1962. On 31 March the total stood at £28,413 million against £28,674 million twelve months previously. The Exchequer was able to repay debt, despite the small overall deficit, principally because the Exchange Equalization Account was acquiring sterling and repaying it to the Exchequer as its holdings of gold and currencies were reduced. Striking changes in the composition of the debt were to be seen in the decline of nearly £1100 million in the total Treasury bill issue, against an increase of £683 million over the previous twelve months; in an increase of

£1200 million in marketable securities, as compared with a decline of £628 million; and a contraction of £363 million in 'other debt in sterling', which had risen by nearly £200 million in 1961–2.

The swing in government finance to marketable securities from floating debt was possible because the market demand for both medium- and longer dated securities was fairly well sustained during the year, the downward trend in interest rates being expected to continue, and the authorities were thus in a position to make substantial funding sales. Indeed, during 1962 'tap' supplies of several new issues in the hands of departments were exhausted within a few months. In May the authorities issued a further tranche, amounting to £300 million, of 5 per cent Treasury Stock 1986–9 at 84½ per cent. This was above the market price for existing stock, and it was reported that the issue was designed to be taken up by the authorities to assist them in retaining control at the long end of the gilt-edged market, official supplies of Funding 5½ per cent having been exhausted.

In June, following reports that departmental holdings of 6 per cent Conversion Stock 1972, through which the authorities had been exerting influence on the market, had run out, an issue of £400 million 5 per cent Exchequer Stock 1967 was made at £98 per cent. In September, a further £500 million of 5½ per cent Treasury Stock 2008–12 was issued at £95 per cent, again largely to replenish official portfolios, the 'tap' for 5 per cent Treasury Stock 1986–9 having been exhausted during the previous week. Later that month it was reported that departmental supplies of 5 per cent Exchequer Stock 1967 had been absorbed and a cash and conversion offer of £400 million of 4 per cent Treasury Stock 1965 was announced. Conversion was offered to holders of the £300 million of 5½ per cent Treasury Bonds, due to mature on 14 November, at par plus a cash payment of 10*s*. per cent. The cash issue of £100 million of the stock at 99½ was oversubscribed by the public on the day of issue; this was believed to be the first occasion for many years previously that this had occurred. It was made known in October that the official 'tap' of 5½ per cent Treasury Stock 2008–12 had run dry.

These substantial issues were accompanied by a reduction in the amount outstanding of Treasury bills issued by tender, which fell by £370 million to £2630 million, the lowest figure for eleven years. Treasury bills issued through the 'tap' also declined steeply by £723 million to £1607 million; the release of £220 million of Special Deposits will have contributed to the decline, but in large measure the reduction probably reflected the departmental absorption of marketable government securities.

In the nine months to mid-December, holdings by the public of marketable government securities rose by £494 million. Including Treasury bills, the total of marketable debt rose by £624 million, and of this the London clearing and Scottish banks and the discount market together accounted for £534 million, £249 million being in bonds and £285 million in Treasury bills. On balance, the discount market increased its holdings of bonds by £32 million and of Treasury bills by £84 million, despite a decline in bill holdings in the three months to June. Overseas central banks and other official institutions added to their holdings of both bonds and Treasury bills in the three months to mid-June, but reduced both by rather more than these increases in the succeeding six months.

Sales of 'national savings' securities made a larger contribution to the Exchequer in the year to end-March 1963 than in 1961–2. Net receipts from national savings as a whole amounted to £309 million including accrued interest, as compared with £176 million in the previous twelve months and the record figure of £385 million in 1959–60. Withdrawals from the Post Office Savings Bank again exceeded deposits, but new investments in ordinary departments of trustee savings banks increased slightly, and in the special investment departments they continued to rise sharply. On 13 March it was announced that the current issues of national savings certificates and defence bonds had been withdrawn and that new series were to be offered.

As bank rate had been reduced, market rates for Treasury bills had fallen, though generally the expectation of changes was reflected in the tenders. By mid-June 1962 the bill rate was below 3¾ per cent, in anticipation of a further reduction in bank rate. When the first release of Special Deposits was made with no change in bank rate, market expectations changed and the bill rate rose to just under 4 per cent. From the end of July the rate fell steadily, and by the beginning of October the margin below bank rate had widened to nearly 1 per cent, with renewed expectations of an early reduction in bank rate. The second release of Special Deposits, again unaccompanied by a change in bank rate, was followed by a sharp rise, of ¼ per cent, in the discount rate. At the beginning of November the decline was resumed, the margin by mid-December having again widened to nearly 1 per cent.

Following a slight increase in December, the bill rate fell by ¼ per cent with the reduction in January of bank rate from 4½ to 4 per cent, and the margin narrowed to under ½ per cent, although it subsequently widened slightly. On 19 March, however, the Bank of England, under the changed arrangements announced when bank rate was reduced, charged 4½ per cent, that is ½ per cent over bank rate, for loans to the discount market, and at the next weekly tender the bill rate rose by about ⅜ per cent, to within ¼ per cent of bank rate. By mid-April 1963 the margin was still little over ¼ per cent. During the year to mid-April, the Bank of England made advances to the discount market on about fifty days, as compared with seventy-six in the previous twelve months; on only the one occasion mentioned was lending at a rate other than bank rate.

An improvement in the prices of government securities persisted throughout last year, most prices reaching their highest levels for several years in October 1962. It was suggested that the gilt-edged market gained strength from uncertainties in the prospects for equities and official indications that a fall in the long-term yield would not be opposed. Then, too, the banks were restoring their holdings of government securities. Among short-term bonds, the yield on $5\frac{1}{2}$ per cent Exchequer Stock 1966 fell fairly steadily, to stand at $4\frac{1}{2}$ per cent in September as compared with $5\frac{1}{2}$ six months previously. After a short-lived rise to around 5 per cent in the following month, the decline was resumed, and at the end of 1962 the yield had fallen again to $4\frac{1}{2}$ per cent. The gross redemption yield in mid-April was $4\frac{3}{4}$ per cent. Yields on medium- and long-dated stocks moved similarly: those on 5 per cent Conversion Stock 1971 and on $3\frac{1}{2}$ per cent Treasury Stock 1979–81 stood at about $5\frac{3}{8}$ per cent in mid-April as compared with $6\frac{1}{4}$ per cent for both stocks a year previously. Yields for both stocks fell sharply at the beginning of July 1962, and, broadly speaking, the decline continued until the end of January.

As is customary, the rates allowed and charged in the banking system followed bank rate closely. The deposit rate of the London clearing banks continued to be fixed at 2 per cent below bank rate, and leading rates moved with bank rate. The large number of borrowing customers, for whom the terms are 1 per cent over bank rate subject to a minimum of 5, then fell to the lowest borrowing rates applicable under such arrangements.

Other lenders, too, reduced their charges. The rate of interest charged on new loans by the Agricultural Mortgage Corporation was reduced to 6 per cent last January. The rates recommended by the Building Societies Association to be applied by members on mortgages, shares and deposits remained unchanged throughout 1962, but nonetheless several societies announced reductions during the second half of the year. Following the cut in bank rate in January, the Association decided to reduce its recommended rates for mortgages from $6\frac{1}{2}$ to 6 per cent and for shares from $3\frac{3}{4}$ to $3\frac{1}{2}$ per cent (tax paid by the society), the change to take effect from the beginning of February for new mortgages and from the beginning of April 'or as soon as possible thereafter' for shares and existing mortgages. As to official rates, the tax-free rate of interest on tax reserve certificates was reduced three times during 1962, and a further reduction, to $2\frac{1}{4}$ per cent, was made in January 1963. The rates at which local authorities borrow through the Public Works Loan Board had been changed seven times since the beginning of April 1962, when they were $6\frac{7}{8}$ per cent for loans of up to fifteen years and $6\frac{3}{4}$ per cent for loans over fifteen years; a rate of $5\frac{3}{4}$ per cent was then applied to all borrowing from the Fund, whatever the term.

With access to the Board restricted, local authorities continued to look elsewhere for funds. Nevertheless, during the year to May 1963 resort to temporary borrowing was less marked, mortgages and stock issues having been more widely used. The authorities' borrowing arrangements were being reviewed by the Treasury. The cost of borrowing from the market, as from the PWLB, fell over the year in line with the general trend of interest rates. By the end of the financial year, mortgage rates were around $5\frac{3}{4}$ per cent, that is, 1 per cent below the rate prevailing twelve months earlier. The downward movement in short rates was less pronounced and less regular; at the end of March the rate on money at seven days' notice stood at $4\frac{1}{2}$ per cent and that for three months at $4\frac{3}{4}$ per cent, as compared with $5\frac{5}{8}$–$5\frac{3}{4}$ and $5\frac{3}{4}$ per cent respectively at the end of March 1962.

The fall in equity prices persisted in the first half of 1962, but some recovery was evident in the summer. Prices tended to weaken as the Common Market negotiations reached a final stage, and improved when they were broken off. During the first quarter of 1963, prices as a whole were little changed, but ordinary share yields were generally somewhat higher than twelve months earlier. After rising to over 6 per cent in June, the yield on the *Financial Times* index fell to about $5\frac{1}{4}$ by January. At the end of the financial year it had fallen to 5 per cent. The 'reverse yield gap' has persisted, although it was almost closed in September, when the yield on the Actuaries Investment Index rose, while that on gilt-edged stocks with the longest date to maturity was falling (see Chart (C), Appendix 3).

According to Midland Bank statistics, the amount of new money raised in 1962 by issues of all kinds of securities was £605 million, as compared with £609 million in 1961. Issues by companies fell by £147 million, but the total for governments and public bodies was almost quadrupled to reach £192 million. The share of company issues represented by ordinary capital fell sharply in 1962, to nearly three fifths of the total, compared with three quarters in the preceding year, and the proportion of fixed interest securities rose to over two fifths, issues of preference capital again being negligible.

10

Uneven Growth

1964 – Rapid Expansion

In the previous article of this annual series, the economic position was described as one in which we were all 'awaiting improvement'. During the next twelve months, to April 1964, the pace of expansion was fast and furious, partly in response to the monetary and fiscal measures of the second half of 1962 and the budget of 1963, but also stimulated by rising demand at home and abroad. In the winter of 1963, unemployment was falling, exports were rising, and the national income was growing at a rate of around 6 per cent per annum, while prices were steady. This rate of growth was well above the objective of 4 per cent put forward by the National Economic Development Council and accepted by the government. Quite early in 1964 doubts were expressed as to the practicability of maintaining expansion at so swift a pace without giving rise to inflationary developments, especially as prices were edging upwards, labour scarcities were reported and the external situation was becoming less favourable.

Despite disturbing similarities with previous occasions when business activity had to be sharply checked to relieve pressure on sterling, this time no corresponding difficulty was evident, and heroic measures were avoided. The raising of bank rate from 4 to 5 per cent at the end of February was a mild and not unexpected application of brakes, the official explanation saying that the rise was designed to help 'to achieve a smooth transition from the present growth rate of 6 per cent, which is possible while we are taking up slack in the economy, to a long-term growth rate of 4 per cent'. A more or less neutral budget in April 1964, after the expansionary pattern followed in the previous year, likewise was intended to represent a gentle restraint on the economy.

Another official reason offered for the increase in bank rate was that it would bring the level of interest rates in Britain more closely into line with those abroad, and thus help to discourage an outflow of short-term funds. In general, sterling had been firm throughout the financial year, although for one or two days in February 1964 official intervention was necessary to support the rate following the publication of disappointing overseas trade returns for the previous month. Nevertheless, as expansion gathered momentum, the overseas trade account moved into deficit and this seemed likely to grow, mainly because of a rise in imports to meet the growing needs of industry. But although the balance of payments was adverse by the third quarter of 1963, sterling proved less vulnerable than hitherto, partly because the authorities had let it be known that they recognized the need to achieve both a higher and more stable rate of growth than in previous years, and were prepared, if necessary, to use the gold and currency reserves, as well as facilities with the International Monetary Fund and other resources, to finance the initial period of strain.

A year before, when the economy had barely recovered from the effects of an exceptionally severe winter, the Chancellor of the Exchequer announced tax concessions amounting in aggregate to about £270 million as well as a substantial rise in government outlays. This general stimulation included special inducements for industry in regions where the incidence of unemployment was particularly high. Here, however, we are concerned with the economy as a whole, and with noting its response to official encouragement. The building industry quickly recovered from the setbacks of the previous months, and by the end of June it was evident that other sectors of the economy also were expanding fairly rapidly. Indeed, during the previous three months, industrial output, after seasonal adjustment, was nearly 1 per cent higher than in the third quarter of 1962, the previous best quarterly level.

Imports as well as exports were rising, but the current account of the balance of payments remained comfortably in surplus. The economy continued to move ahead for the rest of 1963, with national output in the fourth quarter about 8 per cent above the level of a year earlier. Personal consumption and exports were still providing the main stimulus to expansion but public authorities' current expenditure was continuing to rise, and public sector investment was gathering momentum. In the fourth quarter, too, stockbuilding by industry was substantial. Meanwhile the numbers unemployed continued to fall, and although a margin of spare manufacturing capacity still seemed to be available, the Chancellor of the Exchequer put forward the view in February that any remaining slack would be fully taken up in 1964.

Thus in the early weeks of 1964 the economy was in a state of 'vigorous expansion', but already the pace of growth was giving rise to misgivings, and these were heightened when the overseas trade figures for January, showing a large adverse gap, were published. Sterling immediately came under pressure, although it was described by the Bank of England as 'neither very severe nor long-lasting'. Within two weeks bank rate, which had stood at 4 per cent for fourteen months, was raised to 5 per cent, and besides the twin objectives of the move already mentioned, the Bank of England expressed the hope that the increase 'might also lead to a more normal pattern of short-term interest rates' in Britain.

The gross domestic product in 1963 was about 5 per cent higher than in 1962, or 3½ per cent if calculated at constant prices. Industrial production rose similarly, the index of 118·7 (1958 = 100) for 1963 as a whole comparing with 115·0 for 1962. It fell sharply in January 1963, to 109 on a seasonally adjusted basis, but by June had recovered to 118, and thereafter rose steadily to reach 125 in December. The average for the last quarter of the year was 8 per cent above that of the corresponding period of 1962. In the early months of 1964 the index advanced further, and the improvement as compared with a year before became more pronounced; the provisional estimate for February last was 126 against 113 for February 1963.

Comparing 1963 with 1962, industries showing the largest increases in output were chemicals and allied industries, motor vehicles, and paper, printing and publishing; output of gas, electricity and water undertakings also showed a pronounced rise. A sharp fall was recorded for the shipbuilding and marine engineering group, and a slight one, attributable to the weather, for the construction industries. In February of this year, on the evidence of the regular enquiry into industrial trends conducted by the Federation of British Industries, a fair though diminishing margin of industrial capacity remained available to meet further expansion of output.

Personal consumption, valued at constant prices, was nearly 4 per cent higher in 1963 than in 1962, but the upward movement was uneven. For the first seven months the rise in the volume of retail sales was slow, but as the tax reductions announced in the budget began to take effect, they rose sharply in August to a level about 3½ per cent above the average for the first seven months and were well maintained for the rest of the year. Sales of cars were substantially higher than in 1962. The total for hire purchase debt rose in every month from February 1963 onwards, and in February 1964, at £969 million, was £97 million higher than a year before.

Expansion of the economy was reflected in a decline in unemployment. After reaching 878,000 in February 1963, the highest figure for 16 years, the number out of work in Great Britain fell in each of the following five months and by mid-July had been halved, bringing the proportion unemployed down to 2 per cent from nearly 4. The total rose in August, as usual, but thereafter the decline was resumed and persisted until the end of the year, against the seasonal trend. The proportion unemployed in April 1964 was 1·8 per cent, as compared with 2·7 per cent twelve months before.

All parts of the country shared in the improvement, and in some conditions of virtually 'full employment' existed, but disparities between the regions not only persisted but also tended to become somewhat greater. In April 1964 the highest unemployment rates were still those of Northern Ireland (7·5 per cent), Scotland (4·0 per cent), and Northern region (3·6 per cent), by contrast with the Midlands (1·0 per cent) and London and South East (1·1 per cent). As unemployment lessened, shortages of skilled workers were reported from various parts of the country, and in some sectors of industry may have been hindering further expansion of output. The amount of overtime worked rose sharply in course of 1963.

Capital investment began to make substantial headway towards the end of 1963. In the public sector, the total for the second half of the year was already nearly 15 per cent higher than in the corresponding period of 1962, with a further increase in prospect; in the annual white paper on *Public Investment in Great Britain, October 1963* (Cmnd. 2177), published last November, it was estimated that expenditure in 1964–5 would be 7 per cent above the total of £2335 million as planned for 1963–4. Private housebuilding increased during 1963, the number of permanent dwellings under construction for private owners rising from 153,000 to 177,000, and so, too, did investment in shops and offices. Meanwhile the decline in investment by manufacturing industry, which had persisted since the autumn of 1961, seems to have been arrested. For 1963 as a whole, the total of capital expenditure by industry is estimated to have been 4 per cent lower in volume than in the previous year, a rise of 3 per cent reported for the distributive and service industries being more than offset by a fall of 10 per cent for manufacturing industry. In 1964 private fixed investment generally was expected to increase; the survey by the Board of Trade suggested that manufacturing industry would spend 8 per cent more than in 1963.

Up to the third quarter of 1963, industry as a whole was not adding to stocks and work in progress, even though output was rising, but a sharp increase occurred in the last quarter. The trend of production suggested that further increases were likely in 1964.

Reports from industry indicated that early in 1964 businessmen generally were optimistic as to future prospects. Referring to the results of its regular enquiry for the three months to February, the Federation of British Industries reported that 'the marked optimism of the last two returns continues, supported by further strong upward trends in orders and output'. Moreover the margin of unused industrial capacity remained appreciable, but indications of rising costs and prices were more extensive than in previous returns, notably as regards export prices.

Price movements during 1963 were generally modest. As measured by the official index numbers, wholesale prices of manufactured products increased by about 1½ per cent, and of basic materials by nearly 2½ per cent; for retail prices the rise was almost 2 per cent. A substantial number of price increases was reported early in 1964, particularly for engineering products, but for five basic industries – coal, cement, steel, chemicals and oil – it was indicated that it would be possible to keep selling prices stable throughout 1964.

With the slack in employment being taken up, hourly wage rates as a whole rose on average by about 4½ per cent during 1963. In April 1963 the Chancellor of the Exchequer had announced a new 'guiding light' for rises in personal incomes of 3–3½ per cent, and in November he gave a warning that wage settlements above that level could only be justified by 'very strong' special circumstances. In the official *Economic Report* 1963 published in April 1964, however, it was noted that only 'limited progress' had been made 'towards securing acceptance of an incomes policy'.

A number of wages and hours agreements were referred to the National Incomes Commission during the previous twelve months; the Commission's first findings, published in April 1963, described a forty-hour week agreement in the Scottish building industry as being 'contrary to the national interest'. A second report, issued in July, examined the role of profits in an incomes policy and urged companies whose productivity rose by more than 3–3½ per cent a year to reduce prices. According to the *Economic Report 1963*, company profits rose in the last three quarters of 1963, and in the fourth exceeded the previous peak of early 1960.

In June the National Economic Development Council, which has met on a number of occasions throughout the year, published *Export Trends*, the third of its reports on the economy. A progress report for the period up to the end of 1963 was issued in March 1964; at the same time the director-general expressed the view that Britain was now 'well on course' towards attaining the 4 per cent growth target. Also in March, 'liaison committees' were set up for the chemicals, chocolate and sugar confectionery, electronics, machine tools, mechanical engineering and paper and board industries, and others were projected.

A surplus surrendered

The current account of the balance of payments was comfortably in surplus in the first half of 1963, but moved into deficit in the second, to provide a surplus for the whole of the year of £121 million, or £19 million more than in 1962. On long-term capital account, net private investment abroad was sustained at a fairly high level throughout the year; net foreign investment in the United Kingdom was low at the beginning, possibly due to uncertainties over the Common Market negotiations, but recovered thereafter. The balance of official and private long-term capital movements was an outflow of £147 million, as compared with one of £89 million in 1962. Taking into account unidentified transactions, current and long-term capital payments together resulted in a deficit for the year of £155 million against a surplus of £99 million in 1962 (the annual figures in Appendix 2 have been revised: see Tables 1 and 1a).

Exports of goods rose sharply in 1963, especially in the first half, and for the whole year were higher by 8 per cent in value and 6 per cent in volume than in 1962. On the same comparisons imports increased by 7 and 4 per cent respectively, but towards the end of the year they were rising more swiftly than exports. This development was not unexpected; and in his budget speech in April 1963 the Chancellor of the Exchequer had indicated that if it occurred, as a consequence of economic expansion, then a 'perfectly reasonable and sensible' action would be to finance such a deficit out of the reserves or in other ways, rather than take action that would restrict growth. In presenting his 1964 budget, the Chancellor reaffirmed that 'in so far as we are paying for imports that are necessary for economic expansion, we are . . . entitled to regard this as a proper subject for financing through the use of our external credit, so long – and this condition must never be overlooked – as our domestic economy remains sound'.

The better showing of exports in 1963, particularly in the first three quarters, was attributable in part to expansion in world trade, but also to a less unfavourable development of costs and prices than was experienced by some of Britain's principal overseas competitors. The United Kingdom share of world trade in manufactures was just about maintained at the 1962 level, i.e. at 15 per cent, whereas previously it had been falling fairly steadily. Shipments to the sterling area increased particularly sharply in the first quarter, and for the whole year were 8 per cent higher than in 1962. The growth in exports to western Europe, now Britain's largest group of markets, was well maintained for the first nine months, but then levelled out. Rises were recorded for each of the six Common Market countries as compared with 1962, ranging from 7 per cent for West Germany to 31 per cent for France, while for EFTA countries taken as a whole the increase was about 7 per cent, and for the United States 4 per cent. By product, the most notable increases were in exports of cars and machinery.

Among imports, the main increases were recorded for industrial raw materials, especially wool and timber, and some semi-manufactures, for example chemicals, and could be associated with industrial development and the building up of stocks. Shipments from the sterling area, western Europe and North America all contributed to the higher level of imports.

The central gold and convertible currency reserves declined on balance by only £53 million in 1963, notwithstanding a number of special payments, including outgoings of £66 million in December in respect of the North American loans. In June, advances amounting to £89 million made by overseas central banks earlier in the year were repaid. From March to January of this year, the underlying trend of the reserves was upward, but an outflow of £17 million in February, before the bank rate change, was only partly made good in March. At the end of that month the total was £950 million, against £1005 million a year before (see Appendix 2, Table 2). Figures of the composition of the gold and convertible currency reserves were published for the first time for March 1963 and thereafter were issued quarterly; they show that gold usually accounted for nine tenths or more of the total.

The net decline in the reserves in 1963 would have been substantially greater but for the favourable balance of payments situation of the rest of the sterling area taken as a whole. During the year sterling holdings of sterling area countries increased by £165 million, whereas those of the non-sterling area world fell by £34 million, though they were rising over the second half of the year. In detail, western European countries as a whole reduced their net holding of sterling by £141 million in the first quarter of 1963, over one half of this figure being in balances held by Finland, Greece, Spain, Turkey, Yugoslavia and Andorra, which have since continued to maintain lower net holdings. EFTA and EEC countries, by contrast, had by December 1963 built up their net holdings of sterling to levels well above those of a year previously.

In 1963 arrangements were made for the support of sterling following the breakdown of the Common Market negotiations. Over the twelve months to May 1964 sterling has remained firm, except for a day or two towards the end of February last, when official support was given. The spot rate against the dollar fell below parity in August following increases in short-term interest rates in the United States, but at the same time the usual discount on forward sterling virtually disappeared; indeed, for a few days 'one-month' sterling was at a premium against the dollar for the first time for several years. From August onwards the spot rate has remained at slightly under \$2·80.

No special measures have been required to support sterling, but the standby agreement with the IMF, allowing drawings up to the equivalent of \$1000 million in case of need, was renewed for a further year from 8 August 1963. As already noted, on a number of occasions the Chancellor had indicated that Britain would be ready to draw on the reserves and other resources if expansion of the economy should lead to external strains. At the annual meeting of the International Monetary Fund in 1963, he said that there were 'basically three types of situation in which a country may need access to substantial liquid assets'. Recourse to the Fund would be particularly suitable to meet 'serious fluctuations in short-term balance of payments experience – whether on current or capital account – arising from external influences such as abrupt changes in the terms of trade or substantial capital movements'; and in 'the initial phase of a domestic expansion accompanied by substantial restocking of materials'. Where the currency was subject to short-term speculation, however, he thought that the situation 'may best be met by such schemes as the Basle arrangements, the gold pool, and by swap arrangements, with the Fund resources also available'.

Several changes in the UK exchange control arrangements were made during the year under review. Most of these represented an easing of administrative requirements, but an important development was the effective merging of the property dollar and investment dollar markets in April 1964. Under the new regulations, UK residents wishing to purchase property outside the sterling area could use investment dollars or any other 'switch' foreign currency for the purpose, but transactions remained subject to Bank of England permission. Also from the beginning of April, the proceeds of sales of direct investments outside the sterling area could be sold in the investment dollar market, instead of at official rates as previously; the effect of this relaxation would be to increase the supply of investment dollars, and after the announcement the premium on them fell slightly. Previously, it had fluctuated widely, from 6 per cent to over 14 per cent early in 1964.

The Eurodollar came under strain on two occasions towards the end of 1963 as a result of defaults on short-term dollar obligations to some European banks, the first following the failure of a German undertaking, and the second in connection with difficulties in the US vegetable oil market. These developments weakened confidence, and some institutions found it necessary to offer higher rates for funds. The rate on Eurodollar deposits in London at three months' notice moved steadily upwards in 1963, to reach $4\frac{1}{4}$ per cent per annum in December. The rate allowed on Eurosterling deposits in Paris at three months' notice has fluctuated, generally above the Eurodollar rate; at present the rates are around 5 and $4\frac{1}{4}$ per cent respectively.

The first official indication of the size of the Eurodollar market in London was given in an article in the March 1964 issue of the *Quarterly Bulletin* of the Bank of England. This stated that 'in the main, the assets denominated in non-sterling currencies [totalling £1010 million at end 1962] represent Eurodollars on-lent by UK banks, which are offset by a more or less equivalent currency deposit liability under UK short-term liabilities'.

Further evidence was provided during the year of close cooperation between the monetary authorities of the United Kingdom and the United States. The assassination of President Kennedy in November caused little disturbance in exchange markets. Precautionary measures were taken by the Federal Reserve Bank of New York, including intervention to steady the dollar-sterling rate, and the Bank of England stated that it was considering taking action in the market if necessary. At that time the United States used part of a 'swap' facility agreed with the United Kingdom in May 1963, which provides for mutual currency help to be given up to a total of \$500 million if required; previously, the arrangement had been limited to a total of \$50 million. Following the increase in UK bank rate in February, it was disclosed that the United States and the United Kingdom had been in close consultation beforehand.

Meanwhile fresh information – and again from an official source – was provided about the operation of the 'gold pool', another area of international action in which a number of central banks have been cooperating.* In 1960, when the gold market was under strain, the Bank of England, with the full support of the US monetary authorities, had intervened as substantial sellers of gold. Further progress was made in the following year when the central banks of the United States and a number of European countries, including the United Kingdom, agreed to cooperate in a sales consortium for the purpose of stabilizing the gold market. Similarly, a buying syndicate was created in 1962 when a surplus of gold seemed likely. In 1963 the syndicate acquired substantial quantities of gold, and rather more than £600 million was shared out amongst the central banks participating in the pool. According to the Bank of England, 'there is little doubt that the knowledge that the central banks were working together in the gold, as well as in the exchange markets has helped to maintain public confidence in the existing international monetary structure'.

On the wider field of international monetary arrangements, at the IMF meeting last October it was decided to promote immediately studies of 'the outlook for the functioning of the international monetary system and its probable future needs for liquidity'. One such study is being conducted by the Fund itself, and another by the ten countries which are parties to the agreement concluded in December 1961 to augment the Fund's resources.

Monetary measures and banking innovation

By the end of 1962 all official measures to check bank lending had been withdrawn, and none has since been reimposed. Thus throughout the past year the banks have been free to lend and to develop the innovations introduced in 1958. Indeed, the liquidity requirements of the banks have been eased so as not to hinder the availability of finance as the economy has expanded. Moreover, bank rate stayed at 4 per cent from the beginning of 1963 until 27 February 1964, when it was raised to 5 per cent. During the second half of 1963 the total for bank advances showed little change, despite hastening economic recovery, but in the early months of 1964 the customary upswing was pronounced, carrying the aggregate for advances by the London clearing banks in March last to £4379 million, this being 10 per cent higher than a year before. The total of classified advances in Great Britain rose somewhat more swiftly, by 11½ per cent over the year to February 1964, to £4817 million.

The rise in lending to the classifications concerned mainly with industry and trade was less rapid, at just under 8 per cent; in the 'personal and professional' and the 'financial and other' groups, where official restraints had been

* See Bank of England *Quarterly Bulletin*, March 1694, and also p. 336.

marked, expansion was swifter. By amount, the largest increase was in personal and professional lending, but the rate of rise was quickest for the 'financial and other' category, in which is included a wide range of financial undertakings, such as building societies and hire purchase finance companies. Looking more closely at the groups for industry and trade, borrowing by heavy industry was virtually unchanged on balance over the year, notwithstanding a sharp rise during the three months to February 1964, but substantial increases were recorded for textiles and retail trade. Bank lending to agriculture also rose by more than one tenth during the period.

As bank deposits were not growing at the same pace – a point to which we return later – advances absorbed an ever-increasing proportion of banking resources, rising from just over 46 per cent of deposits at the beginning of 1963 to 49 per cent at the end. Indeed, in February 1963 the proportion moved above 50 per cent for the first time since well before the Second World War. The movement into 1964 persisted, with still higher proportions being recorded. Last March advances of the clearing banks taken together were 53 per cent of deposits, and for some the percentage was approaching 55. With the demand for advances pressing hard on available funds, a first step followed the orthodox course of investment sales, so that the ratio of investments to deposits over the year fell from 16 to 14½ per cent in March 1964. In the early months of 1963 investments held by the clearing banks had been reduced by £100 million or so, but thereafter movements were irregular and small, with an upward tendency after August. In February and March of 1964, however, the fall in investments was resumed, with a reduction of £92 million in all, to £1201 million, as compared with £1234 million a year earlier.

Of greater significance and, indeed, of some historical importance, was the next step, namely a reduction by the authorities in the level of the 'liquidity ratio' which the banks were then required to observe. About a year previously the Bank of England had indicated that for the time being it would take a less rigid view of the established minimum level of 30 per cent, and on various occasions one or other of the clearing banks recorded ratios slightly below this level. At the beginning of 1964, when the Exchequer situation was about to move into surplus, the liquidity ratio for the clearing banks as a whole was only 33·2 per cent, as against 34·6 per cent a year before and 36·1 in January 1962.

The likelihood of liquidity pressure had been evident for some time, and, as the authorities were anxious to avoid a restriction in bank credit, in September the banks had been advised of a further relaxation. In October the governor of the Bank of England said that the banks could aim 'to achieve a liquidity ratio of not less than 28 per cent between now and the make-up date in April 1964', and that the Bank 'would see no objection to a gradual move towards . . . a lower figure [than the 30 per cent customary minimum], against which Special Deposits amongst other things, could be applied should the need for them arise'. He noted that the clearing banks were content to work to a lower figure, and added that it was 'clearly in the interests of the authorities to cooperate in ensuring that the banks [were] in a position . . . to sustain . . . economic expansion'. Subsequently, the run to April, as originally indicated, seems to have been quietly extended indefinitely, the March issue of the Bank of England *Quarterly Bulletin* commenting that 'nearly all the banks should be able, without selling more investments, to keep their liquidity ratios above 28 per cent, which has been accepted as a suitable minimum figure for the present'.*

TABLE C3 *London clearing banks, assets ratios (per cent of total deposits)*

	*Total liquid assets**	*Advances**	*Investments*
1938: average for year	29·6	43·0	28·0
1946 ,,	25·2†	17·5	26·4
1952 ,,	34·4	30·3	32·6
1959 ,,	32·9	37·8	26·5
1963 ,,	31·8	50·5	15·6
1964: March	29·7	53·2	14·6

* Some changes in composition were made in 1961.
† Excluding Treasury deposit receipts, equivalent to 29·3 per cent of total deposits.

These and other changes that by then had occurred since 1938 in the distribution of bank assets are set out in Table C3, recording the ratios to deposits of the main items, while fluctuations in deposits and assets since 1959 are summarized in Appendix 2, Table 5. It is noteworthy that the growth in net deposits was greater in amount and more rapid in pace during 1963–4 than in the two preceding financial years, while for current accounts alone the rise has been even swifter; between March 1963 and March 1964 these increased by 9·6 per cent against 5·8 per cent in 1962–3. Relatively, the banking system did not seem to have lost ground quite so noticeably as in previous years. Thus the downward trend in deposits as a proportion of the gross national product, which had been evident since 1947, appeared to have been checked in 1963. Nevertheless, funds continued to be attracted by some other financial institutions in still larger amounts.

* The new methods of regulating bank liquidities introduced in 1971 are discussed in Chapter 5.

In 1959 the Radcliffe Committee drew attention to the holdings of Treasury bills by industrial and commercial undertakings and suggested that the banks could prevent further development of this kind by competing freely for large deposits, though this would mean considerable alteration in money market arrangements and a 'radical change in the business of the discount houses'.* Since then 'outside' holdings of Treasury bills have diminished, though not by reason of competition from the banks. It is other financial institutions that have attracted funds, including the accepting houses; overseas banks operating in this country; the trustee savings banks through their special investment departments, and building societies. The general discussion was widened to embrace interest allowed on savings accounts and hours of opening to the public, and in 1963 the governor of the Bank of England asked whether the 'considerable rigidity in interest rates . . . in the banking world . . . [was] . . . an encouragement to the growth of bank deposits', and whether 'the traditional hours within which bank customers are expected to transact their business . . . [were] . . . in step with demands of potential bank customers' today.

A number of proposals for greater flexibility in rates of interest and other forms of competition had long been under discussion by the banks, and thereafter schemes were brought to a more advanced stage. It is generally known that the banks felt that if higher rates were to be allowed on credit balances, then an increase would also be necessary in lending rates. In a developing situation it did not prove easy to see clearly where the balance of advantage and disadvantage lay, but it was assumed that the various possibilities remained under active consideration. Meanwhile, as has been mentioned, the tide of deposits did not run so heavily against the banking system.

In one important area of the banking service public demands were always growing, and at a rate swifter than other measures of the nation's progress. Transactions activity on bank accounts intensified at an ever-hastening rate. The total for debit clearings passing through the Banker's Clearing House in 1963 was nearly 11 per cent higher than in 1962, with the town clearing rising by about $11\frac{1}{2}$ per cent and the general clearing by just under $7\frac{1}{2}$ per cent. The total for credit clearings was over 15 per cent higher than in 1962, and now represented between $2\frac{1}{4}$ and $2\frac{1}{2}$ per cent of the total debt clearing, and 13 per cent of the general clearing. The Midland Bank Index of Business Turnover was up by 8 per cent in 1963 as compared with 1962, and in the first quarter of this year showed an increase of 20 per cent over the corresponding period of 1963. During the year the gross national product rose by just over 5 per cent.

Other proposals also came to the fore during the year to May 1964, one

* *Report of the Committee on the Working of the Monetary System* (Cmnd. 827), para. 587.

presenting a further whetting of the edge of competition. In February 1964 the trustee savings banks were permitted to undertake current account services, including the issue of cheques, and it was indicated that a cheque scheme might be in operation before the end of 1964. Another measure to reach the statute book, the Protection of Depositors Act, 1963, is designed to protect the public from fraudulent inducements to deposit money, and later regulations were made relating to the form of accounts and the content of advertisements for deposits, including the use of the words 'bank', 'banker' and 'banking'.

In September 1963 the report of the Committee of Inquiry on Decimal Currency (Cmnd. 2145) was published. A majority of the Committee recommended the adoption of a '£-cent-½' system, with a major unit identical with the current £, while a minority proposed a system based on a major unit equal to 10*s*. No indication was then given of the government's attitude to the Committee's proposals.

A further stage was reached on the question of banking hours. An early suggestion that pilot schemes involving experimental closing on Saturday mornings in some areas should be undertaken, was not taken further, but in February 1964 the Committee of London Clearing Bankers announced that it was to examine 'from all angles the practicability of a general Saturday closing of branches, combined as may be appropriate with other changes in opening hours'. A similar statement was made on behalf of the Scottish banks.

Several developments involving particular banks have occurred. In two of them the Midland was concerned, the first being an agreement to establish closer ties with three important European banks, the Amsterdamsche Bank in Holland, the Banque de la Société Générale de Belgique, and the Deutsche Bank in Germany. No exchanges of capital were to be made, but cooperation was to be developed in special fields of activity. Secondly, the Midland, jointly with the Commercial Bank of Australia, the Standard Bank and the Toronto-Dominion Bank, has formed Midland and International Banks Limited, with each of the four contributing capital to the new venture. The new bank stood ready to provide medium- to long-term finance for exports, to participate in the financing of large-scale development projects, and to take part in underwriting business in appropriate circumstances. Subsequently, Westminster Bank and Philip Hill, Higginson, Erlangers, joined with six foreign banking groups in the establishment of a new Spanish industrial bank.

The 1963 budget provided tax concessions aggregating £269 million, and deficits for 1963–4 of £90 million above the line and of £687 million overall were forecast. In the event, an above-the-line surplus of £73 million was recorded, and the net borrowing requirement was £478 million. The annual Exchequer figures in recent years are summarized in Appendix 2, Table 4.

(Transactions affecting the Civil Contingencies Fund are included in the below-the-line items and sinking fund provisions are excluded from ordinary expenditure.)

In presenting his budget for 1964–5, the Chancellor of the Exchequer said that his task was to ensure that 'expansion continues at a rate that can be sustained without inflation'. The purpose of the budget was, therefore, 'to achieve a smooth transition from the recent exceptionally rapid rate of growth to the long-term growth rate of 4 per cent'. His 'best judgement' was that an increase in taxation by the equivalent of £100 million should be 'enough to steady the economy without going so far as to give a definite check to expansion'. The level of savings also was 'fundamental', and a number of changes designed to encourage national savings were proposed.

The budget proposals were increases of about 10 per cent in the duties on tobacco and on alcoholic drinks, estimated to yield an extra £53 million and £44·5 million respectively in 1964–5. As a result of these and other adjustments, the above-the-line surplus was estimated at £67 million for 1964–5, virtually the same as the out-turn for the previous year, and the overall deficit or borrowing requirements was put at £791 million. If sinking fund provisions were omitted from ordinary expenditure, the estimates were for an above-the-line surplus of £109 million and an overall deficit of £749 million. The Chancellor stated that £165 million of the borrowing required arose from the change in arrangements for lending by the Public Works Loan Board to local authorities (see p. 307), but there would be 'an equal reduction in local authority calls on the market'.

He proposed to extend for a further year the power to make surcharges or rebates of up to 10 per cent in respect of revenue duties and purchase tax. The arrangements were to be amended, however, so as to make the 'regulator' more flexible by allowing changes to be made separately in respect of tobacco, alcoholic drink, hydrocarbon oils, and all other revenue duties including purchase tax. The regulator was 'designed to deal with short-term situations'; the increase now proposed in the duties on tobacco and alcoholic drinks was related to 'the long-term growth of public expenditure which calls for higher levels of revenue on a more permanent basis'.

During the year to March 1964, increased government borrowing was required to finance the Exchequer deficit, and the national debt rose from £29,848 million to £30,193 million. At the end of the year, the total for floating debt was £255 million higher than twelve months previously, and that for marketable securities was £224 million higher. Two government stocks together amounting to nearly £1000 million, 3 per cent Exchequer Stock and $4\frac{3}{4}$ per cent Conversion Stock, came to maturity in June 1963. Both maturities had been bought in by the authorities on a substantial scale beforehand, and no conversion offers were made, but issues were marketed in order to replenish the 'tap'. In September £500 million of Exchequer Loan 1968 was placed on offer, and in February of 1964 an issue was made of £400 million of 5¼ per cent Funding Loan 1978–80, largely, it is thought, because official supplies of 5 per cent Exchequer Stock 1976–78, of which £400 million had been offered for cash in April of 1963, had fallen to a low level. In all, therefore, issues of government stock amounted to £1300 million in 1963–4, and maturities to £1000 million. Holdings by the public of marketable government securities rose by £98 million in the nine months to the end of December 1963; in the previous three months they had fallen by £226 million.

Net sales of 'national savings securities' made a smaller contribution to the Exchequer last year than in 1962–3: £39 million against £109 million. For national savings as a whole, net receipts in 1963–4 amounted to £314 million including accrued interest, a few millions more than in the previous year. Balances with the special investment departments of the trustee savings banks again rose appreciably, but withdrawals from the Post Office Savings Bank exceeded deposits, and the Chairman of the National Savings Committee has described the income from national savings certificates and defence bonds as 'disappointing'. Net repayments of tax reserve certificates were again substantial, the total outstanding falling by £60 million to £292 million over the year, but sales of premium bonds were well maintained.

The new encouragements to saving announced in the budget speech took several forms. The limit on holdings of the current issue of national savings certificates was raised from £300 to £600, and that on premium bonds from £800 to £1000. Then on 15 May the current issue of 4½ per cent defence bonds was replaced by an issue of 5 per cent national development bonds, which would qualify for a tax-free bonus of £2 per cent if held for the full term of five years and would be encashable at par on one month's notice. The Chancellor also said that he was putting in hand 'a detailed study' of the possibility of offering 'some form of contractual savings scheme' through the National Savings Movement.

According to preliminary estimates,* the total for personal savings of all kinds in 1963 was about the same as in 1961 and appreciably higher than in 1962. About 9 per cent of disposable income seems to have been saved as compared with 10 per cent in 1961 and 8½ per cent in 1962.

From March 1963, when for the first and only time under the changed arrangements announced in the previous January the Bank of England required the discount market to pay ½ per cent over bank rate for loans from it, until bank rate was raised to 5 per cent in February 1964, the average rate of discount on tender Treasury bills remained unusually close to bank rate. Throughout this period the market had frequently found it necessary to borrow substantial amounts from the central bank, and this helped to maintain the

* *Preliminary Estimates of National Income and Balance of Payments 1963*, Cmnd. 2328.

firmness of short-term rates. In consequence, when the United States Federal Reserve Banks increased their rediscount rates from 3 to 3½ per cent in July 1963 no important movement of short-term funds out of the United Kingdom followed.

When bank rate was raised from 4 to 5 per cent in February 1964, the Bank of England expressed the hope that the change, 'though aimed mainly at moderating the pace of expansion, might also lead to a more normal pattern of short-term rates'; it was not intended, however, to attract short-term funds across the exchanges.* The move had been largely discounted by the market, and at the immediately following tender the Treasury bill rate moved up by only a little more than ½ per cent, while a small margin in favour of London on the covered Treasury bill yield was restored. Subsequently, the average tender rate has moved within a narrow range, at nearly ¾ per cent below bank rate; previously the margin had been around only one quarter.

The rate allowed by the London clearing banks on deposits at seven days' notice was raised by the same amount as bank rate in February, thus maintaining the usual margin of 2 per cent below, and lending rates also were increased correspondingly. Customers of the banks who had been borrowing on the fairly common terms of 1 per cent over bank rate subject to a minimum of 5, accordingly found that the cost of borrowing had again moved above the basic minimum. Meanwhile there have been indications that some banks were exerting upward pressure on their lending rates, as well as on the terms on which credit accounts for particular categories of customers are conducted.

After falling in the early weeks of 1963, prices of government securities subsequently were tending to rise and the downward movement in long-term yields was in accord with official policy. After October, however, long and medium yields were rising until March of this year. According to the Bank of England,† 'official policy did not seek to oppose the rise in yields' which developed during the early months of this period, 'but there were some official purchases on a few occasions when the market was rather thin'.

Among short-term bonds, the yield on 5 per cent Exchequer Stock 1967 fell steadily from the end of March 1963 until October, but by the end of March last had risen to nearly 5 per cent, only a little below the level of a year previously. The movements in other government securities have been similar. In the undated range, the yield on 3½ per cent War Loan declined over the second quarter of 1963, then it fluctuated, and after October was rising; at the end of March last it was about 6 per cent, a little higher than a year earlier and comparing with only 5½ per cent in August 1963.

Changes in 'administered' rates during the year under review have all been upwards. The Agricultural Mortgage Corporation raised its rate of interst on

* *Bank of England Quarterly Bulletin*, March 1964.
† *Quarterly Bulletin*, March 1964.

new loans from 6 to $6\frac{1}{2}$ per cent per annum at the beginning of February 1964, and again to $6\frac{3}{4}$ per cent on 24 April. Late in March the tax-free rate on tax reserve certificates was raised from $2\frac{1}{4}$ to $2\frac{3}{4}$ per cent. The rates at which local authorities borrow through the Public Works Loan Board were unchanged from February 1963 until March 1964, when the rate applying to all new loans, whatever the period, was raised from $5\frac{3}{4}$ to $6\frac{1}{8}$ per cent. This was superseded on 1 April 1964 by new arrangements for charging differential rates of interest, as described below.

Proposed changes in local authorities' borrowing arrangements were outlined in a white paper published last October.* The proposals regarding temporary borrowing were given effect as from 1 April 1964 by a General Consent made under the Control of Borrowing Order, 1958; this establishes limits on temporary debt both for up to three months and for up to twelve months, which must be achieved over the next four years.

For borrowing from the Public Works Loan Board the new arrangements that were introduced did not restore full access such as prevailed before 1955; in the official view recent experience had shown 'that at least the larger authorities can, without undue difficulty, raise a substantial part of their money on the market'. In general, local authorities were to be permitted to obtain a 'quota' of up to 50 per cent of their annual long-term finance from the PWLB, this ratio to be progressively introduced over the succeeding four years. Special provisions apply to small authorities, and the Board would continue to act as 'lender of last resort'. The Public Works Loans Act, 1964, authorized the Treasury to fix differential rates of interest, not only according to the length of the loan but also according to whether repayment was to be at maturity or by instalments, and whether or not the borrowing is within the 'quota' limit. For 'quota' borrowing the rates of interest ranged from $5\frac{1}{8}$ to $5\frac{7}{8}$ per cent.

A development in local authority financing was the issue by Manchester Corporation of two series of one-year bonds. The first of these, of £500,000, was placed with two discount houses in February 1964. This experimental issue, it was thought, might show whether the issue of bonds through the discount market could be developed as an important new form of local authority borrowing. A further issue of £1 million of one-year bonds was made in March. It is still not clear whether a free market for such bonds, involving a readiness on the part of all banks to accept them as security, will develop; an inhibiting factor was that they were not eligible for rediscount or as collateral at the Bank of England.

Prices of industrial securities rose fairly steadily from March 1963 until the end of the year, when the general level was about one fifth higher than twelve months previously. Early in 1964 some sharp declines occurred and

* Local Authority Borrowing, Cmnd. 2162.

subsequent movements were uneven. Early in February 1964 the *Financial Times* index of industrial ordinary shares stood no higher than in the previous September, but at the end of March it was 10 per cent above the level of a year earlier and continued to rise in April. The 'yield' on equities, on the same basis, was about 5 per cent in March 1963; it fell to around $4\frac{1}{2}$ per cent at the end of the year, and by mid-April it had risen to about $4\frac{3}{4}$ per cent. The 'reverse yield gap', comparing equities and $2\frac{1}{2}$ per cent Consols, widened during the twelve months to mid-April, when it was again well over 1 per cent.

According to the statistics regularly compiled by this bank, the amount of new money raised by issues of all kinds of securities was £593 million in 1963, as compared with £605 million in 1962 and £609 million in 1961. In brief, issues by companies last year were £37 million greater than in 1962, but the total for governments and public bodies declined by nearly £50 million. A noticeable development has been the growth in importance of London as an international financial centre and as a capital market for foreign bond issues.

1965 – Sterling Under Attack

In April 1964, the economy was buoyant, business confidence was high, production was rising and investment in industry was gathering pace. But the increase in economic activity, then at a swift rate by comparison with the achievement over the previous decade, had brought misgivings, and the possibility of 'overheating' had led the authorities to apply mild restraints. Bank rate was at 'amber', having been raised from 4 to 5 per cent in February, and the April budget was ostensibly designed to encourage a smooth transition to a somewhat slower rate of growth. In fact, the rise in output was soon halted, while the external trade and payments situation deteriorated, and this, with the uncertainties of an election of a new government, led to a loss of confidence in sterling. During the year to April 1965 preoccupation with the external situation overshadowed some improvement in industrial production and in exports, two aspects of the economy that had proved disappointing for most of 1964.

With a balance of payments deficit of massive proportions for the year already evident, the new government, which had been elected in October, announced a temporary surcharge on many imports and tax and other inducements to promote exports. But the further pressure on sterling was not eased by an autumn budget that extended welfare payments and increased taxation, and only temporary relief was gained towards the end of November by the raising of bank rate to 7 per cent. Two weeks later the governor of the Bank of England requested the banks to give priority to lending for exports and purposes promoting efficiency. Traditional monetary methods of restoring confidence were not sufficient, however, so that considerable use had to be made of international credit facilities, culminating in the arrangement of a credit of $3000 million, mainly at short-term, from eleven central banks, the Bank for International Settlements and the United States Export-Import Bank. It was only then that sales of sterling began to subside, and even so the funds which had been withdrawn did not return.

In December the United Kingdom availed itself of a longer-term credit facility of $1000 million with the International Monetary Fund, and this was used to fund part of the short-term aid already used. Further arrangements were made in the opening months of 1965 for extending these facilities where possible and for replacing part of the short-term debt by longer-term borrowing. Yet the foreign exchange market remained unsettled, with rumours of an impending devaluation of sterling spreading and having to be denied; indeed, the pressure on sterling continued to be felt intermittently until the budget in April.

More generally, some headway had been made in the formulation of an incomes policy; a joint 'statement of intent' on productivity, prices and incomes was signed in December 1964 by representatives of the government, the trade unions and employers, and this was followed in February by a white paper giving details of the machinery and procedures for the introduction of a prices and incomes policy. An independent National Board for Prices and Incomes was formed to which selected price increases, wage claims and settlements were to be referred, and this replaced the National Incomes Commission. Meanwhile, although the overall growth target of 4 per cent per annum in the period to 1966 had been abandoned, the Department of Economic Affairs suggested that output could rise by 25 per cent in the six years to 1970, and this newly formed department was preparing a national plan.

The gross domestic product for 1964 was about 7½ per cent higher than in 1963, or 5½ per cent if calculated at constant prices. The seasonally adjusted index of industrial production, after remaining unchanged at 127 from January to September, then moved ahead, reaching 132 in December; and again the average for the whole of 1964 was 7½ per cent above that of 1963. The largest increases in output over the year were in engineering and the manufacture of electrical goods, in the production of building materials and metal goods, and in the output of timber and furniture.

The rise in production towards the end of 1964 was attributable to a late recovery in exports, and to a rise in consumers' spending. At the same time the volume of stocks held by manufacturers and distributors rose during the year by £425 million, that is by 5½ per cent and £277 million more than in 1963. The bulk of the rise was due to an increase in manufacturers' stocks and work in progress, but wholesalers and retailers also enlarged their stocks. By the close of the year, however, the growth of stockbuilding generally was tending to level out, and in the manufacturing sector it was beginning to decline.

Capital investment rose strongly throughout 1964. Industry's plans for investment during the year were higher on successive forecasts, and they are expected to rise again this year, though probably more slowly. In 1964, gross fixed capital investment, public and private, amounted in total to £5805 million, an increase of nearly one fifth over 1963.

In the labour market, the slack which had been apparent at the end of 1963 was quickly absorbed, with a downward trend in unemployment, a growing number of unfilled vacancies, a high and rising volume of overtime, and a low level of short-time working. The proportion of unemployed in Great Britain as a whole fell from 2·0 to 1·5 per cent during the year, the figures for the London and South East and the Midlands regions dropping below 1·0 per cent. With such pressure on labour supplies, the weekly rates of wages increased on the average in the principal industries and services by 3·7 per cent in 1964; as working hours had been reduced, the rise in hourly rates of wages was by 4·7 per cent. Average earnings in manufacturing and some other industries in October 1964 were $8\frac{1}{2}$ per cent higher than a year earlier.

Prices, too, were moving upwards. The rise of 5 per cent in retail prices during 1964 was, in fact, the largest annual increase since 1961. It was attributable in part to the increased taxes imposed in April 1964 on drink and tobacco and in November on petrol, while higher rents and local rates also contributed to the trend. Wholesale prices of materials were steady during the first six months of 1964, but they rose by about 2 per cent in the second half of the year.

Already in 1963 the current account of the balance of payments had turned into deficit, a surplus in the first half of the year being replaced by a deficit of £50 million in the second half as imports grew to meet the expanding needs of industry. During 1964 it became plain that the rise in exports was failing to match that in imports. Even in the first quarter of 1964 the deficit on visible trade rose to £126 million, from £33 million in the previous quarter. The deficit in the second quarter was almost as high at £108 million. For the half year, with net invisible earnings showing little change, the current account deficit amounted to £114 million, against a surplus of £146 million in the first six months of 1963. This marked deterioration was accompanied by an unusually high net outflow on long-term capital account, partly by way of exceptional investment abroad by oil companies. For the first half of 1964 the deficit on current and long-term capital transactions amounted to £314 million.

In the following months little improvement was seen in the trade figures, and in October, when the government issued a statement on the economic situation, it was estimated that the balance of payments deficit for the whole of 1964, taking current and long-term capital account together, was 'most unlikely to be below £700 million and may well reach £800 million'. Although a considerable improvement was expected in 1965, nevertheless the prospect was still of a deficit at 'an unacceptable level'. In these circumstances the government took immediate steps, including the imposition of a temporary surcharge of 15 per cent on imports, irrespective of origin, but excluding foodstuffs, unmanufactured tobacco and basic raw materials; it also announced a scheme for the granting of rebates to exporters and of other aids. A review of government expenditure was initiated with the intention, among other objectives, of reducing the strain on the balance of payments.

When in December the third quarter's figures became available, a further sharp rise in the visible trade deficit was shown, the current account deficit amounting to £182 million. The net outflow of long-term capital payments was also maintained at an exceptionally high level, and the overall deficit was put at £251 million. Exports improved in the fourth quarter, and the deficit on current and long-term capital transactions was reduced to £180 million.

For the year as a whole, the deficit amounted to no less than £749 million, and was much as was forecast in October. During the early months of 1965 the monthly trade figures generally indicated a growth of exports and moderation in the volume of imports. Nevertheless, speaking at Cardiff at the end of February, the Chancellor of the Exchequer was of the opinion that 'we shall still have a deficit at the end of 1965 even though it will be much smaller than the colossal deficit of last year'.

Thus Britain's foreign trade results were the most disappointing aspect of the economy throughout 1964. While exports rose in value by less than $4\frac{1}{2}$ per cent on the previous year, imports expanded by 15 per cent. And, whereas one half of the rise in the total of exports was accounted for by higher prices, only about one third of the rise in imports was accounted for in this way. The weakness of exports in 1964 was associated with a slower rate of growth in several continental countries. Indeed, the value of Britain's exports to the Common Market as a whole increased by only two per cent as compared with 15 and 17 per cent in the two previous years. Shipments to France and Germany rose by no more than 2 or 3 per cent, while those to Italy fell by 21 per cent. By contrast, trade with most EFTA countries markedly improved; for the United Kingdom's two main outlets in EFTA, Sweden and Denmark, exports rose by 17 per cent and 13 per cent respectively. Exports to some of the main sterling area countries, notably Australia and South Africa, showed encouraging growth in 1964. North America, too, was an expanding market once more, but trade with Soviet bloc countries was disappointing. The most notable increase was in shipments of semi-manufactured goods which rose strongly for the second year running.

Imports into the United Kingdom continued to grow in 1964. More than one half of the increase was in imports of basic materials and semi-manufactures, partly attributable to stockbuilding and to the further growth in economic activity. Imports of capital goods, which comprised two thirds of finished manufactures coming from abroad, continued to rise rapidly; the total for imports of all finished manufacturers rose by 29 per cent in 1964 as compared with 1963, and within this group, consumer goods increased by 23 per cent and 'other mainly capital goods' by 31 per cent. Indeed the most significant change in the pattern of imports over the past few years has been the growth in finished manufactures; in 1964 these accounted for more than 15 per cent of the total import bill against just over 11 per cent in 1960.

It was to the 'disturbing increase' in imports of manufactured goods that the government drew particular attention in its statement in October 1964 on the economic situation, and it was these, and also semi-manufactured items, at which the temporary surcharge was directed. The surcharge was the subject of considerable overseas criticism, and it was said to be in breach of some international agreements, including the EFTA convention; exception was also taken to the way in which it was imposed without prior consultation. Against these charges, the United Kingdom government pleaded the urgent need for effective action. With the subsequent improvement in the trend of visible trade, it was announced that the surcharge would be reduced from 15 to 10 per cent from 27 April 1965.

Pressure on the pound

The continuing deterioration in the trade and payments position had been reflected in a fall in the exchange value of sterling during the spring and summer of 1964. Seasonal pressures added to this, while poor trade figures and political uncertainties associated with the general election and a new government disturbed foreign exchange markets still further. This led to heavy sales of sterling in the autumn and thereafter, necessitating considerable official support.

Earlier in the year steps had been taken to make sure that assistance would be available should it be needed. In May a 'swap' agreement with the United States involving the equivalent of $500 million was extended for a further year, and in August the standby facility with the International Monetary Fund, under which the equivalent of $1000 million was available to be drawn if required, was also renewed for a further year. Some use had been made of the United States swap arrangement in June, this being repaid within a fortnight, but further drawings began to be made at the end of August and again in September as sterling came under pressure. At about this time, a short-term credit of $500 million was arranged with the central banks of Belgium, Canada, France, Italy, the Netherlands, Switzerland and West Germany. This short-term credit and the United States swap facilities were of great assistance in the following months when the sterling crisis became acute; all this borrowing was repaid when the drawing from the IMF of currencies equivalent to $1000 million was made at the beginning of December 1964.

When bank rate was raised to 7 per cent on 23 November, it was stated to be intended 'to place beyond any doubt the government's determination to maintain sterling at its present parity'. This was not the first official affirmation of the intention to keep sterling secure, but references to the willingness to take the necessary measures had led overseas holders of sterling to expect an increase in bank rate on Thursday 19 November. When this did not happen, the outflow of funds increased substantially, leading to the rise in bank rate being announced by the Chancellor of the Exchequer on the following Monday. On the two previous occasions when the bank rate had been raised from 5 to 7 per cent, in September 1957 and July 1961, the pressure on sterling had ended almost immediately. In 1964 it eased only slightly and was then resumed on a large scale.

In these circumstances the Bank of England arranged massive assistance for sterling, facilities being assembled to the extent of $3000 million, mainly at short-term, with the help of eleven central banks – those included in the earlier short-term credit plus the central banks of Austria, Japan and Sweden, and including the Bank for International Settlements and the United States Export-Import Bank. This temporary assistance was arranged with remarkable speed, and announced on 25 November, only two days after the increase in bank rate. As soon as these arrangements were announced, spot sales of sterling subsided, at least for a while, and the spot rate against the US dollar rose above $2·79, but the foreign exchange market remained unsettled. By the end of November, the $500 million available under the US swap arrangements and the $500 million of short-term credit arranged with other overseas central banks had all been fully drawn, and a further $200 million had been used out of the $3000 million credit.

At the beginning of December steps were taken to place part of the short-term aid on a longer-term basis, when the United Kingdom exercised its drawing right under its standby facility with the IMF to draw currencies equivalent to $1000 million. Of the total, the equivalent of $345 million was provided from the Fund's existing holding of currencies and $250 million was obtained by the Fund from the sale of gold. The remaining $405 million was procured through the Fund's General Arrangements to Borrow, under which participating countries lend their currencies in order to supplement the Fund's own resources, should these be insufficient, and if after consultation the participating countries agree on the necessity. With these more permanent credit facilities provided – the IMF drawing is repayable in three years – it was possible to repay the $1000 million outstanding under the initial support arrangements. At the same time Switzerland, which was not a member of the Fund but associated with the General Arrangements to Borrow, provided the United Kingdom with a three-year bilateral credit in Swiss francs equivalent to \$80 million. Of this, \$50 million was used to repay an earlier loan from Switzerland, outstanding since 1961.

By the end of the year, sterling had been supported by short-term aid consisting of \$525 million drawn under the \$3000 million standby credit, and the longer-term credits of \$1000 million from the IMF as well as \$80 million under the three-year Swiss credit. Moreover, payment of principal and interest amounting to £62 million, due in December on the United States and Canadian post-war loans, was deferred in the light of the balance of payments position. To this might be added a contingent liability arising from operations by the Bank of England to support the forward exchange rate on a scale thought to represent a fresh development in policy, though the authorities held at the time that it would be mistaken to regard this action as threatening an abnormal drain on the reserves when the deals matured.

Further short-term aid was taken in January 1965, but in February it was possible to start repaying some of the credits, though a further resort to them became necessary in March. That part of the \$3000 million short-term credit which expired in February was replaced by similar but new facilities available until the end of May. Under an agreement made in February and published as a white paper in March (Cmnd. 2610), the line of credit totalling \$250 million granted by the US Export-Import Bank was available until 25 November 1965, and if the funds were drawn they would be repayable in ten six-monthly instalments beginning two years after the drawing. As a further backing for sterling in the coming months, another drawing was being sought from the IMF. The Chancellor of the Exchequer stated in April that the government was 'liquefying' its holdings of dollar securities so as to provide 'a considerable reinforcement to our reserves'.

For two years the spot rate for sterling against the US dollar had been standing close to the par value of \$2·80, but in May 1964 it began to sag steadily and official intervention was necessary from time to time in order to moderate the fall. The behaviour of forward rates at this time, however, did not suggest loss of confidence in the pound, the weakness of sterling reflecting the deteriorating payments situation, and also the development of tighter monetary conditions in western Europe. By the middle of September the exchange rate had fallen to a little above \$2·78¼ with regular official support being given.

In November, as the crisis of confidence in sterling became severe, the exchange rate was at the customary minimum support level of \$2·78¼. On 20 November, and in the next few days, sales of sterling were, according to official sources, 'massive and growing'; the discount on forward sterling widened rapidly, and the authorities began to give substantial support to forward as well as to spot sterling. With the announcement of the international standby credit on 25 November, spot sales subsided for a while and the rate rose above \$2·79 for the first time since the previous June. Nevertheless, throughout December, with heavy selling of forward sterling, the authorities gave continuing support in the forward market. In January, official support for sterling was still necessary at times, but in the following month an improvement occurred with the publication of better trade figures for January. At this time spot sterling rose to above \$2·79½; it fluctuated for a while, but then began to move downwards again, falling to below \$2·79¼ by the middle of March. The first reactions to the April budget were favourable, and were reflected in an improvement in rates, which was well maintained throughout the month.

Ordinarily the current balance of payments and capital transactions – both long- and short-term – are reflected in monetary movements in short-term reserves and liabilities – that is, predominantly in the official reserves of gold and convertible currencies and overseas holdings of sterling. In times of pressure, international aid was provided in such a way that these two indicators no longer reflected the true monetary position. Thus, because of the massive foreign help given to sterling in the autumn and winter, the fall in the gold and currency reserves, by £122 million during 1964, was fairly small. Nevertheless, at £827 million at the end of December, the total of reserves was more than £350 million below the level of three years earlier (Appendix 2, Table 2). Following a rise of £17 million in the first six months of the year, the reserves fell by nearly £140 million in the second half, and this would have been £62 million greater had not the repayment on the North American loans been deferred.

In the first half of the year, an inflow of short-term funds had shielded the reserves from the mounting payments deficit; moreover, the balance of payments of the overseas sterling area was in surplus, partly for seasonal reasons. In the third quarter the inflow of funds was no longer as large as the deficit, and £125 million had to be found from the reserves and borrowing facilities. By the fourth quarter, overseas holdings of sterling were being sharply reduced, partly because the overseas sterling area was in current deficit, but also because of the flight from the pound. Excluding special assistance, the sterling holdings of non-sterling countries fell by £193 million and those of sterling countries by £175 million. With the aid of £359 million drawn from the IMF, the reduction in the reserves was no more than £80 million. No details are available of monetary movements in the first quarter of 1965, though the reserves showed little change.

In his budget speech in April 1965 the Chancellor announced stricter measures of exchange control and steps to reduce the net outflow of long-term capital by at least £100 million a year. In addition a number of fiscal measures were proposed, including the ending of the special tax treatment of overseas trade corporations. Various aspects of the proposed operation of the corporation tax will also effectively involve higher taxation on some forms of income from overseas.

Prices on the London gold market were influenced by the operations of the central banks' 'gold pool'. Prices of gold were fairly steady throughout the early months of 1964, but demand increased considerably in the autumn with the approach of elections in both the United States and the United Kingdom, and the price rose from about \$35·08 per fine ounce in August to \$35·12 in mid-October and again in mid-December, thus reflecting disquiet about developments in the international currency system.

Shortly after the end of the year the London price had risen to \$35·13, usually regarded as the upper limit. Then it rose higher, influenced by the action of the French authorities in converting part of their US dollar holdings into gold. When the London fixing price reached \$35·19, the US Treasury reaffirmed its determination to maintain the existing price of gold, and the price eased. A strong upward movement reappeared early in February 1965, following criticism by President de Gaulle of the gold exchange standard, and by mid-March the price of gold again reached \$35·18. Subsequently the position became a little easier, though demand remained substantial.

Strains on money and banking

After about two years of freedom from official restrictions on lending, the banks had extended advances and, to ease seasonal pressures in the early months of 1964, the then minimum liquidity ratio requirement was reduced from 30 to 28 per cent; it was later indicated that this new minimum would continue in force for the time being. The raising of bank rate about that time, from 4 to 5 per cent, had been a mild and not unexpected application of the brakes – in the words of the governor of the Bank of England, 'an amber light'. The general economic strategy was to try to obtain a smooth rate of growth, avoiding resort to 'stop-go' measures; for instance in his April 1964 budget speech the Chancellor repeated his view that 'in so far as we are paying for imports that are necessary for economic expansion, we are . . . entitled to regard this as a proper subject for financing through the use of our external credit, so long . . . as our domestic economy remains sound'. But the growing uncertainties that developed in the second half of the year pointed to the need for further monetary measures.

Following an autumn budget, which did little to reassure opinion at home and overseas, bank rate was raised on 23 November to 7 per cent. Whereas earlier in the year bank rate had been used for internal reasons and not 'to attract short-term funds across the exchanges', this later increase was the direct result of pressure on sterling. As noted above, however, this pressure only eased with the announcement of foreign credits, and further monetary action was taken through the banking system.

Early in December the banks were requested by the governor of the Bank of England to give priority to lending to aid exports and productive investment of manufacturing industry, and also to have full regard to the aims of the government on regional development. To make this possible, the banks were asked to curtail facilities made available for purposes such as advances for building and property development, hire purchase undertakings and 'personal and professional' needs, except when such lending served the purposes to which priority was to be given. The governor wrote in similar terms to other financial institutions, making it clear, however, that it was not intended that building society lending in the field of housing for the owner-occupier should be affected.

The background to the governor's request was a rapid expansion in bank advances during 1964, and it was already being questioned whether this could be maintained without an expansion in bank resources. By the autumn the combined liquidity ratio of the banks was little more than 30 per cent, or closer to the new minimum of 28 per cent than was usual at that season. Liquidity pressures arose also from the course of government revenue and expenditure which, as explained below, was involving less borrowing from the market on Treasury bills than had been expected. This was made clear in revised estimates given by the Chancellor in his autumn budget speech, and when moving the second reading of the associated Finance Bill he said that 'the position of the banks is such that they will wish in the coming months to moderate the expansion of their lending in the interests of their liquidity position and the normal seasonal pressure will reinforce this tendency'. Thus the banks were beginning to become more selective in lending, even before the Bank of England's 'directive'.

In these conditions the trend of bank advances changed with the new year. Up to mid-December 1964 advances had been rising each month – on a seasonally adjusted basis – since the easing of the previous credit squeeze in 1962, but in January and February they fell. In March and April, however, a strong upward movement was again evident, leading to a call on 29 April 1965 for Special Deposits to be placed with the Bank of England.

The quarterly classification of advances for February showed, in general, that over the previous three months falls had occurred in the restricted categories, notably personal and professional borrowers, whereas lending to most industrial groups had continued to increase, and particularly advances to heavy industry. These show that the aggregate for all banks increased by £510 million to £5327 million, or by over 10 per cent, in the twelve months to February. All the main groups other than the nationalized industries shared in the rise (see Appendix 2, Table 8).

With bank advances growing at a swifter rate than deposits – though these also were expanding – the proportion of advances for the clearing banks as a whole rose over the year to December from about 50 per cent to 53 per cent of deposits. In his annual statement for 1964, the chairman of the Midland

Bank remarked that 'since the war we have usually felt "comfortable" when [the] proportion [of advances] kept within 50 per cent of deposits, but today for banks generally the ratio is well above this figure, and I should see no reason for uneasiness if it were to rise somewhat further'.

As advances grew, liquidity ratios fell and investments had to be reduced. During 1964 investment holdings of the banks fell by over £100 million, while in the first quarter of this year further reductions amounted to over £130 million, when the inflow of tax payments into the Exchequer was reflected in a comparatively large decline in net deposits, by £187 million as against £104 million in the corresponding period of 1964. In these circumstances the ratio of investments to deposits, which had been nearly 15½ per cent at the end of 1963, had fallen to 13 per cent a year later, and by March 1965 it was down to 12 per cent, the lowest figure since the war.

The clearing banks' holdings of commercial bills, including refinanceable credits, has continued to grow. From a total of £277 million at mid-March 1964, the figure had risen to £343 million by the end of the year, and by March 1965 to £360 million, representing a rise of 30 per cent over the twelve months.

Changes in the distribution of the banks' assets since 1938, and fluctuations in deposits and assets are summarized in Appendix 2, Table 6.

During 1964 all except one of the 'big five' banks made increases in capital, Barclays, Midland and Lloyds by scrip issues and Westminster by both a rights and a scrip issue. The Midland also issued nearly one million shares as a result of its participation in Midland and International Banks, and District Bank issued an additional three million shares to National Provincial, its parent bank. At the end of 1964 the ratio of capital and reserves to deposits for the 'big five' banks ranged between 4½ per cent and 6¾ per cent; on average it was 5½ per cent as compared with 4½ per cent in 1961 and about 3 per cent in 1958.

In the banking system the traditional rates structure was maintained, despite pressure for more aggressive competition for deposits. Thus deposit rate was 2 per cent below bank rate, though since bank rate had been at a high level, deposits were comparatively highly remunerated at 5 per cent. Some rates in the 'parallel' market had, however, run at exceptionally high levels. Although Eurodollars rates in London were generally maintained at between 4 and 5 per cent, for Eurosterling in Paris much higher rates, generally about 7 or 8 per cent, were paid from the beginning of the sterling crisis onwards. Rates in London for short-term borrowing by local authorities also rose to about 7 or 8 per cent, or higher, as noted below.

Subsidiary and associated undertakings of the banks attracted funds by offering the going rates in the market. Thus companies associated with the banks sought funds in this way and more recently other subsidiaries operating in special fields did so. Most of the larger banks formed or joined in subsidiary undertakings covering a wide field of operations, including export finance, and seeking funds at market rates.

For orthodox lending the banks raised the floor for the finest rates, and a rather wider spread was arranged between the various categories of borrowers. Commitment fees, too, became more prevalent.

As throughout the post-war period, the number and amount of cheques passing through bank clearings continued to grow. On a working-day average basis the total for debit clearings was over 17 per cent higher in 1964 than in 1963; the town clearings, which cover a large proportion of purely financial transactions, rose by over 18 per cent and general clearings by nearly 12 per cent. In addition, the total for the more recently introduced credit clearings rose by over 13 per cent, this form of money payment then representing about 13½ per cent of the general clearing.

In March 1965 the Bank of England published, in its *Quarterly Bulletin,* an important study of Clearing House statistics, appropriately processed, which found 'some ground for believing that bank clearings, if used with an understanding of their limitations, can provide some help in assessing the latest developments in the economy'. Another prompt indicator of business activity that had been issued for some years was based upon bank turnover figures. This was the Midland Bank Index of Business Turnover, which for 1964 as a whole was about 14 per cent higher than in 1963. On a seasonally corrected basis, the index fell in the third quarter of 1964, but then recovered strongly, and in the first quarter of 1965 it showed an increase of 11 per cent over the corresponding period of 1964. Since the index was derived from turnover figures it covered cash drawings as well as all cheques, representing a much wider range than simply cheques passing through clearings. Some trustee savings banks were then introducing a cheque book service, the cheques to be cleared through the existing clearing system.

Finance for exports had always been excluded when restrictions were applied to bank lending and, indeed, the banks took a large part in providing fresh facilities for those trading abroad. True the banks' aid continued to take the traditional form of overdrafts and the discount and negotiation of trade bills. Nevertheless, the banks, supported by the Export Credits Guarantee Department and actively encouraged by the Bank of England, developed arrangements for providing medium-term finance for exports.

For shipments of heavy capital goods, often associated with large constructions abroad, longer-term credit might be granted by an exporter's bank, or for exceptionally large projects the commitment was sometimes arranged by a consortium of commercial banks, often organized by a merchant bank. Since the beginning of 1962, the London clearing banks and the Scottish banks provided medium-term financing for major export contracts, such as the export of heavy capital equipment, at a fixed rate of interest, which for credits arranged up to 1967 was set at 5½ per cent per annum. For a time a consortium of insurance companies provided additional finance at a fixed rate of 6½ per cent for the period of any such contract above that provided by the banks. At first the availability of bank funds at the fixed rate of interest was limited to credits of up to five years covered by direct bank guarantees or financial guarantees of the ECGD, but in January 1965 the scope of these arrangements was widened considerably. Then the London clearing banks and the Scottish banks agreed in future to provide funds under both types of guarantee at the fixed rate of 5½ per cent, whatever the length of the credit, thus taking over for new advances the arrangements whereby Insurance Export Finance provided the long end of such credits and offering facilities at highly favourable rates. At the same time the position of the banks was eased by the Bank of England, which extended to the new arrangements its refinancing facilities; broadly speaking, these were available to the banks in respect of payments due in the following eighteen months or for 30 per cent of the loan outstanding, whichever was the greater. Moreover, the Bank of England then stood ready to refinance the whole of the outstanding balance of such export credit five years or more after its origin. The banks, however, would not be able to regard these additional amounts so refinanceable as liquid assets to be included in making up their liquidity ratios, though the Bank of England undertook to see what could be done to assist a bank or banks in particular difficulty as a result of commitments on export credits.

When these arrangements were announced, the ECGD broadened the basis for its direct bank guarantees. Previously these were given for export contracts in respect of United Kingdom capital goods worth not less than £100,000, involving three years' credit or longer, but from January 1965 these guarantees were made available for any contract for manufactures of all kinds, for not less than £50,000, for which three years credit or longer was approved by the Department. The clearing banks similarly extended to these goods their fixed rate of interest arrangements. In April these arrangements were further extended, when the ECGD's minimum period for bank guarantees was changed from three to two years, the percentage cover was increased from 90 to 100 per cent, and the cost of the service was reduced. Moreover, the standard minimum percentage of insurance cover provided by the ECGD was increased from 85 to 90 per cent.

During 1965, two banks developed their services in the United States, the Midland by setting up an agency in New York, to extend the work of the representative's office, and Barclays by applying to open a state bank in California and to establish an agency of Barclays Bank DCO, both in the business area of San Francisco. Then, too, the Standard Bank and the Bank of West Africa proposed to merge their activities. The Standard Bank already had a substantial holding in the Bank of West Africa and other large shareholders included the National Provincial and Westminster Banks. Both decided to exchange their interests for shares in the Standard Bank and to increase their investments in the joint undertaking. At the same time, Lloyds Bank was to dispose of its holding in the Bank of West Africa, while the Midland Bank and the Chase Manhattan Bank acquired an interest in the Standard Bank. The idea was 'to bring together these British and American banking interests (with a possible subsequent widening of the field), in order to launch an international banking organization with wide connections and with particular interest in Africa'.

Nearer home, the Midland Bank announced in March 1965 that it was making an offer for the capital of Northern Bank, which has 132 offices in Northern Ireland and 54 in the Republic of Ireland. The intention was that the Northern Bank should continue to be run as a separate organization, side by side with the Midland and the Belfast Banking Company, for many years past an affiliation of the Midland operating in Northern Ireland.

The budget of April 1964 increased taxation by about £100 million, raising the duties on tobacco and alcoholic drink, and the above-the-line surplus was expected to reach £67 million. Even so, the overall borrowing requirement was then put at £791 million. In October, after the general election, the new government announced an export rebate scheme which it was later estimated would cost £80 million a year at the existing level of exports, and imposed a surcharge on imports of 15 per cent that was expected to bring in about £200 million in a full year. Then in the autumn budget speech a month later, the Chancellor raised the duty on petrol by 6*d.* a gallon and increased national insurance benefits and contributions from March 1965. He also announced an increase in the standard rate of income tax from 7*s.* 9*d.* to 8*s.* 3*d.* from April 1965; the introduction from the next budget day of a capital gains tax covering both short- and long-term gains; and the replacement of income tax and profits tax on companies by a new corporation tax. The revised tax on companies was to apply first to profits of the period immediately following that which formed the basis for tax for the year 1965–6.

In November, the indications were that, before allowing for the tax changes, the overall deficit for the whole of the financial year 1964–5 in fact would have been about £540 million and not £791 million, but allowing for the effect of various new measures the borrowing requirement was expected to be between £400 million and £450 million. In the event an above-the-line surplus of £420 million was recorded, with the net borrowing requirement, at £426 million, close to the November estimate. In Appendix 2, Table 4, where the annual Exchequer figures are summarized, transactions affecting the Civil Contingencies Fund are included in below-the-line items, while sinking fund provisions are excluded from ordinary expenditure, and for these reasons the figures differ from those in the official presentation.

In his 1965 budget the Chancellor took the view that he should reduce the pressure on resources to the extent of £250 million a year, by increases in taxation and prospective reductions in expenditures. He also proposed to reduce the net outflow of long-term capital by at least £100 million a year, by the measures of exchange control and in other ways, as already mentioned. Even so, loans from the Consolidated Fund were expected to rise steeply, largely because of increased lending to local authorities and the nationalized industries, and the borrowing requirement was expected to nearly double at £724 million.

During the year to March, with increased government borrowing required to finance the Exchequer deficit, the national debt rose from £30,226 million to £30,415 million, despite £200 million of surplus sterling funds returned from the Exchange Equalization Account. The nominal total of marketable securities outstanding fell by £390 million over the twelve months, as maturities exceeded new issues. Two stocks totalling £779 million – $4\frac{1}{2}$ per cent Conversion Stock and $2\frac{1}{2}$ per cent Exchequer Stock – came to maturity in May 1964. Substantial official purchases were made of these beforehand and no conversion offers were necessary. In the same month, however, an issue was made of £400 million of $5\frac{3}{4}$ per cent Funding Loan 1987–91 to replenish official portfolios of long-dated stocks. In February last £391 million of 4 per cent Treasury Stock was redeemed on maturity – again substantial official purchases had been made in advance. At about the same time a further £450 million of 5 per cent Exchequer Stock 1967 was issued to replenish official holdings of short-dated stocks. In all, therefore, issues of government stock amounted to £850 million and maturities to £1170 million.

Net sales of 'national savings securities' recovered sharply in the financial year to March, mainly as a result of the introduction last May of 5 per cent National Development Bonds to replace Defence Bonds, various issues of which had been running since 1939. The new bonds were similar to Defence Bonds, but had the attraction of a higher coupon rate, and in the ten and a half months to the end of March, net sales amounted to £152 million, though net redemptions of Defence Bonds totalled £73 million. Net sales of Premium Bonds, at £53 million, were also well maintained in the twelve months to March, but net repayments of tax reserve certificates again were substantial.

For national savings as a whole, net receipts in 1964–5 amounted to £330 million including accrued interest, £16 million more than in the previous year. Balances with the special investment departments of the trustee savings banks again rose sharply, but withdrawals from the Post Office Savings Bank generally exceeded deposits. When bank rate was raised to 7 per cent, the clearing banks, for the first time since the war, raised the rate allowed on the first £250 in savings accounts from 2½ to 3½ per cent. According to preliminary estimates,* the total for 'personal' savings of all kinds last year was nearly £190 million more than in 1963. Nearly 8½ per cent of disposable income seems to have been saved in 1964, as compared with 8 per cent a year earlier and 7¾ per cent in 1962.

The net outcome of the Exchequer deficit, on a rather smaller scale than had been expected, and the movements in other types of borrowing, was that the floating debt rose by £284 million to £5,016 million. Within this total, however, a switch occurred, with tap Treasury bills rising by £754 million, despite the return of £200 million by the Exchange Equalization Account, and bills issued through the tender falling by £500 million. The main cause was the balance of payments deficit, and the pressure on sterling in November.

When bank rate was increased to 5 per cent in February 1964, the discount market readjusted the Treasury bill tender rate. For about a year before, Treasury bill rate had been held unusually close to bank rate, and one of the stated purposes of the change in bank rate had been to widen the differential. Another outcome of the change of policy was that bank rate was not applied at all in money market borrowing for more than a year, from mid-January 1964 to late January 1965, except – as almost invariably – over the half-year periods. Moreover, the market maintained the same tender rate until the middle of May, and obtained satisfactory allotments. Then, in order to regain the initiative against outside tenderers, the discount houses changed their syndicate bid, and thereafter, during June and July, they varied it several times, increasing the average rate from $4\frac{5}{16}$ per cent in February to a little over $4\frac{5}{8}$ per cent by the end of July. The authorities were content at this time to see the bill rate flexible and in the existing circumstances – including a tendency towards tighter money abroad – to see it rise moderately.

In the uncertainties preceding the general election, there was a tendency between August and October for most short-term rates to move upwards, although the discount houses did not change their tender price. Immediately after the election and the publication of adverse trade figures, however, the discount rate was raised to just under 4¾ per cent, and at the next tender, following the raising of bank rate to 7 per cent in November 1964, to just over $6\frac{5}{8}$ per cent. This sudden increase in money and bill rates brought losses to the discount houses, both on their bill and their bond portfolios.

With the receipt by the Exchange Equalization Account of large amounts of sterling as a reflection of the difficulties of sterling, the Exchequer had little need to raise funds from the market by Treasury bills. Indeed, in January, and again in subsequent months, offerings were reduced on occasion to £160 million, the smallest amount since 1952. Yet, no further change was made in the syndicate bid until late in January, even though in most weeks

* *Preliminary Estimates of National Income and Balance of Payments 1959 to 1964* (Cmnd. 2629).

the discount houses obtained only small allotments from the much reduced offerings. Thereafter the syndicate bid was raised repeatedly, and at one time the average bill rate had fallen by more than 5*s*. per cent from its mid-January level. In addition to competition for bills, the discount houses were conscious of the possiblity of a fall in bank rate. The Bank of England was unwilling to see the discount rate brought down, and applied bank rate repeatedly and heavily. Late in March 1965 the discount houses were brought to heel, and the discount rate recovered, but in April it began to fall again. Other short-term rates have also risen more or less in line with the bank rate change in November, the main exception being rates paid by local authorities, to which we refer below.

In the gilt-edged market, prices in 1964 were fairly steady up to the date of the election, apart from a period of weakness in July. After the middle of October, however, they fell sharply, despite official interventions, at times on a substantial scale. A strong recovery at the end of that month was reversed sharply as uncertainties grew, including that as to whether the newly announced capital gains tax would be applied to gilt-edged securities; although the bank rate change and other reassurances about the end of November steadied the market, the improvement was short lived. About the middle of December the publication of further disappointing trade figures added another depressing influence, but an intimation to jobbers in the stock market that the authorities would be prepared to buy at prevailing prices if stock were offered quickly brought about a firmer condition. Towards the end of December sentiment improved, although the market remained quiet until the middle of January 1965 when more encouraging news of the economy helped to stimulate demand. Thereafter prices remained fairly steady, though weakening at times, until the budget, which led to a further marking down of prices, but later some recovery occurred.

One of the results of raising bank rate to 7 per cent was that the yields on gilt-edged securities throughout the whole range of maturities became unusually closely bunched, at around 6½ per cent. Among short-term bonds, the gross redemption yield on 5 per cent Exchequer Stock 1967 fluctuated about the 5 per cent level until July, when it was approaching 5½ per cent. Following the bank rate change in November the yield rose to over 6 per cent and by the end of the year it had risen further to about 6½ per cent. At the end of March 1965 the gross redemption yield was above 6½ per cent, about 1½ per cent above the level a year earlier. The movements in other government securities were similar. In the 'undated' range, the gross flat rate yield on 3½ per cent War Loan rose from about 6 per cent in January 1964 to 6¼ per cent by mid-year; it then fluctuated about this figure for a few months, but rose again towards the end of the year to reach nearly 6½ per cent. At the end of March 1965 it was yielding 6½ per cent.

As in the previous year, changes in administered rates were all upwards. The tax-free rate of interest on new tax reserve certificates was increased from $2\frac{3}{4}$ to $3\frac{1}{2}$ per cent in November, having been raised from $2\frac{1}{4}$ to $2\frac{3}{4}$ per cent the previous March. In addition to substantial changes made in April 1964 to the structure of rates charged by the Public Works Loan Board on new loans to local authorities, the rates themselves were raised on a number of occasions. The government spoke at times of introducing specially favourable interest rates for local authorities and house purchasers, but the only action taken, following the rise in bank rate, was to keep the main PWLB rates unchanged despite the rise in market rates. The Agricultural Mortgage Corporation also increased its rate of interest on new loans from $6\frac{3}{4}$ to $7\frac{1}{4}$ per cent in January this year, following two other upward revisions in rates in the early months of 1964.

Changes in local authority borrowing arrangements, which came into effect in April 1964, are outlined on p. 307. Broadly speaking the new procedure places restrictions on short-term borrowing by local authorities, but gives them greater access to the Public Works Loan Board at government lending rates plus a small service charge. Local authorities will eventually be allowed to obtain up to 50 per cent of their annual long-term finance from the Board, but in the first year it was laid down that each local authority could obtain 20 per cent of its long-term borrowing needs from the Board, or, to help smaller authorities, £50,000, whichever was the greater. This led to far greater borrowing from the Board than at any time since 1955, when local authorities were turned from the Board and required to borrow in the market.

After the 2 per cent rise in bank rate in November, with no change in the Board's 'quota' lending rates, drawings soon accelerated, and less was borrowed in the mortgage market, where rates had risen appreciably. Relief was given to small authorities by raising the amount which an authority could borrow from the Board in 1964–5 to 20 per cent or £100,000, whichever was the greater. Although rates of interest on new loans in excess of quotas were then raised, those for quota borrowing were maintained at the level ruling before the bank rate change. Under the original arrangements, the proportion which could be borrowed from the Board was raised from 20 to 30 per cent at the beginning of this financial year. A further relaxation was announced in the April 1965 budget speech, when the Chancellor proposed that authorities in the less prosperous areas eventually selected under the government's policy of regional development should be allowed to anticipate the final arrangements for all authorities and borrow up to 50 per cent of their long-term money from the Board.

Another alteration in local authority borrowing arrangements was made in July, when the statutory power given to authorities to issue short-term bonds was in effect brought into operation. To ensure orderly marketing arrangements, however, the terms and timing of bonds issued 'to or through the agency of any bank, discount house, issuing house or broker' were made subject to Bank of England approval. In general, a maximum term of five years was applied to these bonds, with the authorities preferring maturities longer than one year, although the local authorities mainly wanted to borrow for as short a period as possible; thus, most issues were for one year. At the same time local authorities were permitted to issue stocks with a minimum life of five years instead of ten years as previously. From July until September, thirty issues of bonds were placed in the market and were granted a Stock Exchange quotation, the total amount involved being about £26 million. Other bonds, probably exceeding £10 million in total, were placed in the discount market and elsewhere, without a Stock Exchange quotation, although rates for them were quoted daily in the financial press.

The uncertain character of the capital market in the months before the election made it necessary to curtail the flow of local authority stock and bond issues, particularly as a number of the early issues of bonds which had been placed in the first instance with jobbers in the Stock Exchange were reported to be slow in moving into the hands of more permanent holders. Consequently, no further issues of stock or bonds were made between October and December, but stock issues were resumed in January 1965 on a considerable scale and bond issues in February. Some of the first one-year bonds, issued by Manchester Corporation under special legislation and placed in the discount market, matured and were renewed.

Some of the risks of short-term borrowing developments came into prominence towards the end of 1964. During the final quarter accepting houses and overseas banks, which were affected by the drain on sterling, sharply reduced their loans to local authorities. Through these and other withdrawals, local authorities came under considerable pressure and were forced to rely more heavily on the Public Works Loan Board and the domestic banks. Over the turn of the year rates were bid up, for one week's or one month's money, to as high as 8 to $8\frac{1}{4}$ per cent. Although the position subsequently eased somewhat, rates continued to be high in relation to other short-term rates. By March funds became scarce again, due in part to the lack of overseas bank money resulting from a request by President Johnson that United States banks and companies should lend less abroad and deposit more of their funds at home. Late in March, rates as high as 9 per cent or more were being quoted for seven-day loans for local authorities, though in April they eased appreciably.

At the beginning of our period, share prices were high and rising, but with gathering doubts as to the course of the economy, and political uncertainties, this trend was halted. After the election, equity markets weakened sharply particularly when the proposals for a new capital gains tax and a corporation tax were announced. By mid-December prices had fallen to their lowest level for that year, but thereafter they fluctuated; the *Financial Times* – Actuaries

Index of 'all-share' equity prices reached 98 in late April 1965, as compared with 95 in mid-December, 109 at the beginning of October and 105 in the previous March. The average 'yield' rose from $4\frac{1}{4}$ per cent in March 1964 to just over 5 per cent in December and to between $5\frac{1}{4}$ to $5\frac{1}{2}$ per cent in March. The 'reverse yield gap', comparing this index of equities with the yield on $2\frac{1}{2}$ per cent Consols, widened to well over 1 per cent in the year to April 1964, but narrowed somewhat with the generally higher yields; in mid-April it was just under 1 per cent.

The London Stock Exchange began for the first time to publish regular statistics of turnover in the gilt-edged and other markets as from the beginning of September 1964. These show that for the period September to December turnover amounted to £6349 million, representing nearly $1\frac{3}{4}$ million bargains. According to statistics regularly compiled by the Midland Bank, the amount of new money raised by issues of all kinds of securities was £508 million in 1964, as compared with £593 million in 1963 and £605 million in 1962. The aggregate of new money raised in 1964 fell from previous high levels owing to a sharp decline in activity in the new issue market in the last quarter of the year. In particular, issues by home companies fell by £46·5 million during the year, while issues in respect of countries outside the Commonwealth increased from £4·5 million to £21 million. London houses and brokers, acting in cooperation with overseas banks, were estimated to have been involved in foreign currency issues in 1964 amounting to well over £300 million.

1966 – Further Uncertainties and Restraints

Between the autumn of 1964 and April 1965 a wide range of measures was taken to restore confidence in the pound and to deal with the external situation generally. Over the twelve months to April 1966 action was again necessary to meet periods of pressure on sterling and to promote continued recovery in the external balance of payments: in particular, further resort was made to overseas short-term credits, exchange controls were extended, new restraints were put on the banks and other lending institutions, hire purchase restrictions were tightened, and measures were taken to check the growth of public sector expenditure.

Some of these developments – which are described more fully below – were associated with renewed and intense pressure on sterling in the summer of last year. More generally, however, progress towards better balance in economic affairs, both at home and abroad, had been uneasy and uncertain. True, the balance of payments was much less unfavourable in 1965 than in 1964, but the deficit on current and long-term capital transactions combined was still formidable. The internal political situation and other developments – for example interest rate movements abroad – had led to hesitancy in exchange markets. And some domestic developments gave cause for concern.

Under the weight of the wide range of restrictive measures, the rate of growth of the economy slowed down appreciably in 1965, although employment remained at a high level. In March 1966, the percentage unemployed was the lowest recorded for that month for ten years, and the number of unfilled vacancies the highest for fifteen; reports of labour shortages have persisted. For the whole year, the gross domestic product, calculated at constant prices, was about 2½ per cent higher than in 1964, less than half the increase recorded between 1963 and 1964. Industrial production, according to the official index, rose by about the same percentage, this comparing with an increase of 7½ per cent for the previous year, but on a seasonally adjusted basis it was running more or less level throughout 1965, a slight downward movement from February to June being balanced by a slight rise thereafter, so that in December the index was at the same level as in January (see Appendix 3, Chart (a)). A similar movement was seen in the index for the manufacturing industries, but the index of construction in the third quarter was two points below the figure recorded in the first.

Investment continued to rise last year, though less rapidly than in either 1964 or 1963. Taken as a whole, gross fixed capital formation was about 4 per cent greater than in 1964. Further marked increases were recorded for private manufacturing industry and the public sector, but only relatively moderate increases for housing and the distribution and service trades. Stockbuilding also continued, but at a slower rate than in 1964.

At current prices, consumers' expenditure was 6 per cent higher than in 1964; calculated at constant prices, the increase was less than 2 per cent, and in the fourth quarter the total was less than 1 per cent higher than in the corresponding period of the previous year. For the whole year the index of retail prices was over 4¾ per cent above that of 1964. An increase of two points in the index in April was associated with changes in indirect taxes in the budget and increases in local authority rates: over the rest of the year the index (16 January 1962 = 100) rose from 112·0 to 114·1, and in March 1966 it stood at 114·6. The relatively slow rise in the index since April 1965 has been attributed in part to the activities of the National Board for Prices and Incomes, but the influence of the Board on wages and earnings has been less apparent. The index number of negotiated wage rates rose by nearly 5 per cent during 1965, and average earnings by nearly 7 per cent.

External imbalance reduced

The final deficit on the balance of payments in 1964 was put at £769 million, the adverse balance on visible trade being £535 million, as compared with less than £100 million in each of the two previous years, and the net outflow on long-term capital account amounting to £363 million, against £162 million in 1963 and under £100 million in 1962. A considerable improvement was recorded in the first half of 1965. For the first three months of the year the deficit on the current and long-term capital accounts combined was £104 million, against £149 million in the corresponding period of 1964, and a further reduction, to £38 million against £171 million, occurred in the second. The main elements in this recovery were a reduction in the adverse visible trade balance and – especially in the second quarter – in the net outflow of private investment.

In the third quarter, however, the position deteriorated. On visible trade, although imports continued to fall, exports also declined, and the deficit was £42 million greater than in the second quarter. The invisibles account, from a surplus of £53 million, moved into deficit to the extent of £18 million. A sharp deterioration occurred on private long-term capital account; although net UK investment abroad was £1 million less than in the previous quarter, a net inflow of only £3 million was recorded in respect of overseas investment in the United Kingdom, as compared with £50 million over the previous three months. The net result was a deficit on current and long-term capital transactions of £210 million.

In the final quarter, movements were again more favourable. The current account swung into surplus for the first time since the second quarter of 1963, and at £25 million it compared with a deficit of £118 million in the previous three months. The trade deficit fell to only £19 million and invisibles also showed a substantial improvement, a surplus of £44 million being recorded. A small surplus was also recorded on private investment account, resulting from a sharp recovery in overseas investment in Britain.

Over the year as a whole, the overall deficit fell by more than one half to £354 million. The current account deficit fell by £270 million, to £136 million; on visible trade alone the reduction was from £535 million to £265 million. Net earnings from invisible items were unchanged at £129 million, and on long-term capital account the net outflow was reduced by £145 million to £218 million last year, most of this improvement being accounted for by net private investment which fell by £110 million.*

A notably encouraging feature of Britain's external transactions in 1965 was the expansion in exports, the trade accounts showing a rise of 7 per cent by value as compared with 1964, following one of slightly over 4 per cent in the previous year. By volume, the increase was nearly 5½ per cent, against 2¾ per cent between 1963 and 1964. Most of last year's increase was in exports of manufactured goods, which rose by nearly 9 per cent by value, and the decline in Britain's share of world trade in these was checked.

Imports rose by only slightly over 1 per cent in value as compared with

* See Appendix 2. Annual figures are given in Tables 1 and 1a (new presentation). The figures are as revised officially from those given above.

15 per cent in 1964, and in volume by less than 1 per cent, as compared with over 11 per cent. The main increase last year was in imports of fuel, while those of food, beverages and tobacco generally declined. Imports of manufactured goods, which had contributed substantially to the rise in the total in 1964, showed little further growth in 1965, an increase of 14 per cent for capital goods being almost offset by a fall of 11 per cent for consumer goods. Up to April, in which month the import surcharge was reduced from 15 to 10 per cent, the volume of imports was at an appreciably lower level than a year before, but over the following six months it was three per cent higher than in the corresponding period of 1964, when the surcharge was not yet being applied. Subsequently, imports of goods subject to it have risen considerably; in the three months November 1965 to January 1966 inclusive, the volume of such imports was 10 per cent higher than in the corresponding period a year before.

Exports to all the main trading areas were higher than in 1964, the largest increase, of 18 per cent, being recorded for North America, with shipments to the United States growing by 23 per cent and to Canada by seven. Shipments to western Europe as a whole rose by 4 per cent. The increase for EFTA countries was almost 7 per cent, but for the Common Market less than 1 per cent, reflecting perhaps the growing tariff disparities between the two trading groups and in particular the further reduction of ten per cent of base levels in tariffs on imports from member countries, which were made by each group with effect from 1 January 1965. Further reductions of ten per cent were made from 1 January 1966.

Trade with the overseas sterling area developed more favourably for the United Kingdom than in 1964, with imports into Britain falling by nearly 4 per cent and exports increasing by 7.

It became known that during the first quarter of 1965, the United Kingdom made further drawings amounting to $415 million on the special short-term facilities aggregating $3000 million made available by eleven central banks, the Bank for International Settlements and the United States Export-Import Bank during the critical days of November 1964. Thus by the end of March 1965 short-term borrowing under these arrangements stood at $940 million and a further $157 million was taken during April.

In May, this borrowing was put on a longer-term basis, as earlier assistance had been, by borrowing from the International Monetary Fund. The United Kingdom had announced in February that it intended to make a further application to the Fund, and on 25 May the equivalent of $1400 million (£500 million) was drawn for repayment by May 1970. At the same time Switzerland provided a parallel credit equivalent to $40 million. From these borrowings the whole of the outstanding short-term debt of $1097 million was repaid, and the balance of $343 million was added to the reserves.

Further resort to short-term borrowing was to become necessary in subsequent months to counter renewed pressures on sterling; all of this was provided from the United States, although in July, in addition, West Germany deposited £41 million as provision for future purchases to offset part of the cost of United Kingdom military expenditure in Germany. In June $360 million was taken from the Federal Reserve Bank of New York under the reciprocal swap arrangement of $750 million. Pressures intensified during July and August, and the balance of the swap facility was drawn. In addition, a further $140 million was made available by the Federal Reserve Bank.

Early in September, when the Bank of England announced that it had entered into new arrangements with ten central banks* and the Bank for International Settlements for the purpose of taking advantage of the improved 'sentiment towards sterling', it seemed that the tide had turned. No details as to amount or period of the new facilities have been disclosed, except that it became known that the Federal Reserve Bank agreed to provide an additional $200 million and the US Treasury a further substantial amount.

Nor was it known at the time to what extent, if at all, these facilities were being 'activated', but in the *Monthly Review* for March 1966 of the Federal Reserve Bank of New York† it is stated that immediately after the announcement of the new support arrangements the Federal Reserve began bidding strongly in the market for sterling; thereafter, 'market forces took over', and intervention by other central banks was not required. Confidence in sterling continued to grow, and during September the reserves rose by £61 million and the supplementary swap assistance of £50 million ($140 million) was repaid.

The recovery was maintained thereafter; in each month up to February, when the last of the short-term assistance was repaid, indebtedness was reduced and additions were recorded to the gold and currency reserves. In February the reserves were further strengthened by taking in the 'liquefied' portion of the official portfolio of dollar securities, amounting to £316 million, while the balance of the United States swap borrowing, by now reduced to £103 million, was repaid. In March, however, the reserves fell by £27 million to £1276 million. This fall was a 'true' one in the sense that no drawings were made on the Federal Reserve swap facility or on any other lines of credit, and it was considered reasonably satisfactory in view of the rise in North American interest rates and the pre-election uncertainties. A further call on the reserves was avoided in December when, as in 1964, the repayments of interest and principal on the United States and Canadian government loans were postponed. The line of credit for $250

* All those that participated in the short-term credit of November 1964, with the exception of the Bank of France.

† *Treasury and Federal Reserve Foreign Exchange Operations*, by Charles A. Coombs.

million opened with the Export-Import Bank in November 1964 and due to expire in November 1965 was extended for a further year.

As indicated on p. 315 arrangements for assistance to sterling have blurred the relationships between recorded movements in the United Kingdom's external monetary situation. In the first half of last year the published reserves rose by £170 million, but over the same period liabilities to the International Monetary Fund and other non-territorial organizations rose by £488 million. Meanwhile net liabilities to other sterling area countries fell by £132 million, mainly reflecting a deterioration in their aggregate balance of payments, and to non-sterling area countries by £60 million. During the second half of the year, external sterling liabilities to countries were rising again, by £38 million to the sterling area and by £158 million to the rest of the world, but the figure for non-territorial organizations was little changed.*

Monthly movements since January 1965 in outstanding indebtedness arising from operations in support of sterling since the autumn of 1964 are shown in Table C4. The figures for the IMF comprise only the drawings referred to above, and take no account of other changes in the United Kingdom's position in relation to the Fund, in particular the special drawing in March of this year to cover the gold content, equivalent to $120 million, of the additional quota due under the arrangements agreed early in 1965.

Before the budget of April 1965, the spot rate for sterling against the United States dollar was around $2·79, but thereafter it improved and was almost at parity early in May, the highest level for nearly a year. By mid-June, however, it had fallen again to $2·79$\frac{1}{16}$, and except for a brief rise late in July remained at around this level until the announcement of new support early in September. This was followed by a sharp rise in the spot rate, which reached parity late in September and early in November stood at $2·80$\frac{1}{2}$, the highest level since January 1963. This was more or less maintained, in a firm market, until a sharp decline was recorded early in March with the announcement of the general election. At this time the authorities were reported to be operating to support the rate. Thereafter the rate remained roughly steady at about $2·79$\frac{1}{2}$. Earlier, the market had seemed to be little affected either by developments in Rhodesia or the raising of the Federal Reserve discount rate in December.

The forward discount on sterling remained fairly substantial throughout most of the year. The three-month forward discount fell slightly from its previous level of about 2 cents between May and August 1965, but it was not until September that it fell below 1 cent. It increased only slightly in March this year, despite the fall in spot sterling. During January and February many of the forward deals made by the authorities towards the end of last year matured, and commitments were then substantially reduced. The authorities

* See Appendix 2, Table 3 (assistance for sterling).

TABLE C4 *Assistance for sterling* (*$m. amounts outstanding at end of period*)

	IMF	Federal Reserve Bank of New York	Other central banks and BIS	Switzerland	Total	Net change over month
1965: Jan.	1000	200	600	80	1880	+275
Feb.	1000	105	600	80	1785	− 95
Mar.	1000	320	620	80	2020	+235
Apr.	1000	280	817	80	2177	+157
May	2400	—	—	120	2520	+343
June	2400	360	—	120	2880	+360
July	2400	525	—	120	3045	+165
Aug.	2400	890	—	120	3410	+365
Sept.	2400	750	—	120	3270	−140
Oct.	2400	700	—	120	3220	− 50
Nov.	2400	550	—	120	3070	−150
Dec.	2400	475	—	120	2995	− 75
1966: Jan.	2400	290	—	120	2810	−185
Feb.	2400	—	—	120	2520	−240
Mar.	2400	—	—	120	2520	—

were again active in the forward market during the year. Indeed, according to the article in the Federal Reserve Bank of New York's *Monthly Review* already referred to, 'large-scale' operations by the Bank of England in the forward market 'were conducted forcefully and with great technical skill'. The rate for security sterling fluctuated with the movements in the spot rate for sterling, generally at a discount of under $\frac{1}{4}$ cent.

Further restrictions on the flow of currency into the investment dollar pool, following those announced in the April budget, were imposed in July: the foreign currency proceeds of life policies, and the assets of immigrants re-designated as residents of the United Kingdom, which were previously treated as investment currency, had to be exchanged at the official rate. In addition, no further foreign exchange was to be made available at the official rate for investment projects outside the sterling area. Between April and September the premium on investment dollars fluctuated between 8 and 15 per cent. Thereafter it rose sharply; in March 1966 it reached nearly 25 per cent and in mid-April was still around 20 per cent.

Following the reintroduction of a separate 'property currency' in April 1965, the premium on the currency from this pool quickly rose to about 25 per cent. Thereafter, in a very thin market the quotation fluctuated between 11 and 35 per cent.

Demand for gold – arising mainly from Chinese purchases, continued doubts about sterling, and the political situation in Asia, notably in Vietnam – remained high for most of the period April to December 1965, and the London price occasionally reached high levels. During the first week of August, the price at the daily fixing rose to \$35·19$\frac{3}{8}$ per fine ounce, but thereafter, with substantial Russian sales, and as confidence in sterling improved, the price eased. In the early part of 1965 the 'sales consortium' arrangements under the gold pool were operating to keep the market supplied at a reasonable price; later, as the pressure of demand eased, the gold supplied by the consortium earlier in the year was fully repaid.

Monetary restraints intensified

In the conditions described earlier, it has not been found possible to ease the monetary restraints imposed in 1964–5; indeed, further restrictions were applied. These began with a call on 29 April 1965 for Special Deposits to be placed with the Bank of England, at the rate of 1 per cent of gross deposits for the clearing banks and $\frac{1}{2}$ per cent for the Scottish banks. Just previously, in his budget speech, the Chancellor of the Exchequer had stated that he would be prepared to reinforce the existing tight and effective control on bank lending 'if it were to prove necessary'. The call for Special Deposits was followed almost immediately by a letter of guidance from the governor of the Bank of England, the first of three sent during the following twelve months. In his letter of May 1965 the governor emphasized that the authorities wished the call for Special Deposits to be fully reflected in the banks' lending policies, and that it should be mitigated as little as possible by the sale of investments. The advice given in the letter of December 1964 as to the direction of lending still stood, and in particular first priority was to be given to the promotion of exports. In addition, however, a quantitative limit was imposed, with a request to the clearing banks not to increase their advances to the private sector at an annual rate of more than about 5 per cent in the twelve months to mid-March 1966, and similar limits were indicated for the totals of their acceptances and purchases of commercial bills. The governor wrote in similar terms to a number of bodies, including the other main banking organizations, asking them to observe a comparable degree of restraint.*

Meanwhile bank rate had been maintained at the 'crisis' level of 7 per cent, to which it had been raised in the previous November, but on 3 June 1965 it was reduced to 6 per cent. It was made clear that the change did not imply any relaxation of credit restrictions, and indeed a tightening of the hire purchase regulations was announced on the same day. Minimum deposits under agreements for most goods were increased, from 20 to 25 per cent for cars and motor cycles, and otherwise generally from 10 to 15 per cent.

* For a fuller account of restrictions imposed up to October 1965 see pp. 46 ff.

A second letter from the governor of the Bank of England to the clearing banks, on 27 July 1965, coincided with the announcement of further measures to limit the growth of demand, principally restraints on the growth of public expenditure and investment and a reduction in the maximum period for hire purchase contracts on most goods from three years to two and a half. The letter to the clearing banks re-emphasized the importance of encouraging exports but stressed that it was equally important to restrain the growth of finance for imports. The banks were therefore asked to scrutinize requests for credit even more carefully than before where it appeared that their purpose might be to facilitate payment for imports, notably of manufactured goods for home consumption or for stockbuilding.

The next request to the clearing banks, sent on 1 February 1966, related to the period after March 1966, when the 105 per cent 'guideline' would have run its course. They were then informed that until further review their advances, acceptances and holdings of commercial bills, taken separately and making allowances for seasonal factors, should not rise above the levels set for March 1966, and once more the guidance as to the direction of lending remained unchanged. To some extent this third 'directive' indicated an intensification of the 'credit squeeze', since little or no scope for expansion of advances was provided even though prices were rising, while the seasonal pattern would imply an absolute reduction in lending from the level fixed for March 1966 of say 4 per cent by December 1966. Other financial institutions were again asked to observe similar restraint.

Also in February, the terms for hire purchase and rental agreements were restricted further: the maximum period for hire purchase contracts on most goods was reduced to two years and the minimum down payment was raised from 15 to 25 per cent. For cars and motor cycles the maximum period was reduced to twenty-seven months, the minimum down payments remaining unchanged. Advance rentals required under hiring agreements were increased from twenty to thirty-two weeks.

When the limit of 5 per cent on the growth of advances to the private sector over the period to March 1966 was imposed in the previous May, difficulties in meeting the official requirement were foreseen in view of commitments under established overdraft limits and the tendency for agreed facilities to be utilized more fully in times of credit stringency. In the event, however, net advances by the clearing banks other than to the nationalized industries rose in the year to March 1966 by only 2½ per cent, from £4638 million to £4757 million; over the nine months to December 1965 the total fell by 2·7 per cent, and the seasonal upswing in the first quarter of 1966 was 5·4 per cent. Gross advances fell from £4854 million to £4764 million between March and November of 1965, and rose by March 1966 to £5008 million.

Gross deposits of the clearing banks rose by £557 million to £9280 million over the year to March 1966, nearly two thirds of the increase being in respect of deposit accounts, the return on which had been relatively high at the customary level of 2 per cent below bank rate. Other outlets for liquid funds, however, had provided even higher returns. During the year, subsidiary and associated companies of the clearing banks, which were not bound by the banks' rate agreement, continued to develop, and new institutions were set up.

As may be seen from Appendix 2, Table 5, the increase in net deposits over the year to March last was appreciably greater than in either of the two previous years, and that in advances substantially smaller. Over the nine months to December 1965 the ratio of advances to gross deposits fell from 55·6 to 50·9 per cent; after the turn of the year, seasonal movements brought about the usual increase but the mid-March ratio of 54·0 per cent compared with 55·6 per cent a year before.

In these conditions, no acute strains on liquidity were experienced, notwithstanding the call for Special Deposits, one half of which was required to be made by 19 May and the rest by 16 June. Although throughout the year the total of market Treasury bills outstanding was lower, and at times substantially so, than in 1964–5, the holdings of the clearing banks rose by more than one half between March 1965 and January 1966, and in March 1966, at £656 million, were £97 million higher than twelve months previously. Total liquid assets rose by £221 million over the year, and the combined liquidity ratio from 29·5 to 30·1 per cent, a comfortably high figure for March. The easing of the liquidity situation was partly the result of the redemption of £976 million of 5½ per cent Exchequer Stock on 15 March, which likewise largely accounted for the fall in the banks' holdings of investments in the first quarter of 1966 to £1111 million. Even so, over the whole of 1965–6, investments rose by £63 million. Prior to the governor's letter of May, with its specific reference to investments, some realizations had taken place to meet pressure on liquidity, but thereafter aggregate holdings were rising up to January 1966 when a peak of £1188 million was reached. The ratio of investments to gross deposits rose correspondingly between April and January, from 11·4 to 12·7 per cent, but by March 1966 it had fallen to 12·0 per cent.

The effects of the qualitative requests to the banks regarding their lending were evident in the regular analyses of advances of the members of the British Bankers' Association by trade and other classifications. In total, they rose by 4·9 per cent or £263 million over the year to February 1966 – less than half the rate of increase over the previous twelve months. Advances to the personal and professional group fell by 7½ per cent, or £74 million, despite an increase of £13 million in the quarter to February 1966; to hire purchase finance companies by 17½ per cent, or £27 million; and to other financial borrowers by 10 per cent, or £16 million. By contrast, advances to industry and trade as a whole rose by 11 per cent, or £382 million; within this group loans to heavy industry rose by 20 per cent.

The requests to the banks to give priority to export finance had been meticulously observed. Indeed, the range of facilities was further widened during the year, with the introduction of a special scheme for financing and underwriting export orders involving short-term credit, thus supplementing the existing arrangements for providing medium-term financing for major export contracts. These, too, were extended; in July the minimum size of contract to which the scheme applies was further reduced, from £50,000 to £25,000, and later the Export Credits Guarantee Department indicated that it was prepared, 'where the banks are agreeable', to waive the new minimum in special cases.

Initially, the new short-term facility arranged in conjunction with the Export Credits Guarantee Department was for credit periods of thirty days or more but less than two years, and applied to credit-insured exports where payment was due against a negotiable instrument, for example a bill of exchange or promissory note. For each insured exporter ECGD would give the exporter's bank a guarantee covering it up to a stated maximum amount outstanding. The banks would advance 100 per cent of the principal value of the bill of exchange relating to the shipment, charging the exporter interest at bank rate with a minimum of 4½ per cent per annum until payment was received. Once the buyer has accepted the bill, the bank would look to him for payment or, should he default, to the ECGD. Thus the exporter would have received cash for his export by the time of shipment and would be freed from the risk of bank recourse at an early stage.

Despite the application of restrictive monetary policies, activity on bank accounts continued to increase, though at a somewhat slower rate than in the previous year. The total value of cheques passing through the Bankers' Clearing House, on a working-day average basis, was 15·2 per cent higher than in 1964, and the number of debit items dealt with, at 545 million, was 4·1 per cent higher. The value of the general debit clearing rose by 6·4 per cent, and the total of credit clearings by 10·6 per cent, these now representing 14·0 per cent of the general clearing.

According to the Midland Bank Index of Business Turnover, the rate of growth of business activity for the country as a whole declined in 1965: the index was 7 per cent higher in 1965 than in 1964, as compared with an increase of 14 per cent between 1963 and 1964. On a seasonally corrected basis the index rose in the second quarter of 1965, but in the fourth quarter was at the same level as in the first; in the first quarter of 1966, however, it rose by 6 per cent.

Progress in developing other channels for transmission of payments was recorded during the year, as an increasing number of trustee savings banks began to operate cheque accounts, while the government decided to go ahead with the setting up of a postal giro system. Another official decision of interest to the banks, though not immediately, was that the United Kingdom should convert to a decimal currency in February 1971; the pound would remain the major unit, divided into 100 cents.

Among the banks themselves, also, important developments in the payments field have taken place. The Midland Group's Cheque Card Service, which came into operation in March 1966, guarantees payment of cheques drawn by cardholders for amounts up to £30 each; and similar facilities are provided with the National Provincial Group's Travel Card, and under the Bankers Card scheme operated by Lloyds and eleven other British and Irish banks. The common purpose of these arrangements is to extend the 'usability' of cheques; that of the Barclaycard scheme, announced by Barclays Bank in January 1966, is the provision of credit card facilities, and so also is the participation of Westminster Bank in the Diners' Club.

Two of the 'big five' acquired other institutions during the year: Lloyds the National Bank of New Zealand, and Midland the Northern Bank with branches throughout Ireland. Both acquisitions resulted in capital increases of the parent bank; and Martins Bank made a one-for-eight scrip issue.

In December the National Commercial Bank of Scotland and the Bank of Ireland made an offer for the share capital of National Bank, which amounted to £17 million in terms of cash and convertible loan stock of the Bank of Ireland. It was agreed that the National Bank would become a wholly owned subsidiary of the National Commercial Bank of Scotland, but would maintain its separate identity and hence its membership of the Committee of London Clearing Bankers; its business in Ireland, however, would be transferred to a subsidiary, National Bank of Ireland, which would become part of the Bank of Ireland group.

During the year Westminster Bank was actively associated with the underwriting and placing of a number of market issues of capital and Midland Bank took an equity participation in European Enterprises Development of Luxembourg.

Table 4 in Appendix 2, showing government receipts and outgoings, has been revised to take account of the changes in classification of items introduced in the Financial Statement published in April 1965. These revise the concept of 'the line', and the expressions 'above the line' and 'below the line' then disappeared from Exchequer terminology; the new distinction is between loans from and repayments to the Consolidated Fund, and other revenue and expenditure.

In the 1965 budget, which was summarized in that year's Survey, a surplus of revenue over expenditure of £544 million was estimated, but 'net consolidated loans' were expected to rise to £1268 million, giving an overall borrowing requirement of £724 million, as compared with an actual figure of

£386 million for the previous year. In fact a surplus of revenue over expenditure of £689 million was recorded for the year and net consolidated fund loans totalled £1265 million, so that the overall borrowing requirement stood at £577 million. This unforeseen rise of £145 million in the surplus resulted in part from a rise in actual income tax receipts over the budget estimate, of £86 million, largely a reflection of increased earnings.

The 1966 budget was due to be opened early in May, after this Survey had gone to press. Before the dissolution of Parliament it was indicated that 'the need for severe increases in taxation' was not foreseen, but that a general tax on betting and gaming, expected to yield £11 million in a full year, would be proposed.

Besides the overall deficit in the year to March 1966 of £576 million, payments to extra-Exchequer funds were required as well as finance for the Exchange Equalization Account. In the outcome, the net borrowing requirement of the Exchequer amounted to £813 million as compared with £190 million in the previous year. Net repayments of non-marketable debt amounted to £231 million, Treasury bills issued through the tender declined by £110 million, and ways and means advances were reduced by £40 million; these movements were more than offset by increases in tap bills of £560 million, of other debt in sterling of £594 million net, and of marketable securities. Thus the floating debt rose during the financial year by £410 million, as compared with an increase of £282 million in the previous twelve months.

The net sum raised on marketable securities over the twelve months was £54 million. In June, in order to replenish official stocks of short- and medium-dated stock, issues for cash were made of £100 million each of 6½ per cent Exchequer Loan 1969 and 6½ per cent Treasury Loan 1976. Holders of 3 per cent Savings Bonds 1955–65, which were due for redemption on 15 August and of which £709 million was outstanding, were invited to convert at par into either or both of the new stocks. Holders of £311 million accepted conversion into the 1969 stock and of £200 million into the 1976 stock. Two further issues were made in 1965: on 27 September official holdings of long-dated stocks were replenished by the issue of £600 million 6 per cent Funding loan 1993 at £96 and on 1 November a further issue was made of short-dated stock, £500 million of 6 per cent Exchequer Loan 1970 at £99. At mid-December, therefore, the nominal total of marketable securities had risen by just over £1100 million, but a reduction of £976 million occurred in March with the redemption of 5½ per cent Exchequer Stock 1966.

Although the nominal total of marketable securities rose by over £1000 million over the nine months to December 1965, sales out of official hands were much smaller. For the six months to September, indeed, the public as a whole disposed of securities to the extent of £20 million, but in the following quarter, as noted in *Economic Report on 1965* issued by the Treasury, the authorities sold no less than £197 million of stock, by far the largest quarterly figure since 1962, and of this £130 million was taken up outside the banking sector.

Net payments in respect of 'national savings securities' exceeded net sales by £172 million in the year to March 1966; the only increase was in receipts from premium bonds. In view of the 'heavy competition' facing the national savings certificate, in March the Chancellor of the Exchequer announced the introduction of a new certificate earning interest, if held for five years, of £4 11*s.* 3*d.* per cent per annum free of tax. The maximum individual holding is 500 units.

For national savings as a whole net receipts in 1965–6 totalled £51 million including accrued interest, or £278 million less than in the previous year. Withdrawals from the Post Office Savings Bank again exceeded deposits, but balances with ordinary departments of trustee savings banks increased, and in the special investment departments they continued to rise sharply. With the rate of interest allowed on tax reserve certificates remaining unchanged, the total of savings held in this form fell by £59 million, the third successive annual fall. The total remaining invested at the end of March was £192 million, as compared with £352 million three years earlier.

The Post Office Savings Bank Act, permitting the Bank to open investment accounts offering a rate of interest higher than the traditional 2½ per cent, was passed in March 1966. The amounts deposited had to be invested by the National Debt Commissioners in government and local authority stock, public sector securities, debentures of companies currently paying dividends, the trustee savings banks and 'designated building societies', and the return to depositors was expected to be 5 per cent per annum. In February the Chancellor stated that he was withdrawing a request made in the summer of 1965 to trustee savings banks not to seek approval from the National Debt Commissioners for permission to pay interest rates above 5 per cent on deposits in special investment departments, and subsequently several increases were announced.

Throughout much of the year the discount houses experienced difficulty in obtaining adequate allotments of Treasury bills at the weekly tender, with supplies of bills relatively low, outside competition keen and the authorities unwilling to see the discount rate brought down. The discount houses continued to find themselves short of Treasury bills after the end of the financial year 1964–5; bids tended to rise throughout April and into May, even though borrowing from the Bank of England frequently became necessary, and the average rate of discount on Treasury bills had fallen to little above 6¼ per cent by the time bank rate was reduced to 6 per cent early in June.

From then until December the discount houses were continuing to attempt to increase their allotment, and the authorities to prevent a fall in the average discount rate by forcing the houses to borrow at bank rate from time to time.

On 15 October the syndicate obtained only 8 per cent of the tender, the lowest allotment since August 1939.

At the end of 1965, following the increase in official United States rates, the average rate of discount was just over $5\frac{1}{2}$ per cent against below $5\frac{3}{8}$ per cent at the beginning of December. The rate fell back slightly in January as the houses tried to obtain a reasonable allotment from the seasonally small amounts of bills offered at the tenders. On 28 January the amount of Treasury bills offered at the weekly tender fell to £150 million, the lowest figure for fourteen years. By the end of February the rate had risen to nearly $5\frac{5}{8}$ per cent, and it remained at around that level up to mid-April.

The discount houses kept their buying rate for prime bank bills high in relation to bank rate, and many of them tended to widen further the margins over the prime bank bill rate at which they would buy and sell best quality trade bills. It was announced in September that the Bank of England had reduced from 50 to 35 per cent the proportion of inland finance bills which, for the time being, it was prepared to accept in its sampling of prime bank bills from the market, and that only one half of this proportion could be hire purchase finance bills. It was also reported that some commercial banks had become more selective in the paper that they were prepared to buy.

The gilt-edged market was subject to a number of uncertainties, among them, early in the year, the effects of the proposed long-term capital gains tax. Late on 26 May 1965 it was announced that for gilt-edged stocks issued before budget day the capital gains taxes would not apply to price movements within the range between the lowest price at which a stock had been issued and the redemption price. Dealings were suspended for a time on 27 May while the implications for prices were being worked out, and when they were resumed later a substantial amount of switching occurred. For the same reason, exceptionally heavy dealings were recorded in 5 per cent Exchequer Stock 1967 in October, when the stock went ex dividend.

Yields throughout the year remained at well over 6 per cent and except for a few weeks early in 1966 on most shorter-dated stocks they were above those on longer-dated. The yield on $3\frac{1}{2}$ per cent Conversion Stock 1969 rose from 6·75 per cent at the beginning of April 1965 to 6·99 per cent in August; by October it had fallen back to 6·45 per cent; at mid-April it stood at 6·75 per cent. At the other end of the market, the yield on $2\frac{1}{2}$ per cent Consols rose steadily from 6·39 per cent in April to 6·71 per cent early in August, but by mid-September it had fallen to 6·11 per cent. An upward trend was then resumed, and at mid-April it stood at 6·69 per cent.

The rates charged on 'quota' borrowing from the Public Works Loan Board remained unchanged throughout the period under review, at between $5\frac{5}{8}$ per cent and $6\frac{1}{8}$ per cent depending upon the period of loan and the method of repayment. No change was made, either, in the tax-free rate of interest – $3\frac{1}{2}$ per cent – allowed on tax reserve certificates. On 26 May 1965 the Agricultural

Mortgage Corporation raised its rate of interest on new loans to 7¾ per cent. The Building Societies Association's recommended mortgage rate has remained at 6¾ per cent, and indications have apparently been given that an increase would not meet with official approval; a number of societies have been charging higher rates. In order to attract sufficient funds, the Association found it necessary to increase in July 1965 the recommended tax-paid rates of interest allowed on shares from 3¾ to 4 per cent, and on deposits from 3½ to 3¾ per cent.

For the financial year 1965–6 local authorities were able to draw 30 per cent of their capital requirements from the Public Works Loan Board, as compared with 20 per cent for the previous year, with the exception that, under the Public Works Loan Act, 1965, local authorities in 'less prosperous areas' were allowed to apply for up to 50 per cent of their long-term requirements. In August, as a consequence of the measures announced in July, the Board decided that local authorities would only be able to draw the balance of their borrowing quota for the year by phased instalments with the proviso that authorities that had already drawn more than one half of their year's quota by late July would not be allowed any further drawings before October. Nevertheless, consolidated fund loans to local authorities in the financial year, at £525 million, exceeded the budget estimate by £165 million.

Substantial sums were again raised by the issue of stocks and short-term bonds. Over the financial year local authorities raised £119 million in new money by stock issues and £80 million by short-term bond issues, and in addition bonds were thought to have been placed with the discount market. With greater resort to the PWLB and the new issue market, demands on the short-term money and mortgage markets generally eased.

A notable development in the field of local authority borrowing was the issue in September by the Manchester Corporation of £3 million of 90-day bills in anticipation of revenue. Under the Manchester Corporation Act 1965 the Corporation's power was extended to cover issues for revenue purposes: previously the Corporation was allowed to issue bills only to finance capital expenditure. The bills are readily negotiable and rediscountable at the Bank of England and they have, therefore, an advantage over other forms of temporary borrowing.

For most of the period the other sections of the Stock Exchange were affected by the same influences as the gilt-edged market. The *Financial Times*–Actuaries Index fell from 98·2 at the end of March 1965 to 92·5in early July; it then rose and by the end of November it stood at 106. Prices fluctuated thereafter and at the end of March 1966 the index stood at 104·8. The average 'yield' rose from 5⅓ per cent at the beginning of the year to 5¾ per cent in early July, but by 31 March 1966 it had fallen to just under 5¼ per cent. The 'reverse yield gap' – the margin by which this index is exceeded by the yield on 2½ per cent Consols – widened in the second half of 1965 and the first quarter of 1966, at the end of which it was over $1\frac{1}{4}$ per cent.

Despite the difficulties facing the market, according to statistics regularly compiled by the Midland Bank, the amount of new money raised by the issue of all securities rose from £508 million in 1964 to over £770 million in 1965, the largest amount ever recorded. Companies raised £503 million, an increase of £89·8 million over 1964, of which £454·6 million or over 90 per cent consisted of debt issues. Despite the rise in new issues the amount of new money raised for overseas was only £6·4 million, as compared with £43·4 million in 1964 and £58·4 million in 1963. In the first quarter of 1966 new money raised in the United Kingdom totalled over £305 million, as compared with £217 million in the corresponding period of 1965. Debt issues accounted for 47 per cent of the £212 million raised by companies.

11

Stagnation and Devaluation

1967 – Resolute Restrictive Measures

In July 1966 a 'squeeze' was applied harder by far than any in Britain's post-war period, and then during the year to April 1967 the recovery of sterling was more convincing than at any time since the loss of confidence that began in 1964. The cost was a moderate recession at home, with a check to growth and business development. The budget of April 1966, broadly neutral in its impact, followed earlier measures intended to relieve pressures in the internal economy and to improve the balance of payments. But abroad the remedies were not regarded as adequate and the seamen's strike with other adverse developments added to growing uncertainties. Then, too, in financial centres overseas a general tightening of monetary conditions was accompanied by high rates of interest. By early July 1966 sterling was again a storm centre in world currencies.

The British government acted resolutely. On 14 July 1966 bank rate was raised by one point to 7 per cent – the second time it had reached what was then regarded as a 'crisis' level in under two years – and additional Special Deposits were called for from the banks. A 'package' of further deflationary measures followed on 20 July, 'to deal not only with the short-run pressure on sterling but also with the underlying economic situation', as the government explained, 'to redeploy resources, both manpower and capacity, according to national priorities, and check inflation'. As an unusual part of the July 'package', the government called for a comprehensive standstill for six months in wages, salaries and other incomes and in prices, followed by a further six months of 'severe restraint'; at first the new 'freeze' was intended to be voluntary, but later some statutory powers of enforcement were taken and used to a limited extent.

Controls imposed on financial institutions by the July measures were wide ranging and also severe. Those affecting the banks are dealt with later. For the rest, hire purchase controls were further strengthened, both as regards minimum deposits and maximum repayment periods and most severely in respect of the purchase of vehicles. For these the minimum deposit was raised from 25 to 40 per cent, and the maximum repayment period reduced from twenty-seven to twenty-four months.

The effects of the July measures – superimposed as they were on earlier ones – were soon apparent. Unemployment rose, industrial production declined and many industrial units were soon operating well below capacity. Business confidence was undermined, but the government held firm to its severe restraints. By the last quarter of 1966 the overall balance of payments was showing a surplus. Indeed, the financial year closed with sterling strong, some external debts repaid and early repayments of others in prospect. The prices and incomes policy was seen to have made reasonable headway, and indices of domestic conditions remained steady. Thus as external conditions improved, this helped to make possible the reduction of bank rate to 6 per cent in two stages, on 26 January and 16 March. In addition, an increase in the rates of the new investment grants was introduced and some minor additions were made to the priority categories for bank lending. It was, then, in a situation that might be called high level stagnation in industrial conditions that the Chancellor introduced the budget of April 1967 which brought virtually no changes, his view being that he 'should not take any substantial action to influence demand just now'. He did, however, remove the direct quantitative restriction on bank advances and foreshadowed a considerable change in methods of monetary regulation, to which we refer later.

Economic growth came virtually to an end in 1966: the gross domestic product at constant prices was only about $1\frac{1}{4}$ per cent higher than in 1965 against increases of $2\frac{1}{2}$ per cent and nearly 6 per cent in 1965 and 1964 respectively. Total industrial output rose by a little under 1 per cent against 3 per cent in the previous year. In important aspects a decline was evident. The official index of industrial production fell by nearly 4 per cent between July and November 1966 and, although it rose slightly in December and January 1967, it was then running below the level of a year earlier.

In these conditions, unemployment rose sharply from the equivalent of a little over 1 per cent of the working population in July to 600,000, or over $2\frac{1}{2}$ per cent, in February 1967, the highest level for nearly four years. Gross fixed capital formation at constant prices was only 1 per cent greater than in 1965. Although the volume of investment in the public sector continued to rise substantially, it fell in the private sector, including manufacturing industry. The decline in the rate of stockbuilding, which became evident in 1965, continued in 1966 notwithstanding a marked increase for manufacturing industry, particularly vehicles, during the second half of the year.

The index of retail prices rose by about 4 per cent during 1966, or at a rate only slightly below that of 1965, even though the 'freeze' was in operation. This was in part because of the imposition of selective employment tax payments, which began in September 1966. However, from November 1966 onwards, when the index (16 January 1962=100) reached 118·1, the rise was relatively slow, with the figure for March 1967 being 118·6. Until the slight thawing of the 'freeze' in January virtually no increases had been recorded in basic weekly wage rates since July 1966. Indeed over the six months to October 1966, the average weekly earnings of male manual workers in manufacturing industry fell for the first time since they began to be recorded in 1959.

Overseas deficit reduced

The overall deficit on balance of payments account, including both current and long-term capital transactions, was provisionally estimated as £189 million in 1966, against £348 million in 1965 and £761 million in 1964. On visible trade account the deficit was reduced considerably to £138 million, but net earnings from 'invisibles' also fell substantially, by £83 million to £77 million, this being the lowest figure since 1947. As a result the adverse balance on current account, at £61 million, was only £48 million lower than in 1965, though it was £332 million better than in 1964. The reduction in the net outflow of long-term capital continued.

Much of the improvement in 1966 was recorded in the final quarter, when an overall surplus of £121 million was achieved. In the first quarter a substantial deficit was attributable to visible trade and a large net outflow on account of long-term capital, both official and private. This capital outflow was halted in the second quarter and was small in the third but the visible trade deficit did not improve. In spite of the removal of the import surcharge at the end of November, imports in the fourth quarter fell by about 6 per cent and exports increased by over 15 per cent, as compared with the third quarter, giving rise to a favourable visible trade balance of £151 million. A net inflow of private investment – the first since the last quarter of 1965 – partially offset a heavy net outflow of capital on official account, attributable partly to the servicing, for the first time since 1963, of the North American loans.

One disappointment was a sharp decline in net invisible earnings. This is the traditional mainstay of Britain's current balance of payments, but it had fallen almost continuously since 1962. It fell to £77 million in 1966 of which only £8 million was earned in the second half of the year. Net private invisible earnings fell slightly to £549 million, but government expenditure abroad rose to £472 million, mostly for military purposes.

As to investment flows, private investment overseas – direct and portfolio – from the United Kingdom amounted to £315 million in 1966, against £356 million in 1965, with direct investment continuing at about the same level. Foreign private investment coming into the United Kingdom rose sharply by £65 million to £266 million, partly as a result of takeover activities of United States firms. In the outcome the excess of United Kingdom private overseas investment was reduced considerably to only £49 million. The sustained gross outflow of direct private investment occurred despite the introduction of corporation tax, which was expected to militate against it, and also despite the introduction last May of a 'voluntary programme' of restraint on such investment in the developed economies of the sterling area – Australia, New Zealand, South Africa and the Republic of Ireland. Companies were asked to postpone for the time being any investment of more than £25,000 a year, and to make every effort to finance projects from local sources rather than in the United Kingdom.

Despite the disruption caused by the seamen's strike, which lasted for six weeks from mid-May, the high rate of increase in exports which became evident in 1965 was generally continued throughout 1966. The value of exports rose by 6½ per cent in 1966, as compared with 7 per cent in the previous year and 5 per cent in 1964. About one half of the increase was accounted for by higher export prices, the volume of exports rising by about 3¼ per cent against an increase of over 5 per cent in 1965.

Imports continued to rise at a moderate pace. The total value of imports grew by 3½ per cent against the exceptionally low increase of 1 per cent recorded in 1965; increased prices accounted for about 1 per cent of the rise. The effects were evident of the seamen's strike and of the early announcement that the government would remove the import surcharge, then at a rate of 10 per cent, at the end of November 1966. Abnormally low figures were recorded for imports in October and November, and although a substantial rise was recorded in December, the total was only at about the same level as the average for the first nine months of the year; imports reached a record level in January 1967 but fell sharply during February and March. It was perhaps significant that imports of goods not subject to the surcharge were showing signs of declining towards the end of 1966.

The rise in imports of manufactured goods, which slowed down appreciably in 1965, began to accelerate again in 1966. Indeed, the increases in imports, apart from fuel, were largely confined to finished and semi-finished manufactures. Only a small increase was recorded in the value of food, drink and tobaçco, and fuels, while basic materials were lower, largely as a result of a marked decline in the last quarter of the year.

Figures for trade with the overseas sterling area were disappointing. Exports to other member countries fell in total – by about 3 per cent as compared with a rise of 7 per cent in 1965 – whilst UK imports from the sterling area also fell fractionally. However, exports to most other trading areas rose substantially; increases of one quarter or more were recorded for the United States, Japan and the east European countries. Exports to western Europe rose by 9 per cent, against 4 per cent in 1965; the total to EFTA countries increased by over 11 per cent and that to EEC countries by 6 per cent. The final tariff reduction on intra-EFTA trade in industrial goods became effective on 1 January 1967.

From May 1966 sterling was adversely affected by recurring bouts of speculative selling in the foreign exchange markets. Reference has been made to the rise in bank rate and the July measures as the principal steps taken at home to deal with the situation. Further government action was designed more directly to ease the balance of payments position. The basic travel allowance for holidays outside the sterling area was reduced to £50 a year from 1 November 1966; a tightening of controls was made over capital transfers by emigrants to countries outside the sterling area; and the limit on cash gifts to residents of those countries was reduced. In addition the government announced that it intended to reduce its own expenditure overseas by £100 million a year by the end of 1967–8. Early in August 1966 the authorities limited the extent to which United Kingdom banks were able to hold short-term funds abroad, by reducing the size of the positions which they were allowed to carry in foreign exchange. Reductions were made both in open positions, which are the uncovered positions that may be carried in foreign currency, and in the amounts of spot exchange which may be held (and temporarily invested abroad) in cover for forward commitments.

Although these various measures were well received in other countries, they were not enough and the operation of saving sterling had to be assisted by aid from monetary authorities abroad, including the central bank facilities made available in September 1965. During March 1966 a special swap transaction, amounting to the equivalent of £54 million, had been entered into with the United States, but the effect of this on the reserves was offset by the reversal of other central bank transactions of earlier months. In June 1966 it was announced that the swap facilities arranged with ten central banks and the Bank for International Settlements in September 1965 were being continued in a different form, which in effect meant that they were available to meet the outcome of lack of confidence in sterling, but not to finance Britain's balance of payments deficit. At the same time a credit facility was concluded independently with the Bank of France, which had not participated in the central banks' arrangements, and the reciprocal swap facilities with the United States were continued.

Further strengthening came in September 1966 when these swap facilities were raised from $750 million to $1350 million and facilities with other central banks were increased by undisclosed amounts; these were a part of more general international arrangements intended to create a broader margin of safety for the stability of the world monetary system. In the words of the *Bank of England Bulletin*, the use of swap facilities 'fluctuated quite widely' during the third quarter of 1966.

In the first four months of 1966 the reserves had increased by £184 million, but this was after bringing in £316 million from the liquidation of the Treasury's dollar portfolio as well as repaying outstanding debts. Thereafter the reserves continued to fall until September, when a small rise occurred, associated with an improved outlook for sterling and the international support arrangements. In October a start was made on repaying the short-term debts to overseas central banks and by the end of March 1967 these had been wholly repaid. A payment was made of £69 million in December 1966 in respect of principal and interest on the North American loans. Nevertheless, the reserves increased by £35 million to £1164 million in the six months to March 1967. It was then announced that the central bank facilities in support of sterling, arranged in the previous June, had been renewed, and it was disclosed that these arrangements, excluding those with the United States and France, amounted to the equivalent of $1000 million.

In his budget speech in April 1967 the Chancellor referred to the 'great improvement in the balance of payments, in international confidence and in our debt position'. He announced that the drawing made from the IMF in the winter of 1964 would be repaid by 2 December 1967, with some payments probably being made before that date; the original amount of £357 million had been reduced to an outstanding figure of £292 million by sterling drawings of other countries. The £28 million borrowed from Switzerland would likewise be repaid by 2 December.

He stated also that it had been decided 'to unify the security sterling and official exchange markets'. The unification came into effect on 12 April 1967; it meant that non-residents buying sterling securities from residents could no longer pay in security sterling but would have to settle in foreign currency or in sterling bought at the rate in the official market. Conversely, non-residents (except residents of Rhodesia) selling sterling securities would receive ordinary external sterling, freely convertible at the official rate. The change did not affect residents of the United Kingdom, but at the same time as announcing the abolition of security sterling the Chancellor stated that he had given instructions for 'a fresh drive against illegal transactions' by United Kingdom residents through the free currency markets in the Persian Gulf and Hong Kong; as a result of this and the unification of the two markets some of the foreign currency which had hitherto been exchanged for security sterling in some free markets abroad was expected to accrue to the reserves. A technical change made at the same time was to extend the list of 'specified currencies' – those which UK residents must on acquisition offer for sale to an authorized dealer – to cover all foreign currencies; all the major currencies were already specified, and to maintain a distinction was 'no longer worthwhile'.

The spot rate for sterling against the US dollar improved early in April 1967 to slightly above the parity of $2·80, the highest level since March 1966.

In the intervening year, the rate has been subject to severe pressures; and despite considerable official support it fell in mid-July and again in early September to about \$2·78$\frac{3}{4}$. A weakness of sterling in the market which had become evident towards the end of February 1966 had continued in the next few months. Net sterling liabilities to non-£ area countries declined markedly during the first half of 1966, although they more than recovered in the third quarter. With the further fall early in July of the spot rate, the forward rate margins began to widen, after having remained fairly close for nearly a year. Following the July measures the spot rate rose above \$2·79 and later forward margins narrowed again.

Throughout the world's monetary centres, interest rates were high during 1966, and continued to rise until the autumn. Thereafter they began to fall, with gathering speed. Although interest rates were high in Britain also, when the cost of forward foreign exchange cover was allowed for they were not always in favour of sterling. A key relationship consists of that between the rates for Eurodollar deposits and those for deposits with United Kingdom local authorities, taking into account forward cover, and this was in favour of dollars throughout 1966, to some extent encouraging an outflow of funds from Britain.

With the falling trend of short-term interest rates – Eurodollar rates reached their peak in November – and the recovery of confidence in sterling, this margin has been reduced, and from the beginning of 1967 it was virtually eliminated. It was this downward trend in rates in other countries which made possible the reductions of the United Kingdom bank rate. The trend was hastened by a meeting arranged in January 1967 by the Chancellor of the Exchequer with the finance ministers of several other countries, including the United States and West Germany, at which it was agreed to collaborate in reducing short-term rates. The first reduction in bank rate followed a few days later. Indeed, to May 1967, central bank discount rates had been reduced in at least seven countries, including the United States, West Germany (three times), Canada, Belgium, the Netherlands and Sweden.

Reductions in lending

A major channel of regulation throughout the past critical year has been the banking system. Higher interest rates increased profit margins but in general banking activities were still more closely restricted. The rise in bank rate in July 1966 was accompanied by a further call for Special Deposits, of 1 per cent of deposits from the clearing banks and $\frac{1}{2}$ per cent from the Scottish, bringing the percentages required to be transferred in this way to the Bank of England to 2 for the clearing and 1 for the Scottish by make-up day in August.

Already, the term of application of the official ceiling on advances to the private sector of 105 per cent, seasonally adjusted, of the level at March 1965, had been extended from the original date of March 1966 to March 1967, and thereafter until further notice. In August 1966 the Bank of England requested the banks to examine the levels of overdraft limits of borrowers in non-priority categories with a view to bringing about early and substantial reductions. As it turned out, this marked the peak of monetary restraints in the period since the end of 1964.

When the July measures were applied, net advances of the clearing banks, unadjusted for seasonal factors, were in fact nearly 6 per cent above the level of March 1965 and, with the expectation of pressures on company liquidity from selective employment tax as well as revised arrangements for the payment of income tax, it appeared that the banks might be confronted with still further demands for advances. Indeed, when SET had been announced in the May 1966 budget, the possibility had been officially envisaged of relaxation of the limit on bank lending to meet transfers by those employers entitled to rebates or premium payments of SET. Later it was announced that no such relaxation would be made.

Nor was it required. The July restrictions had so shaken business confidence that the demand for advances actually fell away, with the result that towards the end of 1966 bank lending was well below the official ceiling and the clearing banks were again making investments. On 1 November the Bank of England publicly reminded borrowers in the priority categories that the banks could be expected to have sufficient funds available in the following months to meet all requests from them, subject to ordinary banking criteria. At various times small extensions were made to priority categories: agriculture, temporary bridging finance for house purchase, and later housebuilding itself.

In his April 1967 budget statement the Chancellor announced that he was moving on to a somewhat different form of monetary regulation. He said that it was 'still necessary to keep the growth of credit within modest bounds', so that he saw 'no reason to vary the present guidance on the direction of lending', but he wished to 'move as rapidly as possible to a less rigid form of overall control'. Accordingly he removed the 105 per cent limit from the clearing and Scottish banks, but clearly intended that credit should remain restricted, as much when provided by the banking system as by other sources. He stated that 'the Special Deposits system will be used in future in a new and more flexible manner, so that a call for Special Deposits should no longer be regarded as a crisis measure but as a routine adjustment to conditions as they develop. The object will be to maintain a continuous control over bank lending'. In this way the clearing banks were relieved, for the time being at any rate, from the observance of the most distasteful – and most constricting – among the numerous ratios that had come to be applied to their activities by the authorities.

It should be noted that regulation by way of liquidity alone is more flexible and acceptable, though it has still to be seen whether it is as effective as direct controls. Even now these ratios – for cash, liquid assets and Special Deposits – remain to be satisfied in ways peculiar to each of them. It has to be recognized, too, that Special Deposits have no term for repayment as, for example, had the Treasury deposit receipts of the war and early post-war years, and ordinarily there is no provision for encashment. Hence what is in effect to operate as a variable liquidity ratio will have at times a top slice of a frozen asset. In considering the effectiveness of the system, it will be recalled that, after introduction in 1958, Special Deposits had to be buttressed first by the return of 'directives' and eventually by quantitative limitation of advances by way of the 'ceiling'. At this second attempt, as previously, the adequacy of the system would depend no doubt upon the way it was operated and tested by the nature of the credit situation that it had to regulate.

If it were possible to operate a system for the banks that was close to a variable liquidity ratio, this could not be so with those lending institutions not required to maintain ratios similar to those of the clearing banks. Thus for other banking institutions the 105 per cent limit was maintained pending the working out of 'suitable new arrangements to secure from them an appropriate degree of restraint in their lending'; for finance houses it might be required for 'a longer period' while the 'special problems' of controlling them were examined.

The effects of the government's measures were evident in the banking figures. Advances of the clearing banks fell over the financial year 1966-7 by £187 million, or by 3·9 per cent, this being the first annual period in which a fall had occurred since 1957–8. By the autumn of 1966 the demand for advances was diminishing and clearly it had not begun to recover when the budget was opened. Net deposits increased by only £47 million or 0·5 per cent in 1966–7, which was barely one tenth of the rise in each of the two preceding years. Indeed, during the fourth quarter of 1966 deposits actually fell slightly, whereas the seasonal expectation was for a substantial rise at that time. This contributed to the slower rate of growth in the money supply during the year to which attention was drawn in the official *Economic Report* on 1966: 'The rise in total money supply, taking deposits and currency in circulation with the public together, was just over 4 per cent, not much more than half the rate of increase in 1965.' With the volume of deposits steady and advances falling, the banks generally maintained their liquidity ratios comfortably above the minimum despite the call for additional Special Deposits in the summer of 1966; the average for the clearing banks for the calendar year 1966 was 31·0 per cent. The ratio of advances to deposits was somewhat lower, at 52·5 per cent for 1966, compared with 53·8 in 1965. In March 1967 it had fallen to 51·7, compared with 54·0 per cent a year earlier and 55·6 in March 1964.

Some idea of changes in demand for advances may be obtained from the quarterly classification, though the series was revised in February 1967. The new classification, published by the Bank of England, was based on the Standard Industrial Classification, and included advances made by all banks operating in Great Britain. Appendix 2, Table 8a shows the figures for the old classification and Table 8a the new classification for February 1967 onwards.

With the reduced demand for advances, the banks increased their investments, the total for the clearing banks rising by £172 million over the year to mid-March to reach £1283 million. The ratio to gross deposits was 13·7 per cent at mid-March 1967, compared with 12·0 in March 1966, thus reversing the steady fall in the past few years. Over the year as a whole, the clearing banks' holdings of Treasury bills fell by £253 million, and in both February and March 1967 the totals were below those for commercial bills (including refinanceable export credits).

For two years, holdings of commercial bills by the banks had been subject, like advances, to a ceiling. Part of the growth in other than Treasury bills was accounted for by purchases of local authority bills, a new development which is discussed later in this chapter.

The restraints operating during 1966 had little effect on the activity on bank accounts. The total value of cheques passing through the Bankers' Clearing House was 10·7 per cent higher than in the previous year, calculated on a working-day basis, compared with a rise of 15·2 per cent in 1965. The general debit clearing rose by 9·2 per cent and credit clearing by 9·1 per cent; the credit clearing now represents about 14·0 per cent of the general clearing.

The Midland Bank Index of Business Turnover, derived from figures of total drawings on current accounts with the Midland Bank, showed that the rate of growth in business activity for England and Wales as a whole declined again in 1966; an increase of 5 per cent was recorded, compared with one of 7 per cent between 1964 and 1965, and 14 per cent between 1963 and 1964. On a seasonally corrected basis the index continued to rise until the second quarter, but fell in the third and again slightly in the fourth. However, the upward movement was resumed in the first quarter of 1967.

As from 1 April 1967, credit transfers between holders of bank accounts could be made free of charge, and improvements were made in the collection account arrangements. A system of direct debiting suitable for use by large organizations receiving frequent payments, whether of fixed or varying amounts, from individuals with bank accounts, was also introduced, on a limited experimental basis at first. Where customers agree to direct debiting, the banks could make transfers from their accounts to those of their creditors on the initiative of the creditors.

In June 1966 the charges levied by the banks in Great Britain were referred to the National Board for Prices and Incomes for consideration in the light of the profits and dividend policies of the banks; the reference was later extended to include banks in Northern Ireland. The Board was excluded from examining aspects of monetary policy, such as changes in bank rate.

Another development of official policy was contained in the Companies Bill. This proposed to give powers to the Board of Trade to make orders reducing or abolishing the exemptions from disclosure of some information in their accounts, which banks and discount houses then enjoyed; such orders might apply to all banking and discount companies or to 'any class' of them, a class being defined by reference to 'any circumstances whatsoever'.

Progress towards a completely mechanized money transmission service by the banks quickened with the placing of large orders for computers and ancillary equipment. Cheque cards and credit card arrangements also continued to develop. Individual banks introduced new facilities, such as unit trusts and payroll services, and some extended their deposit-taking subsidiaries and also their overseas connections.

During the early months of 1967 three undertakings – unconnected with the major banks – which advertised for deposits from the public at comparatively high rates of interest suspended withdrawals; two of them went into liquidation. These developments led to widespread criticism of the adequacy of the Protection of Depositors Act.

The problems of the discount houses arising from the developing shortage of Treasury bills in the market in recent years are examined in Chapter 6. Developments in other short-term markets which grew rapidly and in which the discount houses had begun to participate to a limited extent, are also discussed in that and the following chapter. Both of these trends continued during the year under review. At the same time several innovations were made both by the authorities in their methods of control and by the houses themselves branching out into new activities to offset the difficulties they experienced in the primary money market.

The authorities meanwhile modified their arrangements for influencing the discount market. At the end of June 1966 the Bank of England began to lend money to the market at bank rate overnight. Previously, lending had been for a minimum of seven days and the new technique provided more flexibility in the means of giving help to the market. A further technique was developed in September by the introduction of overnight lending at rates currently ruling in the market, and this type of lending quickly became a commonly used means of giving assistance to the discount houses, either in conjunction with or in place of the previous 'open back door' method of buying bills at the ruling market rate. With developing flexibility in the use of such techniques, various combinations of them, suitable to the circumstances of the day, were used simultaneously.

From May 1966 the Treasury bill tender rate showed a slight upward trend; after the rise in bank rate to 7 per cent in July it reached an all-time record level of just over $6\frac{3}{4}$ per cent during September. During October the rate fell back almost to $6\frac{1}{2}$ per cent in the expectation of a cut in bank rate before the end of the year, but the authorities forced the market into the Bank on numerous occasions, and the discount rate rose almost to $6\frac{3}{4}$ per cent again by the end of November. Thereafter, with rates abroad beginning to ease, the discount rate showed a steady decline, and with bank rate twice reduced it stood well below $5\frac{1}{2}$ per cent at the end of April 1967.

Competition for the small weekly offering of Treasury bills reinforced other downward pressures on the discount rate during the second half of the year under review. For most of October and November 1966, only £150 million of bills were being offered each week, with maturities often considerably in excess of this amount. With the authorities acting to prevent a significant fall in the average rate of discount, the discount houses were unable to raise their agreed bid and were often left with only a small allotment of bills. In the early months of 1967 even smaller amounts were offered, as low as £120 million a week, and at 31 March only £1750 million of tender bills were outstanding, compared with £2180 million at 31 March 1966 and £2290 million at the corresponding date in 1965.

Faced with such a shortage of one of their major assets, the discount houses increased their holdings of 'commercial and other bills', which included those issued by the government of Northern Ireland and some local authorities, and also of local bonds. In addition, several of the houses began to expand their activities into the rapidly developing secondary markets. Some took interests in firms of brokers dealing in the inter-bank or foreign exchange (including Eurodollar) markets; and some obtained Bank of England approval to participate in the market in London dollar certificates of deposit, either as brokers or as principals.

In his budget statement in April 1966, the Chancellor estimated that local authorities would borrow £398 million from the Exchequer in the financial year to March 1967, compared with £525 million in 1965–6. In the event, the budget estimate was exceeded by £120 million, an outcome similar to that of 1965–6. The proportion of their borrowing which local authorities may obtain from the Public Works Loan Board, which it had been intended to raise from 30 to 40 per cent for 1966–7, was kept at 30 per cent; the Board also continued to act as lender of last resort, at higher rates, to those authorities which could not raise the balance of their requirements on the market. For 1967–8 the basis of calculating access to the Board was to be 'actual capital payments during the year less capital receipts and central government grants and loans', and they became entitled to borrow up to 34 per cent of their requirements on this basis. The attempt to restrict temporary borrowing to 20 per cent of outstanding borrowing also continued, and authorities with proportions in excess of this were to be able to borrow from the Board 30 per cent of any funding carried out to bring them nearer this target proportion.

Local authorities continued to make use of the capital market during the year by means of loan stock and short-term bond issues. New issues by local authorities totalled £201 million net in 1966, of which £71 million net was raised by means of short-term bonds, usually of one or two years' maturity. This figure, however, takes no account of the large number of issues made in 1966 to replace maturing ones; the outstanding total of all quoted local bonds was in the region of £160 million in April 1967. In addition, some issues had been placed with the discount market without a quotation.

In the previous chapter we noted the issue by Manchester Corporation of ninety-day bills, issued in anticipation of revenue. Such bills have an advantage over other types of temporary borrowing in that they are readily negotiable and rediscountable at the Bank of England, but few local authorities are empowered to issue them. However, the Greater London Council issued £25 million of bills by tender in November 1966, at a rate of discount only slightly higher than that of Treasury bills. When the issue matured, a further £25 million of bills was issued to replace it.

Prices of government securities were falling during the early months of the year under review, generally reaching their lowest point in August 1966, following the rise in bank rate; at this time most of them were yielding well over 7 per cent. Subsequently prices rose more or less continuously, despite exceptionally heavy funding sales by the government and also some substantial local authority issues. By mid-April 1967, yields ranged from a little over 6 per cent at the short end (even less for those close to maturity) to approaching 6½ per cent on long-dated and undated issues.

Following the budget of May 1966, equity prices climbed steadily until mid-June, but discouraging company news and the impositions of the July measures caused a fall until November. Thereafter, however, they recovered steadily. The yield on industrial ordinary shares, as measured by the *Financial Times*–Actuaries 500 index, rose from around 5 per cent in June 1966 to over 6¼ per cent early in November, but by the end of April 1967 had fallen back to about 5¼ per cent. The 'reverse yield gap' narrowed or temporarily disappeared in November 1966, according to which indicators one uses; thereafter, despite the rising gilt-edged market, it tended to open again as equities also began to rise.

Despite the fluctuations of the market, the amount of new money raised in the United Kingdom in 1966, according to statistics compiled by the Midland Bank, rose from £770·5 million to £856·5 million. Of this total, company issues raised £638 million, compared with £503 million in 1965. Within the company total, issues of equity capital rose from £45·5 million to £142·5 million, mainly as a result of the rights issue of £60 million by British Petroleum early in the year. However, during the early months of 1967 the sums raised by companies were substantially lower.

The revenue surplus for 1966–7 was £738 million, and loans from the Consolidated Fund totalled £1478 million, giving a borrowing requirement of £740 million, or £453 million higher than estimated; it was only heavy sales of government securities that enabled the contraction in the tender Treasury bill issue to continue.

In his April 1967 budget, the Chancellor did not seek to influence demand and made no major tax changes; among the minor changes were the consolidation of the 10 per cent increase in duties imposed by the use of the regulator in the previous July, and the removal of the 10 per cent surcharge on surtax imposed at the same time. He foresaw a decline in the revenue surplus from £738 million to £637 million, and net Consolidated Fund loans were expected to rise from £1478 million to £1580 million. He stressed that about half this expenditure was on 'economic services', and that private capital investment was expected to fall, so that the increased net borrowing requirement – £943 million against £740 million – would not generate excessive demand. However, it was necessary to ensure that it did not 'lead to an unduly large increase in monetary liquidity', by 'raising as much as possible . . . outside the banking system'. Accordingly he made some improvements in the terms of company tax reserve certificates, and increased the limits on holdings of national savings certificates and premium bonds. He also questioned whether it was 'necessarily the best arrangement that so much of the borrowing requirement of local authorities and public corporations is financed in the first instance by the Exchequer', and stated that he had put in hand a review of these arrangements.

Over the financial year, the total national debt outstanding increased by £624 million to £31,964 million, but within the total a good deal of funding took place, the total floating debt falling by £1267 million. The nominal value of marketable securities rose by £1912 million, the result of four issues of government stock which took advantage of the better tone in the gilt-edged market from September. Existing tap stocks having run out, issues were made in October of £700 million of $6\frac{3}{4}$ per cent Exchequer Stock 1971 and £400 million of $6\frac{3}{4}$ per cent Treasury Loan 1990–5. In February 1967, this new long tap was exhausted and the short considerably run down; further issues were made of £400 million of $6\frac{1}{4}$ per cent Exchequer Loan 1972 and £500 million of $6\frac{1}{2}$ per cent Funding Loan 1985–7.

The authorities made net sales of £229 million of stock in the calendar year 1966, despite having to absorb considerable amounts of stock in the early part. The banking sector absorbed £119 million of the total, and the domestic non-banking sector a further £113 million. However, in the last quarter of 1966, with gilt-edged prices rising, net sales amounted to no less than £410 million, and further heavy sales took place in the early months of 1967, exacerbating the shortage of Treasury bills in the market.

The financial year ending in March 1967 was a disappointing one for the national savings movement, particularly as it was celebrating its fiftieth anniversary and had been hoping for a substantial inflow of funds. The new national savings certificate which went on sale early in 1966 proved popular, and net receipts totalled £60 million, compared with net withdrawals of £157 million in the previous year. A new issue of national development bonds was also made, carrying a rate of interest of $5\frac{1}{2}$ per cent, but these were less generally welcomed than the new savings certificate; net repayments, taken together with defence bonds, were £15 million, compared with a net inflow of £7 million in the previous financial year.

A new type of account, the investment account, invested in a way similar to special investment accounts of trustee savings banks, was opened by the Post Office Savings Bank in June 1966. The new account offered a rate of $5\frac{1}{2}$ per cent to depositors already holding a balance of at least £50 in an ordinary account. During the year, net receipts on investment accounts totalled £73 million, but net withdrawals from ordinary accounts amounted to £153 million, compared with £38 million in 1965–6.

For trustee savings banks, deposits in special investment departments, following the removal of the maximum rate of interest of 5 per cent, rose by £62 million, compared with £53 million in the previous year, but deposits in the ordinary departments fell by £41 million, compared with an increase of £14 million in 1965–6. In his 1967 budget speech the Chancellor announced that the trustee savings bank movement was being given permission to set up a unit trust, 'entirely on its own responsibility'.

1968 – The Worst Post-War Year: Crisis and Devaluation

Few would deny that the year to April 1968 was the most eventful in monetary affairs in the preceding post-war period. It included the devaluation of sterling, the subsequent measures – among them an 8 per cent bank rate and the most severe budget since the war – to curb demand on domestic resources, and a crisis in the international payments system. It ended on a more assured note, with reasonable prospects of a substantial turn-round in the balance of payments, which would provide a basis for steadier and faster growth in the domestic economy, and with hopes of more settled conditions in international monetary matters.

The course of affairs in the United Kingdom continued to be dominated by the external situation. In the early months of 1967 the balance of payments position seemed to be improving, and although the budget was broadly 'neutral' in its impact, some selective measures of reflation were thought to be appropriate at a time when unemployment was, by post-war standards, at a particularly high level. Restrictions on bank credit were eased in April; bank rate was reduced from 6 to $5\frac{1}{2}$ per cent in May; hire purchase restrictions were eased in June and August; payments of investment grants were further accelerated; and to assist the development areas a regional employment premium was introduced.

But the improvement in the balance of payments was not maintained, and it deteriorated swiftly in the second half of 1967. Several special factors – including the Middle East war, the effects of the removal of the import surcharge, and dock strikes – contributed to the poor external results, although the fundamental nature of the external imbalance was implicit in the acceptance by the International Monetary Fund of the need to devalue. With the devaluation in November 1967, the trend of official policy was sharply reversed, so as to ensure that the opportunity thus presented of increasing exports and for import-saving was not lost. The change in parity was accompanied by a 'package' of measures to curb home demand on resources.

The main developments preceding the devaluation, the devaluation itself and the associated measures are recorded in Chapter 2. With the approval of the International Monetary Fund the par value of the pound in terms of gold was lowered on 18 November from 2·48828 to 2·13281 grammes, equivalent to a reduction in the exchange rate against the US dollar from 2·80 to 2·40, a devaluation of one seventh, and the new spot dealing limits were set at 2·38 to 2·42.

The contents of the devaluation 'package' followed a familiar pattern. In the weeks before 18 November bank rate had already been raised, in two stages, to 6½ per cent but it was now increased to 8 per cent, the highest level, except for a few days in August 1914, since the crisis in the United States in 1873 and a full 1 per cent higher than at any time in the post-war period; a rigid ceiling was placed on bank advances, with similar restrictions on the activities of other financial institutions; and hire purchase terms on cars were tightened. It was announced, too, that government expenditure would be reviewed, and that payments of export rebates, and selective employment tax premiums (except to manufacturers in the development areas), would be abolished from 1 April 1968. The rate for Corporation Tax for the year 1967–8 was to be raised from 40 to 42½ per cent and this was confirmed four months later in the budget proposals.

Some cuts in planned defence expenditure were announced in November and in the same month a Letter of Intent was sent to the International Monetary Fund in connection with the application for a standby credit (see Appendix 4(a). In this the overriding aim was seen to be an improvement in the balance of payments of 'at least £500 million a year'. In January 1968 wide-ranging reductions in planned government expenditure were announced but these were still insufficient to prevent a substantial increase in the total in 1968–9 and a further rise in 1969–70. The budget itself was brought forward to 19 March. The Chancellor of the Exchequer insisted that 'we must have a stiff budget followed by two years of hard slog', and his proposals, which included the introduction of a firm prices and incomes policy were 'severe'.

In 1967, as in 1966, economic growth was minimal. The gross national product, at £33,924 million, was about 4 per cent higher than a year before but almost all the increase was due to higher prices. Indeed, the index of industrial production was slightly lower, on average, than in 1966, and that for manufacturing industries alone showed a fall of about 1 per cent, notwithstanding some recovery in November and December. The slackening in demand for labour which began in mid-1966 persisted well into 1967, and the number of wholly unemployed in Great Britain, after adjustment for seasonal factors and excluding school leavers, rose from 1·9 per cent of the working population in December 1966 to 2·4 per cent in September 1967. Subsequently the underlying trend was slightly downwards; but at the end of the year under review the level of unemployment remained a little above that of a year before, but so too did the number of unfilled vacancies.

The volume of gross fixed capital formation rose by nearly 5 per cent in 1967 after increasing only fractionally in 1966. The recovery was entirely in the public sector, with marked rises in investment by local authorities – particularly on housing – and public corporations. The fall in investment by manufacturing industry of $6\frac{3}{4}$ per cent, however, was smaller than had been forecast. Only a moderate increase in stocks was recorded in the first half of 1967, and a decline in the second if allowance is made for delays in clearing exports.

On balance over the first nine months of 1967 the index of retail prices rose by less than $\frac{1}{2}$ per cent, but thereafter the upward trend became more pronounced, and the increase for the whole year was about $2\frac{1}{2}$ per cent as compared with 4 per cent in 1966. Following devaluation wholesale prices of basic materials and fuels used in manufacturing industries rose sharply, after having shown little change for nearly two years. Some pressure on wage rates became evident in the second half of 1967 following the ending of the period of severe restraint in June.

External difficulties

The United Kingdom's balance of payments deficit on current and long-term capital account in 1967 was the second largest ever recorded, only exceeded by that of 1964, and marked a drastic reversal of the clear, if irregular, improvement in the two intervening years. The deficit was provisionally estimated at £540 million, against £133 million in 1966 and £342 million in 1965. This outcome was all the more disappointing because of the hopes raised in the last quarter of 1966 and the first quarter of 1967, which saw overall surpluses of £146 million and £3 million respectively, But thereafter the position progressively worsened, with the fourth quarter's deficit, of

£356 million, accounting for about two thirds of the total for the year. The deterioration was on visible trade account, showing a deficit for the year of £650 million, of which nearly one half occurred in the fourth quarter against £147 million in 1966. The adverse balance on government transactions was £449 million, or £12 million less than for the previous year, and the net inflow on account of 'other invisibles' was slightly greater at £585 million, though still somewhat below the 1965 figure. The net outflow of long-term capital again fell markedly, in continuing response to government measures taken earlier.

Although exports were at a high level in the early months of 1967, the upward trend was losing momentum and imports were rising. In the second quarter exports declined, mainly as a result of weakness of demand in some export markets but also reflecting a continued contraction in Britain's share of world markets. Thereafter the external trade figures deteriorated sharply as a result of the Middle East crisis, which involved the closure of the Suez Canal from June 1967 onwards, and dock strikes beginning in September which had a more marked impact on exports than on imports. It has been officially suggested that one half or more of balance of payments deficit may have been attributable to the Middle East crisis, dock strikes, and the effects of the removal of the import surcharge in November 1966 on the timing of import arrivals. The rise in some import prices following devaluation contributed to the deficit in the fourth quarter.

The value of exports fell in 1967 by about $\frac{1}{2}$ per cent – the first annual decline since 1958 – as compared with increases averaging nearly 7 per cent over the four previous years; by volume they fell by $1\frac{1}{2}$ per cent. Imports, both in value and in volume, rose last year by 8 per cent, the increase by value being roughly double the average annual rate of growth over the past decade. Net invisible earnings, which previously had been tending to fall, rose from £116 million in 1966 to £136 million in 1967, with lower government outlays abroad and higher net earnings on private account.

Private overseas investment in the United Kingdom in 1967 exceeded the comparable outflow for the first year since 1962. The net inflow was only £28 million, but this contrasted with an outflow of £20 million in 1966 and much larger ones in 1965 and 1964, of £148 million and £258 million respectively. Gross direct investment abroad in 1967, excluding oil, fell by about £40 million to £244 million, but with the inclusion of 'oil and miscellaneous' and portfolio transactions total private investment abroad was £71 million higher at £363 million. Private investment in the United Kingdom from abroad amounted to £391 million, a record level and an increase of £119 million over 1966. Although direct investment, excluding oil, fell slightly, from £196 million to £185 million, a marked rise was recorded for 'oil and miscellaneous', and net disinvestment in corporate securities, which had been substantial in 1966, fell sharply.

The government announced in January 1968 that the restrictions on direct investment overseas were being eased so as to allow access to official exchange of up to £50,000 or 50 per cent of the total investment for projects outside the sterling area directly concerned with promoting exports of goods or services; the concession applied only where the prospective benefits to the balance of payments equalled or exceeded the total cost of the investment within eighteen months and continued thereafter.

Early in 1967 sterling appeared to have weathered the storm that had blown up during the summer of 1966. By the end of March 1967 Britain's short-term debts to overseas central banks had been repaid and in his budget speech in April the Chancellor had been able to refer to a 'great improvement in the balance of payments, in international confidence and in our debt position'. But this view was short-lived, and by the late summer pressures on sterling were again assuming crisis proportions.

Possibly the main cause of the change of sentiment was the realization that the United Kindom's balance of payments position was not continuing to improve. Then, too, attention was being directed to the possible effects on sterling if membership of the European Economic Community were to be agreed. Moreover, from April 1967 onwards, the tendency for world interest rates to fall was halted and to some extent reversed. In particular, marked rises were recorded in short-term interest rates in the United States and in the Eurodollar market. Events in the Middle East, and the dock strikes, all helped to bring the crisis to a head.

The battle for sterling was hotly contested, and the support given both before and after devaluation makes an interesting chapter in the post-war history of international monetary cooperation, while at the same time serving to show its limitations. Facilities known to have been available to the United Kingdom from overseas banks and international organizations during the months before devaluation included a line of credit of $1000 million from a number of foreign central banks, the United States Treasury and the Bank for International Settlements, for the purpose of offsetting withdrawals of funds; and reciprocal swap arrangements totalling $1350 million with the US Federal Reserve. The full amount available under the US swap arrangement had been used by mid-November, and other lines were also drawn upon. Additionally, in October, a consortium of three Swiss commercial banks made a loan to the UK government of 450 million Swiss francs, and some central banks had agreed to lend a total of $250 million through the Bank for International Settlements, repayable by twelve equal monthly instalments beginning in June 1968, to cover repayment by the United Kingdom of the outstanding amount of the 1964 drawing from the IMF.

International support arranged at the time of, or subsequent to, the devaluation comprised initially a one-year standby facility of $1400 million from the International Monetary Fund, additional credit facilities of some

$1500 million made available by central banks, and an increase to $1500 million in the existing US currency swap arrangements. The previous central bank credit of $1000 million for offsetting fluctuations in sterling balances was later renewed, the French contribution for three months but otherwise for a year from March 1968 onwards, and at the time of the central bank agreement on gold (see p. 366) in March it was announced that further assistance had been given to the United Kingdom authorities which would immediately bring the total of credits still available, including the IMF standby, to $4000 million. This figure excluded the US swap arrangements; some repayments under these were made after devaluation and by the end of December outstanding drawings had been reduced to $1050 million.

The reserves rose steadily during the first four months of 1967 to reach £1216 million, the highest figure of the year. A decline in May of £161 million was more than accounted for by repayments of foreign debts, mainly to the IMF, of £173 million, but the downward trend continued in subsequent months, despite increasing resort to the US swap arrangement and other facilities, and the September total of £976 million was the lowest since the 1964 sterling crisis. An increase in October was more than accounted for by the Swiss bank loan, and a further rise in November was recorded only after adjustment for the new rate of exchange – which had the effect of raising the end-October figure by £167 million – and the inclusion of the realized proceeds of the remainder of the Treasury's portfolio of dollar securities, amounting to £204 million at the new rate.

In December the trend was better; although the total fell by £100 million, this was after the annual repayment of principal and interest on the North American loans. Small increases in January and February 1968 were followed by a slight decline in March, when substantial outlays during the gold crisis were largely offset by an inflow of funds following the budget.

As sterling was under pressure it is, at first glance, surprising to find that the net sterling liabilities rose by £220 million in 1967. However, declines of £151 million for sterling area countries and of £116 million for non-territorial organizations (mainly the repayment to the IMF) were much more than offset by an increase of £487 million for non-sterling countries, arising from the way in which official support is given to sterling. In part, this is extended by central banks holding sterling in excess of their usual requirements, and in 1967 official net holdings rose by £459 million while private holdings fell by £123 million. Neither the figures nor the experience of the foreign exchange market suggest that any considerable reflux of funds occurred in the months following devaluation. The net claims of United Kingdom banks in non-sterling currencies rose by £4 million to £38 million in 1967, but gross liabilities and gross claims each increased from around £3000 million to over £4300 million, indicating continued growth of the Eurocurrency market, though the figures were affected by the devaluation.

In April 1967 the spot rate for sterling against the US dollar rose above the \$2·80 parity for the first time since February 1966, but it remained there for less than a week. It then fell almost continuously and by the end of July was only a little over \$2·78½. From then onwards, despite a few short-lived rallies, the rate again drifted downwards, to \$2·78¼ in November. During this period, considerable official support was being given to the forward as well as the spot market, and the three months' margin varied between ¼ and ¾ of a cent, though widening to 1¼ cents in November.

Following devaluation the spot rate for a time remained firmly at the new official ceiling of \$2·42 but by mid-December it had fallen to only a little over the new parity. It recovered to over \$2·41 in February, but the rush for gold in March and the associated pressure on the dollar had an adverse impact on sterling, the spot rate falling to nearly \$2·39 despite official support. After the budget, however, it rose above par again for a time.

After devaluation the Bank of England generally withheld support from the forward market, and the margin between spot and forward rates widened, at times dramatically. In early March for example the discount on three months' forward sterling was as much as 9 cents in some dealings, but in early April was around 2½ cents.

In the year to April 1968 interest rates seem to have had less influence on the flow of funds than uncertainties concerning exchange parities. Even when bank rate was at 8 per cent against US Federal Reserve discount rates of 4½ per cent, no substantial volume of funds was attracted. Throughout the period, the covered margin was generally in favour of investment in Euro-dollars as against deposits with UK local authorities, although until the beginning of December 1967 it did not exceed 1 per cent. From then onwards however, with the forward discount on sterling fluctuating, it was generally wider, reaching 4 per cent or more. Late in April 1968 it had fallen to between 1 and 2 per cent.

Over the year the rate of interest for three months' Eurodollars in London generally fluctuated between 3 and 6 per cent, though it rose as high as 7 per cent towards the end of November 1967 and again at the time of the March 1968 gold crisis. Early in 1968 a number of central banks and the Bank for International Settlements, which frequently made use of the market as an outlet for their resources, were believed to have provided it with funds so as to moderate movements in rates.

The investment dollar premium fluctuated around 20 per cent in the second quarter of 1967, but then rose to around 30 per cent in November. It rose further in April 1968, and late in the month was around 40 per cent. Because of the devaluation of sterling this is equivalent to a higher figure than previously. Exchange control arrangements, and particularly the 25 per cent surrender requirements, had considerably reduced the flow of investment dollars.

During 1967 the 'gold pool'* was a net supplier to the market, with demands on it towards the end of the year becoming substantial as the movement of gold into private hands intensified. For the second year running the offtake for industrial use and hoarding exceeded the amount of newly mined gold, and world monetary stocks again contracted. Speculative demand rose sharply after sterling devaluation, and intensified in January and February 1968 as pressure on the dollar developed, reflecting growing unease about the external situation of the United States and doubts about the future of the reserve currency arrangements. Early in March, the London gold price was pressing against the effective ceiling price of $35·20 per fine ounce held by the gold pool and demand reached a record level. At the request of the United States authorities the London gold market was closed on Friday 15 March, and this and the following day were also proclaimed Bank Holidays in the United Kingdom, although banks remained open for meeting the domestic cash requirements of customers in sterling; the London foreign exchange market and stock exchanges were closed.

During the same weekend an emergency meeting was held in Washington of the governors of the seven central banks still participating in the gold pool arrangements. The outcome was a decision to abandon the gold pool. Gold would continue to be transferred on the basis of $35 per fine ounce between monetary authorities who undertook no longer to sell, nor necessarily to buy, in the market, thus in effect creating a two-tier system for gold: in the market the price would be free to find its own level. In the United Kingdom, banks and most markets conducted normal business from 18 March but, as part of the agreement, the London gold market remained closed until 1 April. When it reopened on the new basis the dollar price of gold settled down at about $37 per ounce, this comparing with up to $45 that had occasionally been quoted in continental centres during the preceding weeks. The free market price rose to around $38 an ounce following an announcement early in April that South Africa was not intending to sell any gold on the free or official market 'in the near future' and later increased further.

Thus the immediate outcome of the conference was a marked subsidence of speculation in gold and restoration of confidence in existing international monetary arrangements. A contributory factor was the agreement to co-operate more closely than in the past to minimize flows of funds in order to assist exchange stability, and further assistance for sterling was announced as noted on p. 364. At the same time the United States announced a substantial increase in the 'swap' arrangements for mutual support of currencies

* Established in 1961 by a number of central banks, to operate in the London market in order to stabilize the price of gold. The participating countries were the United States, Belgium, Italy, Netherlands, Switzerland, West Germany and the United Kingdom; France also was a member but ceased to take an active part in the pool from July 1967 onwards. See also p. 299.

among fourteen countries including the United Kingdom. Further support for the existing international monetary arrangements came with the meeting of the 'Group of Ten' countries which was held shortly afterwards at Stockholm. The Washington communiqué had given as one reason why it was no longer felt necessary to buy monetary gold from the market, that the existing stock was sufficient 'in view of the prospective establishment of the facility for special drawing rights'.

The annual meeting of the IMF in September 1967 had agreed on a proposal for establishing a new reserve facility to meet the possible need for a supplement to existing international reserve assets; in more detail the plan provided for a means for creating special drawing rights (SDRs) in the Fund, which participating countries would accept as reserves and use for international settlements. At Stockholm in March nine of the 'Group of Ten' member countries – France reserving its decision – agreed to press ahead with plans for the scheme for special drawing rights up to a maximum of 50 per cent of IMF quotas, or $10,500 million. Shortly afterwards the drafting of detailed amendments to the IMF articles of agreement was completed.

Credit again curtailed

When some easing of credit controls had become possible, the ceiling on bank advances – 105 per cent of the March 1965 level – was removed in April 1967, though the banks were asked to continue to observe the selective criteria and it was made clear that only a 'modest' increase in credit would be permitted. At the same time the Chancellor indicated that the system of Special Deposits would be 'used in future in a new and more flexible manner', the object being to 'maintain a continuous control over bank lending'. Financial institutions other than the clearing and Scottish banks remained subject to the ceiling but talks were opened to devise new methods by which their lending activities might be subjected to continuous control. At the end of October 1967 the governor of the Bank of England was able to report that 'good progress' was being made in these discussions. However, in the new situation following the devaluation of sterling, no further progress seemed to have been made with the evolution of new forms of lending control for other financial institutions, and the level of Special Deposits remained unchanged at 2 per cent of gross deposits for the clearing banks and 1 per cent for the Scottish banks.

At the time of devaluation the authorities again resorted to the imposition of a ceiling on lending. Advances in sterling to the private sector were not to rise above the mid-November figure until further notice, except for seasonal reasons, but completely excluded from restraint were medium-term lending at the fixed rate of $5\frac{1}{2}$ per cent for exports and shipbuilding, short-term lending for exports at bank rate and other advances specifically identified as financing exports. Selective criteria for advances within the ceiling were firmly indicated; priority was to be given to finance for production and investment associated with exports and import-saving, and – a noteworthy addition – for the promotion of invisible earnings. Similar restrictions were placed on other financial institutions, and generally for credit made available through commercial bills or through leasing facilities. Presenting his budget in March 1968 the Chancellor of the Exchequer stated that 'the immediate outlook offers no scope for relaxing credit restraint at present' and the banks were asked to continue to observe the ceiling and the existing priorities.

Demand for advances was slow to revive following the withdrawal of the ceiling in April 1967 and by June the net figure for the private sector was still only 1·7 per cent higher than in March 1965. However, a marked increase was recorded in July and from then on the underlying trend was upward, and over the year to March 1968 the total rose by £482 million, or 10·5 per cent, against a fall of nearly 3 per cent in the previous year.

For net deposits the increase over the twelve months was at nearly the same rate, by 9·5 per cent, to reach £9452 million, as compared with only $\frac{1}{2}$ per cent in 1966–7. With this expansion in resources, an increase in investment holdings occurred, of £76 million, or 6 per cent, although as a proportion of deposits they declined slightly on balance from 13·7 to 13·2 per cent. The average investment ratio for 1967, however, at 13·7 per cent, was above that of both the preceding years; this followed a steep decline in the years 1958–65. The average ratio of advances to deposits in 1967 was lower than in 1966 but in each of the first three months of 1968 it was above the corresponding figure for 1967.

The liquidity ratio was tending to fall in 1967 and by March 1968 the combined figure was only 28·7 per cent as compared with 29·5 per cent a year before, with the two largest banks showing no margin above the permitted minimum of 28·0 per cent.

Figures for the banking sector as a whole show some noteworthy features. The total for current and deposit accounts rose by £2710 million to £18,449 million, with about two thirds of the increase accounted for by accepting houses and overseas banks. The amount for this group was swollen by a number of special factors including £232 million because of additions to the list of contributors to the statistics; £168 million for negotiable dollar certificates of deposit, which totalled £249 million at the end of the year; and an undisclosed amount due to the revaluation in terms of sterling, following devaluation, of deposits in non-sterling currencies. Advances of the banking sector rose by £2288 million to £12,409 million, but £1794 million of this increase was for accepting houses and overseas banks and reflected, in part, revaluation of currency lending.

In the classification of bank advances the increase over the three months to February 1968, especially pronounced for overseas residents, was largely attributable to the introduction of new contributors and the revaluation of advances in foreign currencies following devaluation. For nearly all the major categories the totals in February 1968 were appreciably higher than a year before. The relatively rapid rise in lending to personal borrowers during 1967 was not maintained after reimposition of severe restrictions in November.

Further progress was made with the improvement of money transfer services offered by the clearing banks, which were preparing themselves for competition from the National Giro, to be run by the Post Office and scheduled to begin operating later in 1968. The title 'Bank Giro' was given to the banks' money transfer services, which then included direct debiting arrangements, a particularly useful service for large organizations receiving frequent payments, whether of fixed or varying amounts, from holders of bank accounts. Meanwhile the twelve provincial clearing centres, with the exception of the afternoon clearing in Liverpool, were closed on 12 January 1968. Their business had become relatively unimportant, representing little more than 4 per cent of the general debit clearing, and only ½ per cent or so of all clearings. The object of the change was 'to assist in the general streamlining of the banks' money transmission services', since cheques remitted through London may be dealt with as part of the automatic input to the banks' computers.

The use of the banks' transmission services again rose sharply in 1967, mainly because of an increase of over one quarter in the amount passing through the town clearing. Otherwise the total value of cheques and other debit items passing through the general and provincial clearings was only 6·9 per cent higher on a working-day basis than in the previous year as compared with an increase of 9·0 per cent between 1965 and 1966. The growth of the credit clearing also slowed down, from 9·1 to 7·8 per cent, and it continued to represent about 14 per cent of the general clearing. The Midland Bank Index of Business Turnover rose by 5 per cent in 1968, roughly the same rate as in 1966.

Among the major banking events of the year was the publication in May 1967 of the report of the National Board for Prices and Incomes on bank charges. The Board found that bank charges to customers were not excessive, although in times of high bank rate the banks received an 'endowment' element in profits. More generally it was argued that the banks should compete more actively for deposits between themselves and hence with other financial institutions. This view led to the main recommendation that collective agreements on rates of interest allowed on deposits should be abolished, and similarly with the agreements on charges to specified classes of borrowers and on commission charges; the banks individually should publish tariffs of their main charges. It was also suggested that the government should aim at ensuring complete disclosure of profits and reserves as soon as practicable, and that consideration should be given to the imposition of a levy on the 'endowment' element in profits if this persisted. The policy followed by the banks of conducting ancillary activities, such as hire purchase finance, through subsidiary companies rather than directly, was questioned.

Generally the Board's recommendations did not command ready or widespread acceptance and were not at that time carried further, but one sentence in the report proved to be the harbinger of striking changes. The relevant passage was: 'The Bank of England and the Treasury have made it plain to [the Board] that they would not obstruct some further amalgamations if the banks were willing to contemplate such a development. . . . ' Except for National Provincial's acquisition of District Bank in 1962 – following the traditional pattern of a national bank absorbing a largely local bank – the structure of commercial banking had shown little change for half a century; the Treasury Committee on Bank Amalgamations in 1918 had indicated that further mergers might not be in the public interest, as a result of which it was considered that the authorities would resist proposals for amalgamations between major banks.

This interpretation of the official attitude now had to be revised, and within months of publication of the report extensive changes in the banking structure were initiated. First came the announcement towards the end of 1967 by Martins Bank that it was willing to consider the possibility of merging with another bank, but the first positive development was a statement by Westminster and National Provincial Banks on 26 January 1968 that they had agreed in principle to combine, and a holding company, National Westminster, was later formed. Within a fortnight, on 7 February, Royal Bank of Scotland (which owned Glyn, Mills and Williams Deacon's Bank) and the National Commercial Bank of Scotland (in which Lloyds Bank had a shareholding) announced that they were to merge, and on the following day Barclays Bank and Lloyds Bank, both of which had made undisclosed bids for Martins Bank, also announced proposals for merging, the group possibly to include Martins Bank.

The Barclays-Lloyds-Martins proposals were referred to the Monopolies Commission, which was asked to report on them within six months; in addition, the governor of the Bank of England introduced a ban on further merger proposals until after the government had considered the report. In the various announcements stress was laid on the advantages of rationalization of branch networks and on the benefits to be gained from the sharing of computer networks.

Meanwhile the establishment of joint enterprises between banks in different countries continued apace. Around mid-1967 several United Kingdom banks announced their participation in various ventures for the setting up of new European institutions jointly with Continental and sometimes United States banks. The Midland Bank, for example, formed a new company, Banque Européenne de Crédit à Moyen Terme, jointly with Samuel Montagu, Amsterdam-Rotterdam Bank, Deutsche Bank and Société Générale de Banque; two French banks and an Italian bank later participated. The Midland also participated, along with the same Dutch, German and Belgian banks, in two new ventures in New York, and also acquired a one third interest in Montagu Trust, the parent company of Samuel Montagu, merchant bankers.

A year or two earlier it appeared possible that the banks would eventually be required to make full disclosure of their profits, the course recommended by the PIB. Under the provisions of the Companies Act, 1967, this became possible merely by the making of an Order, but, in February 1968 the Minister of State, Board of Trade, stated that 'for the time being it has been concluded that the desirability of giving more information to shareholders is overridden by the arguments against disclosure'. It had been agreed that the banks would be allowed to continue to make undisclosed transfers to and from hidden reserves, but that full details would be given to the Bank of England for onward transmission to the Board of Trade.

Over the year the London money market was subject to considerable shifts in the availability of funds, and to several changes in bank rate. On 4 May 1967 bank rate was lowered from 6 to 5½ per cent, only to be raised again, each time by ½ per cent, on 19 October and 9 November. The exceptionally high rate of 8 per cent established on 19 November 1967 was maintained for over four months; it was not lowered until 21 March 1968, when it was clear that the budget had been reasonably well received, and then only by ½ per cent.

In the summer of 1967 the authorities were pursuing a fairly easy market policy, at the same time showing considerable flexibility in their operations. On only one occasion after bank rate was reduced in May until late September was the market forced to borrow at bank rate, and then only overnight. In this period the government was borrowing heavily on Treasury bills – a sharp reversal of the trend for several years past – and with the discount houses obtaining substantial allocations they were able to rebuild their Treasury bill portfolios, which at times became unduly large. The Middle East crisis caused some unevenness in the flow of funds but the Bank of England closely controlled the situation by concentrating on overnight lending.

Towards the end of September, with short-term money rates abroad rising, the Bank of England was taking a stricter line in the market, and lending at bank rate occurred frequently. Early in November 1967, however, assistance was usually given at market rates, and in the week immediately following devaluation and the sharp increase in bank rate, funds were provided on an 'unprecedented scale', to a net total of £700 million, to relieve the considerable difficulties being experienced by the market, money being extremely scarce as banks called in funds to meet sales of sterling. Subsequently funds continued on the whole to be in short supply, particularly around mid-February 1968 when three months' forward foreign exchange contracts entered into at the time of devaluation reached maturity; substantial official support was given from time to time. While bank rate stood at 8 per cent the London clearing banks, as a concession to the discount market, kept their minimum call money rate 1¾ per cent below it, but reverted to the more usual margin of 1⅝ when bank rate was reduced to 7½ per cent.

In the middle of 1967, with the government borrowing requirement rising and funding sales difficult, the amounts of Treasury bills offered at the weekly tenders began to move upwards from the extremely low levels which had prevailed for over a year. Until the end of 1967, the weekly issues were exceeding £200 million, but because of the seasonal contraction in issues, and the omission of a weekly tender at the time of the gold crisis in March, the amount outstanding at 31 March 1968, at £2050 million, was only £300 million higher than a year before. On some occasions Treasury bill rate has been unusually close to bank rate, and at the beginning of October 1967 it was only 6*d.* per cent below it, the smallest margin recorded in the post-war period.

The London market for negotiable dollar certificates of deposit continued to develop and in January 1968 three of the leading dealers in the secondary market for London dollar CDs announced the formation of the International CD Market Association. Earlier, an impediment to the issue of London dollar certificates of deposit for periods of one year or longer had been removed when the Inland Revenue ruled that banks need no longer deduct income tax from deposit interest paid, and some banks, including Midland and International Banks, placed issues with a maturity of several years. Although accepting houses and overseas banks in London had issued £249 million of dollar certificates at the end of 1967, this represented only 4 per cent of their non-sterling currency deposits. Sterling certificates had yet to appear, but the Finance Bill provided for them to become subject to exchange control, thus removing a technical obstacle to the development of a market in them.

The market for equities was exceptionally buoyant during the year, at times surprisingly so. Sharp rises were recorded shortly before devaluation and following the budget proposals in March 1968, even though these included restraint on dividend increases. The *Financial Times* Industrial Ordinary share index (1 July 1935=100) reached an all-time high of 469·7 in April 1968, bringing it 37 per cent above the level of a year earlier. Yields fell correspondingly, that on the *Financial Times*–Actuaries 500 share index from over 5¾ per cent early in 1967 to under 4½ per cent by December, and subsequently to under 3¾ per cent.

Prices of gilt-edged securities fell fairly sharply in May and June 1967, and then showed little change on balance until coming under renewed pressure in October and November. They fell again at the time of devaluation and by end-March 1968 they were still at about the same levels despite the reduction in bank rate. Yields increased sharply towards the end of the year under review; the redemption yields on most securities were well over 7 per cent.

The total amount of new money raised by the issue of marketable securities in the United Kingdom in 1967, at £672 million, was £185 million less than in 1966, the figure for companies falling by £216·5 million to £422 million, of which debt financing accounted for over four fifths. In the first quarter of 1968 the market was again less active than a year before. The redemption yield on twenty-year industrial debenture and loan stocks was around 8 per cent in April 1968 against 7¼ per cent twelve months earlier, and the 'reverse yield gap' between equities and fixed-interest securities widened considerably.

Net borrowing by local authorities from the central government fell sharply in 1967–8, to only £347 million, against a budget estimate of £480 million and £518 million in 1966–7. The decline was probably largely attributable to the reluctance of local authorities to commit themselves to relatively long-term borrowing at the prevailing high rates of interest, particularly in the early months of 1968, when they were influenced by a change in the Public Works Loan Board interest rate structure following the introduction by the government of new housing subsidy arrangements. From end-May 1967 the Board's rates for all loans, whether within or outside quotas, reflected the appropriate government lending rates, whereas for some time previously rates for quota loans had carried an element of subsidy. The rates on quota borrowing, which had remained unchanged within a range of 5¾ to 6⅛ per cent since August 1964 were increased several times to reach 7⅜ to 7⅝ per cent. Local authorities raised £192 million of new money by market issues in 1967, slightly less than in either of the two previous years. Last year's fall was more than accounted for by a reduction in net new issues of bonds, which declined from £71 million in 1966 to £53 million. The timing of issues of stock was much affected by conditions in the gilt-edged market, none being made in the period October 1967 to January 1968.

With less resort being made to the central government and the stock market, local authorities borrowed heavily from the banking sector. During 1967 its outstanding advances to UK authorities rose from £657 million to £1018 million, or by around £300 million allowing for revisions to the statistics; lending by accepting houses and overseas banks increased by £270 million to £797 million and that by domestic banks by £91 million to £217 million. Demand upon the banks remained heavy in the first quarter of 1968.

Building societies continued to expand their activities rapidly during 1967. The net increase in shares and deposits outstanding rose during the year by £1104 million, against £724 million in the previous year. Net lending on mortgages amounted to £808 million, against £667 million. Even so, their outstanding lending commitments continued to rise, and at the end of the year amounted to £430 million. In the early months of 1968, building societies experienced a falling off in the inflow of funds for lending. In April the Building Societies Association recommended to member societies that the lending rate should be increased from $7\frac{1}{8}$ to $7\frac{5}{8}$ per cent, and the tax-paid rate on share accounts from $4\frac{1}{4}$ to $4\frac{1}{2}$ per cent.

Government expenditure rose sharply over the year to 31 March 1968, and although revenue also rose substantially, the revenue surplus amounted to only £330 million against a budget estimate of £637 million and a surplus of £738 million in 1966–7. Meanwhile, Consolidated Fund lending (net) rose slightly to £1661 million, despite the lower figure for local authorities, giving a borrowing requirement of £1312 million against the estimate of £1032 million. One reason for the growth of revenue, and to a lesser extent of expenditure also, was the inclusion for the first time of a full year's receipts and payments of selective employment tax; gross revenue amounted to £1064 million against £600 million in 1966–7. Reductions in the planned increase in public expenditure, announced in January 1968, were designed to reduce the total for the central government and local authorities, expressed in '1967 survey prices', from £15,378 million to £15,078 million in the financial year 1968–9; the estimated comparable figure for 1967–8 was £14,387 million.

The Letter of Intent given to the IMF (see Appendix 4(a)) indicated that the Exchequer's borrowing requirement would be kept under firm control in 1968–9 and that this would probably entail holding down the total to £1000 million. The 1968 budget proposals in fact provided for a considerably lower figure. Substantial increases in taxation – mainly in indirect taxes – were designed to produce an additional £923 million of revenue in a full year and £775 million in 1968–9, and the borrowing requirement was put at only £364 million; had no changes been made in taxation it would have been about £1139 million. A change made in the accounting arrangements for government lending resulted in most domestic lending transactions passing through a new National Loans Fund. This was to be credited with interest on loans made, and interest payable on the national debt above this figure would be provided from the Consolidated Fund. The profits of the Issue Department of the Bank of England, and changes in the capital of the Exchange Equalization Account, were also to be applied to the National Loans Fund.

To judge from the Exchequer Return the national debt outstanding rose by £1312 million to £33,276 million in 1967–8; the floating debt rose by £1575 million, as compared with a decline of £1267 million in 1966–7. In May 1967, £750 million of $2\frac{1}{2}$ per cent Savings Bonds 1964–7 were redeemed; holders of £516 million accepted an offer to convert into $6\frac{1}{4}$ per cent Exchequer Loan 1972, and holders of £59 million converted into $6\frac{1}{2}$ per cent Funding

Loan 1985–87; the balance of £175 million was redeemed for cash. Later in the year £850 million of 5 per cent Exchequer Stock 1967 was redeemed for cash and in March £498 million of 4 per cent Exchequer Loan 1968 was also redeemed for cash. Issues were much lower than in the previous year. Apart from the conversion issues already mentioned, a new long tap, $6\frac{3}{4}$ per cent Treasury Loan 1995–98, bringing £567 million into the Exchequer, was issued shortly after devaluation and this was followed in February 1968 by an issue of $6\frac{3}{4}$ per cent Exchequer Stock 1973, raising £679 million. The latter issue was to replace official supplies of the short tap, $6\frac{1}{4}$ per cent Exchequer Stock 1972, and of the steel nationalization stock, $6\frac{1}{2}$ per cent Treasury Stock 1971, which had run out. The authorities made net sales of marketable securities amounting to £529 million in the calendar year 1967, well over twice the level recorded a year before. More than one half of sales were to the banking sector. The pattern of sales showed considerable swings; net sales amounted to £600 million in the first quarter and £297 million in the fourth, but net purchases of £324 million and £44 million were made in the second and third quarters respectively.

Net sales of national savings securities as a whole rose somewhat more in 1967–8 than in the previous year, but only because of a decline in repayments. Even though sales of the then current issue of national savings certificates fell sharply, holdings of certificates rose by £55 million, about the same amount as in 1966–7; the maximum individual holding of the current issue was raised from £750 to £1000 from 22 March 1968. Sales of $5\frac{1}{2}$ per cent national development bonds, introduced in 1966, were poor in 1967–8 and, with substantial redemptions of maturing defence bonds, holdings of bonds fell. The national development bond was replaced by a new British savings bond, which came on sale on 1 April 1968. This carried a rate of interest of 6 per cent with a £2 per cent tax-free bonus if held for the full life of five years.

The trustee savings banks continued to extend their services during the year; further banks offered current account facilities and the initial offer was made of units in the TSB Unit Trust. In the ordinary departments repayments continued slightly to exceed receipts, but net savings in the special investment departments rose by £40 million. Some banks raised the rate of interest on investment accounts to 6 per cent. Under the Trustee Savings Banks Act, which received the Royal Assent in February 1968, provision was made for the rate of interest paid to the banks on funds deposited with the National Debt Commissioners to be increased, for giving the banks some powers of investing funds direct, and for reapportioning some expenses between ordinary and special investment departments. Withdrawals from Post Office ordinary accounts exceeded receipts by £153 million in 1966–7 and by a further £114 million in 1967–8. Balances on investment accounts, however, increased by over £60 million, bringing the total invested to about £140 million by end-March 1968.

12

Achieving External Stability

1969 – The Surplus Elusive

The year to April 1968 was described as the most eventful in monetary affairs in the preceding post-war period; that to April 1969 must surely rank as one of the most disappointing. Despite the devaluation, the most severe budget since the war, and a succession of other measures, the current account deficit on the balance of payments for 1968 was the largest ever recorded and further external support for sterling was required. Some progress towards surplus was achieved, but it was uneven and slower than had been hoped. In particular, exports expanded well, assisted by a fairly rapid rise in world trade, but imports remained obstinately at a high level. Other favourable developments were a substantial measure of economic growth with the level of employment well maintained and – towards the end of 1968 – a marked upturn in industrial investment.

But the external situation remained the paramount consideration, and for this reason it was necessary to maintain interest rates at exceptionally high levels, progressively to tighten credit controls, and in these and other ways to reinforce the severe restraints imposed at the time of devaluation and again in the 1968 budget. These last were designed to bring about a reduction of nearly 2 per cent, in real terms, in consumers' expenditure between the second half of 1967 and the second half of 1968. Further pressure was applied at the end of May with in effect a reduction of the ceiling on bank advances. Although retail trade fell sharply from the levels recorded during the pre-budget boom, personal spending was continuing to run above the forecast level and imports remained high. In September the Bank of England *Quarterly Bulletin* judged that the economy had 'departed somewhat from the path foreseen at the time of the budget' and suggested that this had 'delayed until later in 1969 the expected move into surplus of the balance of payments'. Nevertheless, a general improvement in the external situation, and the announcement of the Basle agreement relating to sterling balances, made it possible for bank rate to be reduced by $\frac{1}{2}$ per cent to 7 per cent on 19 September 1968.

From then on, however, with consumption beginning to revive, an uneven improvement in the external trade position, indications that international tensions were building up again, and a check to the downward trend in world interest rates, further restraints were successively imposed. Hire purchase terms on a wide range of goods were made more stringent early in November and later in the same month indirect taxes were increased, an import deposit scheme was introduced, and the banks were asked to reduce further their lending to the private sector. Progress towards the new advances ceiling proved difficult and by February it was clear that it would not be achieved as requested by March. The authorities reinforced the squeeze on 27 February 1969 by raising bank rate a full 1 per cent to 8 per cent.

The course of Exchequer finance in Britain was also pressing on liquidity towards the end of the financial year 1968–9, as import deposits, higher purchase tax and excise duty payments, the special charge on investment incomes, and increased rates of corporation tax and selective employment tax all contributed to a sharp rise in government revenue. The main purpose of the April 1969 budget, in the words of the Chancellor of the Exchequer, was to continue the balance of payments improvement, but to do so in a way 'compatible with the maintenance of economic growth and the requirements of social justice'. The squeeze on consumption was to be continued, and the various proposals were estimated to bring a substantial overall surplus on the Exchequer accounts.

Sterling came under considerable pressure at times during the twelve months to April 1969 and, while giving some indications of growing underlying strength, remained below parity against the US dollar throughout the period. The continued sensitivity of sterling to uncertainties regarding other currencies, notably in May 1968 during the French troubles and at the time of the European currency crisis in November, was disturbing. Other developments too had been of considerable consequence for sterling, quite apart from the rising level of international interest rates, including those on Eurodollars. Modest progress was made in improving international monetary arrangements; the establishment of special drawing rights in the IMF moved nearer, and the two-tier gold system remained in force. A significant development was the funding and underwriting of part of the overseas sterling balances under the Basle agreement of September, and towards the end of 1968–9 central banks took further steps to neutralize the effect on reserves of speculative currency movements.

After a pause in the second quarter, the economy expanded fairly strongly during the second half of 1968. For the whole year gross national product, at £36,358 million, was 5½ per cent higher than in 1967, although in real terms the rise was of the order of 3½ per cent. Industrial production rose by around 4½ per cent as compared with a slight fall in the previous year, and for manufacturing industries alone the increase was about 5½ per cent. The increase in output was somewhat slow to show in terms of unemployment. The underlying trend was upwards until August, but thereafter it was tending to fall until March 1969.

Industrial investment did not at first rise as quickly as expected in 1968 and the rate of growth of investment in the public sector was tending to slow down. For the year as a whole the volume of gross fixed capital formation rose by 3½ per cent in total, as compared with nearly 6¾ per cent in 1967. The volume of industrial stocks and work in progress fell fairly sharply in the first quarter of 1968, but increases were subsequently recorded, particularly in the last quarter.

Retail prices rose sharply, partly because of higher indirect taxation and the effect of devaluation on prices of imported goods. For 1968 the average price level was about 5 per cent higher than in the previous year, or double the increase recorded in 1967; the upward pressure on prices persisted in the early months of 1969. The prices of basic materials and fuels used in manufacturing, which rose steeply in the six months immediately following devaluation, fell on balance over the next six months, but subsequently rose.

The government continued to operate a prices and incomes policy, which included 'a ceiling of 3½ per cent on wage, salary and dividend increases'. Under the Prices and Incomes Act, which received the Royal Assent in July 1968, the government took powers for eighteen months to impose standstills on increases in prices and incomes for up to twelve months. Nevertheless, individual earnings rose fairly sharply. Basic wage rates were under pressure, more especially towards the end of 1968, and the increase over 1967 was nearly 7 per cent while average earnings rose by 8 per cent. Total dividend payments in 1968 showed virtually no increase above the average of the preceding three years.

The elusive external surplus

At the time of devaluation in November 1967 it was hoped that clear evidence of underlying improvement in the balance of payments would appear during the second half of 1968, but progress proved to be much slower than was expected. Imports (including payments for US military aircraft) at £6899 million in 1968 were 11 per cent higher by volume than in 1967, but 22 per cent by value. The increase in import prices in terms of sterling that devaluation brought about did not reduce demand as had been expected. In part, the increase in imports may have been associated with the limited success in controlling rising personal consumption, and also with the increase in domestic stocks from a relatively low level.

Thus the various measures of domestic restraint were to some extent occasioned by, and aimed at, the level of imports. The government remained opposed to direct methods of controlling imports, but in November it introduced the import deposit scheme, a measure of a kind new to Britain. Broadly speaking, import deposits were payable on all imports of goods other than basic foods, feeding stuffs, fuel and raw materials, goods destined for export and some categories of goods imported mainly from developing countries. Importers had to deposit with the Customs and Excise authorities 50 per cent of the value of the goods, in addition to any other duties payable, before the goods could receive Customs clearance. Deposits, on which no interest was paid, were repayable after 180 days. At first, UK importers were permitted to borrow foreign currency or external sterling to pay the deposits, but this facility was soon withdrawn. However, many overseas suppliers extended their credit terms, thus easing the pressure on importers and incidentally benefiting the central reserves.

Exports, by contrast, responded much as had been expected to the advantage given by devaluation, although a major factor was the continued growth in world trade. The value of exports was 23 per cent higher in 1968 than in 1967 and the increase in volume was about 14 per cent. In comparing the figures for the two years allowance must be made for the effects of the dock strikes at London and Liverpool during the final quarter of 1967, but about two thirds of the increase was attributed to other factors. The expansion of exports was widespread geographically, with the value of shipments to the United States rising by 43 per cent, to Latin America by 35 per cent, to the USSR and Eastern Europe by 33 per cent, and to the EEC countries by 24 per cent.

As a result of these movements the visible trade deficit, including payments for military aircraft from the United States, widened from £635 million in 1967 to £796 million in 1968, but a significant improvement occurred between the first and second halves of the year – the deficit falling from £460 million to £336 million – and the position also improved between the third and fourth quarters.

However, the trade figures for the first quarter of 1969 were somewhat disappointing. Exports, seasonally adjusted, averaged £541 million a month, compared with £544 million a month in the previous quarter, and imports were running at a monthly rate of £673 million, compared with £678 million in the fourth quarter of 1968. The visible trade balance (excluding payments for US military aircraft) was provisionally estimated at £43 million a month on average for the quarter, the same level as the estimate for the previous quarter. One major distortion to the figures in the first three months was the dock strike at some United States ports which held up deliveries.

On invisible account, the government net deficit was virtually unchanged at £462 million, despite the deferment of interest payments on the United States and Canadian loans. However, net invisible earnings, excluding government transactions, again rose substantially, from £702 million to £839 million; the bulk of this improvement came from the net earnings of private services. After remaining at around £200 million for several years, these rose to £349 million in 1967 and £481 million in 1968.

The net deficit on long-term capital account was reduced from £116 million in 1967 to £39 million in 1968. This was mainly because official transactions brought in a surplus of £23 million as against a deficit of £57 million in the previous year, partly because of the deferment of £36 million of capital repayments of the North American loans. The net outflow of private investment was almost unchanged at £62 million; investment abroad by UK residents rose from £435 million to £621 million, largely because of heavy portfolio investment, particularly in Australia, while foreign investment in the United Kingdom rose from £376 million to £559 million, largely reflecting takeover and merger activity.

Thus the overall deficit on current and long-term capital accounts combined, at £458 million, showed a reduction of less than £60 million on 1967. Moreover, the 'balancing item', which had been heavily favourable in 1967, was turned into a negative item of £87 million, so that the adverse balance of monetary movements rose from £300 million to £545 million.

The devaluation in November 1967 represented a loss in the value of sterling reserves of overseas countries, in terms of non-devaluing currencies, whether they adjusted their own parities against the pound or not. In view of continuing uncertainties in the early part of 1968, several sterling area countries proceeded further with diversification of their reserves, and in the second quarter the total of sterling balances held by the central monetary institutions fell by over £280 million. A credit against which the United Kingdom could draw to meet a running down of sterling balances had been available from overseas central banks since 1966, but it was now thought desirable to replace this by a more formal arrangement which would ensure a greater degree of stability in sterling area holdings. The representatives of twelve central banks, together with the Bank for International Settlements, agreed in July 1968 to make available a facility of $2000 million, on which drawings could be made over three years, and repayment of which would be due within ten years. The assistance was dependent upon the negotiation by the United Kingdom government of suitable agreements with the governments of the rest of the sterling area for the maintenance of agreed proportions of their reserves in the form of sterling.

By early September sufficient progress had been made for a final decision to be made to set up the facility, under which the United Kingdom is able to make drawings of foreign currencies through the BIS 'as and to the extent that the sterling balances of the overseas sterling area fall below an agreed starting level'. In order to protect the balances of the overseas sterling area countries, the United Kingdom government gave a dollar guarantee covering that part of each country's official sterling reserves which exceeded 10 per cent of its total reserves; in return the individual governments of the overseas sterling area countries agreed to maintain minimum proportions – separately negotiated for each country – of their reserves in sterling. Most guarantees were to remain in force for three years, with provision for a two-year extension by mutual consent.

Initial drawings under the agreement took place to finance reductions which had occurred earlier in 1968 in the sterling balances of the overseas sterling area countries. When these new arrangements were made, it was announced that the assistance provided in 1966 for a similar purpose would be ended by 1971, and $600 million borrowed under this facility would be repaid in eight quarterly instalments beginning in September 1969.

Early in June 1968 assistance was taken from the IMF under the standby arrangement made at the time of devaluation. The drawing, the equivalent of £583 million, was used to repay part of the United Kingdom's indebtedness under short-term facilities, including the drawings made under the swap facility with the Federal Reserve. Nevertheless, further drawings under the swap agreement were made in the second half of the year and at the end of December the total outstanding was $1150 million. A table published in the *Financial Statement and Budget Report 1969–70* showed that, over the five years 1964–8 the United Kingdom had needed to finance a deficit of £3600 million, largely as a result of the current account deficits and a decline in overseas holdings of sterling; of this amount £1100 million had been borrowed from the IMF, £2000 million from other official sources and the balance had been met by a running down of the gold and currency reserves and liquidation of the official dollar portfolio.

The published figures of gold and convertible currency reserves fell over the year to March 1969 by £105 million to £1029 million. The total at the end of September, at £1132 million was virtually the same as six months before but in the fourth quarter it fell month by month to £1009 million. Most of this decline – £115 million out of £123 million – was accounted for by the repayment of medium-term obligations to various overseas creditors, and by the end of March the reserves had risen by £20 million despite further substantial repayments of short-term indebtedness. Official policy was to use currency purchased in the market to pay off obligations to overseas creditors rather than to build up the reserves.

In order to provide an immediate benefit to the reserves, exchange control authority for the use of sterling usance credits to finance trade between countries outside the sterling area was withdrawn in October. No changes were made where a resident of the sterling area was involved as exporter, importer or merchant, where the trade was being financed in currencies other than sterling, or in arrangements for sight drafts.

The total of net overseas sterling liabilities rose by £686 million during 1968. The increase of £542 million in holdings of international bodies reflected mainly the drawing made from the International Monetary Fund in June. Liabilities to other sterling area countries fell by £152 million, primarily as a result of the reductions by the central monetary authorities during the second quarter. Liabilities to non-sterling area countries rose by £296 million, but those to the central monetary authorities alone rose by £662 million, reflecting the manner in which assistance was given to sterling. For other non-sterling area holders of sterling the movement was the other way, with the net claims of United Kingdom residents on them rising by £366 million to £504 million. At the end of the year they held a total of £537 million of sterling but their gross sterling indebtedness amounted to £1041 million; most of this was in respect of commercial bills, which rose during 1968 by over £200 million, presumably reflecting the growth of UK exports and particularly of export credit. The net liabilities of United Kingdom banks in currencies other than sterling, mainly US dollars, rose from £8 million at the end of 1967 to £29 million at the end of December 1968. Both liabilities and claims rose, however, by over £2700 million as the market in Eurodollars continued to grow.

With the United Kingdom balance of payments recovering much more slowly than had been hoped, and recurrent uncertainties in international monetary matters generally, sterling remained below its US dollar parity throughout the year, and at times the Bank of England found it necessary to give support. Speculation against the French franc in May 1968 led to revived doubts about the pound and the rate fell to $\$2{\cdot}38\frac{3}{8}$. In the November 1968 currency crisis sterling came under intense pressure, even though speculation mainly centred on the possibility of a devaluation of the French franc and a revaluation of the Deutschmark. Following heavy intervention by the authorities the London foreign exchange market was closed from 20 to 22 November while consultations took place in Bonn between the finance ministers of the major western countries. In the event, the various measures which were taken did not include any realignment of currency parities, and sterling remained under pressure in the early part of December despite further domestic restraints. However, helped by the improved trade figures for November and by a need on the part of those who were oversold to meet sterling commitments, the rate improved during the remainder of December and into the new year. By the beginning of March the rate had risen to over $\$2{\cdot}39\frac{1}{2}$, the best level since late October; after a brief but sharp fall early in the month the rate steadily improved, and by the middle of April 1969 was again above $\$2{\cdot}39\frac{1}{2}$, but subsequently fell back sharply to $\$2{\cdot}38\frac{1}{2}$.

Following the devaluation of sterling the Bank of England did not appear to intervene in the forward market, and rates fluctuated with market circumstances. At times the discounts on forward sterling were substantial, particularly during June and the early part of July and again in December 1968. In the earlier period, the margin on three months' forward sterling widened to over 4 cents against the US dollar, and although it narrowed in July and remained at more normal levels until November, it then moved to over 2 cents. At the beginning of April 1969, the margin was still 1½ cents, compared with less than ½ cent immediately before the November crisis, and later widened further.

The investment dollar premium continued to fluctuate at historically high levels. At the end of April 1968 it stood at just above 40 per cent and for the most part it fluctuated around that level, but it rose to about 50 per cent or more at times. The Chancellor of the Exchequer announced in his budget speech that one of the restrictions under the voluntary programme of restraint on overseas investment, whereby financial institutions had been asked not to increase their portfolio holdings of foreign currency securities, was to be lifted. Since most such investment must take place through the investment currency market the premium rose quickly from 44½ per cent to 60 per cent, but subsequently it fell back to around 50 per cent.

The rate on three-month Eurodollars rose from around 6½ per cent at the end of April 1968 to 7¼ per cent early in June, but subsequently fell back steadily and was down to 5½ per cent in September. Later movements were generally upwards. For several weeks up to mid-December it was around 7 per cent, but with rising levels of interest rates in a number of centres, and particularly a tightening monetary situation in the United States causing US banks to bid for Eurodollars for repatriation, the three months' rate had reached 8½ per cent by the beginning of March.

Short-term interest rates in London, particularly those in the parallel markets such as that for deposits with local authorities, are strongly influenced by the rate on Eurodollars adjusted for the cost of forward foreign exchange cover. Hence, in large measure, the rise in parallel market rates in the early months of 1969, was one of the reasons given for the increase in bank rate on 27 February. Even so, the difference in yield between Eurodollars and deposits with local authorities, covered forward, remained in favour of Eurodollars, by a varying margin.

The gold marketing arrangements agreed at Washington in March 1968 continued in operation, even though the free market and fixed monetary prices for gold diverged to a much greater extent than was probably foreseen at the Washington Conference. The London market price frequently rose above $40 an ounce, and a steady upward trend after December, brought it up to $42·75 by mid-January, and to $43·6 on 30 April. The newly appointed Secretary to the US Treasury stated in January that the new administration would not change the official dollar price of gold. The terms on which the IMF might buy newly mined gold were not settled during the year although in April South Africa transferred a relatively small amount in accordance with the formalized arrangements for currency purchases. The South African authorities also made sales on the free market from time to time, but that country's balance of payments situation was sufficiently favourable to make gold sales generally unnecessary.

Intensified pressures on the banks

Both fiscal and monetary measures were called in aid to produce a progressively tighter monetary situation and thus to hold back imports and consumer's expenditure. A number of 'requests' were made to the banks to tighten credit; instead of the usually substantial net government borrowing requirement there was a modest repayment of debt; and interest rates rose to unprecedented levels.

The ceiling reimposed on bank advances in sterling to the private sector in November 1967 allowed for no increase except for seasonal reasons, but did not affect fixed-rate medium-term lending for exports and shipbuilding, short-term export lending at bank rate and other advances specifically identified as financing exports. In May 1968 a new ceiling was indicated to the clearing banks, this time covering all lending in sterling to the private sector including credit related to exports and for shipbuilding. They were asked to restrict the total of this lending, after seasonal adjustment, to 104 per cent of the corresponding figure for November 1967 – roughly the level then existing – and within this ceiling priority was to be given to lending for export transactions and for activities directly related to improving the balance of payments, including the promotion of invisible earnings. To make room for the continued expansion of these categories, personal lending and other 'non-priority' borrowing were to be further curtailed. Credit provided through commercial bills and leasing facilities was to be subject to the same restrictions and personal loans for hire purchase transactions were to be on terms no easier than those permitted by the Board of Trade for comparable contracts. Lending to local authorities, which had risen appreciably during the previous half-year, was to return to 'normal levels'. Similar restrictions were placed on other financial institutions, and members of the Finance Houses Association were requested to limit their lending to its level at end-October 1967.

The clearing banks were critical that there had not been 'adequate prior consultation' with them about this requirement, especially as they were committed to a substantial increase in export lending now brought within the control, and this, when advanced, would push lending above the ceiling. Following discussions with the authorities they were allowed a 'reasonable time' in which to reduce other advances. In aggregate their lending was probably again within the permitted figure by mid-August but the governor of the Bank of England stressed that the restrictions would still have to be 'rigorously enforced over the period ahead'.

Following the November currency crisis the Chancellor of the Exchequer announced further restrictions, including the introduction of the import deposit scheme. This was expected to have its effect partly by tightening the internal monetary situation, and the banks were asked not to lend to finance such deposits except in limited special circumstances. Moreover, though fixed-rate lending for exports and shipbuilding, but not other credit for exports, was now once more excluded from the overall ceiling, other clearing bank lending, after allowing for seasonal movements, was to be reduced further to reach 98 per cent of its mid-November 1967 level by mid-March 1969, implying a general contraction of about 2 per cent. Similar restrictions were applied to Scottish banks but the remaining banks – who finance only a small amount of fixed-rate lending – were asked to ensure that by the end of March their controlled lending did not exceed 102 per cent of its level immediately before devaluation, again a reduction of about 2 per cent.

The banks experienced considerable difficulty in meeting this extra requirement, partly because of the unusually heavy demand for advances for tax purposes in the early months of the year, and the import deposit scheme was further reducing company liquidity. At the end of January the authorities requested 'renewed efforts by the banks, bearing results quickly', to which the clearing banks replied that they would 'do their best' to meet the target but that 'no positive assurance' of success could be given. The February figures showed further increases in lending, and bank rate was raised to 8 per cent, partly to support the policy of credit restraint. Some reduction was achieved in March, though lending was still well above the ceiling which had been set for that date, and the banks were allowed some further limited time to make the required reduction. Further progress was made in April 1969.

Advances tended to decline slightly after the first quarter of 1968 and the seasonal rise during the early part of 1969 was less pronounced than in 1967, despite the pressures already noted. Nevertheless clearing bank net advances (excluding those to nationalized industries) rose by £172 million, or 3·4 per cent, to £5239 million during the year to March 1969; for 1967–8 the increase was 10·5 per cent. Net deposits also expanded much more slowly than in the previous year, by £244 million, or 2·6 per cent, to reach a total of £9696 million, as compared with an increase of 9·5 per cent over the previous twelve months. With interest rates remaining high the share of total deposits held in deposit accounts continued to grow and in 1968, on average, it was 40 per cent, with current accounts at 52 per cent. The average ratio of gross advances to gross deposits in 1968, at 50·3 per cent, was virtually the same as for the previous year.

The value of cheques and other debit items passing through both town and general clearings increased by 7·0 per cent during 1968 as compared with an increase of 24·3 per cent a year before. Credit clearings – including items passing through the Inter-Bank Computer Bureau – rose in value by 14·3 per cent against 7·8 per cent in 1967. The National Giro, operated by the Post Office, opened for business on 18 October 1968. At the end of December its deposits amounted to only £10 million, of which £8 million was on government account. The funds were invested with local authorities or in the money market.

The turn-around in government finance in the closing months of 1968–9 brought severe pressure on bank liquidity. The volume of tender Treasury bills in issue was greatly reduced during 1968–9, and clearing bank holdings fell by £61 million. Their holdings of commercial and other bills increased marginally and the proportion of their liquid assets held in the form of call money continued to rise. Special Deposits with the Bank of England were maintained at 2 per cent of gross deposits, the level established in July 1966. The average liquidity ratio in 1968 was virtually the same as in 1967 at 30·5 per cent, and over the twelve months to March 1969 the combined liquidity ratio rose from 28·7 to 29·4 per cent. This increase, however, was only achieved by a substantial reduction in holdings of government securities during the first quarter of 1969, and over the financial year as a whole a net decline of £128 million, or 9·0 per cent, was recorded; during the previous three years the banks had been adding to their portfolios. The proportion of clearing bank investments to total deposits fell only slightly in 1968, but the sales early in 1969 brought the ratio down to 11·7 per cent by mid-March, the lowest figure for three years.

For the banking sector as a whole advances rose by £3396 million to £15,799 million during 1968, but of this increase about three quarters was accounted for by borrowing by overseas residents from accepting houses and overseas and other banks, mainly in non-sterling currencies. Current and deposit account balances of the banking sector increased during 1968 by £3699 million to reach £22,146 million, about two thirds of the increase being accounted for by deposits by overseas residents with the accepting houses and overseas and other banks. Issues of negotiable dollar certificates of deposit by these banks almost doubled during the year, bringing the outstanding total to the equivalent of £597 million.

A market in negotiable sterling certificates of deposit, which had been in preparation for some time, opened on 28 October 1968. Issuers of the certificates included the deposit-taking subsidiaries of the clearing banks, and overseas and merchant banks, with discount houses forming the basis of the secondary market. The Bank of England had previously announced that sterling certificates held by banks would not rank as liquid assets for purposes of liquidity ratios and that banks' liabilities in the form of certificates would be treated as 'ordinary deposit liabilities' for the purpose of Special

Deposits and the Cash Deposits scheme described below. The clearing banks indicated to the discount houses their readiness to hold certificates overnight up to pre-arranged maximum amounts, against call money already lent to each house. Sterling certificates outstanding at the end of December totalled £165 million, about half the deposits coming from UK residents outside the banking sector. By the end of March 1969 the total had reached £261 million, most certificates being for periods of up to three months. From an initial level of around 7 per cent the sterling CD interest rate, for three-month deposits, rose steadily to 8 per cent during December where it remained until late February; following the bank rate increase it rose to over 9 per cent.

Excluding the large increase in advances to overseas residents the main rise in classified advances by the banking sector occurred in the 'manufacturing' sector. Advances to engineering, shipbuilding and vehicles combined rose by £165 million during the three months to February 1969 and by nearly £200 million over the year as a whole. Advances to the 'personal' sector rose between February and November 1968, but declined somewhat over the next three months.

The rapid growth of banks other than the clearing and Scottish banks, both in numbers and deposits, posed problems of control. In 1965 these banks were brought within the scope of the quantitative limit on bank lending, but as they observe widely differing cash and liquidity ratios, a method similar to the Special Deposits scheme applying to clearing and Scottish banks was not appropriate. The terms of a new arrangement – the Cash Deposits scheme – were made public in June 1968. The banks concerned were liable to be called on to make cash deposits with the Bank of England calculated as a percentage of specified deposit liabilities in sterling. Interest at Treasury bill rate would usually have been paid, but a lower rate was possible; the percentage of liabilities deposited would normally but not necessarily have been uniform for all banks within the scope of the arrangements. Deposits would initially be called for a fixed maximum period of six months but the Bank reserved the right to replace deposits by fresh calls. The scheme was never activated.

The Monopolies Commission report on the proposed mergers between Barclays and Lloyds, and Barclays, Lloyds and Martins Banks, was published in July 1968. It concluded by a majority of six to four that a merger involving Barclays and Lloyds could be expected to operate against the public interest and therefore should not be allowed, but that there was a 'strong case' for Martins joining with another bank. After considering representations from the banks concerned, the government accepted the majority conclusions of the Commission. The three banks abandoned their original proposals and Barclays promptly made an offer for Martins, which was accepted. Martins became a subsidiary of Barclays on 1 November 1968.

The merger between the Westminster Bank and National Provincial Bank became operative on 10 July 1968, when each bank took up one half of the ordinary shares of the newly formed National Westminster Bank. Initially the banks retained their individual status but in due course a single branch network was to be operated – taking in also that of the District Bank – and about 400 branches were to be closed. The merger between the National Commercial Bank of Scotland and the Royal Bank of Scotland also became effective in July; the Scottish branches of the new 'National and Commercial Banking Group' took the name of the Royal Bank of Scotland on 1 April 1969. The clearing bank subsidiaries of the Group – National, Williams Deacon's and Glyn Mills – later merged and a new company, Williams & Glyn's Bank, was formed for this purpose.

New opening hours for the Scottish banks came into effect in June 1968, with Saturday closing and late opening between 4.30 and 6 p.m. on Thursdays. In September the clearing banks announced that they would close on Saturday mornings after 1 July 1969. From the same date weekday opening hours were to be extended to 9.30 a.m. to 3.30 p.m., though Town Clearing branches would continue to close at 3 p.m. Discussions with representatives of the staffs on opening for one evening each week were not conclusive and the matter was referred to arbitration.

The clearing banks continued to widen the range of their activities abroad, for example by establishing new representative offices, but no major new formations comparable with those of previous years were announced. New ground was broken at home in September with the establishment by the Midland Bank Finance Corporation and Samuel Montagu jointly of Midland Montagu Industrial Finance, the object of the new company being to provide minority equity finance for successful businesses not yet large enough to have access to the public capital market.

Bank rate had been at $7\frac{1}{2}$ per cent for six months when it was lowered to 7 per cent on 19 September 1968; it was raised to 8 per cent on 27 February 1969. At no time during the twelve months to April 1969 did the Bank of England lend to the money market at bank rate, even overnight; bank rate had not been applied in this market since November 1967. This may have been because, with the increasing tightness of money arising from fiscal policy, the authorities had not needed to exert their influence in this way. The weekly offer of Treasury bills at the tender declined, and the total outstanding at the end of March 1969, at £1350 million, was £700 million lower than a year before. The Treasury bill discount rate was usually only about $\frac{1}{4}$ per cent below bank rate during most of the period, although the margin widened in August in anticipation of the cut in bank rate.

The authorities continued to operate in the money market in a variety of ways, in the earlier part of the year mainly by lending at market rates for short periods, but from towards the end of 1968 rather more by purchases of Treasury bills. With the shortage of Treasury bills, this was not always easy, and in February the authorities added to their range of techniques by purchasing fine bank bills from the discount market at the current market rate. Previously the authorities had only bought sample quantities of such bills regularly in order to examine their quality and type.

During May 1968 the Bank of England gave permission to some discount houses to make a market in foreign currency bills of exchange; this was not, however, granted to houses with interests in foreign currency broking.

When bank rate was raised to 8 per cent the clearing banks increased their minimum rate for call money lent to discount houses by only $\frac{7}{8}$ per cent, thereby widening the margin between the two rates from $1\frac{5}{8}$ to $1\frac{3}{4}$ per cent. A similar pattern operated between November 1967 and March 1968, when bank rate was also 8 per cent.

Other short-term rates were fairly steady in the second quarter of 1968, and were falling from June to early November, but the trend was then reversed. The rate for three-month loans to local authorities fluctuated between 8 and $8\frac{1}{2}$ per cent in the three months to June with the corresponding rate for finance houses $\frac{1}{4}$ to $\frac{1}{2}$ per cent higher. By early November the rate was below 7 per cent for local authorities and just above for finance houses, but by mid-February both had risen by about 1 per cent.

One of the reasons given for the increase in bank rate from 7 to 8 per cent on 27 February was that 'the lowest rate of interest ordinarily charged by the clearing banks on their restricted lending is currently well below yields obtainable on short-term investment in the parallel money markets'. Nevertheless, the increase in bank rate was promptly followed by a broadly similar movement in rates in the parallel markets, so that relationships with clearing bank lending rates remained generally unchanged. The rate for seven-day deposits with local authorities rose from $7\frac{1}{2}$ to $8\frac{1}{2}$ per cent, and the three month rate from 8 to 9 per cent; the three-month finance house rate rose from $8\frac{1}{2}$ to over $9\frac{1}{4}$ per cent. That on three-month sterling certificates of deposit rose from over 8 to over 9 per cent. The inter-bank rate for overnight money fluctuates considerably, but broadly it rose from about 7 to 8 per cent. Rates generally remained at these levels during March and April 1969.

Prices in the gilt-edged market remained on a downward trend throughout most of 1968–9 and especially during the second half of the period, with the largest falls recorded for the longer-dated securities. A sharp decline in prices in May and June 1968 was followed by a recovery of confidence during the late summer, but this was short lived and from late October the market weakened more or less continuously, influenced by such factors as the disappointing course of the balance of payments, the international trend of interest rates and the tight money situation at home. For a period the authorities seemed to be less willing than previously to support the market and prices fell substantially, with yields reaching record levels. By April 1969 yields on short-dated stocks had risen by about 1 per cent to $8\frac{1}{2}$ per cent over the year, but those on longer-dated securities had risen by $1\frac{1}{2}$ per cent to even higher levels. The yield on company debentures and loan stocks had risen to about $9\frac{3}{4}$ per cent.

The market for equities showed considerable fluctuations. The *Financial Times* Industrial Ordinary share index (1 July 1935=100) rose from around 460 in May to an all-time peak of 521·9 on 19 September 1968. Prices weakened during the fourth quarter of 1968, followed in January by a recovery to near the September level, but subsequent weakness brought the index back to around 470 in April 1969. The dividend 'yield' on the *Financial Times*–Actuaries 500 share index at the end of April 1969 was about $3\frac{1}{2}$ per cent as compared with about $3\frac{3}{4}$ per cent a year earlier. In these circumstances the reverse yield gap – between the yield on the *Financial Times*–Actuaries index and that on $2\frac{1}{2}$ per cent Consols – was then over 5 per cent as compared with about $3\frac{1}{4}$ in April 1968 and rather less than 1 per cent in April 1967.

The total of new money raised by the issue of marketable securities during 1968 reached a new peak of £864·3 million, a rise of £192 million on 1967 and nearly £8 million higher than the previous record level in 1966. Company issues increased by well over one half of their 1967 total to reach £676·4 million and with the widening of the yield gap a marked revival in popularity of equity issues was seen. With both equity and fixed interest markets hesitant, many companies have issued convertible securities, though these did not always go well in the market.

In 1968 local authorities again increased their borrowing from the banking sector, by £215 million to £1232 million, but the figure for accepting houses and overseas and other banks rose by £308 million, whereas that for the deposit banks fell by £97 million to only £120 million. Net borrowing by local authorities from central government sources – predominantly the Public Works Loan Board – during 1968–9 reached £469 million, an increase of about one third over the previous year. Interest rates charged for borrowings from the Board – reflecting appropriate government lending rates – were raised during the early part of 1968, and expectations of a subsequent reduction influenced the amount of borrowing. Reductions in the Board's rates came in August, but the trend was soon reversed and by the end of March quota loans were costing around 9 per cent.

With high interest rates and a general weakness in the gilt-edged market, local authorities may have been reluctant to come to the market for funds. During 1968 the total of new money raised by issues of stocks and bonds fell for the third consecutive year to £159 million, against £192 million in 1967, and no stock issues were made after October. By the end of March 1969 local authorities were required to have brought down the total of temporary debt to not more than one fifth of total outstanding loan debt, to complete the funding process begun in 1964. Most local authorities achieved the objective, some well in advance of the target date, but it was believed that a few still had further funding to do.

The inflow of funds to building societies was not maintained at the previous year's high level in 1968, the net increase in shares and deposits of £774 million comparing with £1099 million. Net lending on mortgages, however, was £20 million over the previous year's total at £843 million, but outstanding lending commitments at the end of the year, at £328 million, were well down on the figure for December 1967. A failure to attract adequate funds for lending during late 1968 and the early months of 1969 led the Building Societies Association to increase their recommended rate for mortgages to new borrowers from $7\frac{5}{8}$ to $8\frac{1}{2}$ per cent from 1 April 1969. An increase in rates on share accounts from $4\frac{1}{2}$ to 5 per cent tax paid was also recommended.

Sales of units by unit trusts reached record levels around the turn of the year and in each of the three months December to February net sales amounted to about £33 million. The total value of funds at the end of February 1969 was nearly £1500 million, as compared with £900 million a year before.

A sharp change occurred in the Exchequer position in 1968–9 (see Appendix 2, Table 4). Government expenditure was about £750 million higher than in 1967–8, but reflecting increases in taxation in the 1968 budget and again in November, revenue rose by no less than £2130 million. The Consolidated Fund surplus of £1748 million was, as intended, far larger than that for 1967–8, and as loans from the National Loans Fund fell slightly to £1423 million, a net repayment of debt of £287 million was made, the first year this had been possible since 1950–1 and comparing with a net borrowing requirement of £1312 million in 1967–8. Changes in taxation announced in the budget were expected to bring in an extra £270 million in 1969–70, but after taking account of the buoyancy of the revenue, total receipts were expected to increase by £1445 million to £15,008 million. Expenditure was expected to rise by £936 million to £12,551 million and after taking account of net lending by the National Loans Fund – put at £1631 million for 1969–70 – the government expected to make a net repayment of debt of £826 million.

Plans were announced in February 1969 to encourage nationalized industries to borrow part of their capital requirements abroad, instead of entirely from the Exchequer; several nationalized bodies and the Industrial Reorganization Corporation had been given the necessary borrowing powers. The first borrowing was made by the Gas Council in March, when it arranged to raise the equivalent of £31 million by an issue and a placing of bearer bonds in the West German capital market. The government undertook the exchange risk on one of these, for a premium which offset much of the interest rate advantage. Later BOAC arranged to borrow 30 million Swiss francs from three Swiss banks.

High interest rates elsewhere and buoyant consumer spending affected national savings in the financial year 1968–9. Repayments exceeded receipts by £20 million, whereas in the previous year a net inflow of £85 million was recorded. Total repayments increased by £143 million over the year, receipts by £40 million. Sales of national savings certificates fell sharply and holdings declined by £20 million. The new British Savings Bond, which came on sale on 1 April 1968, attracted £80 million but this was more than offset by repayments of defence bonds and national development bonds. However, net sales of premium bonds almost doubled over the year to give a net addition to public holdings of £81 million.

Changes announced in the budget included an increase of £500 to £1500 in the limit on holdings of the twelfth issue of national savings certificates, and the issue of a new 7 per cent British Savings Bond. The Chancellor also proposed a 'Save as you earn' system of contractual savings which would allow up to £10 a month to be deducted from earnings or saved in other ways. He said that 'the reward for a completed five-year contract would take the form of a terminal bonus, completely free of all tax'. The proposed bonus was '£12 at the end of five years for every £60 saved over the period through subscription of £1 a month' and this would be raised to £24, if the savings were left for a further two years without further subscription.

The trustee savings banks continued to develop their services, but had a poor year for attracting deposits. In the ordinary departments repayments exceeded receipts by £25 million, over twice the figure for 1967–8, and net receipts in the special investment departments were halved to £21 million, although some banks raised the rates offered to 6½ per cent. Withdrawals from Post Office Savings Bank ordinary accounts exceeded receipts by £116 million over the year, an increase of £3 million; net receipts to investment accounts of £54 million were £2 million lower than in the previous year. The rate of interest paid on investment account deposits was raised from 6 to 6½ per cent on 1 October 1968. Plans were announced for raising the limits on deposits in ordinary and investment accounts of the Post Office and trustee savings banks from £5000 to £10,000.

The national debt was reduced by £287 million to £32,989 million during 1968–9, and by a further £50 million if Exchange Equalization Account transactions are included. The floating debt rose by only £346 million, following the increase of £1576 million in 1967–8; in both years overseas operations to support sterling greatly affected the figure, as the counterpart funds of swap arrangements are usually held in tap bills and the total for these rose by nearly £1000 million. On 1 August 1968 £533 million of 3 per cent Funding Stock 1966–68 was redeemed for cash, as was £334 million of 3½ per cent Conversion Stock 1969 on 1 March 1969; substantial lines of both stocks were already in official hands before the redemption dates. No new issues of marketable securities were made during the year, and no conversion operations had taken place since May 1967.

The authorities made net purchases of £506 million of marketable securities during the calendar year 1968, in contrast to sales of £529 million in the previous year. Well over one half of these purchases were from the banking sector with the discount houses providing about two thirds of this total. Net purchases of £14 million in the first quarter were followed by purchases of £500 million in the second and of £405 million in the fourth; only in the third quarter were net sales made, of £413 million.

1970 – Growth Resumed

The devaluation of sterling in November 1967, and the exceptionally severe monetary and fiscal restraints imposed subsequently to restore the external situation, at last began to bear fruit during the year to April 1970. Indeed, a dramatic improvement was seen in the balance of payments, with growing confidence in the pound, and towards the end of 1969 and in the early months of 1970 large inflows of funds from abroad were recorded. These enabled substantial repayments to be made of short-term external indebtedness that had been incurred earlier to support the pound. The strength of sterling contributed to, and was itself consolidated by, more settled conditions in international monetary affairs generally towards the end of the year. Other developments that helped to relieve strains on the system were the devaluation of the French franc in August, the revaluation of the Deutschmark in October, and later the activation of Special Drawing Rights with the International Monetary Fund.

With the improvement in Britain's external situation remaining the principal objective of policy, the various fiscal and monetary restraints on domestic demand were maintained, and the economy grew only slowly. As intended, the main element of expansion was provided by exports, which rose by 9 per cent in volume. Consumers' expenditure in real terms was only about $\frac{1}{2}$ per cent higher in 1969 than in 1968, and public expenditure fell by more than 2 per cent. Private fixed investment, however, rose by 4 per cent, and some stockbuilding occurred. The outcome was that industrial production rose only hesitantly, and the increase in gross domestic product barely exceeded 2 per cent, against over 3 per cent in 1968. The average proportion unemployed in the United Kingdom was 2·4 per cent, the same as in the previous year.

Early in 1969–70 the government gave some exacting undertakings to the International Monetary Fund in connection with an application for a standby credit for $1000 million needed for a rescheduling of overseas debt repayments. The commitments laid down in the Letter of Intent (this is reproduced in Appendix 4(b)) to the Fund included the achievement of an overall balance of payments surplus of £300 million in the financial year 1969–70, and the restriction of 'domestic credit expansion' – a new concept – to the limit of £400 million in the same period. As a result monetary conditions were unusually stringent. Interest rates at times reached exceptionally high levels and bank rate was held unchanged at 8 per cent from 27 February 1969 to 5 March 1970; and liquidity pressures on the private sector, including the banks, intensified.

Despite the emergence of a surplus on the balance of payments during the second half of 1969, the various restraints were fully maintained in order to consolidate the improvement. The reduction of bank rate early in March 1970 was justified on the grounds that it was undesirable to attract 'hot' money from abroad, and was said not to be a signal for an easing of monetary policy. However, substantial increases had been made in foreign travel allowances in January, and although the import deposits scheme was renewed in December 1969 for a further year, the rate was reduced.

The process of gentle relaxation continued in the budget, introduced on 14 April 1970; the Chancellor felt it 'right to give a moderate stimulus to the economy, but to spread this between monetary and fiscal measures'. Bank rate was reduced by a further ½ per cent to 7 per cent and a gradual rise in controlled bank lending of up to 5 per cent in the year to March 1971, was envisaged, though Special Deposits were increased. The Chancellor emphasized that he was not making any general relaxation of credit; he was sceptical of the view that company liquidity was 'excessively low', but in the interests of investment he was anxious to avoid 'an excessive stringency of restraint'. Modest fiscal reliefs were announced so as to speed the prospective rate of growth of the economy from 3 to 3½ per cent between the first halves of 1970 and 1971.

Some months before the ending of the government's statutory control of incomes at the beginning of 1970, it was becoming evident that some wage settlements were exceeding the ceiling for annual increases of 3½ per cent. Wage and salary earnings per employee in the second half of 1969 were about 8 per cent higher than in the corresponding period a year earlier. On the other hand, productivity probably rose at a slower rate in 1969. A white paper on *Productivity, Prices and Incomes Policy after 1969* (Cmnd. 4237), published in December, suggested a 'norm' of 2½–4½ per cent, but subsequent wage claims and settlements were substantially in excess of this range. This development seemed to represent a major threat to the continued success of the whole post-devaluation stategy for management of the economy, and was largely responsible for the 'cautious' budget, in which the Chancellor of the Exchequer had warned that 'incomes cannot for long continue to rise at their present rate' without endangering stability.

External recovery gathers pace

The surplus on the balance of payments which had been looked for as a result of devaluation was slower to appear than had been hoped and expected. But the development of the external situation over the year to April 1970 was highly satisfactory. As figures became available for the first and second quarters of 1969 it became evident that overall the accounts were near to balance, or at worst only slightly in deficit. In the second half of the year it became increasingly clear that a substantial surplus was being earned; indeed, surpluses were even recorded on visible trade account in all but one month from August to March. Net earnings from invisibles were at an historically high level, and for the first time since 1961, a small net inflow of long-term capital was recorded. The 'basic' surplus for 1969 was put at £387 million, as against a deficit of £398 million in 1968, and substantial inflows of short-term capital occurred towards the end of 1969 and in the early months of the following year, enabling large repayments of short-term indebtedness to overseas central banks to be made.

The value of exports rose by 12 per cent in 1969, with the volume increasing by 9 per cent and prices by 3 per cent. In addition to price advantages arising from devaluation, a major factor in export performance was the continued growth in world trade despite the slowing down of the United States economy towards the end of the year. Exports to North America were only about 3 per cent higher than in 1968, and fell sharply in the last quarter. For the EEC and EFTA areas, however, increases of 18 and 22 per cent respectively were recorded. Exports to the overseas sterling area rose by 12 per cent. Imports also rose, but by only 5 per cent, mainly as a result of price increases; and payments for US military aircraft, at £61 million, were at the lowest level since 1966.

The deficit on visible account was reduced to £158 million from £643 million in 1968, and a small surplus was seen in each of the last two quarters. Consideration of the monthly trade figures during the year was complicated following an announcement in June 1969 that exports had been under-recorded in the official statistics for several years to the extent of £10 million or more a month, and subsequently some over-recording of exports was estimated to have taken place.

Among the factors that helped to moderate the rise in imports was the continued operation of the import deposits scheme that had been introduced in November 1968. The Letter of Intent sent to the International Monetary Fund in May 1969 (see Appendix 4(b)) in connection with the application for a standby credit stated that the scheme would be withdrawn as soon as the balance of payments permitted, and the enabling powers were due to lapse in December 1969. However, in November it was decided to retain the arrangement for a further year but with the rate of deposit reduced from 50 to 40 per cent of the invoice value; a further reduction, to 30 per cent, was made at the end of April 1970. From May 1969 onwards, with repayments of deposits made six months previously roughly balancing new deposits, the net amount outstanding settled down at around £550 million; of this, it was stated in November, 30 to 40 per cent had been financed from abroad either by loans or by credits to importers from overseas suppliers. To have abandoned the scheme would thus have led to an outflow from the reserves of £30–40 million a month for six months.

Earnings from 'invisible' transactions again rose markedly in 1969, the gross figure by more than one tenth to £4054 million. The net total was £524 million, against £334 million in 1968 and only £230 million in 1967. In 1967 and 1968 the improvements had mainly reflected increases in the net export of services, but in 1969 the principal factor was a rise in net private sector receipts of interest, profits and dividends, to £801 million against £557 million in 1968. Higher interest rates, an increase in holdings of government securities by overseas residents and the resumption in 1969 of interest payments on the North American loans, all contributed to an increase of nearly £100 million in net public sector payments of interest abroad.

On official long-term capital account a deficit of £95 million was recorded, as compared with a surplus of £21 million in 1968, the swing being mainly attributable to the resumption of North American loan repayments, the payment of two instalments on the subscription to the International Development Association and a marked contraction in net borrowing from the United States Export-Import Bank under the credit for purchases of US military aircraft. On the other side, increased loan receipts came from West Germany under the offset arrangement for the stationing of UK troops there.

Receipts also included for the first time borrowings by nationalized industries and local authorities in foreign currencies from the overseas private sector, to a total of £76 million, but these were not recorded in the 'official' capital account. The Gas Council raised nearly £30 million and the Electricity Council nearly £20 million by bond issues in Germany; they were guaranteed by the Treasury against changes in exchange parities, the charge for the guarantee being included as a loading in the rate of interest. A number of local authorities promoted local acts giving them the power to borrow abroad.

Private investment transactions brought a net inflow of £116 million – the first since 1962 – against an outflow of £110 million in 1968. The most important reasons for this swing were a substantial decline in investment in Australian company securities, and the downturn in prices on the New York Stock Exchange which induced UK investors to switch from long-term to short-term external assets pending reinvestment; the acquisition of such assets would be recorded under the heading 'monetary movements' rather than 'investment'. Outward direct investment again increased in 1969, with reinvested profits accounting for over three fifths of the total. By contrast, inward direct investment was slightly lower than in 1968; take-over activity was at a lower level, and reinvested profits fell because of lower earnings and higher remittances.

The swing in the 'basic balance' (current and long-term capital transactions) from a deficit of £398 million in 1968 to a surplus of £387 million in the following year was accompanied by an even more marked shift in monetary movements. The balance on these, at £569 million, exceeded the basic surplus by £182 million, which thus appears in the accounts as a favourable 'balancing item'; in 1968 the balancing item had been negative to the extent of £145 million. The change was thought to reflect an unwinding of adverse 'leads' and 'lags' in commercial payments and other unidentified inflows of short-term funds.

The net result of the balance of payments as a whole and other flows of funds was that £740 million became available in 1969 for 'official financing transactions', of which £440 million accrued during the fourth quarter alone. Since the reserves rose during the year by £45 million, around £700 million, of short- and medium-term debt was repaid; further progress was made in the early months of 1970. Apart from resumption of payments on the North American loans, priority was given to reducing short-term liabilities outstanding with overseas central banks, repayments to the IMF being largely offset by further drawings.

During the financial year 1969–70 the United Kingdom's total of short- and medium-term overseas debt outstanding was reduced from $7466 million (£3111 million) to $3970 million (£1654 million). It was then about $4100 million (£1700 million) below the peak recorded in December 1968. Of the decline during the fifteen months to March about $300 million was accounted for by net repayments to the IMF. Assistance of the short-term swap variety fell from over $4000 million to $800 million and drawings under the swap facility of $2000 million with the Federal Reserve Bank of New York were all repaid.

Early in 1969, before the balance of payments surplus had materialized, it became clear that some rescheduling of debt repayments would be needed, in particular to meet obligations to the IMF under the 1965 drawing of $1400 million. In June the Fund approved a standby credit of $1000 million, of which one half, or £208 million, was drawn immediately and used to reduce debts with overseas monetary authorities under special arrangements. Earlier in the year £83 million had been repaid to the IMF and a further £82 million was repaid in May, but the net effect of the second quarter's transactions was a drawing of £125 million. Further instalments of £83 million each of the 1965 drawing were repaid in August and November but these were nearly matched by further drawings. In February and March 1970 the last two instalments of the 1965 credit, amounting to £140 million in all, were paid to the Fund, these repayments being partly offset by the drawing in March of £62·5 million from the Fund as the last tranche of the 1969 standby facility, and by the use of Special Drawing Rights. The amount outstanding with the Fund at April 1970 was $2400 million and the next repayment was not due until June 1971.

Substantial progress was made in repayments to the Bank for International

Settlements. The two remaining instalments of a credit arranged at the time of devaluation were paid in the second quarter of 1969, and in September £31 million was paid to the Bank as the first quarterly repayment of £250 million drawn under the 1966 Basle facility in support of fluctuations in the sterling balances. Subsequently the repayments were progressively speeded up, with that due in June 1970 having been met in the preceding February.

Repayments of aid provided by central banks appear to have been only moderate in the first quarter of 1969 but were rather larger in the second, when the drawing under the IMF standby credit was used for this purpose, even though further recourse to central bank facilities was made during the May 1969 currency crisis; during this a special recycling arrangement became operative with West Germany as a counter to speculative movements of funds across the exchanges. In the third quarter also other central banks provided assistance on balance, following the French devaluation and further speculation over a revaluation of the Deutschmark, but this was far more than offset by repayments in the fourth quarter, and these continued at an accelerating rate in the first three months of 1970.

The published figures of gold and convertible currency reserves rose over the year to March 1970 by £100 million to £1129 million, their highest level since September 1968. After falling slightly on balance over the first three quarters of 1969, they rose each month since, but by comparatively modest amounts, most of the inflow of funds being used to repay external debts. A notable addition at the beginning of January 1970 was the first allocation, of \$410 million (£171 million), of Special Drawing Rights, of which \$65 million was transferred to the Fund in February in repayment of debt.

The total of net overseas sterling liabilities fell by £604 million during 1969, but for non-sterling area countries by £860 million; this mostly represented the repayment of central bank aid. Holdings of the sterling area countries recovered by over £200 million, but failed to regain the peak levels reached in 1966. UK sterling claims on non-sterling area countries tended to increase, because of the granting of export credits.

Sterling came under pressure at times during 1969. In May an international currency crisis – not specifically related to sterling – kept the spot rate down to the 'floor' of \$2·38$\frac{1}{4}$, and a considerable amount of support was given. Pressure also developed in August, following the French devaluation, and support was again required but on that occasion the authorities allowed the spot rate to fall to \$2·38$\frac{1}{8}$; the three month discount widened to 8 per cent at an annual rate and it was reported that official support had also been given to the forward market, for the first time since devaluation.

Generally, however, sterling strengthened as the year progressed. In particular, the speculative pressures arising from uncertainties concerning the Deutschmark abated when the West German government suspended maintenance of dealing within official limits from 30 September 1969, and formally revalued by fixing a new parity on 24 October. Sterling benefited from the subsequent withdrawal of funds from West Germany and from a reversal of positions taken up earlier against the pound. Announcements of improved monthly trade and quarterly balance of payments figures also helped to restore confidence. With the rise in the spot rate, which would have been much more pronounced but for official purchases of dollars, forward margins narrowed considerably in October and November and, on some later days, the one month rate stood at a small premium. In the early months of 1970 the spot rate against the US dollar almost consistently stood above the \$2·40 parity.

After the 1969 budget the premium on investment dollars rose to the particularly high level of 60 per cent, but it thereafter began to fall sharply, and by the end of June last was fluctuating around 30 per cent, and in July below 20 per cent. This decline was probably attributable to the fall in prices on some foreign stock exchanges, particularly in New York. With sterling under pressure again in August, the premium rose to a little under 30 per cent. Around the end of the year and in the first two months of 1970 it was in the region of 38 per cent. Subsequently it eased to under 30 per cent.

In the Eurodollar market, the rapid rate of growth experienced in 1968 continued in the first half of 1969 when external liabilities and claims of UK banks in non-sterling currencies grew from £7100 million to £10,500 million. By the end of the year the totals had reached nearly £12,000 million. Some particularly high rates of interest were recorded; for example, the three-month rate reached nearly 13 per cent per annum in June 1969, after banks in the United States had raised their prime lending rates to the record level of 8½ per cent. Rates reached a peak in the summer months, and thereafter tended to fall somewhat irregularly. Various Federal Reserve measures and the general cooling off in the US economy reinforced the downward trend, and by March 1970 the three-month rate was below 9 per cent. The covered margin remained in favour of Eurodollars as against deposits with UK local authorities throughout 1969, sometimes by a substantial amount. However, the gap narrowed later, with the fall in Eurodollar rates and the reduction in the forward margin, and in some weeks early in 1970 a small margin in favour of London appeared.

Conditions in the free market for gold, which was considerably widened by the agreement in Washington in March 1968, reflected the general improvement of confidence in international monetary arrangements (for a fuller account of developments at that time refer to 'Progress in International Monetary Cooperation' in the November 1969 issue of the *Midland Bank Review*). From over \$43 a fine ounce in April 1970 the price fell to \$35 by early December and, at one time in January 1970, to \$34·75, the lowest level since the London market reopened in 1954. Several factors are thought to have caused this change in market conditions. Delay in reaching an agreement over the terms on which the IMF might buy newly mined gold from South Africa – eventually concluded in December 1969 – led to reports that the Republic was being increasingly forced to sell gold on the free market to cover the deterioration in its balance of payments position. The activation of the scheme for Special Drawing Rights also contributed, as did the cost of holding gold. Towards the end of January the free market price recovered to around $35 – the price of the metal for official monetary purposes.

Members of the London bullion market agreed in November 1969, after discussions with the Bank of England, to reduce the amount of silver financed in sterling to a level equivalent to that at the end of 1968; at the same time UK banks and financial institutions were asked 'to conduct their silver operations in a manner to support the arrangement. . . .' Stocks of silver held by UK dealers at home and overseas, and financed in sterling, had risen sharply and it was thought that the new requirement would result in a fairly substantial addition to the official reserves.

Money and credit under continuing restraint

Fiscal and monetary restraints imposed during the previous year were fully maintained in 1969–70, and a new concept for the basis of policy – domestic credit expansion – was introduced. Otherwise, until bank rate was reduced in March 1970, and new arrangements for controlling the growth of bank lending were announced in the following month, changes in the monetary scene were few, and then mainly of emphasis.

Early in 1969 attention was increasingly being directed to the rate at which the money supply was rising, and the Letter of Intent sent to the International Monetary Fund in May gave an undertaking to limit 'domestic credit expansion'. DCE was officially defined as the sum of the public sector borrowing requirement plus bank lending to the private sector less sales of public sector debt to the non-bank private sector. Another definition, arriving at the same result, was to add bank lending – both to the public and private sectors – to any increase in non-bank holdings of notes and coin, and borrowing overseas by the public sector. In effect, then, DCE was the total arrived at after adjusting the increase in money supply by any changes directly arising from an external surplus or deficit. (For further discussion of DCE, and money supply generally, see Chapter 4.)

The undertaking was to limit the growth of DCE to £400 million in 1969–70, against an increase of £1175 million in 1968–9; the course of DCE, and the government's borrowing requirement within it, were to be examined quarterly to see that they were consistent with the intended outcome for the year, and the government undertook to take appropriate action.

The commitment was met with little difficulty, among other reasons because the Exchequer's borrowing requirement was negative and substantial sales of public sector debt to the non-bank sector were made. In the first nine months of the financial year DCE rose by £422 million, but after allowing for seasonal factors was estimated to have contracted by nearly £170 million. The money supply rose by nearly £800 million – or only about £250 million after seasonal adjustment – in the same period; nearly three quarters of this rise came in the last three months of 1969 because of the large inflow of funds from abroad, the effects of which were offset in arriving at the total for DCE. In 1968–9 the money supply increased by £914 million.

The banks continued to be under severe official pressure to restrain their lending to the private sector, one of the components of domestic credit expansion, and the official ceilings imposed on the different groups of financial institutions remained in force unchanged throughout the financial year. Generally, however, the clearing banks were unable to bring the total of their lending subject to control down to 98 per cent of the mid-November 1967 level, the ceiling requirement. Following an increase in advances in May 1969 to a level about 2¾ per cent above the ceiling, the rate of interest paid by the Bank of England on Special Deposits was halved. The clearing banks complained that this 'fine' was 'irrelevant' and would have 'no effect whatsoever on the level of advances' as they were 'already carrying out the government's instructions to the best of our ability'; however, the penalty remained in operation until 15 April 1970.

Following another increase in advances in August 1969, bringing the total to some 4½ per cent above the ceiling, the need to effect a reduction in advances was again stressed, but the communiqué issued after a meeting between the Chancellor of the Exchequer and the bank chairmen made no reference to the ceiling and subsequently, although advances remained above it, the banks were commended for their restraint. The October level of about 4 per cent above the ceiling came to be regarded as the appropriate criterion, though not publicly designated as such. In the event, controlled lending fell in relation to the ceiling in both November and December, but thereafter rose again under the influence of strong seasonal pressures, and in March 1970 was 5½–6 per cent above the '98 per cent' ceiling.

This benchmark was superseded by new arrangements for controlling bank lending announced in the budget speech in April 1970. The existing ceiling was then removed, subject to 'the continuance of close consultation' between these banks and the authorities. It was indicated, however, that sterling lending by both clearing and Scottish banks to the domestic private sector and to overseas borrowers, but excluding fixed-rate lending under special schemes for exports and shipbuilding finance, should not rise in the aggregate by more than about 5 per cent over the year from mid-March 1970. Moreover, the special deposit mechanism was to be used more flexibly in future so as 'to exert a continuing influence over the liquidity and lending capacity of the banks'. In view of the liquidity position at that time, Special Deposits were increased, from 2 to $2\frac{1}{2}$ per cent for the clearing banks and from 1 to $1\frac{1}{4}$ per cent for the Scottish, the increase to be paid to the Bank of England by 6 May.

Institutions coming under the heading 'other banks', i.e. the merchant, overseas and other banks, whose ceiling had previously been 102 per cent of the level immediately before devaluation, were now asked to ensure that individually their controlled lending did not rise by more than 7 per cent over the year to mid-March 1971. It was indicated that failure to follow the official 'guidance' would result in a call for 'cash deposits' under the arrangements worked out in 1967 but not brought into operation. Members of the Finance Houses Association and some other non-member houses were asked to ensure that, over the twelve months commencing 31 March 1970, their lending did not rise by more than 5 per cent.

For all banks and finance houses, the permitted increase in lending was to be directed to finance of exports not covered by the fixed-rate schemes, and of production and investment both in manufacturing industry and agriculture which would help the balance of payments by increased exports, higher invisible earnings or savings in imports. Finance, whether direct of indirect for personal consumption should not increase, and severe restraint should still be applied to finance for imports and import deposits. Banks were also asked not to allow their sterling acceptances outstanding to rise faster than the rates specified for their sterling lending.

Analysis of the banking figures over the year was complicated by the decision of the clearing and Scottish banks to disclose figures of 'true' profits and 'hidden' reserves, beginning with the annual accounts for 1969, and other accounting changes. The banks announced in September 1969 that they had agreed to waive the exemption granted to them under company legislation in the preparation of their accounts, and an order was subsequently made under the Companies Acts withdrawing the exemption. Substantial revisions to accounting procedures followed from this decision and for January and February 1970 only abbreviated composite figures were published. Publication of detailed monthly statements was resumed in respect of March, on the new basis.

Broadly, the effects of disclosure by the clearing banks were to transfer approximately £500 million from gross deposits to published reserves; and to reduce deposits further by about £350 million, and advances by about £35 million, following the adoption of a uniform accounting treatment for cheques in course of collection and items in transit.

The impact of official policies, including that relating to the growth of the money supply and domestic credit expansion, became increasingly marked in the banking figures for 1969. After the slowing down in the rate of growth of net deposits in 1968, a decline of £97 million was recorded in 1969, notwithstanding an increase of £107 million in the fourth quarter attributable to the inflow of overseas funds.

Net advances to the private sector continued to grow, although at only slightly over half the rate of each of the two preceding years. Here again the movement was irregular, as the banks strove with fluctuating success to bring their controlled lending down to the ceiling; the bulk of the increase in advances consisted of fixed-rate lending for exports and shipbuilding, which was outside the control. The average ratio of gross advances to gross deposits in 1969 was 51·5 per cent, slightly higher than in 1968; the proportion for March 1970 was exceptionally high at 59·3 per cent, mainly because of the reduction in the deposits figure.

Special Deposits were maintained at 2 per cent of gross deposits throughout the year, and at times it appeared likely that liquidity pressures would become exceptionally severe. By August 1969 the combined liquidity ratio of the clearing banks had fallen to 28·4 per cent, an unusually low level for that time of the year. Treasury bill holdings, at only £124·5 million, reached their nadir for the post-war period, though they subsequently fell to £77 million in March 1970.

The liquidity position eased later in 1969, and in mid-December the ratio was 32·1 per cent, reflecting the inflow of funds from abroad. Thereafter, the usual seasonal contraction was partly offset by the effects of 'disclosure' and other accounting changes, which probably added about 2 percentage points, and the March figure, of 29·7 per cent, was slightly higher than a year before. In the early part of 1969 especially, pressures on their liquidity made it necessary for the banks to realize investments on a substantial scale. During the year, they fell by £327 million, the first net contraction since 1964, and in December 1969 investments amounted to only 10·3 per cent of gross deposits, as against 13·3 per cent a year before.

Although deposits of the clearing banks declined in 1969, for the banking sector as a whole, they again rose substantially. The net movement was more than accounted for by another marked rise, by the equivalent of £7195 million to £16,539 million, in the foreign currency deposits of the accepting houses, overseas and other banks; sterling deposits of these banks also rose, by £862 million to £5109 million. The new market in sterling certificates of deposit became well established, the total outstanding in December 1969 of £443 million comparing with £165 million a year earlier – a more rapid growth than that of the market for dollar CDs at a comparable stage.

The value of cheques and other debit items passing through the town and general clearings combined continued to increase, by 16·6 per cent during 1969, well over twice the rate of 1968, but below that of 1967. For the general clearing alone, the value of items rose by 10·5 per cent against 14·9 per cent in 1968. Credit clearings were 17·2 per cent higher in 1969 against 14·3 per cent in 1968. Progress of the National Giro since it opened in October 1968 had been slow, although deposits began to increase more rapidly in the last quarter of 1969. Even so, by end-December they amounted to only £36 million, and of this three quarters was held on accounts of the government and public corporations. The minimum deposit needed to open a National Giro account was lowered from £5 to £1. From 1 May 1970 customers of the National Giro were offered access to personal loan facilities with Mercantile Credit. The trustee savings banks began to participate in the direct debiting service at the beginning of 1970.

Movements in advances by the banking sector according to type of borrower in general reflected the operation of the quantitative and qualitative controls. Advances to manufacturing industry rose throughout the year to February 1970, the major part of the increase going to engineering, shipbuilding and vehicles. Advances for 'other production' fell and those to services rose on balance, but the changes were small. In line with official requirements, personal advances suffered a fairly sharp contraction, which would have been even more marked if bridging finance for house purchase had not been included in the list of priority categories. Advances to overseas residents again rose sharply, and accounted for the bulk of the rise in the total; even so, they increased at a slower rate than in the previous year.

The clearing and Scottish banks raised their lending rates – other than the concessionary rates for some exports and shipbuilding – by $\frac{1}{2}$ per cent on 1 October 1969, and banks in Northern Ireland at the beginning of January. The unusual feature of this increase was that it was not associated with a change in bank rate, nor was the deposit rate raised, so that in relation to both the margin was widened. For some time bank lending had been becoming increasingly cheap in relation to other sources of finance so that pressure on bank facilities was intensifying; indeed, some customers had been borrowing from the banks under previously agreed arrangements and placing the money in the complementary markets where, at times, higher rates could be obtained.

The special schemes for medium- and long-term finance for exports and shipbuilding continued to operate, with the fixed rate of interest remaining unchanged at $5\frac{1}{2}$ per cent. In order that this type of finance should not take up a disproportionate amount of the assets of any of the banks, the Bank of England in May 1969 extended its refinancing facilities. Broadly, when the amount of the 'advances' component of such lending came to exceed 5 per cent of the gross deposits of a bank, the excess could be rediscounted with the Bank of England, and by March 1970 the amount refinanced in this way amounted to nearly £40 million.

Further progress was made with previously-agreed mergers of clearing banks. Barclays Bank formally absorbed the business of Martins Bank; and District, National Provincial and Westminster Banks, as formally merged into National Westminster, ceased to operate under their former styles. In

Scottish banking, the Bank of Scotland and British Linen Bank agreed upon a merger, so reducing the number of Scottish banks to three; Barclays Bank, which owned nearly all the share capital of British Linen Bank, took a 35 per cent interest in the new bank. A new subsidiary of National and Commercial Banking Group – Williams & Glyn's Bank – was formed with a view to incorporating the businesses of Glyn, Mills, National Bank and Williams Deacon's Bank. In January 1970, two UK overseas banks, the Standard and Chartered Banks, merged to form a new group.

During the year 1969–70 some bank branches were closed, mostly as a direct consequence of the mergers, and more closures were foreshadowed. The clearing banks introduced new hours of opening on 1 July 1969. Branches ceased to open on Saturdays, but the hours of opening during the week were extended and, for an experimental period of one year, full branches were opened on one selected evening a week from 4.30 to 6 p.m. Members of the Accepting Houses Committee and the British overseas and foreign banks in London also began to close on Saturdays. Bills of exchange falling due on a Saturday were treated as being payable on the next succeeding business day.

Banks issuing their own cheque guarantee cards began to replace them with a new joint, standardized form of card from 1 July 1969. Changes in the coinage in preparation for decimalization in February 1971 brought extra work for the banks. The halfpenny ceased to be legal tender on 1 August 1969 and the half crown on 1 January 1970. A new 50p coin was introduced in October 1969 to replace the 10*s*. note, which was gradually withdrawn from circulation.

The discount market met with some difficulties. Bank rate was maintained at 8 per cent from 27 February 1969 until 5 March 1970 when it was lowered to $7\frac{1}{2}$ per cent; a further reduction, to 7 per cent, was made on 15 April. In general, short-term rates tended to rise until the summer of 1969, and thereafter to ease somewhat. The Treasury bill discount rate, though it is more effectively stabilised by official action than other short market rates, reflected this trend. At times the margin below bank rate was extremely narrow, being less than $\frac{1}{4}$ per cent for most of 1969 and for a time in June less than 0·1 per cent; the Treasury bill rate was then at its highest level for at least 70 years. At these and some other tenders the syndicate received a substantial volume of the bills on offer but at some other times the proportion was extremely low, and on occasion during 1970 it received no allocation of ninety-one-day bills at all.

The overall impact of government finance was a reduction of the amount of outstanding Treasury bills issued by tender by £150 million to £1200 million during the year to 31 March 1970, this following a reduction of £700 million in 1968–9. The amount of bills on offer at the weekly tenders fell to as little as £80 million a week in the second half of February and most of March, the lowest since the war.

The emphasis in official policy towards the market again appears to have been on flexibility so as to ease to some degree the difficult conditions arising from fiscal pressure. Thus the authorities on many occasions lent at market rates or made purchases of commercial and local authority bills as well as Treasury bills. A severe shortage of funds late in July, following a good response to a government stock issue, was relieved by lending at market rates for the unusually long period of eighteen days because insufficient bills of the appropriate maturity were available for purchase by the Bank of England; the purpose was to bridge the period until two government stocks matured in August. Easier conditions tended to prevail towards the end of 1969, but the tax-gathering season produced some extremely tight conditions, particularly in early March. Extensive official support was forthcoming, but on more than one occasion the authorities charged bank rate for lending for a period of seven days, for the first time since October 1967; this was intended to encourage the discount houses to make changes in the disposition of their assets, which was considered to be somewhat long in view of the reduced holdings of Treasury bills.

Despite these strains, the discount houses managed to expand their total assets by more than £150 million to over £1800 million during 1969, following a contraction of over £80 million in 1968. Although their Treasury bill holdings fell, they increased their holdings of other sterling bills (including commercial and local authority bills), government and local authority stocks, sterling certificates of deposit and other assets.

Some especially high rates of interest were recorded in the other short-term money markets – the 'complementary' markets described in Chapter 7 – to which international influences operating through the Eurodollar rate notably contributed. Reflecting its role as intermediary between the various markets, rates in the inter-bank market were particularly volatile. Occasionally 25 per cent or more was commanded for overnight money but rates as low as 1 or 2 per cent were also recorded. On most days, however, rates between 7 and 9 per cent were more common.

In the local authority market, short-term rates moved up by about 1 per cent to around $9\frac{1}{2}$ per cent in May 1969 and remained in this region during much of the summer and autumn. However, both the seven-day and three-month rates eased in November, with the former falling as low as 8 per cent in some days in December with the longer rate at around 9 per cent. Both rates fluctuated sharply at the end of December and early in 1970, and about the beginning of March the seven-day rate rose to unprecedented levels, at times of 15 per cent or more. Subsequently both rates settled down at around 9 per cent. The three-month rate for deposits with finance houses moved broadly around 10 per cent from May to November 1969, but subsequently fluctuated around $9–9\frac{1}{2}$ per cent.

The margin between complementary market rates and the Treasury bill rate, which had increased in 1968–9, widened still further during the following year, and tended to fluctuate substantially. This brought further strain on those institutions in the complementary markets which customarily related their lending rates to bank rate, and some breaks with this practice occurred. For instance, some of the United States banks in London adopted a base rate – not necessarily bank rate but related to their borrowing costs – in arriving at rates to be charged on loans. Again, the annual report of the Finance Houses Association for the year to March 1970 noted that: 'The customary link between bank rate and money market rates has been much weaker over recent months and the cost of money reached much higher levels than would be customary with bank rate at 8 per cent. Bank rate can therefore no longer be taken as a guide to the level of charges which finance houses make for the use of their facilities.'

Prices of stock exchange securities – both equity and gilt-edged – were depressed over much of the year to April 1970 and despite the squeeze on liquid assets new issue activity was restrained. In the gilt-edged market prices fell sharply during the first half of 1969 with the authorities apparently less willing to intervene than previously in the interests of greater control over the money supply. By the end of May most government securities were showing gross redemption yields of over 9 per cent, and the *Financial Times* Index of Government Securities (15 October 1926=100) fell to the all-time low of 64·21 on 11 June 1969. A prolonged recovery followed bringing most yields down to 8½–8¾ for medium and long-dated government stocks and even lower for 'shorts' by the middle of April 1970 to bring the *Financial Times* index nearly 12 per cent above its lowest level. The rise in prices generally persisted despite large funding sales by the authorities.

Prices of equities likewise suffered a sharp setback in the first half of 1969, the *Financial Times* Industrial Ordinary Share Index (1 July 1935=100) falling to 357·4 on 28 July 1969, the lowest level for about two years and more than 30 per cent below the all-time high of 521·9 recorded in September 1968. Uneven recovery brought the index to over 420 for a short period in January 1970, but it later fell and remained below 400. Lower profits earned by some companies and the operation, until the end of 1969, of the officially imposed 3½ per cent ceiling on dividend increases had a moderating influence. In early April the 'yield' on the *Financial Times*-Actuaries 500 share index was around 4¼ per cent, about ¾ per cent higher than a year before. For most of 1969 the amount by which this yield exceeded by that on 2½ per cent Consols – the reverse yield gap – was in the region of 5 per cent although it narrowed slightly in the early months of 1970. Yields on company loan stocks generally followed the trend of gilt-edged; they rose to nearly 11 per cent at the peak in the summer of 1969, but by early April 1970 had fallen to around 10 per cent.

The total of new money raised by issues of marketable securities during

1969 amounted to £733 million – the fourth highest figure on record – although £131 million below the peak level of the previous year. Issues by the public sector, at £141 million, were the lowest since 1964; company issues at £592 million were only slightly lower than in 1968, even though the level of activity fell sharply in the second half of the year. Because of the difficult conditions in the equity market and the high yields which prevailed for fixed-interest securities, many companies resorted to the issue of convertible loan stock.

After an absence of nearly seven months, local authorities returned to the new issue market in May 1969 despite the high level of interest rates. In all, ten stock issues were made in 1969; all had coupons of between 9¼ and 9¾ per cent and all except one were priced below par. Local authorities similarly had to fix high coupons to their bond issues, of 10⅜ per cent in September and early October, although by early in 1970 they had fallen below 9 per cent. On balance during 1969 local authorities increased their borrowing from the banking sector, and especially from the accepting houses, overseas and 'other banks'. Borrowing from the central government also rose. Rates charged on new borrowing from the Public Works Loan Board were changed frequently but remained generally in excess of 9 per cent on quota borrowing, although falling after the turn of the year to around 8½–9 per cent.

Some recovery occurred in 1969 in investment in building societies, the net increase of £920 million comparing with £767 million in 1968. By contrast net lending on mortgages fell by £97 million to £763 million, the lowest total since 1966, and as a result aggregate liquidity increased slightly. Outstanding lending commitments at the end of 1969 were a little higher than a year before. Despite a high level of investment in the early months of 1969, for the whole year sales of unit trusts' units, at £263 million, were about £65 million less than in 1968, but repurchases of units rose. With the decline in share values total funds of the unit trusts amounted to only £1460 million in February 1970 against the record level of £1590 million for January 1969.

The Exchequer surplus recorded in 1968–9, the first since 1950–1, was succeeded by a much larger one in 1969–70. Total revenue rose by £1903 million, while total expenditure rose by £1207 million to provide a Consolidated Fund surplus of £2444 million, against £1748 million in 1968–9. With net lending by the central government, at £1439 million, only slightly higher than in the previous year and well below the budget estimate, a net repayment of debt of £961 million was made, as compared with £287 million in 1968–9; in 1967–8 there was a net borrowing requirement of £1312 million.

The first of a new annual series of white papers on public expenditure was published in December (Cmnd. 4234); covering 1969–70 and the four following years. It was estimated that such expenditure in real terms would rise by about 3½ per cent in 1970–1 and by 3¼ per cent in 1971–2; both movements were thought to be compatible with the objective that the rate of growth of public sector outlays should be consistent with the increase in total domestic resources. In August 1969 the government raised from 8 to 10 per cent the 'test discount rate' used for appraising new investment in the public sector. Further progress was made during the year in the application of cost benefit analysis when considering public sector investment projects.

With a surplus of £961 million on government transactions in the financial year to March 1970, the total national debt outstanding fell to around £33,000 million. The floating debt contracted by nearly £1100 million to £4989 million. Tender Treasury bills provided £150 million of the reduction but the bulk of it was in tap bills, associated with the unwinding of positions under swap arrangements.

Achievement of the official commitment to restrain 'domestic credit expansion' was greatly assisted by the volume of funding sales of government securities to the public other than the banks. In the six months to September 1969, holdings of the banking sector fell by £250 million but other holders took up £150 million of debt. Domestic borrowing was particularly heavy in the fourth quarter of 1969, partly to finance the Exchequer's seasonal deficit and partly because of the inflow of funds from abroad; of the £900 million needed about £350 million came from the non-bank sector and about £550 million from the banks. For 1969 as a whole, despite heavy official purchases in the first quarter, the authorities sold a total of £183 million of gilts after repaying maturing issues aggregating £1131 million; net purchases of £506 million were made in 1968.

Several new issues of gilt-edged securities were made during the financial year 1969–70, whereas none were recorded in the previous year, and some of them attracted a high level of applications from the public. The first issue was £400 million of 9 per cent Treasury Loan, 1994 in July at £96½ per cent, the coupon being the highest ever recorded for a British government security. By October 'tap' supplies of these 'Treasury Nines' were virtually exhausted, and £400 million of 8¾ per cent Treasury Loan 1997 was issued at £95 per cent as the new long tap stock. Two issues with shorter maturity dates were made in January 1970: £200 million of 6¾ per cent Exchequer Loan 1971, issued at £96 6*s*. 3*d*. per cent to replenish official holdings of short-dated stocks; and £600 million of 8½ per cent Treasury Loan 1980–2, at £96 5*s*. per cent, as a medium-dated tap stock. In addition, holders of 3 per cent Savings Bonds 1960–70, which was to mature in September 1970, were offered conversion into the latter stock. Over £1000 million of the 3 per cents was then outstanding but the conversion offer was accepted by holders of only about £260 million. Three issues fell due in August 1969 – 6½ per cent Exchequer Loan 1969, 4½ per cent British Electricity guaranteed stock 1967–9, and a small amount of the similar issue of the South of Scotland Electricity Board – amounting in aggregate to £626 million. All were paid off in cash, as was

£500 million of 6 per cent Exchequer Loan 1970 which matured in March 1970.

With a view to giving the government broker greater flexibility in operations in the gilt-edged market, some changes were made during the year. It was announced in July 1969 that official prices would no longer be quoted for tap stock issues, but that offers from jobbers would be considered. Earlier in the year it was decided that official market operations in gilt-edged securities with less than ninety-one days to maturity would no longer be tied to Treasury bill rate.

The demand from the private sector for gilt-edged securities, the high yields available on other outlets for funds and the effects of the credit squeeze generally, help to explain the poor performance of 'national savings' in the financial year 1969–70, when repayments exceeded receipts by £126 million. Despite the raising in April 1969 of the limit on holdings of the twelfth issue of national savings certificates, sales fell short of total redemptions by £92 million. Similarly encashments of defence bonds, national development bonds and British savings bonds greatly exceeded sales of the latter, even though the rate of interest was raised from 6 to 7 per cent. Premium bonds remained relatively popular, although net sales fell to £48 million from £81 million in 1968–9.

The 'Save as you earn' contractual savings scheme came into operation on 1 October 1969. Under this regular savings of from £1 up to £10 a month are rewarded at the end of five years with a terminal bonus, free of all tax, of £12 for every £60 saved; the tax-free payment is raised to £24 if the savings are left for a further two years, without further subscription. Savings under the SAYE scheme, operated by the Department for National Savings and the trustee savings banks, amounted to only £5·7 million by end-March 1970, but around a quarter of a million contracts had been registered involving a total savings commitment of over £100 million in the next five years. Although the maximum monthly amount that may be saved under the scheme is £10, up to £10 more may be placed with one of the many building societies which have, with official approval, introduced SAYE plans of their own.

The Post Office changed its status from that of a government department to a public corporation on 1 October 1969; the Post Office Savings Bank was then renamed National Savings Bank and the Post Office Register of Government Stock became the National Savings Stock Register. At the same time the maximum daily limit on dealings in stocks on the Register was increased, and commission charges raised slightly. The rate of interest payable on investment accounts with the National Savings Bank was raised from 6½ to 7 per cent, also on 1 October, and the limit on withdrawals on demand from the Bank's ordinary accounts was increased by £10 to £20 at the beginning of 1969. The Chancellor of the Exchequer announced in the budget in April 1970 that the government was proposing to take powers to be able to vary, by order, the rates of interest payable on deposits in the ordinary accounts of the National Savings Bank, in the ordinary departments of the trustee savings banks and in the No. 2 Department of the Birmingham Municipal Bank. However, it was not possible to change existing rates until interest came to be credited for the year 1971.

The withdrawal of funds from NSB ordinary accounts continued in 1969–70 with repayments exceeding receipts by £125 million, or £5 million more than in the previous year; by contrast net receipts were recorded on investment accounts, but at £37 million these were £22 million less than in 1968–9. For the fourth successive year net withdrawals took place from ordinary departments of trustee savings banks, repayments exceeding receipts by £36 million, against £19 million in 1968–9. Despite increases in many of the rates offered there was an outflow of funds from the special investment departments, amounting to £28 million against an inflow of £22 million in the previous year.

1971 – A Sound External Situation

The distinguishing feature of the year, to April 1971, in marked contrast to those that preceded it, was that the external situation ceased to be the dominant consideration in the application of domestic policies. The strong balance of payments situation that had been achieved in 1969, as the devaluation of November 1967 and subsequent measures began to take effect, was well maintained. Indeed, the total inward currency flow – in the new balance of payments presentation – was little short of £1300 million in 1970 against around £750 million in 1969. Most of this improvement was due to investment and other capital movements; nevertheless, the surplus on the current account of the balance of payments also increased by some £200 million, though mainly, it must be said, because of a marked movement in the terms of trade in the United Kingdom's favour.

The substantial currency inflows, which were especially pronounced late in 1970 and continued into 1971, were not entirely welcome. They were the counterpart of massive outflows of short-term funds from the United States, attracted by higher levels of interest rates in the United Kingdom and elsewhere, and following successive reductions in other centres bank rate was eventually lowered by a full point on 1 April 1971, having been held at 7 per cent for over a year. A particularly welcome outcome of the balance of payments situation was the repayment, by end-March 1971, of all outstanding short-term and medium-term debt which had previously been incurred in support of sterling, except for £683 million owing to the International Monetary Fund.

The main causes of disquiet during the year were to be found not in external developments but in the slow growth of the domestic economy on the one hand, and the accelerating rate of wage and price inflation on the other, an unusual and unhappy conjunction. In real terms, output rose by less than 2 per cent in 1970, that is even more slowly than in 1969, but by contrast with the previous year the main expansionary impetus came from consumer's expenditure rather than exports and investment. With output growing at a slower rate than productive potential, unemployment rose steadily throughout the year and in March 1971 amounted to 3·3 per cent of the labour force, as compared with 2·7 per cent twelve months previously.

The reason why, in these conditions, more expansionary policies were not pursued is to be found in the disturbing and accelerating rate of increase in prices and incomes, at a pace without parallel for many years. By March 1971 the index of basic wage rates was 12 per cent higher than a year before, retail prices 9 per cent, and wholesale prices 2 per cent. No specific arrangements designed to control increases in prices and incomes were introduced when statutory restraints lapsed at the end of 1969; indeed, the new government which took office in mid-1970 set its face against the reintroduction of an incomes policy as such, though it exerted pressure on employers in both the public and private sectors to resist blatantly inflationary pay claims.

With costs rising faster than prices, company profits and liquidity remained under considerable pressure. Gross trading profits, before providing for depreciation and stock appreciation, rose by only 1·6 per cent between 1969 and 1970, as compared with increases of 11·8 per cent in wages and salaries and 9·6 per cent for gross domestic product. The rate of business failures increased, and some large companies were involved. In the personal sector incomes rose faster than consumption and prices, and savings expanded.

With containment and then reduction of cost inflation taking first priority in official policy, the few measures of relaxation were modest and mainly directed towards an easing of the pressures on company liquidity, in order to sustain the level of investment. The official lending guidelines were relaxed in March 1970 to permit an increase for the clearing banks over the next twelve months of about 5 per cent; the actual increase was somewhat smaller. However, further calls for Special Deposits were made on them, in April 1970 and again in October. During the year the import deposits scheme was phased out and came to an end in December, though repayment of sums deposited before then remained subject to the six months' delay. In October it was announced that the level of income tax and corporation tax would be reduced for the financial year 1971–2.

The budget in April 1971 was designed to raise the rate of growth of the economy to about 3 per cent, that is the assumed rate of growth of productive potential, though this figure was not expected to be achieved until the first half of 1972. The fiscal changes, again, were to a considerable degree directed to improving the liquidity of the corporate sector, and in indicating that a slightly faster rate of growth of bank lending would be permitted the Chancellor expressed the hope that additional credit would be channelled mainly to companies. So the year 1970–1 ended with the prospect of a somewhat faster rate of growth developing. But in important respects the outlook remained uncertain if not disquieting, notably as regards movements in costs and prices, and the levels of unemployment and investment.

External recovery – another good year

The external situation, following the big improvement in 1969, remained satisfactory in 1970. A surplus was earned on current account, in every quarter, with visible trade itself making a positive contribution in both the first and fourth quarters. Net earnings from invisibles, at £628 million, exceeded the high level recorded in 1969, whilst investment and other capital movements produced an exceptional net inflow of nearly £500 million, contrasting with a small net outflow in 1969. The combined surplus from the current account and investment and other capital flows was put at £1287 million, as compared with a surplus of £743 million in 1969, enabling large repayments of short-term debt to be made to the International Monetary Fund and overseas central banks, and these continued in the first quarter of 1971.

A surplus of £3 million on visible trade in 1970 – the first since 1958 – followed a deficit of £141 million in 1969. Among the factors that helped to produce this exceptional surplus was an improvement in the terms of trade; these averaged 104 for 1970, compared with 101 in 1969 (1961 = 100) and by the end of the year the index had risen to 107. Another factor may have been the import deposits requirement which continued until 4 December, though the rate of deposit was progressively reduced during the year.

The value of exports rose by 12 per cent in 1970, with volume increasing by less than 4 per cent and prices by 8 per cent. With slack conditions in the United States, exports to North America were virtually unchanged, but for the EEC and EFTA areas increases of 15 and 18 per cent respectively were recorded. Exports to the overseas sterling area rose by 9 per cent. Imports rose by 6 per cent in volume, that is nearly twice as fast as exports, and by 9 per cent in value. Analysis of the figures as the year progressed was complicated first by adjustments made for under-recording of exports, and then by the dock strike in June, which considerably distorted the monthly figures in the second half of the year.

Net earnings from 'invisible' transactions amounted to £628 million in 1970, against £578 million in 1969 and £337 million in 1968. The improvement in 1969 was mainly due to an increase of some £230 million in net private sector receipts of interest, profits and dividends but in 1970 it was the outcome of various movements. Against the deterioration of about £60 million in the shipping account and an increase of £15 million in government expenditure overseas, receipts from banking and other financial services rose by some £50 million and net payments of interest by the public sector fell by about £70 million, largely because of reductions in outstanding debts and in the level of interest rates.

The presentation of capital and monetary movements in the balance of payments accounts was substantially altered in 1970, all of them being grouped under a new heading 'investment and other capital flows' (see Appendix 2, Table 1a). These, together with the current balance – presentation of which was not altered – and the 'balancing item', provided a total of currency flows to be financed by changes in the reserves and official debt transactions.

The principal factor in the substantial improvement in the capital account in 1970 was a massive shift in the direction of net short-term movements. Eurodollar borrowing in London for investment overseas (£166 million), other currency transactions of United Kingdom banks (£313 million), increases in the gross sterling balances of overseas countries (£486 million) and other short-term capital movements (£119 million) together produced a net inflow of £1084 million, compared with an inflow of £154 million in 1969. Against this, export credit exceeded import credit by £292 million, some £132 million more than in 1969. The net long-term capital outflow amounted to £293 million, against £9 million in the previous year.

On official long-term capital account net outgoings of £205 million were recorded, as compared with £98 million in 1969. The increase was mainly attributable to the absence of West German offset loans, which amounted to £52 million in 1969, and more net borrowing from the United States Export-Import Bank to finance the purchase of US military aircraft. Net aid lending increased from £60 million to £85 million. Overseas borrowing by public corporations and local authorities was negligible in 1970, compared with £76 million in 1969.

Private long-term investment transactions resulted in a net outflow of £70 million, against a net inflow of £26 million in 1969. Outward direct investment was £47 million lower than in 1969, but that of oil companies rose substantially and portfolio investment overseas also increased. Inward direct investment was little changed though reinvested profits and investment on inter-company account increased. With depressed conditions on the London Stock Exchange, the high level of overseas portfolio investment in UK company securities achieved in 1969 was not maintained in 1970; net investment of £82 million mainly reflected an exceptional inward transaction in the third quarter (offset in UK direct investment overseas), heavier borrowing by UK companies from banks outside the United Kingdom, and new issues in foreign currency by UK companies.

With a total 'currency inflow' of £1287 million and a current account surplus of £631 million, and after taking into account £38 million of increased gold subscriptions to the IMF and the receipt of £171 million as the first allocation of Special Drawing Rights in the Fund, £1420 million became available in 1970 for 'official financing transactions'. The bulk of this was applied to debt repayment; the reserves rose by only £125 million and short- and medium-term official debt was reduced by £1295 million. Part of the reduction in UK indebtedness to the IMF was due to purchases of sterling from the Fund by other countries.

Further progress in repayment of short- and medium-term debt incurred to support sterling was made in the first quarter of 1971, the total outstanding being reduced from £1654 million to £683 million over the year to the end of March 1971. All debt other than that owing to the IMF was paid off, in particular the balance of the large sums borrowed from overseas central banks at various times in the late 1960s. In the third quarter of 1970 Britain made a drawing of $400 million (£167 million) under the swap facility of $2000 million with the Federal Reserve Bank of New York, but this was repaid in the following three months.

In his budget speech in March 1971 the Chancellor of the Exchequer announced that, although the United Kingdom was not obliged to begin making repayments of debt outstanding to the IMF until June, arrangements had been made for an earlier start. The £551 million outstanding in respect of the 1968 drawing had been due to be paid off in eight quarterly instalments beginning in March, but the first four such payments, totalling £285 million, were then made. This brought the level of IMF debt still outstanding to £683 million, comprising the balance of £266 million of the 1968 drawing and £417 million drawn under the 1969 standby facility, on which repayments become due from June 1972.

The fifth and sixth quarterly instalments of £31 million each due to the Bank for International Settlements, on the loan made to finance fluctuations in the sterling balances under the Basle arrangements of June 1966, were paid in advance of their due date in 1970. The last two instalments, amounting to £62 million, were paid off in January 1971, and £16 million still outstanding on a line of credit established with the United States at the same time as the Basle arrangements was cleared in 1971. The balance of short-term debts due to overseas central banks, which at the end of 1968 exceeded £2000 million, was repaid by the end of February 1971.

The published total of gold and convertible currency reserves rose over the year to March 1971 by £253 million to £1382 million, the highest figure ever recorded in terms of sterling, though it was written up by one sixth as a result of devaluation in November 1967 and includes some exceptional receipts such as allocations of Special Drawing Rights in the IMF. At the beginning of January 1971 the reserves were reinforced by the second allocation of SDRs amounting to $300 million (£125 million). During 1970 the total of net short-term overseas sterling liabilities – comprising external banking and money market liabilities in sterling – increased by £362 million, of which £82 million was attributable to non-sterling area countries. Holdings of sterling area countries rose by £279 million to £2053 million; the overseas sterling area had a favourable basic balance of £200 million in its transactions with the rest of the world in the first nine months of 1970.

Sterling was on a declining trend from April to September 1970, the market being affected by the pronounced rise in prices and wages, disappointing trade figures and the dock strike in July. In that month the spot rate fell below \$2·39. Further pressures developed in August, partly as a result of industrial disputes, which had a generally unsettling effect throughout the year, and again in September on suggestions that changes in official exchange rate policy might be agreed at the annual meeting of the IMF. Heavy selling of sterling at one time took the spot rate down to \$2·38$\frac{1}{8}$, and official support became necessary. Subsequently a shortage of sterling and favourable trade figures brought about a sharp recovery to \$2·38$\frac{1}{2}$. Another factor in the recovery was the firm statement by the Chancellor at the annual IMF meeting to the effect that Britain fully supported the system of fixed exchange rates.

For the rest of 1970 and up to the end of the period in 1971 covered by this chapter sterling was on a generally rising trend in spite of continuing concern regarding inflationary pressures and industrial disputes, partly because of the satisfactory balance of payments situation and partly because of the high level of domestic interest rates against a background of falling rates overseas. The spot rate moved above \$2·40 in January and from the beginning of February onwards was never below \$2·41. Indeed at times it was very close to the upper limit of \$2·42, especially in February, and the authorities found it necessary to buy in currency to prevent it going higher.

Otherwise they were willing to allow the rate to rise in order to check an inflow of funds which was presenting difficulties for domestic monetary management. Hence too the reduction of bank rate by 1 per cent on 1 April 1971, which was officially stated to be 'intended to avoid a further widening of the margin between rates in this country and abroad'; it was also said that 'the prospect of another fall in overseas interest rates had been taken into account'. Heavy official sales of gilt-edged securities were made during this period, facilitated by and to some extent offsetting the internal monetary effects of the inflow of funds. The weakness of the US dollar after the beginning of 1971 contributed to the strengthening of the sterling-dollar rate, but sterling was also strong against other currencies.

In August 1970 the market for 'property currency' was merged with the investment currency market, but this had little effect on the premium for investment dollars which continued to fluctuate between 24 and 28 per cent. By October, however, it had moved to between 30 per cent and 36 per cent, largely as a result of a rise in prices on the New York Stock Exchange.

In December permission to borrow foreign currencies for portfolio investment abroad, previously confined to investment trusts and some similar institutions, was extended to 'professional managers of securities', without time limit; on realization of investments, accordingly, any surplus after repayment of the underlying borrowing became exempt from the general 25 per cent surrender requirement, provided it was not exchanged for sterling. These changes lessened the demand for investment dollars, and also produced some uncertainty in the market, the premium falling from 33 per cent before the relaxation was announced to around 20 per cent in January. In mid-April 1971 the premium fell to about 15 per cent, but generally was a little over 20. Subsequently the market was influenced by the possibility of further relaxations and by doubts about the continued strength of US stock market prices.

As Table C5 shows, the London Eurocurrency market continued to develop, though less rapidly than in 1969. External liabilities of UK banks in non-sterling currencies increased by slightly over £3000 million and claims by rather less whereas in 1969 both rose by nearly £5000 million. Growth in 1970 was again mostly in US dollars, but the relative importance of other currencies was on the increase.

The slowing down of the overall rate of growth was mainly due to changes in the Federal Reserve's reserve requirements designed to check borrowing of Eurodollars by the domestic banks, and the raising – to the same end – of Regulation Q limits on rates of interest paid on large domestic time deposits. As a result, UK claims on North America fell by over £1350 million, though liabilities rose by nearly £200 million and net claims fell from just over £3500 million to under £2000 million. The main growth was in business with western Europe; liabilities to holders on the continent rose by over £2300 million and claims by rather more, so that net liabilities declined.

Interest rates fell sharply following the change in US policy and the consequential repatriation of Eurodollars. Rates reached a peak of over 9½ per cent in May and June 1970, but thereafter tended to fall more or less continuously, and by the end of March 1971 the three months' rate was about 5¼ per cent, although it subsequently tended to harden at around 5¾ per cent, in response to policy developments in the United States.

For several years past, the liabilities and claims of UK banks in non-sterling currencies have more or less balanced, and at the end of 1969 net claims amounted to only £12 million. During 1970, however, liabilities rose more rapidly than claims, and at the end of the year were greater by some £460 million. This development was largely explained by the relative willingness of the UK authorities to permit borrowing of foreign currencies by companies through their UK bankers, for switching into sterling for domestic use. By the end of 1970, however, it was becoming less desirable to attract short-term funds from abroad, and it seemed anomalous to some that resort

TABLE C5 *External liabilities and claims of UK banks in non-sterling currencies (£m. end of year)*

	Currency			*Area of holder*		
	Total	*US $*	*Other*	*North America*	*Western Europe*	*Other*
UK liabilities						
1967	4,384	4,038	346	912	2413	1059
1968	7,139	6,404	735	1624	3917	1598
1969	11,994	10,728	1266	2357	6709	2928
1970	15,153	13,086	2067	2552	9045	3556
UK claims						
1967	4,376	3,837	539	1855	1453	1068
1968	7,117	6,245	872	3263	2166	1688
1969	12,006	10,514	1492	5884	3570	2552
1970	14,691	12,189	2502	4528	6270	3893
Net liabilities (−) *or claims* (+)						
1967	− 8	−201	+193	+ 943	− 960	+ 9
1968	− 22	−159	+137	+1639	−1751	+ 90
1969	+ 12	−214	+226	+3527	−3139	−376
1970	−462	−897	+435	+1976	−2775	+337

to finance of this kind be allowed while lending in sterling by UK banks remained restricted. Accordingly in January 1971 this policy was modified. Specific permission became necessary for all new foreign currency borrowing for domestic use; this was then normally given for periods of at least five years, thus effectively confining such borrowing largely to the financing of investment. Also in January it was stated that permission would not normally be granted to residents to borrow sterling or any other scheduled territory currency from non-residents for any purpose.

The free market price for gold, which had fallen to about $35 per fine ounce – the official price for monetary purposes – late in 1969, remained at or near that figure until September 1970. After September the price tended to rise gradually, and then fluctuate in the region of $38 and $39 an ounce. This recovery was attributed largely to growing demand from industrial consumers: little speculative activity had been seen, though the weakness of the US dollar was a growing influence, and trading conditions had been fairly quiet.

Monetary expansion but continued restraint

A change in approach to monetary policy was disclosed in the budget in March 1971 when the Chancellor rejected 'a quantified DCE objective' for the financial year 1971–2 and turned instead to a proposed guideline for the money supply, on the grounds that domestic credit expansion is 'a less relevant indicator when the external position is strong'. He said that, 'given the current growth of incomes, there would be dangers for liquidity and employment if we sought immediately to reduce the growth of money supply to much below 3 per cent per quarter. But this does not mean that I intend the growth of money supply simply to accommodate the going rate of inflation. As the rise in costs and prices is moderated, so the aim will be to slow down the growth of the money supply. . . . I do not want to prejudge this or appear to set a limit to what can be achieved by laying down now a firm objective for money supply for 1971–2 as a whole'. He considered that monetary policy had 'no special magic for dealing with cost inflation', and saw no reason 'to restrict the growth of money supply so as to reduce demand below the level needed to achieve a growth of output in line with the growth of productive potential'.

The measure of changes in the money supply depends to a large extent on the definition adopted (see Chapter 4). For the first three quarters of the financial year 1970–1, the Chancellor quoted M_3, the broadest of the three definitions used in the official statistics. Seasonally adjusted, this showed an average quarterly growth rate of about 3 per cent. Recent figures for each of the series are shown in Table C6. As may be seen, on any definition the money supply rose sharply in 1970, after increasing moderately in 1969. A notable increase in 1970, among the component series of M_3, was recorded for sterling bank deposits of the overseas sector.

A significant rise in bank deposits of residents mainly reflected a substantial increase in lending. Direct control of bank lending was maintained

TABLE C6 *Money supply (£m. end-period)*

	M_1	M_2	M_3 unadjusted	M_3 seasonally adjusted
1968	8492	13,562	15,800	15,561
1969	8471	13,643	16,255	16,028
1970:				
March	8036	13,071	15,690	16,127
June	8504	13,760	16,545	16,773
Sept.	8641	14,035	16,890	17,025
Dec.	9237	14,835	17,777	17,541

M_1 = Notes and coin in circulation and sterling current accounts held by the private sector,
M_2 = M_1 plus sterling deposit accounts of the private sector with the deposit banks and discount houses only.
M_3 = M_2 plus sterling deposit accounts with other banks, all non-sterling deposits of the private sector and all deposits of the public sector.

in 1970–1, though less rigorously than during the previous year. For 1969–70 the clearing banks were asked to bring their restricted lending down to 98 per cent of the November 1967 level, a requirement which in the event it proved impossible to meet. For 1970–1, however, in order to avoid increased pressures on company liquidity, it was proposed to permit a gradual and moderate increase in restricted sterling lending. The indicated increases by March 1971 as compared with March 1970 were 'about 5 per cent' for the clearing and Scottish banks 'in the aggregate' and 7 per cent for other banks calculated individually.

It was further intended to use Special Deposits more flexibly, and a start was made by increasing the call from 2 to $2\frac{1}{2}$ per cent for the clearing banks and from 1 to $1\frac{1}{4}$ per cent for the Scottish banks. This move was interpreted as foreshadowing a change of emphasis away from lending ceilings towards liquidity control (see Chapter 5). In response to a particularly sharp jump in lending in July 1970, however, the Bank of England firmly reminded the clearing and Scottish banks that the guidelines for the year remained in force and requested that all possible steps be taken to abate the growth of lending. A further call for Special Deposits – to $3\frac{1}{2}$ per cent for the clearing banks – was made in the October and the need for continued restraint was reiterated.

From then on, restricted lending by the clearing banks was held below the official guideline, mainly because of the strict control being exercised by the banks, but also, perhaps, to some extent because of a falling off of demand even though company liquidity generally remained under pressure. In March 1971 the lending limits were again raised. In his budget speech, the Chancellor of the Exchequer stated that 'for the time being it would not be inconsistent with our general objectives' if bank lending subject to restriction were to grow at a rate of about $2\frac{1}{2}$ per cent a quarter; accordingly the new limit for the clearing and Scottish banks – again in the aggregate – for the three months ending mid-June 1971 was $7\frac{1}{2}$ per cent above the level at mid-March 1970 after seasonal adjustment, and for the other banks $9\frac{1}{2}$ per cent on the same base date. It was stressed that priorities in lending remained unchanged and, especially, that continued restraint should be observed in personal lending; the additional credit should be provided 'mainly to companies'. This was the first time that 'ceilings' had been fixed for so short a period ahead, and the Chancellor stated that it was possible that something less than the figure of $2\frac{1}{2}$ per cent indicated for the first quarter might be 'more appropriate' later in the year.

Also significant was the renewed indication of the intention to move towards more flexible control arrangements. On a number of occasions the banks themselves have drawn attention to the undesirable features of direct quantitative restrictions, and their views seem to have found increasing acceptance by the authorities. In the 1971 budget speech the Chancellor said, as in effect some of his predecessors had done, that the existing arrangements were 'clearly defective on the score both of flexibility and of scope for competition'. He thought it would be possible to achieve 'more flexible but still effective arrangements basically by operating on the banks' resources', and that any such scheme should be 'capable of influencing the monetary system as a whole and the interplay between the different sources of credit creation'. Such ideas would 'now be fully explored between the authorities and the banks and finance houses'.

Banking statistics show that net deposits were on a marked upward trend in 1970–1, the March to March increase of £1111 million, or 12 per cent, comparing with a fall of £32 million in 1969–70 and an increase of £244 million in 1968–9. Part of the latest year's increase reflected the growth of bank lending and another contributory factor up to September 1970 was net purchases of government securities by the authorities; and in September 3 per cent Savings Bonds 1960–70, of which £758 million was outstanding, were redeemed in cash, giving added impetus to the rise in bank deposits. Official purchases of government stock exceeded sales by some £275 million in the quarter to end-September, but in the following quarter official operations were on balance negligible. In the first quarter of 1971, when net deposits rose by £352 million, a number of abnormal factors were operating; the inflow of funds from abroad was heavy, though large official sales of gilts were also being made; holdings of import deposits were being run down, thus lessening the Exchequer surplus; and the postal strike resulted in delays in making tax payments.

These delays are also thought to have moderated the usual seasonal expansion of lending, but on the figures net advances to the private sector rose over the year to March 1971 by £171 million or 3·1 per cent; on a seasonally adjusted basis, they rose sharply over the three months to July, but therafter showed no pronounced movements either way. Restricted lending – that is, lending by both advances and commercial bills in sterling to the private sector, and excluding the growing amounts of medium- and long-term fixed-rate lending for exports and shipbuilding – followed a broadly similar course. Following the official indication in July that such lending was rising too rapidly the trend after seasonal adjustments was perhaps slightly downwards, and by mid-March 1971 the total was less than 4 per cent higher than in March 1970, as compared with the permitted growth of 5 per cent. No striking changes in the distribution of assets took place.

On balance the banks were sellers of gilt-edged securities in 1970–1, although not to the same extent as in the previous year, their combined portfolios falling by £29 million, against £154 million in 1969–70. In March 1971 the ratio of total investments to gross deposits was 10·2 per cent, as compared with 11·8 per cent twelve months previously. A change in the accounting treatment of investments in bank balance sheets following disclosure at the end of 1969 resulted in an increase of £75 million in total investments of the clearing banks, of which £60 million was in respect of British government securities.

By contrast with investments, liquid assets rose substantially during the year and at no time were the clearing banks under liquidity pressure despite further calls for Special Deposits. Initially, this was due to the effects of accounting changes made previously which reduced gross deposits and added perhaps 1½ percentage points to the combined liquidity ratio. Subsequently, particularly in the quarter to end-September, the volume of liquid assets was swollen by substantial reductions in holdings of government stocks by holders outside the banking sector, which were reflected in a marked increase in the volume of Treasury bills held within it, and in the final quarter of the year by the heavy inflow of funds from abroad. The average liquidity ratio of the banks for 1970 was 31·7 per cent, compared with 30·1 per cent in 1969, and in March 1971 it stood at 32·4 per cent, compared with 29·7 per cent a year earlier.

The increases in Special Deposits called in April 1970 – raising them from 2 to 2½ per cent for the clearing banks and from 1 to 1¼ per cent for the Scottish banks – were the first changes since July 1966. At the same time payment of the full rate of interest, which had been halved in June 1969, was restored. In line with the intention of making the system more flexible, on 29 October 1970 a further call was made of 1 per cent of Special Deposits from the clearing banks, and ½ per cent from the Scottish, bringing the totals to 3½ per cent and 1¾ per cent respectively, the highest levels reached since the scheme was first introduced.

During 1970 the total deposits of the group shown in the official statistics as 'accepting houses, overseas banks and other banks in the United Kingdom' rose from £21,647 million to £27,528 million. By far the major part of this increase was in deposits denominated in currencies other than sterling, as described earlier. Sterling deposits rose from £5108 million to £6456 million, the increase of £1348 million being rather higher than that for the clearing banks; issues of sterling certificates of deposit accounted for £647 million of the increase and the total of these certificates stood at £1089 million at the end of December. Movements in the main assets and liabilities are shown in Table C7. Call money rose by £320 million, reflecting in the main the increase in lending to the discount market referred to later in this chapter. Advances increased by £173 million, of which about two thirds was made in the quarter to end-June 1970, and the authorities in consequence reminded some of the banks that the request for restraint made in March still stood.

Total classified advances rose by £4249 million, or 39 per cent over the year to February 1971, but lending, largely in foreign currencies, to overseas residents by non-clearing banks accounted for £2908 million of the increase. Otherwise the main growth was in lending to manufacturing industry, which rose by nearly a quarter. Advances to personal borrowers rose appreciably

TABLE C7 *Selected assets and liabilities in sterling of 'accepting houses and overseas and other banks' (£m. end of period)*

	*Current and deposit accounts**	*Balances with other UK banks*	*Money at call and short notice*	*Loans to local authorities*	*Sterling bills discounted*	*British government securities*	*Advances*	*Other assets*
1968	4247	1123	255	1104	171	461	1405	297
1969	5108	1567	249	1338	154	430	1466	455
1970: June	5848	1699	353	1670	146	398	1583	735
Dec.	6456	1747	569	1727	170	354	1639	968

* Including sterling certificates of deposit.
(Later figures appear in Table A15, p. 134.)

between May and August 1970, and over the twelve months by nearly one fifth.

The National Giro continued to make progress during 1970, but total deposits, mainly from the public sector, remained small in relation to those of other institutions, at £58 million. During the year, public sector deposits rose by £11 million to £37 million and private sector deposits by £11 million to £21 million. The bulk of its resources were lent in various ways to local authorities. At that time the future of Giro became uncertain since the government declined to sanction its continuance until satisfied that it could be run at a profit.

The returns of the Bankers Clearing House showed that the value of items passing through the town and general debit clearings in 1970 was £772,464 million and the number of articles 727·1 million. Credit clearing was £14,391 million by value and the number of items was 188·1 million. These figures did not represent the total amounts transmitted through the banking system, and in particular they did not include the internal clearings of the individual banks. Accordingly, because of the various banking mergers effected in 1970, comparisons with the 1969 figures were not meaningful. The clearing house began collecting internal figures to be made available for the first time in 1971. In the first quarter of 1971, the value of internal debit clearings was £46,834 million, or about 18 per cent of the total debit clearing. The value of internal credit clearing, at £10,042 million for the first quarter, accounted for 70 per cent of the total credit clearing. A better measure of current account activity was provided by the Midland Bank Index of Business Turnover (1968 = 100), which was unaffected by the changes in the clearing figures. The index rose from 111 in 1969 to 128 in 1970, an increase of over 15 per cent.

After prolonged representations by the banks, the authorities gave their concurrence to an increase from 5½ to 7 per cent in the rate of interest charged by the banks on new fixed-rate guaranteed lending for exports and shipbuilding as from 1 October 1970.* At the same time, the rate on bill and open account business for guaranteed export credit of up to two years was increased from bank rate to ½ per cent above it.

The banks were not only becoming increasingly concerned – up to October – at the relatively low rate of interest applicable to the medium- and long-term lending under the export and shipbuilding schemes; another source of anxiety was the growing volume of such lending, which was pre-empting an increasing proportion of deposit resources. This was occurring despite refinancing facilities available at the Bank of England. For credits agreed for two years or more the Bank of England stood ready to refinance up to 30 per

* Details of the export credit schemes were given in 'Export Finance from the Banks', in the August 1962 issue of the *Midland Bank Review* and in the 'Annual Monetary Survey' for 1965 (see Chapter 10); the arrangements for shipbuilding were described in 'The Changing Shape of British Shipping', a *Review* article in November 1970.

cent of the amount outstanding in respect of each eligible transaction or, for export finance transactions, the amount repayable within eighteen months, if this should be the greater; accordingly each bank showed these amounts as liquid assets and the remainder as advances. The position was that the Bank of England would actually refinance either of these two portions to the extent that it exceeded 5 per cent of gross deposits. In practice, therefore, for any individual bank the total of lending under the schemes need not exceed 10 per cent of its gross deposits. Beyond that point the lending would be taken over by the Bank of England, and the banks collectively were then very near it; for a year or so past a number of them have been refinancing part of such sums included as advances.

Further structural developments occurred during the year, especially in the international field. At home, the merger of the three clearing banks in the National and Commercial Banking Group, to form Williams and Glyn's Bank, took effect in September 1970, and the Bank of Scotland and British Linen Bank formally merged on 1 March 1971. In Northern Ireland, the Belfast Banking Company and Northern Bank, both subsidiaries of the Midland Bank, merged under the title of Northern Bank from the beginning of July 1970. A notable merger announced in overseas business was that of Lloyds Bank Europe with the Bank of London and South America to form a new company, Lloyds and Bolsa International, in which Lloyds Bank would hold slightly over one half of the capital. Among banks registered in London but whose main activities were abroad, the merger between the Australia and New Zealand Bank and the English, Scottish and Australian Bank was completed, and in April 1971 it was announced that Barclays Bank Limited was to bid for that portion of the capital of Barclays Bank DCO that it did not already hold.

The attractions of 'secondary banking' in London also produced several new developments during the year. County Bank, a wholly owned subsidiary of National Westminster Bank, doubled its capital from £4 million to £8 million, and that of Barclays Bank (London and International) was increased from £5 million to £10 million. Lloyds Bank incorporated a new wholly owned subsidiary, to be known as Lloyds Associated Banking Company, to operate as a short- and medium-term finance company.

New 'consortia banks' involving British interests were established in London and abroad. These included the Orion Group, specializing in large-scale Eurocurrency issues of up to ten years' duration, in which National Westminster Bank participated; Bank of America Limited, jointly owned by Bank of America and Kleinwort Benson; London Multinational Bank, in which the British member, Baring Bros., took a 20 per cent interest; and United International Bank, in which Williams and Glyn's Bank acquired a $12\frac{1}{2}$ per cent interest. Overseas, the Midland Bank, along with the three European banks with which it had developed specially close links since

1963, formed European Banks' International Company based in Brussels, for the purpose, among others, of managing joint ventures. Midland also took a $17\frac{1}{2}$ per cent interest in Euro-Pacific Finance Corporation, based in Melbourne.

An important event in the banking calendar was the change to decimal currency on 15 February 1971. The changeover was achieved smoothly as a result of the long and thorough preparations that had been made. The operation took place in the middle of the postal strike, but the dislocation which this might have caused was avoided by a clearing operation which had long been planned, involving the use of special transport arrangements. The banks were closed to the public for two days – 11 and 12 February – during which time all items in the pipeline were cleared and all balances converted to decimals, so that the banks reopened on 15 February for business as usual. The withdrawal of some of the old notes and coinage had taken place in advance, and on D-day the last three of the new decimal coins were put into circulation – those for 2p, 1p and $\frac{1}{2}$p. A welcome benefit to banking which came at the time of decimalization was the freeing of cheques from stamp duty as from 1 February.

In September 1970, the Bank of England amended the exchange control regulations to enable holders of cheque cards, issued by several of the clearing banks, to use them in various countries outside the scheduled territories to cash cheques of up to £30. This enabled British cardholders to obtain the benefits of the Eurocheque scheme, under which banks in several countries cash cheques for cardholders from other participating countries.

For the discount houses 1970–1 proved a rather better year than the previous one. The foundations of this improvement were the two reductions in bank rate in March and April 1970 bringing it down from 8 to 7 per cent. The beneficial effects of the reductions were supplemented by a large expansion in the market's total assets in the second half of 1970.

After April, the authorities were concerned to prevent any further rapid fall in short-term rates, and the Treasury bill rate was held fairly steady from May 1970 until February 1971; indeed, for twenty-one weeks from mid-August until mid-January the discount houses' weekly tender bid remained unchanged, a period of unprecedented stability in times of active monetary policy. By contrast market pressures were bringing lower rates at the short end of the gilt-edged market, and yields at the end of the year were substantially lower than at the beginning.

A major factor in the market's favour was a considerable increase in the volume of Treasury bills issued through the tender. At 31 March 1971 the amount of tender bills outstanding was £1780 million, £590 million higher than a year earlier, compared with reductions of £150 million in the previous year and £700 million in 1968–9. In March and April the syndicated bid on several occasions was too low to secure any bills, whereas throughout most of the year the houses obtained substantial proportions of the totals allotted. The banks were not keen buyers and, as a result, the aggregate of Treasury bills held by the eleven houses at 31 December 1970, at £876 million, was over twice as high as a year earlier and was by far the largest holding shown since the figures, which go back to 1951, were first made available. Margins between Treasury bill yields and borrowing costs were, however, generally narrow.

Principally due to this rise in holdings of Treasury bills the market's total assets rose to a new peak, of £2354 million, at the end of 1970. Holdings of bonds fell over the year by over £200 million to £160 million, but those of other sterling bills rose by £68 million to £697 million and sterling CDs by £171 million to £268 million. Dealings in foreign currency acceptances and dollar CDs made a useful contribution to profits. In April 1971 the Bank of England removed the rule that discount houses which had affiliations with deposit brokers were debarred from dealing as principals in the markets in dollar CDs and foreign currency acceptances.

The pattern of market borrowings also showed a notable change. Lending by the clearing banks increased by about £100 million to over £1400 million over the year, but their share of the market's total borrowed funds fell from 75 per cent to 62 per cent. The increased participation of the 'accepting houses, overseas banks and other banks' group and of lenders outside the banking sector was probably due to the decline in the relative attractiveness of yields in the 'complementary' markets.

In the pursuit of short-term stability of interest rates, the Bank of England followed an active and flexible policy of market intervention. A new series of figures showed that official assistance in the market in the year to 9 December amounted in total to £4716 million, against £3765 million in the previous year. Assistance mainly took the form of purchases of Treasury bills, but other sterling bills were purchased, particularly early in the year before the market had built up its portfolio of Treasury bills. Advances at bank rate were generally made overnight but in January 1971 the market was required to borrow for seven days.

The main influence on rates in the 'complementary' markets has been the almost uninterrupted decline since May 1970 in the Eurodollar rate, reflecting movements in overseas financial centres, and especially New York. The three-month rate for inter-bank deposits fell from around 9½ per cent to 7½ per cent during 1970, and broadly comparable declines were recorded in the markets for local authority and finance house deposits. As a result, the margin of 'complementary' market rates above the Treasury bill rate, which had been wide during 1969, fell to more normal levels.

Even so, the increasing tenuousness of the link between bank rate and the Treasury bill rate on the one hand and rates in the 'complementary' markets on the other was given practical recognition by the Finance Houses Association, with the introduction of a new Base Rate reflecting the trend of the cost of three-month deposits in the inter-bank market. This was offered as an alternative to bank rate as the basis for the determination of rates charged by FHA members on industrial and commercial lending. When introduced on 1 September 1970 the rate was 8 per cent; it was reduced to 7½ per cent on 1 November, but was again raised to 8 per cent on 1 March.

In 1970–1, as in 1969–70, the public sector showed a surplus of the order of £4500 million on current account, but capital receipts fell short of expenditure by more than this and the net outcome was an overall deficit of £617 million, compared with £598 million in the previous year. On the Exchequer accounts, Consolidated Fund revenue again exceeded expenditure and net loans from the Consolidated Fund taken together, though by much less than in 1969–70.

As in the preceding two years, the total of floating debt outstanding was further reduced, from almost £5000 million to around £4300 million. This reduction, however, was entirely in tap Treasury bills, large quantities of which had been issued in connection with previous support operations for the pound. Treasury bills issued through the tender rose over the year and at the end of March £1780 million was outstanding compared with £1190 million a year earlier; thus the declining trend of recent years was reversed.

The increase in the nominal amount of marketable securities outstanding was principally due to the large inflows of funds into this country in the first quarter of 1971, attracted by the relatively high rates of interest available in London. The demand for gilt-edged stocks exhausted the government broker's supply of tap stocks on a number of occasions, and, in the first four months of 1971, four issues to an aggregate nominal amount of £2300 million had been made. During January, a further tranche of £600 million of Treasury Loan 1976, and a further £500 million of Treasury Loan 1994, were issued; in February £600 million of Exchequer Stock 1976 was issued; and in March £600 million of Treasury Loan 1992–6. Earlier in the financial year, £300 million of Treasury Loan 1974, and £600 million of Treasury Loan 1984–6 had been absorbed by the market. The largest redemption during the year was that of the widely held 3 per cent Savings Bonds 1960–70. The 6½ per cent Treasury stock 1971, of which £528 million nominal was outstanding, was redeemed in January 1971.

Local authorities raised more new money last year against stocks and bonds than they had in 1969. The total was £154 million, compared with £137 million a year earlier. Eleven stock issues raised £108 million and all except one were priced below par with coupons between 9 and 9¾ per cent, giving a rather lower average redemption yield than issues in 1969. The yield on yearling bonds fell more sharply, from 9½ per cent at the end of 1969 to just over 8 per cent at the end of 1970, and to little more than 7 per cent last month. During 1970 local authorities increased their borrowing from the banking sector by £341 million, principally from the accepting houses, overseas and 'other' banks. Borrowing from the central government rose by £145 million in the financial year 1970–1, compared with £56 million in 1969–70. Rates charged on new borrowing from the Public Works Loan Board were again subject to frequent change; for quota borrowing, those at the shorter end of the range were slightly reduced on balance to around 7½–8 per cent over the year to March 1971. The rates for longer borrowing, however, rose slightly on balance from around 9 per cent to 9½ per cent; loans of over twenty-five years had been quoted at 10 per cent in December. Short-term rates in the local authority market generally fell on balance. That for seven-day money was around 7½ per cent in April 1970, and below 7 per cent in April last; the three-months' rate fell over the same period from 7¾ to 6¾ per cent.

Personal incomes were rising faster than expenditure in 1970; the savings ratio – as a proportion of disposable income – is provisionally put at 8·2 against 7·6 per cent for 1969. The increased liquidity of the personal sector was reflected in the figures for various forms of saving. In 1970–1 the total invested in 'national savings', excluding accrued interest, rose by £121 million, compared with a fall of £198 million in 1969–70. The new decimal issue of national savings certificates, first made available in October and yielding 5¾ per cent per annum free of tax if held for four years, proved popular, and for the first time in several years sales of certificates exceeded repayments in the second half of 1970–1. Both the National Savings Bank and the trustee savings banks fared better than in 1969–70, though deposits on ordinary account in the National Savings Bank fell by nearly £100 million. Sales of British savings bonds and premium savings bonds, though less than in 1969–70, made modest contributions to the general rise in national savings. Net receipts from the 'Save as you earn' scheme in 1970 – its first full year of operation – were only £21 million. The number of SAYE contracts is now over 350,000, excluding those with building societies.

In his 1971 budget speech the Chancellor announced a number of changes in terms all designed to encourage 'national savings'. The maximum holding of the decimal savings certificate was raised from £500 to £1000; the tax-free bonus on British savings bonds, if held for five years, was increased from £2 to £3 per cent; a monthly prize of £50,000 on premium bonds was introduced and the maximum holding of these bonds increased from £1250 to £2000; and the upper limit of the monthly payment under the SAYE scheme is to be raised from £10 to £20 from next September.

Earlier, following the Finance Act, 1970, the rate of interest on deposits in ordinary accounts with the National Savings Bank, the trustee savings banks and the No. 2 Department of the Birmingham Municipal Bank was raised from 2½ to 3½ per cent. This was the first time that any of these rates had been altered, the National Savings Bank rate having stood at 2½ per cent for well over a century. Provision is to be made in the 1971 Finance Act to raise the annual amount of interest from these sources which is exempt from income tax from £15 to £21 – that is, the interest on a deposit of £600, as before. It was announced in February this year that the Birmingham Municipal Bank was to make available, through United Dominions Trust, loans of £100 and upwards to depositors; the rate of interest will be 9 per cent per annum on the initial amount. A year ago Mercantile Credit began offering personal loan facilities to National Giro account holders.

Both investment in building societies and lending by them rose to unprecedented levels in 1970. The net increase in shares and deposits was £1462 million, compared with £895 million in 1969. Net lending on mortgages, which had turned down in 1969, totalled £1036 million, an increase of £254 million on the previous year. At end-December last, aggregate liquidity was higher than for some years past, but outstanding lending commitments had also risen markedly and liquidity began to fall in the first two months of 1971. Indeed, with the failure of Rolls Royce in February, one building society experienced sudden and exceptional withdrawals of funds, but these were short lived.

The uncertainty evident in the equity market continued to affect the unit trust movement unfavourably, particularly in the second half of 1970. For the whole year sales of units totalled £171 million, £92 million less than in 1969 and barely half the peak sales recorded in 1968. Despite the employment of a higher proportion of funds in short-term assets the downward drift of share prices caused total funds to fall for the second consecutive year; the market value was £1398 million at end-December last, compared with £1412 million in 1969 and £1482 million in 1968. Some improvement was shown in the opening months of this year, though sales remained low.

Prices of equities, as measured by the *Financial Times*-Actuaries all-share index, were at much the same level at the end of April 1971 as a year earlier; the intervening fluctuations generally reflected uncertain market conditions. In the gilt-edged market the trend was better with the *Financial Times* index of prices of government securities rising to its highest levels since the end of 1968. Prices rose steadily from June to August 1970 and thereafter showed little movement until a sharp but temporary break occurred in late October; this was attributed to uncertainties over the future course of monetary policy, arising from a statement by the Chancellor on economic policy, and was checked by the announcement of increased calls for special deposits from the banks. Recently prices have again been on an upward trend, despite heavy funding sales. During January, turnover in gilts on the stock exchange exceeded £5000 million, considerably higher than in any month since figures were first published in 1964. Yields on gilt-edged remained fairly high until the end of 1970, when they were generally around the same levels as nine months before, but in the first three months of this year have tended to fall by around $\frac{1}{2}$ per cent, especially for medium- and long-dated stocks. During

1970, yields on the shorter-dated stocks had been falling much more than those on the longer-dated ones, and a significant gap between long and short rates opened up for the first time for some years.

The *Financial Times* industrial ordinary share index (1 July 1935 = 100), which had risen above 420 in January 1970, fell to 315·4 in June, but thereafter rose sharply and almost touched 380 at the beginning of October. With growing uncertainty about the business outlook the trend was reversed and by the end of November the index was back almost to its June levels. By the beginning of March the index was at a four-year low point of 305·3 but recovered to 386·2 at end-April 1971. The dividend yield on the industrial ordinary index was around 4 per cent at the end of April 1971 having fluctuated during the year between 4½ and 5½ per cent. The interest rate on twenty-year company debentures has generally remained between 10 and 11 per cent. Within this range it was well above the rate on bank advances, thus adding to the difficulties of the banks in their efforts to persuade customers to fund borrowing.

Resort to the market was also inhibited by the uncertain trends in the equity market. For most of 1970, the figures compiled by the Midland Bank of new money raised by issues of marketable securities were running at levels below those of the corresponding period a year earlier, and the total of new money raised, at £539 million, was the lowest since 1964 and nearly £200 million lower than in 1969. Preference and ordinary capital raised less than £70 million combined, the lowest figure since 1965. However, the total sums raised by new issues began to recover in the later months of 1970, and the improvement seems to have continued into 1971.

SECTION D

Appendices

APPENDIX 1

A Chronology of major events in monetary policy April 1957 to December 1971

(*See p. 453 for period of office of Chancellors of Exchequer and governors of the Bank of England.*)

1957

9 April — The Chancellor of the Exchequer in his budget statement announced that a Committee of Inquiry would be established under the chairmanship of Lord Radcliffe, 'to inquire into the working of the monetary and credit system and to make recommendations'.

Banks were asked to 'keep credit within bounds', although 'some increase in the level of advances may result from the provision of bank finance for purposes of the highest priority'. A letter had been sent to the Capital Issues Committee (CIC) asking that when dealing with applications for bank advances referred to it, the Committee should consider not only the purpose of the advance but also whether bank borrowing was the appropriate method of finance. Consent was not to be recommended unless it was satisfied that it was 'a strictly temporary and short bridging operation, pending the completion of funding arrangements', or that exceptional features made the raising of funds from other sources impossible.

19 September — Bank rate was raised from 5 to 7 per cent. The increase was made necessary by speculation against sterling, but was required also to support internal measures, based on the 'control of the money supply', to combat inflation. The clearing banks were told that the average level of bank advances during the ensuing twelve months was to be held at the average level for the preceding twelve months. Government expenditure was to be limited and the CIC was asked to take 'a more restrictive and critical attitude towards applications to borrow', particularly for large amounts.

8 October — The Chancellor of the Exchequer said that government policy was 'to halt the increase in the supply of money . . . whether it be new money or existing money travelling rather faster'.

29 October — The banks were told that in calculating the total level of advances they could exclude medium-term advances guaranteed by the Export Credits Guarantee Department.

1958

6 January — Mr Thorneycroft, Chancellor of the Exchequer, resigned following differences of opinion as to the level of government expenditure. The new Chancellor, Mr Heathcoat Amory, stated that there would be 'no change in the government's economic or financial policy'.

21 February — The first report of the Council on Prices, Productivity and Incomes supported the measures taken in September 1957 and welcomed 'the stress laid by the authorities on the importance of re-establishing their effective control over the quantity of money'.

20 March — Bank rate was reduced from 7 to 6 per cent. This reduction did not imply any general relaxation in monetary policy.

15 April — The Chancellor of the Exchequer, in the budget speech, said that the banks would have to continue to hold down the level of advances, except for 'any projects for sound development in areas where unemployment is substantially above the average'.

22 May — Bank rate reduced from 6 to 5½ per cent; it was not to be taken as a 'green light' for the economy to reflate.

19 June — Bank rate was reduced from 5½ to 5 per cent.

3 July	The Chancellor announced the withdrawal, as from the end of July, of the limitation on the total of bank advances. He hoped in future to dispense with quantitative requests, but announced a new temporary system of 'Special Deposits'. A new order raised the CIC exemption limit from £10,000 to £50,000. The CIC no longer had to concern itself with the appropriateness of bank finance for capital purposes, and was free to take 'a longer view' of proposals.
25 July	Barclays Bank took a substantial minority interest in United Dominions Trust. Several other links between banks and instalment credit finance houses were announced in the next few weeks.
14 August	Bank rate was reduced from 5 to $4\frac{1}{2}$ per cent.
5 September	The Chancellor of the Exchequer stated that the personal loans schemes recently introduced by the banks and the resulting competition in consumer credit were 'in line with the general spirit of the government's policy'.
17 September	The Bank of England informed insurance companies that they were free to develop their own investment policies.
16 October	The governor of the Bank of England said that the 'closer connection between the banking system and the hire purchase industry was in the public interest' and 'will help to strengthen the economy'.
29 October	Having been eased in the previous month, all remaining restrictions on hire purchase and rental terms were removed.
20 November	Bank rate was reduced from $4\frac{1}{2}$ to 4 per cent. This was officially described as a 'technical adjustment'. The clearing banks' minimum lending rate to the discount market was reduced by only $\frac{3}{8}$ per cent to $2\frac{3}{8}$.

1959

5 February	Control of borrowing and of new capital issues was lifted by a general consent given under the Control of Borrowing Order, 1958. Specific consent was still required for bonus issues of redeemable securities, for borrowing by local authorities and for transactions by persons resident outside Britain.
19 August	The report of the Radcliffe committee on the working of the monetary system (Cmnd. 827) was published (see 9 April 1957).

12 November — The Chancellor of the Exchequer and the governor of the Bank of England both said that although recent expansion of credit had been helpful to the economy, it would need watching if it continued much longer at the same pace.

26 November — Following the proposals in the Radcliffe Report, the Chancellor of the Exchequer announced a new procedure for conveying the Chancellor's approval of bank rate changes. New arrangements were to be introduced for coordinating Treasury and Bank of England policy in place of the standing committee recommended in the Radcliffe Report.

1960

21 January — Bank rate was raised from 4 to 5 per cent, primarily for domestic reasons.

12 February — The governor of the Bank of England said that because the economy had become somewhat overheated, new facilities granted by the banks should be curtailed a little.

4 April — The Chancellor of the Exchequer said that 'we have reached the stage where we should be cautious about further extension of credit'.

28 April — The Bank of England made the first call for Special Deposits, at the rate of 1 per cent of gross deposits for the clearing banks and ½ per cent for Scottish banks, to be made on or before 15 June (see Appendix 2, Table 7). The Chancellor of the Exchequer gave details of hire purchase controls, to be reimposed on the following day. The object of those measures was not to halt expansion but to put 'a slight brake on its rate'.

23 June — Bank rate was raised by 1 to 6 per cent; and further calls for Special Deposits, raising them to 2 per cent for clearing banks and 1 per cent for Scottish, were made by the Bank of England. Investment in the public sector for the financial year 1961–2 was to be held 'at the level of the current programme for the present year'.

20 October — Both the Chancellor of the Exchequer and the governor of the Bank of England said that credit restrictions would be eased as soon as it was safe to do so, and that Special Deposits had 'proved a useful addition to our monetary armoury'.

27 October — Bank rate was reduced from 6 to 5½ per cent, for external reasons only.

8 December Bank rate was reduced by a further $\frac{1}{2}$ per cent to 5 per cent, again for external reasons.

1961

12 January The first issue of the *Bank of England Quarterly Bulletin* was published.

20 January Control over hire purchase terms was eased.

9 February The governor of the Bank of England stated that monetary policy had achieved to a considerable extent, its objectives in 1960, having contributed to preventing an 'overboiling' of the economy in the spring and to maintaining confidence in sterling; it had also had some influence in redirecting bank credit from consumption to investment.

17 April The Chancellor of the Exchequer announced proposals for two new 'economic regulators' to reduce dependence on monetary and credit restrictions: one to impose a surcharge, or grant a rebate of up to 10 per cent on excise duties and purchase tax, and the other to levy a charge on employers based on the number of employees.

20 July The report of the committee of inquiry into the control of public expenditure noted the damaging effects of 'stop-and-go' monetary policy.

25 July Measures announced by the Chancellor of the Exchequer to restrain the economy and to 'form the basis for a long-term improvement in the balance of payments' included an increase in bank rate from 5 to 7 per cent; calls for further Special Deposits, making the cumulative total 3 per cent for clearing banks and $1\frac{1}{2}$ per cent for Scottish, and the imposition of a surcharge of 10 per cent of the existing rates of customs and excise duties and purchase tax.

The impact of the call for Special Deposits was intended to fall on advances. The clearing and Scottish banks were asked to be 'particularly severe' on borrowing proposals related to personal consumption, including finance for hire purchase and speculative property development. Other banks, including foreign and overseas banks, accepting houses and insurance companies, were also asked to observe similar restraints in their lending policies.

The Chancellor also called for a 'pause' in increases in wages, salaries and dividends, and asked local authorities to 'hold back' all but essential expenditure.

3 August	The banks began to reduce advances to hire purchase finance companies in accordance with an official request.
10 August	The Bank of England asked hire purchase finance houses not to seek finance for further expansion from sources other than the banks.
5 October	Bank rate was reduced from 7 to 6½ per cent. The reduction was, according to the Chancellor, 'a little and very limited thaw', and the credit restrictions and other measures were to continue.
2 November	Bank rate was reduced from 6½ to 6 per cent, because of the improvement of sterling.
1962	
8 March	Bank rate was reduced from 6 to 5½ per cent, in view of the strength of sterling and the improved general economic situation.
22 March	Bank rate was lowered from 5½ to 5 per cent; the change reflected the continued strength of sterling.
31 March	'Pay pause' ended.
9 April	It was announced in the budget that the surcharge on customs and excise duties was to be ended but that most basic tax rates would be increased to preserve the revenue.
26 April	Bank rate was reduced from 5 to 4½ per cent, as a result of the continuing strong position of sterling.
4 May	The first issue of *Financial Statistics* was published.
31 May	It was announced that Special Deposits of the clearing banks were to be reduced from 3 to 2 per cent, and of the Scottish banks from 1½ to 1 per cent in June. The banks were told that the release would 'only permit of a limited relaxation of restraints'. In lending policies priority was still to be given to finance of exports and of production which would aid exports.
5 June	Slight relaxation of hire purchase controls.
26 July	A National Incomes Commission to be established.
27 September	It was announced that Special Deposits were to be reduced in October from 2 to 1 per cent for the clearing banks and from 1 to ½ per cent for the Scottish banks.

3 October — Formal selective restrictions on lending by banks and other financial institutions were withdrawn, though they were asked to pay special attention in lending policies to exports and the promotion of business in those areas of the country where resources were not being fully used.

The Chancellor of the Exchequer said that public investment was to be increased in the coming year, and that the major objective was 'to achieve a higher and more stable rate of economic growth'.

23 October — Reductions were made in some minimum hire purchase deposits requirements.

6 November — The rate of purchase tax on sales of new cars was reduced.

29 November — The remaining Special Deposits of the clearing and Scottish banks – 1 per cent and ½ per cent of gross deposits respectively – to be released in December.

1963

1 January — The 45 per cent general purchase tax level was reduced to 25 per cent.

3 January — Bank rate was reduced from 4½ to 4 per cent, in view of the domestic economic situation and the strong position of sterling.

The Bank of England informed discount houses that in future, when lending to the market for periods of seven days or more, it might charge bank rate, or ½ to 1 per cent over bank rate, at its discretion.

4 February — The government accepted the 4 per cent growth target proposed by the National Economic Development Council.

3 April — The Chancellor of the Exchequer gave as the theme of his budget 'expansion without inflation, and the achievement of the 4 per cent growth target'. He announced reductions in taxation; the prospect was for an above-the-line deficit, the first forecast since 1946, as well as the customary 'overall' deficit. Power was to be sought to operate the surcharge or rebate on customs and excise duties for a further year.

16 October — The governor of the Bank of England said that the clearing banks had been informed that they should aim to achieve a liquidity ratio of not less than 28 per cent in the period up to mid-April 1964.

1964

31 January	The Chancellor of the Exchequer said that the existing rate of economic expansion was higher than could be maintained in the long run, and that the rise in prices and costs should be moderated.
27 February	Bank rate was increased from 4 to 5 per cent, to bring short-term interest rates in the United Kingdom more closely into line with those overseas.
14 April	The main purpose of the budget, which raised some taxes, was to achieve a smooth transition from the present exceptionally rapid rate of growth to the long-term growth rate of 4 per cent.
26 October	Restrictive measures of the new Labour government included a temporary surcharge of 15 per cent on all imports other than foodstuffs and raw materials.
11 November	An autumn budget contained increases in duties on oil products including petrol and in national insurance contributions and benefits.
23 November	Bank rate was raised from 5 to 7 per cent to 'maintain sterling at its present parity'.
8 December	The governor of the Bank of England wrote to the chairman of the Committee of London Clearing Bankers suggesting that the rate of increase of lending should be reduced, and that the banks should give priority in lending to exports and to the strengthening of productive investment by manufacturing industry; they should also have regard to the government's regional development policies. Lending for property development, hire purchase and 'professional and personal' needs should be restrained. Similar letters were sent to other banking institutions, and associations representing insurance companies, building societies and finance houses.

1965

6 April	In the budget the standard rate of income tax was raised from 7*s*. 9*d*. to 8*s*. 3*d*., and corporation tax and capital gains taxes were introduced.
27 April	The import surcharge (see 26 October 1964) was reduced to 10 per cent.

29 April	The Bank of England called for Special Deposits at the rate of 1 per cent for the clearing banks and $\frac{1}{2}$ per cent for the Scottish banks.
5 May	The Bank of England asked the banks not to increase their lending to the private sector by more than 5 per cent over the year to March 1966. Other financial institutions including hire purchase finance companies received similar requests; special emphasis was placed on lending for the promotion of exports.
3 June	Bank rate was reduced from 7 to 6 per cent; but initial deposits for hire purchase transactions were raised.
27 July	Measures to assist external situation contained: a reduction in the maximum period of repayment for hire purchase contracts for some goods; cuts in public investment and expenditure; restriction of private building; reductions in finance for imports to be provided by banks.
1966	
17 January	The system of tax incentives for investment was replaced by one of investment grants.
1 February	Banks were asked to continue lending ceiling announced on 5 May 1965 (i.e. increase to be kept to 5 per cent over March 1965 figure) until further notice (see 12 July 1966).
7 February	Hire purchase controls were intensified.
8 February	The Chancellor of the Exchequer stated that restriction of public sector investment would continue.
3 May	The main feature of the budget included the introduction of the selective employment tax and the fixing of the initial rate of corporation tax at 40 per cent.
12 July	The Chancellor of the Exchequer announced that the 105 per cent limit on bank advances would remain in force at least until the end of March 1967. He also said that there would be no general arrangements to ease the effects of the selective employment tax by relaxing the limit on bank lending.
14 July	Bank rate was increased from 6 to 7 per cent and calls made on the clearing and Scottish banks for additional Special Deposits of 1 per cent and $\frac{1}{2}$ per cent respectively.

20 July — Further measures to deal with the economic situation included a voluntary standstill on wages, salaries and prices for six months, followed by a further six months of 'severe restraint'. Hire purchase controls were tightened. Some taxes were raised and public investment at home and overseas was to be reduced.

10 August — The Bank of England stressed to the clearing banks the need for an immediate review of existing advances and limits to secure early and substantial reductions in non-priority lending in order to provide funds for essential purposes within the 105 per cent ceiling.

1 November — The Bank of England stated that the banks would have 'sufficient resources . . . to meet all those demands of the priority categories of borrowers which satisfy normal banking criteria. Among these, exports take first place followed by lending in support of productive investment by manufacturing industry and agriculture.' Temporary bridging finance for house purchase was also of special importance at a time when the redeployment of labour needed to be encouraged.

1967

23 January — The Chancellor of the Exchequer stated that he had been informed by the banks that they were ready 'to give help by way of bridging facilities' for projects in development areas, 'pending receipt of payments due from government sources'. They would also 'adopt a generous attitude to applications for borrowing for the purpose of promoting business' in the areas, would be 'willing to accept that borrowing may be for a longer term than they would ordinarily allow', and on occasion would be prepared 'to take more than the normal risk'.

26 January — Bank rate was reduced from 7 to $6\frac{1}{2}$ per cent. The reduction had been made possible 'by the recent reductions in interest rates and in monetary pressures in other important centres and the lessening of pressure on the domestic economy'.

6 February — The Chancellor of the Exchequer announced that lending to finance housebuilding would be regarded as a priority category for bank advances.

16 March — Bank rate was reduced from $6\frac{1}{2}$ to 6 per cent as the result of the continued easing of monetary conditions in other countries and maintenance of the strength of sterling.

11 April — The main monetary changes in the budget were as follows: (i) the ceiling on advances of the London clearing and Scottish banks was removed, but Special Deposits were to be used more flexibly; (ii) the 105 per cent limit was to continue to apply to the lending of other banking institutions and finance houses pending the formulation of further arrangements; (iii) a relaxation was made in some hire purchase controls.

4 May — Bank rate was reduced by $\frac{1}{2}$ per cent to $5\frac{1}{2}$ per cent; it followed a lowering of central bank discount rates in other financial centres.

7 June — The hire purchase controls on cars were relaxed.

30 August — Further relaxations of hire purchase were announced for cars, furniture and other consumer durables.

19 October — Bank rate was raised by $\frac{1}{2}$ per cent to 6 per cent. The change was in response to external pressures on sterling and higher interest rates abroad.

9 November — Bank rate was increased by $\frac{1}{2}$ per cent to $6\frac{1}{2}$ per cent in response to pressures on sterling and the rising trend in US interest rates.

18 November — Sterling was devalued from \$2·80 to \$2·40. Bank rate was raised to 8 per cent and banks were asked to limit lending in sterling to the private sector to the amount lent in mid-November until further notice, but all lending for exports and medium-term lending for shipbuilding was excluded from the control. Other measures included a new priority in bank lending for production for exports and imports savings; the strengthening of hire purchase controls on cars, and the raising of corporation tax from 40 to $42\frac{1}{2}$ per cent.

13 December — All institutions providing finance for instalment buying of goods subject to hire purchase controls were asked to exercise restraint in making personal loans.

1968

16 January — Substantial cuts in planned public expenditure were announced.

26 January — Westminster and National Provincial Banks stated that they had agreed in principle to combine and the newly formed National Westminster became operative on 10 July 1968 (see Appendix 5(c)).

8 February	Barclays Bank and Lloyds Bank also announced proposals for merging, the group possibly to include Martins Bank. Later, the Monopolies Commission, in a majority decision, found that a merger involving Barclays and Lloyds could be expected to operate against the public interest. This recommendation, accepted by the government, led to the banks abandoning their plan.
19 March	In the budget substantial increases in taxation were announced, including a new one-year tax charge on investment incomes.
21 March	Bank rate was reduced from 8 to 7½ per cent in the light of 'international and domestic considerations'.
23 May	The Bank of England issued a new notice to the clearing banks on lending policy, designed to achieve 'a greater reduction in lending to non-priority borrowers'. The ceiling was amended to cover all lending to the private sector, including finance for exports and shipbuilding. The banks were asked to keep their lending within 104 per cent of the November 1967 level, and the finance houses to bring their lending within 100 per cent of the end-October 1967 level.
14 June	The Bank of England published details of the scheme for regulating the volume of lending of non-clearing banks by way of a fresh scheme, including calls for 'Cash Deposits' with the Bank of England.
30 August	The Bank of England issued a statement re-emphasizing the need for further reductions in bank advances for non-essential purposes.
2 September	The selective employment tax was increased by 50 per cent.
19 September	Bank rate was reduced from 7½ to 7 per cent in response to the continued strength of sterling following the Basle agreement and the August trade figures. Domestic restrictive credit policy was to continue.
17 October	The governor of the Bank of England said that more attention should be paid to control of the money supply.
18 October	The National Giro opened for business.
1 November	Hire purchase controls were tightened. Martins Bank became a subsidiary of Barclays Bank.

22 November — New measures to control consumer expenditure and improve the balance of payments were announced. Purchase tax and excise duties were raised by 10 per cent. An import deposit scheme was introduced for imports of most manufactures, the rate being 50 per cent. Lending by clearing and Scottish banks to the domestic private sector was to be reduced to 98 per cent of the November level by mid-March 1969, but medium-term finance for exports and for shipbuilding was excluded. Priorities, broadly as before, were stressed. Other banks were asked to restrict advances to 102 per cent of end October 1967 level.

1969

14 February — Nationalized industries were encouraged by the government to borrow part of their capital requirements abroad.

27 February — Bank rate was increased from 7 to 8 per cent.

15 April — The budget included increases in the selective employment tax and corporation tax.

2 June — Following a sharp increase in bank advances, the Bank of England imposed a 'fine' on the clearing banks by reducing by one half the rate of interest paid on Special Deposits. The penalty continued to operate until 15 April 1970.

11 September — At a meeting between the Committee of London Clearing Banks and the Chancellor of the Exchequer it was made clear that there could be no relaxation of the credit squeeze.

1 October — The London clearing and Scottish banks raised their lending rates by $\frac{1}{2}$ per cent, although there had been no change in bank rate.

4 December — The import deposit scheme was extended for another year but the rate was reduced to 40 per cent (see 22 November 1968).

1970

5 March — Bank rate was reduced from 8 to $7\frac{1}{2}$ per cent.

14 April — In his budget statement the Chancellor announced that bank rate would be reduced by $\frac{1}{2}$ per cent to 7 per cent with effect from 15 April. In place of the existing ceiling arrangements on bank lending an increase would be allowed by the clearing banks and Scottish banks of 5 per cent over the twelve months to March 1971 in the aggregate of their lending subject to restrictions. Other banks individually were permitted increases of 7 per cent over the same period. The banks were

asked to direct any increased lending towards the finance of exports and of production and investment which would contribute to the balance of payments. Special Deposits would be used more freely in future and would be raised on 6 May from 2 to 2½ per cent for the clearing banks and from 1 to 1¼ per cent for Scottish banks.

1 May — The rate for import deposits was reduced to 30 per cent (see 4 December 1969).

27 July — Bank lending rose sharply and the banks were officially reminded of the restrictions.

1 September — The rate for import deposits was reduced to 20 per cent (see 1 May 1970).

The Finance Houses Association introduced a 'base rate' to which lending rates could be linked, rather than using bank rate.

27 October — Reduction in planned government expenditure was announced. Corporation tax and income tax were to be reduced, and investment grants abolished.

29 October — Special Deposits were raised to 3½ per cent for the clearing banks and 1¾ per cent for the Scottish banks.

4 December — The import deposit scheme was abolished.

1971

12 January — Following a sharp rise in foreign currency borrowing from non-residents by UK companies for use at home, exchange control measures were tightened. Henceforward specific application had to be made for all such foreign currency borrowing, with permission only normally given if repayment was due after more than five years.

15 February — Decimal currency was introduced. Following the success of the operation, the transitional period of dual currency working was brought to an end on 31 August 1971, much sooner than had been expected.

24 March — The report of the Crowther Committee on consumer credit was published. It recommended the abolition of official control over hire purchase terms and extensive changes in the law governing consumer credit.

30 March — The Chancellor of the Exchequer proposed substantial tax reductions in his budget statement, including cuts in corporation tax and selective employment tax, and the abolition of the short term capital gains tax. Proposals for future tax reform included the replacement of purchase tax and SET with a value added tax, and the introduction of a single graduated personal tax.

Restraint on bank lending to the restricted categories was eased; the total was to be allowed to grow at about $2\frac{1}{2}$ per cent of the March 1970 figures in the second quarter of 1971. In future it was hoped to operate on the banks' resources rather than by directly guiding their lending; discussions were to be held between the authorities and the banks and finance houses.

1 April — Bank rate was reduced from 7 to 6 per cent, 'consistent with the requirements of domestic monetary policy' and taking into account 'the prospects of a further fall in overseas interest rates'.

15 April — Lloyds, National Westminster and Midland banks announced that they were to launch jointly a credit card.

20 April — It was announced that the Bank of England had given permission for discount houses to be involved both as principals and brokers in foreign currency deposits.

29 April — National Westminster Bank introduced a medium-term fixed-interest loan scheme for the smaller business.

14 May — The Bank of England consultative document on *Competition and Credit Control* was published (see Appendix 4(e)). It proposed the abolition of the banks' interest rate agreements and the maintenance by all banks of a fixed percentage of their sterling deposit liabilities in specified reserve assets. Ceilings on bank lending were to be removed when the new arrangements became operative, but the authorities were to reserve the right to make qualitative requests.

At the same time the authorities stated that with immediate effect they would not in future generally support the market in gilt-edged securities with a life of one year or more to redemption.

28 May — The governor of the Bank of England in a speech in Munich forecast more frequent changes in bank rate, and the use of Special Deposits and open-market operations to influence the level of interest rates.

5 July	The rates of selective employment tax were halved.
15 July	The Confederation of British Industry announced that it had asked its large company members to give a pledge to avoid price increases or to limit unavoidable ones to 5 per cent over the year ahead.
19 July	Reflationary measures announced by the Chancellor of the Exchequer included the removal of hire purchase restrictions, reductions in purchase tax rates, and a two-year increase in the initial tax allowances on capital equipment and plant.
21 July	Proposed regulations were published for the discount market under the Bank of England's new credit control system; they included a requirement that 50 per cent of the houses' funds should be in public sector debt. Recognized discount houses were to continue to have exclusive lender of last resort facilities at the Bank of England.
16 August	The London gold and foreign exchange markets were closed following the announcement that the United States had suspended the official convertibility of the dollar into gold or other reserve assets, and had imposed an import surcharge. The gold market in London reopened on 17 August, but the foreign exchange market remained closed until 23 August when sterling was allowed to float with a lower support level of \$2·38 against the US dollar but no upper limit.
31 August	Several new exchange control measures were introduced to discourage inflows of funds from abroad, but slight relaxations were announced in mid-September 1971.
2 September	Bank rate was reduced from 6 to 5 per cent in view of 'the present strength of Britain's external position and the current uncertainties in the international monetary situation'.
10 September	The Bank of England issued a notice to banks and finance houses concerning the new approach to credit control (see Appendix 4(g)) which had been outlined in May 1971. A Bank of England paper, *Reserve Ratios and Special Deposits* (see Appendix 4(h)), gave details of the new reserve assets requirements which became operative on 16 September for the London clearing and Scottish banks, although other banks were allowed until the end of the year to comply fully with

the new $12\frac{1}{2}$ per cent minimum 'reserve assets ratio'; existing ceilings on lending were removed. For instalment credit finance houses the ratio was set at a minimum of 10 per cent and they were allowed one year to build up gradually to this position. Special Deposits outstanding were repaid to the London clearing and Scottish banks, but the system was retained and extended to include other banks and finance houses. From 16 September the banks abandoned their interest rate agreements and from 1 October rates were to be related not to bank rate but to a base rate as established by each individual bank. The clearing banks subscribed for about £750 million of three new short-dated government stocks specially issued to absorb excess bank liquidity.

Changes affecting the London discount market were similar to those outlined in the previous July. In addition the market was no longer to tender for Treasury bills at an agreed price, although it would continue to ensure that the total amount of the weekly offering was covered by applications.

1 October — The Midland Bank began paying more than the former CLCB seven-day deposit rate on deposits of between £10,000 and £25,000 placed with a new money market division. On 15 October Barclays Bank reduced its base rate for lending from 5 to $4\frac{1}{2}$ per cent.

7 October — Exchange control regulations were introduced to restrict or prohibit purchases by non-residents of the sterling area of a wide range of securities.

17 November — The Minister of Posts and Telecommunications announced that the National Giro was to remain in operation, but a substantial reshaping was to be made of the service, and charges were to be increased.

2 December — The government announced that the tax reserve certificate scheme was to be withdrawn by stages.

14 December — The Chancellor of the Exchequer announced that all outstanding post-war credits, thought to total up to £130 million, were to be repaid beginning in April 1972.

19 December — Following the discussions in Washington of the Finance Ministers of the Group of Ten, the United Kingdom accepted a new parity or 'middle rate' of \$2·60571 to the pound, with

a maximum permitted margin of fluctuation of 2·25 per cent on either side, representing an effective revaluation of sterling in terms of the dollar of 8·57 per cent, but an unchanged official gold parity. Other leading currencies were similarly revalued against the dollar at varying rates. The Canadian dollar, however, was to continue to float. The United States stated that, subject to Congressional approval and the satisfactory conclusion of short-term international trade negotiations, it proposed to change the official dollar price of gold from $35 to $38 a fine ounce. These various measures were widely regarded as only an interim solution to international currency problems pending agreement on more far-reaching reforms to the world monetary system.

20 December The Bank of England removed the special foreign exchange controls introduced earlier in the year to deter speculative inflows.

'The Authorities' since 1957

Chancellors of the Exchequer in office

G. E. P. Thorneycroft	January 1957 – January 1958
D. H. Amory	January 1958 – July 1960
J. S. B. Lloyd	July 1960 – July 1962
R. Maudling	July 1962 – October 1964
L. J. Callaghan	October 1964 – November 1967
R. H. Jenkins	November 1967 – June 1970
I. N. Macleod	June 1970 – July 1970
A. P. L. Barber	July 1970 –

Governors of the Bank of England in office

Sir C. F. Cobbold	Appointed 1 March 1949 – resigned 30 June 1961 (re-elected twice)
Lord Cromer	1 July 1961 – 30 June 1966
Sir Leslie O'Brien	1 July 1966 – re-elected 1971 for a second five-year period

APPENDIX 2

Statistics

TABLE 1 *United Kingdom balance of payments 1959–1969 (£m.)*

	1959	*1960*	*1961*	*1962*	*1963*	*1964*	*1965*	*1966*	*1967*	*1968*	*1969*
Current account											
Imports*	3639	4138	4043	4095	4362	5005	5054	5255	5674	6916	7202
Exports and re-exports	3522	3732	3891	3993	4282	4486	4817	5182	5122	6273	7061
Visible balance*	−117	−406	−152	−102	− 80	−519	−237	− 73	−552	−643	−141
Government services and transfers (net)†	−227	−282	−332	−360	−382	−432	−447	−470	−464	−462	−458
Other invisibles (net)	+489	+423	+480	+574	+576	+556	+607	+586	+705	+786	+1015
Current balance	+143	−265	− 4	+112	+114	−395	− 77	+ 43	−312	−319	+416
Long-term capital											
Balance	−255	−192	+ 68	− 98	−149	−354	−197	−106	−139	−103	− 31
Balance of current and long-term capital	−112	−457	+ 64	+ 14	− 35	−749	−274	− 63	−451	−422	+385
Balance of monetary movements	+134	+158	− 39	− 89	+104	+760	+242	+ 89	+250	+503	−664
Balancing item	− 22	+299	− 25	+ 75	− 69	− 11	+ 32	− 26	+201	− 81	+279

* Including payments for US military aircraft.
† Payments and receipts of interest, profits and dividends by the government are included in 'Other invisibles'.
Source: United Kingdom Balance of Payments 1970 (HMSO, August 1970)

TABLE 1a *United Kingdom balance of payments (new presentation) 1959–71 (£m.)*

	1959	*1960*	*1961*	*1962*	*1963*	*1964*	*1965*	*1966*	*1967*	*1968*	*1969*	*1970*	*1971*
Currency flows and official financing													
Current account balance*	+152	−255	+ 6	+122	+124	−376	− 52	+ 83	−298	−288	+443	+611	+952
Investment and other capital flows	−108	+286	−316	− 3	−107	−299	−322	−556	−573†	−1005†	− 97	+562	+1847
Balancing item	− 26	+294	− 29	+73	− 75	− 20	+ 21	− 74	+200	−117	+397	+114	+429
Total currency flow	+ 18	+325	−339	+192	− 58	−695	−353	−547	−671	−1410	+743	+1287	+3228
Allocation of Special Drawing Rights												+171	+125
Gold subscription to IMF	− 58	− 32						− 44				− 38	
	− 40	+293	−339	+192	− 58	−695	−353	−591	−671	−1410	+743	+1420	+3353
Financed as follows:													
Official borrowing drawn (+) or repaid (−)	− 79	−116	+370	−375	+ 5	+573	+599	+625‡	+556‡	+1296	−699	−1295	−1817
Official reserves (drawings on, +; additions to, −)	+119	−177	− 31	+183	+ 53	+122	−246	− 34	+115	+114	− 44	−125	−1536

* Figures for current account balance differ from those shown in Table 1 because of late revisions to official statistics.
† Includes Exchange Equalization Account losses on forward dealings (− £105 million in 1967 and − £251 million in 1968).
‡ Includes transfer of official dollar portfolio to reserves (+ £316 million in 1966 and + £204 million in 1967).
Source: United Kingdom Balance of Payments 1971 (HMSO, August 1971)

TABLE 2 *United Kingdom reserves and liabilities* 1959–1970 (£m., end of period)*

	United Kingdom	*Overseas sterling liabilities (net)*				
End of	*Gold and currency reserves*	*£ area countries*	*non-£ area countries*	*International organizations*	*Total*	*External banking and money market liabilities*
1959	977	2691	682	705	4078	
1960	1154	2463	1312	549	4324	
1961	1185	2616	768	958	4342	
1962*	1002	2653	682	605	3940	
1962*	1002	2430	733	606	3769	
1963	949	2592	670	627	3889	3084
1964	827	2591	714	991	4296	3049
1965	1073	2593	775	1481	4849	2994
1966	1107	2595	885	1655	5135	2946
1967	1123	2448	1336	1540	5324	2700
1968	1009	2311	1626	2082	6019	2414
1969	1053	2529	763	2123	5415	2438
1970	1178					2813

* The statistical series, Overseas Sterling Holdings, was replaced in 1963 by a new series entitled 'External Liabilities and Claims in Sterling', with figures for 1962 provided for both. The new figures were more comprehensive than before with additional reporting institutions, and claims and liabilities were arranged under different headings (see *Bank of England Quarterly Bulletin*, June 1963). Figures on the old basis for the years 1959–62 were officially revised to bring them as far as possible into line with the later series. The official series was further radically revised in conception in 1970, then becoming restricted to external banking and money market liabilities in sterling as shown in the last column of the Table 2; figures on the new basis were given back to 1963 only.

Sources: Bank of England Quarterly Bulletin, Bank of England Statistical Abstract and *Financial Statistics.*

TABLE 3 *Assistance for sterling *1959–1971* (£m.)

End of	*Borrowing with a sterling counterpart*					*Foreign currency deposits*	*Total*†	*US dollar equivalent*‡ (\$*m.*)
	IMF	*Swiss loan*	*FRB swap arrangement*	*Other*	*Total*			
1959	116	—	—	—	116	—	116	325
1960	—	—	—	—	—	—	—	—
1961	370	—	—	—	370	—	370	1040
1962	—	—	—	—	—	—	—	—
1963	—	—	—	—	—	—	—	—
1964 June	—	—	5	—	5	—	5	15
Sept.	—	—	12	—	12	59	71	200
Dec.	357	28	71	45	501	72	573	1605
1965 Mar.	351	28	114	151	644	100	744	2083
June	851	42	129	53	1075	—	1075	3012
Sept.	851	42	268	97	1258	—	1258	3523
Dec.	846	42	169	115	1172	—	1172	3283
1966 Mar.	880	42	—	133	1055	—	1055	2956
June	868	42	54	148	1112	—	1112	3113
Sept.	867	42	143	489	1541	18	1559	4364
Dec.	861	42	125	439	1467	14	1481	4148
1967 Mar.	835	42	—	152	1029	—	1029	2884
June	665	14	81	129	889	—	889	2490
Sept.	656	14	232	457	1359	—	1359	3804
Dec.	628	17	438	791	1874	193	2067	4961

TABLE 3 (*contd.*)

End of	*Borrowing with a sterling counterpart*					*Foreign currency deposits*	*Total†*	*US dollar equivalent‡ ($m.)*
	IMF	*Swiss loan*	*FRB swap arrangement*	*Other*	*Total*			
1968 Mar.	628	17	458	1174	2277	320	2597	6233
June	1211	17	—	1472	2700	402	3102	7446
Sept.	1176	14	167	1502	2859	281	3140	7536
Dec.	1134	11	480	1527	3152	211	3363	8071
1969 Mar.	1000	4	458	1493	2955	156	3111	7466
June	1125	—	427	1222	2774	244	3018	7243
Sept.	1115	—	458	1203	2776	285	3061	7346
Dec.	1104	—	271	1139	2514	150	2664	6394
1970 Mar.	1000	—	—	654	1654	—	1654	3969
June	992	—	—	469	1461	—	1461	3506
Sept.	985	—	167	459	1611	—	1611	3866
Dec.	970	—	—	399	1369	—	1369	3286
1971 Mar.	683	—	—	—	683	—	683	1640
June	675	—	—	—	675	—	675	1619
Sept.	415	—	—	—	415	—	415	997

* UK official short- and medium-term borrowing from abroad.
† Including foreign currency deposits.
‡ Calculated $2·80 = £1 to end-September 1967, and $2·40 = £1 from end-December 1967.
Source: Bank of England Statistical Abstract, to end-1969; later figures from *Bank of England Quarterly Bulletin*.

TABLE 4 *UK Central government receipts and outgoings 1958–9 to 1971–2 (£m.)*

Fiscal year	*Ordinary revenue*	*Ordinary expenditure*	*Net below-the-line expenditure*	*Combined surplus (+) or deficit (−)*
1958–59	5,480	5,064	553	−138
1959–60	5,631	5,205	700	−275
1960–61	5,934	5,747	536	−349
1961–62	6,645	6,195	626	−176
1962–63	6,794	6,400	416	− 22
1963–64	6,890	6,776	551	−437
1964–65*	7,727	7,265	846	−384
	Ordinary revenue	*Ordinary expenditure*	*Net consolidated fund loans*	*Combined surplus (+) or deficit (−)*
1964–65*	8,157	7,713	830	−386
1965–66	9,144	8,456	1265	−577
1966–67	10,279	9,541	1478	−740
1967–68*	11,855	11,525	1661	−1331
	Ordinary revenue	*Ordinary expenditure*	*Net lending from the National Loans Fund*	*Combined surplus (+) or deficit (−)*
1967–68*	11,227	10,871	1744	−1312
1968–69	13,363	11,615	1423	+287
1969–70	15,266	12,822	1439	+961
1970–71	15,843	14,086	1560	+203
1971–72	16,897	15,499	1965	−567

* The system of government accounting was changed in the year 1964–5, and again in the year 1967–8 when figures on the old and the new bases were given, as above.

Sources: Government finance accounts published in the *London Gazette*; *Financial Statistics*.

TABLE 5 *Fluctuations in bank liabilities and assets, quarterly, 1959–1972 (£m.)*

Clearing banks		*Net deposits**	*Public sector assets*			*Net advances to private sector*	*Commercial bills*
			Investments	*Other†*	*Total*		
1959	2nd qtr	+143	−118	+124	+ 6	+149	+ 9
	3rd qtr	+252	− 31	+139	+109	+144	− 6
	4th qtr	+320	− 70	+136	+ 65	+187	+ 34
1960	1st qtr	−359	−229	−282	−511	+194	− 11
	2nd qtr	+111	−123	+ 85	− 38	+123	− 8
	3rd qtr	+ 88	− 62	+125	+ 63	+ 56	− 14
	4th qtr	+187	− 24	+ 70	+ 46	+ 85	+ 24
1961	1st qtr	−118	− 85	−262	−347	+125	+ 58
	2nd qtr	+216	−102	+187	+ 85	+144	+ 14
	3rd qtr	− 44	− 36	+185	+149	−179	+ 28
	4th qtr	+ 24	+ 71	+113	+184	−109	− 3
1962	1st qtr	−125	− 23	−255	−278	+166	+ 20
	2nd qtr	+164	+ 91	+ 23	+114	+ 25	+ 3
	3rd qtr	+ 74	+ 48	+ 33	+ 81	+ 27	—
	4th qtr	+179	+ 81	—	+ 81	+ 78	− 9
1963	1st qtr	−140	− 83	−395	−478	+333	+ 42
	2nd qtr	+173	− 32	+123	+ 93	+ 62	+ 5
	3rd qtr	+157	+ 24	+109	+133	+ 37	− 19
	4th qtr	+221	+ 50	+ 81	+130	+ 23	+ 9
1964	1st qtr	−104	− 84	−304	−388	+254	+ 50
	2nd qtr	+134	+ 18	+ 28	+ 46	+ 49	+ 10
	3rd qtr	+260	− 3	+ 83	+ 80	+173	− 7
	4th qtr	+215	− 39	+ 27	− 12	+100	+ 68
1965	1st qtr	−187	−131	−155	−286	+133	+ 17
	2nd qtr	+233	− 1	+173	+172	+ 16	+ 3
	3rd qtr	+156	+ 7	+130	+137	− 18	+ 18
	4th qtr	+224	+117	+173	+290	−100	− 8
1966	1st qtr	− 79	− 74	−180	−254	+245	− 9
	2nd qtr	+ 34	+ 5	+ 17	+ 22	− 12	+ 5
	3rd qtr	+156	+ 4	+278	+282	−149	− 2
	4th qtr	− 3	+ 59	+ 54	+113	−171	+ 25
1967	1st qtr	−139	+102	−367	−265	+162	+ 7
	2nd qtr	+339	+ 71	+149	+220	+ 91	+ 9
	3rd qtr	+250	+ 16	+169	−185	− 5	+ 15
	4th qtr	+202	+ 25	+124	+149	+ 25	− 16
1968	1st qtr	+ 40	− 47	−277	−324	+369	+ 21
	2nd qtr	+ 74	− 46	+ 40	− 6	− 43	+ 52
	3rd qtr	+288	+ 56	+289	+345	− 37	− 30
	4th qtr	+ 84	+ 52	+ 47	+ 99	− 19	− 7

TABLE 5 (*contd.*)

Clearing banks	Net deposits*	Public sector assets			Net advances to private sector	Commercial bills
		Investments	Other†	Total		
1969 1st qtr	−201	−202	−274	−476	+271	− 3
2nd qtr	− 43	− 55	+ 37	− 18	− 77	+ 38
3rd qtr	+ 41	− 60	− 55	−115	+126	+ 36
4th qtr	+107	− 18	+238	+220	−165	+ 13
1970 1st qtr	− 62	− 21	−490	−511	+407	+ 66
2nd qtr	+127	− 41	+ 96	+ 55	+ 2	+ 44
3rd qtr	+382	− 42	+296	+254	+ 84	+ 21
4th qtr	+249	− 14	+337	+323	−121	+ 25
1971 1st qtr	+352	+ 68	−138	− 70	+206	+ 57
2nd qtr	− 50	+ 59	−108	− 49	− 48	+ 85
3rd qtr	+428	+763	−484	+279	+ 69	+157
4th qtr	+1131	+ 60	+118	+178	+957	+ 40
1972 1st qtr	+484	−159	−275	−434	+1121	− 68
Financial years						
1958–59	+241	−209	−140	−350	+524	+ 3
1959–60	+324	−448	+117	−331	+674	+ 26
1960–61	+ 71	−294	+ 18	−276	+348	+ 60
1961–62	+195	− 91	+230	+139	+ 29	+ 60
1962–63	+276	+137	−339	−202	+464	+ 37
1963–64	+448	− 42	+ 8	− 34	+377	+ 46
1964–65	+422	−155	− 18	−173	+456	+ 88
1965–66	+534	+ 63	+320	+368	+119	+ 4
1966–67	+ 47	+172	− 18	+151	−170	+ 35
1967–68	+831	+177	+165	+229	+480	+ 29
1968–69	+244	−128	+102	− 39	+172	+ 12
1969–70	− 32	−154	−270	−424	+291	+152
1970–71	+1111	− 29	+591	+562	+171	+147
1971–72	+1193	+723	−372	+351	+2099	+215

* Total deposits, less items in transit and balances with, and cheques in course of collection on, other banks.

† Treasury bills, money at call and short notice, Special Deposits and advances to nationalized industries.

TABLE 6 *Clearing banks asset ratios 1938, 1946, 1958–1971 (per cent of gross deposits)*

Average for year	*Total liquid assets†*	*Gross advances**	*Investments*
1938	29·6	43·0	28·0
1946	25·2‡	17·5	26·4
1958	34·0	29·0	32·4
1959	32·9	37·8	26·5
1960	31·8	*44·7*	19·5
1961	33·0	47·0	15·2
1962	33·5	46·7	15·7
1963	31·8	50·5	15·6
1964	30·3	52·7	14·3
1965	30·7	53·8	12·1
1966	31·0	52·5	12·1
1967	30·6	50·4	13·7
1968	30·5	50·3	13·2
1969	*30·1*	*51·9*	*11·3*
1970§	31·7	51·9	11·2
1971 March§	32·4	54·9	10·2

* Some change in composition was made in 1961.

† Excluding Special Deposits. Details of calls and releases of Special Deposits are given in Table 7, p. 465.

‡ Excluding Treasury deposit receipts, equivalent to 29·3 per cent of total deposits.

§ Not strictly comparable with earlier figures due to accounting changes associated with disclosure of 'true' profits.

TABLE 7 *Special Deposits of London clearing banks* with Bank of England 1960–1971*

Date of		*Call or release (−)*		*Cumulative total*	
Announcement	*Transfer*	*% of gross deposits*	*£m.†*	*% of gross deposits*	*£m.†*
1960 28 April	by 15 June	1	70	1	70
23 June	by 20 July	½	35	1½	105
	by 17 August	½	38	2	143
1961 25 July	by 16 August	½	38	2½	185
	by 20 September	½	36	3	221
1962 31 May	on 12 June	−½	36	2½	185
	on 18 June	−½	36	2	149
27 September	on 8 October	−½	38	1½	113
	on 15 October	−½	38	1	75
29 November	on 10 December	−½	39	½	38
	on 17 December	−½	38	nil	nil
1965 29 April	by 19 May	½	44	½	44
	by 16 June	½	43	1	87
1966 14 July	by 20 July	½	47	1½	140
	by 17 August	½	49	2	189
1970 14 April	by 6 May	½	51	2½	247
29 October	by 11 November	1	108	3½	366
1971 10 September	by 15 September	−3½	393	nil	nil

* For the Scottish banks the percentage rate has throughout been one half of that of the clearing banks and the cumulative total for Scotland on 11 November 1970 was £19·6 million. Special Deposits were not called from Northern Irish banks.

† The amounts fluctuate in accordance with movements in gross deposits and hence the figures for calls and releases do not necessarily correspond with the amount outstanding at the previous change.

Source: Financial Statistics

TABLE 8 *Classified advances of members of British Bankers' Association* 1946, 1958–1966 (£m., February of each year)*

	1946	*1958*	*1959*	*1960*	*1961*	*1962*	*1963*	*1964*	*1965*	*1966*
Agriculture and fishing	67	212	259	325	371	367	412	458	505	523
Heavy industry	84	286	342	401	583	645	704	712	849	1018
Textiles	22	112	108	135	151	165	171	200	224	221
Food, drink and tobacco	57	129	177	196	213	207	215	228	270	314
Other industry and manufacture	107	322	394	517	612	702	777	839	949	1072
Services (including retail trade)	99	211	288	398	442	452	536	598	624	655
Total industry and trade	435	1271	1568	1971	2371	2538	2814	3035	3421	3803
Public utilities	7	54	76	78	78	85	90	89	53	63
Local government	79	75	95	90	91	79	76	79	91	74
Personal and professional	240	320	437	638	691	672	794	946	1007	933
Financial and other	88	222	292	467	487	476	551	667	755	717
Total	848	1941	2467	3243	3717	3850	4325	4817	5327	5590
Total clearing banks only	n.a.	1632	2080	2765	3153	3233	3608	4044	4472	4665

* The figures relate to all advances made by member banks of the British Bankers' Association through offices located within Great Britain, irrespective of the borrowers' country of residence. Advances exclude bills discounted and foreign bills negotiated or bought and also 'internal' accounts. Members of the B.B.A. comprise the London clearing banks and the Scottish banks; most of the Northern Ireland banks and the other deposit banks; and most members of the British Overseas and Commonwealth Banks Association (see Table 8a for later figures on different basis).

Source: Bank of England Statistical Abstract No. 1, 1970

TABLE 8a *Classified advances of the banking sector* (£m., February of each year)*

	1967	*1968*	*1969*	*1970*	*1971*	*1972*
Manufacturing						
Food, drink and tobacco	241	285	306	372	445	427
Chemicals	214	215	241	268	322	337
Metal manufacturing	197	192	195	151	219	173
Engineering, shipbuilding and vehicles	1059	1152	1350	1,707	2,163	2,105
Other manufacturing	525	562	660	723	827	762
Total	2236	2406	2751	3,221	3,976	3,804
Other production						
Agriculture, forestry and fishing	474	490	528	504	528	575
Mining and quarrying	81	91	118	93	121	150
Construction	345	371	389	408	471	608
Total	900	952	1035	1,005	1,120	1,333
Services						
Transport and communications	162	181	181	248	304	301
Public utilities and local government	167	233	166	198	219	247
Distribution	694	757	840	811	816	1,042
Other services	471	529	624	591	656	825
Total	1494	1700	1811	1,848	1,995	2,415
Financial	773	902	947	966	1,129	1,828
Personal	820	967	978	888	1,048	1,641
Overseas residents	1046	1577	2382	2,960	5,868	6,455
Total	7629	8484	9905	10,887	15,136	17,475
Total clearing banks only	4575	5030	5292	5,437	6,006	7,330

* Covers all banks in Great Britain that contribute to the official banking sector figures. This analysis is based so far as possible on the Standard Industrial Classification and although some headings are the same as in the former BBA series (see Table 8) the contents of most are not identical. This classification compares advances, both in sterling and foreign currencies, provided by banks to their customers, but, unlike the earlier series, lending to overseas residents is shown separately. Funds placed through the specialized financial markets with other banks or with local authorities or finance houses are excluded.

Source: Financial Statistics

TABLE 9 *Interest rates at selected dates*

	1959	*1960*				*1961*			*1962*				*1963*		*1964*	
	30 June	*30 Jan.*	*24 June*	*29 Oct.*	*10 Dec.*	*29 July*	*7 Oct.*	*4 Nov.*	*10 Mar.*	*24 Mar.*	*28 Apr.*	*6 Oct.*	*5 Jan.*	*27 Sept.*	*28 Feb.*	*24 Dec.*
Bank rate*	4·00	5·00	6·00	5·50	5·00	7·00	6·50	6·00	5·50	5·00	4·50	4·50	4·00	4·00	5·00	7·00
Treasury bills†	3·45	4·54	5·68	5·09	4·48	6·69	6·12	5·43	5·02	4·45	4·05	3·62	3·56	3·67	4·31	6·63
Defence/national development/ British savings bonds‡	5·00	5·00	5·00	5·00	5·00	5·00	5·00	5·00	5·00	5·00	5·00	5·00	5·00	4·50	4·50	5·00
National savings certificates§*	4·20	4·20	4·20	4·20	4·20	4·20	4·20	4·20	4·20	4·20	4·20	4·20	4·20	3·79	3·79	3·79
Local authorities' deposits (7 days' notice)	—	—	5·81	5·50	5·13	7·50	6·69	6·07	6·00	5·75	4·88	4·13	4·13	4·25	4·81	8·00
Eurodollars (3 months)	—	—	—	—	—	—	—	—	—	—	—	3·94	3·75	4·00	4·00	4·88
Inter-bank (sterling overnight rate)‖	—	—	—	—	—	—	—	—	—	—	—	—	—	—	—	6·25
Government securities:																
'Medium-term' – a representative stock	5·21	5·40	5·98	5·97	6·06	6·53	6·47	6·09	6·22	6·24	6·22	4·78	5·04	4·83	5·53	6·47
'Irredeemable' – 2½ per cent Consols	4·76	5·18	5·68	5·45	5·63	6·57	6·44	6·35	6·25	6·17	6·10	5·58	5·56	5·43	6·08	6·32
Long-term loans:																
Public Works Loan Board	5·75	5·88	5·88	6·13	6·13	6·25	7·00	7·00	6·75	6·75	6·75	6·38	5·88	5·75	5·75	6·00
Agricultural Mortgage Corporation	5·50	5·50	6·00	6·50	6·50	7·00	7·50	7·50	7·50	7·50	7·50	7·00	6·50	6·00	6·50	6·75

	1965		1966		1967					1968		1969		1970		1971	
	11 June	*31 Dec.*	*8 July*	*30 Dec.*	*10 Mar.*	*28 Apr.*	*5 May*	*21 Oct.*	*24 Nov.*	*22 Mar.*	*20 Sept.*	*28 Feb.*	*13 June*	*6 Mar.*	*24 Apr.*	*30 Apr.*	*29 Oct.*
Bank rate*	6·00	6·00	6·00	7·00	6·50	6·00	5·50	6·00	8·00	7·50	7·00	8·00	8·00	7·50	7·00	6·00	5·00
Treasury bills†	5·60	5·53	5·81	6·53	5·86	5·41	5·23	5·73	7·55	7·14	6·61	7·71	7·91	7·33	6·77	5·68	4·27
Defence/national development/ British savings bonds‡	5·00	5·00	5·00	5·50	5·50	5·50	5·50	5·50	5·50	5·50	6·00	6·00	7·00	7·00	7·00	7·00	7·00
National savings certificates§*	3·79	3·79	4·56	4·56	4·56	4·56	4·56	4·56	4·56	4·56	4·56	4·56	4·56	4·56	4·56	5·74	5·74
Local authorities' deposits (7 days' notice)	6·10	6·25	6·13	7·25	6·50	6·13	5·75	6·00	8·06	8·69	7·38	8·50	8·44	11·00	7·50	6·31	4·56
Eurodollars (3 months)	5·00	5·25	6·38	6·56	5·50	4·75	4·75	5·63	7·00	6·63	5·88	8·50	11·44	9·25	8·50	6·25	5·13
Inter-bank (sterling overnight rate)‖	5·56	5·75	6·44	7·00	5·94	5·88	4·56	5·72	7·88	9·75	7·06	8·56	9·25	7·63	5·75	4·50	4·50
Government securities:																	
'Medium-term' – a representative stock	6·83	6·68	7·18	6·74	6·45	6·38	6·38	7·04	7·25	7·30	7·50	8·50	9·50	8·54	9·26	8·54	7·45
'Irredeemable' – 2½ per cent Consols	6·63	6·46	6·98	6·65	6·37	6·36	6·39	6·92	7·09	7·13	7·35	8·48	9·57	8·35	9·18	9·15	8·67
Long-term loans:																	
Public Works Loan Board	6·00	6·00	6·00	6·00	6·00	6·00	6·00	7·00	7·38	7·38	7·63	8·50	9·50	8·75	8·75	9·13	8·13
Agricultural Mortgage Corporation	7·75	7·75	7·75	8·50	8·50	7·50	7·50	7·75	8·00	8·50	8·25	9·25	10·25	10·25	9·75	10·25	8·50

* Throughout the period, until 1 October 1971, the rate paid by the London clearing banks on deposits at 7 days' notice remained at 2 per cent below bank rate

† Average discount rate at weekly tender

‡ Excluding any tax-free bonus payable on maturity

§ Cumulative rate, free of tax, if held for full term (5 to 7 years according to issue)

‖ Rates are generally for the last Friday of the month and therefore do not necessarily correspond with the date at the head of the column.

TABLE 10 *Changes in UK bank rate* since 1951*

Date of change		*Amount of increase or decrease*	*New rate (%)*	*Date of change*		*Amount of increase or decrease*	*New rate (%)*
1951	8 November†	+ ½	2½	1962	8 March	− ½	5½
1952	12 March	+1½	4		22 March	− ½	5
1953	17 September	− ½	3½		26 April	− ½	4½
1954	13 May	− ½	3	1963	3 January	− ½	4
1955	27 January	+ ½	3½	1964	27 February	+1	5
	24 February	+1	4½		23 November	+2	7
1956	16 February	+1	5½	1965	3 June	−1	6
1957	7 February	− ½	5		14 July	+1	7
	19 September	+2	7	1967	26 January	− ½	6½
1958	20 March	−1	6		16 March	− ½	6
	22 May	− ½	5½		4 May	− ½	5½
	19 June	− ½	5		19 October	+ ½	6
	14 August	− ½	4½		9 November	+ ½	6½
	20 November	− ½	4		18 November	+1½	8
1960	21 January	+1	5	1968	21 March	− ½	7½
	23 June	+1	6		19 September	− ½	7
	27 October	− ½	5½	1969	27 February	+1	8
	8 December	− ½	5	1970	5 March	− ½	7½
1961	26 July	+2	7		15 April	− ½	7
	5 October	− ½	6½	1971	1 April	−1	6
	2 November	− ½	6		2 September	−1	5

* The minimum rate at which the Bank of England stands ready to lend at last resort to a discount house which has the privilege of access to the Discount Office of the Bank either by rediscounting bills of approved quality or by lending against the security of such bills or of short-dated government securities.

† Prior to 1951 bank rate had remained unchanged at 2 per cent since being lowered from 3 per cent on 26 October 1939.

Source: Financial Statistics

TABLE 11 *The Price of Gold 1958–1971 (per fine ounce)*

	*Sterling price at daily fixing**		*US dollars (mid point of daily range)*	
	Highest £ *s. d.*	*Lowest* £ *s. d.*	*Highest*	*Lowest*
1958	12.10.11 (July)	12. 8. 8½ (January)	35·14	34·99
1959	12.10. 9 (September)	12. 8.11¾ (April)	35·14½	35·05
1960	13.10. 0 (October)	12. 9. 9½ (April)	38·25	35·06½
1961	12.14.11 (January)	12. 9. 8¼ (November)	35·82½	35·06
1962	12.11. 3¼ (October)	12. 9. 1¼ (March)	35·20	35·07
1963	12.10.11¾ (September)	12. 9. 9¾ (January)	35·12	35·05½
1964	12.12. 4¾ (October)	12.10. 6 (May)	35·13	35·06
1965	12.12. 3 (August)	12.10. 3¾ (November)	35·19½	35·09
1966	12.12. 5¾ (September)	12.10. 6½ (January)	35·20	35·11½
1967	14.13. 2¾ (December)	12.11. 2 (April)	35·21	35·14½
1968	17.17. 2 (May)	14.11. 6¼ (January)	42·60	35·13¾
1969	18. 6.11 (March)	14.12. 0 (December)	43·82½	35·00
1970	16. 8. 0½ (October)	14. 9. 6½ (January)	39·19	34·75
	£ p	£ p		
1971	18 162 (August)	15 592 (January)	43·94	38·27½

* Since 1 April 1968 two 'fixings' have taken place each day in the London market instead of one previously. At the same time the London price began to be quoted in US dollar terms instead of sterling. Following the Washington Agreement of March 1968 a two-tier gold price system was introduced with the official price for transactions between central banks held at $35 a fine ounce.

Source: Annual Bullion Reviews of Samuel Montagu

APPENDIX 3

Charts illustrating monetary and economic background 1958-1971

The charts are based on series appearing regularly in the *Midland Bank Review*, except where otherwise stated. They are quarterly averages of monthly figures, when available, plotted at mid-quarter. All index numbers have been put on the base of average 1958 = 100. Where figures are seasonally adjusted this is stated.

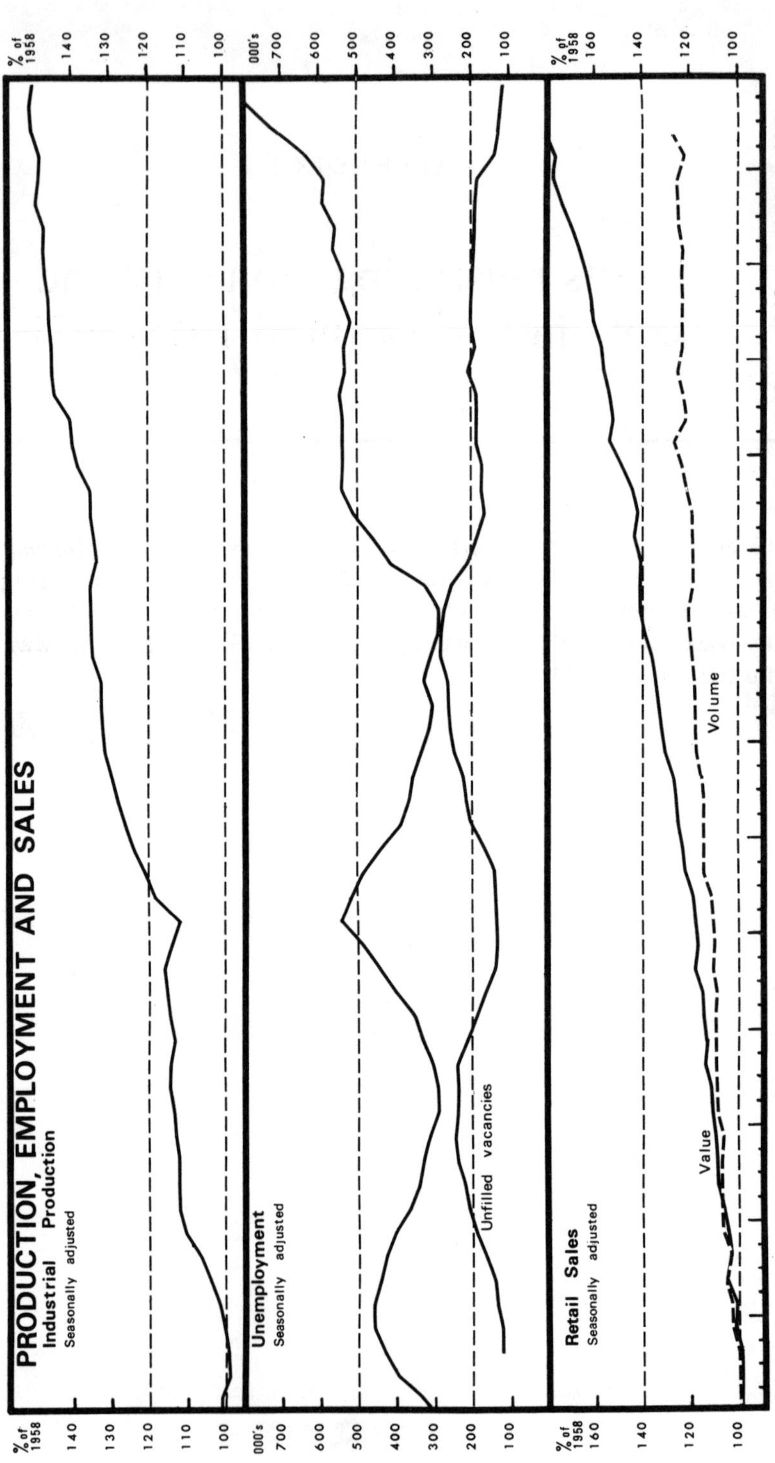

PRODUCTION, EMPLOYMENT AND SALES
Industrial Production
Seasonally adjusted
% of 1958
140
130
120
110
100
Unemployment
Seasonally adjusted
000's
700
600
500
400
300
200
100
Unfilled vacancies
Retail Sales
Seasonally adjusted
% of 1958
160
140
120
100
Value
Volume
1958
1959
1960
1961
1962
1963
1964
1965
1966
1967
1968
1969
1970
1971

Chart (a)

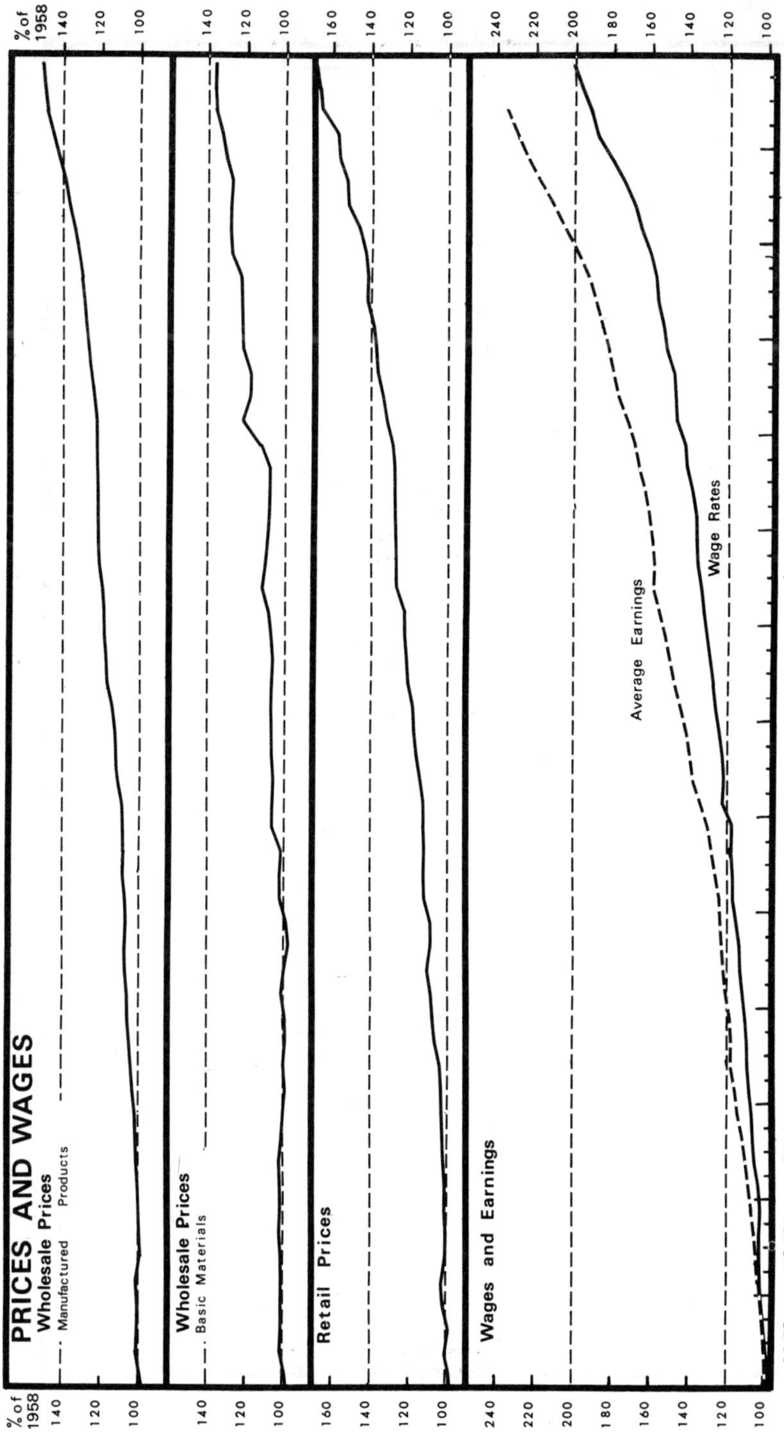

PRICES AND WAGES
Wholesale Prices
Manufactured Products
Wholesale Prices
Basic Materials
Retail Prices
Wages and Earnings
Average Earnings
Wage Rates
% of 1958
1958
1959
1960
1961
1962
1963
1964
1965
1966
1967
1968
1969
1970
1971

Chart (b)

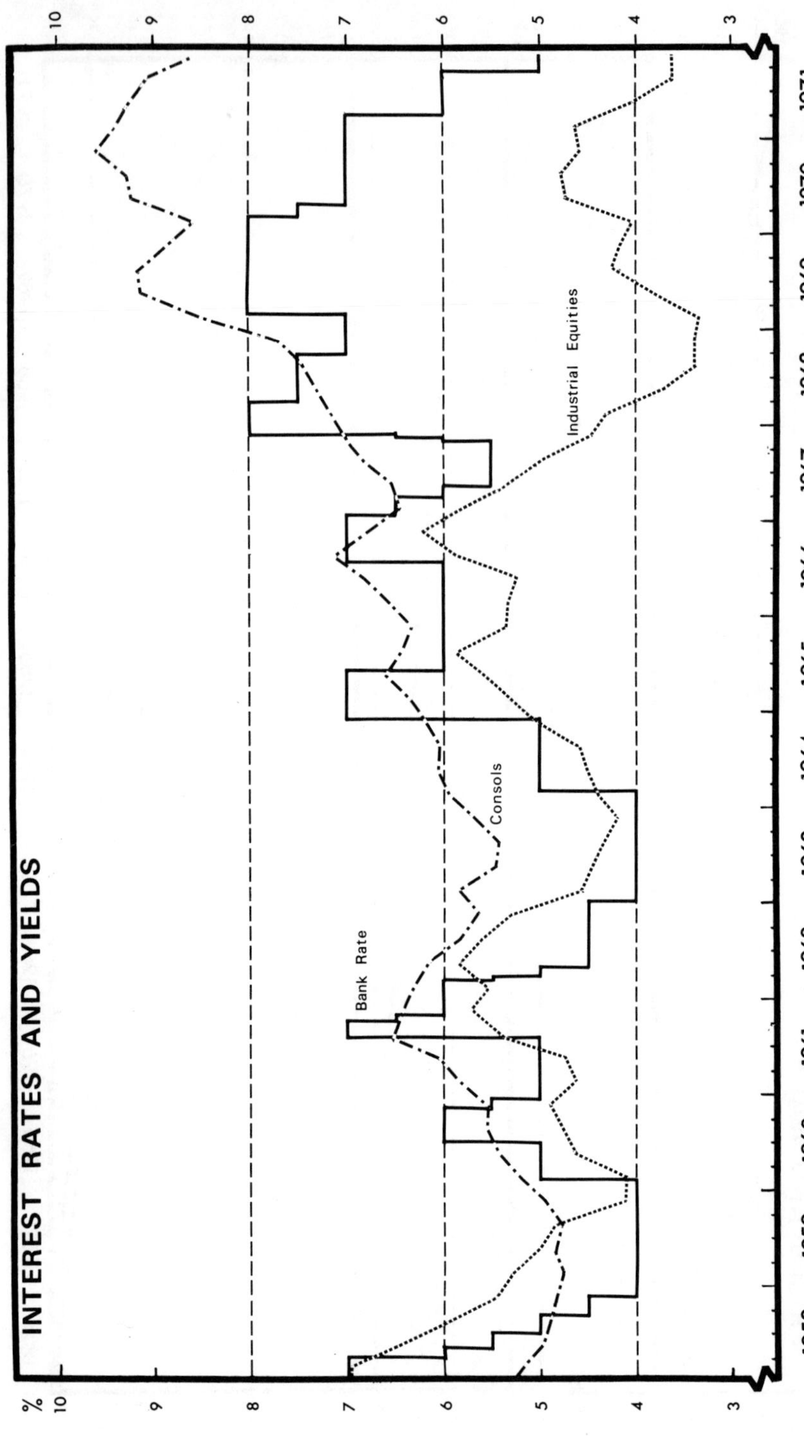

INTEREST RATES AND YIELDS
%
10
9
8
7
6
5
4
3
Bank Rate
Consols
Industrial Equities
1958
1959
1960
1961
1962
1963
1964
1965
1966
1967
1968
1969
1970
1971

Chart (c)

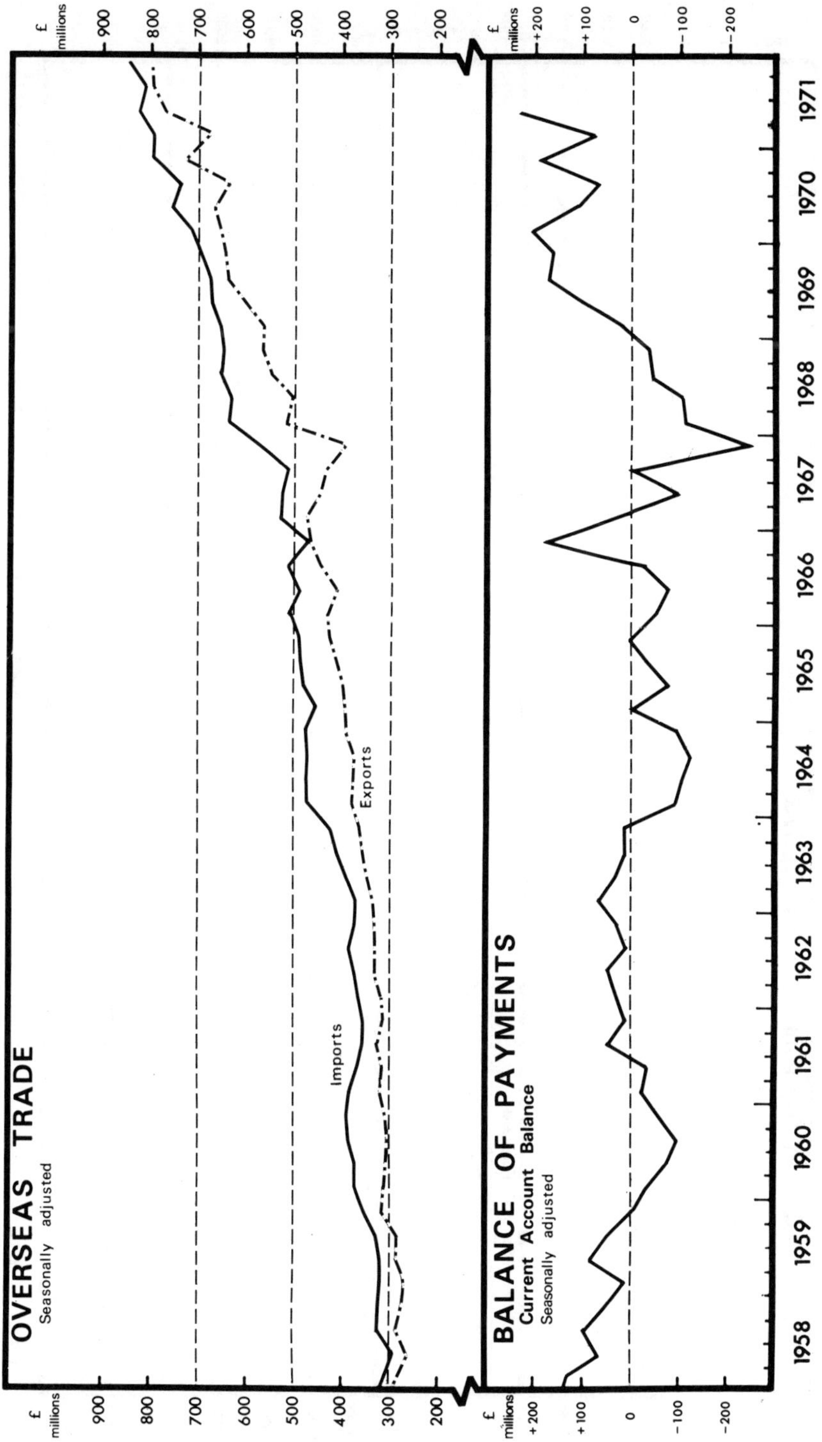
OVERSEAS TRADE
Seasonally adjusted
Imports
Exports
BALANCE OF PAYMENTS
Current Account Balance
Seasonally adjusted
£ millions
900
800
700
600
500
400
300
200
+200
+100
0
-100
-200
1958
1959
1960
1961
1962
1963
1964
1965
1966
1967
1968
1969
1970
1971

Chart (d)

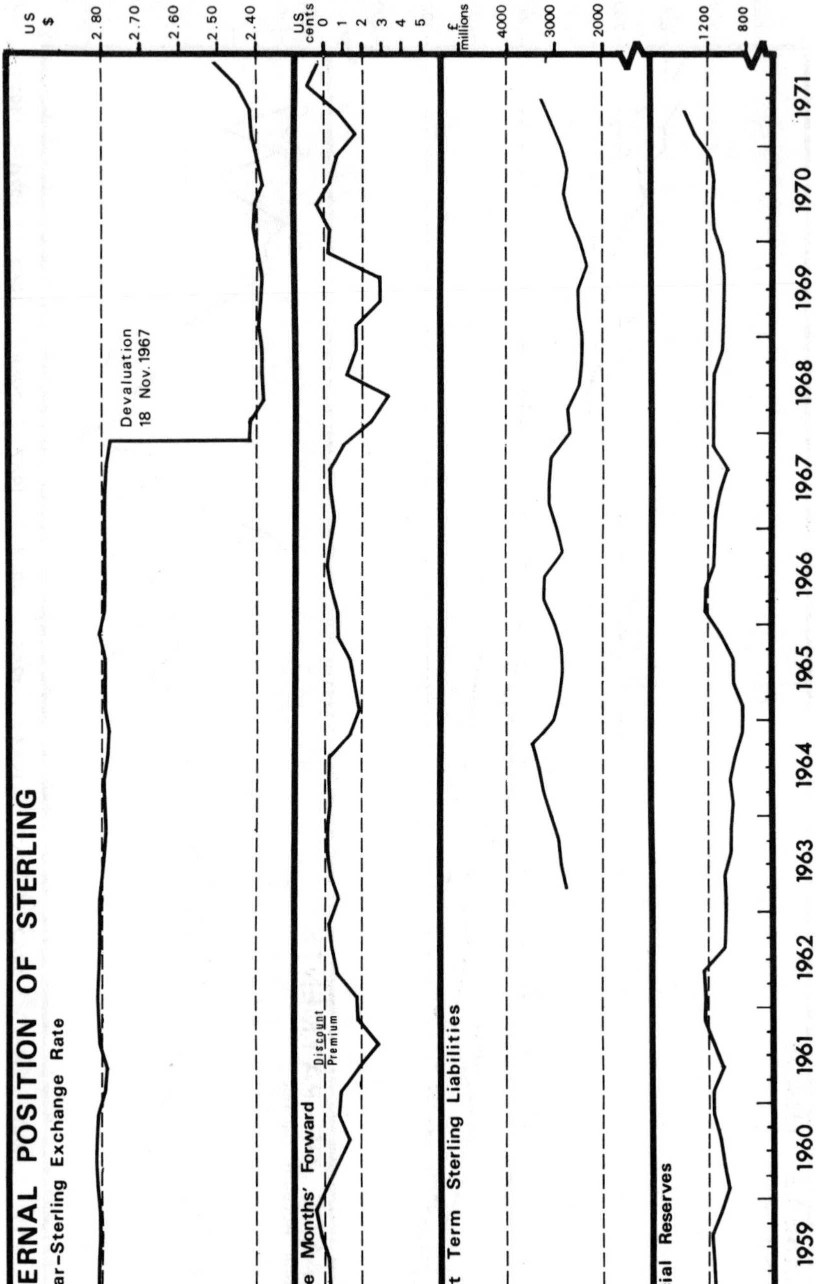

EXTERNAL POSITION OF STERLING
Dollar-Sterling Exchange Rate
Devaluation
18 Nov. 1967
Three Months' Forward
Discount
Premium
Short Term Sterling Liabilities
Official Reserves
US $
2.80
2.70
2.60
2.50
2.40
US cents
0
1
2
3
4
5
£ millions
4000
3000
2000
1200
800
1958
1959
1960
1961
1962
1963
1964
1965
1966
1967
1968
1969
1970
1971

Chart (e)

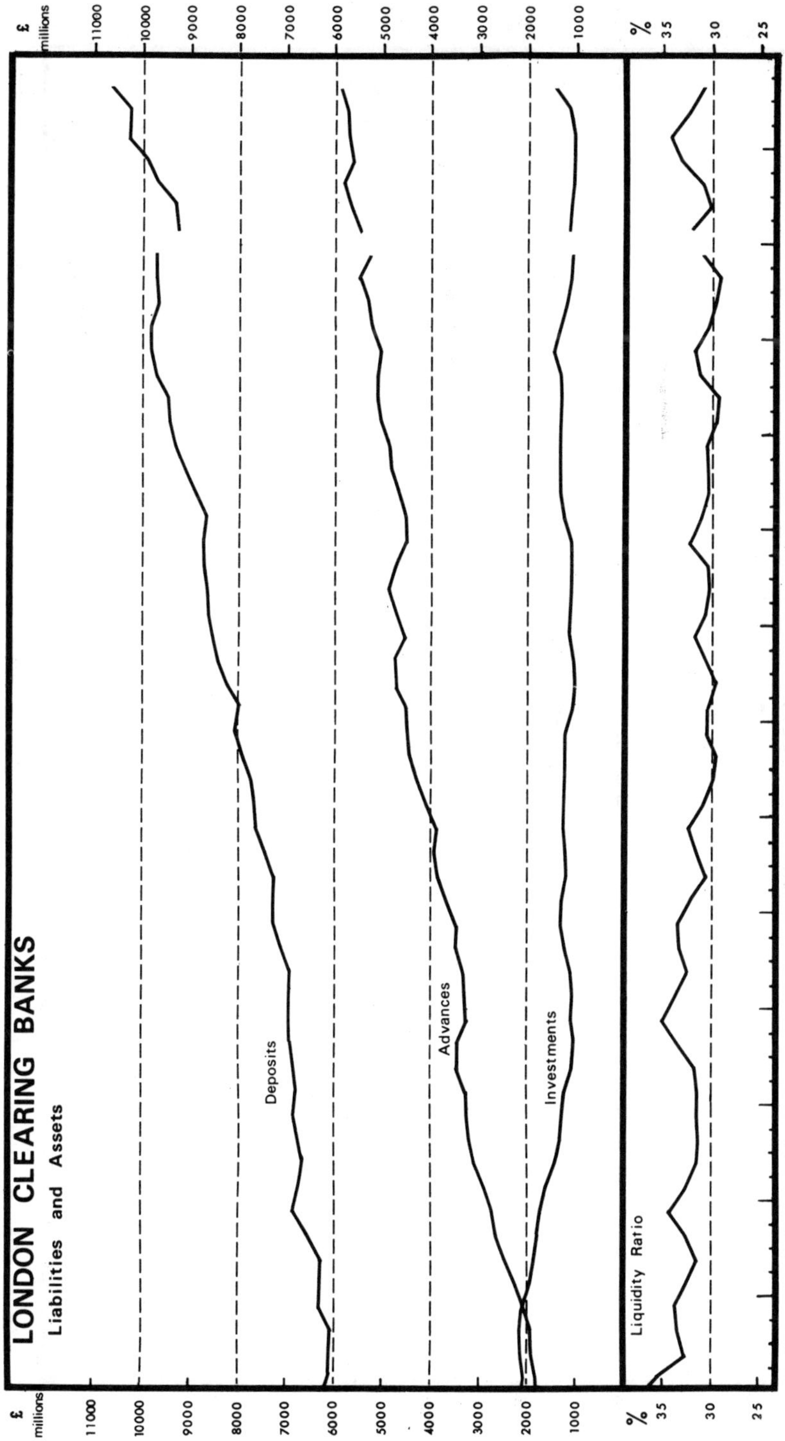

LONDON CLEARING BANKS
Liabilities and Assets
£ millions
11000
10000
9000
8000
7000
6000
5000
4000
3000
2000
1000
Deposits
Advances
Investments
%
35
30
25
Liquidity Ratio
1958
1959
1960
1961
1962
1963
1964
1965
1966
1967
1968
1969
1970
1971

Chart (f)

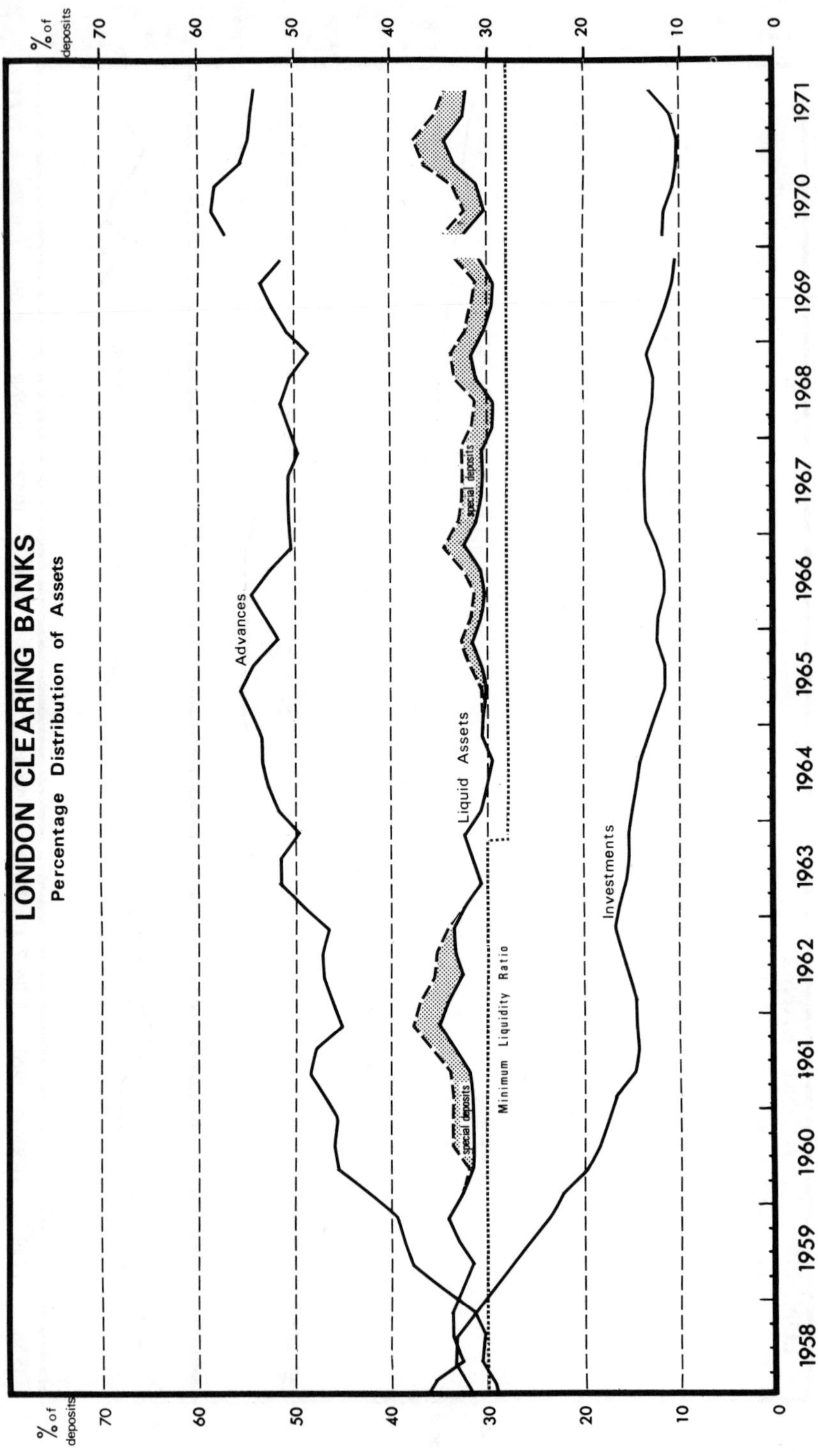

LONDON CLEARING BANKS
Percentage Distribution of Assets
Advances
Liquid Assets
special deposits
special deposits
Minimum Liquidity Ratio
Investments
% of deposits
70
60
50
40
30
20
10
0
1958
1959
1960
1961
1962
1963
1964
1965
1966
1967
1968
1969
1970
1971

Chart (g)

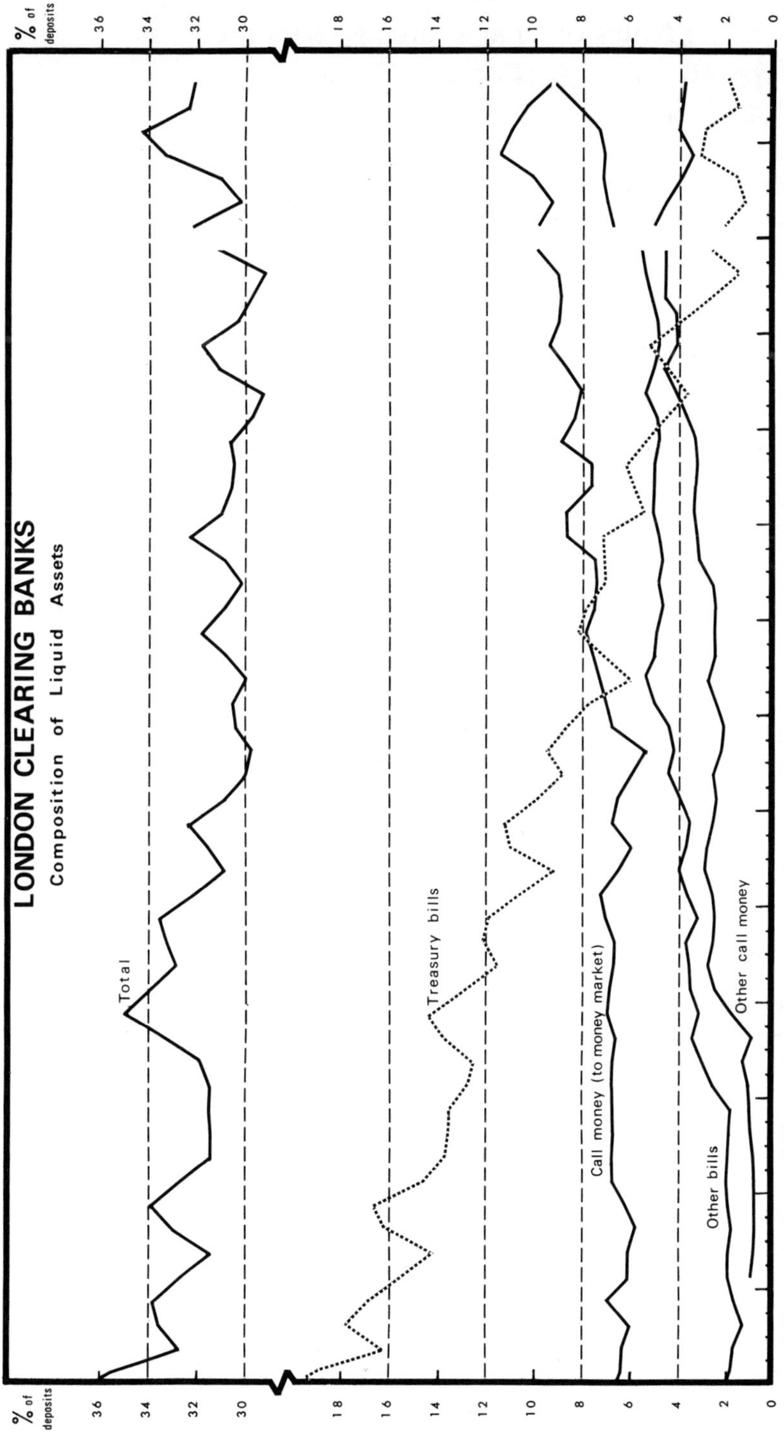
LONDON CLEARING BANKS
Composition of Liquid Assets
% of deposits
36
34
32
30
18
16
14
12
10
8
6
4
2
0
Total
Treasury bills
Call money (to money market)
Other bills
Other call money
1958
1959
1960
1961
1962
1963
1964
1965
1966
1967
1968
1969
1970
1971

Chart (h)

Notes on charts, giving series used

CHART (a) *Production, employment and sales (all figures seasonally adjusted)*	*Sources*
Industrial production *Index numbers for the UK of industrial production for all industries.*	Central Statistical Office
Unemployment *Numbers registered as wholly unemployed, excluding school leavers, in Great Britain.*	Department of Employment
Unfilled vacancies *Numbers of adult vacancies notified to employment exchanges in Great Britain.*	Department of Employment
Retail sales *Value and volume index numbers for all kinds of business in Great Britain.*	Department of Trade and Industry

CHART (b) *Prices and wages*	*Sources*
Wholesale prices *Manufactured products – home market sales, UK.* *Basic materials – basic materials and fuel used in UK manufacturing industry.*	Department of Trade and Industry
Retail prices, UK	Department of Employment
Average earnings *Average weekly earnings of all manual workers in Great Britain, twice yearly enquiry, plotted at mid-April and mid-October.*	Department of Employment
Wage rates *Basic weekly wage rates – average for all workers in all UK industries and services.*	Department of Employment

CHART (c) *Interest rates and yields*	*Sources*
Bank rate – plotted at actual dates.	Bank of England

$2\frac{1}{2}$% Consols *Gross flat yield based on daily means of middle-opening and middle-closing prices, ignoring tax and gross accrued interest.*	Bank of England
Industrial equities *Yields based on daily* Financial Times – *Actuaries share indices, with figures to 1963 derived from Actuaries' Investment indices.*	*Financial Times* Institute of Actuaries Faculty of Actuaries

CHART (d) *UK overseas trade (all figures seasonally adjusted)*	*Sources*
Imports *Value of imports c.i.f., excluding deliveries of but including payments for US military aircraft and missiles.*	Department of Trade and Industry
Exports *Value of exports f.o.b., including re-exports.*	Department of Trade and Industry
Balance of payments *Net surplus or deficit on current account, quarterly figures.*	Central Statistical Office

CHART (e) *External position of sterling*	*Sources*
Dollar-sterling exchange rate *Middle-closing spot rate and three months' forward margin; premium indicates forward dollars are at a premium against sterling.*	Bank of England
Short-term sterling liabilities *Official end-quarter figures of external banking and money market liabilities in sterling, published from 1963, and plotted at end-quarter.*	Bank of England
Official reserves *As published*	HM Treasury, Bank of England

CHART (f) *London clearing banks – liabilities and assets*

Figures from 1970 onwards are not comparable with those for

earlier years because of accounting changes. Source: Committee of London Clearing Bankers.

Net deposits

Current, deposit and other accounts, less items in transit and cheques in course of collection on other banks, etc.

Advances

Advances to customers and other accounts excluding items in transit.

Investments

As published.

Liquidity ratio

Percentage of liquid assets (see Chart g) to gross deposits.

CHART (g) *London clearing banks – percentage distribution of assets*

Figures from 1970 onwards are not comparable with those for earlier years because of accounting changes. Assets expressed as percentages of gross deposits. Source: updated from chapter 'Clearing Banks' by J. E. Maycock in *Money in Britain 1959–69*, edited by D. R. Croome and H. G. Johnson (Oxford University Press, 1970), p. 168.

Advances

Advances to customers and other accounts, including items in transit.

Liquid assets

Liquid assets plus Special Deposits (Special Deposits being distinguished by the shaded area).

Investments

As published.

CHART (h) *London clearing banks – composition of liquid assets*

Figures from 1970 onwards are not comparable with those for earlier years because of accounting changes. Source: updated from chapter 'The Nature and Uses of Bank Liquidity' by J. E. Wadsworth in *Monetary Theory and Monetary Policy in the 1970s*, edited by G. Clayton, J. C. Gilbert and R. Sedgwick (Oxford University Press, 1971), p. 206.

Breakdown of liquid assets into components:

Treasury bills, call money (to money market), other bills (including refinanceable credits), other call money, and total – all expressed as percentages of gross deposits. Cash, then maintained at 8 per cent of deposits, is not shown on the chart.

APPENDIX 4

Monetary documents

(*a*) *Letter of Intent of 23 November 1967*

My dear Mr Schweitzer,

I am setting out in this letter a statement of the policies and intentions of the government of the United Kingdom.

The UK government reached their decision to seek the International Monetary Fund's agreement to a reduction in the parity of the pound sterling in the light of their latest periodic review of the position and prospects of the UK economy, including the outlook for the balance of payments, to the end of 1968.

The government's main objectives of policy remain the achievement and maintenance of a strong balance of payments, together with a high rate of economic growth which will make for full employment.

So far as the balance of payments is concerned, the government's aim, at the new rate of exchange which has been concurred in by the Fund, is an improvement of at least £500 million a year. On present prospects for world trade this should mean a surplus in the second half of 1968 at an annual rate of at least £200 million. Beyond that there should be a further substantial rise in the surplus as the full benefits of the change in the UK's competitive position are felt.

At the same time as they took their decision on the rate of exchange, the government decided that measures should be taken as and when required to free resources from domestic use on the scale necessary to secure the improvement referred to in paragraph 4 above.

As the Fund Board will be aware, calculations of the effect of a change in the parity of a currency, and still more of the timing of such effects, are necessarily extremely speculative. This makes it difficult to decide precisely, in the initial stages, on the scale and timing of the measures that are required to make sure that the improvement in the competitive position is not lost through insufficient capacity at home being available to meet the expected increase in demand as it builds up over time.

The government is satisfied that the measures announced on 18 November 1967 will bring about a sufficient shift in resources in the coming months to go a very long way towards achieving the improvement needed to achieve their balance of payments objectives. These measures – details of which are annexed to this letter – will together with the effect on purchasing power at home of the devaluation itself, lead to a reduction of home demand by about £750 million to £800 million below what would otherwise have been the case.

The government is fully aware of the possibility that further measures will be needed to maintain the momentum towards the balance of payments improvement referred to in paragraph 4 above. They intend to take further action once it becomes apparent that such action is required to secure the necessary balance of payments surplus.

The next review of the position and prospects of the UK economy and balance of payments will, in the normal course of business, be carried out in February 1968. At this time it should be possible to assess more accurately than can be done at present the effects of the decisions announced on 18 November 1967. In the light of the review, the government will make a decision on the precise nature of any further action required. They will be happy to consult with the managing director on the results of this review, and again after the further reviews which are planned for July and November 1968.

Fiscal policy will continue to play the most important role in making room for the needed improvement in the balance of payments. It is the government's intention to ensure that the Exchequer's borrowing requirement for the financial year beginning 1 April 1968 is kept under firm control. So far as can be seen at present, this entails holding down the borrowing requirement to not more than £1000 million – the appropriateness of which estimate and the measures necessary to ensure that it is achieved will be reviewed with the managing director in accordance with the timetable specified in paragraph 9.

The steps that have already been taken and will continue to be taken give rise to the expectation at present that bank credit expansion will be sufficiently limited to ensure that the growth of money supply will be less in 1968 than the present estimate for 1967, both absolutely and as a proportion of GNP, despite the expected substantial recovery of reserves. It continues to be the government's policy to meet its own needs for finance as far as possible by the sale of debt to the non-bank public and interest rate policy will be used to this end. In the consultations mentioned in paragraph 9, the actual course of bank credit in relation to the expected course will be taken into account in determining appropriate policy actions.

The government's object will be to ensure, in cooperation with the TUC and CBI, that the policy for prices and incomes measures up to the requirements of the new situation. It will be the government's intention to maintain the policy set out in the White Paper, *Prices and Incomes Policy after 30 June 1967* (Cmnd. 3235), under which there is no entitlement to a 'norm' or standard increases in pay, and increases in pay and prices have to be justified against criteria of the national interest which are equally relevant to the new situation. There is no criterion for any pay increases related to changes in the cost of living. To support the application of the policy, the vetting arrangements will be strengthened in order to ensure that the rise in wages and salaries does not exceed what the economy can afford over the next twelve months.

The government has already started talks with management and unions on alternative ways of achieving this objective.

The government is determined to maintain the new parity without resort to any additional restrictions on current payments or intensification of the present restrictions. The government, moreover, intends to abolish all remaining restrictions on current transfers and payments as soon as the balance of payments allows. Similarly, as the balance of payments strengthens, the government will consider what relaxations can be made in the present restrictions on capital transfers.

The government are convinced that the above measures will lead to a strong balance of payments. It is important, however, for the stability of the international monetary system to establish confidence in the new parity from the start. The government therefore requests a standby of $1·4 billion from the Fund to carry out its economic aims, both domestic and external, which it believes are fully in conformity with the aims of the Fund.

Before making purchases under this requested standby arrangement with the International Monetary Fund the government of the UK will consult with the managing director on the particular currencies to be purchased from the Fund.

The government believe that the policies here outlined are adequate to achieve the economic goals described in this letter. If, however, present policies should turn out to be inadequate, the government is firmly determined to take such further measures as may be necessary to achieve these goals. If, in the opinion of the government of the UK or managing director of the Fund, the policies are not producing the desired improvement in the balance of payments, the government of the UK will consult with the Fund, during the period of the standby arrangement and as long thereafter as the Fund holdings of sterling exceed 125 per cent of quota, to find appropriate solutions.

Yours sincerely,

J. CALLAGHAN

(*b*) *Letter of Intent of 22 May 1969*

Dear Mr Schweitzer,

The government of the United Kingdom hereby requests of the International Monetary Fund a standby arrangement under which for a period of one year the United Kingdom will have the right to purchase from the Fund currencies of other members in exchange for sterling in an amount equivalent in total to $1000 million. The government intends to make an immediate drawing of the equivalent of $500 million. Before making a request for a further purchase under the standby arrangement, the government will consult with the Fund and reach understanding regarding the circumstances in which such purchases may be made. Before making purchases under the requested standby arrangement, the government will consult with the managing director on the particular currencies to be purchased from the Fund.

2. The purpose of this standby is to support the government's economic objectives and policies. It will facilitate the repayments of external debt now falling due, including the scheduled repurchases of sterling from the Fund in respect of the 1965 drawing by the United Kingdom, and will assist in maintaining stability in the international monetary system.

3. In accordance with the normal practice of the Fund in regard to applications for standby facilities, I summarize in this letter the government's main economic objectives and policies, as set forth in my budget speech on 15 April 1969 and other recent statements of policy.

4. As I said in my budget speech, it is the government's policy to do everything necessary to put the United Kingdom balance of payments on a secure and healthy basis, as an essential means to sustained growth and prosperity. The budget was designed to continue and strengthen the balance of payments strategy which the government has been pursuing. The objective is to obtain a substantial and continuing balance of payments surplus.

5. Strong action has been taken, and the balance of payments has already improved considerably. Progress has not been as large or rapid as the government wished but the government intends it to continue and strengthen. The government is taking and will continue to take the action necessary to this end. The growth of public expenditure and private consumption is being limited so that there is room for the desired substantial and continuing balance of payments surplus to develop. The intention is to make sure that the turnround in the structure of the United Kingdom economy gains full momentum. Substantial further progress is intended and expected during the next year. In the financial year ending in March 1970 the objective is to obtain a surplus of at least £300 million on the current and long-term capital account of the balance of payments.

6. Public expenditure for both 1968–9 and 1969–70 is running within the totals announced by the government in January 1968 (Cmnd. 3515). In 1968–9 aggregate expenditure is estimated to have increased in real terms over the previous year by 4·1 per cent. This was within the announced limit of 4·75 per cent. For 1969–70 public expenditure will again be held within the totals announced in January 1968 which allowed for an increase of 1 per cent in real terms over the planned level for 1968–9; the increase over the actual outturn for 1968–9 will be larger.

7. The full year yield of the increases in direct and indirect taxation made in the 1968 budget, in November 1968, and in the 1969 budget, is in total some £1500 million. The central government borrowed £1331 million net in 1967–8. In 1968–9 the central government borrowing requirement (excluding receipts from import deposits) was about £70 million. In 1969–70, the central government's accounts (again excluding import deposits) are intended to be in surplus by at least £850 million, and the current estimate is of a surplus approaching £1000 million, an improvement of more than £1000 million over the previous financial year.

8. As was also stated in the budget speech, the government attaches the greatest importance to monetary policy, which provides an essential support to fiscal policy. The rise in money supply in 1968 of £986 million was broadly in line with the growth of GNP; but the increase in credit in the economy was too high, and the government intends not to permit credit to be supplied to the economy on anything like this scale in 1969–70.

9. The government will therefore watch closely the development of domestic credit expansion during the year. The government's objectives and policies imply a domestic credit expansion for the private and public sectors in the year ending 31 March 1970 of not more than £400 million, compared with some £1225 million in 1968–9. It is the government's policy to ensure that the course quarter by quarter of domestic credit expansion as a whole, and of the central government borrowing requirement within it, is consistent with the intended result for the year as a whole, and to take action as appropriate to this end.

10. The statutory powers relating to prices and incomes policy introduced in the exceptional circumstances following devaluation continue in effect until the end of 1969. Thereafter the powers of Part II of the 1966 Prices and Incomes Act will be activated, and will be used to defer, in appropriate cases, the implementation of a pay settlement or price increases for three to four months in the context of a reference to the Prices and Incomes Board. Further guidance to negotiators will be issued in a new white paper later in the year.

11. The government is confident that its present policies will strengthen sterling as an integral part of the international monetary system. Freedom of international trade and current payments continues to be an aim of policy to which the government attaches great importance. It is the government's policy to maintain the present degree of trade liberalization, and to abolish as soon as the balance of payments allows the restrictions which it currently maintains on travel expenditure and small cash gifts, and also the import deposit scheme.

12. The government believes that the policies set forth in this letter are adequate to achieve the objectives of its programme, but will take any further measures that may become appropriate for this purpose. The government will consult with the Fund from time to time, in accordance with the regular policies of the Fund on such consultation, about the course of the United Kingdom economy and any further measures affecting the balance of payments that may be appropriate.

Yours sincerely,

ROY JENKINS

(*c*) *Text of a letter from the Chancellor of the Exchequer* (*R. A. Butler*) *to the governor of the Bank of England* (*C. F. Cobbold*) *published in* The Times *on 26 July 1955*

I should be glad if you would urgently call the attention of the British Bankers Association and other bodies concerned to the statement which I have just made in the House of Commons on the economic situation of the country.

The essential need of the moment is for a reduction in the total demand on the country's resources. Only a part of that demand is financed by bank advances; but it is an important part and one which, with the cooperation of the banks, can be readily affected by the granting or withholding of credit.

In such circumstances I have no doubt that the banks will agree that it is their duty to reduce the amount of bank credit below what they would be glad to give in less difficult times. Indeed, the necessary reduction in demand is unlikely to be achieved unless the total of bank advances is reduced below its present level.

It is for the banks to decide what steps they must take to make this policy effective. But I look for a positive and significant reduction in their advances over the next few months.

(*d*) *Copy of notice from the Bank of England giving guidance on bank lending – 1968*

NOTICE

CREDIT RESTRICTION

In November 1967 banks were asked to hold down most of their lending in sterling to the private sector and to borrowers abroad to the level then current. At that time it was not possible to foresee with any relability the rate of growth in lending directly related to exports which would be needed over the immediately ensuing months; and such lending was therefore not brought within the quantitative limit then requested. Because the prospective growth of exports is now clearer, it has become possible to make an adequately reliable estimate, for the months ahead, of the growth in bank lending directly related to exports. Accordingly, the authorities have concluded that the administration of credit restrictions can both be simplified and made more effective by accommodating all lending directly related to exports, and to the financing of shipbuilding (under the special scheme relating thereto) within a new overall ceiling on bank lending to the private sector and overseas.

The authorities have also decided that the restrictions requested last November should be modified so as to achieve a greater reduction in lending to non-priority borrowers than has so far taken place and at the same time to leave sufficient room for lending for exports and for activities directly related to improving the balance of payments.

The clearing bank figures for May published this morning show, after seasonal adjustment, that the total of their lending in sterling to the private sector and to borrowers abroad, including export finance and other hitherto exempted categories, now stands at about 104% of the level reached in November 1967. These banks are asked not to allow this lending to exceed this percentage figure until further notice. All other banks should restrict their lending to the same percentage increase over November 1967.

Within this new ceiling and subject to normal banking criteria, banks are asked to give priority to lending for export transactions, to finance for production and investment necessary to sustain increased exports, for the promotion of invisible earnings or, as in the case of agriculture, for securing a saving in imports. The banks will need to make room for such lending within the new ceiling by curtailing lending to persons and for other non-priority purposes. They are asked especially to intensify restrictions on the granting of credit associated with imports of manufactured goods for home consumption or imports for stock accumulation.

Banks are asked to apply the restrictions set out above both to credit given through loans and overdrafts and also to credit given through commercial bills and leasing facilities.

Personal loans where related to the purchase of goods subject to hire purchase terms control should be on terms no easier than those permitted by the Board of Trade for hire purchase contracts.

The authorities have noted that lending to local authorities by the London clearing and Scottish banks, through advances, has risen appreciably since last November, largely because of switching from other forms of short-term finance. The banks are asked to ensure that such lending returns to normal levels.

Bank of England
23 May 1968

(*e*) *Copy of Bank of England consultative paper issued in May 1971*

COMPETITION AND CREDIT CONTROL

1. The Chancellor of the Exchequer announced in his budget speech that the authorities wished to explore with the banks and finance houses the possible development of new techniques of monetary policy, with the objective of combining an effective measure of control over credit conditions with greater scope for competition and innovation. He said: 'I believe it should be possible to achieve more flexible but still effective arrangements basically by operating on the banks' resources rather than by directly guiding their lending.'

2. This paper sets out some proposals to this end as a basis for discussion.

3. In recent years the authorities have paid particular attention to certain categories of lending in sterling by banks and finance houses who have been asked and have agreed to observe quantitative limits on that lending. In practice these limits have been applied individually to most of the banks and finance houses affected and consequently have impeded competition and innovation so that the efficient have been prevented from growing and the less efficient have been helped to maintain the level of their business. Competition in the banking system is at present also limited by the agreements between the Bank of England and the London and Scottish clearing banks which require these groups, but not other banks, to hold certain specified classes of assets to an amount not less than a fixed percentage of their deposit liabilities (the cash and liquidity ratios). In addition, the London and Scottish clearing banks adhere to collective agreements fixing the rates which they pay on deposits and setting minimum rates charged on advances.

4. The authorities, for their part, propose that the impediments to competition arising from the existing liquidity and quantitative lending controls should be replaced by other means of influencing bank and finance house lending in sterling, including the application of a reserve ratio across the whole banking system. It would be part of these proposals that when the changes are introduced, the London and Scottish clearing banks should abandon their collective agreements on interest rates (subject to the proviso in paragraph 15 below about the terms offered on savings deposits).

5. The techniques of monetary policy now proposed would involve less reliance on particular methods of influencing bank and finance house lending and more reliance on changes in interest rates, supported by calls for Special Deposits on the basis of a reserve ratio across the whole of the banking system. There would be similar arrangements for deposit-taking finance houses.

6. For the banking system it is proposed to modify the Special and Cash Deposits scheme so as to put banks on a common basis so far as the operation of these schemes is concerned. The Special Deposits scheme provides for calls for deposits by the Bank of England to whatever extent the authorities deem necessary for the purposes of credit control and for payment of interest on such deposits close to the Treasury bill rate. Its effectiveness rests in part on the agreement by the London and Scottish clearing banks, mentioned above, to hold certain specified assets to an amount not less than a fixed percentage of their deposit liabilities. The Cash Deposits scheme places a narrow limit on the extent to which the Bank of England may call for deposits but allows the Bank in certain circumstances to pay a low or even nil rate of interest on outstanding deposits. No agreement exists with the banks participating in the Cash Deposits scheme regarding any minimum ratio of specified assets. The effectiveness of the Cash Deposits scheme rests predominantly on guidance being given by the authorities, which in practice may differ little from requests for quantitative restrictions.

7. It is now proposed that all banks should:

(i) hold not less than a fixed percentage of their sterling deposit liabilities in certain specified reserve assets;

(ii) place such amount of Special Deposits with the Bank of England as the Bank may call for from time to time.

The proposal that all banks should observe a minimum reserve assets ratio is intended to provide the authorities with a known firm base for the operation of monetary policy.

8. It is proposed that the reserve assets should comprise cash at the Bank of England and certain assets which the Bank will normally be prepared to

convert into cash. The principal assets which would qualify for inclusion are balances with the Bank of England (other than Special Deposits), British government and Northern Ireland government Treasury bills, money at call with the London Money Market,* British government securities with a year or less to run to maturity, local authority bills eligible for rediscount at the Bank of England and, up to a proportion of deposits to be specified, commercial bills eligible for rediscount at the Bank of England. The Bank will wish to discuss with the London clearing banks the understanding which for the future should govern the level of their balances with the Bank within the reserve ratio. It is not proposed that notes in tills should be included in the ratio because they are held mainly as a stock-in-trade to meet the needs of the banks' customers.

9. The amount of reserve assets to be held by banks would be calculated by reference to their sterling deposits obtained outside the banking system, including sterling resources acquired by switching foreign currencies into sterling.

10. The objective of putting banks on a common basis leads to a strong presumption that the reserve ratio in 7 (i) above should be uniform for all banks. It is recognized that there is a wide diversity of business between banks in the United Kingdom but in that part of their business which involves the taking of sterling deposits and their employment in sterling assets – which is all that the present proposals seek to control – the similarities of function are more important than the dissimilarities. Moreover, according different treatment to different parts of the banking system would be difficult to reconcile with the objectives of the proposals in this paper, and would impede the authorities in making uniform calls for Special Deposits.

11. A preliminary examination suggests that a uniform reserve ratio as defined above could be set close to the average practice of the banking system in recent years without causing inequity or undue disturbance arising from banks needing to rearrange their portfolios. Such an average would suggest a ratio of $12\frac{1}{2}$ per cent of relevant deposit liabilities. In addition, it would be for consideration from time to time what level of Special Deposits was required. The need for a call for Special Deposits would be determined by the authorities, in the light of monetary conditions generally, including the behaviour of total sterling lending by all banks, and of the intention of the authorities to maintain adequate control. The amount of Special Deposits to be placed with the Bank of England might be calculated by reference to all or only some of the banks' liabilities to which the reserve ratio would be applied. In particular, a call could be related to domestic or to overseas

* The exact definition of this item is to be agreed in the light of discussions. It is not proposed to include money placed in the inter-bank or local authority temporary money markets.

deposits, or the rate of call might be different for domestic and overseas deposits. The rate or rates of call would be the same for all banks; and all deposits called would bear interest at a rate equivalent to the Treasury bill rate.

12. Problems would be likely to arise in moving from the existing methods of control to the arrangements just described. Where reserve assets were appreciably below the prescribed ratio, there would be problems of adjustment for the banks concerned. Where reserve assets were appreciably above the prescribed ratio, there would be problems for the authorities in ensuring maintenance of adequate control over monetary conditions. Special provisions to meet each set of problems would need to be devised and agreed.

13. In the context of the above proposals it has been decided to restrict the extent of the Bank of England's operations in the gilt-edged market. With immediate effect, these will be conducted on the following general basis:

- (i) the Bank will no longer be prepared to respond to requests to buy stocks outright, except in the case of stocks with one year or less to run to maturity;
- (ii) they reserve the right to make outright purchases of stock with more than a year to run solely at their discretion and initiative;
- (iii) they will be prepared to undertake, at prices of their own choosing, exchanges of stock with the market except those which unduly shorten the life of the debt;
- (iv) and will be prepared to respond to bids for the sale by them of 'tap' stocks and of such other stocks held by them as they may wish to sell.

This modification by the Bank of their mode of operation in the gilt-edged market represents a return towards the position in the market which they occupied up to some ten years ago. In the present context, it will help to limit, further than can be achieved solely by alterations in the Bank's dealing prices, fluctuations in the resources of the banking system arising from official operations in the gilt-edged market. It is being put into effect now so that it can be taken into account in discussions of the proposals on credit control outlined in this paper. More generally , it is considered appropriate to accompany changes in credit control intended to allow greater freedom of competition in the banking system with lesser intervention by the authorities in the gilt-edged market so as to leave more freedom for prices to be affected by market conditions and for others to operate if they so wish.

14. Notwithstanding the abandonment of quantitative ceilings, and the adoption of the above proposals, the authorities would continue to provide the banks with such qualitative guidance as may be appropriate. For example,

so long as hire purchase terms control remains in force, banks will be asked that personal loans related to the purchase of goods subject to terms control should be made on terms no easier than those permitted by the Department of Trade and Industry for hire purchase contracts.

15. The greater freedom afforded to banks by the above proposals might lead them to compete for individuals' savings at present invested in public sector debt or in the finance of housing. The impact of such competition on savings banks and building societies would need careful consideration and the Bank of England would wish to discuss this matter with the banks. It might be that a need would be recognized, for example, to observe some limits on the terms offered for savings deposits. The need for such limits would be open to reconsideration in the light of changed circumstances.

16. The members of the London Discount Market Association are not parties to either the Special Deposits or the Cash Deposits schemes; separate proposals are therefore being made to the Association to ensure that their operations do not undermine the authorities' arrangements with the banks.

17. The Bank of England would wish to discuss with the Finance Houses Association arrangements for their members parallel with those for banks proposed above. The Bank would wish to discuss this question also with those finance houses not members of the Association who have been receiving the Bank's requests for credit restriction.

18. Some amendments to and amplification of existing statistical information provided by banks and finance houses would be required to put the arrangements proposed above into practice. It would be essential for the authorities to receive this modified information, accurately compiled, promptly each month.

Bank of England
May 1971

(*f*) *Copy of a Bank of England press notice on the Discount Market, July 1971*

The Discount Market

In the document entitled *Competition and Credit Control* published by the Bank of England in May [see Appendix 4(e)], it was stated that separate proposals would be made to the members of the London Discount Market Association for modifications to official techniques of monetary policy. These proposals have now been made and are being discussed with the Association.

In the document published in May it was stated that it would be part of the changes proposed by the authorities that the London and Scottish clearing banks should abandon their collective agreements on interest rates. The proposed changes also have implications for the agreements between the market and the clearing banks on tendering for and purchase of Treasury bills and on competition for non-bank funds by the market; and for the agreements which at present exist among the members of the market. The future of these agreements is under discussion.

The Bank have told the Association that they wish to maintain their existing mode of operation in the short-term money market. The Bank have therefore asked the market to agree to continue to apply each week for an amount of Treasury bills sufficient to cover the amount of bills offered at the tender; and have said that, if this agreement is forthcoming, they will be prepared to continue to confine to the market their extension of last resort facilities in the form of lending or purchases of eligible paper (apart, of course, from the usual direct purchases of bills from the banks in the day-to-day management of the money market and any facilities accorded by the Bank to money and discount brokers). The Bank have stated that when they extend last resort facilities by lending, they would require the houses to provide part of the collateral, up to a minimum proportion to be agreed, in the form of Treasury bills.

The authorities need to ensure that they have adequate influence over credit extended by the discount market whether on the basis of funds borrowed from the banking system or of funds borrowed outside the banking system. In framing the proposals put to the market, the Bank have sought to move away from the existing system of quantitative controls and to devise arrangements which would allow members of the market freedom to compete. They have also borne in mind that their proposal that money at call with the Market shall qualify without limit as a reserve asset for banks in satisfaction of the minimum requirement enhances the special place of the market in official techniques of monetary control.

In the Bank's view their objectives can be met by obtaining the agreement of members of the market to hold a stated minimum proportion of their funds in public sector debt,* conforming closely with the present average practice for the market as a whole, namely 50 per cent, and this has been proposed to them.

The Bank recognize that when their proposals on credit control are accepted and put into effect, members of the market could be approached by banks with requests to engage in very short-term transactions designed to substitute 'window dressing' arrangements for genuine observance of their minimum

* British government and Northern Ireland government Treasury bills, local authority bills and bonds and British government, British government-guaranteed and local authority stocks with not more than five years to run to maturity.

reserve ratio obligation. The Bank have therefore asked each house to give a firm undertaking that they would not in any circumstances be prepared wittingly to engage in such transactions; and have said that they would reserve the right to call at any time for full information on the conduct of each House's book.

The Bank will, of course, continue to be concerned that the size of each House's total business bears an appropriate relationship to their capital and reserves.

Bank of England
21 July 1971

(g) *Copy of Bank of England notice to banks and finance houses*

Credit Control - The New Approach

Changes in the techniques of monetary policy and banking practice, as agreed with the banks and finance houses following discussion of the proposals set out in the Bank of England's paper *Competition and Credit Control* will be put into effect from 16 September 1971. The requests about lending made in the Bank's Notice of 30 June 1971 and earlier Notices will lapse after 15 September 1971.

An outline of the new arrangements is set out in the attached paper *Reserve Ratios and Special Deposits.* From 16 September (except where individual transitional arrangements have been agreed) banks will maintain a $12\frac{1}{2}$ per cent reserve ratio day by day and will place such Special Deposits with the Bank of England as may be called for from time to time. Outstanding Special Deposits (made by the London and Scottish clearing banks) will be repaid on 15 September.

The London clearing banks have agreed, as part of the transition to the new arrangements, to subscribe for a total of some £750 million of the three stocks which, it has been announced today, will be issued by HM government on 15 September.

Further discussions are to take place about the application of the new arrangements to banks in Northern Ireland.

From 16 September instalment credit finance houses having eligible liabilities of £5 million or more will commence building up a 10 per cent reserve ratio (to be achieved within twelve months); they will also place such Special Deposits with the Bank of England as may be called for from time to time. These arrangements are also outlined in the attached paper.

Bank of England
10 September 1971

(*h*) *Copy of Bank of England pamphlet on the new arrangements for the control of credit, September* 1971

Reserve Ratios and Special Deposits

Following discussions by the Bank of England with the banking associations and with individual banks on the Bank's paper *Competition and Credit Control* which was published last May, agreement has been reached on new arrangements for the control of credit which will come into effect from 16 September. In future the banks will observe (day by day) a uniform minimum reserve ratio of 12½ per cent of 'eligible liabilities' and will place such Special Deposits with the Bank (on a uniform basis, related to eligible liabilities) as may be called for from time to time. This gives effect to the basic principles of the arrangements outlined in *Competition and Credit Control*, but in the course of the discussions a number of clarifications and modifications of detail to the original proposals have been agreed. The main features of the scheme are described in the following sections.

Eligible liabilities are defined as the sterling deposit liabilities of the banking system as a whole, excluding deposits having an original maturity of over two years, plus any sterling resources obtained by switching foreign currencies into sterling. Inter-bank transactions and sterling certificates of deposit (both held and issued) will be taken into the calculation of individual banks' liabilities on a net basis, irrespective of term. Adjustments will be made in respect of transit items.

Eligible reserve assets will comprise balances with the Bank of England (other than Special Deposits), British government and Northern Ireland government Treasury bills, company tax reserve certificates, money at call with the London money market, British government stocks with one year or less to final maturity, local authority bills eligible for rediscount at the Bank of England and (up to a maximum of 2 per cent of eligible liabilities) commercial bills eligible for rediscount at the Bank of England.

Eligible money at call with the London money market will comprise funds placed with members of the London Discount Market Association, with certain other firms carrying on an essentially similar type of business (the discount brokers and the money trading departments of certain banks traditionally undertaking such business) and with certain firms through whom the banks finance the gilt-edged market, namely the money brokers and jobbers. In order to constitute an eligible reserve asset, funds placed with these firms must be at call (or callable, if not explicitly at call) and must be secured (in the case of the jobbers, on gilt-edged securities).

Special Deposits, when called, will be a uniform percentage across the banking system, normally of each bank's total eligible liabilities; further consideration will be given to the possibility of different rates of call relating to overseas deposits. Calls and repayments will normally be announced on a Thursday with the announcement of bank rate. Amounts called will be rounded to the nearest £5000 and will be adjusted monthly to take account of changes in eligible liabilities as reported to the Bank. Special Deposits will bear interest at a rate equivalent to the Treasury bill rate.

Interest rates. The London and Scottish clearing banks will abandon their collective agreements on interest rates as part of the new arrangements. In the light of discussions held with the banks, the authorities see no need, at least in present circumstances, to seek to limit the terms offered by the banks for savings deposits to protect the position of the savings banks and building societies.

Transitional arrangements. The problems of adjustment mentioned in *Competition and Credit Control* are being met in two ways. Firstly, after allowing for the repayment of existing Special Deposits it was apparent that the reserve asset holdings of the London clearing banks over and above the prescribed minimum level would be quite out of proportion to their present and immediately prospective level of lending. These banks have therefore agreed to subscribe for some £750 million of three new government stocks, maturing respectively two, three and six years hence, to be issued concurrently with the repayment of outstanding Special Deposits. Secondly, individual banks whose holdings of reserve assets have hitherto been well below the prescribed ratio have been given the opportunity of agreeing with the Bank appropriate transitional periods (not extending beyond the end of the year) during which their reserve asset holdings may be built up gradually to the prescribed level.

Northern Ireland banks. The new arrangements apply in principle to all banks in the United Kingdom. However, in the Bank's discussions with the Northern Ireland Bankers' Association, members of that Association, while accepting in principle the application to them of a reserve asset ratio, have represented that the unmodified application to them of the ratio now agreed with other banks in the United Kingdom would present certain difficulties peculiar to the branch-banking system in Northern Ireland. The difficulties arise, *inter alia*, from the fact that the system is operated by banking companies who, in varying degrees, also operate the branch-banking system in the Republic of Ireland. In acknowledging these difficulties, the Bank have accepted that further and detailed discussions must take place before a reserve asset ratio can be agreed with banks in Northern Ireland. In addition, the authorities acknowledge that the application of specific credit policy measures to Northern Ireland should, in the future as in the past, take account so far as practicable of such special economic conditions as may prevail there.

The money market. Agreement has been reached with the London Discount Market Association on the basis of the Bank's proposals published in July. Members of the Association will continue to apply each week for a total amount of Treasury bills sufficient to cover the amount of bills offered at the tender. They will also maintain at least 50 per cent of their funds in defined categories of public sector debt. The Association have informed the Bank that, from the introduction of the new arrangements, they will no longer tender for Treasury bills at an agreed price. The discount brokers outside the Association will continue to participate in the Treasury bill tender and will maintain a similar minimum ratio of public sector debt, as will the money trading departments of certain banks (which will be treated separately from the rest of their business for this purpose). The Bank will continue to confine to the money market access to last resort lending facilities.

The categories of public sector debt to be included in the ratio will be British government and Northern Ireland government Treasury bills, company tax reserve certificates, local authority bills and bonds, and British government, British government-guaranteed and local authority stocks with not more than five years to run to maturity.

Finance houses. Agreement has been reached with members of the Finance Houses Association (and with certain individual houses outside the Association) on a scheme for instalment credit finance houses which take deposits, parallel to that agreed with the banks.

The Bank understand that some of these houses wish to seek full recognition as banks [in particular, under Section 25 (2) of the Protection of Depositors Act]; all houses obtaining such recognition will be treated as banks for reserve ratio and Special Deposit purposes. The parallel scheme will apply in principle to all other instalment credit finance houses (whether members of the Finance Houses Association or not), although houses having eligible liabilities of less than £5 million will be exempt so long as they remain below this limit.

In all essentials the scheme for finance houses closely follows that for the banks. Eligible liabilities, as for the banks, will exclude deposits having an original maturity of over two years; however, as the houses remain outside the banking system, amounts borrowed from banks will also be excluded, so that the liability to hold reserve assets and make Special Deposits is not applied twice to the same funds. The required minimum reserve asset ratio will be 10 per cent instead of 12½ per cent, but the definition of eligible reserve assets will be the same. Calls for Special Deposits will normally be at the same rate as calls on the banks, but the Bank will have the right in certain defined circumstances to call Special Deposits from the finance houses at a higher rate. In no circumstances, however, will the total of reserve assets and Special Deposits represent a higher proportion of eligible liabilities for the finance houses than for the banks. Finance houses participating in these arrangements will be allowed a transitional period of twelve months in which holdings of reserve assets may be built up in stages to the required level.

Banking statistics. On the third Wednesday of each month (and at end-quarters) each bank will complete a new return detailing its eligible liabilities, eligible reserve assets and reserve ratio position. For the time being these returns will be additional to present banking statistical returns. The definitions of the various items making up eligible liabilities and eligible reserve assets have been developed with the assistance of representatives of banking associations at a number of statistical working party meetings. It is intended that a permanent statistical committee should develop from this working party, in order to provide a forum at which longer-term problems concerning the collection of banking statistics may be examined. The new arrangements for monetary control envisage more uniform treatment of all groups of banks, and it will be necessary to achieve greater standardization and uniformity in various types of returns now made by different categories of banks. At the same time it is hoped that fuller discussions will enable the authorities' needs for statistical information to be coordinated more closely with the banks' own requirements.

Bank of England
September 1971

APPENDIX 5

Banking Structure

(*a*) *Companies treated as banking or discount companies*

Part I

The following companies may be treated as banking or discount companies for the purposes of schedule 8 to the Companies Act, 1948 (as amended), as at 31 December 1970.

Alexanders Discount Company Ltd	5
Allen, Harvey & Ross Ltd	5
American Express International Banking Corporation	10
Anglo-Israel Bank Ltd	8
Anglo-Portuguese Bank Ltd	8
Antony Gibbs & Sons Ltd	4
Arbuthnot Latham & Co. Ltd	4
Australia and New Zealand Banking Group Ltd	6
Banco de Bilbao	8
Banco de Santander	8
Banco Espanol en Londres S.A.	8
Bankers Trust Company	5
Bank of Adelaide, The	6
Bank of America National Trust & Savings Association	10
Bank of Cyprus (London) Ltd	7
Bank of India Ltd	7
Bank of London & South America Ltd	7
Bank of Montreal	8
Bank of New South Wales	6
Bank of New Zealand	6
Bank of Nova Scotia, The	7
Bank of Tokyo Ltd, The	8
Banque Belge Ltd	8
Banque Belgo-Congolaise S.A.	8
Banque de l'Indochine	8
Barclays Bank D.C.O.	7
Baring Brothers & Co. Ltd	4
British and Continental Banking Company Ltd	8
British and French Bank Ltd	8
British Bank of the Middle East, The	7
Brown, Shipley & Co. Ltd	4
Canadian Imperial Bank of Commerce	7

Cater Ryder & Company Ltd 5
Chartered Bank, The 7
Charterhouse, Japhet Ltd 4
Chase Manhattan Bank, N.A., The 10
C. Hoare & Co. 3
Clive Discount Company Ltd 5
Commercial Bank of Australia Ltd, The 6
Commercial Banking Company of Sydney Ltd, The 6
Commercial Bank of the Near East Ltd, The 8
Crédit Industriel et Commercial 8
Crédit Lyonnais 8

Eastern Bank Ltd, The 7

First National Bank of Boston 10
First National Bank of Chicago, The 10
First National City Bank 10

Gerrard and National Discount Co Ltd. 5
Gillett Brothers Discount Company Ltd 5
Guinness Mahon & Co. Ltd 4

Habib Bank (Overseas) Ltd 8
Hambros Bank Ltd 4
Hill, Samuel & Co. Ltd 4
Hongkong and Shanghai Banking Corporation, The 7

Ionian Bank Ltd 9
Italo-Belgian Bank 8

Jessel, Toynbee & Co. Ltd 5
J. Henry Schroder Wagg & Co. Ltd 4

Keyser Ullmann Ltd 9
King & Shaxson Ltd 5
Kleinwort Benson Ltd 4

Lazard Brothers & Co. Ltd 4
Leopold Joseph & Sons Ltd 9
Lewis's Bank Ltd 3
Lloyds Bank Europe Ltd 7

Manufacturers Hanover Trust Company 10
Mellon National Bank and Trust Company 10
Mercantile Bank Ltd 7
Midland and International Banks Ltd 9
Morgan Grenfell & Co. Ltd 4
Morgan Guaranty Trust Company of New York 10
Moscow Narodny Bank Ltd 8

National and Grindlays Bank Ltd 7
National Bank of Australasia Ltd, The 6
National Bank of Greece S.A. 8
National Bank of New Zealand Ltd, The 6
National Commercial & Glyns Ltd 9
National Discount Company Ltd, The 5
Netherlands Bank of South Africa Ltd 8
N. M. Rothschild & Sons Ltd 4
Norman & Bennett Ltd 11

Ottoman Bank 7

Provincial Bank of Ireland Ltd, The 3

Rea Brothers Ltd 4
Royal Bank of Canada, The 7

Samuel Montagu & Co. Ltd 4
Sanwa Bank Ltd, The 8
Seccombe, Marshall & Campion Ltd 5

S. G. Warburg & Co. Ltd	4
Singer & Friedlander Ltd	9
Slater, Walker Ltd	9
Smith, St. Aubyn & Co. Ltd	3
Société Générale pour Favoriser le Developpement du Commercè et de l'Industrie en France S.A.	8
Standard Bank Ltd, The	7
Standard Bank of West Africa Ltd	7
State Bank of India	7
Swiss Bank Corporation	8
Swiss-Israel Trade Bank	8
Toronto-Dominion Bank, The	7
Union Bank of Switzerland	8
Union Discount Company of London Ltd, The	5
United Bank Ltd	7
Westminster Foreign Bank Ltd	7
Wm. Brandt's Sons & Co. Ltd	4
Yorkshire Bank Ltd	3

Part II

The companies listed in Part I, and the following additional companies, may be treated as banking or discount companies for the purposes of the Protection of Depositors Act, 1963 (as amended), as at 31 December 1970.

Algemene Bank Nederland	8
Bank of Scotland	2
Banque de Paris et des Pays-Bas, S.A.	8
Barclays Bank Ltd	1
British Linen Bank	2
Clydesdale Bank Ltd	2
Clydesdale Bank Finance Corporation Ltd	9
County Bank Ltd	9
Coutts & Co.	1
International Commercial Bank Ltd	9
Irving Trust Ltd	5
Johnson Matthey Bankers Ltd	9
Lloyds Bank Ltd	1
Lombard Banking Ltd	9
Midland Bank Ltd	1
Midland Bank Finance Corporation Ltd	9
National Westminster Bank Ltd	1
Rothschild Intercontinental Bank Ltd	9
Royal Bank of Scotland Ltd, The	2
Williams, Glyn & Co.	9
Williams & Glyn's Bank Ltd	1

Source: Department of Trade and Industry, *Companies in 1970* (HMSO, 1971).

The number shown against each bank indicates the type of bank, according to the classification for official statistic purposes, as quoted in *Notes and Definitions* to *Financial Statistics* (April 1970 edition):

1 Clearing banks
2 Scottish banks
3 Other deposit banks
(1–3: Deposit banks)
4 Accepting houses

5 Discount houses
6 Australasian banks
7 Other British Overseas and Commonwealth banks
8 Foreign banks, affiliates and other overseas banks
9 Other banks
10 American banks
11 Discount broker

(*b*) *Major subsidiary and associated banks of the clearing banks, at 31 December 1970**

Barclays Bank
Bank of Scotland
Banque de Bruxelles S.A.
Barclays Bank S.A.
Barclays Bank D.C.O. (since renamed Barclays Bank International)
Barclays Bank (London and International) Ltd
Barclays Bank Trust Company Ltd
Barclays Export Finance Company Ltd
Barclays Overseas Development Corporation Ltd
Barclays Unicorn Ltd
United Dominions Trust Ltd
Yorkshire Bank Ltd

Coutts & Co.
Coutts Finance Co.

Lloyds Bank
Bank of London and South America Ltd, Lloyds Bank Europe Ltd (have since merged to form Lloyds & Bolsa International Bank Ltd)
Exporters' Refinance Corporation Ltd
Lewis's Bank Ltd
Lloyds and Scottish Ltd
National and Commercial Banking Group Ltd
National and Grindlays Holdings Ltd
The National Bank of New Zealand Ltd
Yorkshire Bank Ltd

Midland Bank
Banque Européenne de Crédit à Moyen Terme
Clydesdale Bank Ltd
Forward Trust Ltd
European-American Banking Corporation
European-American Bank & Trust Company
Midland and International Banks Ltd
Midland Bank Executor & Trustee Company Ltd
Midland Bank Finance Corporation Ltd
Montagu Trust Ltd
Northern Bank Ltd

* For a comprehensive schedule of the subsidiary and affiliated interest of the major banks of the world see: *Who Owns What in World Banking* (Banker Research Unit, pp. 225).

National Westminster Bank
Centre-File Ltd
County Bank Ltd
Coutts & Co.
Isle of Man Bank Ltd
Lombard Banking Ltd, North Central Finance Ltd (have since merged to form Lombard North Central)
Orion Bank Ltd
Orion Termbank Ltd
The Diners Club Ltd
Ulster Bank Ltd
Westminster Hambro Trust Managers Ltd
Yorkshire Bank Ltd

Williams & Glyn's Bank
St Margaret's Trust Ltd
Williams, Glyn & Co.
Williams & Glyn's Trust Company Ltd

(*c*) *Mergers between major deposit banks of the United Kingdom 1959 – 1971*

Year	*Participants*	*Name of new bank or group*
1959	Commercial Bank of Scotland merged with National Bank of Scotland	National Commercial Bank of Scotland
1962	National Provincial Bank took over District Bank	District Bank retained its identity until the merger between National Provincial and Westminster Banks in 1968 was fully implemented on 1 January 1970
1965	Midland Bank acquired the share capital of Northern Bank	Northern Bank continued to operate under its own name
1968	National Provincial Bank, together with its subsidiary District Bank, combined with Westminster Bank	National Westminster Bank (full integration of the banks began in January 1969 and was completed a year later)
	Barclays Bank acquired the share capital of Martins Bank with effect from 1 November 1968*	Barclays Bank, after completion of merger in December 1969

* Earlier in the year plans for a merger of Barclays, Lloyds and Martins Bank were abandoned following an adverse report from the Monopolies Commission.

	National Commercial Bank of Scotland merged with The Royal Bank of Scotland	Both National Commercial Bank of Scotland and The Royal Bank of Scotland became subsidiaries of the holding company, National and Commercial Banking Group, which also owns the share capital of Williams & Glyn's Bank (see below): National and Commercial Bank of Scotland and The Royal Bank of Scotland began trading under the name of the latter from 1 April 1969
1970	Belfast Banking merged with Northern Bank, both being subsidiaries of Midland Bank.	Northern Bank
	Glyn, Mills The National Bank Williams Deacon's Bank	Williams & Glyn's Bank
	The British Linen Bank Bank of Scotland	Bank of Scotland after merger became fully effective on 1 March 1971

APPENDIX 6

Articles of monetary interest published in the *Midland Bank Review* 1958-71 and not reprinted

ECONOMIC CONDITIONS

Banking and Finance (each issue February 1967 onwards) A regular article comprising a short commentary on the general business situation, quoting the latest Midland Bank Index of Business Turnover figures (see below), and giving special attention to developments in financial markets; a number of charts illustrating the course of business conditions in the United Kingdom; and a section entitled 'Government and Business' summarizing official developments of significance to industry and trade. 'Government and Business' and the charts appeared regularly as separate features until November 1966.

Midland Bank Index of Business Turnover (February 1960, May 1963, May 1965) The Index was introduced in May 1958, and revised in February 1960; seasonal corrections were applied in May 1963; regional figures were presented for the first time in May 1965. A separate index for Northern Ireland was introduced in the issue of August 1967.

MONEY AND BANKING

New Capital Issues Statistics (annually in February) Commentary on the Midland Bank statistics which are issued monthly:

'Smoothing out the Tax Flow' (November 1958) A study of figures relating to the irregular inflow of taxes on income and profits, and its reactions upon the banking situation.

'Corporate Investment in Equities' (February 1959)

'Capital Issues Control: Dead or Dormant?' (February 1960)

'Analysis of "The Reverse Gap"' (May 1960) An examination of the change in relations between basic yield on fixed-interest-bearing and equity investment in a number of countries in recent years.

'More Light on British Banking' (August 1961) Improvements in banking statistics and new series.

'Gold Over a Decade – Supplies and Marketing since 1954' (November 1964)

'Swings and Roundabouts in Bank Figures' (February 1965) Further improvements in banking statistics.

'Meeting the Silver Shortage' (August 1965)

'Modern Means of Moving Money' (February 1966) A study of ways of making money payments through the commercial banks, savings banks and post office.

'Capital Markets in Europe' (May 1966) A summary of the conclusions reached in an examination of some European capital markets undertaken by the Economic Research Group of the Amsterdam-Rotterdam Bank, Deutsche Bank, Midland Bank and the Société Générale de Banque.

'Britain's Stock Exchanges since the War – A Story of Adaptation and Innovation' (November 1968)

'Taxation of Capital Gains in the United Kingdom – A General Survey' (February 1971)

'European Monetary Cooperation' (February 1971) A summary of an article which appeared in the first issue of the *EBIC Bulletin*, a publication of the European Banks' International Company whose members comprise Amsterdam-Rotterdam Bank, Deutsche Bank, Midland Bank and Société Générale de Banque.

'The Cost of Bank Finance – A Comparative Study' (August 1971) Shortly before the ending of the agreement between the London clearing banks on the minimum 'blue chip' interest rate for lending to first-class borrowers, banking structures, lending practices and interest rates charged on bank lending in France, West Germany, Italy, the Netherlands, the United States and Japan were described in detail in this article.

PUBLIC SECTOR FINANCE

'The Nuisance of Stamp Duties' (May 1959) This means of raising revenue was introduced from Holland in 1694 and has altered very little in broad outline since then.

'Borrowing by Local Authorities – Further Sources of Funds' (November 1961) Examines developments in local authority borrowing after 1954, and in particular discusses ways in which authorities sought to attract finance after restrictions had been placed on access to the Public Works Loan Board.

'Non-Marketable Debt and the Exchequer' (November 1962) The contribution to financing the Exchequer of non-marketable forms of borrowing, including national savings securities, tax reserve certificates, terminable annuities, and external transactions.

'Current Budgets of Local Authorities' (February 1964)

'Profits Taxes – Purposes and Prospects' (August 1964)

'Financing the Nationalized Industries' (August 1968)

'The Development of Purchase Tax' (August 1969)

FOREIGN TRADE, EXCHANGE AND PAYMENTS

'The Position of Sterling: Background Material' (August 1960)

'GATT in the World Today' (February 1961)

'Sterling as a "Key" Currency, (August 1963),

'Britain's Tariff Today and Tomorrow' (November 1963)

'Exchange Control in Britain Today' (February 1964)

'Farewell to the Surcharge – Two Years of Trial – and Error?' (November 1966)

'Tariffs and Trade Patterns – A Résumé of Recent Developments and Trends' (May 1968)

'The Retreat from Bretton Woods – The Story So Far' (November 1971)

Index